COMPUTERS

INFORMATION TECHNOLOGY IN PERSPECTIVE

ELEVENTH EDITION

Larry Long
and
Nancy Long

PEARSON

Prentice
Hall

Pearson Education International

Vice President/Publisher: Natalie Anderson
Executive Acquisitions Editor: Jodi McPherson
Senior Marketing Manager: Emily Williams Knight
Senior Editorial Project Manager: Kristine Lombardi Frankel
Assistant Editor: Melissa Edwards
Editorial Assistants: Jodi Bolognese and Jasmine Slowik
Marketing Assistant: Danielle Torio
Development Editor: Joyce Nielsen
Senior Media Project Manager: Cathi Profitko
Production Manager: Gail Steier de Acevedo
Senior Project Manager, Editorial Production: Tim Tate
Associate Director, Manufacturing: Vincent Scelta
Manufacturing Buyer: Tim Tate
Design Manager: Maria Lange
Art Director: Pat Smythe
Associate Director, Multimedia Production: Karen Goldsmith
Manager, Print Production: Christy Mahon
Print Production Liaison: Ashley Scattergood-Tooey
Interior Design: Ray Cruz
Cover Design: John Romer
Infographics: Kenneth Batelman
Illustrator (Interior): Black Dot Group
Full Service Composition: Black Dot Group/An AGT Company
Printer/Binder: Von Hoffmann Corporation
Cover Printer: Phoenix Color Corporation

Pearson Education LTD.
Pearson Education Australia PTY, Limited
Pearson Education Singapore, Pte. Ltd
Pearson Education North Asia Ltd
Pearson Education, Canada, Ltd
Pearson Educación de Mexico, S.A. de C.V.
Pearson Education–Japan
Pearson Education Malaysia, Pte. Ltd
Pearson Education Upper Saddle River, New Jersey

10 9 8 7 6 5 4 3 2 1
ISBN 0-13-121780-1

To our children,
Troy and Brady,
The motivation for all we do.

CONTENTS OVERVIEW

CONTENTS

SPECIAL INTEREST SIDEBARS

PREFACE TO THE STUDENT

Welcome to the computer and information technology revolution. You've taken the first step toward information technology (IT) competency, the bridge to an amazing realm of adventure and discovery. Once you have read and understood the material in this text and have acquired some hands-on experience with computers, you will be poised to play an active role in this revolution.

- You'll be an intelligent consumer of PCs and related products.
- You'll be better prepared to travel the Internet and take advantage of its wealth of resources and services.
- You'll become a participant when conversations at work and school turn to computers and technology.
- You'll be better able to relate your computing and information processing needs to those who can help you.
- You'll know about a wide variety of software and services that can improve your productivity at work and at home; give you much needed information; expand your intellectual and cultural horizons; amaze you, your family, and your friends; and give you endless hours of enjoyment.

Achieving IT competency is the first step in a lifelong journey toward greater knowledge and interaction with more and better applications of IT. IT competency is your ticket to ride. Where you go, how fast you get there, and what you do when you arrive are up to you.

LEARNING AIDS

Each chapter contains several helpful learning aids that can help you understand and retain information technology concepts and terminology. The two-page chapter opening has two learning aids:

- *Learning Objectives*. The learning objectives give you a target for learning for each numbered section.
- *Why This Chapter Is Important to You*. This learning aid serves two purposes. First, it provides an overview of chapter content and, second, it offers compelling reasons why learning the material can help you achieve important life goals.

The body of the chapter has a learning aid at the beginning and end of each numbered section.

- *Why This Section Is Important to You*. Each section begins with a statement that answers the question, "Why do I need to know this?" There is a natural motivation to learn when you know the "Why?"
- *Section Self-Check*. These objective questions (multiple-choice and true-false) are designed to test and reinforce your knowledge of the section's content. Answers for these questions are provided at the back of the book.

The end-of-chapter material includes an extensive array of learning aids.

- *Chapter Summary*. Every boldface term is included in a section-by-section summary of the chapter.
- *Key Terms*. Key terms are listed in alphabetical order with cross-references to the pages where the terms are introduced.
- *Matching*. Here you match a word or a phrase to 15 terms or concepts from the chapter. Answers to this matching exercise are provided at the back of the book.
- *Chapter Self-Check*. The Chapter Self-Check, which is organized by numbered section, is an extension of the Section Self-Check; that is, it contains more of the same types of questions to assess your understanding of the material. Answers to these exercises are provided at the back of the book.

- *IT Ethics and Issues.* Several scenarios introduce important information technology ethical considerations and issues. Each scenario has discussion questions that encourage critical thinking and/or promote a lively in-class debate.

- *Discussion and Problem Solving.* These questions invite group discussion or individual/group problem solving related to concepts presented in the chapter.

- *Focus on Personal Computing.* Each chapter has exercises designed to expand your personal computing horizons, all within the context of chapter content.

- *Online Exercises.* The Long and Long Companion Website invites you to go online and explore the wonders of the Internet through a comprehensive set of Internet exercises. These entertaining exercises invite you to learn more about the topics in this book and to do some serendipitous (just-for-fun) surfing.

Computers is supported by a comprehensive mixed-media learning assistance package. The Long and Long Companion Website at **www.prenhall.com/long** includes *Online Exercises, Web Projects, Internet Links,* an *Interactive Study Guide,* and much more—all designed to help you learn about computers and information technology. Other online learning tools are described in the Preface to the Instructor.

YOU, COMPUTERS, AND THE FUTURE

Whether you are pursuing a career as an economist, a social worker, a politician, an attorney, a dancer, an accountant, a computer specialist, a sales manager, or virtually any other career, the knowledge you gain from this course ultimately will prove beneficial. Keep your course notes and your book; they will prove to be valuable references in other courses and in your career.

Even though computers are all around us, we are seeing only the tip of the information technology iceberg. You are entering the IT era in its infancy. Each class you attend and each page you turn offers a learning experience that takes you one step closer to an understanding of how computers and IT are making the world a better place in which to live and work.

PREFACE TO THE INSTRUCTOR

Everything seems to be changing—at home, at work, during leisure, and in education. The forces behind this change, computers and information technology (IT), are the reason we now live in an interconnected society. *Computers,* 11th edition, captures this paradigm shift in societal trends in a way that instills in students an urgent desire to learn and to play an active role in this technology revolution.

MEETING THE CHALLENGES OF TEACHING INTRODUCTORY IT COURSES

The introductory IT course has its teaching challenges. Throughout the term we are historians, scientists, and, on occasion, sociologists. In the same course we now toggle between lecture, lab, and, for some, distance learning via the Internet. If that's not enough, we teach an ever-increasing amount of material to students with a wide range of career objectives and technical abilities. *Computers* and its extensive teaching/learning system are written and designed to give you what you want and need to meet these challenges.

OBJECTIVES FOR THE ELEVENTH EDITION OF COMPUTERS

We had these primary objectives as we began writing this eleventh edition of *Computers.*

- *Make content relevant to the student.* Throughout the book, we make learning about IT a very personal experience. Each chapter begins with "Why This Chapter Is Important to You" and each major section begins with "Why This Section Is Important to You."

- *Motivate the student to learn.* The text and all supplements are written in a style that remains pedagogically sound while communicating the energy and excitement of IT to the student. We want the information in this book to be absorbed, retained, and enjoyed.

- *Present the right content at the right level for IT competency.* We cover only that material which is appropriate for *modern* IT competency. We feel an obligation to present topics at depths consistent with introductory learning. Our focus is on information that will have an impact on the student's ability to cope with the IT revolution.

- *Create content that reflects the state-of-the-art of the technology.* We are committed to maintaining our position as the most current IT concepts book available.

- *Streamline the presentation of material.* We have streamlined the presentation, eliminating those boxed items that may be interesting, but are not critical to chapter concepts or IT competency. This streamlining effort is in response to faculty and students who tell us they want a book that presents important material in a straightforward manner without extraneous clutter. The result is a cleaner, more easily absorbed presentation.

- *Present IT ethics in more depth.* An appreciation for IT ethics has emerged as a core topic for college graduates. A chapter is devoted to IT ethics. Each chapter has several *IT Ethics and Issues* scenarios with probing discussion questions designed to spur lively in-class discussions. Also, the *Discussion and Problem Solving* section has numerous engaging discussion questions on IT issues.

- *Cover the Internet in a way that reflects its true impact on society.* Chapters 3 and 9 are devoted to the Internet, and the Net is mentioned or discussed hundreds of times throughout the book. We are an interconnected society and it is our obligation to present the breadth of Internet applications, examine timely Internet issues, and gaze into the future of the Net.

- *Give professors plenty of flexibility.* The text and its mixed-media teaching/learning system are organized to permit maximum flexibility in course design and in the selection, assignment, and presentation of material.

- *Emphasize personal computing.* Students enjoy personal computing, so we take every opportunity to relate terms and concepts to their personal computing experiences.
- *Make this edition transition friendly. Computers,* 11th edition, was written to enable a smooth, seamless transition for those colleges moving from previous editions of *Computers.*

COMPUTERS IS AN ANNUAL EDITION

Computers is updated annually, and each year we make thousands of changes to bring *Computers* abreast with a rampaging technology. Just look at what has happened in one year since the last edition.

- Instant messaging emerged as a major communications tool in the corporate world.
- Open source software development is going mainstream.
- Broadband has reached critical mass in many geographic areas enabling the widespread implementation Net-based applications such as video-on-demand, grid computing, and videoconferencing.
- Chip technology has gone from microns to nanometers.
- De facto standards have emerged for rewritable DVD and short-range wireless communications.
- Home networking has become commonplace.
- Internet gaming has exploded.
- New IT ethics issues, such as the use of facial recognition systems, have emerged.
- People routinely check their e-mail and chat via cell phones.
- Hard disk storage capacities have doubled.
- The Internet is the conduit for most international calls.

CHANGES IN THE ELEVENTH EDITION

One reason that *Computers* has remained the choice of thousands of your colleagues through ten editions is because we try very hard to evolve with your needs and give you the features you need to teach successful courses. In that regard, this edition has several very visible changes.

- *Reorganized to meet emerging IT educational needs.* A number of changes have been made to the overall organization of the book. To provide a better fit for the semester format, the full book now has a Getting Started section and 12 chapters, one less than the 10th edition. "Going Online" is moved from Chapter 7 to Chapter 3. The Brief edition, which was previously the Getting Started plus 10 chapters, is now the Getting Started plus eight chapters.
- *Expanded "Getting Started" section.* Unique to introductory IT books, the very visual Getting Started section is expanded, to help jumpstart the student's personal computing experience and enable leveling of IT understanding. This popular section introduces the essential information students need to get them up and running—hardware basics, GUI/operating system concepts, file management, networking and Internet access concepts, and an introduction to using word processing, e-mail, Internet browser, and instant messaging software.

THE CRYSTAL BALL

- *Expanded end-of-chapter material.* The chapter review materials are significantly enhanced from previous editions. The *Chapter Summary* and *Discussion and Problem Solving* elements are continued and several new aids are added, including *Key Terms* (with page references), *Matching, Chapter Self-Check* (a supplement to *Section Self-Checks*), *IT Ethics and Issues* (scenarios and discussion), *Focus on Personal Computing* (hands-on PC exercises), and *Online Exercises* (references to the companion Web site).

PERSONAL COMPUTING

- *New margin elements: The Crystal Ball and Personal Computing.* These short, to-the-point sidebars give students some solid advice on how to prepare for the future and get the absolute most of their personal computing experience. Both are written in first person by author Larry Long. *The Crystal Ball* offers author predictions on information technology from 3 to 10 years into the future. The Crystal Ball looks to the future on many topics, such as health care and personal communications. *Personal Computing* contains tips, hints, and recommendations that can enhance the student's personal computing experience.

A COMPUTERS EDITION FOR EVERY COURSE

Computers comes in two editions.

- *The Brief Edition.* Eight *core chapters,* plus a *Getting Started* section at the beginning of the book, introduce students to the world of information technology: concepts relating to interaction with computers; fundamental hardware, software, and communications concepts; going online (the Internet and its applications); and IT ethics and issues. The brief book includes three colorful *IT Illustrated* modules: computer history, the making of integrated circuits, and a PC buyer's guide.

- *The Full Edition.* The full edition has four additional chapters. The student is introduced to the cyberworld, from e-commerce to Web site development. A *two-chapter* sequence introduces students to the various types of information systems and includes an overview of the latest approaches to system development. The focus of the last chapter is the future: IT careers, robotics, and future IT applications.

THE COMPUTERS TEACHING/LEARNING SYSTEM

Computers, 11th edition, continues the Long and Long tradition of having the most comprehensive, innovative, and effective support package on the market. The book is but one component of a comprehensive *mixed-media teaching/learning system* that is designed to give you maximum flexibility in course design and instruction. Use these resources to offer IT competency education in whatever formats meet your student and curriculum needs.

TOOLS FOR ONLINE LEARNING
A wealth of online learning tools are available to facilitate the teaching/learning process.

Long and Long Companion Website: www.prenhall.com/long

The Companion Website is customizable with real-time news, headlines, and current events and it offers a variety of activities and services, including downloadable supplements. These resources complement student learning.

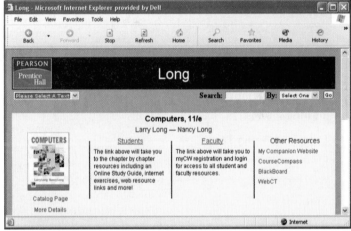
Long and Long Companion Website

- *Internet Exercises.* The Internet exercises encourage students to explore more fully IT competency topics while familiarizing themselves with the Internet. Each chapter has an Internet exercise for each of the special interest sidebars as well as an additional 2-4 exercises focusing on chapter specific topics and real-world issues.

- *Interactive Study Guide.* The Interactive Study Guide helps the student learn and retain concepts presented in the text. The student can choose from four skills quizzes: multiple choice, true or false, matching, or essay. A summary report is returned to the student within seconds. After completing a quiz, the student has the option of routing the answers to his or her e-mail address and/or to that of the instructor.

- *Online End-of-Chapter Materials.*

- *Web Resources.* Additional web resources include Careers in IT, Technology Updates, Technology Buying Guide, crossword puzzles, a Web Guide and much, much more.

- *Instructor Downloads.* The Companion Website includes many helpful password-protected faculty resources. These resources are dynamic, ever changing, and include supplementary exercises, the image library, videos, animations, the instructor's manual and Test Bank in Word and PDF format, and PowerPoint presentations.

The instructor's resources are also available on the instructor's one-stop CD-ROM called Present IT. The new IRCD/Present IT is a comprehensive, user-friendly, Instructor's Tool that is all you need to prepare and present powerful lectures to your students. You can easily customize your own lecture presentation selecting from dynamic PowerPoints, images, videos, animations, and more.

Image Library

- *Instructor's Manual (IM)*. The *Instructor's Manual* is available in Microsoft Word and PDF format and is available in hard copy, as well. The *Instructor's Manual* contains teaching hints, references to other resources, selected images, lecture notes, key terms with definitions, solutions to review exercises, and much more.

- *PowerPoint Slides*. Several hundred colorful and illustrative PowerPoint slides are available for use with Microsoft PowerPoint. The chapter-by-chapter PowerPoint slides can be customized easily to meet lecture needs.

- *Windows PH Test Gen and Test Item File. Windows PH Test Gen* is an integrated PC-compatible test-generation and classroom-management software package. The package permits instructors to design and create tests, to maintain student records, and to provide online practice testing for students. The accompanying *Test Item File* contains thousands of multiple-choice, true/false, matching, and essay questions.

Additional media resources include an image library, animations, and brand new TECH TV videos, giving motion and additional meaning to the student's learning experience.

Online Course Development and Management

Prentice Hall provides the content and support you need to create and manage your own online course in *WebCT, Blackboard,* or Prentice Hall's own *CourseCompass™*. These online course development tools, along with embedded Long and Long content, offer you and your colleagues all the advantages of a custom-built program, but without the hassle. If you are considering offering all or part of your course via distance learning, then these tools can help you create, implement, and deliver a high-quality online course or course component with relative ease. If you already offer an online course, then these tools can assist you in formalizing your course.

Online Learning: WebCT and Blackboard

These Web-course tools give you the flexibility to customize your online course by integrating your custom material with content from *Computers,* 11th edition. Content includes lecture material, exercises, individual student projects, team projects, homework assignments, additional testing questions and all resources found on the Companion Website. Whether you are off and running or this is your first online course, these ready-to-go online course resources can save you countless hours of preparation and course administration time.

- *CourseCompass™ at* **www.coursecompass.com**. CourseCompass™ is a dynamic, interactive online course management tool powered by Blackboard. Best of all, Prentice Hall handles the hosting, the technical support, and the training so you can focus on your course by creating the best teaching and learning environment for both you and your students.

- *Blackboard at* **www.prenhall.com/blackboard**. Prentice Hall's abundant online content, combined with Blackboard's popular tools and interface, results in robust Web-based courses that are easy to implement, manage, and use—taking your courses to new heights in student interaction and learning.

- *WebCT at* **www.prenhall.com/webct**. Course-management tools within WebCT include page tracking, progress tracking, class and student management, gradebook, communication, calendar, reporting tools, and more.

Train and Assess IT

With Prentice Hall's *Train and Assess IT* software program, you can experience the more challenging computer topics anywhere you have access to a computer and/or the Internet. Delivered over the Web or on CD-ROM, the labs present an interactive, multimedia look into the world of computer concepts. The training component offers computer-based training that a student can use to preview, learn, and review computer concepts (Inside the Box, The Internet—Connecting from Home, PC Troubleshooting Basics, Working with Graphics, Security and Privacy, and many more), Windows concepts, and Microsoft Office applications (Word, Excel, PowerPoint, Access, and Outlook). Each lab takes about 20 minutes to complete. Built-in prescriptive testing suggests a study path based on student test results. The assessment component provides performance-based assessment to evaluate the students understanding of specific computer/IT skills.

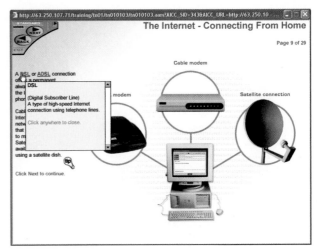

Train and Access IT

EXPLORE IT at www.prenhall.com/phit

A Web and CD-ROM-based training program for computer competency, *EXPLORE IT,* includes a variety of interactive multimedia training modules, including Troubleshooting, Programming Logic, Mouse and Keyboard Basics, Databases, Building a Web Page, Hardware, Software, Operating Systems, Building a Network, and more.

Finally, there is the author link. If you have questions regarding the book, resources, package, or course planning, contact us directly (Prentice Hall representatives can provide contact information).

LARRY LONG, PH.D.   NANCY LONG, PH.D.

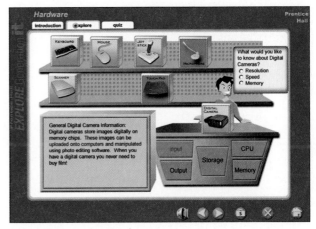

EXPLORE Generation IT Lab

ACKNOWLEDGMENTS

Any introductory book, especially this 11th edition of *Computers* and its many mixed-media ancillaries, is a major undertaking involving many talented people. Each year, my friends and colleagues at Prentice Hall do a magnificent job of articulating the focus of the book, supporting us during the writing process, and, ultimately, blending over a thousand separate elements of text and imagery into a beautiful and effective college textbook. These professionals should be very proud of *Computers,* for it is their book, too. Jodi McPherson, Natalie E. Anderson, Melissa Edwards, and Jasmine Slowik comprise a magnificent editorial team. The quality of the production is evident and for that we thank Kristine Lombardi Frankel, Gail Steier de Acevedo, Tim Tate, Vinnie Scelta, and their colleagues. Cathi Profitko, Karen Goldsmith, Christy Mahon, and their colleagues do wonders with our Web and mixed-media supplements. The art and design is beautiful, thanks to Pat Smythe, Maria Lange, Kenneth Batelman, Ray Cruz, and John Romer. Our book is made all the better with continuous feedback from Emily Knight and Daneille Torio in marketing. In addition, we would like to thank Joyce Nielsen, Sandy Reinhard, and Caryl Wenzel for their diligence in the development and production process.

We would like to thank those who created key ancillaries for *Computers*: *Delores Pusins* of Hillsborough Community College (Interactive Study Guide and Test Item File), *Frank Futyma* of Columbus Technical Institute (Instructor's Resource Manual), *Nancy Surynt* of Stetson University (PowerPoint slides), and *Sherry Thorup* of Middle Tennessee State University (content for WebCT and Blackboard online courses).

The feedback from numerous college professors, both invited and voluntary, has proven invaluable in refining this new edition to better serve their course needs. We would like to extend our heartfelt gratitude to these professors for their insight on this and previous editions of *Computers*.

Amir Afzal, Strayer College
Sally Anthony, San Diego State University
Gary R. Armstrong, Shippensburg University
Suzanne Baker, Lakeland Community College
Dr. David Bannon, Wake Technical Community College
Michael J. Belgard, Bryant and Stratton College
Harvey Blessing, Essex Community College
Amanda Bounds, Florida Community College at Jacksonville
Wayne Bowen, Black Hawk Community College
Jeanann Boyce, University of Maryland
Shira L. Broschat, Washington State University
Sandra Brown, Finger Lakes Community College
Michael Brown, DeVry Institute of Technology, Chicago
Roy Bunch, Chemeketa Community College
Don Cartlidge, New Mexico State University (emeritus)
Stephanie Chenault, The College of Charleston
Carl Clavadetscher, California Polytechnic State University, Pomona
Eli Cohen, Wichita State University
William Cornette, Southwest Missouri State University
Nancy Cosgrove, University of Central Florida
Cheryl Cunningham, Embry-Riddle Aeronautical University
Marvin Daugherty, Indiana Vocational Technical College
Joyce Derocher, Bay de Noc Community College
Wendell Dillard, Arkansas State University
Barbara Ellestad, Montana State University
Dan Everett, University of Georgia
Ray Fanselau, American River College
Shirley Fedorovich, Embry-Riddle Aeronautical University
J. Patrick Fenton, West Valley College
Dr. Diane Fischer, Dowling College
Barry Floyd, California Polytechnic State University, San Luis Obispo
Dr. Charles Foltz, East Carolina University
James Frost, Idaho State University

Jorge Gaytan, University of Texas, El Paso
Dr. Homa Ghajar, Oklahoma State University
Kirk L. Gibson, City College of San Francisco
Randy Goldberg, Marist College
Tom Gorecki, Charles County Community College
Timothy Gottlebeir, North Lake College
Nancy Grant, Community College of Allegheny County
Rob Murray, Ivy Tech State College
Nancy Grant, Community College of Allegheny County South Campus
Ken Griffin, University of Central Arkansas
Vernon Griffin, Austin Community College
Don Hall, Manatee Community College
Cindy Hanchey, Oklahoma Baptist University
Nancy Harrington, Trident Technical College
Wayne Headrick, New Mexico State University
Grace C. Hertlein, California State University
Shirley Hill, California State University
Seth Hock, Columbus State Community College
Fred Homeyer, Angelo State University
Peter Irwin, Richland College
James Johnson, Valencia Community College
Cynthia Kachik, Santa Fe Community College
Dr. M. B. Kahn, California State University at Long Beach
Dr. Adolph Katz, Fairfield University
Robert Keim, Arizona State University
Michael A. Kelly, City College of San Francisco
Helene Kershner, SUNY, Buffalo
Constance K. Knapp, Pace University
Suzanne Konieczny, Marshall University
Doug K. Lauffer, Community College of Beaver County
Sandra Lehmann, Moraine Park Technical College
Michael Lichtenstein, DeVry Institute of Technology, Chicago
Rajiv Malkan, Montgomery College
Ruth Malmstrom, Raritan Valley Community College
Dennis Martin, Kennebec Valley Vocational Technical Institute
LindaLee Massoud, Mott Community College
Gary Mattison, Strayer College
William McDaniel, Jr., Northern Virginia Community College at Alexandria
Michael A. McNeece, Strayer College
Dori McPherson, Schoolcraft College
William McTammany, Florida Community College at Jacksonville
Gloria Melara, California State University at Northridge
Mike Michaelson, Palomar College
Thomas H. Miller, University of Idaho
Domingo Molina, Texas Southmost College
Margaret J. Moore, Coastal Carolina Community College
Joseph Morrell, Metropolitan State College of Denver
Carol Mull, Asheville-Buncombe Technical Community College
Patricia Nettnin, Finger Lakes Community College
Edward Nock, DeVry Institute of Technology, Columbus
Lewis Noe, Ivy Technical Institute
Anthony Nowakowski, State University of New York College at Buffalo
Frank O'Brien, Milwaukee Technical College
Alvin Ollenburger, University of Minnesota
Anne L. Olsen, Wingate College
Dr. Emmanuel Opara, Prairie View A&M University
Beverly Oswalt, University of Central Arkansas
Michael Padbury, Arapahoe Community College

Rick Parker, College of Southern Idaho
Verale Phillips, Cincinnati Technical College
James Phillips, Lexington Community College
Nancy Roberts, Lesley College
Behrooz Saghafi, Chicago State University
Dr. John Sanford, Philadelphia College of Textiles and Science
Ruth Schmitz, University of Nebraska at Kearney
Judy Scholl, Austin Community College
Al Schroeder, Richland College
Marian Schwartz, North Central Technical College
Mark Seagroves, Wingate College
John F. Sharlow, Eastern Connecticut State University
Bari Siddique, Texas Southmost College
Richardson Siebert, Morton College
Robert Spear, Prince George's Community College
John Stocksen, Kansas City Kansas Community College
Carl Ubelacker, Cincinnati State Technical and Community College
Dr. Diane Visor, University of Central Oklahoma
Thomas Voight, Franklin University
Henry Wardak, Everett Community College
Lynn Wermers, North Shore Community College
Dr. Joseph Williams, University of Texas at Austin
Larry B. Wintermeyer, Chemeketa Community College
Floyd Jay Winters, Manatee Community College.

Finally, we wish to thank the professionals from over 100 companies who have contributed resources (information, photos, software, and images) to this book and its supplements.

ABOUT THE AUTHORS

Dr. Larry Long and **Dr. Nancy Long** have written more than 30 books, which have been used in hundreds of colleges throughout the world. Larry is a lecturer, author, consultant, and educator in the information technology fields. He has served as a strategic-level consultant to most major types of industries and has over 25 years of classroom experience at IBM, the University of Oklahoma, Lehigh University, and the University of Arkansas. Nancy has teaching and administrative experience at all levels of education.

COMPUTERS

INFORMATION TECHNOLOGY
IN PERSPECTIVE

GETTING STARTED

This Getting Started section is designed to give you a quick start on your personal computing adventure. The emphasis here is on the essentials in the five areas listed below. Depending on your level of understanding and experience with computers and information technology, you may decide to carefully study this Getting Started section, skim it, or skip it altogether.

The personal computer (PC) is a bit of a mystery to the technology novice, but PCs aren't as complex as you might have thought. They have only four basic components: processor, input, output, and storage. Each PC can be outfitted with a variety of processors, many different types of input and output (I/O), and a wide array of storage devices. This section introduces common I/O and storage devices.

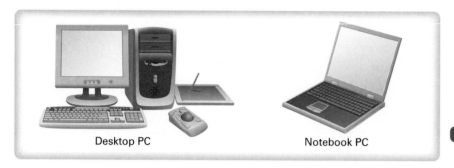

Desktop PC   Notebook PC

FIGURE GS-1
Personal Computers

THE DESKTOP AND NOTEBOOK PC

Most personal computers are either *desktop PCs* or *notebook PCs* (see Figure GS-1). The desktop PC can be found in every company and in most homes. The notebook PC, sometimes called a laptop PC, is a self-contained portable PC designed for use by mobile people. Reasonably powerful desktop PCs can be purchased for under $1,000. Expect to pay a premium for portability. A notebook PC might cost twice as much as a desktop PC with similar capabilities. Generally, desktop PCs outsell notebook PCs 2 to 1; however, that is changing, as more and more people are choosing notebook PCs. We can expect this trend to continue as the price of notebook PCs falls and notebook PC capabilities approach those of desktop PCs.

Microphone

Speakers
(Stereo Sound)

Video Camera

Image Scanner

Multimedia
All personal computers are equipped with a microphone for audio input and speakers for audio output. The inexpensive video camera is a common multimedia input peripheral on desktop PCs.

A TYPICAL PC SYSTEM

A wide range of peripheral devices (input/output and storage devices) can be attached to a PC's system unit. Figure GS-2 shows devices commonly configured with PCs.

Common Input Devices
The two most common input devices are the mouse and keyboard. All PCs have *keyboards* for entering text and commands. The most commonly used *point-and-draw device* is the *mouse*; however, other devices can aid you in navigating around the system, moving objects, and in drawing applications. For example, many notebook PCs come with touchpads. Generally, to select an item, move the cursor (a moveable pointer) over the item (perhaps an OK button or the name of a program) and click (tap) the left mouse button. To open (or choose) an item, double-click (two rapid taps) the left button. Right-clicking (tapping the right mouse button) causes a context-sensitive menu to be displayed.

FIGURE GS-2
PC Peripheral Devices

Monitor   Printer

Common Output Devices
The results of processing are displayed on a *monitor*. The *printer* produces printed (hard copy) output, such as a report.

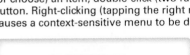

Keyboard   Mouse

The System Unit
The *system unit* houses the *motherboard*, a single circuit board that includes the *processor*, *RAM* (memory for programs and data during processing), and *other electronic components*. The *electronic bus* on the motherboard provides the electronic path through which the processor communicates with memory/storage components and the various input/output peripheral devices. Permanent storage on *hard disk* and *interchangeable disks/discs* is encased in the system unit, too.

Modem

Hard disks   CD-ROM/DVD-ROM   DVD+RW/CD-RW Combination Drive   Floppy disk (diskette)

Communications
The *modem*, which may be internal (within the system unit) or external, provides a link to the Internet via a regular telephone line connection.

Storage
The typical PC will have three types of permanent storage. the permanently installed *hard disk* is housed in the system unit and contains data and programs which are read and transferred to RAM for processing. New programs are installed to hard disk and updated data are written to hard disk. The system unit will also have a floppy disk *drive* and either a *CD-ROM* or *DVD-ROM* drive. The *floppy disk (diskette)*, which can be either low or high capacity, can be inserted into the floppy disk drive as needed for read/write operations. High-capacity CD-ROM disks are inserted into their respective drives as needed for read-only operations. Most commercial programs are distributed on CD-ROM.

THE MICROSOFT WINDOWS OPERATING SYSTEM

Software refers to a collective set of instructions, called programs, which can be interpreted by a computer. The programs cause the computer to perform desired functions, such as word processing, the generation of business graphics, or flight simulation. At the center of the software action is the operating system. It controls everything that happens in a computer. We interact with the PC via its user-friendly, "point-and-click" graphical user interface (GUI). The operating system manages, maintains, and controls computer resources and is, therefore, considered system software. In contrast, applications software describes those programs that address a particular user application, such as word processing or e-mail. Microsoft Windows operating systems are installed on about 90% of the PCs in the world. The most widely used operating systems are Windows 95, Windows 98, Windows Me, Windows 2000, and Windows XP. Windows XP, the current version, is the basis for the examples used in this book. "Windows" is used as a collective reference to all Microsoft Windows operating systems, all of which are in common use.

FIGURE GS-3
**System
Start-up**

THE BOOT PROCEDURE

The *system startup* procedure on almost any computer is straightforward—flip the on/off switch on the processor unit to *on*. It is good practice to turn on needed input/output devices before turning on the processor. When you *power up* you also *boot* the system. See Figure GS-3.

1. Turn on the PC to begin the boot process.

2. A program permanently stored in a ROM (read-only memory) chip is run automatically. The ROM-based start-up program performs a system check to verify that RAM, electronic complements, and input/output (I/O) devices are operational. During the system check, the PC manufacturer's name, the name of the college/company, or something else is displayed on a splash screen. If everything checks out, the program searches for the disk containing the operating system, usually the systems permanently installed hard disk. During the search process, you might hear the computer attempt to read from the diskette drive or the CD-ROM/DVD-ROM drive.

3. Upon finding the operating system (usually on the hard disk), the ROM program loads it from disk storage to RAM. Once loaded to RAM, the operating system takes control of the system.

4. Either the Windows welcome screen (shown here) or the classic Windows logon dialog box appears and requests that you choose a user account and enter a password. The logon procedure identifies you to the computer system and, possibly, a computer network and verifies that you are an authorized user. Modern PCs allow you to set up a computer with several user accounts, each of which can be personalized with regard to desktop appearance, favorite Internet sites, password-protected folders and files, and so on.

5. The Windows boot/logon procedure ends with the presentation of your personalized desktop. The Windows GUI is easily customized. Just click the right button on the mouse anywhere on the desktop and click *properties*.

THE SHUT DOWN PROCEDURE

Unlike electrical appliances, computers are not simply turned off when you're done using them. You must shut down your computer in an orderly manner. Shutting down involves a normal exit (click File, then Exit in the application menu) from all active applications programs before shutting off the power. All applications programs have an exit routine that, if bypassed, can result in loss of user data and problems during later sessions (see Figure GS-4).

FIGURE GS-4
System Shut Down

Start
Click the Start button to display the Start Menu.

Shut Down
Select *Shut Down* from the *Start Menu*.

Turn Off
The *Turn Off Computer* (or *Shut Down Windows*) dialog box appears on the desktop. A *dialog box* is a window that asks you to enter further information. Select *Turn Off*, or, if you wish to restart, select *Restart*. Selecting *Restart* causes the system to shut down and then reboot automatically. On legacy Windows (9X and Me) systems, click the down arrow at the right of the drop-down list and select *Shut down*. Click the *OK* button to end your PC session.

FIGURE GS-5
The Add Hardware Wizard

WINDOWS WIZARDS

A utility called a wizard is one of the most helpful features of the Windows operating system (see Figure GS-5). A wizard is a series of interactive dialog boxes that guide you through a variety of system-related processes, such as setting up a network, adding hardware, or troubleshooting a problem. Wizards also are available to help you with numerous applications-related operations, such as sending a fax (via your PC), creating a Web site, publishing a Web site, preparing a resume, writing a newsletter, creating a bar graph, preparing a business plan presentation, setting up a database, and so on. The wizard may ask you to choose from available options or enter specific information at each step. Click Next to proceed through the steps and click Finish when the operation is completed.

RUNNING AN APPLICATION FROM THE WINDOWS DESKTOP

The foundation of the Windows graphical user interface is the Windows desktop. Any installed application can be launched (or run or started or opened) from the Windows desktop (see Figure GS-6).

Shortcut Icon
Click or double-click (tap left mouse button once or twice) on a shortcut icon (with embedded arrow) to run the program represented by the icon.

Desktop
The screen upon which Start button, icons, windows, and so on are displayed is known as the *desktop*.

Background
The desktop background can be a color or a user-selected image, such as this sunset image.

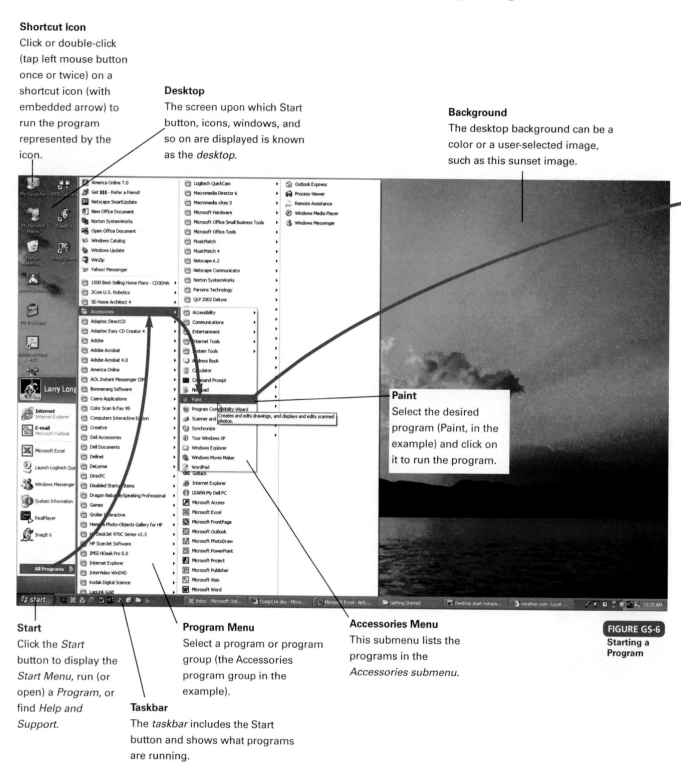

Paint
Select the desired program (Paint, in the example) and click on it to run the program.

Start
Click the *Start* button to display the *Start Menu*, run (or open) a *Program*, or find *Help and Support*.

Program Menu
Select a program or program group (the Accessories program group in the example).

Accessories Menu
This submenu lists the programs in the *Accessories submenu*.

Taskbar
The *taskbar* includes the Start button and shows what programs are running.

FIGURE GS-6
Starting a Program

Menu Bar

The *menu bar* lists the menus available for that application. Select *File*, then *Open* to open and display a particular file, in this case "Horseshoe at Niagara Falls with rainbow.jpg."

Minimize Button, Maximize/Restore Button, Close Button

– Click the Minimize button to shrink the active window to a button in the taskbar.

▢ or ▣ Click the Maximize/Restore button to fill the screen or restore the window to its previous size.

✗ Click the Close button to close (exit) the program.

Title Bar

The title bar at the top of each window shows the name of the program and current document.

Pop-Out Menu

Choosing a menu option with an arrow () displays a pop-out menu.

Pull-Down Menu

A menu bar selection is pulled down.

Toolbar

Most applications have one or more toolbars that contain a group of rectangular graphics, each of which represents a frequently used menu option or command. Generally, toolbars display related user options (for example, formatting or database) and can be displayed horizontally or vertically (shown here) on the perimeter of the work area, or it can float over the work area.

Application Window

Applications, such as Paint, are run in rectangular application windows.

DATA AND FILE MANAGEMENT

Data are the fuel for all information technology applications. Understanding these fundamental data and file management concepts will enable you to grasp the critical relationship between data, information, and computers. Data (the plural of datum) are just raw facts. Data are all around us. Every day we generate an enormous amount of data. Information is data that have been collected and processed into a meaningful form. Simply, information is the meaning we give to accumulated facts (data).

HIERARCHY OF DATA ORGANIZATION

Many types of software, including popular *spreadsheet* (shown here) and database software, let you assemble random pieces of data in a structured and useful manner. The principles of data management, which are new to most people taking this course, include the terms and concepts associated with the *hierarchy of data organization*. Each succeeding level in the hierarchy is the result of combining the elements of the preceding level (see Figure GS-7).

Records

A *record* is a description of an event (for example, a sale, a hotel reservation), an item (for example, a part or product), a person (for example, an employee or customer), and so on. Related fields describing an event or an item are logically grouped to form a record. These records contain fields that might be found in a typical employee record, as well as their values for Alvin Adams and other employees.

Bits and characters

In a computer system, a *character* (A, B, C, 1, 2, and so on) is represented by a group of *bits* (1s and 0s) that are configured according to an *encoding system*, such as *ASCII*. The combination of bits used to represent a character is called a byte. In ASCII, a C is represented inside a computer as 01000011, and a 5 is represented as 00110101. Audio, video, graphics, and all other types of data and information are stored as combinations of bits, as well.

0,1

Bits are configured to represent

11000001 = A

Characters (bytes) are combined to form

Alvin Adams

Fields are logically grouped to form

Alvin Adams, 820 Tioga Ave., NYC, etc.

Records containing related data elements are termed

Files are reorganized and logically integrated to achieve a

Alvin Adams, etc.; Mary Birch, etc.; ...Zak Zakery, etc.

Database

FIGURE GS-7
Levels in the Data Hierarchy

Employee master; Inventory master; Customer master; Supplier master, etc.

The database

The *database* is the integrated data resource for an *information system*. In essence, a database is a collection of files that are in some way logically related to one another. That is, one file might contain logical links that identify one or more files containing related information.

WORKING WITH FILES

In personal computing, the spreadsheet is the most popular software tool for organizing, storing, and manipulating data. After you enter data into this "Employee Master" Excel spreadsheet file, the file can be easily sorted, searched, and revised (fields edited, records added and deleted, and so on), copied, sent via the Internet, and manipulated to produce information and graphs. In the example shown in Figure GS-8, records are sorted by last name. This spreadsheet could just as easily be sorted by ID, zip code, job classification, or any other field (in either ascending or descending order). Note that the "Marital Status" field is *coded* for ease of data entry and to save storage space.

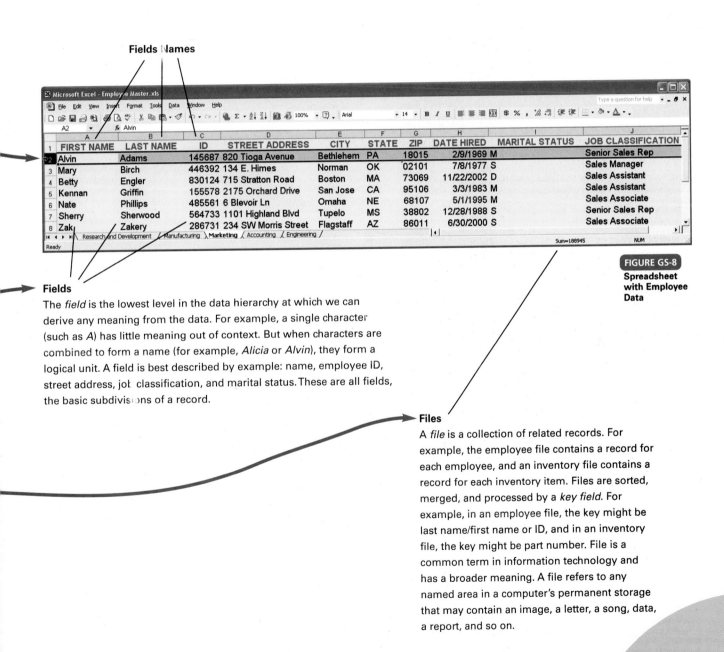

Fields Names

FIGURE GS-8

Spreadsheet with Employee Data

Fields

The *field* is the lowest level in the data hierarchy at which we can derive any meaning from the data. For example, a single character (such as *A*) has little meaning out of context. But when characters are combined to form a name (for example, *Alicia* or *Alvin*), they form a logical unit. A field is best described by example: name, employee ID, street address, job classification, and marital status. These are all fields, the basic subdivisions of a record.

Files

A *file* is a collection of related records. For example, the employee file contains a record for each employee, and an inventory file contains a record for each inventory item. Files are sorted, merged, and processed by a *key field*. For example, in an employee file, the key might be last name/first name or ID, and in an inventory file, the key might be part number. File is a common term in information technology and has a broader meaning. A file refers to any named area in a computer's permanent storage that may contain an image, a letter, a song, data, a report, and so on.

GOING ONLINE

Not too many years ago, computers were simply number crunchers, printing payroll checks and processing accounts receivable. Today, they are that and much more, including tools for communication. Most existing computers are linked to a network of computers, often within an organization or a department, that share hardware/software resources and information. Home networks are becoming increasingly popular. Computer networks can be linked to one another, enabling the interchange of information between people in different companies or on different continents. Most personal computers are linked to a network and/or have ready access to the ultimate network, the Internet, which links millions of computers and networks and billions of people in every country in the world.

NETWORKS

A *local area network* (*LAN*) connects personal computers and other types of terminals and input/output devices in a suite of offices, a college laboratory, or a building (see Figure GS-9). Networks can be as small as a home network or large as an enterprise network serving thousands of knowledge workers. No two networks are the same.

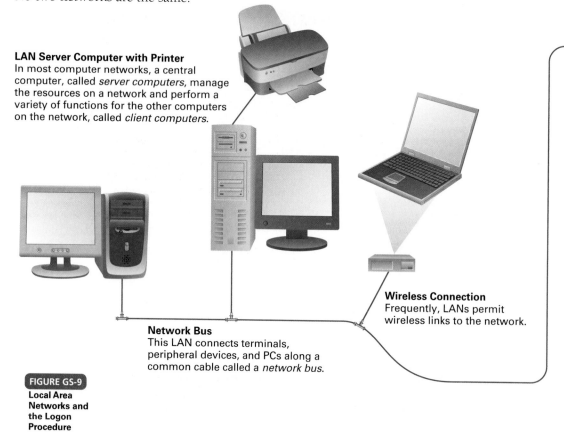

LAN Server Computer with Printer
In most computer networks, a central computer, called *server computers*, manage the resources on a network and perform a variety of functions for the other computers on the network, called *client computers*.

Wireless Connection
Frequently, LANs permit wireless links to the network.

Network Bus
This LAN connects terminals, peripheral devices, and PCs along a common cable called a *network bus*.

FIGURE GS-9
Local Area Networks and the Logon Procedure

Wiring Hub

Multiple PCs can be connected
to a hub, which is connected
to the network bus.

Client Computers

The server computers perform a variety
of functions for the other computers on
the network, called client computers.

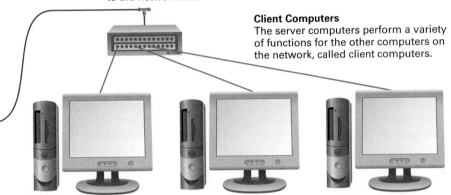

Logon Procedure

Before you can "go online" and use network resources you must logon to the network. You
do this by opening the software that establishes the link to the Internet (see below) and
entering a *user ID* and *password*. the user ID (also called *user name*) is your electronic
identifier and may be known by your friends and colleagues. The password, however, is
yours alone to protect and use. The user ID identifies you for personal communications,
such as e-mail, and it identifies you to the server computer. The password lets you gain
access to the network and it's resources. Typically, the user ID is your name in a standard
format, often the first name or it's first initial in combination with the last name (jansmith,
jan_smith, jsmith, smithj). The password is any combination of contiguous characters
(gowildcats, fyhi2001), which may or may not be case sensitive. To help protect the
confidentiality of your password, an asterisk (*) is displayed for each character entered. It's
a good idea to change your password frequently

"Connect" Dialog Box

In Windows, use the "Connect" dialog
box to logon to an Internet service
provider (ISP) via a dialup connection.
Enter user name (user ID) and
password. You will need an ISP profile
(ArkansasUSA in the example) with
connection settings, including the
telephone number.

THE INTERNET AND INTERNET ACCESS

The Internet is a worldwide collection of interconnected networks. The Net actually comprises millions of independent networks at academic institutions, military installations, government agencies, commercial enterprises, Internet support companies, and just about every other type of organization.

Cyberspace is an amazing place. When you go online, you have access to literally billions of pages of information, from research materials to classic literature to reference material for almost anything to images of planets, people, and places. You can get a weather forecast for any place in the world, get real-time stock quotations, and listen to live radio broadcasts from Japan, Australia, Mexico, and most other countries. You can communicate directly with people from every country in the world via many communication applications, including e-mail, instant messaging, and videophone. You can tap the advice of experts in finance, health care, law, and many other fields. You will have no trouble finding a pick-up Internet-based video game. You can view live video broadcasts of important events. You can view the draws of any juniors tennis tournament, determine the progress of your UPS package, or read the news shortly after it happens. You can travel to almost anywhere via images, video, and inviting descriptions. Also, the Internet is the biggest market in the world, where you can buy and sell almost anything.

Typically, people connect to the Internet via a commercial information service, an ISP, or a local area network (LAN) with Internet access (see Figure GS-10).

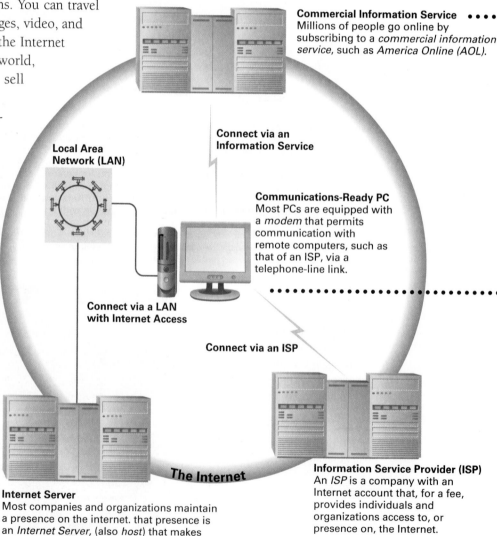

Commercial Information Service
Millions of people go online by subscribing to a *commercial information service*, such as *America Online (AOL)*.

Connect via an Information Service

Local Area Network (LAN)

Communications-Ready PC
Most PCs are equipped with a *modem* that permits communication with remote computers, such as that of an ISP, via a telephone-line link.

Connect via a LAN with Internet Access

Connect via an ISP

The Internet

FIGURE GS-10
Getting on the Internet

Internet Server
Most companies and organizations maintain a presence on the internet. that presence is an *Internet Server*, (also *host*) that makes content available over the internet.

Information Service Provider (ISP)
An *ISP* is a company with an Internet account that, for a fee, provides individuals and organizations access to, or presence on, the Internet.

AMERICA ONLINE (AOL)

AOL and other commercial information services offer a wide range of online services via their own user interface software (AOL 8.0 shown here) over their proprietary network. Plus, AOL offers access to the worldwide Internet. When you *sign on* to AOL, you enter a *screen name*, the AOL user ID, and your *password*. AOL offers 20 "channels" (topic areas), such as music, travel, and news, plus myriad services such as real-time stock quotes.

Channel	Capacity	
Regular telephone lines	POTS 56K bps	DSL 256 K bps to 9 M bps downstream (receiving information) 256 K bps to 1.5 M bps upstream (sending information)
Cable modem (Over Cable TV lines)	400 K bps to 10 M bps	
Digital Satellite (Requires satellite dish)	400 k bps to 1.5 M bps downstream 56 k bps to 1.5 M bps upstream	

Communications Channel

A variety of communications channels carries digital signals between computers. The *channel capacity* (or *bandwidth*) is the number of bits (on/off electrical signals) a channel can transmit per second. Most people link to the Internet via *plain old telephone service* (POTS) at a maximum speed of 56 K bps (thousands of bits per second). This table shows the higher speed connections, some measured in M bps (millions of bps), being made available at reasonable prices. ISPs can tell you which channels are available in your city. Satellite service is available throughout the lower 48 states in the United States.

Internet Browser

You tap the resources of the Internet via Internet browser software, such as *Netscape* (shown here) or *Internet Explorer*. This National Park Service Web site provides information for people planning a visit to the Mount Rushmore National Memorial, including a map of the park (inset).

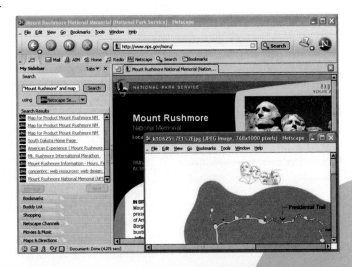

COMMON INTERNET APPLICATIONS

The Internet has many applications. Three of the most popular applications are browsing and searching the World Wide Web using an *Internet browser* and communicating with others via *e-mail* and *instant messaging*.

Internet Browser

Internet browsers let you retrieve and view the Internet's ever-growing resources as well as interact with Internet server computers. A browser runs on your PC and works with another program on an Internet server computer to let you "surf the Internet" (see Figure GS-11).

The Menu Bar

The menu bar at the top of the user command interface is used to select file options (print, save, and so on), to select edit options (including copy, cut, and paste), and to set and change a variety of options.

The Toolbar

Most of your interaction is with the buttons in the toolbar and the hyperlinks in the Web pages. These navigation buttons are common to browsers:

- **Back.** Go to the last site visited.
- **Forward.** Go forward to the next site in the string of sites you have viewed.
- **Stop.** Stop the transfer of information.
- **Refresh.** Reload the current page from the server.
- **Home.** Go to your default home page, usually your college or company.
- **Search.** Go to your default search site, usually a major portal.
- **Favorites/bookmarks.** A list of sites you visit frequently.

Hyperlinks

Hyperlinks in a form of hypertext (a colored, underlined word or phrase), hot images, or hot icons, permit navigation between Web pages on the Internet. Click on a hyperlink to jump (link) to another place in the same page or to another Web site. The cursor changes to a pointing hand when positioned over a hyperlink.

Internet Portal

Often, Internet sessions begin at an Internet portal, such as Yahoo! (shown here). A *portal* is one of millions of Internet destinations, called a *Web site*. A portal offers a broad array of information and services, including a *menu tree* of categories and a *search engine* that lets you do keyword searches for specific information on the Internet.

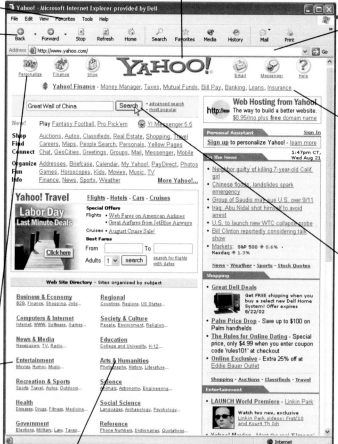

FIGURE GS-11
Using a Browser

Browsing the Net

Poking around the Internet with no particular destination in mind is called browsing. An Internet portal with its menu tree of categories (see example) is always a good place to start. You may navigate through several levels of categories before reaching the pages you want. For example, if you select "Arts & Humanities," Yahoo! lists 26 categories from which to choose (in alphabetical order). Selecting "Humanities" under "Arts & Humanities" presents 17 subcategories and links to several general humanities sites. Selecting "Literature" gives you another set of subcategories and appropriate links, including "Electronic Literature." Drilling down into Electronic Literature presents you with numerous links to sites that contain Mark Twain's "Adventures of Huckleberry Finn" (with illustrations) and thousands of other online books.

Search Results

The typical search results in a list of hyperlinks to Web sites that meet your search criteria ("Great Wall of China"). If you don't get results, try other search criteria and/or another search engine (Google, Lycos, HotBot, Ask Jeeves, MSN, and so on).

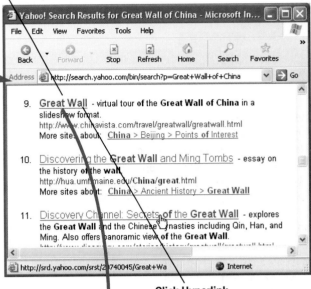

URL Bar

The current *URL* is displayed is this box. The URL is the Internet equivalent of an address. We use browsers to go to and view content at a particular address on the Internet. The home page address for Yahoo! (shown here) is

http://www.yahoo.com/

and for the White House the home page address is

http://www.whitehouse.gov/.

Each Web server's address begins with *http://* and is followed by a unique *domain name*, usually the name of the organization sponsoring the Internet server. The domain name is usually prefaced by www to designate a *World Wide Web* server. What follows the domain name is a *folder* or *path* containing the resources for a particular page. The White House tours URL is

http://www.whitehouse.gov/WH/Tours/visitors_center.html.

Key in an address and press Enter to go to a different Web site.

Web Site Pages

Information on the Internet's *World Wide Web* (the Web) is viewed in *pages*. The Web is the Internet's main application for on-demand distribution of information. The first page you will normally view is the site's *home page*.

Searching the Net

The Internet has billions of pages. There are two basic approaches to finding something on the Internet: *searching* and *browsing*. Each major portal has a *search engine* to help you find the information or service you need. Enter one or more keywords that describes what you want, such as "Great Wall of China" in the example.

Click Hyperlink

Click on one or more of the resulting hyperlinks to go to a site (Discovery Channel, in the example).

E-Mail

E-mail lets you send electronic mail to and receive it from anyone with an Internet e-mail address (see Figure GS-12). This is done with e-mail client software, such as Microsoft Outlook (shown here), or with Web-based e-mail via a browser.

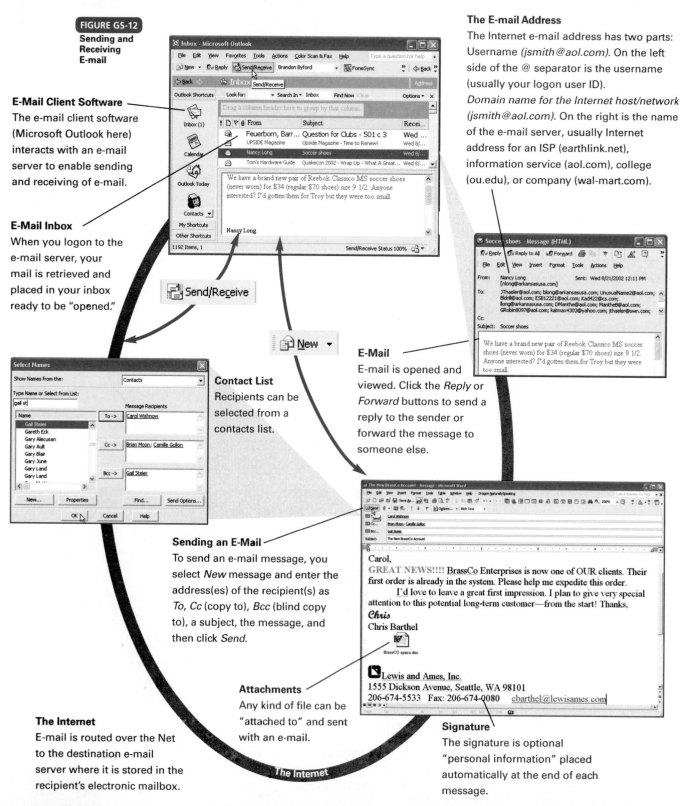

FIGURE GS-12
Sending and Receiving E-mail

E-Mail Client Software
The e-mail client software (Microsoft Outlook here) interacts with an e-mail server to enable sending and receiving of e-mail.

E-Mail Inbox
When you logon to the e-mail server, your mail is retrieved and placed in your inbox ready to be "opened."

The E-mail Address
The Internet e-mail address has two parts: Username (*jsmith@aol.com*). On the left side of the @ separator is the username (usually your logon user ID). *Domain name for the Internet host/network (jsmith@aol.com)*. On the right is the name of the e-mail server, usually Internet address for an ISP (earthlink.net), information service (aol.com), college (ou.edu), or company (wal-mart.com).

Contact List
Recipients can be selected from a contacts list.

E-Mail
E-mail is opened and viewed. Click the *Reply* or *Forward* buttons to send a reply to the sender or forward the message to someone else.

Sending an E-Mail
To send an e-mail message, you select *New* message and enter the address(es) of the recipient(s) as *To*, *Cc* (copy to), *Bcc* (blind copy to), a subject, the message, and then click *Send*.

Attachments
Any kind of file can be "attached to" and sent with an e-mail.

The Internet
E-mail is routed over the Net to the destination e-mail server where it is stored in the recipient's electronic mailbox.

Signature
The signature is optional "personal information" placed automatically at the end of each message.

Instant Messaging

Both instant messaging (IM) and e-mail enable personal communication via the Internet but they have significant differences. Instant messaging allows messages to be sent and displayed in real-time (instantly), where e-mail is stored until retrieved by the recipient. Instant messaging allows text-based conversations with several friends, plus you can talk to them or have video conversations. IM is used extensively in the business world, as well, because workers are informed immediately when their colleagues go online and are available.

The Windows Messenger client software (shown in Figure GS-13) works with the .NET Messenger Service to deliver a variety of services, including file sharing, setting up online meetings or Internet games, sending text messages to cell phones, viewing programs simultaneously, and doing whiteboarding. To participate in instant messaging, you must sign up with one of the instant messaging services and install its client software. Yahoo! and AOL offer popular messaging services. Instant messaging conversations can be between people on opposite ends of the world or between a father at the office and his son at home (illustrated here).

Sign In/Sign Out
Choose Sign In (in the File menu) to inform others who have you on their contact list that you are online. Choose Sign Out to end a session.

Online/Not Online
This area shows which of your contacts are online and which are not. Click on a contact to send a request to begin a conversation. A Windows Wizard guides you through the steps for adding contacts to your list.

Status
The status area indicates whether you are online (signed in) or offline (signed out).

Video Conversation
If your system is configured with a video camera, the person on the other end of the conversation can view the video in real-time. The picture-in-picture option lets you see both the send and receive images. Click start/stop talking or start/stop camera to add/end audio and/or video in the conversation.

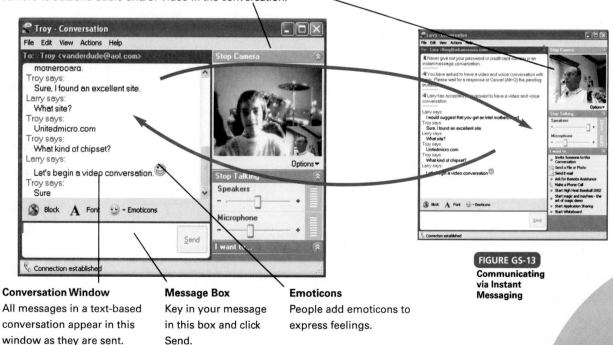

FIGURE GS-13
Communicating via Instant Messaging

Conversation Window
All messages in a text-based conversation appear in this window as they are sent.

Message Box
Key in your message in this box and click Send.

Emoticons
People add emoticons to express feelings.

The four most popular applications of personal computing are word processing, gaming, Internet-based personal communications (e-mail and instant messaging), and Internet browsers. Word processing and gaming are the focus of this section.

Save Document
If you wish to work with the document later, you will need to save it to disk storage for later recall (File, Save).

OPEN DOCUMENT
To recall a document from disk storage, click *File*, *Open*, and then go to the desired folder.

Format Document
Click Format to pull down a menu with a variety of formatting options, including Font (typeface, size, and attribute) and Paragraph presentation.

Text Cursor
Move the text cursor with the mouse and then click to reposition the blinking text entry cursor.

Insert Images
You can insert images (*Insert*, *Picture*, *Clip Art*, or *From File*), such as the barn, and then resize and/or reposition them anywhere within the document.

Help
Click on *Help* to learn more about word processing and its features.

The Document
One or more word processing documents can be opened and displayed (at least, in part) in the work area.

Entering Text
The newsletter shown here demonstrates many of word processing's features (columns, integration of images, text boxes, footers, varying style, size, and color of fonts, and so on). However, to create a simple document, you simply open a new document (*File, New* in the main menu) and begin entering text from the keyboard at the text cursor position.

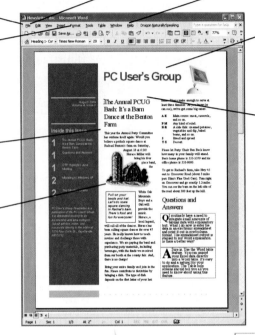

WORD PROCESSING

Word processing software, such as Microsoft Word (shown in Figure GS-14), lets you create, edit (revise), and format documents, which can be printed, displayed, posted to the Internet as Web pages, e-mailed as Microsoft Word attachments, faxed, and so on. The term document is a generic term that refers to whatever is currently displayed in a software package's extended work area (the area in a window below the title bar or toolbar and all that can be viewed by scrolling vertically and horizontally in the same work area). Once you create a document, you give it a name and save it to disk storage as a file, for example, "Newsletter.doc" (see the document name in the title bar).

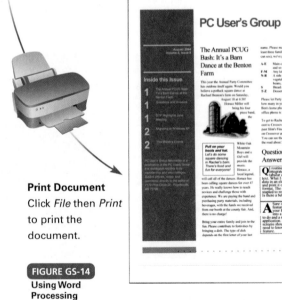

Print Document
Click *File* then *Print* to print the document.

FIGURE GS-14
Using Word Processing

GAMING CATEGORIES

Gaming is so pervasive in personal computing that you should be aware of the scope and types of games. Computer games are rated by the Entertainment Software Rating Board and given one of six ratings, ranging from "early childhood" to "adults only." Games can be placed in the nine categories and all but the puzzle category are shown in Figure GS-15.

Action/Adventure

A large group of games place players in a fantasy world such as in *Jedi Knight II: Jedi Outcast* from Lucas Arts. In this genre, players run, leap, or climb to find entryways that let them progress to the next level. Along the way, they unlock mysteries so they can continue their journey and overcome evil people to reach an objective.

Strategy

In strategy games, such as *Warcraft III-Reign of Chaos* from Blizzard, players become leaders who must collect and use their resources wisely to overcome their opponent, sometimes alien invaders.

RPG (Role Playing Game)

In RPG games, players take on a specific role, where they are at the epicenter of a fantasy that may involve war, betrayal, and faith, such as in *Neverwinter Nights* from BioWare. In their journey, players attain new skills and abilities by winning battles.

Edutainment

These games combine gaming and learning. In their quest to find the international sleuth, Carmen Sandiego, players learn about history, geography, and other topics.

Racing

In racing games, such as *NASCAR 4* by Sierra, players "drive" cars, motorcycles, spaceships, jet skis, snowmobiles, and so on to win races in a variety of venues.

Sports and Recreation

In this category of games, players play video versions of almost any type of sport or recreational game, from hockey (*NHL 2001* from EA Sports shown here) and baseball to darts and fishing. Players become batters, quarterbacks, and so on and swing the bat or throw the ball.

Simulation

In simulation games, the game scenario allows players to operate in a simulated environment, such as piloting an airplane, or be a part of a life-like situation, such as living in and working in a simulated city.

Traditional

Many traditional board, card, and casino-type games are now available in video-game formats. Shown here is Bridge, one of many card games in *Hoyle Card Games* from Sierra.

Chapter 1

Learning Objectives

Once you have read and studied this chapter, you will have learned:

- How information technology **influences our** society and you at work, at home, **and at play** (Section 1-1).

- What it means to achieve IT competency **and** become an active participant in **our information** society (Section 1-2).

- How local and worldwide **computer networks** impact businesses and society **(Section 1-3).**

- Essential hardware, software, **and computer** system terminology that will **enable you to begin** your information technology **learning adventure** with confidence (Section 1-4).

- The relative size, scope, uses, **and variety of** available computer systems **(Section 1-5).**

- The fundamental components **and capabilities** of an IT system (Section 1-6).

- A variety of enterprise **computing and personal** computing applications (Section 1-7).

THE TECHNOLOGY REVOLUTION

Why this chapter is important to you

Welcome! To the computer revolution, that is. We'll be using this "Why This Chapter is Important to You" space to make this book very personal—to show you why studying computers, information technology, and personal computing is important to you, now and in the future. We're all members of a rapidly maturing information society. In this dynamic new society, people at home and in schools, institutions, and businesses are engaged in an ever-growing partnership with computers and information technology, called *IT*. Whether we like it or not, for good or bad, computers and technology are part of just about everything we do, during both work and play. And the fact is, computers will play an even greater role in our lives next month and in years to come.

In the 1960s, mainstreamers considered people who had anything to do with computers, especially the techies who actually touched them, to be different, even a little weird. Through the 1970s, computer-illiterate people led happy and productive lives, not knowing the difference between a system bug and a byte. Well, those days are gone.

Today we're all part of an exploding information society—you, us, and the rest of the world. Computer-knowledgeable people are considered mainstream, even cool in some circles. The rest are on the outside looking in. By reading this book and taking this course, you're telling your family, friends, and, perhaps, your colleagues at work that you want to participate—to be an insider.

It's amazing how achieving information technology competency can help you keep in touch, help you learn, help make many of life's little chores easier and more fun, and help you earn more money. Upon successful completion of this course, you will be information technology competent. In most fields, this competency is considered critical to *getting* and *keeping* a good job. Your adventure into this amazing world of technology begins right here. Have fun!

WHY THIS SECTION
IS IMPORTANT
TO YOU

We now live in an information society where most adults are considered knowledge workers. Your contribution to society is only enhanced when you appreciate the scope and influence that information technology has on our society.

1-1 Our Information Society

Where will you be and what will you be doing in the year 2010? This is a tough question even for IT futurists, who are reluctant to speculate more than a year or so into the future. Things are changing too quickly. A stream of exciting new innovations in **information technology** (**IT**) continues to change what we do and how we think. We use the term *IT* to refer to the integration of computing technology and information processing.

Most of us are doing what we can to adapt to this new **information society** where **knowledge workers** channel their energies to provide a wealth of computer-based information services. A knowledge worker's job function revolves around the use, manipulation, and broadcasting of information. Your knowledge of computers will help you cope with and understand today's technology so you can take your place in the information society—at work, in the home, and during your leisure time.

THE TECHNOLOGY REVOLUTION: TODAY

In an information society, the focus of commerce becomes the generation and distribution of information. This technological revolution is changing our way of life: the way we live, work, and play. The cornerstone of this revolution, the *computer,* is transforming the way we communicate, do business, and learn.

Personal computers, or **PCs**, offer a vast array of *enabling technologies* that help us do all kinds of things, many of which you may never have imagined or dreamed possible (see Figure 1-1).

FIGURE 1–1

PORTABLE SHOPPING SYSTEM
Information technology is changing our lives in many ways. For example, many retail establishments give customers access to a Portable Shopping System that lets shoppers save time by scanning the bar codes of goods as they shop rather than queuing at checkouts. Before starting purchases, customers take a hand-held bar code scanner out of a dispenser rack. The customer scans goods as they are placed in the basket, and the corresponding price appears on the portable scanner's screen. The system gives the customer a running total of the amount of the purchase. After shopping, the customer puts the scanner in the rack and gets a bar-coded ticket detailing the items purchased. This ticket is scanned at the check out. Customers pay as usual, receive their receipt, and are on their way.

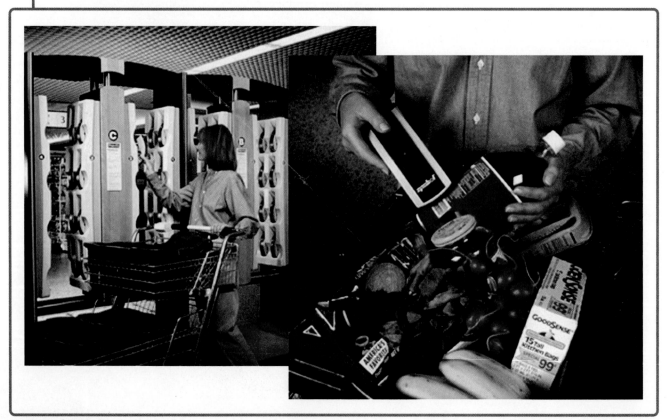

Courtesy of Symbol Technologies, Inc.

At Work

Millions of people can be "at work" wherever they are as long as they have their portable personal computers—at a client's office, in an airplane, or at home (see Figure 1-2). The *mobile worker's* personal computer provides electronic links to a vast array of information and to clients and corporate colleagues, across town or across the country. It even has maps that pinpoint your location to help you navigate the streets of the world.

Tasks that used to take hours, even days, now can be completed in minutes with the aid of IT. Rather than dictating to a machine for transcription by a secretary, managers can simply dictate messages *directly* to their computers. The managers can then send them electronically to their colleagues in a fraction of a second. Marketing reps can prepare convincing presentations, complete with sound, video, and visual effects, in a tenth the time it took a generation ago. Attorneys who used to spend days combing through legal documentation in preparation for trial now use keyword searches to identify applicable books, documents, and cases in a matter of minutes. The managers' messages are timelier, the marketing reps' presentations are more effective, and attorneys can be confident that they haven't missed anything.

At Home

The typical home has at least one personal computer and often several. Millions of people now depend on their PCs to help them with all kinds of tasks: communicating with relatives, preparing the annual Christmas newsletter, doing homework, managing the family investment portfolio, sending greeting cards, and much, much more. The home PC is a family's link to the **Internet,** a worldwide network of computers, with its marvelous resources and applications. People link to the Internet to learn which bank offers the best mortgage rate, to send their congressperson a message, to order tickets to the theater, to learn about the Renaissance period, to visit the virtual Smithsonian Museum, to get a good deal on a new car, to shop for new shoes, to order a pizza, or simply to browse the day away.

Already, a third of the population is looking to the Internet first for their news. The British have introduced *Ananova,* a very likable virtual newscaster, who reads the news as any human newscaster

---

FIGURE 1–2   **TECHNOLOGY IN OUR JOBS**
Twenty-five years ago, college curricula in architecture, accounting, nursing, and, even, engineering included relatively little study in the area of computers and information technology. Today, knowledge workers in the office and on the shop floor rely on information technology for everything from product inspection to cost analysis. The computer has dramatically changed the way people in hundreds of professions do their jobs.

Courtesy of Sun Microsystems, Inc.

would, except she does so in English, French, German, or Italian—your choice. She is a bit unusual having the characteristics of an animated character, green tinted hair, and big eyes. Ananov's voice is synthesized speech created from scanning electronic text for the various stories she "reads."

A home may not only have several PCs, but it may have a variety of special-function computers. Many of these can be programmed by you to perform specific tasks, such as recording a movie on a VCR. We have small computers, called **microprocessors,** in VCRs, automobiles, air-conditioning systems, dishwashers, telephone answering systems, and in many more devices and appliances, including pet food dispensing devices. Computers are all around us—all the time.

At Play

The computer and information technology have had a dramatic impact on our leisure activities. Sure, we still have fun, as we always have, but it's different now. Increasingly, we communicate with our friends and relatives via the Internet through **electronic mail** (**e-mail**) and **instant messaging** (**IM**). Both electronic mail and instant messaging (see "Getting Started" for an overview) allow us to send and receive information (text, audio, and video) via computer-to-computer hookups. Millions of people spend hours "chatting" with other people from around the globe on just about any subject from Elvis sightings to romance, often people they don't know and may never hear from again. Chat is an Internet application that allows you to enter a virtual chat room and converse in real time (at the present) with people who are linked to the Internet. You can chat by keying in and/or speaking what you want to say.

Gaming is another major application of computers (see "Getting Started" for an overview). The software enables virtual worlds to be created within computers where gamers engage in mortal combat, immerse themselves in a virtual city, or work through a labyrinth for clues to save the world. Gamers can compete alone, with others on the same computer, or with others around the world. A gamer can play solitaire or play chess with a grand master in Russia.

Today's personal computers have sophisticated audiovisual systems that allow you to listen to CDs or play the latest hit song retrieved from the Internet. If listening to the music isn't enough, you can view the music video, as well. People routinely watch DVD movies on their PCs.

Sports fanatics have found a home on the Internet. The Internet is filled with information and statistics on literally thousands of teams from junior soccer to major league baseball. Avid fans enjoy viewing real-time statistics and analysis on their PC while watching the game on television. The really serious fan may be involved in a running chat session before, during, and after the game. No longer is the true fan cut off from the game because it's not televised or played on local radio stations. Most major radio stations are broadcasting over the Internet as well as the airwaves, making their signal available worldwide. Generally, if an important game is on the radio, you can listen to it from wherever you are.

FIGURE 1–3 The Internet Appliance
The Compaq iPAQ Home Internet Appliance is representative of the many products being developed for the technology revolution. The iPAQ is especially designed to let you surf the Internet. You can use it to do online shopping, send/receive electronic mail (e-mail), perform banking transactions, or make a telephone call. Most Internet appliances are designed to run right out of the box. Simply plug in the power and telephone cord and you are ready to communicate.

THE TECHNOLOGY REVOLUTION: TOMORROW

Tomorrow, the next wave of enabling technologies will continue to cause radical changes in our lives (see Figure 1-3). For example, if you're in the market for a new home, you will be able to "visit" any home for sale in the country from the comfort of your own home or office via computer. All you will need to do is tell the computer what city to look in and then enter your search criteria (price range, house style, and so on). The electronic realtor will then list those houses that meet your criteria, provide you with detailed information on the house and surrounding area, and then offer to take you on a tour of the house—inside and out. After the virtual tour, you will be able to "drive" through the neighborhood, looking left and right as you would in your automobile. Such systems may seem a bit futuristic, but much of the available real estate in the United States can be viewed on your computer. Systems that permit neighborhood drive-throughs are under active development!

Each day new applications, such as a national multilist for real estate, are being created. Already, votes are being cast online. How long will it be before our PC is the voting booth? Doctors are beginning to make house calls via telemedicine. We continue to march toward a cashless society. It may be inevitable that the stock markets of the world will be open continuously, enabling individuals to buy and sell securities directly. The infrastructure that supports these applications is sometimes called the **information superhighway**. It encompasses a network of electronic links that eventually will connect virtually every facet of our society, both public (perhaps the local supermarket) and private (perhaps Aunt Minnie's recipes).

LOOKING BACK A FEW YEARS

To put the emerging information society into perspective, let's flash back a half century and look *briefly* at the evolution of computing (see Figure 1-4).

- A little over 50 years ago, our parents and grandparents built ships, kept financial records, and performed surgery, all without the aid of computers. Indeed, everything they did was without computers. There were no computers!

- In the 1960s, mammoth multimillion-dollar computers processed data for those large companies that could afford them. These computers, the domain of highly specialized technical gurus, remained behind locked doors. In "the old days," business computer systems were designed so a computer professional served as an intermediary between the **user**—someone who uses a computer—and the computer system.

FIGURE 1–4

A WORLD WITHOUT COMPUTERS
The industrial society evolved in a world without computers. The advent of computers and automation has changed and will continue to change the way we do our jobs. In the automobile industry, those assembly-line workers who used to perform repetitive and hazardous jobs now program and maintain industrial robots to do these jobs.

GM Assembly Division, Warren, Michigan
Courtesy of Ford Motor Company

- In the mid-1970s, computers became smaller, less expensive, and more accessible to smaller companies and even individuals. This trend resulted in the introduction of personal computers. During the 1980s, millions of people from all walks of life purchased these miniature miracles. Suddenly, computers were for everyone!

- Today, most Americans have at least one computer at home or work that is more powerful than those that processed data for multinational companies during the 1960s. The widespread availability of computers has prompted an explosion of applications. At the individual level, we can use our PCs to go on an electronic fantasy adventure or hold an electronic reunion with our scattered family. At the corporate level, virtually every business has embraced information technology. Companies in every area of business are using IT to offer better services and gain a competitive advantage.

THIS COURSE: YOUR TICKET TO ADVENTURE

You are about to embark on a journey that will stimulate your imagination, challenge your every resource, from physical dexterity to intellect, and alter your sense of perspective on technology. Learning about computers is more than just education. It's an adventure!

Gaining a solid understanding of information technology, computers, and personal computing is just the beginning—your IT adventure lasts a lifetime. Information technology is changing every minute of the day. Every year, hundreds of new IT-related buzzwords, concepts, applications, and computing devices will confront you. Fortunately, you will have established a base of IT knowledge (information technology competency) upon which you can build and continue your learning adventure.

SECTION SELF-CHECK

1-1.1 The term used to describe the integration of computing technology and information processing is: (a) information technology, (b) information handling, (c) software, or (d) data tech.

1-1.2 A person whose job revolves around the use, manipulation, and dissemination of information is called: (a) an office wunderkind, (b) a knowledge worker, (c) a data expert, or (d) an info being.

1-1.3 Mail sent electronically is called: (a) snail mail, (b) quick mail, (c) e-mail, or (d) e-news.

WHY THIS SECTION IS IMPORTANT TO YOU

In our information society, information technology (IT) competency is now considered a job-critical skill. This section points you in the right direction to help you with your first step toward IT competency.

THE CRYSTAL BALL:
One Computer Per House Home networking in the multi-PC home is becoming increasingly common. Will PCs proliferate throughout the house like telephones and TVs? Probably not–it would be too expensive to maintain the hardware and software for this many PCs. Within the near future, the typical household will have a single multiprocessor computer system that serves a variety of networked workstations throughout the home and, possibly, controls some processes, such as heating/cooling and lighting. Each workstation will be configured to fit its applications and/or users. For example, the workstation in the bedroom might include a large wall-mounted monitor for on-demand movie/TV viewing and the kitchen might have a touch-screen monitor.

1-2   Rx for Cyberphobia: Information Technology Competency

Not too long ago, people who pursued careers in almost any facet of business, education, or government were content to leave computers to computer professionals. Today these people are knowledge workers and computers are an integral part of what they do. In less than a generation, **information technology competency** (**IT competency**) has emerged in virtually any career from a *nice-to-have skill* to a *job-critical skill*.

WHAT IS INFORMATION TECHNOLOGY COMPETENCY?

If you're afraid of computers, information technology competency is a sure cure. IT competency will allow you to be an active and effective participant in the emerging information society. You and other IT-competent people will:

● *Feel comfortable using and operating a computer system.*

● *Be able to make the computer work for you.* The IT-competent person can use the computer to solve an endless stream of life's problems, from how to pass away a couple of idle hours to how to increase company revenues.

● *Be able to interact with the computer—that is, generate input to the computer and interpret output from it.* **Input** is data entered to a computer system for processing. **Output** is the presentation of the results of processing (for example, a printed résumé or a tax return).

● *Be comfortable in cyberspace.* Cyberspace is a nonphysical world made possible by a worldwide network of computer systems. Once in cyberspace, you can communicate with one another and literally travel the virtual world, visiting Walt Disney World in Florida, the Louvre Museum in Paris, and a million other interesting places.

● *Understand the impact of computers on society, now and in the future.* Automation is having such a profound impact on society that we must position ourselves to act responsibly to ensure that these changes are in the right direction.

● *Be an intelligent consumer of computers and computer equipment, collectively called* **hardware.** Smart computer shoppers save a lot of money, usually getting what they need, not what someone else says they need.

● *Be an intelligent consumer of software and other nonhardware-related computer products and services.* **Software** refers to a collective set of instructions, called **programs**, which can be interpreted by a computer. The programs cause the computer to perform desired functions, such as flight simulation (a computer game), the generation of business graphics, or word processing.

- *Be conversant in the language of computers and information technology.* In this book, you will learn those terms and phrases that not only are the foundation of computer terminology but also are very much a part of everyday conversation at school, home, and work.

Anyone who has achieved information technology competence is quick to tell you what a difference this IT knowledge has made in his or her life. Often it is the difference between getting a job or a promotion. It may open new lines of communication. It may help you save thousands of dollars each year in your purchases.

Businesses know about the importance of computer competency, too. A common complaint among management is that workers are all falling behind the technology. With only 15% of the workforce considered to be IT-competent, management is looking for ways to increase the competency of workers and therefore the overall productivity of companies. For example, several companies provide personal computers and Internet service to all employees—for their homes. Company management hopes that employees will embrace the technology in their homes and carry that understanding to the workplace.

This book is about building IT competency. Once you have completed this course you will join the ranks of those who have no fear of working, living, and playing in the information society. There is one catch, however, in that your information technology competency is valid only for one point in time. The pursuit of IT competency is a never-ending one because IT is always changing (see Figure 1-5).

FIGURE 1–5 Getting Smaller
The circuitry on this relatively recent network card is now contained in a single chip on the right. The world of electronics is getting smaller. We now carry our computers. Some people wear them around their waist. It's inevitable that even greater power and capability will be contained in a wristwatch-type computer that will listen and speak to us.

Photo courtesy of Hewlett-Packard Company

REASONS TO BECOME IT-COMPETENT

There are many reasons that people opt to become IT-competent. These motivations to learn can be grouped into five broad categories.

- *Personal.* Much of the world's information is now in digital format and made available to those with IT knowledge and access to a PC and the Internet. Whether it is reviewing the London bus routes for vacation planning or studying horticulture via distance learning, people are finding that information technology is enhancing their lives. It can help us pursue our hobbies, like genealogy and gardening, provide us with critical medical information, help us learn more about political candidates, and help us organize our family finances. Generally, people are aware of impressive claims for the potential benefits of IT, and they want to enjoy those benefits, both at home and at work.

- *Workplace.* Each day information technology is becoming an increasingly important part of what we do in the workplace. Strategic use of information technology has emerged as a competitive weapon for those companies whose employees recognize and use the potential of IT. There are relatively few jobs that do not require some level of IT understanding. For example, only a few years ago the retail clerk simply learned how to use the cash register. Now that cash register is a point-of-sale (POS) terminal that links the salesperson to inventory systems, order tracking, and other business systems. Every company has problems. Computers along with their software have emerged as the solution tools of the new century. The greater the percentage of employees that can use these tools, the more effective and profitable the company can be.

- *Education.* Information technology opens new doors for education. Millions of people are now learning everything from agriculture to zoology via self-based, interactive, computer-based courses—both stand-alone and Internet-based. The computer is proving to be an effective teaching tool in enhancing traditional methods in kindergarten through higher education to continuing education for professionals. Many colleges now offer degrees whereby the student never sets foot on a physical college campus. This alternative to traditional education is blending well in the information society because it gives people the flexibility to pursue education at their own pace on their own schedule. However, to be an effective learner in this new era of education, IT competency is required.

- *Societal.* Many of the most prominent public issues being debated revolve around the use and implementation of technology. IT competency is necessary to fully understand the ethical issues being debated, such as a national database, electronic money, computer viruses, privacy of personal information, computer monitoring, **spam** (unsolicited e-mail), censorship on the Internet, biometric identification via scanning at public venues, and so on. It is critical that we be informed so that we better understand the potential risks posed by IT-related changes to our social values, freedoms, and economic interests.

- *Curiosity.* Naturally, there is simple curiosity about how this powerful and pervasive technology works.

THE COMPUTER PROFICIENCY DIGITAL DIVIDE

In the United States an estimated 120 million people are considered knowledge workers because they routinely work with computers. However, the vast majority of these people, over 100 million, would not be considered information technology competent! The fact that these people routinely use computers but are not IT-competent is referred to as the "computer proficiency digital divide." Most people use their PCs for only one or two applications, such as word processing or e-mail, or they are trained to work with a specific system, such as accounting, airline reservations, or inventory management. Many of the latter become quite good at the specialized systems but may find no need or time to learn personal computing applications that would let them help their children with their homework, do research, or scan a child's image for grandmother.

Many people believe themselves to be IT competent because they are personal computing veterans or use computers at work. Some are and some are not, mostly because their realm of exposure to IT is limited. Here is a simple test you can use to assess your level of IT competence. Can you describe five critical IT ethics issues facing our information society? Which port is faster, the USB or the 1394? Why is it necessary to run a disk defragmenter? What type of wiring is used in a typical home network? Name three top-level domain Ids other than .com and .edu. In cybertalk, BRB means what? What do TIF, PNG, and JPG files have in common? Describe five time- and/or money-saving personal computing applications for the home other than gaming, word processing, and Internet-based applications. Why would you filter information in an enterprise information system? How might an intelligent agent make your life a little easier? Given your circumstances, which broadband solution would be best for you—DSL, cable, or satellite? These are just a few of the hundreds of points of knowledge that come with IT competency. If you fell short on a few of these, don't worry, because IT competency is a clear objective of this book and this course.

1-2.1	To be IT-competent, you must be able to write computer programs. (T/F)
1-2.2	Generally, what is the presentation of the results of processing called: (a) output, (b) printout, (c) outcome, or (d) download?
1-2.3	Hardware refers collectively to computers and computer equipment. (T/F)

1-3   The Net Connection

Through the 1980s, computers were known for their ability to bring data together to produce information. Today, computers also bring people together, from all over the world, opening the door for improved communication and cooperation.

OUR GLOBAL VILLAGE

In 1967 Marshall McLuhan said, "The new electronic interdependence recreates the world in the image of a global village." His insightful declaration is now clearly a matter of fact. At present, we live in a *global village* in which computers and people are linked within companies and between countries (see Figure 1-6). Over 80% of all classrooms and 98% of all libraries in United States are linked to the Internet and, therefore, the world. To put this in perspective, consider that it took decades for this kind of acceptance for the telephone.

The global village is an outgrowth of the **computer network.** Most existing computers are linked electronically to a network of one or more computers to share hardware/software resources and information. When we tap into a network of computers, we can hold electronic meetings with widely dispersed colleagues, retrieve information from the corporate database, and even work simultaneously on the same design project.

On a more global scale, computer networks enable worldwide airline reservation data to be entered in the Bahamas and American insurance claims to be processed in Ireland. People in Hong Kong, Los Angeles, and Berlin can trade securities simultaneously on the New York Stock Exchange and other exchanges around the world. Computer networks can coordinate the purchases of Korean electronics, American steel, and Indonesian glass to make cars in Japan, and can then be used to track sales of those cars worldwide. Lotteries are no longer confined to a state, or even the nation. Internet-based lotteries draw players from the entire world, paying huge pots to the winners. We can track every point in every match at the U.S. Open Tennis Tournament as they are played.

Thanks to computer networks, we are all part of a global economy, in which businesses find partners, customers, suppliers, and competitors around the world. The advent of this global economy is

FIGURE 1–6

THE GLOBAL VILLAGE
Computer-based communication is turning the world into a global village. We can communicate electronically with people on the other side of the world as easily as we might have a conversation with a neighbor.

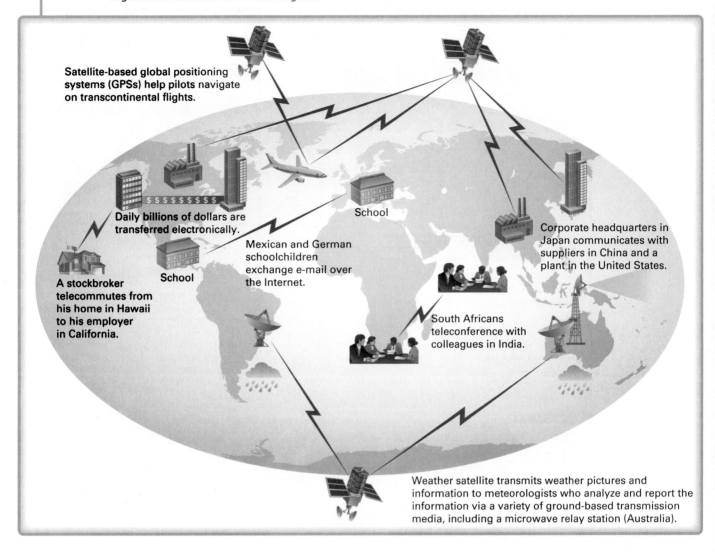

Satellite-based global positioning systems (GPSs) help pilots navigate on transcontinental flights.

Daily billions of dollars are transferred electronically.

School

Mexican and German schoolchildren exchange e-mail over the Internet.

A stockbroker telecommutes from his home in Hawaii to his employer in California.

School

Corporate headquarters in Japan communicates with suppliers in China and a plant in the United States.

South Africans teleconference with colleagues in India.

Weather satellite transmits weather pictures and information to meteorologists who analyze and report the information via a variety of ground-based transmission media, including a microwave relay station (Australia).

changing society across the board, often in subtle ways. For example, customer service may continue to improve as companies realize how quickly a single irate customer can use the Internet to broadcast messages vilifying a company or a particular product to millions of potential customers. Computers, related hardware, and software products are especially vulnerable to such customer attacks. If a product does not stand up to advertised capabilities, the computing community will quickly expose its shortcomings to potential buyers. This same level of scrutiny will ultimately be applied to other products and services. For example, there are hundreds of **newsgroups**, essentially interactive electronic bulletin boards, devoted exclusively to discussions of restaurants in various cities and countries. In these cities and countries, you can be sure that frequent diners know which restaurants offer good food and value and which ones do not. These and thousands of other special-topic newsgroups can be found on the Internet.

THE INTERNET: MILLIONS OF INTERCONNECTED NETWORKS

The Internet, also known simply as **the Net,** is a worldwide network of computers that has emerged as *the* enabling technology in our migration to a global village. It connects millions of computers in millions of networks in every country in the world. All colleges are on the Net; that is, they have an Internet account. The same is true of the vast majority of businesses. Because these organizations have established links to the Internet, people in these organizations can access the Internet. Individuals with PCs can access the Internet, too. If you have access to a computer at a college computer lab or at work, the PCs are probably "on the Net."

FIGURE 1–7 THE INTERNET AND AOL

INTERNET SHOPPING

Most people subscribe to an internet service provider (ISP) to get on the Internet. Once online, you can shop the electronic malls of the information superhighway to find exactly what you want, whether it's an 11-in-1 electronic survival kit or a home.

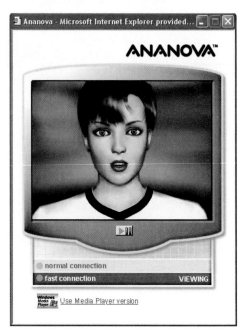

VIRTUAL NEWS

You also can listen to the news read by Ananova, a virtual newscaster, who reads the news in four different languages.

AOL

Most of the rest join America Online (AOL), the most popular online information service. AOL lets you go on the Internet, plus it has 20 interest areas from which to choose, and a variety of other services. Shown here is the Welcome screen, which usually announces "You've got mail" when you "sign on," the weather forecast for the Virgin Islands, the e-mail list and an e-mail, the buddy list (which alerts you when one of your buddies signs on so you can chat), and Internet Radio.

Getting Connected

Typically, individuals gain access to the Internet by subscribing to an **Internet service provider** (**ISP**) (see Figure 1-7). For a monthly fee, you can link your PC to the ISP's computer, thus gaining access to the Net. The monthly cost ranges from $20 to $100, depending on the speed of the connection. An ISP is a company with an Internet account that provides individuals and organizations access to, or presence on, the Internet. Another way to get on the Net is to subscribe to a commercial **information service,** such as **America Online** (see Figure 1-7). **AOL** has over 30 million subscribers. AOL and other commercial information services have one or several large computer systems that offer a wide range of information services over their proprietary network, which, of course, is linked to the worldwide Net. AOL services include up-to-the-minute news and weather, electronic shopping, e-mail, chat rooms, and much more. Most types of services provided by AOL are available to people who go online via an ISP. However, AOL packages them with an easy-to-use interface. AOL is sometimes referred to as an "ISP with training wheels."

The services and information provided by the Net and information services are **online;** that is, once the user has established a communications link between his or her PC, the user becomes part of the network. Most individuals at home use a regular telephone line in conjunction with a device called a modem to link to the Internet. A **modem** permits communication with remote computers via a telephone-line link. When online, the user interacts directly with the computers in the information network to access desired information and services. Other ways to link with the Internet are presented in Chapter 7, "Networks and Networking." When the user terminates the link, the user goes **offline**.

The Internet emerged from a government-sponsored project to promote the interchange of scientific information. This spirit of sharing continues as the overriding theme over the Internet. For example, aspiring writers having difficulty getting read or published can make their writing available to millions of readers, including agents and publishers, in a matter of minutes. Unknown musicians also use the Internet to gain recognition. *Surfers* on the Internet (Internet users) wanting to read a story or listen to a song, **download** the text or a digitized version of a song (like those on CDs) to their personal computer, then read it or play it through their personal computer. Popular **MP3 players,** the next generation Walkmans, can store and play digital music in MP3 format, a method of storing CD-quality music using relatively little memory (see Figure 1-8). Downloading is simply transmitting information from a remote computer (in this case, an Internet-based computer) to a local computer (in most cases, a PC). Information (perhaps a story or a song) going the other way, from a local computer to a remote computer, is said to be **uploaded.**

This spirit of sharing has prompted individuals and organizations all over the world to make available information and databases on a wide variety of topics. This wonderful distribution and information-sharing vehicle is, of course, a boon for businesses. Thousands of publishers, corporations, government agencies, colleges, and database services give Internet users access to their information—some provide information gratis and some charge a fee. Each year, more and more businesses are looking to the Internet as a vehicle to generate revenue.

The Web and Other Internet Applications

The Internet and the World Wide Web (the Web) are used interchangeably, as are the Net and the Web, but they are not the same. The Internet is a global network of computers and transmission facilities. It is the tool that enables a variety of amazing applications. E-mail, instant messaging, and newsgroups are a few of the many applications supported on the Internet. Perhaps the most important Internet application is the **World Wide Web** because it is this application, often called **the Web,** that lets us view the information on the Internet. The information, which may be graphics, audio, video, animation, and text, is viewed in **Web pages.** Other Internet applications, such as chat, videophone (see Figure 1-9), and gaming, are presented and illustrated in Chapter 3, "Going Online."

Services and capabilities of the Internet and commercial information services are growing daily. For example, a hungry traveler on the Internet can now order a pizza via the Net from a large number

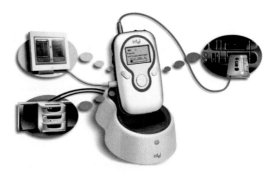

FIGURE 1–8 MP3 Player
There is a revolution under way in the way music is packaged, delivered, and played. Millions of MP3 songs are downloaded each day over the Internet and played on PCs or on MP3 players, like this Intel Pocket Concert Audio Player. You can load it up with four hours of music and take it anywhere. The unit is easily connected to your PC, home stereo, or auto stereo.

Photo courtesy of Intel Corporation

FIGURE 1–9 The Videophone Now a Reality
These schoolchildren in India are videoconferencing with children in the United States. This type of videophone link lets you check out a blind date, attend a virtual family reunion, speak with your business associate in another city, or say good night to your kids "in person" while away on a business trip. To make videophone calls, you need videophone software, an analog or digital camera, a PC, Internet access, and a link to a standard telephone line.

Photo courtesy of Intel Corporation

of online pizza delivery services. It works pretty much like a telephone order, except you enter the information on your PC, and it is routed immediately to the pizza shop nearest you. Usually, the order is displayed for the pizza chef within seconds. Of course, you can't download a pizza—it has to be delivered in the traditional manner. Already you can order almost any consumer item from tulips to trucks through the electronic malls.

Services available from the publicly available Internet and the subscription-based information services play a major role in shaping our information society. We'll discuss both in considerable detail throughout the book. Figure 1-10 presents an overview of popular Internet applications in seven dif-

FIGURE 1–10 **OVERVIEW OF POPULAR INTERNET APPLICATIONS**

PERSONAL COMMUNICATIONS

E-mail	Sand/receive personal and work-related electronic mail
Instant messaging	Real-time text, audio, and/or video communication
Chat	Normally, text-based interaction among groups of people in virtual chat rooms

BROWSING AND SEARCHING FOR INFORMATION

News	Newspapers, television stations, magazines, Internet portals, and other sites offer up-to-the-minute state, local, national, and international news, as well as topic-specific news, such as the stock market analysis and results
Sports	All professional leagues and teams, as well as all colleges, provide continuously-updated sports information and statistics to complement major sports news organizations, such as ESPN
Weather	Up-to-the-minute weather and weather forecasting is available for any city or region
Research for school or job	Billions of pages of information are available on almost any subject
Travel information	A breadth of information is available for tens of thousands of destinations, including cities, specific sites, resorts, and so on, including how to get there
Medical information	The Net has a plethora of medical data, advice, and information

DOWNLOADING AND FILE SHARING

Images and video	These include any kind of still image, from NASA space shots to family baby photos and a variety of brief videos from music videos to family clips
Music	Millions of songs are downloaded and shared, both legally and illegally, each day
Movies	That legal and illegal downloading/sharing of commercial and private movies is growing

STREAMING MEDIA

Video clips	News events, movie trailers, sports highlights, and so on
Audio	Speeches, radio station broadcasts, electronic greeting-card songs, and so on, are streamed over the Net
Movies	On-demand movies may someday threaten the existence of the video store

ONLINE TRANSACTIONS

Online shopping	Shop and buy almost anything on Internet, from groceries to automobiles
Online auctions	Bid on any of thousands of new and used items on the virtual auction block or place your own items up for auction
Online banking	Most bricks-and-mortar banking transactions can be down be done online
Making reservations	All types of travel reservations, including airline, train, hotel, auto rental, and so on, can be made online
Stock trading	Stocks can be bought and sold online
Gambling	Place real bets on virtual casino games and win/lose real money

ENTERTAINMENT

Multiplayer gaming	Play bridge or fight galactic battles with other Net-based gamers
Serendipitous browsing	Surf the Net just for fun to see where it leads you
Adult content	Adult entertainment is a major dot.com industry
Hobbyist	All popular hobbies are supported by sites that contain information and related activities

ferent categories: personal communications, browsing and searching for information, downloading and file sharing, streaming media, online transactions, and entertainment.

SECTION SELF-CHECK

1-3.1	A global network called the Internet links millions of computers throughout the world. (T/F)
1-3.2	A computer network links computers to enable the: (a) linking of terminals and HDTV hookups, (b) sharing of resources and information, (c) distribution of excess processor capabilities, or (d) expansion of processing capabilities.
1-3.3	When the user terminates the link with a commercial information service, the user goes: (a) offline, (b) on-log, (c) out-of-site, or (d) online.

1-4 The Basics: Hardware, Software, and Computer Systems

Almost everyone in our information society has a basic understanding of what a computer is and what it can do. This book is designed to add depth to what you already know.

HARDWARE BASICS

At the heart of any **computer** is its **processor,** *an electronic device that can interpret and execute programmed commands for input, output, computation, and logic operations.* The size of an actual PC processor, a computer's main piece of hardware, is about the size of a matchbook. Smaller ones like those used in VCRs and automobile ignition systems are about the size of your fingernail. Because of their size, processors frequently are referred to as microprocessors. Generally, the terms *processor* and *microprocessor* are used interchangeably.

To many people, computers are somewhat mystical, out of their range of comprehension. But computers aren't as complicated as you might have been led to believe. A **computer system** has only four basic components: *input, processor, output,* and *storage* (see Figure 1-11). Note that the processor, or computer, is just one component in a computer system. It gives the computer system its intelligence, performing all *computation* and *logic* operations. In everyday conversation, people simply say "computer" when they talk about a computer system. We'll do this as well throughout this book.

Each of the components in a computer system can take on a variety of forms. For example, *output* (the results of processing) can be routed to a televisionlike **monitor,** audio speakers (like those on your stereo system), or a **printer** (see Figure 1-11). The output on a monitor or the sounds from the speakers, which are temporary, are called **soft copy.** Printers produce **hard copy,** or printed output that can be physically handled, folded, and so on. Data can be entered to a computer system for processing (input) via a **keyboard** (for keyed input), a microphone (for voice and sound input), or a **point-and-draw device,** such as a **mouse** (see Figure 1-11).

Storage of data and software in a computer system is either *temporary* or *permanent.* **Random-access memory** (**RAM,** rhymes with "*ham*") provides temporary storage of data and programs during processing within solid-state **integrated circuits.** Integrated circuits, or **chips,** are tiny (about .5 inch square) silicon chips into which thousands of electronic components are etched. The processor is also a chip. Permanently installed and interchangeable **magnetic disks** provide permanent storage for data and programs (see Figure 1-11). Because the surface of circular, spinning disks is coated with easily magnetized elements for read/write operation, such as nickel, they sometimes are called *magnetic disks.* Information is read from and written to a variety of disks. **Optical disc** storage media that looks like audio CDs is either read only or read/write. Note the difference in spelling between magnetic *disks* and optical *discs.* A computer system is comprised of its internal components (for example, RAM and special features), the various storage devices, and its input and output **peripheral devices** (printer, monitor, mouse, and so on).

SOFTWARE BASICS

Software refers to any program that tells the computer system what to do. Of course, there are many different types of software. The more you understand about the scope and variety of available software, the more effective you will be as a user. Actually, understanding software is a lot like being in a big house—once you know its layout, you're able to move about the house much easier.

Once but a cottage, this house of software is almost a mansion. Software falls into two categories, system and applications software.

FIGURE 1–11

THE FOUR FUNDAMENTAL COMPONENTS OF A PERSONAL COMPUTER SYSTEM
In a personal computer system, the storage and processing components are often contained in the same physical unit. In the illustration, the interchangeable disk/discs-storage medium is inserted into the unit that contains the processor.

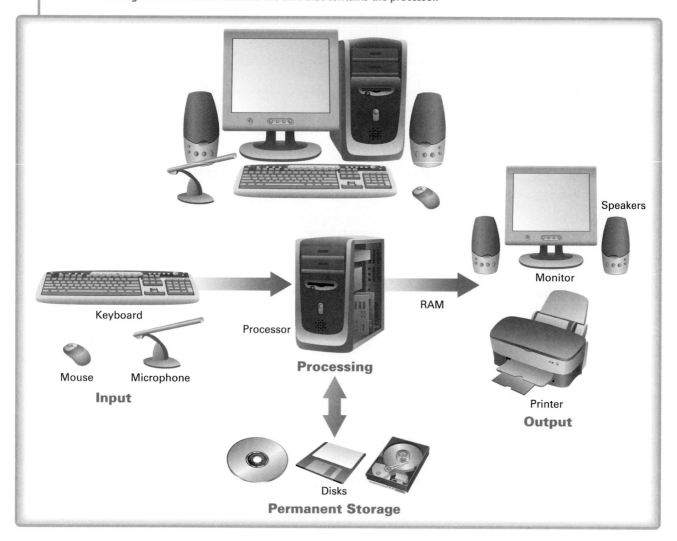

Speakers

Monitor

RAM

Keyboard

Processor

Mouse   Microphone

Processing

Input

Printer

Output

Disks

Permanent Storage

● *System software.* When you turn on the computer, the first actions you see are directed by system software. **System software** programs take control of the PC on start-up, and then play a central role in everything that happens within a computer system by managing, maintaining, and controlling computer resources.

● *Applications software.* **Applications software** is designed and created to perform specific personal, business, or scientific processing tasks, such as word processing, tax planning, or interactive gaming. We'll visit every room in the house by the time you finish this book.

COMPUTER SYSTEMS BASICS

General-purpose computers capable of handling a variety of tasks can be found in a range of shapes, from cube-shaped to U-shaped to cylindrical to notebook-shaped. However, the most distinguishing characteristic of any computer system is its *size*—not its physical size, but its *computing power.* Loosely speaking, size, or computing power, is the amount of processing that can be accomplished by a computer system in a certain amount of time, usually a second.

At one end of the power spectrum is the low-end personal computer that costs less than $500 and at the other is the powerful **supercomputer** that may cost more than an office building. The personal computer, as the name implies, serves one person at a time. In contrast, a super-computer can handle the processing needs of thousands of users at a time or perform processing that would take thousands of PCs.

Over the past five decades computers have taken on as many handles as there were niche needs. Terms like *mainframe computer* and *minicomputer* were popular in the 1970s and 1980s. Today, computers are generally grouped in these categories: notebook PCs, desktop PCs, wearable PCs, handheld computers, thin clients, workstations, server computers, and supercomputers. Give desktop PCs a slight edge in power over notebook PCs, but, generally, the two types offer similar computing capabilities. Wearable PCs are worn by the user, about the waist, head, or on the arm, providing the ultimate in mobile processing. The workstation is a notch above the top desktop PCs, offering individuals the performance they need for demanding scientific and graphics applications. In most computer networks, one or more central computers, called **server computers,** manage the resources on a network and perform a variety of functions for the other computers on the network, called **client computers,** which usually are PCs or workstations. PCs, workstations, and thin clients are linked to the server computer to form the network. **Thin clients** are somewhat less than full-featured PCs (thin) and they are clients of (dependent on) server computers for certain resources, such as storage and some processing.

Any general-purpose computer, a notebook PC to a supercomputer, can be a server computer. But manufacturers build a special class of computers, called server computers, which are designed specifically for the server function. There are small ones for small businesses and larger ones to handle network needs for multinational companies. We should emphasize that these categories of computers are relative. What people call a personal computer system today may look like a workstation at some time in the future and be called by an entirely different name.

PCs, workstations, "servers," and supercomputers are computer systems. Each offers many **input/output,** or **I/O,** alternatives—ways to enter data into the system and to present information generated by the system. All computer systems, no matter how small or large, have the same fundamental capabilities—*input, processing, output,* and *storage.* Keep this in mind as you encounter the computer systems shown in Figure 1-12. In keeping with conversational computerese, we will drop the word *system* when discussing the categories of computer systems. Remember, however, that a reference to any of these categories (for example, supercomputer) implies a reference to the entire computer system.

The differences in the various categories of computers are very much a matter of scale. Try thinking of a *supercomputer* as a *wide-body jet* and a *personal computer* as a *commuter plane.* Both types of airplanes have the same fundamental capability—they carry passengers from one location to another. Wide-bodies, which fly at close to the speed of sound, can carry hundreds of passengers. In contrast, commuter planes travel much slower and carry fewer than 50 passengers. Wide-bodies travel between large international airports, across countries, and between continents. Commuter planes travel short distances between regional airports. The commuter plane, with its small crew, can land, unload, load, and be on its way to another destination in 15 to 20 minutes. The wide-body may take 30 minutes just to unload. A PC is much like the commuter plane in that one person can get it up and running in just a few minutes. One person controls all aspects of the PC. The supercomputer is like the wide-body in that a number of specialists are needed to keep it operational. No matter what their size, airplanes fly and carry passengers and computers process data and produce information. Besides obvious differences in size, the various types of computers differ mostly in how they are used. Section 1-5 should give you insight into when and where a particular system might be used.

FIGURE 1–12 CATEGORIES OF COMPUTERS

Personal Computer
(notebook PC and desktop PC)

Handheld Computer

Thin Client

Wearable PC

Workstation

Server Computer

Supercomputer

1-4.1	Supercomputers have greater computing capacity than personal computers. (T/F)
1-4.2	A printer is an example of which of the four computer system components: (a) input, (b) output, (c) processor, or (d) storage?
1-4.3	Which component of a computer system executes the program: (a) input, (b) output, (c) processor, or (d) storage?

PERSONAL COMPUTING: Desktop or Notebook? The choice for the primary PC usually is between a *desktop PC* and a *notebook PC*. Generally, the choice between the two PCs hinges on two considerations: *need for portability* and *cost*. If your lifestyle demands portability in personal computing and you are willing to pay up to twice as much for the same computing capability as a comparable desktop PC, then you should seriously consider a notebook PC. You'll always pay a premium price for mobile computing. If cost is a concern and portability isn't, the desktop PC is for you. If gaming is an issue, notebooks do games, but not as well as desktops.

1-5 Personal Computers to Supercomputers

Every day, more computers are sold than existed in the entire world 35 years ago. Back then, most medium to large companies had a computer, but they came in only one size—big. They filled large rooms, even buildings. Today, computers come in a variety of sizes. In this section we take a closer look at these popular categories of computers: personal computers (notebook PCs, desktop PCs, and wearable PCs), handheld computers, thin clients, workstations, server computers, and supercomputers.

PERSONAL COMPUTERS: UP CLOSE AND PERSONAL

In 1981, IBM introduced its **IBM PC** and it legitimized the personal computer as a business tool. Shortly after that, other manufacturers began making PCs that were 100% compatible with the IBM PC; that is, they basically worked like an IBM PC. Most of today's personal computers (over 80%) evolved from these original PC-compatibles. Long removed from the IBM PC, they are also called **Wintel PCs** because they use the Microsoft *Windows 9x/Me/2000/XP* (a collective reference to Microsoft *Windows 95, Windows 98, Windows Millennium (Me), Windows 2000*, or *Windows XP*) control software and an Intel Corporation or Intel-compatible processor. Each of the Microsoft Windows family of **operating systems** controls all hardware and software activities on Wintel PCs. Operating systems form the foundation of the system software category of software.

The Wintel PC represents the dominant PC platform. A **platform** defines a standard for which software is developed. Specifically, a platform is defined by two key elements:

- The processor (for example, Intel® Pentium III®, Intel® Celeron™, Intel Pentium 4®, Intel Itanium™, Intel McKinley™, Motorola® PowerPC®, AMD Athlon, and so on)

- The operating system (for example, Windows® XP, Windows Me, Mac® OS X, Unix®, Linux, Lindows, and so on)

Generally, software created to run on one platform is not compatible with any other platform. Most of the remaining personal computers are part of the Apple *Power Mac®*, *PowerBook®*, or *iMac*™ line of computers. These systems use the *Mac® OS X* operating system and are powered by Motorola® *PowerPC®* processors.

One person at a time uses a PC. The user turns on the PC, selects the software to be run, enters the data, and requests the information. The PC, like other computers, is very versatile and has been used for everything from communicating with business colleagues to controlling household appliances. The personal computer is actually a family of computers, some are small and portable and some are not meant to be moved. The most common PCs, the notebook and desktop, have a full keyboard, a monitor, and can function as stand-alone systems (see Figure 1-13).

Notebook PCs

Until recently, people in the business world often purchased two PCs, a **notebook PC** for its portability and a **desktop PC** for its power and extended features. Early notebook PCs simply didn't have the power or the capabilities of their desktop cousins. That has changed. Now, notebook PCs offer desktop-level performance. These powerful notebook PCs let people take their "main" computer with them wherever they are, at work, at home, or on vacation. Each year, an increasing percentage of people choose to buy notebook PCs as their only PC. Today, close to half of all personal computers purchased for use in businesses are notebooks. That percentage continues to increase.

Notebook PCs are light (a few pounds up to about eight pounds), compact, and portable. It's easy to fold them up and take them with you. Notebook PCs, which also are called **laptop PCs**, are about the size of a one-inch-thick notebook. They have batteries and can operate with or without an external power source, on an airplane or a wilderness trail.

High-end notebook PCs can run circles around some desktop PCs. Some user conveniences, however, must be sacrificed to achieve portability. For instance, input devices, such as keyboards and point-and-draw devices, are given less space in portable PCs and may be more cumbersome to use.

FIGURE 1–13 PERSONAL COMPUTERS: DESKTOPS AND NOTEBOOKS

THE IMAC DESKTOP

Apple computer pioneered the all-in-one concept with its original see-though iMac in 1998. This iMac, which has a 10.6-inch footprint, was completely redesigned in 2002 with a flat screen that "floats" in mid-air, allowing for ease of adjustment. The new iMacs, which are designed to be the center of our emerging digital lifestyle, have a SuperDrive™ that permits playing and creating custom CDs and playing DVDs. Under the hood, the iMac sports an impressive list of features, including a powerful processor, plenty of memory, stereo sound, and network and Internet capabilities.

Courtesy of Apple Computer, Inc.

NOTEBOOK PC

When searching for a personal computer, this executive identified portability and flexibility as her primary criteria, so she chose a laptop PC. Laptop users can now ask for SuperDisk drives (shown here) to be built into new notebooks for convenient, interchangeable, and high-capacity storage (over 100 million characters of data on a SuperDisk the size of a traditional floppy disk).

Photo courtesy of Imation Corporation

DESKTOP PC

This Dell Dimension tower system can sit under, beside, or on top of a desk. This home office system is configured with a large-screen monitor, an ink jet printer, a flatbed scanner, a digital video camera, and a satellite modem (atop the system unit) for high-speed Internet. The system has five speakers, including a woofer, and an uninterruptible power source (UPS) for backup if power is interrupted.

Long and Associates

FUTURISTIC CONCEPT PCS

Intel Corporation is working with PC manufacturers to build better, simpler, and more effective personal computers. Shown here are several Intel Concept PCs that showcase the possibilities and benefits of drastically redesigned, legacy-free, easily upgradeable personal computers. These concept PCs provide a glimpse into the future of mobile PCs. The concept PCs include features that enable the always on, always connected vision, include seamless wireless connectivity capabilities, enhanced security, ease of use, as well as Tablet PC/notebook PC functionality. The futuristic concept PCs have small external displays that can show a calendar, phone numbers, or incoming e-mail so the user does not have to open and boot up the system to obtain this information. The systems have fingerprint recognition biometrics to ensure they are truly personal.

Photo courtesy of Intel Corporation

Generally, notebook PCs take up less space and, therefore, have a smaller capacity for permanent storage of data and programs. Laptop battery life can be as little as a few hours for older models to 20 hours for state-of-the-art rechargeable lithium batteries.

Many notebook PC buyers purchase a **port replicator,** too. Also called a **docking station,** the port replicator lets you enjoy the best of both worlds—portability plus the expanded features of a desktop PC. The notebook PC, which supplies the processor and storage, is simply inserted into or removed from the port replicator, as needed. The process takes only a few seconds. The port replicator can be *configured* to give the "docked" notebook PC the look and feel of a desktop PC. Once inserted, the notebook can use the port replicator *ports* and whatever is connected to them. **Ports** are electronic interfaces through which devices like the keyboard, monitor, mouse, printer, image scanner (to enter images to the system), and so on are connected. Port replicators also provide bigger speakers and an AC power source. Some provide a direct link to the corporate network.

Desktop PCs

The ubiquitous desktop PCs are not considered portable because they rely on an outside power source and are not designed for frequent movement. The desktop PC's **system unit,** which contains the processor, disk storage, and other components, may be placed in any convenient location (on a nearby shelf, on the desk, or on the floor). The system unit for early desktop PCs was designed to lay flat on a desk to provide a platform for the monitor. Today's *tower* system unit with its smaller *footprint* (the surface space used by the unit) has made the early models obsolete. The desktop PC's footprint continues to dwindle as the tower shrinks and more users opt for the space-saving flat-panel monitors.

Configuring a PC: Selecting the PC's Components

PC users often select, configure, and install their own system. The configuration of a PC or what you put into and attach to your computer can vary enormously. Common configuration options are shown in Figure 1-14.

Nowadays, the typical off-the-shelf PC is configured to run multimedia applications. **Multimedia applications** integrate text, sound, graphics, motion video, and/or animation. Computer-based encyclopedias, such as *Grolier Multimedia Encyclopedia,* and games, such as Broderbund's Carmen Sandiego series, provide a good example of multimedia applications. The encyclopedia can take you back to July 20, 1969, and let you see motion video of the *Apollo 11* lunar module *Eagle* landing on the moon at the Sea of Tranquility. If you wish, you can listen to Commander Neil Armstrong proclaim, "That's one small step for [a] man, one giant leap for mankind" as he steps on the moon. Of course, the electronic encyclopedia contains supporting text that explains that he intended to say "a man." The typical PC includes the following components.

- *Motherboard.* The **motherboard** is a single circuit board that includes the processor and other electronic components. It provides the path through which the processor communicates with memory components and the various I/O peripheral devices. The motherboard is housed in the system unit.
- *Keyboard.* The keyboard is the primary text input device.
- *Point-and-draw device.* The point-and-draw device, which is usually a mouse on desktop PCs, aids in navigation around the system, in moving screen objects, and in drawing applications.
- *Monitor.* The monitor is the display that provides *soft copy* (temporary) output.
- *Printer.* The printer lets the system produce *hard copy* (printed) output.
- *Hard disk.* PCs have a permanently installed high-capacity **hard-disk drive** for permanent storage of data and programs.
- *Floppy disk drive.* PCs usually have a traditional **floppy disk drive** into which an interchangeable **diskette,** or **floppy disk,** is inserted. The system may be configured with an additional higher-capacity interchangeable disk drive, as well.
- *CD-ROM or DVD-ROM drive.* Typically, the PC will have either a read-only **CD-ROM drive** or the newer **DVD-ROM drive** into which an interchangeable **CD-ROM,** which looks like an audio CD, is inserted. The DVD-ROM drive accepts all DVD format discs, as well, including **DVD-Video** for playing movies. Some models are configured with a rewritable option, either **CD-RW** and/or **DVD+RW.**
- *Microphone.* The microphone allows audio input to the system.
- *Speakers.* The speakers provide audio output.

Virtually all PCs, both desktop and notebook, give users the flexibility to configure the system with a variety of storage and I/O peripheral devices. Of course, most or all extra peripherals are left at the office/home when a notebook goes mobile. A PC system is configured by linking any of a wide variety

FIGURE 1–14

THE PERSONAL COMPUTER AND COMMON PERIPHERAL DEVICES
A wide range of peripheral devices can be connected to a PC. Those shown here and others are discussed in detail in later chapters.

Digital camera

Wand scanner

Scanner

Video camera

Image processing
(input)

Microphone

Sound
(input and output)

Speakers (stereo sound output)

LCD projection panel (used in conjunction with an overhead projector)

Data/video projector

Plotter

Desktop page printer

Hard-copy output

Monitor (input/output)
Touch screen (input)
Keyboard (input)

Uninterruptible power supply (UPS) to enable clean, steady power

Point-and-draw devices
(input)

Mouse   Trackball

Digitizer tablet and crosshair

Touchpad

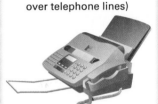
Modem (data communication over telephone lines)

Facsimile (fax) machine

Telephone

Personal digital assistant and laptop PC (computer to computer)

Communications
(remote input/output)

Read/write optical laser disk

3.5-inch diskette and SuperDisk

CD-ROM/DVD DVD+RW/CD-RW

Hard disk

Tape backup unit (TBU)

Zip disk

Secondary storage

of peripheral devices to the processor component. Figure 1-14 shows the more common storage and peripheral devices that can be configured with a PC. Many other peripherals can be linked to the "typical" PC, including video cameras, telephones, image scanners, other computers, security devices, and even a device that will enable you to watch your favorite television show on the PC's monitor.

Wearable PCs

Thousands of mobile workers could benefit from using a computer if only the computer were lighter, freed their hands, and didn't tether them to a desk or a power outlet. Now a new generation of **wearable PCs** promises to extend the trend begun by notebook and handheld computers.

Wearable computers, long a staple of science fiction, are here. In an effort to create truly personal computers that meld a computer and its user, designers have divided the wearable PC's components into cable-connected modules that fit into headsets, drape across shoulders, hang around the neck, and fasten around the waist, forearm, or wrist. Lightweight (two pounds or less), the components are covered in soft plastic and strapped on with Velcro.

Manufacturers of these wearable PCs combine existing or emerging technologies to create customized PCs for specific types of workers. The TLC (Tender Loving Care) PC for paramedics is a good example. At an accident scene, speech-recognition software lets the paramedic dictate symptoms and vital signs into a slender microphone hanging from a headset. The computer, draped across the medic's shoulders like a shawl, compares this data to a CD-ROM medical directory in the shoulder unit. The computer then projects possible diagnoses and suggested treatments onto the headset's miniature display. The TLC unit improves upon the two-way radio medics now use to communicate with emergency-room doctors. Instead of describing symptoms over a two-way radio, medics could use a trackball-operated video camera and body sensor strapped to their palm to *show* doctors the patient's condition. The video and additional data would be beamed to the doctors by a satellite link. Headphones would let the medics get feedback and additional advice from the waiting doctors.

Certainly, the trend is toward increasingly smaller PCs. Some say that an emerging trend is toward increasingly wearable PCs. If this trend holds, it's inevitable that vendors will be as concerned with fashion as they are with functionality. Power and size have always been critical elements of PCs, but now design is of growing importance. We may be entering an era of fashion wars where we may have to upgrade our PC to keep up with the latest fashion fad! With everyone drawing from essentially the same pool of microprocessors, is it possible that technical innovation may someday take a back seat to fashion?

Perhaps the most intriguing concept in wearable computers is the Body Net. The Body Net will be a network of wearable computers strategically located over the body. For example, the shoe-based computer might detect your location, and then transmit appropriate location-specific information for viewing on your eyeglasses computer. Perhaps within the decade, the PC will become as much an essential part of one's wardrobe as an indispensable business tool.

HANDHELD COMPUTERS: A COMPUTER IN HAND IS BETTER THAN . . .

Handheld computers are just that, computers that can be held in your hand. Handheld computers come in various form factors to address a variety of functions. The term **form factor** refers to a computer's physical shape and size. Computers, especially handheld computers and notebook PCs, continue to take on new form factors, often with unique features and capabilities. For example, one form factor integrates a cellular phone with a handheld computer. Another enables a notebook to be converted to a pen-based computer with handheld-like functionality.

Palmtop PC, personal digital assistant (PDA), connected organizer, personal communicator, mobile business center, and Web phone are just a few of the many names for handheld computers. Handheld computers weigh only a few ounces, can operate for days on their batteries, and can fit in a coat pocket or a handbag. As with notebooks, handheld computers must sacrifice some user convenience to achieve portability. The keyboards on those that have keyboards are miniaturized, making data entry and interaction with the computer difficult and slow. The display screen on some pocket PCs is monochrome (as opposed to color) and may be difficult to read under certain lighting situations.

Handheld computers are becoming increasingly important as the nature of information technology applications becomes ever more mobile. The increase in the number of handheld computers in use is a by-product of our information society's transformation to a mobile, geographically dispersed workforce that needs fast, easy, remote access to networked resources, including e-mail. Some handheld computers have built-in wireless communications capabilities that give their users immediate access to the Internet, colleagues, and clients, and needed information, virtually anytime, anywhere. Interaction with handheld computers can be via an electronic pen (handwritten text and graphics), by touching the keys on an on-screen keyboard, by keying on a reduced-key keyboard, or by speech (see Figure 1-15).

FIGURE 1–15 HANDHELD AND WEARABLE COMPUTERS

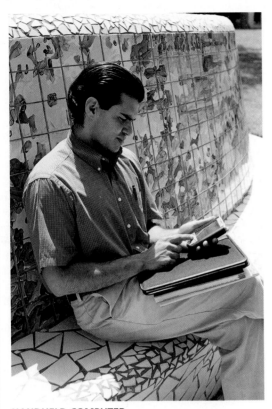

HANDHELD COMPUTER

The Compaq iPAQ Pocket PC and its accessories give people access to the Internet and important business and personal information at any given time, in any given place. This palm-sized computer can store thousands of addresses, years of appointments, to-do items, memos, and e-mail messages. The executive can use a stylus or a screen-based keyboard to enter data. Also, it's easy to exchange information with a desktop or notebook PC.

Reprinted with permission of Compaq Computer Corporation. All Rights Reserved.

POCKET PC WITH KEYBOARD

This HP Pocket PC delivers the power, speed, and flexibility needed by people on the go. This miniature computer, which can fit in a purse or a coat pocket, can run the same applications as its notebook and desktop cousins. This handheld computer is shown with the HP e-copier, which can be moved over any hard copy document to produce an electronic copy (image) of anything from a business card to a flip chart.

Photo courtesy of Hewlett-Packard Company

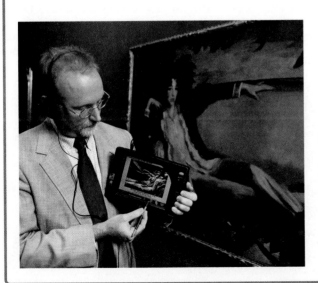

WEARABLE PC

This communications maintenance man uses a hands-free, paperless computer system while performing his duties. Xybernaut's wearable PC, the Mobile Assistant, is worn on a belt or shoulder strap and includes a display worn on the head like a headset. The wearable PC is a voice-controlled personal computer that frees workers from bulky manuals. This man simply navigates to needed information by voice interface, and then glances at the display.

Courtesy of Xybernaut

PCS IN MUSEUMS

People visiting the Whitney Museum of American Art can take a self-guided interactive gallery tour with the assistance of a handheld PC. The pen-based PCs are loaded with multimedia information keyed to the artworks. Viewers of this 1916 portrait of Gertrude Vanderbilt Whitney, by Robert Henri, can hear the artist's letter written to Gertrude Whitney to arrange the sitting, listen to period chamber music, and look at photographs of Gertrude Whitney's palatial childhood home.

Photo courtesy of Intel Corporation

Mobile workers have found handheld computers that use an electronic pen, also called a **stylus,** in conjunction with a combination monitor/drawing pad to be very useful. These types of handheld computers, which are sometimes called **pen-based computers,** may or may not have a small keyboard. Users can select options, enter data via the on-screen keyboard, and draw with the pen. Pen-based computers often are designed for a particular application. For example, United Parcel Service (UPS) couriers use pen-based handhelds when they ask you to sign for packages on a touch-sensitive display screen with an electronic stylus. Coca-Cola and Pepsi-Cola distributors equip their salespeople with handheld computers, which enable them to manage their territories better.

Handheld computers with their improved input technology are making a big splash, as mobility and being connected become requirements for knowledge workers. Handhelds are improving each year in their ability to interpret handwritten text. Current technology demands that the user enter the alphanumeric information according to some basic rules. One rule might be that each letter has a particular starting point. For example, the user begins at the top to enter an "i" (see Figure 1-16). Handwritten characters are interpreted by handwriting-recognition software and then entered into the system. Insurance agents and claims adjusters who need to work at accident or disaster scenes have found handheld computers more suitable to their input needs, which may include entering both text and drawings. **Speech-recognition software**, which allows the user to enter spoken words into the system, is being integrated into high-end handheld computers. Speech recognition can be much faster than handwritten input, but it's impolite to talk to your computer during a meeting.

Generally, handheld computers support a variety of **personal information management (PIM)** systems. A PIM might include appointment scheduling and calendar, e-mail, fax, phone-number administration, to-do lists, tickler files, "Post-it" notes, diaries, and so on. Some handhelds can support a variety of PC-type applications, such as spreadsheets and personal financial management. Also, handhelds are designed to be easily connected to other computers and printers for data transfer, network access, and printing. Accessories for handhelds include a full-sized keyboard.

There are as many applications for handheld computers as there are organizations and functions. For example, a growing application for handhelds is emerging in the doctor's office, where the handheld may make the doctor's prescription pad a thing of the past. Thousands of doctors are using handheld computers to help them when they prescribe drugs. The doctor can ask the system to list applicable drugs for a particular medical condition. After selecting a drug, the system checks for possible drug interactions with other drugs the patient might be taking and it lists possible side effects. The system even makes recommendations relative to the patient's insurance coverage. Upon completion of the *e-prescribing* process, the prescription is e-mailed directly to the druggist. The automation of the prescribing process is expected to give a boost to health-care quality considering that over 100,000 people die and 2 million people are hospitalized because of drug side effects and prescription errors.

Handhelds, though, are not all business. You can use them to play interactive games, chat with friends on the Internet, listen to downloaded MP3 music (as you would on a Walkman), or read a good **electronic-book (e-book)**. Or, if you prefer, you can kick back, don your head set, and let the computer's **text-to-speech software** read the e-book to you!

FIGURE 1–16

HANDWRITTEN INPUT
These Graffiti characters, which are similar to capital letters, are the basis for entering handwritten data into Palm handheld computers. All characters are entered with a single stroke and most people learn the strokes in minutes. The dot indicates where to begin the stroke for a particular character. Numbers and letters are entered in separate areas.

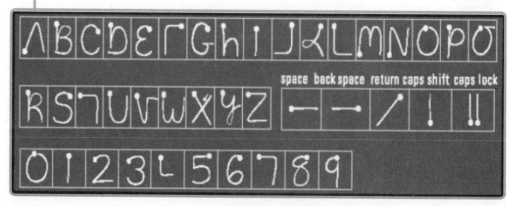

THIN CLIENTS: IN NETWORKS, THIN IS IN

In contrast to the conventional PC, the *thin client* is designed to function only when it is linked to a server computer (normally part of an organization's internal network of computers). The thin client looks similar to a PC (see Figure 1-17) but has several major differences. First, it has a relatively small processor and considerably less RAM (internal storage) than modern personal computers. Second, it does not have a permanently installed disk. And, it is less expensive than a stand-alone PC.

The thin client depends on a central network server computer to do much of its processing and for permanent storage of data and information. Here is the way a thin client works: The network computer user has access to a wide range of applications. However, the software applications and data are downloaded as they are needed to the thin client from a network's central computer. Whether or not to buy into the thin client concept is one of the major debates in the information technology community. Exchanging PCs for thin clients will eliminate the expensive and time-consuming task of installing and maintaining PC-based software, but it will make all thin clients dependent on the server computer. If the server goes down, all thin clients depending on it go down.

FIGURE 1–17 Thin Clients
In some companies, thin clients, such as this Sun Ray 1 Appliance, have replaced PCs in the workplace. Thin clients are so named because they are somewhat less than full-featured PCs (thin) and they are clients of (dependent on) server computers for certain resources.

Courtesy of Sun Microsystems, Inc.

WORKSTATIONS: HOT RODS

What looks somewhat like a desktop PC but isn't? It's a *workstation,* and it's very fast (see Figure 1-18). Speed is one of the characteristics that distinguish workstations from PCs. In fact, some people talk of workstations as "souped-up" PCs, the hot rods of computing. The workstation is for "power users"—engineers doing design work, scientists and researchers who do "number crunching," graphics designers, creators of special effects for movies, and so on. Although high-end desktop PCs may not perform as well as workstations, they are used for these applications, as well.

The workstation's input/output devices also set it apart from a PC. A typical workstation will sport a large-screen color monitor capable of displaying graphics at very high-resolutions. **Resolution** refers to the clarity of the image on the monitor's display. For pointing and drawing, the workstation user can call on a variety of specialized point-and-draw devices that combine the precision of a gun sight with the convenience of a mouse. Add-on keypads can expand the number of specialized *function keys* available to the user.

FIGURE 1–18 Workstation
This high-powered workstation is used for video editing and adding visual effects and animation for television programming and for films.

Courtesy of Autodesk, Inc.

The capabilities of today's high-end PCs are very similar to those of low-end workstations. In a few years, the average PC will have the capabilities of today's workstation. Eventually the distinctions between the two will disappear, and we will be left with a computer category that is a cross between a PC and a workstation. Time will tell whether we call it a PC, a workstation, or something else.

SERVER COMPUTERS: CORPORATE WORKHORSES

Most computers, including PCs and workstations, exist as part of a network of computers. At the center of most networks is one or more server computers (see Figure 1-19). In this section, we discuss the relationship between the server and its client computers. First, however, let's get some historical perspective.

Centralized Computing: A Bygone Era

Through the 1980s, huge mainframe computers performed most of the processing activity within a computer network. Back then, the shared use of a centralized mainframe offered the greatest return for the hardware/software dollar. Today, PCs and workstations offer more computing capacity per dollar than do mainframe computers. This reversal of hardware economics has caused IT professionals to rethink the way they design and use computer networks.

During the era of centralized mainframe computers, users communicated with a centralized host computer through dumb terminals that had little or no processing capability. The mainframe performed the processing for all users, sometimes numbering in the thousands. Now, the trend in the design of computer networks is toward *client/server computing*.

Client/Server Computing: Computers Working Together

In **client/server computing**, processing capabilities are distributed throughout the network, closer to the people who need and use them. A *server computer* supports many *client computers*.

- A *server computer*, which can be anything from a PC to a supercomputer, performs a variety of functions for its client computers, including the storage of data and applications software.
- The *client computer*, which is typically a PC, a workstation, or a thin client, requests processing support or another type of service (perhaps printing or remote communication) from one or more server computers.

In the client/server environment, both client and server computers perform processing to optimize application efficiency. For example, the client computer system might run a database application *locally* (on the client computer) and access data on a *remote* (not local) server computer system. In client/server computing, applications software has two parts—*the front end* and *the back end*.

- The client computer runs **front-end applications software**, which performs processing associated with the user interface and applications processing that can be done locally (for example, database and word processing).
- The server computer's **back-end applications software** performs processing tasks in support of its client computers. For example, the server might accomplish those tasks associated with storage and maintenance of a centralized corporate database.

FIGURE 1–19 Server Computer
This Sun server computer system includes disk storage in the unit, a backup fault-tolerant server, and several rack-mounted server computers. The system is capable of serving hundreds of client computers.

Courtesy of Sun Microsystems, Inc.

In a client/server database application (see Figure 1-20), users at client PCs run front-end software to *download* (server-to-client) parts of the database from the server for processing. Upon receiving the requested data, perhaps sales data on customers in the mid-Atlantic region, the client user runs front-end software to work with the data. After local processing, the client computer may *upload* (client-to-server) updated data to the server's back-end software for processing. The server then updates the customer database. The database application is popular in client/server computing, but the scope and variety of applications are growing daily.

Many people share the server computer's processing capabilities and computing resources. Server computers are usually associated with **enterprise systems**—that is, computer-based systems that service departments, plants, warehouses, and other entities throughout an organization. For example, human resource management, accounting, and inventory management tasks may be enterprise systems handled by a central server computer. Typically, users communicate with one or more server computers through a PC, a workstation, a thin client, or a **terminal**. A terminal has a keyboard for input and a monitor for output. Terminals are standard equipment at airline ticket counters. The traditional terminals that have no onboard intelligence, that is, no processor, are being replaced with thin clients. Depending on the size of the organization, a dozen people or 10,000 people can share system resources (for example, information, software, and access to the Internet) by interacting with their PCs, terminals, workstations, thin clients, handheld computers, and other communications devices.

Client/server environments with heavy traffic, such as America Online or a large company, might use a **proxy server computer**. This computer sits between the client PC and a normal server, handling many client requests and routing only those requests that it cannot handle to the real server. The proxy server improves overall performance by reducing the number of tasks handled by the real server. Proxy servers also are used as filters to limit outside access to the server and to limit employee

FIGURE 1-20 A WALKTHROUGH OF A CLIENT/SERVER DATABASE APPLICATION

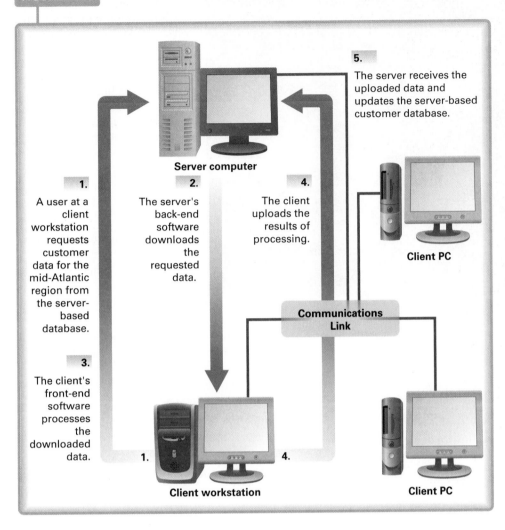

5.
The server receives the uploaded data and updates the server-based customer database.

Server computer

1.
A user at a client workstation requests customer data for the mid-Atlantic region from the server-based database.

2.
The server's back-end software downloads the requested data.

4.
The client uploads the results of processing.

Client PC

Communications Link

3.
The client's front-end software processes the downloaded data.

1.

4.

Client workstation

Client PC

access to specific Web sites. In Chapter 7, "Networks and Networking," we'll introduce several other special-purpose server computers that can be used to improve overall system efficiency.

SUPERCOMPUTERS: PROCESSING GIANTS

During the early 1970s, administrative data processing dominated computer applications. Bankers, college administrators, and advertising executives were amazed by the blinding speed at which million-dollar mainframe computers processed their data. Engineers and scientists were grateful for this tremendous technological achievement, but they were far from satisfied. When business executives talked about unlimited capability, engineers and scientists knew they would have to wait for future enhancements before they could use computers to address truly complex problems. Automotive engineers were still not able to create three-dimensional prototypes of automobiles inside a computer. Physicists could not explore the activities of an atom during a nuclear explosion. A typical scientific job involves the manipulation of a complex mathematical model, often requiring trillions of operations to resolve. During the early 1970s, some complex scientific processing jobs would tie up large mainframe computers at major universities for days at a time. This, of course, was unacceptable. The engineering and scientific communities had a desperate need for more powerful computers. In response to that need, computer designers began work on what are now known as supercomputers (see Figure 1-21).

Supercomputers primarily address **processor-bound applications**, which require little in the way of input or output. In processor-bound applications, the amount of work that can be done by the computer system is limited primarily by the speed of the computer. Such applications involve highly complex or vastly numerous calculations, all of which require processor, not I/O, work.

Categories of Computer Systems

* Personal computer (PC)
  * Notebook PC
  * Desktop PC
  * Wearable PC
* Handheld computer
* Thin client (works with server computer)
* Workstation
* Server computer
* Supercomputer

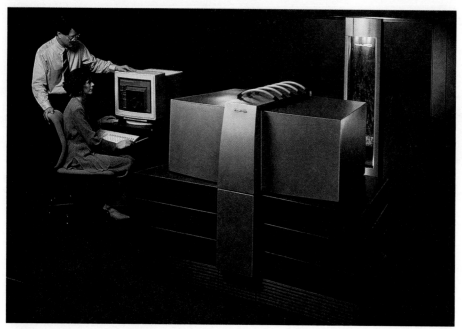

FIGURE 1–21 Supercomputer
The CRAY T90™ supercomputer is one of the most powerful general-purpose computers. General-purpose computers are capable of handling a wide range of applications.

Courtesy of E-Systems, Inc.

Supercomputers are known as much for their applications as they are for their speed or computing capacity, which may be 100 times that of a typical corporate server computer (see Figure 1-22). IBM is just finishing up work on Blue Gene, a supercomputer with over a million processors that will perform 1 million billion (10^{15}) math operations per second. These are representative supercomputer applications:

- Supercomputers enable the simulation of airflow around an airplane at different speeds and altitudes.

- Auto manufacturers use super-computers to simulate auto accidents on video screens. (It is less expensive, more revealing, and safer than crashing the real thing.)

- Meteorologists employ super-computers to study how oceans and the atmosphere interact to produce weather phenomena such as El Niño. It is hoped that eventually supercomputers will help meteorologists make earlier and better forecasts, especially concerning the paths of hurricanes and tornadoes and for flash floods and snowstorms.

- Supercomputers are being used to solve how the proteins are formed in the human body. IBM's Blue Gene is expected to take one year to calculate how a typical protein folds itself into a specific shape that determines its function in the body.

- Hollywood production studios use supercomputers to create the advanced graphics used to create special effects for movies such as *Star Wars Episode II: Attack of the Clones* and for TV commercials.

- Supercomputers sort through and analyze mountains of seismic data gathered during oil-seeking explorations.

- Medical researchers use supercomputers to simulate the delivery of babies.

SECTION SELF-CHECK

1-5.1	The power of a PC is directly proportional to its physical size. (T/F)
1-5.2	Workstation capabilities are similar to those of a low-end PC. (T/F)
1-5.3	What has I/O capabilities and is designed to be linked remotely to a host computer: (a) terminal, (b) printer, (c) port, or (d) mouse?
1-5.4	A notebook PC can be inserted into which of these to enable functionality similar to a desktop PC: (a) slate, (b) port hole, (c) runway, or (d) port replicator?
1-5.5	Spoken words are entered directly into a computer system via: (a) key entry, (b) OCR, (c) Morse code, or (d) speech recognition.
1-5.6	A client computer requests processing support or another type of service from one or more: (a) sister computers, (b) server computers, (c) customer computers, or (d) IT managers.

1-6 Computer System Capabilities

Now that we know a little about the basic types of computer systems, let's examine what a computer can and cannot do. First, let's talk about one of the computer's most significant capabilities—manipulating data to produce information.

PROCESSING DATA AND PRODUCING INFORMATION

Information as we now know it is a relatively new concept. Just 50 short years ago, *information* was the telephone operator who provided directory assistance. Around 1950, people began to view information as something that could be collected, sorted, summarized, exchanged, and processed. But only during the last two decades have computers allowed us to begin tapping the potential of information (see Figure 1-23).

Computers are very good at digesting data and producing information. For example, when you order a cross-country bicycle from an Internet-based *e-tailer,* an online retailer, the data you enter to the system (name, address, product ID) are entered directly into the e-tailer's computer. When you run short of cash and stop at an automatic teller machine, all data you enter, including that on the magnetic stripe of your bankcard, are processed immediately by the bank's computer system. A computer system eventually manipulates your **data** to produce **information.** The information could be an invoice sent to you via e-mail for the bicycle or a statement from the bank reflecting your withdrawal.

Traditionally, we have thought of data in terms of numbers (account balance) and letters (customer name), but recent advances in information technology have opened the door to data in other formats, such as visual images. For example, dermatologists (physicians who specialize in skin disorders) use digital cameras to take close-up pictures of patients' skin conditions. Each patient's record (information about the patient) on the computer-based **master file** (all patient records) is then updated to include the digital image. During each visit, the dermatologist recalls the patient record, which includes color images of the skin during previous visits. Data can also be found in the form of sound. For example, data collected during noise-level testing of automobiles include digitized versions of the actual sounds heard within the car.

FIGURE 1–22 Supercomputer Application
At Phillips Petroleum Company this Cray Research supercomputer is used to analyze huge amounts of seismic/geological data gathered during oil-seeking explorations. The company uses the computer for many other processor-intensive applications.

Photo courtesy of Phillips Petroleum Company

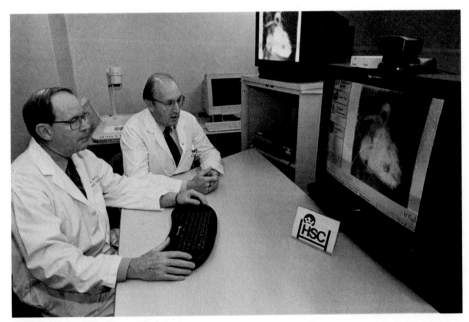

FIGURE 1–23 The Knowledge Worker
Today, we belong to an information society where we are "knowledge workers." For example, doctors are knowledge workers. These doctors use computers and communications technology to practice telemedicine, that is, providing health care remotely over communications links.

Photo courtesy of Intel Corporation

The relationship of data to a computer system is much like the relationship of gasoline to an automobile. Data provide the fuel for a computer system. Your car won't get you anywhere without gas, and your computer won't produce any information without data. It's all about data.

COMPUTERS IN ACTION: A PAYROLL SYSTEM

To get a better idea of how a computer system actually works, let's look at how it might do the processing of a *payroll system*. Just about every organization that has employees and a computer maintains a computer-based payroll system. The payroll system enables input and processing of pertinent payroll-related data to produce payroll checks and a variety of reports. The payroll system walkthrough in Figure 1-24 illustrates how data are entered into a network of personal computer systems

FIGURE 1–24 **A WALKTHROUGH OF A LAN-BASED PAYROLL SYSTEM**
This step-by-step walkthrough of parts of a LAN-based payroll system (three client PCs and a server) illustrates input, storage, processing, and output.

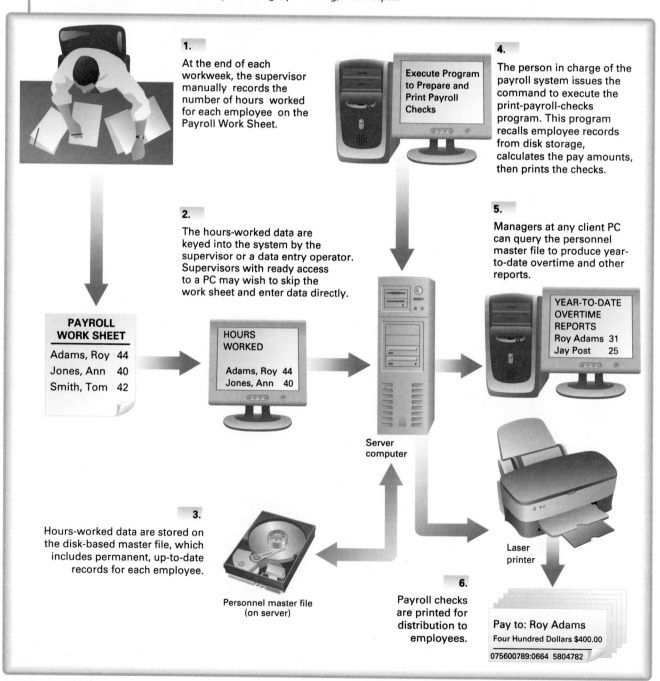

1.
At the end of each workweek, the supervisor manually records the number of hours worked for each employee on the Payroll Work Sheet.

2.
The hours-worked data are keyed into the system by the supervisor or a data entry operator. Supervisors with ready access to a PC may wish to skip the work sheet and enter data directly.

3.
Hours-worked data are stored on the disk-based master file, which includes permanent, up-to-date records for each employee.

4.
The person in charge of the payroll system issues the command to execute the print-payroll-checks program. This program recalls employee records from disk storage, calculates the pay amounts, then prints the checks.

5.
Managers at any client PC can query the personnel master file to produce year-to-date overtime and other reports.

6.
Payroll checks are printed for distribution to employees.

Execute Program to Prepare and Print Payroll Checks

PAYROLL WORK SHEET
Adams, Roy 44
Jones, Ann 40
Smith, Tom 42

HOURS WORKED
Adams, Roy 44
Jones, Ann 40

Server computer

Personnel master file (on server)

YEAR-TO-DATE OVERTIME REPORTS
Roy Adams 31
Jay Post 25

Laser printer

Pay to: Roy Adams
Four Hundred Dollars $400.00
075600789:0664 5804782

and how the four system components (input, processing, output, and storage) interact to produce payroll checks and information (in our example, a year-to-date overtime report).

In the walkthrough of Figure 1-24, the payroll system and other company systems are supported on a **local area network** (**LAN**). A LAN connects PCs or workstations that are relatively near one another, such as in a suite of offices or a building. The typical LAN employs client/server computing where data and applications software are on the server. In Figure 1-24, client PCs throughout the company are linked to a server computer.

WHAT CAN A COMPUTER DO?

Computers perform two operations: input/output operations and processing operations.

Input/Output Operations: Read and Write

Within a computer system, information is continuously moved from one part of the system to another. The processor controls this movement. It interprets information from the keyboard (a tapped key), moves it to memory and eventually to the monitor's display, the printer, or perhaps a stored file. This movement is referred to as input/output, or I/O for short. In performing input/output operations, the computer *reads* from input and storage devices, and then *writes* to output and storage devices.

Before processing begins, *commands* and/or *data* must be "read" from an input device and/or storage device. Typically, user commands and data are entered on a *keyboard* or via *speech recognition* (spoken words entered to the computer system), or they are retrieved from storage, such as a magnetic disk. Once commands and data have been processed, they are "written" to a magnetic disk or to an output device, such as a monitor or printer.

Input/output (I/O) operations are shown in the payroll-system walkthrough example in Figure 1-24. Hours-worked data are entered by a supervisor, or "read," into the computer system (Activity 2). These data are "written" to magnetic disk storage for recall later (Activity 3). Data are "read" from the personnel master file on magnetic disk, processed (Activity 4), and "written" to the printer to produce the payroll checks (Activity 6).

Processing Operations: Doing the Math and Making the Decisions

Any two computers instructed to perform the same operation will arrive at the same result because the computer is totally objective. Computers can't have opinions. They can perform only *computation* and *logic operations programmed by human beings*.

Computation Operations

Computers can add (+), subtract (−), multiply (*), divide (/), and do exponentiation (^). In the payroll system example of Figure 1-24, an instruction in a computer program tells the computer to calculate the gross pay for each employee in a computation operation. For example, these calculations would be needed to compute gross pay for Ann Jones, who worked 40 hours this week and makes $15 per hour:

Pay = 40 hours worked * $15/hour = $600

The actual program instruction that performs the above calculation might look like this:

PAY = HOURS_WORKED * PAY_RATE

The computer would then recall values for HOURS_WORKED and PAY_RATE from the personnel master file and calculate PAY.

Logic Operations

The computer's logic capability enables comparisons between numbers and between words. Based on the result of a comparison, the computer performs appropriate functions. In the example of Figure 1-24, Tom Smith and Roy Adams had overtime hours because they each worked more than 40 hours (the normal workweek). The computer must use its *logic capability* to decide if an employee is due overtime pay. To do this, hours worked are compared to 40.

Are hours worked > (greater than) 40?

For Roy Adams, who worked 44 hours, the comparison is true (44 is greater than 40). A comparison that is true causes the difference (4 hours) to be credited as overtime and paid at time and a half. The actual instruction that would perform the logical operation might look like this:

IF HOURS_WORKED > 40 THEN PAY_OVERTIME

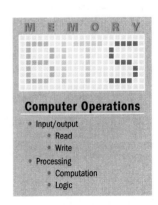

Computer Operations

- Input/output
  - Read
  - Write
- Processing
  - Computation
  - Logic

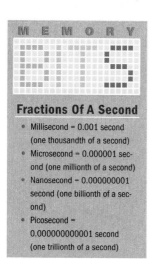

MEMORY BITS

Fractions Of A Second

- Millisecond = 0.001 second (one thousandth of a second)
- Microsecond = 0.000001 second (one millionth of a second)
- Nanosecond = 0.000000001 second (one billionth of a second)
- Picosecond = 0.000000000001 second (one trillionth of a second)

THE COMPUTER'S STRENGTHS

In a nutshell, computers are fast, accurate, consistent, and reliable; plus, they aid in communications and can store huge amounts of data. They don't forget anything, and they don't complain.

Speed

Computers perform various activities by executing instructions, such as those discussed in the previous section. These operations are measured in **milliseconds**, **microseconds**, **nanoseconds**, and **picoseconds** (one thousandth—*milli*, one millionth—*micro*, one billionth—*nano*, and one trillionth—*pico* of a second, respectively). To place computer speeds in perspective, consider that a beam of light travels down the length of this page in about one nanosecond. During that time a large server computer can perform the computations needed to complete a complex tax return.

Accuracy

Computers are amazingly accurate, and their accuracy reflects great *precision*. Computations are accurate within a penny (see Figure 1-25), a micron (a millionth of a meter), a picosecond, or whatever level of precision is required. Errors do occur in computer-based systems, but precious few can be directly attributed to the computer system itself. Most can be traced to a program logic error, a procedural error, or erroneous data. These are *human errors*.

FIGURE 1–25

TRILLIONS OF DOLLARS TRADED WITHOUT ERROR
At the New York Stock Exchange, literally trillions of dollars' worth of securities are routinely bought and sold with nary a penny lost, a testament to the accuracy of computers. Visitors to its Internet Web site can learn about trading and view the trading floor via continuous 360 degree scans from different perspectives. Shown here is a pan of the floor from the famous bell platform where trading is signaled to be open and closed.

Courtesy of the New York Stock Exchange

Consistency

Baseball pitchers try to throw strikes, but often end up throwing balls. Computers always do what they are programmed to do—nothing more, nothing less. If we ask them to throw strikes, they throw nothing but strikes. This ability to produce the consistent results gives us the confidence we need to allow computers to process *mission-critical* information (information that is necessary for continued operation of an organization, a space shuttle, and so on).

Reliability

Computer systems are the most reliable workers in any company, especially when it comes to repetitive tasks. They don't take sick days or coffee breaks, and they seldom complain. Anything below 99.9% *uptime*, the time when the computer system is in operation, is usually unacceptable. For some companies, any *downtime* is unacceptable. These companies provide **backup computers** that take over automatically should the main computers fail.

Communications

Computers can communicate with other computers, and, by extension, with us. Using physical and wireless links, computers are able to share resources, including processing capabilities, all forms of data and information, and various peripheral devices (printers, scanners). This communications capability has enabled the formation of computer networks within an organization and the emergence of the worldwide Internet network. These networks have certainly made communications between people easier and timelier.

Memory Capability

Computer systems have total and instant recall of data and an almost unlimited capacity to store these data, images, audio, video, or whatever can be digitized. A typical server computer system may have trillions of characters and millions of images stored and available for instant recall. A typical PC may have immediate access to billions of characters of data and thousands of images. To give you a benchmark for comparison, this book contains approximately 2 million characters and about 500 images.

Comparing Computer and Human Capabilities

The capabilities of computers and human beings are often compared because our information society is continually making decisions about whether a particular task is best done by a computer or a human. It's not always an obvious decision.

Human output (speech) is slow, maybe 120 words per minute for fast talkers, where computers talk in gigabytes per second. We recognize images (pattern recognition) more quickly than the fastest supercomputers. Computers struggle with pattern recognition. It's estimated that our memory is measured in terabytes (trillions of bytes), right up there with the best of computers. Computers do a much better job, however, of recalling stored information. They are 100% accurate in presenting stored information, which is seldom the case with humans. Computers can learn. So can we, but we do a much better job of applying what we learn to life situations.

The most significant difference between computers and humans is that we think. Computers do only what we tell them to do. And, at least for the foreseeable future, we remain in control.

1-6.1	The operational capabilities of a computer system include the ability to do both logic and computation operations. (T/F)	
1-6.2	Downtime is unacceptable in some companies so they have backup computers. (T/F)	
1-6.3	Which of the following would be a logic operation: (a) TODAY<BIRTHDATE, (b) GROSS-TAX-DEDUCT, (c) HOURS*WAGE, or (d) SALARY/12?	

1-7   How Do We Use Computers?

This section provides an overview of potential computer applications, which should give you a feel for how computers are affecting your life. These applications are presented in two parts, *enterprise computing* and *personal computing*. These applications, however, are but a few of the many applications presented throughout the book.

ENTERPRISE COMPUTING

Enterprise computing comprises all computing activities designed to support any type of organization: a company, a government entity, a university, and so on. Enterprise applications are in three groups: *information systems, process/device control,* and *science, research, and engineering.*

Information Systems

The bulk of existing computer power is dedicated to **information systems.** This includes all uses of computers that support the administrative aspects of an organization, such as airline reservation systems, student registration systems, hospital patient-billing systems, and countless others (see Figure 1-26). We combine *hardware, software, people, procedures,* and *data* to create an information system. A computer-based information system provides an organization with *data processing* capabilities and the knowledge workers in the organization with the *information* they need to make better, more informed decisions.

During any given day we are likely to interact with and/or cause activity within a variety of information systems. You interact directly with a bank's information system when you withdraw money from an ATM (automatic teller machine). When you purchase an item, the retail store updates its inventory and records the sale data. The credit card company updates its records to reflect the purchase and, possibly, debits that amount from your bank account. Each time you use your cellular phone, data are collected and passed around to information systems of cooperating phone companies, as needed. The first stop on a trip to the library is usually the PC linked to the library's information system.

Information systems process personal data on an ongoing basis, often without our knowledge. As you read this, some organization's information system has identified you as a target of commerce and will be sending you an unsolicited e-mail, called spam, or a printed brochure in the near future. A utility company may be processing your monthly invoice. Another information system might have determined that you are due a rebate on your city income taxes. Take a look around you today and be mindful of when you (or your personal information) are part of information systems.

Process/Device Control

Within an enterprise, the number of applications for computer-based **process/device control** is growing rapidly. For example, computers control every step in the oil-refining process and they control thousands of devices from air conditioners to theme park rides (see Figure 1-27). Computers that control processes accept data in a continuous **feedback loop.** In a feedback loop, the process itself generates data that become input to the computer. As the data are received and interpreted by the computer, the computer initiates action to control the ongoing process. An automated traffic-control system is a good example of the continuous feedback loop in a computerized process-control system. Have you ever driven an automobile through a city with an automated traffic-control system? If so, you would soon notice how the traffic signals are coordinated to minimize delays and optimize traffic flow. Traffic sensors are strategically placed throughout the city to feed data continuously to a central computer on the volume and direction of traffic flow (see Figure 1-28). The computer-based control system that activates the traffic signals is programmed to plan ahead. That is, if the sensors locate a group of cars traveling together, traffic signals are then timed accordingly.

S88E5107 1998:12:10 09:33:22

FIGURE 1–26 NASA Information System
Each launch of the space shuttle creates enormous activity in the NASA-based information system that supports the shuttle and the International Space Station. Astronauts, like this one, have ready access to onboard computers, which are linked to the NASA computers. The onboard systems provide ongoing feedback to ground-based scientists during space experiments. The information system encompasses everything from monitoring space resources (fuel, oxygen, and so on) to more earth-based concerns such as inventory and logistics.

Courtesy NASA

Server-sized process-control computers monitor and control the environment (temperature, humidity, lighting, security) inside skyscrapers. These computer-controlled skyscrapers are often referred to as "smart" buildings. At the other end of the process-control spectrum, tiny "computers on a chip" are being embedded in artificial hearts and other organs. Once the organs are implanted in the body, the computer monitors critical inputs, such as blood pressure and flow, and then takes corrective action to ensure stability of operation in a continuous feedback loop.

Computers control **industrial robots** that perform the materials handling duties in huge warehouses. These robots, which navigate about the warehouse without human intervention, pick and place inventory items in bins under computer control. In automobile assembly facilities, computer-controlled robots do the welding and the painting, and they keep the assembly line moving.

FIGURE 1–27 Jurassic Technology
The entertainment industry relies on computers and information technology to enliven experiences, often by using computers to control process and devices. Technology makes it possible for us to go back in time and experience the Jurassic period. At Universal Studios Hollywood theme park, the Jurassic Park River Adventure ride is completely automated.

Photo courtesy of Intel Corporation: Photo by Dana Fineman-Appel, Hollywood, California

Science, Research, and Engineering

Engineers and scientists routinely use the computer as a tool in *experimentation, design,* and *development.* There are at least as many science and research applications for the computer as there are scientists and engineers. One of these applications is **computer-aided design** (**CAD**), which involves

FIGURE 1–28 **AN AUTOMATED TRAFFIC-CONTROL SYSTEM**
In a continuous feedback loop, street sensors provide input to a process-control computer system about the direction and volume of traffic flow. Based on their feedback, the system controls the traffic lights to optimize the flow of traffic.

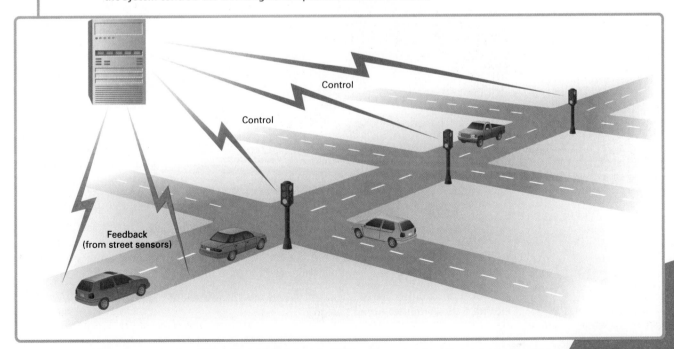

using the computer in the design process (see Figure 1-29). CAD systems enable the creation and manipulation of an on-screen graphic image. CAD systems provide a sophisticated array of tools, enabling designers to create three-dimensional objects that can be flipped, rotated, resized, viewed in detail, examined internally or externally, and much more. Photographs in this chapter and throughout the book illustrate a variety of CAD applications, such as automobile design and architectural design.

PERSONAL COMPUTING

Personal computing, an environment in which one person controls the PC, takes in everything from 3-D games, to going online, to computer-based education, to music composition. A seemingly endless number of software packages add variety to the personal computing experience (see Figure 1-30). The growth of personal computing has surpassed even the most adventurous forecasts of a decade ago. It's not uncommon for companies to have more personal computers than they do telephones. At home, each family member wants his or her own PC. With most PCs now part of a network or linked to the Internet, the reach of personal computing applications is virtually unlimited.

Buying a PC: The PC Investment

The personal computing adventure begins when you acquire a PC. Let's put this purchase into perspective. The typical home PC is used 10 to 50 hours a week. It's not passive like a TV. We interact with it to have fun, be informed, and do the chores of life. As any PC owner will tell you, the PC quickly becomes a major part of what you do. The cost of a PC reflects its importance in your life and home. PCs have emerged as the third most expensive item for the typical family—right behind homes and automobiles. For those families that do not own a home or an automobile, their PC(s) may be their biggest expense.

Living the personal computing adventure can run into serious money—quickly. But you need to weigh that cost against the enormous benefits of having one PC or, perhaps, a few PCs around the house. Given the potential of the PC and the impact it can have on your life and those around you, the PC remains one of the best investments you can make.

Most of the things we own are single-function items. Our automobiles take us from point A to point B. The only variation in functionality is the level of comfort the rider experiences. The dish-

FIGURE 1–29 Computer-Aided Design
This engineer uses computer-aided design (CAD) software to design automobiles.

Courtesy of Sun Microsystems, Inc.

washer washes dishes. Some of our household items are multifunction, like the kitchen sink, a Swiss Army knife, and the umbrella. The PC, however, is a general-purpose device capable of performing an almost endless variety of tasks. Any PC purchased with purpose and invigorated with imagination is well worth its cost—and then some.

PC Applications Galore

A variety of domestic and business applications form the foundation of personal computing. Domestic applications include everything from personal finance to education to entertainment to reference (see Figure 1-31). PC software is available to support thousands of common and not-so-common personal and business applications.

The Software Suite

Software suites are bundles of complementary software that include, to varying degrees, several or all of the productivity software mentioned in this section. The various programs within a given software suite have a

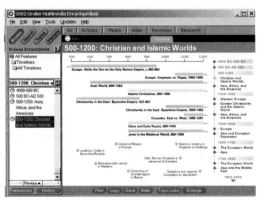

FIGURE 1–30 The Personal Computing Experience
Personal computing provides a much richer experience than just a few years ago. After receiving a box of chocolates for Valentine's Day, this man immediately called his fiancée to show his appreciation. Through a videophone Internet hookup, she is able to see and hear his expression of joy. She sent him a digital image of her with the roses she received from him.

Photo courtesy of Intel Corporation

common interface and are integrated for easy transfer of information among programs. Examples in the book are from Microsoft Office, the most widely used software suite (see Figure 1-32). Corel WordPerfect Office and Lotus SmartSuite are the other major suites. Most new PCs are sold with a software suite installed on the system.

Over the history of personal computing, these software suite applications have formed the foundation for personal computing in the home and in the business world.

- *Word processing.* **Word processing software** enables users to create, edit (revise), and format documents in preparation for output (for example, printing, displaying locally or over the Internet, faxing, or sending via e-mail).

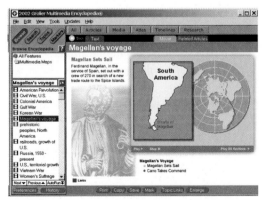

FIGURE 1–31 The Multimedia Encyclopedia
The multimedia encyclopedia is a good place to start your multimedia PC adventure. The *Grolier Year 2002 Multimedia Encyclopedia* (shown here) contains timelines (see illustration), millions of words, thousands of images, almost hundreds of videos, and hours of audio telling and showing us about thousands of persons, places, and things. The CD-ROM encyclopedia uses the full capabilities of multimedia to enrich the presentation of information. "Thumbing" through an encyclopedia will never be the same.

The Grolier Multimedia Encyclopedia copyright © 2002 by Grolier Interactive Inc.

MICROSOFT OFFICE

FIGURE 1–32

The Microsoft Office software suite includes (clockwise from top left) PowerPoint (presentation), Word (word processing), Excel (spreadsheet), Access (database), and, in the center, Outlook (personal information management).

- *Presentation.* **Presentation software** lets you create professional-looking images for group presentations, self-running slide shows, reports, and for other situations that require the presentation of organized, visual information. The electronic images may include multimedia elements, such as sound, special effects, animation, and video.

- *Spreadsheet.* A **spreadsheet** is simply a table of values, numbers, names, and so on. **Spreadsheet software** lets you work with the rows and columns of data in a spreadsheet. Spreadsheet software can summarize columns of data and perform a variety of statistical and financial operations on data. When values change, all other affected values are changed automatically.

- *Database.* **Database software** permits you to create and maintain a database and to extract information from the database. In a database, data are organized for ease of manipulation and retrieval.

- *Desktop publishing.* **Desktop publishing software** allows you to produce camera-ready documents (ready to be printed professionally) from the confines of a desktop. People routinely use desktop publishing software to create newsletters, advertisements, procedures manuals, and many other printing needs.

- *Communications.* **Communications software** is a family of software applications that enables you to send e-mail and faxes, tap the resources of the Internet via **Internet browsers,** and link your PC with a remote computer.

- *Personal information management.* **PIM software,** mentioned earlier in the chapter, is an umbrella term that encompasses a variety of personal management and contact information programs. A particular PIM package might include calendar applications (appointment scheduling and reminders), communications applications (e-mail and fax), and databases that help you organize your phone numbers, e-mail addresses, to-do lists, notes, diary entries, and so on.

These software packages have demonstrated millions of times that they can save you time and money and, generally, make life more convenient.

Building a Software Portfolio

A **software portfolio** is simply the mix of software that you have on your computer. The software suite and other software that might be installed on your computer at the time of purchase provide a good start to growing your portfolio to meet your personal computing needs and goals. With over a

THE CRYSTAL BALL:
PC Prices In the early 1970s, an "electronic" calculator that performed only the basic arithmetic functions cost between $300 and $500, about the price of today's desktop PC. Most people have at least one. I paid $12,000 for my first PC in 1978, roughly the cost of a BMW at the time. Today, a good calculator is a ubiquitous consumer item and can be purchased for under $20. By 2010, the PC (or whatever its emergent form factor will be called) will be an inexpensive consumer item priced at less than a quarter of its current inflation-adjusted cost. Plus, you can bet that they will be continuously online and small enough such that we carry them with us wherever we go.

half-million free and commercial software packages on the market, there is personal computing support for just about any application and the boldest imagination.

One of the hottest areas of personal computing growth is in the area of graphics and multimedia. This growth has been spurred by the availability of inexpensive support hardware, such as digital cameras and image scanners. People are finding a plethora of home and family software that can help them create their own calendars, greeting cards, and banners, help them prepare and file their tax returns, help them design a room or a house, help them manage their finances, and much more. Personal computing has opened a new world in personal communication, enabling video phone conversations between neighbors and friends on the other side of the world. Personal computing has redefined reference materials. We now find encyclopedias and comprehensive dictionaries on CD-ROM or the Internet. The easily accessible Internet has white pages and Yellow Pages for the entire United States. The road atlas is now electronic and dynamic, highlighting for us the best route to our destination.

Students at all levels, from kindergarten to professional adult education, are embracing personal computing as a new approach to learning. Computer-based education and online classes will not replace teachers any time soon, but educators agree that CD-ROM-based *computer-based training* (*CBT*) and *Internet-based distance learning* are having a profound impact on traditional modes of education. Available programs and online courses can help you learn keyboarding skills, increase your vocabulary, study algebra, learn about the makeup of the atom, practice your Russian, learn about computers, and much more. Colleges and even high schools offer thousands of courses online via distance learning. You can now get an MBA, a law degree, and a bachelor's degree in most disciplines without attending a single traditional classroom lecture.

There are thousands of commercial applications created specifically to tickle our fancy and entertain us. You can play electronic golf. You can buy a computer chess opponent in the form of a board, chess pieces, and a miniature robotic arm that moves the pieces (you have to move your own pieces). You can "pilot" an airplane to Paris and battle Zorbitrons in cyberspace.

The amount of computing capacity in the world is doubling every two years. The number and sophistication of personal computing applications are growing at a similar pace. Tomorrow, there will be applications that are unheard of today.

1-7.1	More computing capacity is dedicated to information systems than to CBT. (T/F)
1-7.2	The foundation of personal computing over the last decade has been 3-D computing games. (T/F)
1-7.3	Which of the following is not a software suite: (a) Borland's Business Suite, (b) Corel WordPerfect Office, (c) Lotus SmartSuite, or (d) Microsoft Office?
1-7.4	The PC is considered to be what type of device: (a) single function, (b) multifunction, (c) special-purpose, or (d) general-purpose?

CHAPTER SUMMARY

1-1 OUR INFORMATION SOCIETY

In an **information society**, **knowledge workers** focus their energies on providing myriad information services. The knowledge worker's job function revolves around the use, manipulation, and dissemination of information. Learning about computers is an adventure that will last a lifetime because **information technology (IT)**, the integration of computing technology and information processing, is changing daily.

The computer revolution is transforming the way we communicate, do business, and learn. This technological revolution is having a profound impact on the business community and on our private and professional lives. For example, increasingly, we communicate with our colleagues at work through **electronic mail (e-mail)** or with our friends through **instant messaging (IM)** and **chat** rooms. Sometimes you may get unsolicited e-mail, called **spam.**

In this century we can anticipate traveling an **information superhighway,** a network of high-speed data communications links, that eventually will connect virtually every facet of our society. Today, millions of people have a **personal computer (PC)**. This widespread availability has resulted in an explosion of applications for computers. At home, people may connect to the **Internet,** a worldwide network of computers. Home appliances may also include **microprocessors.**

Through the 1970s, **users** related their information needs to computer professionals who would then work with the computer system to generate the necessary information. Today, users work directly with their PCs to obtain the information they need.

1-2 Rₓ FOR CYBERPHOBIA: INFORMATION TECHNOLOGY COMPETENCY

Information technology competency (IT competency) is emerging as a universal goal in our information society. IT-competent people know how to purchase, set up, and operate a computer system, and how to make it work for them. The IT-competent person is also aware of the computer's impact on society and is conversant the language of technology.

Software refers collectively to a set of machine-readable instructions, called **programs,** that cause the computer to perform desired functions. Computers and computer equipment, which accept **input** and provide **output,** are called **hardware.**

The fact that many people routinely use computers but are not IT-competent is referred to as the "computer proficiency digital divide."

1-3 THE NET CONNECTION

We now live in a global village in which computers and people are linked within companies and between countries. Most existing computers are part of a **computer network** that shares resources and information.

The Internet links almost a billion users in a global network. **The Net** can be accessed by people in organizations with established links to the Internet and by individuals with PCs, often via **Internet service providers (ISPs)**. Often this is done with a **modem,** a device that permits communication with remote computers via a telephone-line link. Commercial **information services,** such as **America Online (AOL)**, offer a wide range of information services, including up-to-the-minute news and weather, electronic shopping, e-mail, and much more. When the user terminates this **online** link, the user goes **offline.** Internet

users can **download** text or a digitized version of a song directly to their PC, then read it or play it through their PC. **MP3 players** can store and play digital music recorded in MP3 format. Information is **uploaded** from a local computer to a remote computer. The **World Wide Web,** or **the Web,** is an Internet application that lets us view Internet **Web pages.** Another application, **newsgroups,** provides electronic bulletin boards. Generally, Internet applications can be placed into these categories: personal communications, browsing and searching for information, downloading and file sharing, streaming media, online transactions, and entertainment.

1-4 THE BASICS: HARDWARE, SOFTWARE, AND COMPUTER SYSTEMS

At the heart of any **computer** is its **processor,** an electronic device capable of interpreting and executing programmed commands for input, output, computation, and logic operations.

Output on a computer can be routed to a **monitor** or a **printer.** The output on a monitor is temporary and is called **soft copy.** Printers produce **hard copy** output. Data can be entered via a **keyboard** or a **mouse,** a **point-and-draw device.**

System software plays a central role in everything that happens within a computer system from start-up to shutdown. **Applications software** performs specific personal, business, or scientific processing tasks.

Random-access memory (RAM) provides temporary storage of data and programs during processing within solid-state **integrated circuits,** or **chips.** Permanently installed and interchangeable **magnetic disks** and **optical discs** provide permanent storage for data and programs. A computer system can include a variety of **peripheral devices.**

The differences in the various categories of computers are a matter of computing power, not its physical size. Today, computers are generally grouped in these categories: notebook PCs, desktop PCs, handheld computers, **thin clients,** workstations, **server computers,** and **supercomputers.** Server computers manage the resources on a network and perform a variety of functions for **client computers.** All **computer systems,** no matter how small or large, have the same fundamental capabilities— *input, processing, output,* and *storage.* Each offers many **input/output,** or **I/O,** alternatives.

1-5 PERSONAL COMPUTERS TO SUPERCOMPUTERS

In 1981, IBM introduced its **IBM PC,** defining the original PC-compatible machine, now also called a **Wintel PC** because of its use of Microsoft Windows **operating systems** and the Intel processors. The Apple iMac and Power Mac, with their Mac OS X and Motorola PowerPC processors, is the other major **platform.** Computers come in a variety of physical and computing sizes. Most personal computers are either **notebook PCs** (also called **laptops**) or **desktop PCs.** Many notebook PC buyers purchase a **port replicator,** called a **docking station,** for portability plus the expanded features of a desktop PC. **Ports** are electronic interfaces through which devices like the keyboard, monitor, mouse, printer, image scanner, and so on are connected. The desktop PC's **system unit** contains the processor, disk storage, and other components. Many mobile workers are benefiting from using a **wearable PC.**

The typical off-the-shelf PC is configured to run multimedia applications. **Multimedia applications** combine text, sound, graphics, motion video, and/or animation. The typical multimedia-configured PC includes a **motherboard**; a keyboard and a point-and-draw device for input; a monitor and a printer for output; a **hard-disk drive** and a **floppy disk drive** into which an interchangeable **diskette**, or **floppy disk**, is inserted; a **CD-ROM drive** into which an interchangeable **CD-ROM** is inserted; a **DVD-ROM** drive that accepts all DVD format discs, such as **DVD-Video** for playing movies; and a microphone and a set of speakers for audio I/O. Some models have rewritable **CD-RW** and/or **DVD+RW**.

Palmtop PC, personal digital assistant (PDA), connected organizer, personal communicator, mobile business center, and Web phone are just some of the names for **handheld computers**. A handheld can have a variety of physical shapes and sizes, referred to as its **form factor**. **Pen-based computers** which may or may not have small keyboards, make use of an electronic pen, call a **stylus**, to do such tasks as selecting options, entering data (via handwritten characters), and drawing. Keying can also be accomplished via an onscreen keyboard. **Speech-recognition** software, which allows the user to enter spoken words into the system, is being integrated into high-end handheld computers. Handheld computers support a variety of **personal information management** (**PIM**) systems, including appointment scheduling and to-do lists. You may also be using handhelds to read a good **electronic-book** (**e-book**) via the computer's **text-to-speech software**.

The thin client computer is designed to function only when it is linked to a server computer.

The workstation's speed and input/output devices set it apart from a PC. A typical workstation will have a high-**resolution** monitor and a variety of specialized point-and-draw devices. A common use of workstations is for engineering design.

In **client/server computing**, processing is distributed throughout the network. The client computer requests processing or some other type of service from the server computer. Both client and server computers perform processing. The **proxy server computer** sits between the client and server, intercepting client requests to improve overall system performance. The client computer runs **front-end applications software**, and the server computer runs the **back-end applications software**.

Server computers are usually associated with **enterprise systems**; that is, computer-based systems that service entities throughout the company. Typically, users communicate with one or more server computers through a PC, a workstation, a thin client, or a **terminal**. Supercomputers primarily address **processor-bound applications**.

A computer system manipulates your **data** to produce **information**. The permanent source of data for a particular computer application area is sometimes called a **master file**.

1-6 COMPUTER SYSTEM CAPABILITIES

A **local area network** (**LAN**) connects PCs or workstations in close proximity. The LAN's server computer performs a variety of functions for other client computers on the LAN.

Computer system capabilities are either input/output or processing. Processing capabilities are subdivided into computation and logic operations.

Computers perform input/output (I/O) operations by reading from input and storage devices and writing to output devices.

The computer is fast, accurate, consistent, and reliable, and aids in communications and has an enormous memory capacity. Computer operations are measured in **milliseconds, microseconds, nanoseconds**, and **picoseconds**. When downtime is unacceptable, companies provide **backup** computers that take over automatically should the main computers fail.

1-7 HOW DO WE USE COMPUTERS?

Enterprise computing comprises all computing activities designed to support any type of organization: a company, a government entity, a university, and so on. Enterprise applications are in three groups: information systems, process/device control and science, research, and engineering.

● *Information systems.* The computer is used to process data and produce business information. Hardware, software, people, procedures, and data are combined to create an **information system**.

● *Process/Device Control.* In computer-based **process/device control**, processes accept data in a continuous **feedback loop. Industrial robots** perform many jobs from materials handling to painting without human intervention.

● *Science, research, and engineering.* The computer is used as a tool in experimentation, design, and development. **Computer-aided design** (**CAD**) involves using the computer in the design process.

The PC is used for **personal computing** by individuals for a variety of business and domestic applications, including such productivity tools as **word processing software, presentation software, spreadsheet software, database software, desktop publishing software, communications software**, including **Internet browsers**, and personal information management software. **Software suites** are bundles of complementary software that may include several or all of these common productivity software packages. A **spreadsheet** is a table of values, numbers, names, and so on. A **software portfolio** is the mix of software that you have on your computer.

KEY TERMS

form factor (p. 40)
front-end applications software (p. 44)
handheld computer (p. 40)
hard copy (p. 33)
hard-disk drive (p. 38)
hardware (p. 26)
IBM PC (p. 36)
industrial robot (p. 53)
information (p. 47)
information service (p. 31)
information society (p. 22)
information superhighway (p. 25)
information system (p. 52)
information technology (IT) (p. 22)
information technology competency (IT
 competency) (p. 26)
input (p. 26)
input/output (I/O) (p. 35)
instant messaging (IM) (p. 24)
integrated circuit (p. 33)
Internet (p. 23)
Internet browser (p. 56)
Internet service provider (ISP) (p. 31)
keyboard (p. 33)
knowledge worker (p. 22)
laptop PC (p. 36)
local area network (LAN) (p. 49)
magnetic disk (p. 33)
master file (p. 47)
microprocessor (p. 24)

microsecond (p. 50)
millisecond (p. 50)
modem (p. 31)
monitor (p. 33)
motherboard (p. 38)
mouse (p. 33)
MP3 player (p. 31)
multimedia application (p. 38)
nanosecond (p. 50)
newsgroup (p. 29)
notebook PC (p. 36)
offline (p. 31)
online (p. 31)
operating system (p. 36)
optical disc (p. 33)
output (p. 26)
pen-based computer (p. 42)
peripheral device (p. 33)
personal computer (PC) (p. 22)
personal computing (p. 54)
personal information management (PIM)
 (p. 42)
picosecond (p. 50)
platform (p. 36)
point-and-draw device (p. 33)
port (p. 38)
port replicator (p. 38)
presentation software (p. 56)
printer (p. 33)
process/device control (p. 52)

processor (p. 33)
processor-bound application (p. 45)
programs (p. 26)
proxy server computer (p. 44)
random-access memory (RAM) (p. 33)
resolution (p. 43)
server computer (p. 35)
soft copy (p. 33)
software (p. 26)
software portfolio (p. 56)
software suite (p. 55)
spam (p. 27)
speech-recognition software (p. 42)
spreadsheet (p. 56)
spreadsheet software (p. 56)
stylus (p. 42)
supercomputer (p. 34)
system software (p. 34)
system unit (p. 38)
terminal (p. 44)
text-to-speech software (p. 42)
the Net (p. 29)
thin client (p. 35)
uploaded (p. 31)
user (p. 25)
wearable PC (p. 40)
Web page (p. 31)
Wintel PC (p. 36)
word processing software (p. 55)
World Wide Web (the Web) (p. 31)

MATCHING

1. Modem
2. Industrial robots
3. Text-to-speech
4. Newsgroups
5. Hardware
6. Software
7. Peripheral devices
8. MP3
9. Backup computers
10. Stylus
11. 1000 nanoseconds
12. Form factor
13. Hard copy
14. Processing operations
15. Master file

a. electronic pen
b. printed output
c. reading e-books
d. size and shape
e. all patient records
f. music file
g. take over when computers fail
h. monitor and printer
i. computation and logic operations
j. 1 microsecond
k. programs
l. computing equipment
m. interactive electronic bulletin boards
n. telephone-line link
o. welding and painting

CHAPTER SELF-CHECK

1-1.1 A person who uses a computer is called a: (a) user, (b) client, (c) software consumer, or (d) utilizer.

1-1.2 Which of these is not a means of personal communication on the Internet: (a) electronic mail, (b) instant messaging, (c) instanotes, or (d) chat?

1-1.3 Because of incompatible video formats, it is not yet possible to view DVD movies on a PC. (T/F)

1-2.1 What causes computers to perform desired functions: (a) programs, (b) soft copy, (c) instruction lists, or (d) procedures?

1-2.2 Data entered to a computer system for processing would be: (a) output, (b) throughput, (c) input, or (d) dataput.

1-2.3 Unsolicited e-mail is knows as: (a) ham, (b) bologna, (c) RAM JAM, or (d) spam.

1-3.1 Uploading on the Internet is transmitting information from an Internet-based host computer to a local PC. (T/F)

1-3.2 The Internet is also known as: (a) the Bucket, (b) the Global Interface, (c) the Net, or (d) Cybernet.

1-3.3 Individuals gain access to the Internet by subscribing to a(n): (a) PSI, (b) ISP, (c) IPS, or (d) SPI.

1-4.1 Output on a monitor is soft copy and output on a printer is hard copy. (T/F)

1-4.2 Of the different types of computers, only personal computers offer a variety of I/O alternatives. (T/F)

1-4.3 Applications software takes control of a PC on start-up and then controls all system software activities during the computing session. (T/F)

1-4.4 Integrated circuits are also called: (a) slivers, (b) chips, (c) flakes, or (d) electronic sandwiches.

1-4.5 Thin clients are like PCs but with more features. (T/F)

1-5.1 The four size categories of conventional personal computers are miniature, portable, notebook, and business. (T/F)

1-5.2 Server computers usually are associated with enterprise systems. (T/F)

1-5.3 Supercomputers are oriented to what type of applications: (a) I/O-bound, (b) processor-bound, (c) inventory management, or (d) word processing?

1-5.4 What is the name given those applications that combine text, sound, graphics, motion video, and/or animation: (a) videoscapes, (b) motionware, (c) multimedia, or (d) anigraphics?

1-5.5 The trend in the design of computer networks is toward: (a) distributed transmission, (b) client/server computing, (c) CANs, or (d) centralized mainframe computers.

1-6.1 On a LAN, the client computer stores all data and applications software used by the server computer. (T/F)

1-6.2 A microsecond is 1000 times longer than a nanosecond. (T/F)

1-6.3 In a LAN, a server computer performs a variety of functions for its: (a) client computers, (b) subcomputers, (c) LAN entity PC, or (d) work units.

1-6.4 An Internet-based online retailer is called a(n): (a) online tailer, (b) net-tailer, (c) e-tailer, or (d) cybertailer.

1-6.5 Supercomputers outperform humans when it comes to pattern recognition. (T/F)

1-7.1 Desktop publishing refers to the capability of producing camera-ready documents from the confines of a desktop. (T/F)

1-7.2 What type of computing comprises all computing activities designed to support an organization: (a) personal, (b) enterprise, (c) industrial, or (d) professional?

1-7.3 Computers that control processes accept data in a continuous: (a) infinite loop, (b) data highway, (c) data traffic pattern, or (d) feedback loop.

1-7.4 The PC productivity tool that manipulates data organized in rows and columns is called a: (a) database record manager, (b) presentation mechanism, (c) word processing document, or (d) spreadsheet.

1-7.5 The typical home PC is used 10 to 50 hours a week. (T/F)

1-7.6 Which PC productivity tool would be helpful in writing a term paper: (a) word processing, (b) presentation, (c) spreadsheet, or (d) communications?

1-7.7 Various programs within a given software suite have a common interface. (T/F)

IT ETHICS AND ISSUES

THE SPAM DILEMMA

As we all know, Spam is a popular Hormel meat product. By some unlucky quirk of fate unsolicited e-mail was given the same name—spam. To Netizens, citizens of the Internet, spam is the Internet equivalent of junk mail and those dreaded telemarketing calls. To the senders of junk e-mail, spam is simply bulk e-mail, usually some kind of advertisement and/or an invitation to try some service or product. Spam may be unsolicited religious, racial, or sexual messages, as well. Such messages can be especially irritating. Generally, Internet users loathe spamming because spammers (those who send spam) use the shotgun approach, broadcasting their message to large numbers of people. Inevitably, enough of these messages find a welcome audience, prompting spammers to send more spam.

Those who receive e-mail consider their e-mail boxes a personal and costly resource. They feel that spam wastes their time, violates their electronic mailbox, and in some cases insults their integrity. On the other hand, spammers cite free speech and the tradition of a free flow of information over the Internet as justification for broadcasting their messages. Spam renews the conflict between free speech and the individual's right to privacy.

Discussion: *Currently, laws favor the spammers; that is, there is little an individual can do to thwart the barrage of junk mail, other than ask his or her ISP to filter spam whenever possible. Do you believe legislation should be enacted to control unsolicited e-mail over the Internet or do you favor industry self-regulation? Explain.*

Discussion: *What are the costs associated with spam? Who pays for spam?*

Discussion: *What are the benefits associated with spam? Who derives the most benefit from spam?*

SHOULD PC OWNERSHIP BE AN ENTRANCE REQUIREMENT FOR COLLEGES?

As the job market tightens, colleges are looking to give their students a competitive edge. With computer knowledge becoming a job prerequisite for many positions, hundreds of colleges have made the purchase of a personal computer a prerequisite for admission (see Figure 1-33). Personal computers are versatile in that they can be used as stand-alone computers or they can be linked to the college's network, the Internet, or other personal computers in a classroom. At these colleges, PCs are everywhere—in classrooms, lounges, libraries, and other common areas.

Wouldn't it be great to run a bibliographic search from your dorm room or home? Make changes to a report without retyping it? Run a case search for a law class? Use the computer for math homework calculations?

Instead of making hard copies of class assignments, some instructors key in their assignments, which are then "delivered" to each student's electronic mailbox. At some colleges, student PCs are networked during class, enabling immediate distribution of class materials. Students can correspond with their instructors through their computer to get help with assignments. They can even "talk" to other students at connected colleges.

Discussion: *If your college does not require PC ownership for admission, should it? If it does, should the policy be continued?*

FIGURE 1–33 The Interactive Networked Classroom
Owning a PC is a prerequisite for admission to the University of Oklahoma's College of Engineering. OU students shown here use PCs with wireless technology that lets them connect to the Internet anywhere within the engineering complex. During class, students and the instructor can easily create a wireless local area network to link all PCs. Students can do the same for a linked study group.

Courtesy of Sooner Magazine, University of Oklahoma

Discussion: *What could students, professors, and college administrators do that they are not doing now (without a PC ownership requirement) if the entire campus were networked and every student were required to have a notebook PC?*

HATE SITES ON THE INTERNET

How do some consumers voice grievances about companies, products, and services? How do some people voice their disgust over a rock group, a political organization, or even a university? They publish their thoughts, warts and all, on the Internet, usually on their own Web page. Just enter the keyword *hate* or *sucks* into an Internet search facility and see how many hits it gets. Anyone or anything is a potential target.

Some of this hate venom may be deserved, but perhaps it isn't. The Internet is a powerful voice that can be used to call attention to flaws in a company's products or services. It can also be used to vilify individuals who may simply be doing their jobs, effectively and legally.

Discussion: *Some experts in the field of Internet monitoring say that the best response to hate site venom is no response. How would you respond if one or more Internet sites mounted an unjustified attack on your company's products? How would you respond to an unjustified personal attack?*

Discussion: *Visit a Web site that is dedicated to denouncing someone, something, an idea, or an organization. Is the content fair and is it appropriate for the Internet? Explain.*

DISCUSSION AND PROBLEM SOLVING

1-1.1 Information technology has had far-reaching effects on our lives. How have the computer and IT affected your life?

1-1.2 Discuss how the complexion of jobs will change as we evolve from an industrial society into an information society. Give several examples.

1-1.3 Contrast these Internet applications: e-mail, instant messaging, and chat.

1-1.4 Think back and discuss your earliest remembrances of computers. Compare those computers to today's.

1-2.1 What is your concept of information technology competency? In what ways do you think achieving information technology competency will affect your domestic life? Your business life?

1-2.2 At what age should information technology competency education begin? Is society prepared to provide IT education at this age? If not, why?

1-2.3 What would be your number one reason to become IT competent?

1-2.4 Do you consider yourself IT competent? Why or why not?

1-3.1 Comment on how information technology is changing our traditional patterns of personal communication.

1-3.2 If you are a current user of the Internet, describe four Internet services that have been of value to you. If not, in what ways do you think the Internet might be a benefit to you?

1-3.3 What might you want to download over the Internet?

1-3.4 Which three Internet applications listed in Figure 1-10 are most appealing to you? Why?

1-4.1 List as many computer and information technology terms as you can (up to 30) that are used in everyday conversations at the office and at school.

1-4.2 Describe an ideal applications software package that might help you meet your personal or business information processing needs.

1-4.3 RAM, magnetic disks, and optical discs enable storage of data on a computer system. Why don't we simplify and have just one of these options?

1-5.1 If you could purchase only one personal computer, which would you buy, a notebook PC or a desktop PC? Why?

1-5.2 Explain circumstances that would cause you to order a port replicator with a notebook PC.

1-5.3 Speculate on how one of these professionals would use a handheld computer: a police officer, an insurance adjuster, a delivery person for a courier service, or a newspaper reporter.

1-5.4 Management at a large company with 1000 three-year-old PCs, all on a network, is debating whether to replace the PCs with thin clients or with new PCs. Each has its advantages. What would you consider to be the single most important advantage for each option?

1-5.5 Give at least two reasons why a regional bank might opt to buy six server computers rather than one supercomputer.

1-5.6 Lots of people wear their PCs. Speculate on why they wear them.

1-5.7 What would be your ideal form factor for a handheld computer?

1-5.8 Speculate on two supercomputer applications not mentioned in the book.

1-5.9 Discuss the relationship between the server computer and its client computers.

1-6.1 Compare the information processing capabilities of human beings to those of computers with respect to speed, accuracy, reliability, consistency, communications, and memory capability.

1-6.2 Within the context of a computer system, what is meant by *read* and *write*?

1-6.3 Identify and briefly describe five computation and five logic operations that might be performed by a computer during the processing of college students throughout the academic year.

1-6.4 Every company has records on computer-based master files or in a database. Describe three types of master files.

1-7.1 The use of computers tends to stifle creativity. Argue for or against this statement.

1-7.2 Comment on how computers are changing our traditional patterns of recreation.

1-7.3 Of the productivity software described in this chapter, choose the two that will have (or currently have) the most impact on your productivity. Explain why you chose these two.

1-7.4 Explain why software packages in a software suite are complementary.

1-7.5 The dominant software suite is Microsoft Office, in its various versions. However, some analysts claim that alternative software suites are as good as or better than it is. Under what circumstances would a company with 5000 PCs opt to go with a Microsoft competitor?

1-7.6 Pick an enterprise you know and list as many of its computing activities as you can, categorizing them as an information system, a process/device control application, or a science, research, and engineering application.

FOCUS ON PERSONAL COMPUTING

1. Go exploring and find out more about your PC (or the one in your college lab). Go to the "Accessories" group on the programs listing (click *Start, All Programs,* and highlight *Accessories*). Every Windows-based PC comes with some interesting and helpful programs. Open at least six Accessories group programs. Give a brief explanation of each and include your assessment of its applicability to your personal computing needs. The Accessories group includes a calculator, a graphics application, a sound recorder, and many more programs.

2. Continue your discovery adventure and run at least three more programs that are not in the Accessories group or a Microsoft Office program (Word, Excel, PowerPoint, and so on). Give a brief explanation of each program and include your assessment of its applicability to your personal computing needs.

INTERNET EXERCISES @ www.prenhall.com/long

1. The Online Study Guide (multiple choice, true/false, matching, and essay questions)
2. Internet Learning Activities
   - The Global Village
   - Personal Computers
   - Handheld Computers
   - Workstations
   - Server Computers
   - Supercomputers
   - Computer History
3. Serendipitous Internet Activities
   - At the Movies

THE HISTORY OF COMPUTING

The history of computers and computing is of special significance to us, because many of its most important events have occurred within our lifetime. Historians divide the history of the modern computer into generations, beginning with the introduction of the UNIVAC I, the first commercially viable computer, in 1951. But the quest for a mechanical servant—one that could free people from the more boring aspects of thinking—is centuries old.

Why did it take so long to develop the computer? Some of the "credit" goes to human foibles. Too often brilliant insights were not recognized or given adequate support during an inventor's lifetime. Instead, these insights would lay dormant for as long as 100 years until someone else rediscovered—or reinvented—them. Some of the "credit" has to go to workers, too, who sabotaged labor-saving devices that threatened to put them out of work. The rest of the "credit" goes to technology; some insights were simply ahead of their time's technology. Figure 1-34 illustrates an abbreviated history of the stops and starts that have given us this marvel of the modern age, the computer.

Figure 1–34 — JOURNEY THROUGH THE HISTORY OF COMPUTING

3000 B.C.: THE ABACUS
The abacus is probably considered the original mechanical counting device (it has been traced back 5000 years). It is still used in education to demonstrate the principles of counting and arithmetic and in business for speedy calculations.

Long and Associates

1623–1662: BLAISE PASCAL
Although inventor, painter, and sculptor Leonardo da Vinci (1425–1519) sketched ideas for a mechanical adding machine, it was another 150 years before French mathematician and philosopher Blaise Pascal (1623–1662) finally invented and built the "Pascaline" in 1642 to help his father, a tax collector. Although Pascal was praised throughout Europe, his invention was a financial failure. The hand-built machines were expensive and delicate; moreover, Pascal was the only person who could repair them. Because human labor was actually cheaper, the Pascaline was abandoned as impractical.

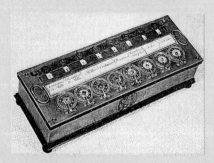

1642: THE PASCALINE
The Pascaline used a counting-wheel design: Numbers for each digit were arranged on wheels so that a single revolution of one wheel would engage gears that turned the wheel one tenth of a revolution to its immediate left. Although the Pascaline was abandoned as impractical, its counting-wheel design was used by all mechanical calculators until the mid-1960s, when they were made obsolete by electronic calculators.

3000 • B.C. City of Troy first inhabited   1639 • First North American printing press

1801: JACQUARD'S LOOM

A practicing weaver, Frenchman Joseph-Marie Jacquard (1753–1871) spent what little spare time he had trying to improve the lot of his fellow weavers. (They worked 16-hour days, with no days off!) His solution, the Jacquard loom, was created in 1801. Holes strategically punched in a card directed the movement of needles, thread, and fabric, creating the elaborate patterns still known as Jacquard weaves. Jacquard's weaving loom is considered the first significant use of binary automation. The loom was an immediate success with mill owners because they could hire cheaper and less skilled workers. But weavers, fearing unemployment, rioted and called Jacquard a traitor.

Courtesy of International Business Machines Corporation. Unauthorized use not permitted.

1793–1871: CHARLES BABBAGE

Everyone, from bankers to navigators, depended on mathematical tables during the bustling Industrial Revolution. However, these hand-calculated tables were usually full of errors. After discovering that his own tables were riddled with mistakes, Charles Babbage (1793–1871) envisioned a steam-powered "difference engine" and then an "analytical engine" that would perform tedious calculations accurately. Although Babbage never perfected his devices, they introduced many of the concepts used in today's general-purpose computer.

Courtesy of International Business Machines Corporation. Unauthorized use not permitted.

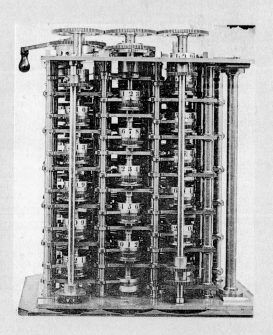

1842: BABBAGE'S DIFFERENCE ENGINE AND THE ANALYTICAL ENGINE

Convinced his machine would benefit England, Babbage applied for—and received—one of the first government grants to build the difference engine. Hampered by nineteenth-century machine technology, cost overruns, and the possibility his chief engineer was padding the bills, Babbage completed only a portion of the difference engine (shown here) before the government withdrew its support in 1842, deeming the project "worthless to science." Meanwhile, Babbage had conceived of the idea of a more advanced "analytical engine." In essence, this was a general-purpose computer that could add, subtract, multiply, and divide in automatic sequence at a rate of 60 additions per second. His 1833 design, which called for thousands of gears and drives, would cover the area of a football field and be powered by a locomotive engine. Babbage worked on this project until his death. In 1991 London's Science Museum spent $600,000 to build a working model of the difference engine, using Babbage's original plans. The result stands 6 feet high, 10 feet long, contains 4000 parts, and weighs 3 tons.

New York Public Library Picture Collection

1801 • Thomas Jefferson elected President   1838 • Samuel F. B. Morse develops Morse Code

1816–1852: LADY ADA AUGUSTA LOVELACE

The daughter of poet Lord Byron, Lady Ada Augusta Lovelace (1816–1852) became a mentor to Babbage and translated his works, adding her own extensive footnotes. Her suggestion that punched cards could be prepared to instruct Babbage's engine to repeat certain operations has led some people to call her the first programmer. Ada, the programming language adopted by Department of Defense as a standard, is named for Lady Ada Lovelace.

The Bettmann Archive/BBC Hulton

1860–1929: HERMAN HOLLERITH

With the help of a professor, Herman Hollerith (1860–1929) got a job as a special agent helping the U.S. Bureau of the Census tabulate the head count for the 1880 census—a process that took almost eight years. To speed up the 1890 census, Hollerith devised a punched-card tabulating machine. When his machine outperformed two other systems, Hollerith won a contract to tabulate the 1890 census. Hollerith earned a handsome income leasing his machinery to the governments of the United States, Canada, Austria, Russia, and others; he charged 65 cents for every 1000 people counted. (During the 1890 U.S. census alone, he earned more than $40,000—a fortune in those days.) Hollerith may have earned even more selling the single-use punched cards. But the price was worth it. The bureau completed the census in just 22 years and saved more than $5 million.

Courtesy of International Business Machines Corporation. Unauthorized use not permitted.

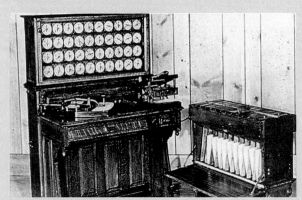

1890: HOLLERITH'S TABULATING MACHINE

Hollerith's *punched-card tabulating machine* had three parts. Clerks at the U.S. Bureau of the Census used a hand punch to enter data onto cards a little larger than a dollar bill. Cards were then read and sorted by a 24-bin sorter box (right) and summarized on numbered tabulating dials (left), which were connected electrically to the sorter box. Ironically, Hollerith's idea for the punched card came not from Jacquard or Babbage but from "punch photography." Railroads of the day issued tickets with physical descriptions of a passenger's hair and eye color. Conductors punched holes in the ticket to indicate that a passenger's hair and eye color matched those of the ticket owner. From this, Hollerith got the idea of making a punched "photograph" of every person to be tabulated.

Courtesy of International Business Machines Corporation. Unauthorized use not permitted.

1924: IBM'S FIRST HEADQUARTERS BUILDING

In 1896 Herman Hollerith founded the Tabulating Machine Company, which merged in 1911 with several other companies to form the Computing-Tabulating-Recording Company. In 1924 the company's general manager, Thomas J. Watson, changed its name to International Business Machines Corporation and moved into this building. Watson ran IBM until a few months before his death at age 82 in 1956. His son, Thomas J. Watson, Jr., lead IBM into the age of computers.

Courtesy of International Business Machines Corporation. Unauthorized use not permitted.

1883 • Brooklyn Bridge completed in New York City   1923 • Vladimir Zworykin patents first television transmission tube

1920s–1950s: THE EAM ERA

From the 1920s throughout the mid-1950s, punched-card technology improved with the addition of more punched-card devices and more sophisticated capabilities. The *electromechanical accounting machine (EAM)* family of punched-card devices includes the card punch, verifier, reproducer, summary punch, interpreter, sorter, collator, and accounting machine. Most of the devices in the 1940s machine room were "programmed" to perform a particular operation by the insertion of a prewired control panel. A machine-room operator in a punched-card installation had the physically challenging job of moving heavy boxes of punched cards and printed output from one device to the next on hand trucks.

1903–1995: DR. JOHN V. ATANASOFF AND HIS ABC COMPUTER

In 1939 Dr. John V. Atanasoff, a professor at Iowa State University, and graduate student Clifford E. Berry assembled a prototype of the *ABC* (for *Atanasoff Berry Computer*) to cut the time physics students spent making complicated calculations. A working model was finished in 1942. Atanasoff's decisions—to use an electronic medium with vacuum tubes, the base-2 numbering system, and memory and logic circuits—set the direction for the modern computer. Ironically, Iowa State failed to patent the device and IBM, when contacted about the ABC, airily responded, "IBM will never be interested in an electronic computing machine."

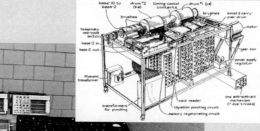

1942: THE FIRST ELECTRONIC DIGITAL COMPUTER: THE ABC

A 1973 federal court ruling officially credited Atanasoff with the invention of the automatic electronic digital computer. The original ABC was dismantled decades ago. Ames Laboratory at Iowa State University used notes and drawings to reconstruct this working replica of Atanasoff and Berry's history-making invention.

1939–1945 • World War II

1944: THE ELECTROMECHANICAL MARK I COMPUTER

The first electromechanical computer, the *Mark I*, was completed by Harvard University professor Howard Aiken in 1944 under the sponsorship of IBM. A monstrous 51 feet long and 8 feet high, the Mark I was essentially a serial collection of electromechanical calculators and was in many ways similar to Babbage's analytical machine. (Aiken was unaware of Babbage's work, though.) The Mark I was a significant improvement, but IBM's management still felt electromechanical computers would never replace punched-card equipment.

Courtesy of International Business Machines Corporation. Unauthorized use not permitted.

1946: THE ELECTRONIC ENIAC COMPUTER

Dr. John W. Mauchly (middle) collaborated with J. Presper Eckert, Jr. (foreground) at the University of Pennsylvania to develop a machine that would compute trajectory tables for the U.S. Army. (This was sorely needed; during World War II, only 20% of all bombs came within *1000 feet* of their targets.) The end product, the first fully operational electronic computer, was completed in 1946 and named the *ENIAC* (Electronic Numerical Integrator and Computer). A thousand times faster than its electromechanical predecessors, it occupied 15,000 square feet of floor space and weighed 30 tons. The ENIAC could do 5000 additions per minute and 500 multiplications per minute. Unlike computers of today that operate in binary, it operated in decimal and required 10 vacuum tubes to represent one decimal digit.

The ENIAC's use of vacuum tubes signaled a major breakthrough. (Legend has it that the ENIAC's 18,000 vacuum tubes dimmed the lights of Philadelphia whenever it was activated.) Even before the ENIAC was finished, it was used in the secret research that went into building the first atomic bomb at Los Alamos.

U.S. Army

1951: THE UNIVAC I AND THE FIRST GENERATION OF COMPUTERS

The first generation of computers (1951–1959), characterized by the use of vacuum tubes, is generally thought to have begun with the introduction of the first commercially viable electronic digital computer. The Universal Automatic Computer (*UNIVAC I* for short), developed by Mauchly and Eckert for the Remington-Rand Corporation, was installed in the U.S. Bureau of the Census in 1951. Later that year, CBS News gave the UNIVAC I national exposure when it correctly predicted Dwight Eisenhower's victory over Adlai Stevenson in the presidential election with only 5% of the votes counted. Mr. Eckert is shown here instructing news anchor Walter Cronkite in the use of the UNIVAC I.

The UNIVAC I just celebrated its golden anniversary (50 years). Forty-six companies and government agencies, including General Electric, DuPont, and the Internal Revenue Service, paid over $1 million for the UNIVAC I, a "walk-in" computer. The maintenance crew had to go inside the computer regularly to change burnt out vacuum tubes (the system had over 5000 of them). The 30-ton system's internal memory was a little more than 10Kb, less than a printed page worth of characters.

Courtesy of Unisys Corporation

1954: THE IBM 650

Not until the success of the UNIVAC I did IBM make a commitment to develop and market computers. IBM's first entry into the commercial computer market was the *IBM 701* in 1953. However, the *IBM 650* (shown here), introduced in 1954, is probably the reason IBM enjoys such a healthy share of today's computer market. Unlike some of its competitors, the IBM 650 was designed as a logical upgrade to existing punched-card machines. IBM management went out on a limb and estimated sales of 50—a figure greater than the number of installed computers in the entire nation at that time. IBM actually installed 1000. The rest is history.

Courtesy of International Business Machines Corporation. Unauthorized use not permitted.

1947 • Chuck Yeager breaks sound barrier   1953 • Hillary and Norgay climb Mt. Everest

1907–1992: "AMAZING" GRACE MURRAY HOPPER

Dubbed "Amazing Grace" by her many admirers, Dr. Grace Hopper was widely respected as the driving force behind COBOL, the most popular programming language, and a champion of standardized programming languages that are hardware-independent. In 1959, Dr. Hopper led an effort that laid the foundation for the development of COBOL. She also helped to create a compiler that enabled COBOL to run on many types of computers. Her reason: "Why start from scratch with every program you write when a computer could be developed to do a lot of the basic work for you over and over again?"

To Dr. Hopper's long list of honors, awards, and accomplishments, add the fact that she found the first "bug" in a computer—a real one. She repaired the Mark II by removing a moth that was caught in Relay Number II. From that day on, every programmer has *debugged* software by ferreting out its *bugs,* or errors, in programming syntax or logic.

The late Rear Admiral Hopper USN (ret) served the United States Navy and its computer and communications communities for many years. It's only fitting that a Navy destroyer is named in her honor.

Official U.S. Navy Photo

1958: THE FIRST INTEGRATED CIRCUIT

If you believe that great inventions revolutionize society by altering one's lifestyle or by changing the way people perceive themselves and their world, then the integrated circuit is a great invention. The integrated circuit is at the heart of all electronic equipment today. Shown here is the first integrated circuit, a phase-shift oscillator, invented in 1958 by Jack S. Kilby of Texas Instruments. Kilby (shown here in 1997 with his original notebook) can truly say to himself, "I changed how the world functions."

Texas Instruments Incorporated

1959: THE HONEYWELL 400 AND THE SECOND GENERATION OF COMPUTERS

The invention of the transistor signaled the start of the second generation of computers (1954–1964). Transistorized computers were more powerful, more reliable, less expensive, and cooler to operate than their vacuum-tubed predecessors. Honeywell (its *Honeywell 400* is shown here) established itself as a major player in the second generation of computers. Burroughs, UNIVAC, NCR, CDC, and Honeywell—IBM's biggest competitors during the 1960s and early 1970s—became known as the BUNCH (the first initial of each name).

Courtesy of Honeywell, Inc.

1957 • *Sputnik* launched

1963: THE PDP-8 MINICOMPUTER

During the 1950s and early 1960s, only the largest companies could afford the six- and seven-digit price tags of *mainframe* computers. In 1963 Digital Equipment Corporation introduced the *PDP-8* (shown here). It is generally considered the first successful *minicomputer* (a nod, some claim, to the playful spirit behind the 1960s miniskirt). At a mere $18,000, the transistor-based PDP-8 was an instant hit. It confirmed the tremendous demand for small computers for business and scientific applications. By 1971, more than 25 firms were manufacturing minicomputers, although Digital and Data General Corporation took an early lead in their sale and manufacture.

1964: THE IBM SYSTEM/360 AND THE THIRD GENERATION OF COMPUTERS

The third generation was characterized by computers built around integrated circuits. Of these, some historians consider IBM's *System/360* line of computers, introduced in 1964, the single most important innovation in the history of computers. System/360 was conceived as a family of computers with *upward compatibility;* when a company outgrew one model it could move up to the next model without worrying about converting its data. System/360 and other lines built around integrated circuits made all previous computers obsolete, but the advantages were so great that most users wrote the costs of conversion off as the price of progress.

1964: BASIC—MORE THAN A BEGINNER'S PROGRAMMING LANGUAGE

In the early 1960s, Dr. Thomas Kurtz and Dr. John Kemeny of Dartmouth College began developing a programming language that a beginner could learn and use quickly. Their work culminated in 1964 with BASIC. Over the years, BASIC gained widespread popularity and evolved from a teaching language into a versatile and powerful language for both business and scientific applications. True BASIC is the commercial version created by Kemeny and Kurtz which now runs without change on nine popular operating systems.

1964 • Beatlemania develops in the U.S.

1969: ARPANET AND THE UNBUNDLING OF HARDWARE AND SOFTWARE

The year 1969 was a big one for important technological achievements. Astronaut Neil A. Armstrong descended the ladder of the *Apollo 11* lunar module making the first step by man on another celestial body. Also in 1969, a U.S. Department of Defense's Advanced Research Project Agency (ARPA) sponsorship of a project, named ARPANET, was underway to unite a community of geographically dispersed scientists by technology. The first official demonstration linked UCLA with Stanford University, both in California. Unlike the moon landing, which had live TV coverage throughout the world, this birth of the Internet, had no reporters, no photographers, and no records. No one remembered the first message, only that it worked. By 1971, the ARPANET included more than 20 sites. Ten years later, the ARPANET had 200 sites. In 1990, ARPANET evolved into what we now know as the Internet.

Also in 1969, International Business Machines (IBM) literally created the software industry overnight when it *unbundled* its products. At the time, IBM had the lion's share of the world market for computers. Software, maintenance, and educational services were included (bundled) with the price of the hardware. When IBM unbundled and sold software separately, the software industry began to flourish.

Courtesy of NASA

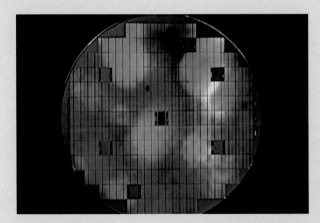

1971: INTEGRATED CIRCUITS AND THE FOURTH GENERATION OF COMPUTERS

Although most computer vendors would classify their computers as fourth generation, most people pinpoint 1971 as the generation's beginning. That was the year large-scale integration of circuitry (more circuits per unit of space) was introduced. The base technology, though, is still the integrated circuit. This is not to say that two decades have passed without significant innovations. In truth, the computer industry has experienced a mind-boggling succession of advances in the further miniaturization of circuitry, data communications, and the design of computer hardware and software.

Courtesy of International Business Machines Corporation. Unauthorized use not permitted.

1969 • *Apollo 11* lands on moon

1975: MICROSOFT AND BILL GATES

In 1968, seventh grader Bill Gates and ninth grader Paul Allen were teaching the computer to play monopoly and commanding it to play millions of games to discover gaming strategies. Seven years later, in 1975, they were to set a course that would revolutionize the computer industry. While at Harvard, Gates and Allen developed a BASIC programming language for the first commercially available microcomputer, the MITS Altair. After successful completion of the project, the two formed Microsoft Corporation, now the largest and most influential software company in the world. Microsoft was given enormous boost when its operating system software, MS-DOS, was selected for use by the IBM PC. Gates, now the richest man in America, provides the company's vision on new product ideas and technologies.

Courtesy of Microsoft Corporation

1981: THE IBM PC

In 1981, IBM tossed its hat into the personal computer ring with its announcement of the IBM Personal Computer, or IBM PC. By the end of 1982, 835,000 had been sold. When software vendors began to orient their products to the IBM PC, many companies began offering *IBMPC compatibles* or *clones*. Today, the IBM PC and its clones have become a powerful standard for the personal computer industry.

Courtesy of International Business Machines Corporation. Unauthorized use not permitted.

1977: THE APPLE II

Not until 1975 and the introduction of the *Altair 8800* personal computer was computing made available to individuals and very small companies. This event has forever changed how society perceives computers. One prominent entrepreneurial venture during the early years of personal computers was the Apple II computer (shown here). Two young computer enthusiasts, Steven Jobs and Steve Wozniak (then 21 and 26 years of age, respectively), collaborated to create and build their Apple II computer on a makeshift production line in Jobs' garage. Seven years later, Apple Computer earned a spot on the Fortune 500, a list of the 500 largest corporations in the United States.

Courtesy of Apple Computer, Inc.

1982: MITCHELL KAPOR DESIGNS LOTUS 1-2-3

Mitchell Kapor is one of the major forces behind the microcomputer boom in the 1980s. In 1982, Kapor founded Lotus Development Company, now one of the largest applications software companies in the world. Kapor and the company introduced an electronic spreadsheet product that gave IBM's recently introduced IBM PC (1981) credibility in the business marketplace. Sales of the IBM PC and the electronic spreadsheet, Lotus 1-2-3, soared.

1976 • United States 200th birthday   1983 • Compact disc (CD) introduced for recorded music

1984: THE MACINTOSH AND GRAPHICAL USER INTERFACES

In 1984 Apple Computer introduced the Macintosh desktop computer with a very "friendly" graphical user interface—proof that computers can be easy and fun to use. Graphical user interfaces (GUIs) began to change the complexion of the software industry. They have changed the interaction between human and computer from a short, character-oriented exchange modeled on the teletypewriter to the now familiar WIMP interface—Windows, Icons, Menus, and Pointing devices.

Courtesy of Apple Computer, Inc.

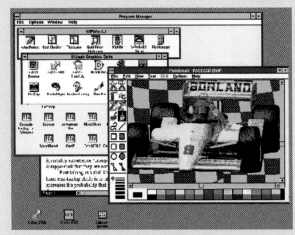

1985–PRESENT: MICROSOFT WINDOWS

Microsoft introduced Windows, a GUI for IBMPC-compatible computers in 1985; however, Windows did not enjoy widespread acceptance until 1990 with the release of Windows 3.0. Windows 3.0 gave a huge boost to the software industry because larger, more complex programs could now be run on IBMPC compatibles. Subsequent releases, including Windows 95, Windows 98, Windows 2000, and Windows XP made personal computers even easier to use, fueling the PC explosion of the 1990s.

1993: THE PENTIUM PROCESSOR AND MULTIMEDIA

The IBM PC-compatible PCs started out using the Intel 8088 microprocessor chip, then a succession of ever more powerful chips, including the Intel 80286, 80386, or 80486 chips. But not until the Intel Pentium (shown here) and its successors, the Pentium Pro and Pentium II, did PCs do much with multimedia, the integration of motion video, animation, graphics, sound, and so on. The emergence of the high-powered Pentium processors and their ability to handle multimedia applications changed the way we view and use PCs.

Photo courtesy of Intel Corporation

1989: THE WORLD WIDE WEB

Former Swiss physicist Tim Berners-Lee invented the World Wide Web, an Internet application that allows us to view multimedia Web pages on the Internet. Berners-Lee and a small team of scientists conceived HTML (the language of the Internet), URLs (Internet addresses), and put up the first server supporting the new World Wide Web format. The World Wide Web, one of several Internet-based applications, came of age as Web traffic grew 341,634% in its third year, 1993. The "Web" was unique and inviting in that it enabled "Web pages" to be linked across the Internet. Today, the World Wide Web is the foundation for most Internet communications and services.

Courtesy of CERN

1989 • Berlin Wall falls

1993: THE INTERNET BROWSER

The 1995 bombing of the Murrah Federal Building in Oklahoma City stirred the emotions of the people throughout the world. This picture by Liz Dabrowski, staff photographer for The Oklahoma Daily (the student voice of the University of Oklahoma in Norman), speaks volumes about what happened and reminds us that we must never forget. In retrospect, we now view 1993 through 1995 as turnaround years for the Internet when millions of people began to tune into it for news of the bombing and other events and for a wealth of other information and services. A number of Internet browsers were introduced during this time, including the Prodigy (a commercial information service) browser shown here and Netscape Navigator. These browsers enabled users to navigate the World Wide Web with ease.

1996: THE HANDHELD COMPUTER

The PalmPilot handheld computer was introduced and signaled to the world that you could place tremendous computing power in the palm of your hand. Now millions of people rely on PalmPilots and other similar handhelds for a variety of personal information management applications, including e-mail.

3Com and the 3Com logo are registered trademarks. PalmIII™ and the PalmIII™ logo are trademarks of Palm Computing, Inc., 3Com Corporation, or its subsidiaries.

1996: U.S. STAMP COMMEMORATES HALF CENTURY OF COMPUTING

The dedication of this U.S. Postal Service stamp was unique in that it was the first to be broadcast live over the Internet so that stamp collectors throughout the world could see and hear the ceremony. The USPS issued the stamp to commemorate the 50th anniversary of the ENIAC (the first full-scale electronic computer) and the 50 years of computer technology that followed. The dedication was held at Aberdeen Proving Ground, Maryland, the home of the ENIAC. In 1999, the U.S. Postal Service granted permission to E-stamp Corporation to issue electronic stamps, stamps sold over the Internet that can be printed along with the name and address on an envelope (shown here). This entrepreneurial effort reminds us that in the new millennium, anything that can be digitized will eventually be distributed over the Internet.

Courtesy of E-Stamp Corporation

1995 • Bombing of the Murrah Federal Building in Oklahoma City

2001 • September 11 terrorist attack on the United States

SECTION SELF-CHECK

1. Lady Ada Lovelace suggested the use of punched cards to Charles Babbage during the 19th century. (T/F)

2. According to a federal court ruling, John Atanasoff is credited with the invention of the automatic electronic digital computer. (T/F)

3. The first significant use of binary automation was Blaise Pascal's Pascaline. (T/F)

4. The first family of computers with upward compatibility was introduced in 1964 by IBM. (T/F)

5. The Internet evolved from ARPANET, a U.S. government sponsored project. (T/F)

6. The first commercially viable computer was introduced in: (a) 1937, (b) 1951, (c) 1978, or (d) 1984.

7. The punched card tabulating machine used in the 1890 census was invented by: (a) Babbage, (b) Gates, (c) Hollerith, or (d) Kapor.

8. The first operational electronic computer was named the: (a) ENIAC, (b) UNIVAC III, (c) IBM 650, or (d) Monrobot.

9. The first integrated circuit was invented in what decade: (a) 1940s, (b) 1950s, (c) 1960s, or (d) 1970s?

10. Apple Computer was started by two young computer enthusiasts in what decade: (a) 1940s, (b) 1950s, (c) 1960s, or (d) 1970s?

chapter

2

Learning Objectives

Once you have read and studied this chapter, you will have learned:

- The purpose and objectives of an operating system, the program that controls all activities within a computer system, plus common operating system platforms (Section 2-1).

- The fundamental concepts and terminology associated with the Windows operating environment (Section 2-2).

- The function and uses of software suite applications (word processing, presentation, spreadsheet, database, and personal information management) (Section 2-3).

- An overview of popular personal computing software including graphics, home and family, education and edutainment, reference, and business and financial (Section 2-4).

SOFTWARE

Why this chapter is important to you

Computing has a language all its own—*computerese*. Operating system terms and concepts contribute mightily to computerese. Fortunately, many of the words and phrases are simply old words being applied to software concepts (for example, *menus, background,* and *help*). Some terms evolved out of the need to abbreviate verbal and written communication (for example, *GUI* and *plug-and-play*). When you consider that the sum total of computing knowledge is doubling every two years, it is no wonder that its language is filled with buzzwords, acronyms, and the like. Even with its shortcomings, computerese provides a surprisingly efficient way to communicate. Our challenge is to learn these terms, then to keep up with the inevitable changes.

To be conversant with a personal computer, you must know your way around its operating system, such as the popular Microsoft Windows operating systems. Once you have read and studied this chapter, you'll be better prepared to interact effectively with the Windows environment, something that most knowledge workers do for several hours each day.

Also in this chapter is an introduction to applications software that is commonly used in business and the home, including software associated with software suites and a variety of popular personal computing applications. In this chapter you will learn that almost anything involving the manipulation of text and images can be done more easily and professionally with word processing software. You'll learn that you can prepare professional-looking visual aids that can bolster the effectiveness of any presentation. You'll learn how spreadsheet and database software can help you organize, analyze, and present all kinds of information. Perhaps, most importantly, you will learn that many personal computing tools exist for work and home that can save you lots of time, make you more productive, and help you present yourself in a more professional manner.

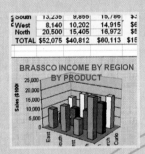

When we go out to a movie we see only a few of those responsible for making the film—the actors. We don't see the director, the producers, the writers, the editors, and many others. Perhaps it's because of this visual link that we, the audience, tend to become adoring fans of glamorous actors. We tend to forget the others involved in the film, even the director who is the person who ties it all together and makes it happen. It's much the same with software. As software users, we tend to shower our praise on that which we see most often—the *applications software.* However, *system software,* like the film director, stays in the background and ties it all together. The most prominent of these behind-the-scenes players is the operating system.

The *operating system* and its **graphical user interface** (**GUI**), both system software, are at the heart of the software action (see Figure 2-1). All other software depends on and interacts with the operating system, the software that controls everything that happens in a computer. Its graphical user interface provides a user-friendly interface to the operating system. *System software* takes in those programs that manage, maintain, and control computer system resources. That includes a variety of **utility programs** that are available to help you with the day-to-day chores associated with personal computing (such as disk and file maintenance) and to keep your system running at peak performance. *Applications software* describes those programs used by the end user for a particular application, such as word processing or tax planning. Figure 2-1 illustrates examples of and the relationship between system and applications software.

Just as the processor is the nucleus of the computer system, the *operating system* is the nucleus of all software activity (see Figure 2-1). Microsoft Windows, Mac OS X, UNIX, Linux, and LindowsOS are popular operating systems for PCs and workstations. The operating system is actually a family of *system software* programs that monitor and control all I/O and processing activities within a computer system. One of the operating system programs, often called the **kernel,** loads other operating system and applications programs to RAM, the PC's main internal memory, as they are needed. The kernel is loaded to RAM on system start-up and remains *resident*—available in RAM—until the system is turned off. Typically, the kernel is responsible for task/process management and for memory/disk management.

If you purchase a PC off-the-shelf, you get whatever operating system is installed. Upgrading an operating system to a new version is not difficult and existing user files remain compatible. However, changing to an entirely different operating system can be cumbersome. When you order a PC, you may have several operating systems from which to choose. One might be business-oriented (set up for business networking) and one might be less expensive and more appropriate for home computing.

All hardware and software are under the control of the operating system. Among other things, the operating system:

- Determines how valuable RAM is allotted to programs
- Performs tasks related to disk and file management
- Sets priorities for handling tasks
- Manages the flow of instructions, data, and information to and from the processor

OPERATING SYSTEM OBJECTIVES

The operating system is what gives a *general-purpose computer,* such as a PC or a company's Internet server computer, its flexibility to tackle a variety of jobs. Most *dedicated computers,* such as those that control devices (dishwashers, car ignition systems, and so on) and arcade games, are controlled by a single-function program and do not need a separate operating system.

One of the best ways to understand an operating system is to understand its objectives. These objectives are listed and explained in Figure 2-2. All operating systems are designed with the same basic objectives in mind. However, server and PC operating systems differ markedly in complexity and orientation. On the server, *multiuser operating systems* coordinate a number of special-function processors and monitor interaction with hundreds, even thousands, of terminals and PCs in a network. Most PC operating systems are designed to support a *single user on a single PC* and enable optional *networking with other computers.*

FIGURE 2–1

RELATIONSHIP BETWEEN THE OPERATING SYSTEM, THE GUI, AND APPLICATIONS SOFTWARE

The operating system coordinates all software activity within a computer system. Our interaction with the operating system is through the graphical user interface, the GUI. Utility programs help you and the operating system manage system resources. With applications software packages, such as spreadsheet and expert systems, we can address a variety of problems. For example, a manager can use spreadsheet software to create *templates* (models) for summarizing sales and maintaining the office's fixed inventory. A knowledge engineer can use expert system software to create a loan evaluation system to assist a bank's loan officers in making better, more consistent decisions.

FIGURE 2–2   OBJECTIVES OF AN OPERATING SYSTEM

OPERATING SYSTEM OBJECTIVES

1. *To facilitate communication between the computer system and its users.*	Users issue system-related commands via the graphical user interface (GUI).
2. *To facilitate communication among computer system components.*	The operating system controls the movement of internal instructions and data between I/O peripheral devices, the processor, programs, and storage.
3. *To facilitate communication between linked computer systems.*	The operating system enables linked computers to communicate.
4. *To maximize throughput.*	System resources are employed to maximize throughput.
5. *To optimize the use of computer system resources.*	The operating system is continually looking at what tasks need to be done and what resources are available to accomplish these tasks; then it makes decisions about what resources to assign to which tasks.
6. *To keep track of all files in disk storage.*	The operating system enables users to perform such tasks as making backup copies of disks, erasing disk files, making inquiries about files on a particular disk, and preparing new disks for use. The operating system also handles many file- and disk-oriented tasks that are transparent (invisible) to the end user (for example, keeping track of the physical location of disk files).
7. *To provide an envelope of security for the computer system.*	The operating system can allow or deny user access to the system as a whole or to individual files.
8. *To monitor all systems capabilities and alert the user of system failure or potential problems.*	The operating system is continually checking system components for proper operation.

ALLOCATING SYSTEM RESOURCES

We all must live within our means, and the same goes for computers. A conscientious shopper can stretch the value of a dollar, and a good operating system can get the most from its limited resources, especially its processor. Operating systems get the most from their processors through **multitasking**, the *concurrent* execution of more than one program at a time. Actually, a single computer can execute only one program at a time. However, its internal processing speed is so fast that several programs can be allocated "slices" of computer time in rotation, making it appear that several programs are being executed at once.

The great difference in processor speed and the speeds of the peripheral devices makes multitasking possible. The speed of a 22-page-per-minute printer doesn't come close to pushing the processor of a low-end PC. The computer's processor is continually waiting for peripheral devices to complete such tasks as retrieving a record from disk storage or printing a report. During these waiting periods, the processor just continues processing other programs. The operating system ensures that the most appropriate resources are allocated to competing tasks in the most efficient manner.

Modern personal computing is done in a multitasking environment, where one or more programs run concurrently and are controlled and assigned priorities by the operating system. For example, you can prepare a graphics presentation in PowerPoint while downloading a new MP3 song via the Internet. The **foreground** is that part of RAM containing the active or current program (PowerPoint in this example) and is usually given priority by the operating system. Other lower-priority programs, such as the MP3 download in the example, are run in the **background** part of RAM. The operating system rotates allocation of the processor resource between foreground and background programs, with the foreground programs receiving the lion's share of the processor's attention.

THE USER INTERFACE

To appreciate the impact of graphical user interfaces (GUIs), it helps if you know what preceded them.

Text-Based Software

Through the 1980s, the most popular microcomputer operating system was **MS-DOS.** The *MS* is short for *Microsoft* and *DOS* is an abbreviation for *disk operating system,* meaning that it is loaded from disk. MS-DOS was strictly *text-based, command-driven* software. That is, we issued commands directly to DOS (the MS-DOS nickname) by entering them on the keyboard, one character at a time. For example, if you wished to issue a command to copy a word processing document from a hard disk to a floppy disk for your friend, you might have entered the following command via the keyboard at the DOS prompt (C:\>).

copy c:\myfile.txt a:\yourfile.txt

Command-driven DOS, in particular, demanded strict adherence to command **syntax,** which are the rules for entering commands, such as word spacing, punctuation, and so on (see Figure 2-3).

GUI-Based Software

Operating systems let you key in text commands or select commands by "pointing and clicking" with a mouse. Most people prefer the user-friendly, graphics-oriented environment—the graphical user interface (see Figure 2-3), or GUI (pronounced "*G-U-I*" or "*gooey*").

GUI users interact with their computers by using a pointing device (perhaps a *mouse* on desktop PCs or a *touchpad* on notebook PCs) and a keyboard to issue commands. Rather than enter a command directly, you choose from options displayed on the screen. The equivalent of a syntax-sensitive operating system command is entered by pointing to and choosing one or more options from menus or by pointing to and choosing a graphics image, called an **icon.** An icon is a picture that represents a processing activity or a file. For example, the file folder icon represents processing activities associated with file management. Users might drag an item to the "trash can" icon to delete a file from disk storage.

GUIs have eliminated the need for us to memorize and enter cumbersome commands. For example, in GUIs all we have to do to copy a file from one disk to another disk is to reposition the file's icon from one area on the screen to another.

PC OPERATING SYSTEMS AND PLATFORMS

In Chapter 1, we learned that the *processor* and an *operating system* define a *platform.* Software created to run on a specific platform will not run on other platforms. The typical computer system, large or

---

FIGURE 2–3 **TEXT-BASED AND GRAPHICS-BASED INTERFACES**
MS-DOS (shown here), the primary PC operating system for the first 15 years of personal computing, has a text-based, command-driven interface. Windows XP has a graphical user interface (GUI) in which files can be dragged with a mouse between disk icons. Each has its pros and cons. For example, MS-DOS demands knowledge of syntax, but the GUI may require more operations (myfile.txt would need to be renamed to yourfile.txt after the drag operation to accomplish the same operation as shown in MS-DOS).

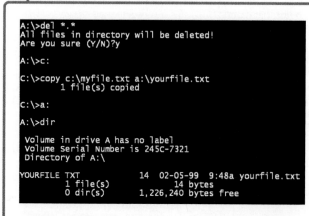 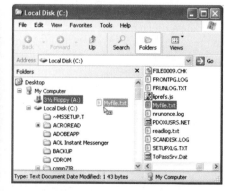

small, runs under a single platform. However, some can run several platforms. A *multiplatform computer* runs its *native* platform and *emulates* other platforms.

The selection of a platform is important because it sets boundaries for what you can and cannot do with your computer system.

PC Platforms Overview

In the server computer environment, choosing a platform is the responsibility of IT specialists. Typically, in the PC environment, you—the individual user—are responsible for selecting the platform. The following discussion focuses on the most common personal computing environments—those developed for PC-compatible computers.

The PC/Windows Platforms: 95, 98, Me, NT, 2000, XP, and CE.

Most personal computer users choose the *Wintel* platform, which combines one of the Microsoft Windows operating systems with an Intel-compatible processor. Windows 95, 98, Me, NT, 2000, XP, and CE are installed on millions of PCs. A major advantage of the Windows 9x/Me/2000/XP family is its ability to run 32-bit programs, that is, programs that use the full 32-bit data paths in the processor. (MS-DOS and the original Windows are 16-bit operating systems.) All members of the Windows family have a similar look and feel.

- *Legacy Versions of Windows: Windows 95, Windows 98, Windows Me, Windows NT, and Windows 2000.* **Windows 95, Windows 98,** and **Windows Me** (Millennium Edition) operating systems are older version of Windows, but are still widely used in the home and in both small and large business. These legacy Windows operating systems emerged from MS-DOS, the original text-based Microsoft operating system, which ruled the PC-compatible environment for the first decade of personal computing. **Windows NT** was the first Windows operating system to divorce itself from the limitations of MS-DOS, thus beginning a new era for PCs. **Windows 2000** was the successor to Windows NT.

- *Modern PC Operating Systems: Windows XP.* **Windows XP** is the version of Windows beyond Windows Me and Windows 2000. In developing Windows XP, Microsoft merged the strengths of Windows 2000 (standards-based security, manageability, and reliability) with the best features of Windows Me (Plug and Play and easy-to-use user interface). Windows XP is the future of the PC/Windows family of operating systems and reflects a push by Microsoft for all Windows users to migrate to Windows XP.

  Windows XP is a powerful client operating system that is emerging as the choice for businesses doing client/server computing. Windows XP, the client-side operating system, works with **Windows 2000 Server** or the newer **Windows .Net Server**, the server-side portion of the operating system (which runs on the server computer) to make client/server computing possible. Windows XP comes in two versions: **Windows XP Professional**, for businesses requiring local area networking capabilities and a high level of security, and **Windows XP Home Edition**, for home and small business users. Microsoft offers **Windows XP 64-Bit Edition** for use on high performance 64-bit workstations.

  Windows operating systems have many features, such as **plug-and-play,** which permits users to plug in a peripheral device or an add-on circuit board into an external port or into a slot on the motherboard, even when the PC is running. The operating system also permits **home networking,** the linking of PCs in a home or small office to share information and resources.

  Wintel platforms are *mostly* **backward compatible,** that is, they allow programs written for earlier Microsoft platforms to be run on modern systems. Because Windows XP is so radically different from earlier operating systems, however, a considerable number of programs designed for older platforms will not run under Windows XP.

  Windows XP is among the new wave of client/server platforms supporting LAN-based *workgroup computing*. Workgroup computing allows people on a network to use the network to foster cooperation and the sharing of ideas and resources. Groupware, such as instant messaging, calendars, brainstorming, and scheduling, is developed to run under workgroup platforms.

- *Windows CE.* The **Windows CE** operating system is designed for handheld and pocket PCs (see Figure 2-4). Its look and feel are similar to those of the other members of the family. Windows CE users can share information with other Windows-based PCs and they can connect to the Internet.

FIGURE 2–4 The Windows CE Platform
This pocket PC runs the Windows CE operating system and has full Internet connectivity. You can check stock quotes from the airport, send an e-mail from a taxi, or read the news from almost anywhere, anytime.

Courtesy of Sun Microsystems, Inc.

The Macintosh/Mac OS X Platform

The Apple family of microcomputers (including the Macintosh, PowerBook, iMac, eMac, and iBook computers) and its operating system, **Mac OS X** (see Figure 2-5), define another major platform. About one in every 10 PCs runs under this platform. The Apple line of microcomputers is based on the Motorola family of microprocessors. One inviting feature of Apple's Mac OS X is that it can be adjusted to fit the user's level of expertise.

Linux, UNIX, and LindowsOS

Linux is a spin-off of the popular **UNIX** multiuser operating system that has been around for decades (see Figure 2-5). The open source operating system was developed over the last decade via a world-wide consortium of developers, all working on the same code. **Open source software** is software for which the actual source programming code (the instructions) is made available to users for review and modification. Linux runs on a number of hardware platforms, including those using Intel and Motorola processors. Because Linux is made available for free over the Internet and is generally regarded to be an excellent operating system, it continues to grow in popularity. Web servers and e-mail servers throughout the world rely on Linux. The significance of the amazing growth of this operating system is that it has the potential to become a competitor to Microsoft Windows client and server programs. With a price tag close to zero and many devoted developers throughout the world, we can expect it to continue to grow in worldwide acceptance. Also, the fact that major technology companies, such as IBM, are creating products that use and can work with Linux helps fuel Linux acceptance. Linux runs on handheld computers, too.

FIGURE 2–5

OPERATING SYSTEMS: WINDOWS XP, LINUX, AND MAC OS X
The interfaces for three popular PC operating systems are shown here. Windows XP represents the Windows family of operating systems. Linux is the open source operating system and Mac OS X is used with Apple computers.

WINDOWS XP

LINUX

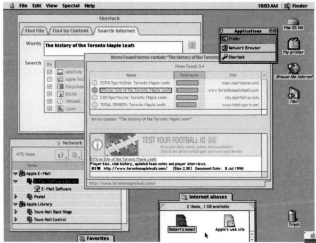

Screen shot copyright 2001 Red Hat, Inc. All rights reserved. Reprinted with permission from Red Hat, Inc.

APPLE MAC OS X

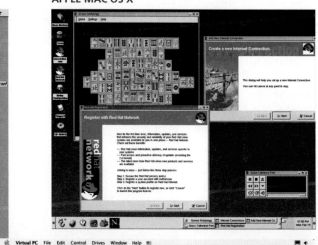

APPLE MAC OS X, EMULATING MICROSOFT WINDOWS OPERATING SYSTEMS (XP, 2000, AND 98)
Courtesy of Connectix

PC Platforms

- Legacy PC-Compatible
  - MS-DOS
  - MS-DOS with Windows
  - Windows 95 and Windows 98
  - Windows Me (Millennium Edition)
  - Windows 2000
- Current PC-compatible
  - Windows XP (Home and Professional versions)
  - Windows CE (handheld and pocket PC)
- Apple Mac OS X
- UNIX, Linux, and LindowsOS

THE CRYSTAL BALL:
Open Source Software Explosion
Open source software is made available to the public in source code format (the actual instructions) and is free of licensing restrictions. Open source software is a team effort where people from all over the world work together for the joy of achievement to create the software, as they did with Linux, the most popular non-Windows operating system. To date, most open source software has been system software; however, I expect this to change dramatically as the world-wide structure for the creation and development of this type of software begins to mature. Expect open source software in all areas to emerge as a viable software alternative in home and office within this decade.

LindowsOS, a commercial Linux-based operating system for PCs, has a Windows-like interface and offers file-level compatibility with many popular Windows-based applications, such as Word and Excel. These selling points and its inviting price tag have prompted industry analysts to predict that LindowsOS may soon surpass Mac OS X to become the second most installed commercial PC operating system.

Platform Problems

Many companies purchase and maintain a fleet of automobiles for use by employees. Companies routinely exchange entire fleets of Chevrolets for Fords (and vice versa) without any loss of functionality. Employees simply come to work in a Chevy and drive away in a Ford. The fleet decision doesn't commit a company over the long term. The choice of a computer platform, however, does.

When you decide on a particular platform, you begin to purchase and create resources for that platform. The investment required in selecting a platform demands a long-term commitment—at least five years. This type of commitment makes choosing a platform at the individual or company level a very important decision (see Figure 2-6).

All companies have platform problems, although some have fewer problems than others. Those that standardize on platforms can enjoy the benefits of easily shared resources (from data to printers). Those that do not must do some work to achieve interoperability. **Interoperability** refers to the ability to run software and exchange information in a **multiplatform environment** (a computing environment of more than one platform). *Enabling technologies* that allow communication and the sharing of resources between different platforms are called **cross-platform technologies.** Multiplatform organizations use cross-platform technologies, both hardware and software, to link PCs, workstations, networks, and so on. Multiplatform environments are more the rule than the exception in medium-sized and large organizations. Whenever possible, companies try to minimize the number of platforms used in the company. The fewer the number of platforms, the less the hassle and expense associated with installing and maintaining cross-platform technologies.

FIGURE 2–6 Installing the Operating System
At this Gateway Corporation assembly plant, workers install the operating system, then test all facets of system operation. Most of Gateway's PCs are custom-built to user specifications, with the user often selecting from several operating system options.

Courtesy of Gateway, Inc.

UTILITY PROGRAMS

System software, which includes the operating system and its GUI, is applicationsindependent. Generally, system software supports the operation and maintenance of the PC's hardware, software, and files. A wide variety of system software *utilities* are available to help you with the day-to-day chores associated with personal computing (disk and file maintenance, system recovery, security, backup, virus protection, and so on) and to keep your system running at peak performance. Figure 2-7 gives you a sampling of common utilities programs you might use to enhance your personal computing environment.

SECTION SELF-CHECK

2-2 Windows Concepts and Terminology

The Microsoft Windows family of operating systems dominates the PC-compatible environment throughout the world. The Microsoft master plan has all Windows users eventually migrating to Windows XP so that we can partake of the Windows "experience" (XP stands for "experience"). Most new PCs come with a Windows XP operating system installed on the hard disk. Windows XP Home Edition works well in the home or a small business, but Windows XP Professional, with its security and networking capabilities, is better suited for businesses with networking on a local area network (LAN). All PC/Windows platforms have a similar look and feel.

The terms, concepts, and features discussed in this section generally apply to Windows 9x/Me/2000/XP; however, the examples are based on Windows XP. The name *Windows* describes basically how the software functions. The GUI-based Windows series runs one or more applications in **windows**—rectangular areas displayed on the screen. The Windows operating system series has introduced a number of concepts and terms, all of which apply to the thousands of software packages that have been and are being developed to run on the Windows platforms.

HELP: F1

Books, like this one, and tutorial software are complementary learning tools. Hands-on activities with Windows or any other software package are essential to learning. The explanations in the following sections will make more sense once you begin working with Windows. We recommend that you visit your college's PC lab and run Help to learn more about your Windows operating system.

Help is readily available.

- *Help for Windows.* All you have to do is click *Start*, then *Help and Support* for operating system help (Figure 2-8). This feature provides online access to comprehensive, continually updated support information, including FAQs (frequently asked questions) and solutions to common problems. The Windows Help capabilities include step-by-step tutorials that lead you through numerous common Windows procedures, such as how to set up home networking or how to use the mouse. Help also includes troubleshooters.

- *Help for any applications program.* Click on *Help* in the main menu at the top of the application window.

FIGURE 2–7   UTILITY SOFTWARE

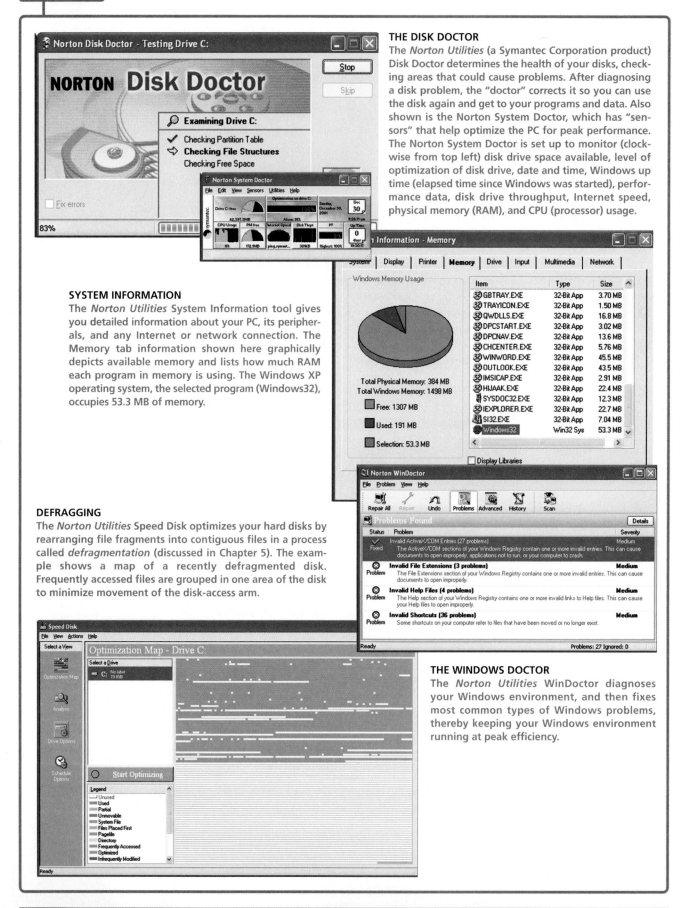

THE DISK DOCTOR

The *Norton Utilities* (a Symantec Corporation product) Disk Doctor determines the health of your disks, checking areas that could cause problems. After diagnosing a disk problem, the "doctor" corrects it so you can use the disk again and get to your programs and data. Also shown is the Norton System Doctor, which has "sensors" that help optimize the PC for peak performance. The Norton System Doctor is set up to monitor (clockwise from top left) disk drive space available, level of optimization of disk drive, date and time, Windows up time (elapsed time since Windows was started), performance data, disk drive throughput, Internet speed, physical memory (RAM), and CPU (processor) usage.

SYSTEM INFORMATION

The *Norton Utilities* System Information tool gives you detailed information about your PC, its peripherals, and any Internet or network connection. The Memory tab information shown here graphically depicts available memory and lists how much RAM each program in memory is using. The Windows XP operating system, the selected program (Windows32), occupies 53.3 MB of memory.

DEFRAGGING

The *Norton Utilities* Speed Disk optimizes your hard disks by rearranging file fragments into contiguous files in a process called *defragmentation* (discussed in Chapter 5). The example shows a map of a recently defragmented disk. Frequently accessed files are grouped in one area of the disk to minimize movement of the disk-access arm.

THE WINDOWS DOCTOR

The *Norton Utilities* WinDoctor diagnoses your Windows environment, and then fixes most common types of Windows problems, thereby keeping your Windows environment running at peak efficiency.

FIGURE 2–7 continued

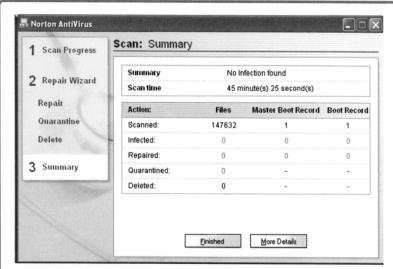

VIRUS PROTECTION
Norton AntiVirus, a popular virus vaccine, scans your disk drive(s) for viruses at system startup. Also, it monitors your PC for any activity that might indicate that a virus is at work in your system. It alerts you to problems, and then removes the virus. Each month, more viruses are added to a list of thousands that float around cyberspace. The LiveUpdate feature lets you periodically download protection from new viruses.

INTERNET PRIVACY PROTECTION
Internet Explorer gives users the option to set the level of Internet privacy protection. Sliding the selector up increases the level of privacy protection and sliding it down minimizes privacy protection to the point that all cookies are accepted. A cookie is personal information given to your Internet browser by a Web server. The cookie is stored on your disk and sent back to the server each time you access the Web site.

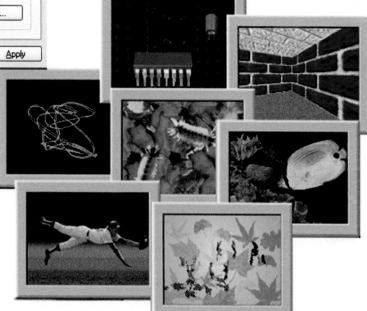

SCREEN SAVERS
A screen saver program takes over the display screen when there is no key or mouse input for a specified time, say 10 minutes. Originally, screen savers were designed to eliminate ghosting, the permanent etching of a pattern on a display screen. The newer monitors do not have this problem, but people love screen savers for their visual appeal, and they hide their work from snoopers when they leave the work area. As shown here, there is a screen saver for everyone and every mood. Screen savers fill the display with constantly moving images or animation until you tap a key or move the mouse.

FIGURE 2–8

THE WINDOWS HELP FEATURE
The Help and Support feature lets you find help by scanning a *hierarchical list by topic.* Click on the *Index* button to search an index similar to one you would find in a book (but without page references). Enter a topic in the *Search* box to search the help files by keyword. Click on the *Support* button for Internet-based Windows XP help and technical support and other valuable help resources.

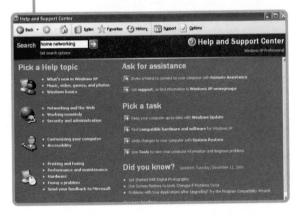

● *Context-sensitive help.* Tap the *F1* key to get *context-sensitive help;* that is, help that relates to the window, object, or whatever is active at the time.

Generally, Help offers you several ways to find the information you need. Most Windows and applications help features will offer these options.

● *Contents.* Use the *Contents* list when you want to look through categories.

● *Search.* You can search for a word or phrase (for example, type "printer").

● *Index.* If you prefer, you can scroll through a book-style alphabetical *Index* to locate the item of interest.

NON-WINDOWS AND WINDOWS APPLICATIONS

Any software application that does not adhere to the Microsoft Windows standard is a **non-Windows application.** Most non-Windows applications will run under Windows, but these software packages do not take advantage of the many helpful Windows features. Generally, non-Windows programs are older software created for MS-DOS.

Programs that adhere to Windows conventions are **Windows applications.** These conventions describe:

● Type and style of window

● Arrangement and style of menus

● Use of the keyboard and mouse

● Format for screen image display

Virtually all new software for the PC environment is designed to run on the Windows platform. The GUI for Windows versions of Word, Quicken, Adobe Illustrator, and all other Windows applications have the same look and feel. *When you learn the Windows GUI, you also learn the GUI for all Windows-based software packages.*

CLICKING, DOUBLE-CLICKING, AND DRAGGING

The Windows GUI uses both a keyboard and a point-and-draw device for input. The point-and-draw device is often a mouse, but with so many notebooks being purchased, it is increasingly a touchpad or some other such device.

When performing operating system functions in Windows, you can opt for the *single-click mode* or the traditional *double-click mode* of Windows 95. Single-click mode is primarily for general Windows operations and may not be available in many applications. Figure 2-9 summarizes the differences between the two modes of clicking.

Right-clicking (tapping the right button on a mouse set up for right-handed use) causes a *context-sensitive menu* to be displayed. The resulting menu relates to the window, object, or whatever the mouse pointer is on at the time of the right-click.

Press and hold the left button to **drag** across the screen. When using a graphics software program, you specify the type of object you want to draw, then drag the mouse pointer across the screen to create the object. When using a word processing program, you highlight a block of text by dragging the mouse pointer from the beginning to the end of the text block. In a GUI, you can point to an object, perhaps an icon, then drag (move) it to a new position. Click and drag operations in a graphics software package are demonstrated in Figure 2-10.

THE DESKTOP

The Windows screen upon which icons, windows, and so on are displayed is known as the **desktop.** The Windows desktop, which is introduced in *Getting Started,* may contain these items (see Figure 2-11).

● *Background.* The background can be anything from a single-color screen to an elaborate image, such as the shoreline in Figures 2-11.

● *One active window.* The **active window** displays the application being currently used by the user.

FIGURE 2–9   CLICKING AND RIGHT-CLICKING FOR WINDOWS OPERATING SYSTEMS

Windows Task	Double-Click Mode (tap the primary button, the left button for right handers, in rapid succession)	Single-Click Mode (tap the primary button)
Select an item	Point and click on item (an icon, a file-name, a taskbar program, and so on).	Point to item.
Open (or choose) an item	Double-click on the item.	Click on the item.
Select a range of items	Click the first item in a group of items, press and hold the Shift key, then **click** the last item (for example, files or words in a paragraph).	Point to the first item in a group of items, press and hold the Shift key, and then **point to** the last item in the group.
Select multiple individual items	Click any item in a group, press and hold the Ctrl key, and then **click** other individual items in the group.	Point to any item in a group, press and hold the Ctrl key, and then **point to** other individual items in the group.
Drag-and-drop item	Point to an item, press and hold the mouse button, and drag the item to new location.	Same as double-click mode.
Display a context-sensitive menu of tasks or options	Point to Item and Right-Click (tap the secondary button, the right one for right handers)	

FIGURE 2–10   **THE MOUSE AND THE MOUSE POINTER**
In the example, a computer artist repositions the mouse pointer on the sun, and then moves the sun image from the left to the right side of the screen.

1. The graphics cursor, or pointer, is initially at Position 1 on the display screen. The artist moves the mouse up (toward monitor) to position the pointer over the image to be moved (Position 2).

2. The artist clicks (taps the left mouse button) on the sun image to highlight the area containing the sun image (rectangular box).

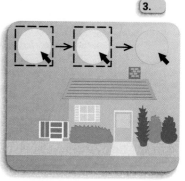

3. The artist drags the image to the desired location (Position 3) by pressing and holding the mouse's left button and moving the mouse. The artist releases the button to complete the drag operation.

FIGURE 2-11

THE WINDOWS DESKTOP
The appearance of this Windows XP desktop depends on the user's application mix and visual wishes at a particular time. Windows enables sophisticated multitasking, that is, running several programs at one time. This feature allows you to work on a word processing document while backing up files and checking e-mail on the Internet. The taskbar lists all open applications. To personalize the desktop, right-click anywhere on the desktop, select Properties, and then change the color scheme, the background, the resolution, or other desktop features.

Network Neighborhood
If your PC is on a LAN, the *My Network Places* icon provides ready access to its resources.

Plug-and-Play
Windows XP provides support for plug-and-play and USB peripherals. This means your system can grow with your computing needs with considerably less effort on your part. All you have to do to add a new device, such as a video camera, is "plug" and "play" it.

Icons and Shortcuts
Program icons, files, and folders (groups of related files) can be displayed directly on the desktop. The *My Computer* icon provides access to all files and folders. An icon with a tiny arrow is a shortcut or a pointer to a file.

Recycle Bin
Deleted items remain in the *Recycle Bin* until you empty it.

Start Button
A handy Start button provides easy access to most of the Windows tools and commonly used applications.

Active Desktop Content
You can add Internet-based "active content" to your desktop as you would a program icon. Active content, such as a stock ticker or the local weather (shown here), changes on your screen.

Internet Explorer
The Windows XP *Internet Explorer* is an integrated file management tool and Web browser. It redefines user-friendliness, especially in the Web page format shown here, where files and folders are shown hierarchically and pictorially, as in the case of these photo album folders. Windows enables descriptive names for files and folders.

Taskbar
The *Taskbar* keeps you abreast of active applications. A button on the taskbar represents each of the open applications you see on the desktop. Just click on the application button to switch to that application. The *Quick Launch Bar* on the left gives you single-click access to user-selected programs. The *System Tray* on the right displays the icons of programs that are loaded on system start up, such as speaker controls, maintenance schedulers, and antivirus protection.

DOS Window
Windows XP eliminates the need for MS-DOS (the original PC-compatible operating system), but offers complete backward compatibility for all MS-DOS and Windows 3.x software.

- *One or more inactive windows.* **Inactive windows** display applications that are running but not being used by the user.
- *Icons.* These small pictures represent programs and other Windows elements.
- *Internet-based active content.* The desktop can display real-time Internet content, such as the weather or stock prices.
- *Various bars showing processing options.* These bars make it easier for you to navigate between applications.

People usually customize their desktops to reflect their personalities as well as their processing and information needs, so no two desktops are the same.

The Taskbar

Typically, a Windows session begins with the **Start button** in the taskbar. The **taskbar,** which can be displayed all the time or hidden, as desired, shows what programs are running and available for use. Click the *Start* button in the taskbar to display the Start menu and open the door to the resources on your PC. An application window can be opened in several ways, but usually people point and click on the desired application icon in the *Programs* option on the Start menu (see Figure 2-12). Highlighting the Programs option presents a pop-out menu with either application options or folders containing other options. A Windows **folder** is a logical grouping of related files and/or subordinate folders.

The Window

Figure 2-13 shows a typical rectangular Windows **application window.** An application window contains an **open application** (a running application), such as Paint or Word. Several applications can be open or running simultaneously, but there is only one *active window* at any given time. Application commands issued via the keyboard or the mouse apply to the active window. The active window's title bar (at the top of each application) is highlighted. There is no active window in Figure 2-11 because the user has clicked on the Start button to open another program. The elements of an application window are: the workspace, the scroll bars, the title bar, the menu bar, the toolbar, the ruler bar, and the corners and borders. Each is described in the following sections and illustrated in Figure 2-13.

Workspace

The application **workspace** is the area in a window below the title bar, menu bar or toolbar. Everything that relates to the application noted in the title bar is displayed in the workspace. In the

FIGURE 2–12

THE START MENU WITH POP-OUT MENUS
The *Start* menu *All Programs* option is selected, prompting a display of available programs. The *Norton SystemWorks* folder and then the *Norton Utilities* subfolder are highlighted, causing its contents (11 applications) to be displayed. Note that recently accessed programs/folders are highlighted.

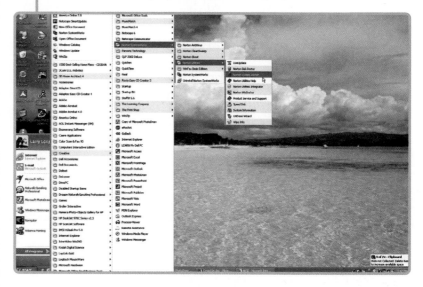

FIGURE 2–13

ELEMENTS OF AN APPLICATION WINDOW
In this example display, the workspace in this *Microsoft PhotoDraw* application has two open document windows, both showing processor chips. The top window, which is the active document window, contains an image of the Intel 8088 processor— the one used in the original 1981 IBM PC. A pan and zoom thumbnail of this image (bottom left) outlines what portion of the image is visible in the document window. The bottom document window shows a state-of-the-art Intel chip.

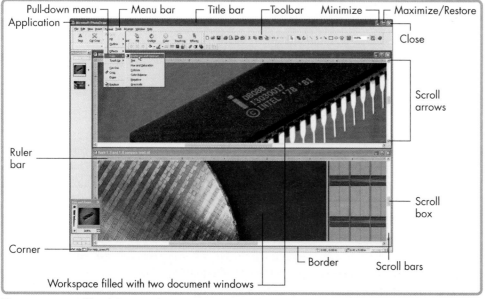

Photo courtesy of Intel Corporation

example in Figure 2-13, two **document windows** are displayed in the parent application window's workspace. Both are photo images and each is shown in a document window. The workspace of a word processing program might contain one or more word processing documents. If only one file/document is displayed in the workspace, then its filename appears in the title bar. If multiple files/documents are displayed, then filenames appear in the title bars of their windows.

When document content is more than can be displayed in a window, the window is outfitted with **vertical** and/or **horizontal scroll bars** (see Figure 2-13). Each bar contains a **scroll box** and two **scroll arrows.** Use the mouse or keyboard to move a box up/down or left/right on a scroll bar to display other parts of the application. This movement is known as **scrolling.**

Title Bar

The horizontal **title bar** at the top of each window runs the width of the window from left to right (see Figure 2-13). The elements of the title bar include the *application icon, window title, Minimize button, Maximize/Restore button, Close button,* and the *title area.* Point and click (or drag) on these elements to change the presentation of the window.

- *Application icon in title bar.* The application icon is a miniature visual representation of the application and is displayed on the left end of the title bar.

- *Window title.* The title bar displays the title of the application ("Microsoft PhotoDraw" in Figure 2-13).

- *Minimize, Maximize/Restore, and Close buttons.* Point and click on the Minimize button (▬), the Maximize (to full screen) or Restore (to a window) button (☐ or ⎘), or the Close button (✖) at the right end of the title bar in Figure 2-13.

- *Title area.* To *move* a window, the user simply points to the window title bar and drags the window to the desired location.

Menu Bar

The menu bar for an application window runs the width of the window just below the title bar (see Figure 2-13). The menu bar lists the menus available for that application. Choosing an option from the menu bar results in a pull-down menu. The *File, Edit, View,* and *Help* menus are available for most applications. Other menu options depend on the application. When you select an item from the menu bar, a subordinate **pull-down menu** (see Figure 2-13) is "pulled down" from the selected menu bar option and displayed as a vertical list of menu options.

Certain conventions apply to user interactions with any menu.

- *Only the undimmed options can be chosen.* Dimmed options are not available for the current circumstances. For example, the *Copy* option would not be available in an *Edit* menu if nothing had been selected to be copied.

- *Corresponding shortcut keys are presented next to many options in Windows menus.* The **shortcut key** is a key combination (for example, Alt+F4 to *Exit* and Ctrl+C to *Copy*), to issue commands within a particular application without activating a menu.

- *Choosing a menu option followed by an arrow (▶) results in a pop-out menu.* The *Color* menu option on Figure 2-13 demonstrates the resulting **pop-out menu.**

- *A user-recorded check mark (✓) to the left of the menu option indicates that the option is active and applies to any related commands.* For example, many programs have a toolbar, a ruler, and a status bar that are hidden or displayed depending on whether or not these items are checked in the *View* menu.

- *There are three ways to choose a menu option.*
  1. Point and click the mouse on the option.
  2. Tap the Alt key to activate the current menu bar. This lets you select an option via keyboard. Enter the underlined letter key, called a **mnemonic** (pronounced *"neh MON ik"*), of the menu option in combination with the Alt key on a keyboard (Alt+o for the *Format* menu in Figure 2-13). Press the underlined letter of a pull-down menu option to choose that option (*l* for *Color* in Figure 2-13).
  3. Once the menu is activated (by mouse click or keyboard), you can use the keyboard arrow keys to select (highlight) the desired option and press the Enter key to choose it.

- *Choosing a menu option followed by an ellipsis (. . .) results in a dialog box.* A pop-up **dialog box** typically asks the user to make further choices or enter additional information.

You'll encounter a variety of menus, including the pop-up and floating menus. The context-sensitive **pop-up menu** is displayed when you right-click the mouse. The pop-up menu gives you options appropriate for whatever you're doing at the time. The **floating menu** "floats" over the display and can be dragged with a mouse to any position on the work area.

You can use a hotkey to issue a few special commands without going through a menu. Tapping the **hotkey,** which is typically a key combination, causes some function to happen in the computer, no matter what the active menu or application (Alt+PrintScreen captures the image of the active window so you can save, display, or print it).

Toolbar

A software package's menu bar is but the tip of a hierarchy of menus that may contain as many as 200 menu item options. You might work with a software package for years and not choose some of these options. You might use others every day. **Toolbars** have been created to give you ready access to these frequently used menu items. Toolbars contain multiple buttons with graphics that represent related menu options or commands (see Figure 2-13). To execute a particular command, simply click on the button. The graphics on the buttons are designed to represent actions of the command. You can customize your toolbars to meet your processing needs.

Ruler Bar

Typically, the **ruler bar** shows the document window's content relative to the printed page. The default usually is inches and standard letter-sized paper (see Figure 2-13).

Corners and Borders

To resize a window, use a mouse and point to a window's border or corner. The mouse pointer changes to a double arrow when positioned over a border or corner. Drag the border or corner in the directions indicated by the double arrow to the desired shape.

The Dialog Box

You will encounter scores of dialog boxes in Windows (such as the Display Properties dialog box) and in user applications. Often, you, the user, must okay or revise entries in the *dialog box* before you can continue with a particular operation. The dialog box may contain any of these elements (see Figure 2-14).

- *Tabs.* The tabs enable similar properties to be grouped within a dialog box (for example, *Appearance* and *Screen Saver*).

- *Text box.* Enter text information in the text box or accept the displayed default entry.

- *Command buttons.* Point and click on the OK command button to carry out the command with the information provided in the dialog box.

FIGURE 2-14 **ELEMENTS OF A DIALOG BOX**
Many common dialog box elements are shown in the Display Properties dialog box. Not shown are the option button and scroll bar adjustment elements.

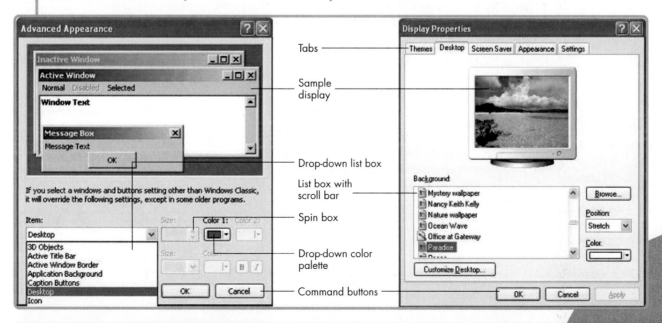

- *List boxes*. A list box displays a list of available choices for a particular option.
- *Drop-down list boxes*. The drop-down list box is an alternative to the list box when the dialog box is too small for a list box to be displayed.
- *Drop-down palette*. The drop-down palette displays a matrix of available font, line, or fill colors.
- *Option buttons*. Circular buttons, called option buttons, preface each item in a list of mutually exclusive items (only one can be activated). Point and click a button to insert a black dot in the button and activate the option.
- *Scroll bar adjustment*. The scroll bar adjustment enables users to change options, such as the speed at which the cursor blinks or speaker volume.
- *Spin box*. The spin box lets you adjust a numerical setting by keying in the desired number or clicking the up or down arrow to "spin" to the desired number.

Icons

Icons, the graphical representation of a Windows element, play a major role in the Windows GUI. Commonly used icons include *application icons*, *shortcut icons*, *document icons*, and *disk drive icons*. The **Explorer** window in Figure 2-15 shows the use of these icons. Use the Explorer to perform file management tasks such as creating folders, copying files, moving files, deleting files, and other tasks related to folder and file management. In Windows, named folders are created to hold document and program files.

Application Icons

The **application icon** is included on a minimized application button in the taskbar and on the title bar in a window. It is usually a graphic rendering of the software package's logo.

Shortcut Icons

A **shortcut icon** to any application, document, or printer can be positioned on the desktop, in a folder, or in several other places. The shortcut icon has an arrow in its lower left corner. Shortcuts are clicked (or double-clicked) to begin an application.

FIGURE 2–15

THE WINDOWS EXPLORER
The Windows Explorer makes resources on the computer readily accessible to the user. The plus sign to the left of the icon indicates that the item has subordinate folders. Click the disk or folder icon to show its content or double-click on an application icon to open the application. Positioning the mouse pointer over an applications icon (as shown here) highlights the icon and causes a hint, details, or explanation to be displayed in the status bar at the bottom of the window.

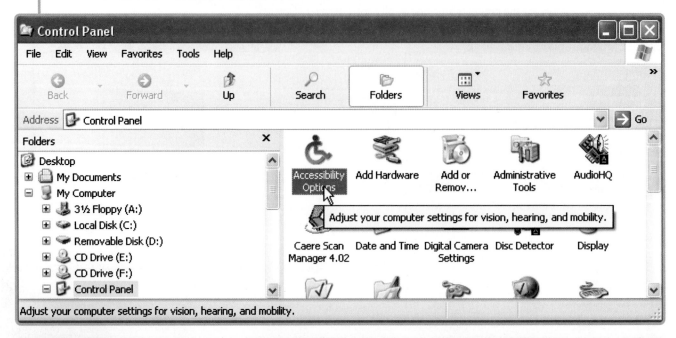

Document Icons

The active document window, which is a window within an application window, can be minimized to a **document icon** within an application's workspace.

Disk Drive Icons

The **disk drive icons** graphically represent several disk drive options: floppy, hard, network (hard), removable disk (for example, Zip disk drive), and CD-ROM (including DVD and CD-RW). The floppy (A), hard disk (C), Zip disk (D), and CD-ROMs (E, a DVD and F, a CD-RW) icons shown in Figure 2-15 resemble the faceplates of the disk drives or show the type of storage media.

Viewing Windows

The Windows environment lets you view multiple applications in windows on the desktop display. Once open, a window can be resized, minimized (and restored), maximized (and restored), and closed.

Essentially, any applications software for the Windows environment can be:

● Viewed and run in a window, the shape and size of which is determined by you, the user

● Run full-screen (maximized), that is, filling the entire screen, with no other application windows or icons showing

When multiple applications are running, the user can use the *Move* and *Resize* capabilities to arrange and size the windows to meet viewing needs.

Within a given application window, such as Microsoft Excel, multiple document windows can be sized, shrunk, and arranged by the user within the workspace. As an alternative, the user can request that the document windows be automatically presented as **cascading windows** or **tiled windows,** which are illustrated in Figure 2-16.

Switching Between Windows

In the Windows environment, users can open as many applications as available RAM will permit. The active window is always highlighted in the **foreground.** When located in the foreground all parts of the window are visible. Other open windows are in the **background,** or behind the foreground (see Figure 2-11). These terms describe RAM concepts, too. To switch between open applications, point and click anywhere on the desired inactive window or on the desired application button in the taskbar. You can also use the Alt+Tab shortcut key to toggle between application windows.

Terminating an Application and a Windows Session

Perform three operations before ending a Windows session.

1. *Save your work.* The *Save* option in the *File* menu updates the existing file to reflect the changes made during the session. The *Save As* option allows users to save the current file under another filename.

2. *Close all open windows.* After saving your work, exit a Windows application through its menu bar (*File* then *Exit*) or by pointing and clicking the Close button in the title bar.

FIGURE 2–16

ARRANGEMENT OF WINDOWS
Here, four open applications are tiled on the Windows XP desktop (clockwise from top left: *Microsoft PhotoDraw, Outlook, Internet Explorer,* and *Microsoft Visio*). The applications, as well as documents within an application's workspace, can be presented as tiled documents (in top left Microsoft PhotoDraw images) or cascading (bottom left Visio documents are overlapped such that all title bars are visible).

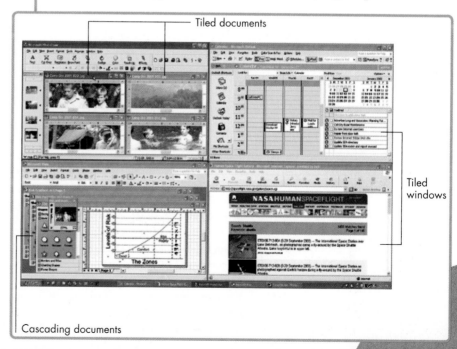

Tiled documents

Tiled windows

Cascading documents

3. *Shut down Windows.* Click *Start* in the taskbar, and then select *Turn Off Computer* (or *Shut Down*). The shut down process is illustrated in Getting Started.

SHARING INFORMATION AMONG APPLICATIONS

The Windows environment offers several methods for sharing information: the Clipboard, and object linking, and object embedding.

The Clipboard: Copy, Cut, and Paste

One of the most inviting aspects of the Windows environment is the ability to copy and move information (text, graphics, sound clips, video clips, or a combination) within and between applications. The most common method of sharing information among applications is to use the Windows **Clipboard** and the *Edit* option in the menu bar. Think of the Clipboard as a holding area for information. The information in the Clipboard can be en route to another application, or it can be copied anywhere in the current document. *Edit* is an option in the menu bar of most Windows applications. Choosing *Edit* results in a pull-down menu from the menu bar. Options common to most Edit menus are *Cut, Copy, Paste,* and *Delete*. The **source application** and **destination application** can be the same, or they can be entirely different applications.

The procedure for transferring information via the Clipboard is demonstrated in Figure 2-17. This example illustrates the *Copy* procedure. Choosing the *Cut* option causes the specified information to be removed from the source application and placed on the Windows Clipboard. Whether *Copy* or *Cut* is chosen, the Clipboard contents remain unchanged until the next copy/cut operation, so you can paste the Clipboard contents as many times as needed.

Object Linking and Embedding: OLE

Another way to link applications is through **object linking and embedding,** or **OLE.** Loosely, an **object** is an item within a Windows application that can be individually selected. The object can be a block of text, all or part of a graphic image, or even a sound or video clip. OLE gives us the capability to create a **compound document** that contains one or more objects from other applications. A document can be a word processing newsletter, a *Microsoft Visio* drawing, a spreadsheet, and so on. The object originates in a **server application** and is linked to a destination document of a **client application.** For example, when a Visio (server application) drawing (object) is linked to a Word (client) note (destination document), the result is a compound document (see Figure 2-18).

OLE Object Linking

OLE lets you *link* or *embed* information. When you link information, the link between source and destination documents is *dynamic*; that is, any change you make in the source document is reflected in the destination document. To link an object, follow the copy/paste procedure, except select *Paste Special* in the *Edit* menu, then choose the *Paste Link* option button in the dialog box.

The capabilities of object linking are demonstrated in Figure 2-18. Linking doesn't actually place the object into the destination document—it places a pointer to the source document (a disk-based file). In linking, the object is saved as a separate file from the source document. Linking is helpful when the object is used in several destination documents because when you change the source, it is updated in all documents to which it is linked.

OLE Object Embedding

When you embed information, you insert the actual object, not just a pointer. Whereas linking is dynamic, embedding is not. To embed an object, choose the *Paste* option button in the *Paste Special* dialog box. You can change the source within the destination document, but the original (if there is one) is unchanged. A source document is not required in object embedding.

2-2.1	In the Windows environment, the active window is highlighted in the background. (T/F)
2-2.2	The Close button in a Windows application is indicated with a letter Y. (T/F)
2-2.3	Which is not considered a common menu format: (a) floating, (b) pop-out, (c) pop-up, or (d) pop-down?
2-2.4	The shortcut key for Copy is: (a) Alt+C, (b) Shift+C, (c) Tab+C, or (d) Ctrl+C.
2-2.5	Which of these would not be found in a dialog box: (a) list boxes, (b) tabs, (c) television buttons, or (d) text boxes?
2-2.6	In OLE, the object originates in a server application. (T/F)

FIGURE 2–17

COPY AND PASTE VIA THE CLIPBOARD
This walkthrough demonstrates the procedure for transferring information among multiple Windows applications: Paint (a paint program), Word (a word processing program), and an Internet-based encyclopedia. In the example, the Eiffel Tower image in a Paint document is marked and copied (to the Clipboard), then pasted to a Word document. Supporting text in the online *Encarta Encyclopedia* is marked and copied to the same Word document via the Clipboard.

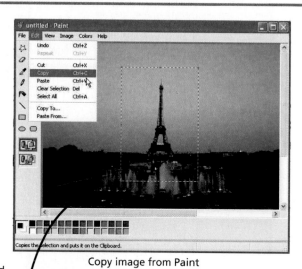

Copy image from Paint

1. *Mark the information.* Drag the select cursor (the Pick tool in Paint) from one corner of the information to be copied to the opposite corner of the area and release the mouse button. The information to be transferred is highlighted.

2. *Copy the marked information to the Clipboard.* Choose Edit in the source application's (Paint) menu bar to display the options. Choose Copy to place the specified information on the Windows Clipboard, leaving the source application unchanged.

Paste to Word

3. *Switch to the destination application and place the graphics cursor at the desired insertion point.*
4. *Paste the marked information.* Choose Edit in the destination application's (Word) menu bar to display the applicable options. Choose the Paste option to copy the contents of the Clipboard to the cursor position in the destination application.

Copy text from Encarta

5. *Mark the information.* Highlight the information to be copied in the source application (Encarta Encyclopedia).
6. *Copy the marked information to the Clipboard.*

Paste to Word

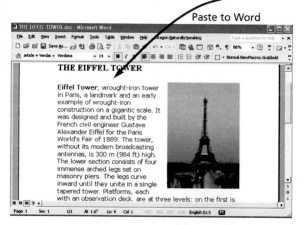

7. *Switch to the destination application and place the graphics cursor at the desired insertion point.*
8. *Paste the marked information.*

FIGURE 2–18

OBJECT LINKING
The map image is linked to a Word document (left) to create a compound document. The original object did not include the school image or the stop sign image. The image was modified in *Microsoft Visio* (middle) within the context of the Word document, and the linked object was updated automatically in Word (right).

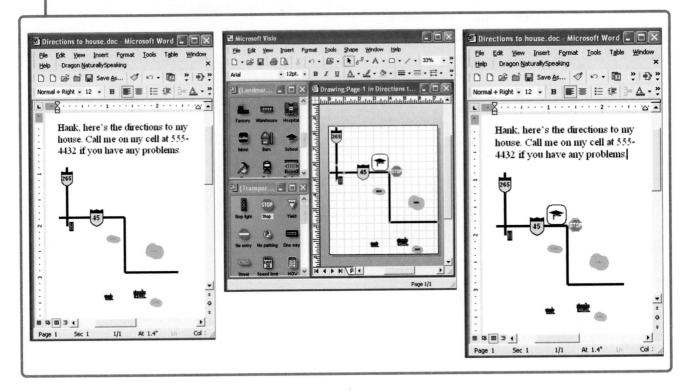

2-3 Productivity Software: The Software Suite

Software suites, such as Microsoft Office, Corel WordPerfect Office, and Lotus SmartSuite, are introduced in Chapter 1. These suites are made up of several complementary applications that can include word processing, presentation, spreadsheet, database, personal information management, desktop publishing, and communications (Internet-related) software. Most new PCs are sold with a full or partial software suite installed on the system. This section is designed to give you an overview of the general functionality and capabilities of the first five on this list.

WORD PROCESSING: THE MOST POPULAR PRODUCTIVITY APPLICATION

At work, at home, at school, and even during leisure activities, we spend much of our time writing. Whether an e-mail, a party announcement, a report, a diary entry, or a newsletter, all can be made easier and more presentable through the use of word processing software.

Word Processing Concepts and Features

Word processing software lets us create, edit (revise), and format documents in preparation for output. Output can be a document that is printed, displayed on a monitor, faxed, e-mailed, or, perhaps, posted to the Internet for worldwide access.

Word processing is the perfect example of how automation can be used to increase productivity and foster creativity. It reduces the effort you must devote to the routine aspects of writing so you can focus your attention on its creative aspects. For example, a *spelling checker* checks your grammar and spelling, an *online thesaurus* helps you find the right word, and a *grammar and style checker* highlights grammatical concerns.

Creating a Document

You'll probably learn the process and techniques of preparing a word processing document in a lab or, perhaps, via interactive computer-based training. To create an original document, such as a résumé (see Figure 2-19), you simply begin entering text from the keyboard and, as needed, enter formatting commands that enhance the appearance of the document when it is printed or displayed (spacing, italics, and so on). You can insert images, such as the photo in Figure 2-19, then resize and/or reposition them anywhere within the word processing document. Once you are satisfied with the content and appearance of the document, you are ready to print, send, or display it.

Formatting a Document

You format a word processing document by specifying what you wish the general appearance of the document to be when it is printed. Typically, the preset format, or *default settings,* fit most word processing applications. For example, the size of the output document is set at letter size ($8\frac{1}{2}$ by 11 inches); the left, right, top, and bottom margins are set at 1 inch; tabs are set every $\frac{1}{2}$ inch; and line spacing is set at 6 lines per inch. The default font might be 12 point Times New Roman. Times New Roman is one of dozens of available **typefaces** you can use in documents. A typeface refers to a set of characters of a particular design (Courier, Futura Book, Old English, and so on are typefaces). A **font** is described by its typeface, its height in points (8, 10, 14, 24, and so on; there are 72 points to the inch), and its presentation attribute (regular, **bold**, *italic*, underline, and so on).

What You Can Do with Word Processing: The Features Package

Typically, text is entered in a word processing or other type of document via *keyboard* or *speech recognition.* In speech recognition, you simply speak into a microphone and the words are interpreted by speech-recognition software and entered in the document. Word processing packages are **WYSIWYG** (pronounced "*WIZ e wig*"), an acronym for "What you see is what you get." This means that what you do to a document, whether entering text or inserting an image, is reflected on the screen showing you what the document will look like when it is printed. Word processing software has many features that help you create exactly what you want. The specifics of these features are left to the hands-on lab, but Figure 2-20 gives you a good visual summary of word processing features and capabilities. All word processing programs come with a healthy supply of prepackaged electronic images called **clip art.**

FIGURE 2–19

WORD PROCESSING RÉSUMÉ
The new Microsoft Office XP suite offers a more streamlined appearance and many new features, such as the "Ask a Question" box that now appears in the toolbar of every Office XP application. Also, notice the *language bar* displayed over the title bar. The language bar enables you to use the *speech recognition* feature in Office XP. This feature lets you dictate text and perform commands by simply talking to your PC. Mallory Brooks used this feature in conjunction with Microsoft Word to help her make a good first impression with prospective employers. The result is this professional-looking résumé that emphasizes her strengths. The use of color adds flair to any document.

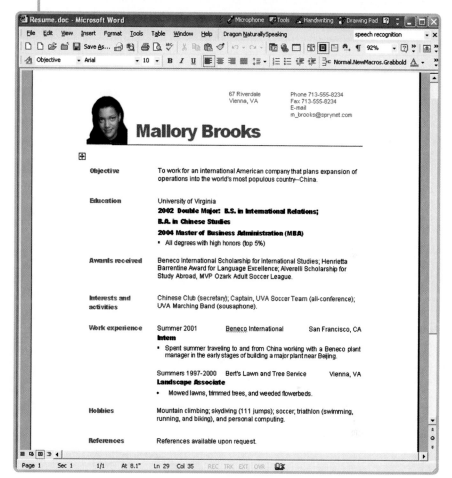

Putting Word Processing to Work

Word processing is extremely versatile, offering you a wide range of capabilities. Here are a few more applications for word processing. You will find many more as you gain experience with this, the most used of all software applications.

● *Merging documents with a database.* Word processing software allows you to merge data in a database with the text of a document. The most common use of this capability is the *mail-merge* feature. The mail-merge example is a good illustration of the use of **boilerplate** text. Boilerplate is existing text that can be reused and customized for a variety of word processing applications.

- *Electronic documents.* Many companies are opting to put their reference materials in electronic, rather than printed, documents. Electronic versions of product catalogs, procedures manuals, personnel handbooks, and so on are now common in the business community. They are easier to create, maintain, and distribute.
- *Creating Web pages.* If you can create a word processing document, you can create a Web page on the Internet. Any word processing document can be saved in Web page format.

FIGURE 2–20

WORD PROCESSING FEATURES OVERVIEW

This word processing document illustrates features common to most word processing software. Note that you can create special effects with the *drawing tool* and *border* features. The *watermark* feature lets you add a drawing, a company logo, headline-sized text (such as the "PRIORITY" in this example), or any image behind the printed document text. In the electronic world, documents are "networked" with hyperlinks (references to different sections of an electronic document or to other related electronic documents on the local computer or on the Internet). Even the *callouts,* which label the features, are a word processing feature. Not shown is the *editing* feature that lets you add editorial remarks and make corrections to an original document. This feature is helpful when several people review a document prior to publication.

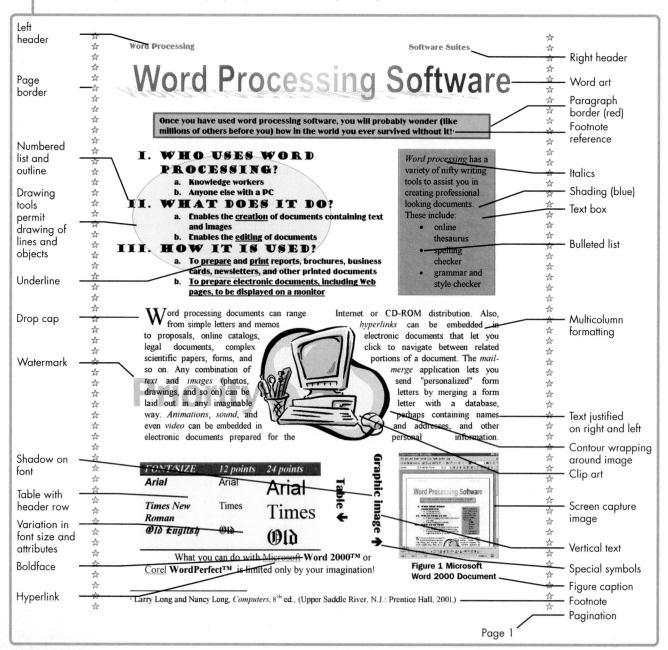

Word Processing versus Desktop Publishing Software

Word processing can handle most document generation tasks, but those organizations that need to produce complicated documents to be printed professionally use desktop publishing software. With desktop publishing software you can create *camera-ready documents* (ready to be printed professionally) such as newsletters, brochures, user manuals, pamphlets, flyers, restaurant menus, periodicals, greeting cards, graduation certificates, and thousands of other printed and published items. The flyer for a school fund-raiser in Figure 2-21 was produced with Microsoft Publisher. The image highlighting the various objects illustrates how desktop publishing documents are composed of rectangular *frames,* text, and images that can be resized and repositioned to meet layout needs. In contrast to word processing, wherein the emphasis is on inserted objects within the running text, desktop publishing emphasizes the overall *document composition.* Various types of *frames* (objects) are pulled together and laid out on a page.

PRESENTATION SOFTWARE: PUTTING ON THE SHOW

Many studies confirm that people who use *presentation software* to create presentations are perceived as being better prepared and more professional than those who do not. Judicious use of this software can help you persuade people to adopt a particular point of view, whether at the lectern or the pulpit. Typically, presentation software is used in conjunction with an LCD projector that projects images onto a screen for all to see.

Presentation software lets you create highly stylized images for group presentations of any kind, to create self-running slide shows for PC-based information displays at trade shows, for class lectures (offline or online), and any other situation that requires the presentation of organized, visual information (see Figure 2-22). The software, such as Microsoft PowerPoint, gives you a rich assortment of tools to help you create a variety of charts, graphs, and images and to help you make the presentation.

Follow these steps to prepare a presentation using presentation software.

1. *Select a template.* Presentation software comes with many handy **templates.** Generically, a template is a form, mold, or pattern used as a guide to making something. All productivity software packages have templates to give us a leg up when creating documents. Templates

FIGURE 2-21

DESKTOP PUBLISHING
Word processing software is sufficient for most home and business document preparation tasks, but desktop publishing software may be needed for the more sophisticated tasks that require camera-ready copy for professional printing jobs.

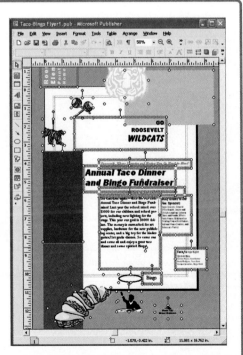

FIGURE 2-22

POWERPOINT SLIDE SORTER VIEW
Microsoft PowerPoint helps you prepare and present slides for presentations. PowerPoint has a variety of slide templates from which you can choose. You can work with the entire presentation or with a single chart (see Figure 2-23). Slides are easily rearranged by simply dragging a slide to a new position.

FIGURE 2-23

POWERPOINT TRI-PANE VIEW
The PowerPoint tri-pane view shows the *slide, outline,* and *notes* so you can work with all the elements of the presentation at once.

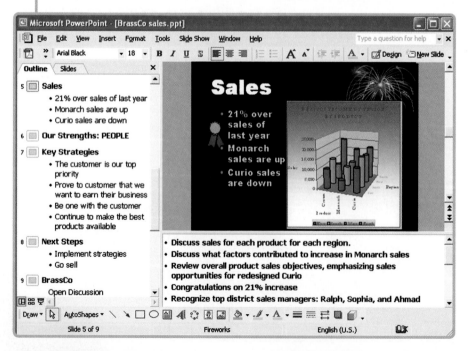

can be real time-savers. (In word processing, there are templates for business letters, faxes, memos, reports, and so on.) PowerPoint, the industry standard for presentation software, has two types of templates: *design templates* and *content templates*. Design templates are predesigned formats and complementary color schemes with preselected background images you can apply to any content material (the outline) to give your slides a professional, customized appearance. A **slide** is one of the images to be displayed. A design template was used to create the presentation "look" shown in Figure 2-22. Content templates go one step further and suggest content for specific subjects (for example, business plan, project overview, employee orientation, and many others).

2. *Create an outline for the presentation.* PowerPoint's tri-pane view lets you view the *slide, outline,* and *notes* at the same time (see Figure 2-23). This view makes it easy to add new slides, edit text, and enter notes while creating a presentation. The outline feature helps you organize your presentation material into a multilevel outline. What you include in the outline is automatically formatted into slides based on the selected design template. In the slides, the main points (first-level headings in the outline) become slide titles and their subordinate items become subheadings and subpoints. Each software package produces its own unique files. However, with so much overlap in functionality between popular productivity software, files can be imported from one type of software to another. When we **import** a file, we convert it from its foreign format to a format that is compatible with the current program. For example, people frequently import Microsoft Word outlines into the PowerPoint outline feature. Microsoft Excel spreadsheets can be imported directly into the PowerPoint chart feature. When we **export** a file, we convert a file in the current program to a format that can be read directly by another program.

3. *Compile and create other nontext resources.* Text alone, no matter how well formatted, may fall short of what is needed for a quality presentation. A good slide presentation will include

some or all of the following: *photo images, charts* and *graphs,* original *drawings,* a variety of eye-catching *clip art, audio clips,* and even *full-motion video* captured with a digital camera. Obviously, not all presentations will comprise every capability, but at a minimum, there is clip art available for every presentation situation (for example, the blue ribbon in Figure 2-23). It's a good idea to use audio to introduce or highlight critical points. For example, a slide on a new employee bonus plan can be introduced with the *ka-ching* sound of a cash register.

With presentation software, you can create a variety of charts from data imported from a spreadsheet or a database, or you can enter the data into a PowerPoint table. Usually the data needed to produce a graph already exist in a spreadsheet or a database. Among the most popular charts are *pie charts* and *bar charts.* You have many other charting options, including *line charts, bubble charts, range charts, doughnut charts,* and *area charts,* each of which can be presented in two or three dimensions and annotated with *titles, labels,* and *legends.*

Besides traditional business charts, presentation software allows you to prepare *organization charts* showing the hierarchical structure of an organization (see Figure 2-24) and *maps* showing demographic information in context with geographic location.

4. *Integrate resources.* Once all text and visual resources have been compiled, it is time to integrate them into a visually appealing presentation. Typically, people work from the slides generated from the outline, inserting clip art, charts, and so on as needed. Some slides may include only a title and images, such as the sixth slide in Figure 2-22. The PowerPoint *slide sorter* view gives you an overview of the presentation. The slide sorter shows thumbnail images to enable the viewing of all or much of a presentation in sequence on a single screen. A **thumbnail** is a miniature display of an image or perhaps a page (document or Web). The slide sorter makes it easy to add or delete slides and to rearrange them to meet presentation needs.

5. *Add special effects.* With PowerPoint, you can give the audience a little candy for the eyes and ears. For example, the current graph or image can be made to *fade out* (dissolve to a blank screen) while the text is fading in. An applause sound can be played when a particular image or element is displayed. PowerPoint offers a variety of transitions and sounds, each of which adds an aura of professionalism while helping to hold the audience's attention. Also, text and objects can be animated. For example, text and objects can be made to fly in from the perimeter of the screen a word or a letter at a time.

6. *Add notes.* Each slide in a presentation can have corresponding notes (see Figure 2-23). Frequently, people make notes for themselves to help them remember to make key points during a presentation.

7. *Deliver the presentation.* A PC-based presentation can be made to an individual or a small group on a single PC, or it can be projected onto a large screen. Or, it can be fashioned as a self-running information center where screens are preset to display in a timed sequence. Or, the entire presentation can be saved as Web pages and posted to the Internet.

Whether you're preparing a report, a speech, a newsletter, or any other form of business, academic, or personal communication, it pays—immediately and over the long term—to take full advantage of presentation software.

SPREADSHEET SOFTWARE: THE MAGIC MATRIX

A spreadsheet is simply a grid for entering rows and columns of data. The typical home or office has scores of applications for organizing tabular information. Instructors' grade books are good uses for spreadsheet software, with student names labeling the rows, quizzes labeling the columns,

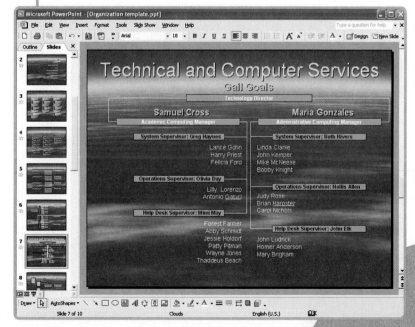

FIGURE 2–24

POWERPOINT ORGANIZATION CHART
PowerPoint 2002, shown here, has new collaboration and animation features that PowerPoint users will find inviting.

FIGURE 2–25 Spreadsheet in Space
On this space walk, Astronauts Steven L. Smith and John M. Grunsfeld are replacing gyroscopes contained inside the Hubble Space Telescope. The typical space shuttle is filled with notebook PCs. Astronauts rely heavily on spreadsheet software to organize and analyze data collected from a variety of activities.

Courtesy of NASA

and scores being the entries. Think of anything that has rows and columns of data and you have identified an application for spreadsheet software: income (profit-and-loss) statements, personnel profiles, demographic data, home inventories, and budget summaries, just to mention a few (see Figure 2-25).

Spreadsheet Concepts and Features

We will use the March sales summary, shown in Figure 2-26, to demonstrate spreadsheet concepts. The national sales manager for BrassCo Enterprises, a manufacturer of an upscale line of brass coat hanger products (the Crown, the Monarch, and the Curio), compiles monthly sales summaries using a spreadsheet software template. The template, simply a spreadsheet model, contains the layout and formulas needed to produce the summary illustrated in Figure 2-26. The manager entered only the data for the current month (the sales amounts for each salesperson for March) and the spreadsheet template performed all of the necessary calculations (the totals and the commissions).

Organization: Rows and Columns

Spreadsheets are organized in a tabular structure with rows and columns. The intersection of a particular row and column designates a **cell**. As you can see in Figure 2-26, the rows are numbered, and the columns are lettered.

Data are entered and stored in a cell. During operations, data are referred to by their **cell address**, which identifies the location of a cell in the spreadsheet by its column and row, with the column designator first. For example, in the monthly sales summary of Figure 2-26, C4 is the address of the column heading for product Crown, and D5 is the address of the total amount of Monarch sales for R. Rosco ($30,400).

In the spreadsheet work area (the rows and columns), sometimes called a *worksheet*, a movable highlighted area "points" to the *current cell*. The current cell is highlighted with either a different background color or a dark border (see the dark border around cell A1, the current cell, in the first example in Figure 2-26). This highlighted area, called the **pointer**, can be moved around the spreadsheet with the arrow keys or the mouse. The address and content of the current cell are displayed in the cell content portion of the spreadsheet above the work area (sometimes called the *formula bar*). The content or value resulting from a formula of each cell is shown in the spreadsheet work area.

Spreadsheets can be large, sometimes thousands of rows and hundreds of columns. When document content is more than can be displayed in a window, you can simply scroll vertically or horizontally through the spreadsheet.

Ranges: Groups of Cells

Many spreadsheet operations ask you to designate a **range** of cells. These are highlighted in Figure 2-26: *cell range* (a single cell); *column range* (all or part of a column of adjacent cells); *row range*; and *block range* (a rectangular group of cells). A particular range is indicated by the addresses of the endpoint cells separated by a colon, such as the row range C14:E14.

Cell Entries

To make an entry in the spreadsheet, simply move the pointer to the appropriate cell, and key in the data. The major types of entries are *label* entry, *numeric* entry, and *formula* entry shown in Figure 2-26. A label entry may be a word or a phrase that occupies a particular cell. In Figure 2-26, "NAME" in cell A4 is a label entry, as is "COMMISSION" in G4.

In Figure 2-26, the dollar sales values in the range C5:E10 are *numeric*. The dollar sales values in the ranges F5:G10 and C12:G12 are results of *formulas*. Cell F5 contains a formula, but it is the numeric result (for example, 61150 in Figure 2-26) that is displayed in the spreadsheet work area. With the pointer positioned at F5, the formula appears in the cell contents box. The formula value in F5 computes the total sales made by the salesperson in row 5 for all three products (that is, total sales is =C5+D5+E5). The actual numeric value appears in the spreadsheet work area (see Figure 2-26).

Spreadsheet formulas use standard notation for **arithmetic operators:** + (add), – (subtract), * (multiply), / (divide), ^ (raise to a power, or *exponentiation*). In Microsoft Excel, formulas begin with an equals sign (=). The formula in F5 computes the total sales for R. Rosco. The range F6:F10 contains similar formulas that apply to their respective rows (=C6+D6+E6, =C7+D7+E7, and so on). For example, the formula in F6 computes the total sales for G. Mann. The last image in Figure 2-26 provides a summary of the actual unformatted cell contents for all cells.

FIGURE 2-26

SPREADSHEET TEMPLATE SHOWING A MONTHLY SALES SUMMARY
Spreadsheets can be formatted to better portray the information (for example, the use of color, font size, and shading). Also, note that the spreadsheet drawing tool lets you draw lines and highlight elements of the spreadsheet. The red markings are included here to help illustrate spreadsheet concepts.

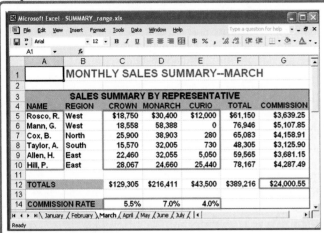

SPREADSHEET RANGES
The highlighted cells in this spreadsheet illustrate the four types of ranges: cell (G12), column (A5:A10), row (C14:E14), and block (C5:E10).

COPYING FORMULAS
The actual content of F5 is the formula in the cell contents box (=C5+D5+E5). The result of the formula (61150) appears in the spreadsheet at F5, formatted as currency ($61,150). In creating the spreadsheet template for the monthly sales summary, the national sales manager for BrassCo entered only three formulas (see cell contents summary below).

- The formula in F5 to sum the product sales for each salesperson was copied to the range F6:F10.
- The formula in G5: =$C$14*C5+$D$14*D5+$E$14*E5 to compute the commission for each salesperson was copied to the range G6:G10.
- The formula in C12: =SUM(C5:C10) to sum the sales for each product was copied to the range D12:G12.

COPYING FORMULAS THAT INCLUDE ABSOLUTE CELL ADDRESSES
Each of the commission computation formulas in the range G5:G10 has the same multipliers—the commission rates in the range C14:E14. Because the *relative* positions between the commission formulas in G5:G10 and the commission rates in C14:E14 vary from row to row, the commission rates are entered as *absolute* cell addresses. If the contents of a cell containing a formula are copied to another cell, the relative cell addresses in the copied formula are revised to reflect the new position (perhaps a new row), but the absolute cell addresses are unchanged. Notice in the cell contents summary below how the absolute addresses ($C$14, $D$14, and $E$14) in the copied formulas (G6:G10) remained the same in each formula and the relative addresses were revised to reflect the applicable row. If a dollar sign precedes the letter and/or number in a cell address, such as $C$14, the column and/or row reference is absolute.

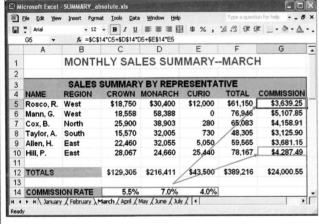

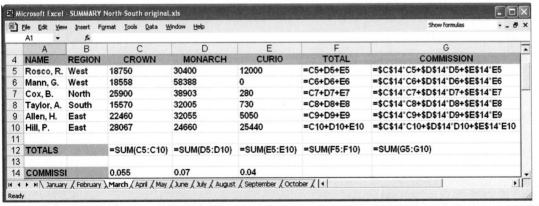

CELL CONTENTS SUMMARY
This cell contents summary illustrates the actual content of the cells in the above spreadsheet. To switch between displaying formulas and their values, press Ctrl+` (grave accent).

FIGURE 2–27

SPREADSHEET GRAPHS
Microsoft Excel, shown here, makes it easier to link data to Internet-based applications. Regional income for each of the three products (range C4:E7) are graphically illustrated in this three-dimensional bar chart.

Spreadsheets offer users a variety of predefined operations called **functions.** To use a function, simply enter the desired function name and enter one or more arguments. The **argument,** which is placed in parentheses, identifies the data to be operated on. The "compute the sum" function, SUM, in C12 in Figure 2-26 (see cell contents summary) adds the numbers in the range C5:C10 and displays the result in C12. Other spreadsheet functions include trigonometric functions, square roots, comparisons of values, manipulations of strings of data, computation of net present value and internal rate of return, and a variety of techniques for statistical analysis.

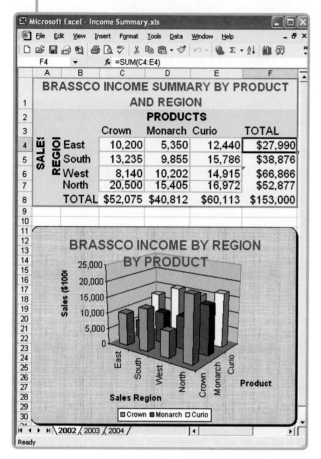

Spreadsheet Graphics

Spreadsheet packages let you generate a variety of charts from spreadsheet data. The spreadsheet template in Figure 2-27 presents an Income Summary by Product and Region for BrassCo. The income figures for each region (the range C4:E7) are plotted by product in a three-dimensional bar chart. To put spreadsheet data into a chart, the BrassCo VP needed only to respond to a series of prompts from the spreadsheet program. The first prompt asked him to select the type of graph to be generated. He then identified the source of the data, entered labels and titles, and so on. The resulting graph permits him to better understand the regional distribution of income by product.

DATABASE SOFTWARE: A DYNAMIC DATA TOOL

Hundreds and maybe even thousands of databases contain information about you. The typical knowledge worker interacts with databases all day long. These are good reasons to learn more about databases. Database software lets you enter, organize, and retrieve stored data. With Microsoft Access, featured here, and other database software packages you can:

- Create and maintain a database (add, delete, and revise records)
- Extract and list information that meets certain conditions
- Make inquiries (for example, "What is the total amount owed by all customers in Alabama?")
- Sort records in ascending or descending sequence by key fields (for example, alphabetical by last name)
- Generate formatted reports with subtotals and totals

These are the basic features. They have other features as well, including spreadsheet-type computations, presentation graphics, and programming.

Database Software and Spreadsheet Software: What's the Difference?

Both database and spreadsheet software packages let you work with data as rows and columns in a spreadsheet and as records in a database. Spreadsheet software gives you greater flexibility in the manipulation of rows and columns of data. Everything relating to spreadsheet-based data is easier with spreadsheet software—creating formulas, generating charts, what-if analysis (for example, "What if revenue increases by 10% next year?"), and so on. Database software offers greater flexibility in the organization and management of records within a database. Everything relating to a database is easier with database software—queries (requests for information), data entry, linking databases, report generation, programming to create information systems, and so on.

In short, spreadsheet packages are great number crunchers and are very helpful for small database applications. Database software packages may be too cumbersome for any serious number crunching, but they are terrific for creating any kind of personal or business information system.

Spreadsheet Organization

- Tabular structure
  - Numbered rows
  - Lettered columns
- Row/column intersect at cell
- Cell address locates cell
- Pointer highlights current cell
- Common cell entry types
  - Label
  - Numeric
  - Formula

Database Concepts and Features

The concepts and features of database software packages are very similar. The Microsoft Access example in this section is generally applicable to all database software.

Creating a Database with Database Software

In a database, related *fields,* such as student, course ID, and major, are grouped to form *records* (for example, a student record in the STUDENTS table in Figure 2-28). PC-based database packages use the *relational* approach to database management, which organizes data into *tables* in which a *row* is equivalent to a *record* that contains *fields* (set apart by columns). As you can see, the database *table* is conceptually the same as a *file.* One or more tables comprise a **relational database,** which refers to all of the tables in the database and the relationships between them.

The best way to explain the concepts of database software is by example. The chairperson of the Computer Information Systems (CIS) department uses Microsoft Access to help her with record-keeping tasks and to provide valuable information. She has created an education database with two tables: COURSE and STUDENT (see Figure 2-28). The COURSE table contains a record for each course offered in the CIS Department. Each record (row) in the COURSE table contains the following fields:

- COURSE ID
- COURSE TITLE
- TYPE of course (lecture, lab, or lecture/lab)
- INSTRUCTOR name
- CREDIT hours awarded for completion of course

The STUDENT table contains a record for each student who is enrolled in or has taken a CIS course. The table has only a few students to enable ease of demonstration of concepts, but it works just the same with hundreds of students. Each record contains the following fields:

- STUDENT (name of student; last name first)
- COURSE ID (provides a link to the COURSE table)
- MAJOR
- DATE ENROLLED
- STATUS (course status: incomplete [I], withdrew [W], or a grade [A, B, C, D, E, or F])

No single field in the STUDENT table uniquely identifies each record. However, the combined STUDENT and COURSE ID fields do identify each record. Therefore, to access a particular record in the STUDENT table, the chairperson must specify both the STUDENT and COURSE ID (for example, Targa, Phil, CIS 330). The COURSE and STUDENT tables can be linked because they have the COURSE ID field in common.

The first thing you do to set up a database table is to specify its structure by identifying the characteristics of each field in it. This structuring is done interactively, with the system prompting you to enter the field name, the field type, and so on. For example, in the first row of Figure 2-29

FIGURE 2–28 **EDUCATION DATABASE: COURSE TABLE AND STUDENT TABLE**
The Microsoft Access Education database is comprised of these two tables. The COURSE table contains a record for each course offered by the Computer Information Systems Department. The STUDENT table contains a record for each student who is enrolled in or has taken a course. The COURSE ID field links the two tables.

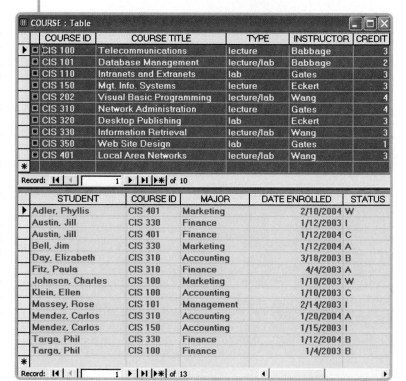

FIGURE 2–29 **STRUCTURE OF THE EDUCATION DATABASE**
This display shows the structure of the COURSE and STUDENT tables of the education database of Figure 2-28. The COURSE record (left) has four text fields and one number field. The STUDENT record has four text fields and one date/time field.

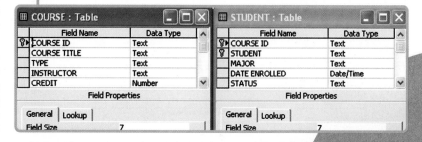

FIGURE 2–30 — DATA ENTRY SCREEN FORMAT

The screen format for entering, editing, and adding records to the COURSE table is illustrated.

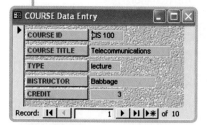

the *field name* is COURSE ID; the *data type* is "text"; and the *field size,* or field length, is seven positions. The field names for the COURSE and STUDENT tables are listed at the top of each table in Figure 2-28 (COURSE ID, COURSE TITLE, TYPE, and so on). Content for a *text* field can be a single word or any **alphanumeric** (numbers, letters, and special characters) phrase. For *number* field types, you can specify the number of decimal positions that you wish to have displayed (none in the example because credit hours are whole numbers).

Once you have defined the structure of the database table, you are ready to enter the data. The best way to enter data is to create a *screen format* that allows convenient data entry. The data entry screen format is analogous to a hard-copy form that contains labels and blank lines for you to fill in (for example, a medical questionnaire). Data are entered and edited (added, deleted, or revised) one record at a time with database software, just as they are on hard-copy forms. Figure 2-30 shows the data entry screen format for the COURSE table.

FIGURE 2–31 — QUERY BY EXAMPLE

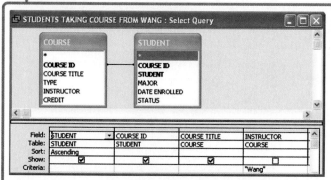

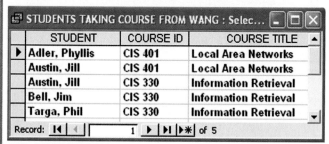

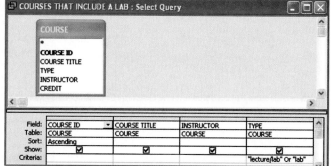

QBE: ONE CONDITION

The department chairperson wanted a listing of all students taking courses from Professor Wang. She requested a list of all courses that meet the condition INSTRUCTOR=*Wang* (see Figure 2-28). All records that meet this condition (see criteria query box shown here) are displayed in the answer window in ascending alphabetical order by student name. She selected only three fields to be included in the results display (checked boxes in figure). Notice that the query needed information from both tables.

QBE: USING LOGICAL OPERATORS

To produce the results shown here, the department chairperson set up her query by example to select only those courses that include a lab; that is, the criteria is (course) TYPE=*lab* OR *lecture/lab* (see Figure 2-28). The OR operator can be applied between fields (see example) or within fields. Only the COURSE table is needed for the query.

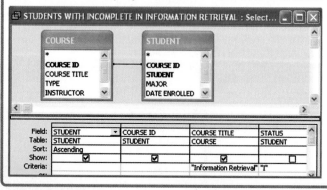

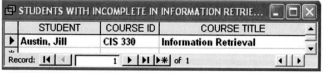

QBE: TWO CONDITIONS

The query in this example is set up to list those students who have an incomplete (STATUS=*I*) in the course entitled Information Retrieval (COURSE ID=*Information Retrieval*). The query requires the use of both tables in the database.

Query by Example

Database software also lets you retrieve, view, and print records based on **query by example.** In query by example, you set conditions for the selection of records by composing one or more example *relational expressions.* A relational expression normally compares one or more field names to numbers or character strings using the **relational operators** (= [equal to], > [greater than], < [less than], and combinations of these operators). Several conditions can be combined with **logical operators** (*AND, OR,* and *NOT*). Figure 2-31 demonstrates three types of query by example—one condition, using logical operators, and two conditions.

Sorting: Rearranging Records

The records in a database table also can be sorted for display in a variety of formats. For example, the COURSE table in Figure 2-28 has been sorted and is displayed in ascending order by COURSE ID. To obtain this sequencing of the database records, the department chairperson selected COURSE ID as the *key field* and *ascending* (versus descending) as the sort order. To get a presentation of the COURSE table sorted by COURSE ID within INSTRUCTOR, she needs to identify a *primary sort field* and a *secondary sort field.* Secondary sort fields are helpful when duplicates exist in the primary sort field (for example, there are three records for INSTRUCTOR=Gates). She selects INSTRUCTOR as the primary sort field, but she wants the courses offered by each INSTRUCTOR to be listed in ascending order by COURSE ID (see Figure 2-32).

Generating Reports

A database is a source of information, and database software helps you get the information you need. A *report* is the presentation of information derived from one or more databases. The simple listings of selected and ordered records in Figure 2-31 are "quick and dirty" reports. Such reports are the bread and butter of database capabilities and can be easily copied or imported into word processing or desktop publishing documents.

Database software allows you to create customized reports and to design their *layout.* This design capability allows you to change spacing and to include titles, subtitles, column headings, separation lines, and other elements that make a report more readable. Managers often use this capability to generate periodic reports, such as the Course Status Summary report shown in Figure 2-33.

Database: The Next Step

The database capabilities illustrated and discussed in this section merely "scratch the surface" of the potential

FIGURE 2–32

COURSE TABLE SORTED BY COURSE ID WITHIN INSTRUCTOR
This display is the result of a sort operation on the COURSE table with the INSTRUCTOR field as the primary sort field and the COURSE ID field as the secondary sort field. Notice that the COURSE ID field entries are in alphabetical order by instructor; that is, the three "Gates" records are in sequence by COURSE ID (CIS 110, CIS 310, and CIS 350).

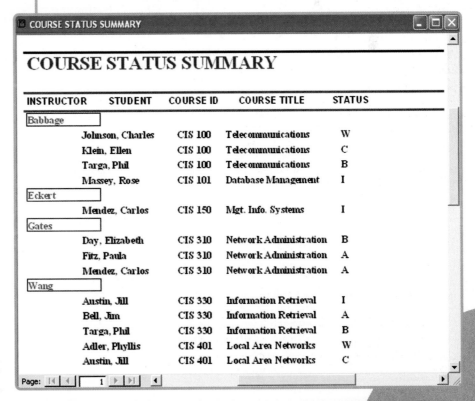

FIGURE 2–33

CUSTOMIZED REPORT
To obtain this Course Status Summary report, the CIS Department chairperson needed both the COURSE and STUDENT tables of Figure 2-28 from the education database.

of database software. For example, with relative ease, you can generate sophisticated reports that involve subtotals, calculations, and programming. In addition, data can be presented as a graph. You can even change the structure of a database (for example, add another field). Database software's programming capability has enabled users to create thousands of useful information systems, including student information systems, inventory management systems, hospital patient accounting systems (see Figure 2-34), and cinema management systems.

PERSONAL INFORMATION MANAGEMENT SOFTWARE

Personal information management or *PIM* software is a catch-all phrase that generally refers to messaging and personal information management software that helps you manage your messages, appointments, contacts, and tasks. PIM software, such as Microsoft® Outlook®, may include *calendar* applications for appointment scheduling and reminders; communications applications such as *e-mail, phone dialer,* and *fax;* and *databases* for organizing telephone numbers, e-mail addresses, to-do lists, notes, diary entries, and so on. Figure 2-35 gives you an overview of Microsoft Outlook personal information management software.

TEMPLATES: GETTING HELP WITH GETTING STARTED

Just as there is no reason to reinvent the wheel, there are relatively few circumstances where we must start from scratch to create a document, database, or presentation. Much of what we want to do has already been done before, whether it's an expense statement spreadsheet, a fax form, or an important market report presentation. Each of the major productivity software packages offers a variety of templates to help you get a head start on your projects. A template is simply a document or file that is already formatted or designed for a particular task. You add the content.

FIGURE 2–34 Databases Part of Our Daily Routine
Data management is part of our daily lives at home and at work, whether we use computers or not. This paramedic dons a Xybernaut wearable PC during emergencies, giving her immediate access to a comprehensive medical troubleshooting database.

Courtesy of Xybernaut

FIGURE 2–35 | MICROSOFT OUTLOOK: PERSONAL INFORMATION MANAGEMENT SOFTWARE
Microsoft® Outlook® is a handy time-management tool that you can use on your own or as part of a group.

STARTING THE DAY
Microsoft Outlook's *Outlook Today* gives you a snapshot of your day. It lists how many new e-mail messages you have, your appointments for the week, and your tasks. It is the best place to get an overview of your day and the week ahead.

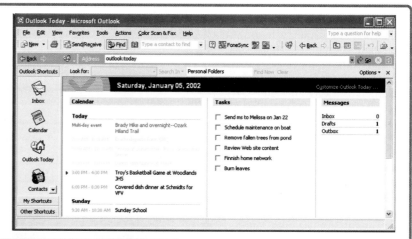

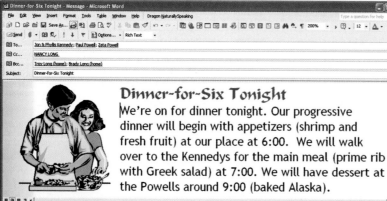

CREATE AND SHARE INFORMATION
The foundation application of PIM software is e-mail. Outlook offers a variety of ways to make your e-mail messages stand out. You can get fancy and write your e-mail on "Stationery" (shown here). You can also add pictures, fonts, and colors to add emphasis to your message. Instant messaging is integrated within the Office XP version of Microsoft Outlook, but not in previous versions of Office.

FIGURE 2–35 continued

KEEPING YOUR APPOINTMENTS

Microsoft Outlook gives you a variety of views for your appointments, including a monthly overview and a daily hour-by-hour listing of appointments (both shown here). It also reminds you of your scheduled appointments and meetings. Appointments can be color coded to indicate the type of appointment, such as important (red), personal (green), or telephone call (yellow). When used on a LAN, Microsoft Outlook helps you schedule meetings by checking the calendars of other participants. People in a workgroup can view nonprivate portions of each other's schedule for the purpose of scheduling meetings. And with PIM software, you will never miss another birthday or anniversary because it keeps track of annual events and recurring events (weekly, monthly, and annual).

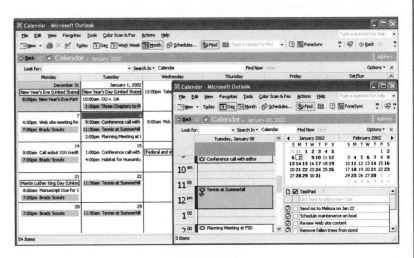

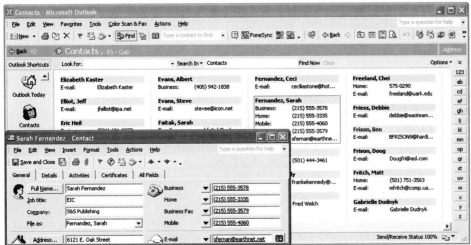

PERSONAL CONTACT INFORMATION

Use PIM software to store the names, phone numbers, and addresses of friends and business colleagues, and any other information that relates to the contact (birthday or anniversary date) in a contacts folder. Just click a button to address a meeting request, e-mail message, or task request to the contact. You can also have Outlook dial the contact's phone number. Outlook will time the call and keep a record in the Journal, complete with the notes you take during the conversation.

THE TO-DO LIST

You can use Microsoft Outlook to manage what you have to do each day. Use it to prioritize your tasks, set reminders for deadlines, and update your progress. Outlook also tracks repeating tasks. When used in a LAN workgroup, use this feature to assign tasks to others and monitor their progress.

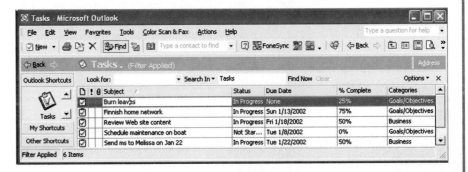

FIGURE 2–36

TEMPLATES FOR EVERY OCCASION
Microsoft Office (shown here) offers a wide variety of templates, including forms for articles of incorporation (Word) and a "motivating a team" presentation (PowerPoint).

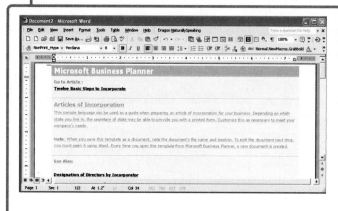
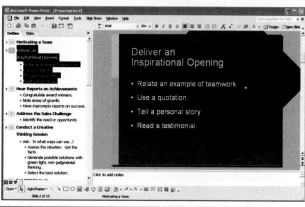

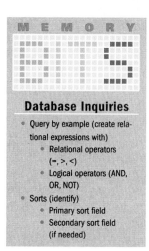

Database Inquiries

- Query by example (create relational expressions with)
  - Relational operators (=, >, <)
  - Logical operators (AND, OR, NOT)
- Sorts (identify)
  - Primary sort field
  - Secondary sort field (if needed)

- *Word processing templates.* Word processing software may come with templates for brochures, e-mail messages, letters, Web pages, faxes, articles of incorporation (see Figure 2-36), memos, calendars, résumés, directories, manuals, and even academic theses.

- *Spreadsheet templates.* In spreadsheets, you have templates for expense statements, purchase orders, grade books, and for many other row-and-column documents.

- *Database software.* Database software includes templates for many database applications such as asset tracking, contract management, inventory control, order entry, resource scheduling, students and classes, video collections, wine lists, and so on.

- *Presentation software templates.* Presentation software offers templates for a presentation on motivating a team (see Figure 2-36), business plan, financial overview, employee orientation, project overview, marketing plan, training program, and even one for communicating bad news.

    Judicious use of templates and other canned and automated resources can save you a lot of valuable time.

2-3.1	Preset format specifications are referred to as concrete settings. (T/F)
2-3.2	Which of these terms is not normally associated with the default settings on word processing software: (a) merge sequence, (b) document size, (c) margins, or (d) font?
2-3.3	Word processing packages are WYSIWYG. (T/F)
2-3.4	An image to be displayed in a PC-based presentation is called a slide. (T/F)
2-3.5	A pattern used to facilitate the creation of a slide presentation is called a: (a) guide word, (b) demographic datum link, (c) template, or (d) hyperlink.
2-3.6	When we convert a file from its foreign format to a format that is compatible with the current program, we: (a) import the file, (b) export the file, (c) bypass the file, or (d) link the file.
2-3.7	D20:Z40 and Z20:D40 define the same spreadsheet range. (T/F)
2-3.8	Panning a spreadsheet to view different parts of the document is called: (a) slipping, (b) scrolling, (c) rolling, or (d) grid pasting.
2-3.9	If the formula =B1+B2-B3 in cell B4 was copied to cell C4, the formula in C4 would be: (a) =B1+B2-B3, (b) =C1+C2-C3, (c) =A1+A2-A3, or (d) =-B1-B2+B3.
2-3.10	If the COURSE database table in Figure 2-28 is sorted in descending order by COURSE ID, the third course record would be Local Area Networks. (T/F)
2-3.11	Database files are sorted, merged, and processed by: (a) a key field, (b) an ISBN, (c) columnar index, or (d) a lock entry.
2-3.12	Which record(s) would be selected from the COURSE table in Figure 2-28 for the condition TYPE=lecture/lab: (a) 100, 330, 110, 401, (b) 101, 202, 330, 401, (c) 202, 150, 320, 350, or (d) 110, 150, 320, 350?
2-3.13	PIM software includes all but which of the following: (a) to-do lists, (b) virus list, (c) notes, or (d) diary entries?

2-4 | Applications Software for Your PC

Word processing software, presentation software, spreadsheet software, browser, e-mail, and gaming software are wonderful applications for PCs. Indeed, you could become a happy PC user and never venture far from the capabilities of these high-use applications. However, there is a lot more to personal computing than these applications. Indeed, there are over a half-million commercial software packages and downloadable shareware (copyright software for which the author requests a small fee for its use), freeware, and public-domain software. **Shareware** is copyright software that can be downloaded for free, but its use is based on an honor system where users pay a small fee to the author(s) for using it. **Freeware** is copyright software that can be downloaded and used free of charge. **Public-domain software** is not copyrighted and can be used without restriction.

GRAPHICS SOFTWARE

A dollar may not buy what it used to, but a picture is still worth a thousand words. *Graphics software* enables the creation, manipulation, and management of computer-based images. With graphics software you can issue a command to draw a blue square. Issue another command and suddenly the square is bigger, smaller, rotated, squeezed, stretched, or even "painted" with different colors and textures. Graphics software helps you create line drawings, company logos, maps, clip art, blueprints, flowcharts, or just about any image you can visualize. You can even touch up red eyes in photographs.

Graphic images can be maintained as **bit-mapped graphics, vector graphics,** or in a **metafile** format. In bit-mapped graphics, the image is composed of patterns of dots called *picture elements*, or **pixels**. The term **raster graphics** is also used to describe *bit-mapped* images. In vector graphics, the image is composed of patterns of lines, points, and other geometric shapes (vectors). The metafile format is a class of graphics that combines the components of bit-mapped and vector graphics formats. The naked eye cannot distinguish one method of graphics display from another; however, the differences are quite apparent when you try to manipulate images in the various formats.

Bit-Mapped Graphics

Bit-mapped graphics, displayed as dot patterns, are created by graphics paint software (see Figure 2-37), digital cameras, fax machines, scanners, and when you capture an image on a screen. The term *bit-mapped* is used because the image is projected, or "mapped," onto the screen based on binary bits. Dots, or pixels, on the screen are arranged in rows and columns. The typical PC monitor displays over a million pixels in rows and columns (for example, in 1024 rows and 1280 columns). Each dot or pixel on a monitor is assigned a number that denotes its position on the screen grid (120th row and 323rd column) and its color.

As with all internal numbers in a computer system, the numbers that describe the pixel attributes (position and color) are binary bits (1s and 0s). The number of bits needed to describe a pixel increases with the monitor's resolution and the number of colors that can be presented (from 256 colors in 8-bit color mode to 32-bit true color mode with millions of colors). Images are stored according to a **file format** that specifies how the information is organized in the file. Most of the popular programs that create graphic images have their own file formats. The bit-mapped file format for a specific file is noted by its filename extension (for example, AuntBertha.bmp or CompanyLogo.gif). These are a few of the many commonly used graphics formats.

THE CRYSTAL BALL:
Software Updates Overnight A major headache for businesses and individuals is keeping software up-to-date. Software and hardware vendors post downloadable updates to the Internet to correct oversights in programming, address security concerns, and add improvements that permit the software to work seamlessly with other new software and devices. The typical PC is filled with software that needs periodic updating. Already, some IT companies alert you when updates are available or they upload and install the updates automatically. This is the beginning of a trend. Within a few of years, users will demand and get software that is updated automatically via the Internet, probably overnight.

- *BMP.* **BMP** is the most common format used in the Microsoft Windows environment.
- *GIF.* **GIF,** a patented format, is used in Web pages and for downloadable online images.
- *TIFF and TIF.* **TIFF,** or **TIF,** is the industry standard for high-resolution bit-mapped images used in print publishing.
- *PCX.* **PCX** was introduced for PC Paintbrush (distributed with Windows) but is supported by many graphics packages and by scanners and faxes.
- *PNG.* **PNG** provides a patent-free replacement for GIF.
- *JPEG or JPG.* **JPEG,** or **JPG,** is commonly used on Web pages and in digital photography.

Vector Graphics

Vectors, which are lines, points, and other geometric shapes, are configured to create the vector graphics image. The vector graphics display, in contrast to the bit-mapped graphics display, permits the user to work with objects, such as a drawing of a computer. Computer-aided design (CAD) software, which is used by engineers and scientists, uses vector graphics to meet the need to manipulate individual objects on the screen. Figure 2-38 illustrates a vector graphics image. Notice how the

FIGURE 2-37

PAINT: A PAINT PROGRAM
Paint software provides you with a sophisticated electronic canvas for the creation of bit-mapped images. Because the canvas is a bit map, you must erase or draw over any individual part with which you are dissatisfied.

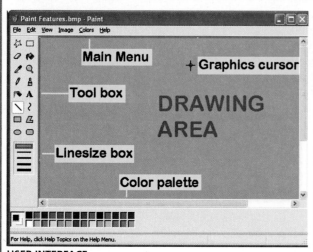

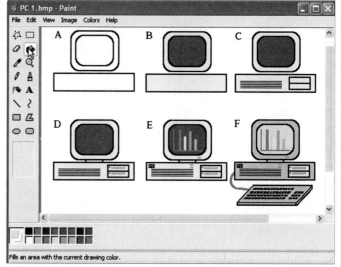

USER INTERFACE

The user interface for Paint, which is distributed with Windows, is representative of paint programs. The parts of the interface include:

- *Drawing area.* The image is created in this area.

- *Graphics cursor.* A point-and-draw device, such as a mouse, is used to move the graphics cursor to draw images and to select options. When positioned in the drawing area, the graphics cursor takes on a variety of shapes, depending on the tool selected.

- *Main menu.* Pull-down menus appear when any of the items in the main menu bar are selected.

- *Tool box.* One of the tools in the tool box is active at any given time. Use the tools to draw; to move, copy, or delete parts of the screen; to create geometric shapes; to fill defined areas with colors; to add text; and to erase.

- *Linesize box.* This box contains the width options for the drawing line.

- *Color palette.* This box contains colors and patterns used with the drawing tools.

CREATING AN IMAGE

This screen shows the steps in creating an image of a PC.

- *Step A.* The *box* and *rounded box tools* are used to create the outlines for the monitor and the processor unit. Notice that the *text tool* (denoted by "A" in the tool box) is used to label the steps.

- *Step B.* The area containing the bit-mapped image created in Step A was *copied* to position B, and then the *paint fill tool* was used to fill in *background colors.* The image in each of the following steps was created from a copy of the image of the preceding step.

- *Step C.* The *line tool* is used to draw the vents on the front of the processor unit. Drag the graphics cursor from one point to another and release the mouse button to draw the line. The two box areas for the disks were created with the box and line tools.

- *Step D.* When the *brush tool* is active, the *foreground color* is drawn at the graphics cursor position. Use the brush tool for freehand drawing, such as the addition of the pedestal for the monitor. The disk slots and the disk-active lights were drawn with the line tool.

screen portion of the overall image is actually made up of many objects. Think of a vector graphics screen image as a collage of one or more objects.

Vector graphics images take up less storage space than do bit-mapped images because vector graphics are defined in geometric shapes, each of which can define the attributes of many pixels. Vector graphics images provide more flexibility in that individual objects within the drawing can be resized, moved, stretched, and generally manipulated without affecting the rest of the drawing. **CGM** and **EPS** are widely supported vector graphics file formats. A popular metafile format, **WMF,** is used for exchanging graphics between Windows applications.

HOME AND FAMILY SOFTWARE

Over half the homes in America have at least one PC. Many have one for the parent's home office and one for the kids. Some have home networks, linking all home computers. Today, a wide range of software is available for these home PCs that can help us with the many activities of day-to-day living, as well as some of the chores of life. Figure 2-39 illustrates but a few of the thousands of software applications that you might find around the home. For example, home *legal advisers* assist you with the creation of a variety of legal documents, from wills to lease agreements. Trip planning software has detailed information on thousands of stops along the route to any destination in the United States. Medical software is a staple around the home PC. Software is available that is specifically designed for personal advocacy; that is,

MEMORY

Graphic Images

- Bit-mapped (raster) graphics
  - Image as pixels
  - Bit-mapped image
- Vector graphics
  - Image as line patterns and geometric shapes
  - Permits manipulation of objects within image
- Metafiles
  - Combination of bit-mapped and vector

FIGURE 2–37 continued

- *Step E*. A logo (upper-left corner of processor box) and a bar graph are added. The *PC* in the black logo box was drawn one pixel at a time. The *zoom* feature explodes a small segment of the draw area to enable the user to draw one pixel at a time (see the next screen).

- *Step F*. In this final step, the yellow color is *erased* to gray. Paint software permits the user to selectively switch one color for another within a user-defined area or in the entire drawing area. The keyboard was *tilted* for a three-dimensional look.

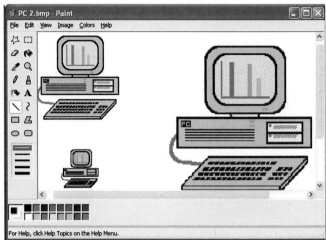

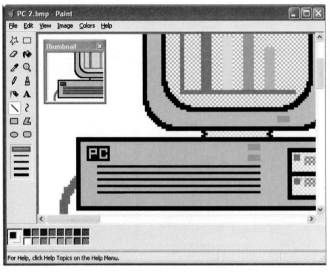

THE SHRINK/GROW FEATURE

The PC image in the upper left corner was copied from Step F above. The original image was selected with the *pick tool*, and then copied to the Clipboard. The Clipboard contents were then loaded to a clean drawing area. The PC image in Step F is reduced and enlarged with the shrink/grow feature of paint software. Notice that image resolution suffers when the image is shrunk or enlarged (for example, the disk slots).

ZOOM FEATURE

In the illustration, the paint software user has zoomed in on the upper-left corner of the processor box in the completed PC image (Step F). Each square is a pixel.

FIGURE 2–38

ADOBE ILLUSTRATOR: A DRAW PROGRAM

Adobe® Illustrator®, shown here, is a vector graphics program. The user draws, then integrates objects to create the drawing. This drawing is made up of several vector objects. Some of the many objects that make up the drawing are moved and highlighted to demonstrate what makes up a vector graphics drawing. In the exploded example, each object is highlighted in blue. Adobe Illustrator's interface is similar to Paint's (see Figure 2-37); however, its drawing features are much more sophisticated.

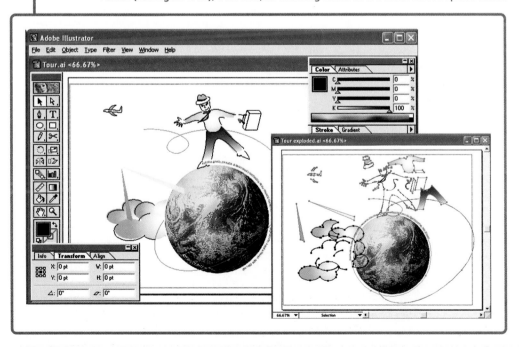

PERSONAL COMPUTING:

The Worth of the Software Bundle
One of the greatest challenges in choosing between alternative PCs is appraising the worth of the preinstalled software. PC vendors want the quality or variety of their software bundle(s) to either confuse the buyer or be the difference maker, depending on the quality of their offerings. The bundled software frequently is the biggest variable in the PC-purchase decision process. A PC vendor may advertise the worth of their software as $800, but the real value is its "street price," which is probably no more than $50 or $60.

it helps you make your point to government agencies, political action groups, politicians, and any other organization or individual you wish to influence. There are software packages designed to help college-bound students and their parents find and secure financial aid. And when they graduate, résumé creation software packages can help them put their best foot forward when looking for a job.

Of course, a plethora of software packages has emerged for hobbyists. No matter what your hobby, you are sure to find software that helps you with some aspect of your hobby. For example, tennis software helps you match statistics, create tournament draws, and figure rankings. There are packages for gardeners/landscapers, astronomers, astrologists, bicycling enthusiasts, UFO watchers, golfers, fishing fans, and for many more.

FIGURE 2–39   **HOME AND PERSONAL SOFTWARE**

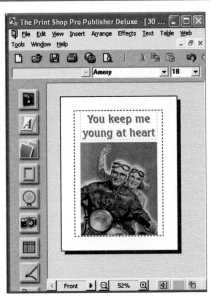

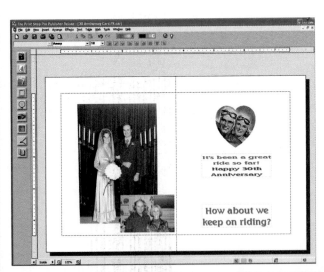

BECOME YOUR OWN PRINTER

All too often, the local greeting card store has cards and announcements for everyone except you. When you want something special, try doing it yourself with *The Print Shop 12* (a product of Broderbund). This software helps you create personalized greeting cards (shown here), banners, business cards, letterheads, certificates, calendars, announcements, invitations, and more. The software offers hundreds of templates from which to choose, one of which is shown here. Only the picture images on the inside were added. If you wish, you can easily create your own from scratch.

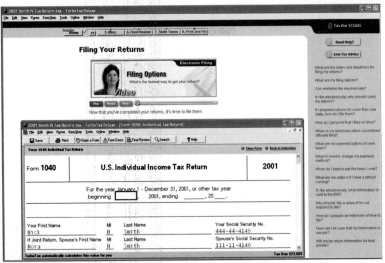

HELP WITH TAXES

Millions of people now prepare their own taxes with tax preparation software, such as *Quicken® TurboTax* (shown here). The interactive software guides you, step-by-step, through the process, answering your questions and making suggestions as needed. Upon completion, you are given the option of filing your return the traditional way (via the postal service) or electronically.

FIGURE 2–39 continued

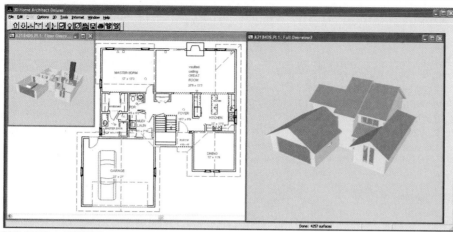

BUILDING A HOUSE?

Are you considering remodeling your current home or building a new one? Then perhaps your first stop should be *3D Home Architect*™ (a product of Broderbund). With this software you can create a floor plan and even see what it might look like by requesting a 3-D external view. You can create a three-dimensional design of your kitchen, play with decorating ideas throughout the house, and even "walk through" the inside of the house to see if the design is what you want.

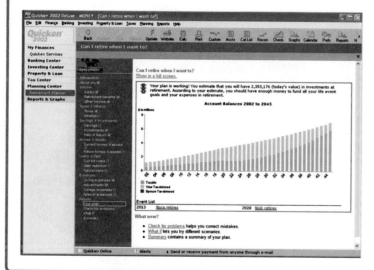

FINANCIAL PLANNING FOR THE FUTURE

Quicken® Retirement Planner guides you step-by-step through the creation of a personalized retirement plan. Use it to plan for retirement, college expenses, buying a vacation home, and much more. The program assists you in deciding how much you should save and where to invest your savings. It also tracks your progress and can generate a variety of helpful reports and graphs.

EDUCATION AND EDUTAINMENT SOFTWARE

Emerging technologies are prompting fundamental changes in education. The *static, sequential* presentation of books has been the foundation for learning since Gutenberg. Now, however, we are beginning to see *dynamic, linked,* and *interactive technology-based* resources in virtually every discipline. When coupled with online distance learning and personal interaction of the traditional classroom environment, such resources offer a richer learning environment. We need to restate that computer-based education will not replace the classroom or teachers anytime soon, but those who have tried it agree that CBT (computer-based training) will have a dramatic impact on the way we learn.

Educational software is experiencing an explosion of acceptance in our homes and schools. Computer-based educational resources take many forms and are being embraced by young and old alike. Students can learn anatomy by taking virtual tours of the body. Students can travel through the Milky Way to Cassiopeia and other constellations while an electronic teacher explains the mysteries of the universe. Millions of elementary age students are getting one-on-one instruction on keyboarding skills. Chemistry students are doing lab exercises with bits and bytes rather than dangerous chemicals. Some innovative software packages tease the mind by inviting students to learn the power of logic and creativity.

It did not take long for education software developers to combine *education* and *entertainment* into a single learning resource. This *edutainment software* gives students an opportunity to play while learning. Figure 2-40 provides a few examples of education and edutainment software.

REFERENCE SOFTWARE

As soon as the technology gurus figured out that audio CDs could hold 650 MB of digital data, the CD-ROM was born. Almost immediately after the introduction of the CD-ROM, books, dictionaries, encyclopedias, newspapers, corporate manuals, and thousands of other printed materials were being translated to digital media, namely the CD-ROM. Now that CD-RW (rewritable) is reasonably priced, we at home and in small offices can create our own CD-ROM-based reference material, too.

Computer-based reference material is much more than simply text on a disk. It is searchable and interactive. Attorneys no longer spend days pouring over scores of cases to prepare for trials. Keyword searches can result in a display of applicable cases within seconds.

FIGURE 2–40 **EDUCATION AND EDUTAINMENT SOFTWARE**

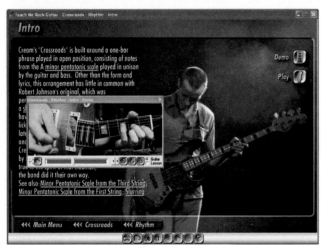

PLAYING ROCK GUITAR
Voyetra's Teach Me Rock Guitar™ provides an easy, step-by-step method for learning rock guitar. The Animated Fretboard shows you the fingerings on the guitar neck in real time as you play. You can even jam with the band!

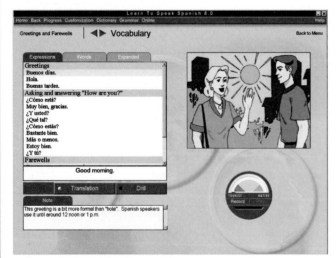

LEARN TO SPEAK SPANISH
Computers and their software have proven to be effective teachers of languages. The Spanish software gives instruction and practice in real-world conversations.

THE eBOOK
This device, the Rocket eBook™ holds the equivalent of a semester's worth of college textbooks (about 4000 pages of text and images). You can read or study it as you would a print book, making margin notes, underlining special passages, and bookmarking pages. The eBook is searchable, too.

Courtesy of NuvoMedia, Inc.

Just about any frequently used printed reference material is available on CD-ROM, or it is being considered for CD-ROM publication. We can get detailed geographic information, multilingual dictionaries, state, and federal census information, specific entrance requirements for thousands of colleges, Fortune 500 financial information, and much more. Figure 2-41 illustrates a variety of CD-ROM-based reference materials.

FIGURE 2–41 REFERENCE SOFTWARE

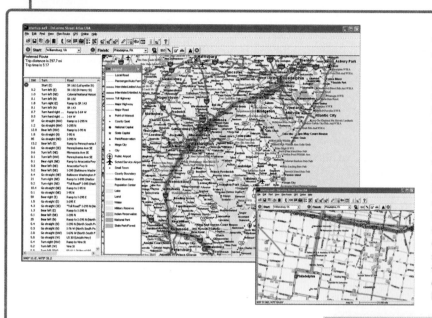

NEVER BE LOST AGAIN

With *Street Atlas USA*® 9.0 by DeLorme you will never be lost again. Incredibly detailed maps help you take the effort out of trip planning. Street Atlas USA 9.0 is a seamless map of the entire country. It offers detail, street address search power, and door-to-door routing. Just identify your start (Williamsburg, Virginia) and finish (Philadelphia, Pennsylvania) points and the software calculates and then displays the best route (in purple). You can zoom in for street-level maps (downtown Philadelphia in the example) that can include as much or little information as you wish, from specific types of restaurants to historical sites. The program also interfaces with global positioning systems (GPSs) to pinpoint your location on the map display and to guide you to your destination, prompting you visually and verbally as to when and where to turn.

HOME MEDICAL ADVISOR

Home Medical Advisor™ is a practical guide to symptom diagnosis and preventive care. You can even talk to a "video" doctor to get answers to detailed questions (shown here) and then receive possible diagnoses and treatments. Hundreds of videos show you exactly what to expect if you are scheduling an eye exam, planning surgery, or having a baby. You can analyze potentially harmful interactions of more than 8000 over-the-counter and prescription drugs. Find expert emergency advice and video demonstrations right when you need them—instantly!

INTERACTIVE COOKBOOK

All the ingredients for planning and preparing perfect recipes and meals are mixed into one program, Compton's® *Complete Cookbook*™. All of the 2000 plus recipes come with step-by-step instructions, color pictures, detailed nutritional facts, and tips from top chefs. To make planning a snap, the software provides a "smart shopping" list and a menu planner.

BUSINESS AND FINANCIAL SOFTWARE

There are literally thousands of PC-based business and financial-oriented software packages for the home and small office. In the business community, there are software packages specifically designed for physicians' clinics, construction contractors, CPAs, churches, motels, law offices, nonprofit organizations, real estate companies, recreation and fitness centers, restaurants, and just about any other organization that has administrative information processing needs. Some business-oriented software for smaller companies can run on a single PC, and other packages are designed for the LAN client/server environment so information can be shared among workers. At home, millions of people now keep family financial records on a PC. Figure 2-42 shows several business/financial software examples.

SECTION SELF-CHECK

2-4.1 Another term for bit-mapped graphics is: (a) raster, (b) vector, (c) faster, or (d) geometric.

2-4.2 Which of these software applications would not be considered a common application for home use: (a) greeting cards, (b) tax preparation, (c) morphing, or (d) trip planning?

2-4.3 It is technologically possible for people at home to put their own reference material on CD-ROM by using what technology: (a) CD-RW, (b) audio CD, (c) VHS, or (d) PCMCIA.

2-4.4 Tax preparation software lets you file taxes electronically. (T/F)

2-4.5 Mapping systems can interface with global positioning systems to pinpoint your location on a map. (T/F)

FIGURE 2–42 BUSINESS SOFTWARE

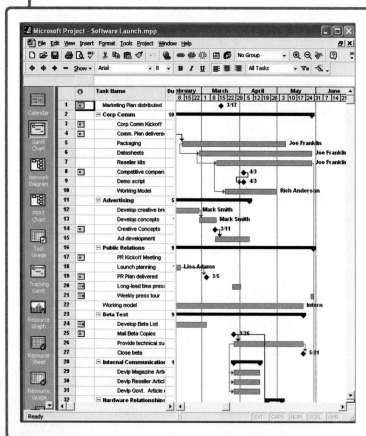

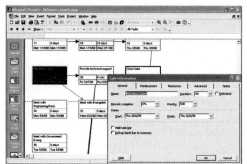

PROJECT MANAGEMENT

Microsoft's *Project* is a great tool for anyone who oversees a team, plans a budget, juggles schedules, or has deadlines to meet. Project management software helps you plan and track your projects more effectively so you can identify and respond to conflicts before they happen.

FIGURE 2–42 continued

BUSINESS AND HOME FINANCES

Anyone who has attempted to balance a sadly out-of-kilter checkbook or consolidate tax information will appreciate *Quicken®* (Quicken software is made and owned by Intuit). Industry analysts refer to Quicken as a "killer app," an application with such useful capabilities that it alone can justify the expense of a computer. This financial management system helps you, personally, or it can help a company manage bills, bank accounts, investments, tax records, assets and liabilities, and much more. You can even write your checks online and all the details are automatically entered into your checkbook register (see example), thereby eliminating duplicate entries. Just print on check stock (see example) designed for your printer, sign, and send. Many avid Quicken users keep track of everything from credit-card purchases to stock transactions. The money trail summarized by Quicken gives these people and companies some insight into what is happening at home and in its businesses. Quicken offers users a variety of reports and graphs (see itemized categories report).

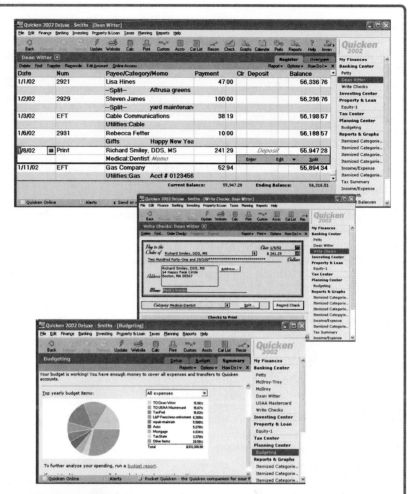

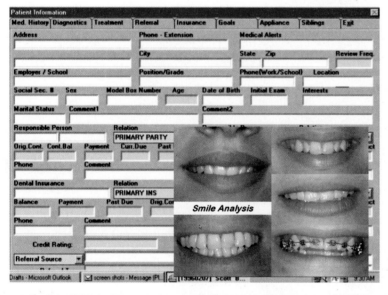

Smile Analysis

APPLICATION-SPECIFIC SOFTWARE: DENTISTRY

For those in almost any business, information technology plays a role in its operation. With Dr. Richard Roblee, an expert in aesthetic dentistry and orthodontic techniques and interdisciplinary therapy, it is critical to his practice and philosophy of treatment. Dr. Roblee relies on several patient information systems to help him, his staff, and his patients track progress, sometimes for years. The client database houses all critical client information, including dental history (both descriptive and visual) and treatment plan.

Courtesy of Dr. Richard Roblee,
D.D.S., M.S.; IDT Systems, Inc.
roblee@idt-network.com

2-1 THE OPERATING SYSTEM

The operating system and its **graphical user interface (GUI)** are the nucleus of all software activity. One of the operating system programs, called the **kernel,** loads other operating system and applications programs to RAM as they are needed. **Utility programs** are a type of system software.

All operating systems are designed with the same basic objectives in mind. Perhaps the most important objectives are to facilitate communication between the computer system and the people who run it and to optimize the use of computer system resources.

Operating systems get the most from their processors through **multitasking**—the concurrent execution of more than one program at a time. High-priority programs run in the **foreground** part of RAM and the rest run in the **background.**

Through the 1980s, the most popular microcomputer operating system, **MS-DOS,** was strictly *text-based, command-driven* software that required strict adherence to command **syntax.** The trend now is toward GUIs that use graphical **icons.** All modern operating systems have adopted the GUI concept.

A processor and an operating system define a platform, a standard for which software packages are developed. The modern PC/Windows platforms include PC-compatible computers with **Windows 95, Windows 98, Windows Me** (Millennium Edition), **Windows NT, Windows 2000, Windows XP,** or **Windows CE** (for handheld and pocket PCs). Windows XP, the client-side operating system, works with **Windows 2000 Server** or the newer **Windows .Net Server,** the server-side portion of the operating system to make client/server computing possible. Windows XP comes in two versions—**Windows XP Professional** and **Windows XP Home. Windows XP 64-Bit Edition** is designed for high-performance 64-bit workstations. Windows operating systems have many features, such as **plug-and-play** and **home networking.** Wintel platforms are *mostly* **backward compatible.**

The Apple family of microcomputers and **Mac OS X** define another major platform.

Linux, a spin-off of the popular **UNIX** operating system, is a popular operating system for a variety of computers. Linux is **open source software.** The Linux-based **LindowsOS** has file-level compatibility with many Windows-based applications.

System software, which includes the operating system and utility software, is applications-independent. Utility software is available to help you with disk and file maintenance, system recovery, security, backup, virus protection, and other system-related tasks.

Those companies that do not standardize on a platform must work to achieve **interoperability,** which refers to the ability to run software and exchange information in a **multiplatform environment.** Enabling technologies that allow communication and the sharing of resources between different platforms are called **cross-platform technologies.**

A wide variety of system software *utilities* can help with personal computing tasks, such as disk and file maintenance, system recovery, security, backup, and virus protection.

2-2 WINDOWS CONCEPTS AND TERMINOLOGY

The Windows *Help and Support* capabilities include step-by-step tutorials that lead you through numerous common procedures.

The GUI-based Windows series runs one or more applications in **windows**—rectangular areas displayed on the screen.

Any software application that does not adhere to the Microsoft Windows standard is a **non-Windows application.** Programs that adhere to Windows conventions are **Windows applications.**

The Windows GUI relies on a point-and-draw device, such as a mouse, to click and **drag.**

The screen upon which icons, windows, and so on are displayed is known as the **desktop.** The **active window** displays the application being currently used by the user. **Inactive windows** display applications that are running but not being used by the user.

Typically, a Windows session begins with the **Start button** in the **taskbar.** An active application window can be minimized to a button in the taskbar. You may open a Windows **folder,** which contains a logical grouping of related files and/or subordinated folders, to obtain a work file.

A rectangular **application window** contains an **open application** (a running application). Several applications can be open, but there is only one active window at any given time.

Everything that relates to the application noted in the title bar is displayed in the **workspace.** Several **document windows** can be displayed in the parent application window's workspace.

When document content is more than can be displayed in a window, the window is outfitted with **vertical** and/or **horizontal scroll bars,** each with a **scroll box** and two **scroll arrows** to enable **scrolling.**

The horizontal **title bar** at the top of each window has these elements: application icon, window title, Minimize button, Maximize/Restore button, Close button, and the title area.

When you select an item from the menu bar, a subordinate **pull-down menu** is "pulled down." Use the left/right or up/down arrow keys to enter the **mnemonic,** or use the mouse to position the mouse pointer at the desired option. Further selection may result in a menu or a pop-up **dialog box.** A **pop-out** menu results when you choose a menu option followed by a right-pointing arrow. The context-sensitive **pop-up menu** is displayed when you right-click the mouse. The **floating menu** "floats" over the display. The **shortcut key** and the **hotkey** help speed up interaction on the keyboard.

Toolbars, containing rectangular graphics, give you ready access to frequently used menu items. The **ruler bar** shows the document window's content relative to the printed page.

The Windows **Explorer,** which can include commonly used icons such as **application icons, shortcut icons, document icons,** and **disk drive icons,** performs file management tasks such as creating folders, copying files, moving files, deleting files, and other folder/file-related tasks.

The Windows environment lets you view multiple applications that can be resized, shrunk, and arranged by the user within the workspace. Or, they can be arranged as **cascading windows** or **tiled windows.**

The active window is always highlighted in the **foreground.** Other open windows are in the **background.** These terms describe RAM concepts, too.

The most common method of sharing information among applications is to use the Windows **Clipboard** and the *Edit* option in the menu bar. The **source application** and **destination application** for a copy or move operation can be one and the same or they can be entirely different applications.

Applications can be linked through **object linking and embedding,** or **OLE.** An **object** is an item within any Windows application that can be individually selected. We can create **compound documents** that contain one or more objects from other applications. The object originates in a **server application** and is linked to a destination document of a **client application.**

OLE lets you *link* or *embed* information. When you link information, the link between source and destination documents is dynamic. When you embed information, you insert the actual object, not just a pointer.

2-3 PRODUCTIVITY SOFTWARE: THE SOFTWARE SUITE

Word processing lets you create text-based documents into which you can integrate images. When you format a document, you are specifying the size of the page to be printed and how you want the document to look when printed. The preset format, or *default settings,* may fit your word processing application. A **font,** which refers to the style, appearance, and size of print, is described by its **typeface.** Most word processing packages are considered **WYSIWYG,** short for "What you see is what you get." The find and replace features make all word processing documents searchable. **Clip art** is prepackaged electronic images stored on disk to be used as needed.

Word processing has a variety of features that enable users to enhance the appearance and readability of their documents, including footnoting, numbered and bulleted lists, outline, drawing tools, borders, integration of images, multicolumn text, and more. Word processing software provides the capability of merging data in a database with the text of a document. The *mail-merge* application is an example. Here you merge a *database file* with a *form file.* **Boilerplate** text is existing text that can in some way be reused and customized for a variety of word processing applications.

You can convert word processing documents to create Web pages on the World Wide Web (the Web), the primary application used for viewing information on the Internet.

Word processing can handle most document generation tasks, but those organizations that need to produce complicated documents to be printed professionally use desktop publishing software to create *camera-ready documents.*

Presentation software enables you to create a wide variety of visually appealing and informative presentation graphics. These steps are used with presentation software: (1) *Select a template.* Microsoft's PowerPoint offers both *design templates* and *content templates.* (2) *Create an outline for the presentation.* PowerPoint's tri-pane view lets you view the *slide, outline,* and *notes* at the same time. **Import** content from other programs directly into PowerPoint slides. **Export** PowerPoint slides to other programs. (3) *Compile and create other nontext resources.* A slide presentation may include text, photo images, charts and graphs, original drawings, clip art, audio clips, and even full-motion video. Among the most popular charts are the pie and bar charts. Presentation software also permits the preparation of organization charts and maps. (4) *Integrate resources.* The PowerPoint *slide sorter* view gives you an overview of the presentation via **thumbnail** images. (5) *Add special effects.* With PowerPoint you can have an image fade out, be wiped away, show animation, or add sound, to name a few. (6) *Add notes.* (7) *Deliver the presentation.*

Spreadsheet software provides an electronic alternative to thousands of traditionally manual tasks that involve rows and columns of data. The intersection of a particular row and column in a spreadsheet designates a **cell.** During operations, data are referred to by their **cell addresses.** The **pointer** can be moved around the spreadsheet to any cell address. To make an entry, to edit, or to replace an entry in a spreadsheet, move the pointer to the appropriate cell.

The four types of **ranges** are a single cell, all or part of a column of adjacent cells, all or part of a row of adjacent cells, and a rectangular block of cells. A particular range is depicted by the addresses of the endpoint cells (for example, C5:E10).

Three major types of entries to a cell are label, numeric, and formula. Spreadsheet formulas use standard programming notation for **arithmetic operators.** Spreadsheets offer predefined operations called **functions.** Each function includes one or more **arguments** that identify the data for the operation.

Different people can use a spreadsheet template over and over for different purposes. If you change the value of a cell in a spreadsheet, all other affected cells are revised accordingly. Spreadsheet packages also can let you generate a variety of charts from spreadsheet data.

Database software lets you enter, organize, and retrieve stored data. Both database and spreadsheet software packages enable us to work with tabular data and records in a database. Database software uses the **relational database** approach to data management. Relational databases are organized in tables in which a row is a record and a column is a field.

In database software, the user-defined structure of a database table identifies the characteristics of each field in it. Related fields are grouped to form records. Content for a *text* field can be a single word or it can be any **alphanumeric** (numbers, letters, and special characters) phrase.

Database software also permits you to retrieve, view, and print records based on **query by example.** To make a query by example, users set conditions for the selection of records by composing a relational expression containing **relational operators** that reflects the desired conditions. Several expressions can be combined into a single condition with **logical operators.**

Records in a database can be sorted for display in a variety of formats. To sort the records in a database, select a primary sort field and, if needed, a secondary sort field. Database software can create customized, or formatted, reports.

Personal information management, or PIM, refers to messaging and personal information management software. PIM software helps you manage your messages, appointments, contacts, and tasks.

Each of the major productivity software packages offers a variety of templates to help you get a head start on your projects. A template is simply a document or file that is already formatted or designed for a particular task.

2-4 APPLICATIONS SOFTWARE FOR YOUR PC

There are over a half-million commercial software packages and downloadable **shareware, freeware,** and **public-domain software.**

Graphics software facilitates the creation, manipulation, and management of computer-based images. Graphic images are presented as **bit-mapped graphics** (file formats include **BMP, GIF, TIFF** or **TIF, PCX, PNG,** and **JPEG** or **JPG**), **vector graphics** (**CGM** and **EPS**), and **metafiles** (**WMF**). In bit-mapped graphics, or **raster graphics,** the image is composed of patterns of dots (pixels). In vector graphics, the image is composed of patterns of lines, points, and other geometric shapes (vectors). The metafile is a class of graphics that combines the components of bit-mapped and vector graphics formats. Paint software, which works with bit-mapped images, provides the user with an electronic canvas.

A wide range of software is available for home PCs that can help us with the many activities of day-to-day living. Popular home applications include greeting cards and banners, tax preparation, and edutainment. Edutainment software combines education and entertainment into a single software package. Most of the reference material distributed on CD-ROM is commercial (for example, encyclopedias) or proprietary; however, with CD-RW we can create our own CD-ROM-based reference material. A wide variety of PC-based business and financial-oriented software packages are available for the home and small office.

KEY TERMS

active window (p. 88)
alphanumeric (p. 108)
application icon (p. 94)
application window (p. 91)
argument (p. 106)
arithmetic operator (p. 104)
background (program/window) (p. 95)
background (RAM) (p. 79)
backward compatible (p. 81)
bit-mapped graphics (p. 113)
BMP (p. 113)
boilerplate (p. 99)
cascading windows (p. 95)
cell (p. 104)
cell address (p. 104)
CGM (p. 114)
client application (p. 96)
clip art (p. 99)
Clipboard (p. 96)
compound document (p. 96)
cross-platform technology (p. 84)
desktop (p. 88)
destination application (p. 96)
dialog box (p. 92)
disk drive icon (p. 95)
document icon (p. 95)
document window (p. 92)
drag (p. 88)
EPS (p. 114)
Explorer (p. 94)
export (p. 102)
file format (p. 113)
floating menu (p. 93)
folder (p. 91)
font (p. 99)
foreground (program/window) (p. 95)
foreground (RAM) (p. 79)
freeware (p. 113)
function (p. 106)
GIF (p. 113)

graphical user interface (GUI) (p. 78)
home networking (p. 81)
horizontal scroll bar (p. 92)
hotkey (p. 93)
icon (p. 80)
import (p. 102)
inactive window (p. 90)
interoperability (p. 84)
JPEG (JPG) (p. 113)
kernel (p. 78)
LindowsOS (p. 84)
Linux (p. 82)
logical operator (p. 109)
Mac OS X (p. 82)
metafile (p. 113)
mnemonic (p. 92)
MS-DOS (p. 80)
multiplatform environment (p. 84)
multitasking (p. 79)
non-Windows application (p. 88)
object (p. 96)
object linking and embedding (OLE) (p. 96)
open application (p. 91)
open source software (p. 82)
PCX (p. 113)
pixels (p. 113)
plug-and-play (p. 81)
PNG (p. 113)
pointer (p. 104)
pop-out menu (p. 92)
pop-up menu (p. 92)
public-domain software (p. 113)
pull-down menu (p. 92)
query by example (p. 109)
range (p. 104)
raster graphics (p. 113)
relational database (p. 107)
relational operator (p. 109)
ruler bar (p. 93)

scroll arrow (p. 92)
scroll box (p. 92)
scrolling (p. 92)
server application (p. 96)
shareware (p. 113)
shortcut icon (p. 94)
shortcut key (p. 92)
slide (p. 102)
source application (p. 96)
Start button (p. 90)
syntax (p. 80)
taskbar (p. 90)
template (p. 101)
thumbnail (p. 103)
TIFF (TIF) (p. 113)
tiled windows (p. 95)
title bar (p. 92)
toolbar (p. 93)
typeface (p. 99)
UNIX (p. 82)
utility program (p. 78)
vector graphics (p. 113)
vertical scroll bar (p. 92)
window (p. 85)
Windows .Net Server (p. 81)
Windows 2000 (p. 81)
Windows 2000 Server (p. 81)
Windows 95 (p. 81)
Windows 98 (p. 81)
Windows applications (p. 88)
Windows CE (p. 81)
Windows Me (p. 81)
Windows NT (p. 81)
Windows XP (p. 81)
Windows XP 64-Bit Edition (p. 81)
Windows XP Home Edition (p. 81)
Windows XP Professional (p. 81)
WMF (p. 114)
workspace (p. 91)
WYSIWYG (p. 99)

MATCHING

1. Windows CE	a. move object with mouse
2. alphanumeric	b. Alt+F4
3. a spinoff of UNIX	c. copyrighted software
4. arithmetic operator	d. operating system for handhelds
5. relational database	e. tables in a database
6. freeware	f. Linux
7. JPG	g. described by typeface
8. graphical user interface	h. contains object from another application
9. range	i. common Web file format
10. background (windows)	j. grouping of related files
11. drag	k. numbers and letters
12. compound document	l. add (+) and subtract (−)
13. font	m. defined area in a spreadsheet
14. folder	n. GUI
15. shortcut key	o. location of inactive windows

CHAPTER SELF-CHECK

2-1.1 MS-DOS is a state-of-the-art operating system. (T/F)

2-1.2 All computers, including computers dedicated to a particular application, have operating systems. (T/F)

2-1.3 A GUI is: (a) text-based, (b) graphics-based, (c) label-based, or (d) paste-based.

2-1.4 The Macintosh family of PCs is unique in that it does not need an operating system. (T/F)

2-1.5 A computing environment that runs more than one platform is what type of environment: (a) high platform, (b) low platform, (c) multiplatform, or (d) cross-platform?

2-1.6 UNIX is a subset of Windows 2000 Server, a more sophisticated operating system. (T/F)

2-1.7 The future of the PC/Windows family of operating systems is: (a) Windows Me, (b) Windows 98, (c) Windows XP, or (d) Windows NEXT.

2-1.8 The operating system for the Apple iMac is: (a) OS Mac, (b) iMac OS, (c) Mac OS X, or (d) The Mac BOSS.

2-1.9 Which of these is a spin-off of the popular UNIX multiuser operating system: (a) Bendix, (b) Linux, (c) Linus, or (d) Lucy?

2-1.10 The proper use of utility software can help keep a PC running at peak efficiency. (T/F)

2-1.11 The universal use of virus vaccine software over the past decade has done away with the threat of computer viruses. (T/F)

2-1.12 To eliminate the possibility of ghosting on modern monitors, the use of screen savers is essential. (T/F)

2-1.13 Which of the following would not be considered utility software: (a) virus protection, (b) backup, (c) file maintenance, or (d) gaming?

2-1.14 The process that rearranges file fragments into contiguous files is called: (a) unfragging, (b) file filling, (c) folder folding, or (d) defragmentation.

2-2.1 Any software application that does not adhere to the Microsoft Windows standard is a non-Windows application. (T/F)

2-2.2 The cascading windows option fills the workspace in such a way that no document window overlaps another. (T/F)

2-2.3 A Windows folder can contain either files or subordinated folders, but not both. (T/F)

2-2.4 Which of these is a point-and-draw device: (a) printer, (b) CD-ROM, (c) mouse, or (d) scanner?

2-2.5 Document windows are displayed in the parent application window's: (a) system window, (b) title bar, (c) scroll area, or (d) workspace.

2-2.6 Object linking does not actually place the object into the destination document. (T/F)

2-2.7 What kind of document contains one or more objects from other applications: (a) hyperlinked, (b) composite, (c) complex, or (d) compound?

2-2.8 To embed an object, choose the Paste Link option button in the Paste Special dialog box. (T/F)

2-3.1 An online thesaurus can be used to suggest synonyms for a word in a word processing document. (T/F)

2-3.2 Boilerplate text is existing text that can in some way be reused and customized for a variety of word processing applications. (T/F)

2-3.3 Desktop publishing documents are composed of rectangular: (a) windows, (b) boxes, (c) doors, or (d) frames.

2-3.4 What refers to a set of characters of a particular design: (a) calligraph, (b) stencil, (c) typeface, or (d) keyface?

2-3.5 The height of a 36-point letter is: (a) one-fourth inch, (b) one-half inch, (c) 1 inch, or (d) 2 inches.

2-3.6 In desktop publishing, the emphasis is on overall document composition, not the running text as in word processing. (T/F)

2-3.7 Presentation software allows users to create charts, graphs, and images for use during presentations. (T/F)

2-3.8 The presentation software slide sorter view lets users add or delete slides and rearrange them to meet presentation needs. (T/F)

2-3.9 Audio clips are an example of a nontext resource for presentation software. (T/F)

2-3.10 A typical slide in a slide presentation would not include: (a) photo images, charts, and graphs, (b) clip art and audio clips, (c) content templates, or (d) full-motion video.

2-3.11 Which of these is a presentation software special effect: (a) fade out, (b) thumbnail, (c) notes, or (d) export file?

2-3.12 The term spreadsheet was coined at the beginning of the personal computer boom. (T/F)

2-3.13 The intersection of a particular row and column in a spreadsheet designates a cell. (T/F)

2-3.14 Spreadsheet software works only with numbers and does not generate charts. (T/F)

2-3.15 A model of a spreadsheet designed for a particular application is sometimes called a template. (T/F)

2-3.16 The spreadsheet pointer highlights the: (a) relative cell, (b) status cell, (c) current cell, or (d) merge cell.

2-3.17 Data in a spreadsheet are referred to by their cell: (a) box, (b) number, (c) address, or (d) code.

2-3.18 Which of these is not a range in a spreadsheet: (a) block range, (b) row range, (c) column range, or (d) grazing range?

2-3.19 Database software gives you greater flexibility in the manipulation of rows and columns of data than does spreadsheet software. (T/F)

2-3.20 AND and OR are relational operators. (T/F)

2-3.21 In a database, related fields are grouped to form records. (T/F)

2-3.22 The definition of the structure of a database table would not include which of the following: (a) field names, (b) field sizes, (c) data types, or (d) pointer cell.

2-3.23 The relational operator for greater than or equal to is: (a) > OR =, (b) < AND = , (c) < NOT = , or (d) < OR =.

2-3.24 Which record(s) would be selected from the COURSE table in Figure 2-28 for the condition TYPE=lecture/lab: (a) 100, 330, 110, 401, (b) 101, 202, 330, 401, (c) 202, 150, 320, 350, or (d) 110, 150, 320, 350?

2-3.25 Which record(s) would be selected from the STUDENT table in Figure 2-28 for the condition STATUS=complete AND MAJOR=marketing: (a) Targa, Phil/330, (b) Targa, Phil/100, (c) Johnson, Charles/100, (d) Bell, Jim/330?

2-3.26 Which of these is normally not associated specifically with database terminology: (a) table, (b) query by example, (c) relational, (d) audio clip?

2-3.27 Personal information management is concerned with messages, appointments, contacts, and tasks. (T/F)

2-3.28 Which of these is messaging and personal information management software: (a) IMP, (b) PIM, (c) MIP, or (d) IPM?

2-3.29 A template is simply a document or file that is already formatted or designed for a particular task. (T.F)

2-4.1 In bit-mapped graphics, the image is composed of patterns of: (a) vectors, (b) pictures, (c) dots, or (d) objects.

2-4.2 Which type of graphics software package provides a computer-based version of the painter's canvas: (a) draw, (b) paint, (c) illustrator, or (d) sketch?

2-4.3 What class of graphics combines the components of bit-mapped and vector graphics formats: (a) metafiles, (b) raster files, (c) text files, or (d) MIDI files?

2-4.4 Which of the following pairs of file formats are used in Web page design: (a) JPG and BMP, (b) TIF and PCX, (c) JPG and GIF, or (d) TIF and PNG?

2-4.5 Which of the following is not a characteristic of education software: (a) linked, (b) sequential, (c) interactive, or (d) dynamic?

2-4.6 Which type of software gives the student an opportunity to play while learning: (a) education, (b) entertainment, (c) edutainment, or (d) fun-and-learn?

2-4.7 In the interactive learning environment, we learn: (a) primarily within workgroups, (b) at our own pace, (c) by the schedule in a syllabus, or (d) only at night.

2-4.8 Which of the following is not a characteristic of reference material on CD-ROM: (a) searchable, (b) interactive, (c) multimedia, or (d) limited to public domain content?

2-4.9 Which of these software packages would not be considered a business-specific application: (a) physician's clinic, (b) fitness center, (c) real estate, or (d) nationwide telephone directory?

2-4.10 Project management software helps you plan and track your projects more effectively. (T/F)

IT ETHICS AND ISSUES

THE QUALITY OF SOFTWARE

The software market is highly competitive even though Microsoft dominates the operating system and productivity software markets. Competition and other market pressures have forced software vendors, including Microsoft, into rushing their products to market, bugs and all. Some industry observers have argued that the quality of software is declining with an increasingly higher percentage of bugs being left intact within commercial software. The end result of this rush to market is that customers lose time and money coping with annoying bugs. Information technology and those who make software decisions are putting pressure on software vendors to raise the quality of their software. Generally, they want a clean product, even if they have to wait for it.

Discussion: *What can software vendors do within the context of competition and economic reality to improve software quality?*

Discussion: *What can those who buy commercial software do to improve software quality?*

COUNTERFEIT SOFTWARE

In some countries, counterfeit software far outnumbers legitimate proprietary software. Counterfeit software is software that is illegally mass produced from copies of the original manufacturer's software and packaged for retail sales. Counterfeit software may look very much, or exactly, like that distributed by the product's manufacturer. Until recently it was believed that most of this activity was offshore (outside the United States); however, a counterfeit ring that had produced and sold millions of dollars worth of counterfeit Microsoft was uncovered in California. The sophisticated operation included commercial CD-ROM duplicators, color printing presses, packaging machines, and everything else needed to create the illusion of a legitimate software package worthy of a certificate of authenticity.

Discussion: *What would be appropriate punishment for the owner of a company that produced and sold over $50 million worth of counterfeit copyright software? For someone who knowingly sold the counterfeit products to legitimate retail outlets? For someone who worked on the counterfeit company's production line?*

Discussion: *What can be done to protect intellectual property from counterfeit operations that is not already being done?*

Discussion: *What, if any, punishment should be given a student who uses CD-RW capability to make a duplicate copy of Microsoft Office, and then gives it to his or her friend. What about the friend who installs and uses the pirated copy of Microsoft Office?*

Discussion: *Does widespread abuse of copyright laws have any impact on incentives for creating intellectual property, such as software? Explain.*

DISCUSSION AND PROBLEM SOLVING

2-1.1   Some people contend that the traditional text-based, command-driven operating system interface has some advantages over the modern graphical user interface. Speculate on what these advantages might be.

2-1.2   Multitasking allows PC users to run several programs at a time. Describe a PC session in which you would have at least two applications running at the same time.

2-1.3   Why is the selection of a platform such an important decision to an organization?

2-1.4   A popular platform for the handheld and pocket PCs is Windows CE. Why don't these devices use Windows 98/Me/2000/XP like other personal computers?

2-1.5   How often should you run virus vaccine software to scan your PC system for viruses?

2-1.6   Discuss the consequences of not performing routine disk maintenance with utility software.

2-2.1   Describe the Windows desktop. Where would you put the taskbar—at the top, at the bottom, or on one of the sides? What else would you do to personalize your desktop?

2-2.2   List and briefly describe four elements of the Windows application window.

2-2.3   In the Windows environment, how is an item, such as an application program or a menu option, selected with a mouse? How is the item opened?

2-2.4   Describe the relationship between a Windows menu bar, a pop-out menu, and a menu item followed by an ellipsis (. . .).

2-2.5   There are two camps when it comes to learning a software package. Some prefer to read the instructions carefully before attempting to create a document. Others prefer to begin using the software, tapping context-sensitive help as needed. In which camp would you feel most comfortable? Why?

2-2.6   Describe three situations in which you might use the Clipboard to copy or move information within or between applications.

2-2.7   Some organizations may delay their migration from an earlier version of Windows to the most recent version of Windows for several years. What do they lose and what do they gain by delaying this decision?

2-2.8   Software vendors list minimum system requirements (processor speed, amount of RAM, etc.) to run their software. Frequently, however, a minimal PC may not permit any real user interaction with the software (too slow, poor graphics, and so on). Why don't vendors publish more realistic system requirements for their software?

2-2.9   Briefly describe at least one advantage gained by dynamically linking information via OLE. Give an example of when object linking might be appropriate.

2-3.1   List five ways that you might use word processing software at school or work. And five more ways at home.

2-3.2   Name five format considerations for a word processing document.

2-3.3   What is meant when a document is formatted to be justified on the right and on the left? Give three examples where type of justification is used.

2-3.4   Customer-service representatives at BrassCo Enterprises spend almost 70% of their day interacting directly with customers. Approximately one hour each day is spent preparing courtesy follow-up letters based on boilerplate text, primarily to enhance goodwill between BrassCo and its customers. Do you think the "personalized" letters are a worthwhile effort? Why or why not?

2-3.5   Identify at least one print document in each of the following environments that would be more effective if distributed as an electronic document: federal government, your college, and any commercial organization. Name five types of charts that can be created with presentation software and illustrate three of them. Describe a situation in which you may need to export a presentation software file to a different type of document (for example, word processing). Do the same for importing a file into a presentation software file.

2-3.6 Create a series of bulleted text charts (manually or with presentation software) that you might use to make a presentation to the class on the capabilities and benefits of presentation software.

2-3.7 Identify three applications for spreadsheet software. Then for each application describe the layout specifying at least three column entries and, generally, what would be contained in the rows.

2-3.8 Use the examples in this section as your guide, and create a formula that might be used in one of the spreadsheet applications you identified in the above question (or another of your choosing). Briefly describe the entries in the formula.

2-3.9 Give an example of four types of ranges. Also, list an alternative way to define the range A4:P12.

2-3.10 Describe the relationship between a field, a record, and the structure of a database table.

2-3.11 If you were asked to create a PC-based inventory management system for a privately owned retail shoe store, would you use spreadsheet software, database software, or both? Why?

2-3.12 Describe two types of inquiries to a student database that involve calculations.

2-3.13 Under what circumstances is a graphic representation of data more effective than a tabular presentation of the same data?

2-3.14 Give examples and descriptions of at least two other fields that might be added to the record for the STUDENT table (Figure 2-28).

2-3.15 Name two possible key fields for an employee file. Name two for an inventory file.

2-3.16 Use appropriate relational and logical operators to set conditions for displaying STUDENT, COURSE TITLE, and MAJOR for all courses completed by marketing or accounting majors that include a lecture. Illustrate the results showing column headings and the appropriate entries sorted by student.

2-3.17 Describe how you might use personal information management software at home.

2-3.18 Describe how you might use personal information management software at work. Which PIM component would be most helpful to you?

2-4.1 Why do you suppose there are so many different graphics file formats? Why doesn't the graphics industry standardize a single format for bit-mapped graphics and a single format for vector graphics?

2-4.2 If you have a PC, list the three home and family software packages in your software portfolio that are most important to you. What home and family packages would you like to add to your portfolio?

2-4.3 What home and family software packages would you like to add to your software portfolio during your first year of PC ownership?

2-4.4 Would you feel comfortable creating common legal documents, such as wills and bills of sale, with legal software without input from an attorney? Explain.

2-4.5 Some children spend more time playing computer-based games than they do attending school. Would you limit your child's time at playing games? If so, how much time each day would be appropriate?

2-4.6 For centuries, the book has been the primary resource for learning. How do you feel about exchanging that tradition for computer-based learning resources that are dynamic, linked, and interactive?

2-4.7 What do you think about integrating entertainment with education software for elementary age children? How about doing this with education software for adults?

2-4.8 Identify at least three printed reference documents you have used in the past that might be improved if made available as CD-ROM-based reference software. Explain why each would be better in electronic format.

2-4.9 A diminishing number of attorneys choose to use printed law books. Would you prefer to retain the services of an attorney who prefers books or one who prefers using electronic media? Explain.

2-4.10 If you work in a business, briefly describe the personal computing software (other than office suite software) that is most useful to you in your job.

FOCUS ON PERSONAL COMPUTING

1. Begin a personal computing session. In Windows, click on *Start* then *Help and Support* in any version of Windows, and then choose options that tell you more about the Windows operating system. For example, Windows XP has "Windows Basics" which tells you how to perform core Windows tasks, search for information, protect your computer, and keep Windows up-to-date. Spend a few minutes learning more about Windows and list four things you learned that you did not know before.

2. Use paint software, such as Paint or Paintbrush (in legacy versions of Windows), to create an image of your choice. Use at least five different paint software features in the creation of the image. Discuss the capabilities and limitations of Paint.

3. Go to a local PC software store, or, if you have access to the Internet, go online and navigate to a software e-tailer, such as Amazon.com (www.amazon.com). Identify at least one commercial software package in each of these categories: graphics, home and family, education, and reference. Which would you purchase first to begin building your software portfolio? Why? How about second? Why?

1. The Online Study Guide (multiple choice, true/false, matching, and essay questions)
2. Internet Learning Activities
   - Operating Systems
   - The Windows Environment
   - Word Processing
   - Spreadsheet/Database
   - Graphics
3. Serendipitous Internet Activities
   - Humor
   - Hotels and Restaurants
   - Money Management

chapter

3

Learning Objectives

Once you have read and studied this chapter, you will have learned:

● The scope of the online world and some of its many opportunities, plus Internet concepts, including how to go online and the makeup of an Internet address (Section 3-1).

● How you can use Internet browsers to access a wealth of information on the Internet (Section 3-2).

● The scope of Internet resources and the various types of Internet applications, including the World Wide Web, FTP, e-mail, instant messaging, newsgroups, and videoconferencing (Section 3-3).

GOING ONLINE

Why this chapter is important to you

The Internet is a new door in our lives that was simply not there a few years ago. In this chapter you'll learn about online information services and the Internet, what you'll need to do to get on, what you'll find when you get there, and how you travel to what seems to be an endless variety of cybersites.

To say that the Internet has had a profound impact on our lives is truly an understatement. What we do at work, how we work, how we learn, and what we do during leisure time have changed dramatically during the short-lived public Internet era. The virtual classroom, where students can attend classes online, is remaking our college and university system. Each year millions more people choose to telecommute to work from their homes. Many more people make their résumé available to millions by posting it to the Internet, then using searchable jobs databases to find employment throughout the world. Many people stay connected to the Internet all day long, taking advantage of its latest resources to get help with many daily activities—planning a vacation, getting the best deal on an airline ticket, communicating with friends via e-mail or instant messaging, and so on. More and more, we rely on the Internet to get our news and weather, and even to play games with other cybersurfers.

For those of you who have not had an opportunity to browse the Internet, this chapter should unlock the door to information and services that can stagger your imagination. The typical response from a first-time visitor to the Internet, called a newbie, is something like "Wow, I had no idea!"

WHY THIS SECTION
IS IMPORTANT
TO YOU

Once on the Internet, you can talk with and even see friends in Europe, send Grandma a picture, schedule a meeting with your coworkers, pay your utility bills, play games with people you've never met, listen to a live radio broadcast of your favorite sporting event, or conduct research for a report. That's seven reasons for you to learn more about the Internet and going online. There are hundreds more in this section, this chapter, and this book.

E-mail, which is now familiar to most people, is one of the bright stars shining in cyberspace (see Figure 3-1). Now imagine being able to explore an entire universe with millions of interesting stars offering thousands of helpful databases, forums for discussions on everything from autos to Zimbabwe, online chat, free downloadable files of every conceivable type, countless free and pay-for-use information services, real-time (as it happens) statistics on sporting events, the latest music videos, college courses and degrees, real-time stock quotes, new and classic electronic books (e-books), the biggest mall in the world, and so much more (see Figure 3-2). That's *the Internet*.

INTERCONNECTED NETWORKS

The Internet is a worldwide collection of *inter*connected *net*works. It's actually composed of millions of independent networks at academic institutions, military installations, government agencies, commercial enterprises, Internet support companies, and just about every other type of organization. Many individuals and families maintain a presence on the Internet, too. Indeed, just about every company and organization has a presence on the Internet. If not, they are in the process of creating a presence.

Just how big is the Internet? The Net links over a million networks with Internet host server computers in every country in the world. Each host computer, an Internet server computer, is connected to the Internet 24 hours a day. Thousands more link up to this global network each month.

The number of people using the Internet is now in the billions. Within the decade, the whole world may be wired, as every country has made access to the Internet a priority, including third world countries. Developed countries are moving toward universal access where every citizen will have ready access to the Net. In America, over 99% of the schools have Internet access that is made available to students. The Internet has created this global village, for we now live in a community of the world.

ARPANET TO THE INTERNET

A lot happened in 1969, including the first landing on the moon, and Woodstock, the culture-defining three-day rock festival. Amidst all of this activity, the birth of what we now know as the Internet went virtually unnoticed. A small group of computer scientists on both coasts of the United States were busy creating a national network that would enable the scientific community to share ideas over communications links. The government-sponsored project, named ARPANET, was to unite a community of geographically dispersed scientists by technology. By 1981, the ARPANET linked 200 sites. A few years later, this grand idea of interconnected networks caught on like an uncontrolled forest fire, spreading from site to site throughout the United States. Other countries wanted in on it, too. In 1990, ARPANET was eliminated, leaving behind a legacy of networks that evolved into the Internet. At that time, commercial accounts were permitted access to what had been a network of military and academic organizations.

What we now know as the Internet is one of the federal government's success stories. Although the Internet, along with its policies and technologies, is now pushed along by market forces, the United States government remains active in promoting cooperation between communications, software, and computer companies.

FIGURE 3–1 The Internet Is Changing Our Way of Life
Ten years ago, virtually all U.S. mail was processed by the U.S. Postal Service (shown here at the San Diego Post Office). Today, several hundred e-mails (see inset) are sent via the Internet for each letter processed by the Postal Service. That ratio has increased dramatically since the events of September 11, 2001. Many organizations changed their policies to encourage more extensive use of electronic communications when terrorist began mailing letters and packages containing the bacterium that causes anthrax.
Courtesy of Lockheed Martin Corporation

WHO GOVERNS THE INTERNET?

When the ARPANET was conceived, one objective of its founders was to create a network in which communications could continue even if parts of the network crashed. To do this, it was designed with no central computer or network. This is still true today. The U.S. Internet *backbone*, the major communications lines and nodes to which thousands of host computers are connected, crisscrosses the United States with no node being the central focus of communications.

Unlike AOL, CompuServe, and other information services, the Internet is coordinated (not governed) by volunteers from many nations serving on various advisory boards, task groups, steering committees, and so on. There is no single authoritative organization. The volunteer organizations set standards for and help coordinate the global operation of the Internet. Each autonomous network on the Internet makes its own rules, regulations, and decisions about which resources to make publicly available. Consequently, the people who run these independent networks are reinventing the Internet almost daily.

FIGURE 3–2 Videoconferencing
Others throughout the world were able to "attend" this presentation at the annual Intel Developer Forum via Internet-based videoconferencing.

Courtesy of Intel Corporation

Any person or organization desiring to connect a computer to the Net must register its **domain name** (for example, ibm.com, yahoo.com, and so on) and computer. The domain name is usually the name of the organization, an abbreviation of the name, or a something similar. The Internet is transitioning to a privatization of the domain name registration process. Now, if you or your company would like to secure a domain name, you would contact any of a number of domain name registration service providers from around the world. In the past, InterNIC, a government-funded organization, provided registration services for the Internet community. Collectively, these organizations keep track of the computers connected to the Net (site names and addresses). They also provide assistance to users concerning policy and the status of their existing registrations. Registered Internet hosts must pay an amount based on Internet usage to support the Internet's backbone.

CONNECTING TO THE INTERNET: NARROWBAND AND BROADBAND

A variety of communication channels, some made up of wires and some without wires, carry digital signals between computers and over the Internet. Each is rated by its *channel capacity* or **bandwidth,** which refers to the amount of digital information that can be pushed through the channel. Bandwidth or channel capacity is the number of bits a line can transmit per second. Domestic channel capacities vary from 56,000 **bits per second** (**bps**), or 56 K bps (thousands of bits, or kilobits, per second), to 9 M bps (millions of bits, or megabits, per second). Commercial channels carry up to 622 M bps.

Channels with high bandwidth are called *broadband*. A channel with a low bandwidth is called *narrowband*. Broadband and narrowband channels are analogous to interstate highways and county roads, respectively. The former carry considerably more traffic, bits, or automobiles, than the latter. The generic term for high-speed Internet access is **broadband access.**

Narrowband: Dialup Service

A dialup link is a temporary connection established by using a modem to dial up the number of the Internet service provider's (ISP's) remote computer (over a regular telephone line). Dialup access is available to anyone with **POTS**—plain old telephone services. When you call the telephone company and request a telephone line, it installs POTS. This narrowband service is in just about every home and business in the United States. This analog line permits voice conversations and digital transmissions with the aid of a modem. Traditional modem technology permits data transmission up to 56 K bps (thousands of bits per second).

PERSONAL COMPUTING:
Broadband vs. Narrowband For about double the monthly subscription cost of dialup Internet access you can have broadband access at 20 to 30 times the speed. The click-and-view Internet (broadband) is a different world than the click-and-wait Internet (at 56 K bps). Broadband changes your perspective on what you can do on the Internet. When you can go more places in less time, you become a cyberexplorer. You don't hesitate to download a 3 MB demo song from a new album. You can enjoy streaming video at broadband resolutions (near TV quality). You tend to take advantage of more online services. Plus, broadband access can be enjoyed by everyone in the family via home networking. If your pocketbook will allow, broadband offers a truly different Net experience.

Broadband: Fast Internet Service

For most of the public Internet era, dialup service was the only option. Now millions are enjoying broadband access, which is 15 to 30 times faster than narrowband access. As anyone who is familiar with click-and-wait narrowband access can attest, Internet access via broadband offers an entirely different experience. A Web page that might take one minute to load at narrowband speeds takes only three seconds on a broadband line.

Broadband opens the door for some amazing applications. Applications include support for full-motion video, videoconferencing, high-speed transfer of graphics, and real-time applications involving a group of online participants. Broadband has become popular for telecommuters who work at home but need to be networked to their office's computer system.

Broadband is "always on," so there is no need to dial up and logon. Generally, the broadband access fee is about double that of narrowband. The most common broadband options are, in order of popularity, cable, DSL, satellite, and wireless.

- *Cable.* Cable television systems originally were designed to deliver television signals to subscribers' homes. However, cable companies everywhere are updating their analog cable infrastructure to enable delivery of digital service that offers crystal-clear television signals and high-speed Internet access. Initially, cable Internet access companies are offering 1 M bps (megabits per second) up to 10 M bps service, significantly faster than POTS service and only slightly more expensive. A 1 M bps channel capacity is very inviting to the millions of people who are chugging along at 56 K bps over POTS lines. Linking to cable TV for Internet access requires that you be a cable subscriber and have a *cable modem*.

- *DSL.* Another technology, **DSL (Digital Subscriber Line)**, has made it possible to receive data over POTS lines at 1.5 to 9 M bps (the **downstream rate**). In a few years, the downstream rate will be 52 M bps. The **upstream rate** (sending) is 128 K bps to 1.5 M bps. Like cable, DSL requires a special *DSL modem*; however, it can share an existing telephone line such that voice conversations and digital transmission can occur at the same time. Cable access was the first widely available broadband service and is leading the way, but DSL is rapidly closing the gap as it is made available to new markets.

- *Satellite.* Broadband Internet access via cable or DSL is not universally available, even for people living in some metropolitan areas. However, satellite service is available to anyone in America with a southern exposure to the sky and the necessary equipment, a digital *satellite dish* and a *satellite modem*. Digital satellite access offers downstream speeds of 400 K bps to 1.5 M bps and upstream rates of 56 K bps to 1.5 M bps.

Satellite has a built-in lag in response time of about a quarter of a second, because of the time it takes the signal to travel to the satellite and back (about 47,000 miles). For most Internet activities, this latency is not a problem, but it can cause problems for real-time interaction, such as in online multiplayer gaming. Also, satellite access may not be available when the cloud cover is dense (thunderstorms). The latency problem and its dependence on weather make satellite Internet access a good choice only when cable and DSL Internet service are not available.

- *Wireless.* Wireless communication lets users take their PC and a link to a LAN (and therefore the Internet) with them to the classroom, conference room, the boss's office, poolside, or wherever they want to go within the limited range of the wireless link. For example, hundreds of colleges make wireless LANs available to students and professors from wherever they might be on campus. Access points, which are hardwired to a central server computer, are scattered throughout campus to extend the reach of the wireless LAN. The **access points** are communications hubs that enable users of PCs and other devices with wireless capabilities to link with the campus LAN via short-range radio waves. The most popular standard used for short-range wireless communication is **Wi-Fi** (*wireless fidelity*), a name given to the **IEEE 802.11b** communications standard. Wi-Fi permits wireless transmission at 11 M bps up to about 300 feet from an access point. The **IEEE 802.11a** communications standard permits a transmission rate of 54 M bps, but more access points are needed since the effective range is only 50 feet. Each wireless device must be equipped with a **wireless LAN PC card** or equivalent device to transmit and receive radio signals.

THE LINK TO THE INTERNET

The online world offers a vast network of resources, services, and capabilities. To go online, people at home with PCs generally subscribe to a commercial information service, such as America Online (AOL), or open an account with a company that will provide access to the Internet, an ISP. When at the office or school, people usually go online via a direct link on the organization's local area network or LAN.

Making the Internet Connection

The three most popular ways to connect your PC to the Internet are introduced in Getting Started and discussed in detail in this section. To go online, you will need to connect your PC to the global network we call the Internet.

Connect via an Information Service Gateway

One way to gain access to the Internet is to subscribe to a commercial information service, such as America Online. This connection method is a popular choice for people working from their home or small business and for those who wish to link their home PC to the Internet. AOL and the other major information services are themselves large self-contained networks. Each provides an electronic *gateway* to the Net; that is, you are linked to the information services network that, in turn, links you to the Internet.

Commercial information services have an array of powerful server computer systems that offer a variety of online services, from hotel reservations to daily horoscopes. About one-third of the American households with PCs subscribe to America Online (AOL) and other major information services, such as CompuServe, an AOL subsidiary, or MSN (Microsoft Network), a Microsoft service. Generally, other information services such as LEXIS-NEXIS, Dow Jones Business Information Service, and DialogWeb cater to niche markets, providing specific services to customers with special information needs (legal, financial, and so on). Information services have grown at a rate of 30% per year since 1990 and there is still plenty of room to grow.

To take advantage of information services, you need a communications-equipped PC (that is, one with a modem and communications software) and a few dollars. Most services have a *monthly service charge*. The monthly service charge for the most popular services is usually a flat rate of $20 to $30 for unlimited usage. Initially, you get:

● *Communications software.* Some information services, such as AOL, give you communications software packages designed specifically to interface with their information service network. Others rely on Internet browsers to deliver the service.

● *A user ID and password.* To obtain authorization to connect with the online information service, you need to enter your user ID and a password to **logon,** or make the connection with the server computer. The **user ID,** sometimes called a **screen name** for AOL users, identifies the user during personal communications and it identifies the user to the server computer. The **password** is a word or phrase known only to the user. When entered, it permits the user to gain access to the network or to the Internet.

● *A user's guide.* A user's guide provides an overview of services and includes telephone numbers that can be dialed to access the information service's private network.

Figure 3-3 takes you on a brief visual tour of America Online, the most popular information service. This walkthrough figure shows you a few of the well-traveled roads on this stretch of the information highway, but it does not begin to show the true breadth and scope of America Online (or any other major information service). Existing services are updated and new services are added on AOL and all of the other information services every day.

AOL is often the choice of Internet newbies. **Newbies** are what seasoned Internet surfers (those who regularly travel or "surf" from Internet site to Internet site) call novice Internet users. Newbies like AOL because it offers a user-friendly interface to a wealth of AOL and Internet services and information. In contrast, an ISP simply offers Internet access. Finding and retrieving Internet resources is up to the subscriber.

Connect via an Internet Service Provider

Most Internet users make the connection via a low-speed **dialup connection** or a high-speed **broadband connection** (via cable, DSL, satellite, or wireless) through an Internet service provider. Satellite service is widely available, but DSL and digital cable may or may not be available in your area; however, these high-demand services are being installed at a breakneck pace throughout America and in many other countries. An *ISP* is an organization that provides individuals and other organizations with access to, or presence on, the Internet. ISPs usually are commercial enterprises, but they can be colleges, churches, or any organization with an Internet account and willingness to share or sell access to the Internet. There are thousands of Internet service providers, ranging from local elementary schools making unused line capacity available to students and parents to major international communications companies, such as AT&T and Sprint.

ISPs do not offer the extended services made available by commercial information services, such as CompuServe and AOL, to their customers. What you get is access to the Internet. Services similar to what AOL offers its members are readily available to anyone with Internet access; however, those services and information are not as conveniently packaged.

FIGURE 3–3   **TOURING AMERICA ONLINE**

COMPUTER CENTER
The AOL Computer Center is among the most active areas. PC enthusiasts can chat for hours about any subject relating to hardware or software. This AOL channel lets you download any of thousands of programs.

SIGN ON TO AMERICA ONLINE
American Online 8.0 software, shown here, provides the interface for over 30 million AOL users. When you sign on to America Online you enter a screen name, usually an alias, like SkyJockey or PrincessLea, and a password. The software dials the AOL number, makes the connection, and displays the AOL main menu (see example), which is divided into 20 channels. You can also sign on to AOL via an ISP/LAN Internet connection.

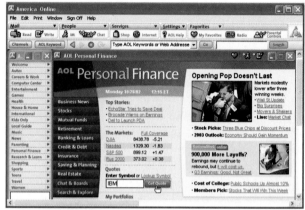

PERSONAL FINANCE
Get up-to-the-minute quotes on stocks, securities, bonds, options, and commodities. A wealth of financial information and services are available for the asking.

Direct via Network Connection

A direct connection to the Internet via a local area network generally is preferable to a dialup link because it normally gives you faster interaction with the Internet. With a direct LAN connection, your PC is linked directly to the Internet via a local area network. A LAN will normally have a broadband link to the Internet, which is shared by the users on the LAN. Depending on the size of the LAN and the extent of Internet usage, the LAN may be connected to a DSL line (up to 9 M bps), a **T-1 line** (1.544 M bps), or a **T-3 line** (44.736 M bps). A faster connection means shorter waits between Internet interactions and the responses. A dialup connection can take from 15 seconds to about 45 seconds to establish, whereas a direct connection via a LAN is "always on." To have a direct connection, your PC must be connected to a LAN that has a link to an Internet host. This is the case with most businesses and college computer labs.

There is a good chance that your college or company's computer network is linked to the Internet. Obtaining access may be as easy as asking your boss, instructor, or the network administrator to assign you an Internet address (user ID) and password.

TCP/IP and Packets

The *Transmission Control Protocol/Internet Protocol* (*TCP/IP*) is the communications protocol that permits data transmission over the Internet. Any operating system (for example, Window or Mac OS) comes with the software needed to handle TCP/IP communications. Communications over the Net are built around this two-layer protocol. A *protocol* is a set of rules computers use to talk to each other.

FIGURE 3–3 continued

PEOPLE CONNECTION
People "enter" AOL chat rooms, the most popular service on AOL, and talk with real people in real time. It's like having a conference call, except the people involved key in their responses. You can "listen in" or be an active part of the electronic conversation. The scrolling conversation on the left is for "The Coffee House," one of the many "Friends" rooms. Also, you can send an instant message to "buddies" who happen to be online, too. Of course, you can send e-mail to anyone in the world who has an e-mail address.

ENTERTAINMENT
The Entertainment channel offers movie reviews, TV guide listings, photos of celebrities, and songs from any style of music, and much more.

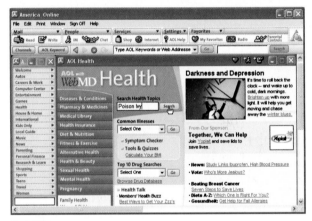

HEALTH
You can learn about nutrition and dieting, health and beauty, alternative medicine, HMOs, treatments for various illnesses, treatments for common health problems, and much more at the Health channel.

The *Transmission Control Protocol* (the TCP of the TCP/IP) sets the rules for the packaging of information into **packets**. Each message, file, and so on to be sent over the Internet is disassembled and placed into packets for routing over the Internet. The *Internet Protocol* (the IP of the TCP/IP) handles the address, such that each packet is routed to its proper destination. Here is how it works. When you request a file from an Internet server computer, the TCP layer divides the file into one or more packets, associates a number with each packet, and then routes them one-by-one through the IP layer. Each packet has the same destination *IP address*, but the packets are independent of one another as they travel through the Internet and may take different paths to their destination. A packet may pass through a number of servers and routers before reaching its destination. At the destination, the TCP layer waits until all the packets arrive, reassembles them, and then forwards them to users as a single file.

Each **point-of-presence** (POP) on the Internet, such as an Internet service provider, has a unique **IP address** that consists of four numbers (0 to 255) separated by periods (for example, 206.28.104.10). A POP is an access point to the Internet. An ISP may have many POPs for use by their subscribers. Typically, when a user logs on to an ISP, the user's computer is assigned a temporary IP address, called a **dynamic IP address.** By assigning IP addresses as they are needed, the number of IP addresses needed to serve customers is minimized since not all customers are online at any given time.

When you dial up an ISP's local POP, your dialup connection generally is made through a **PPP** (**Point-to-Point Protocol**) connection to an Internet host. Once a TCP/IP connection is established, you are on the Internet, not an information service gateway. The TCP/IP protocol is different from the protocol used within the AOL and CompuServe networks. Their Internet gateways enable communication between the information services' native communications protocols and TCP/IP.

Going Online without a PC

You don't have to have a PC to connect to the Internet. Access to the Internet is becoming so much a part of our lives that engineers are finding new ways to give us Internet access. Cyberphobics and those who don't want to purchase a PC can gain access in other ways. The most popular devices are those associated with TV. Some new TVs have built-in modems, Web browsers, and e-mail software. Or, if you don't need a new TV, these capabilities can be purchased in the form of a set-top box and linked to existing TVs. Each TV option comes with a remote keyboard for input.

Entrepreneurs are becoming very imaginative about delivery of Internet service. There's even a plug-in cartridge that turns a Sega video game into a Web browser. The telephone Internet appliance is another path to Internet access. Such devices are used primarily for checking e-mail. Some cellular phones with small embedded displays, called data phones, let you tap into the Internet (see Figure 3-4). Some ISPs offer an **Internet appliance**, such as Intel Corporation's Dot.Station, with subscription to the service. An Internet appliance is an inexpensive communications device with a monitor and keyboard that is primarily for families that do not have a PC. The typical Internet appliance integrates access to the Internet, e-mail, a built-in telephone, and home organization applications.

FIGURE 3–4 The Internet on a Phone
The Internet is now available via a variety of devices, including the telephone. This woman is using her Nokia cellular phone to access services and text information over the Internet. The data phone even lets you check and send e-mail. Communication is at 14.4 K bps, relatively slow for graphics, but fast for text on its small display (96 × 65 pixels).

Courtesy of Nokia

RETRIEVING AND VIEWING INFORMATION ON THE INTERNET

Once you have established an Internet connection, you're ready to explore the wonders of the Internet—almost. To do so, you need to open a *client program* that will let you retrieve and view Internet resources. A **client program** runs on your PC and works in conjunction with a companion **server program** that runs on the Internet host computer. The client program contacts the server program, and they work together to give you access to the resources on the Internet server. Client programs are designed to work with one or more specific kinds of server programs (for example, the Microsoft Internet Explorer client software works with the companion Internet Explorer server software). A single server computer might have several different server programs running on it, so that it works with multiple clients.

An *Internet browser* is one kind of client. Browsers are application software that present you with a graphical user interface (GUI) for searching, finding, viewing, and managing information over any network. Microsoft Internet Explorer and Netscape are the two most popular browsers. Both are used in the examples throughout this book. Most information on the Internet is accessed and viewed in the workspace of browser client programs. You give the browser an Internet address, called the **URL**, and it goes out over your Internet connection, finds the server site identified in the URL, then downloads the requested file(s) for viewing on your browser. The operation of browsers is discussed later in this chapter.

THE INTERNET ADDRESS: URL

The URL, or **uniform resource locator** (pronounced "U-R-L" or sometimes "*earl*") is the Internet equivalent of a postal service street address. Just as postal addresses are interpreted from general to specific (country, state, city, to street address), URLs are interpreted in the same manner. The URL gives those who make information available over the Internet a standard way to designate where Internet elements, such as server sites, documents, files, newsgroups, and so on, can be found. Let's break down one of the following URLs from a proposed companion Internet site for this book (see Figure 3-5).

FIGURE 3–5
THE URL WEB ADDRESS
A Web page is accessed by its URL or Uniform Resource Locator.

http://www.prenhall.com/long/11e/main.html			
http:	**www.prenhall.com**	**long/11e**	**main.html**
World Wide Web access method or protocol.	Address, or the domain name, of server at the Internet host site. It will always have at least two parts, separated by dots.	The name of the folder (Long) and, if needed, the subordinate folder (11e) on the server computer's disk that contains the html (Web) document or file to be retrieved.	The name of the document to be retrieved and displayed, in this case an html Web page. This could be a jpg file, pdf file, or some other type of file.

- *Access method or protocol—**http:**//www.prenhall.com/long/11e/main.html*. That portion of the URL before the first colon (*http* in the example) specifies the access method or protocol. This indicator tells your client software, your Internet browser, how to access that particular file. The *http* tells the software to expect an **http (HyperText Transport Protocol)** file. Http is the primary access method for interacting with the Internet. Other common access methods include *ftp* (File Transfer Protocol) for transferring files, and *news* for newsgroups. When on the Internet, you will encounter URLs like these.

ftp://ftp.prenhall.com (Prentice Hall ftp site)

http://www.yahoo.com (Internet portal and search engine)

news://alt.tennis (tennis newsgroup)

- *Domain name—http://**www.prenhall.com**/long/11e/main.html*. That portion following the double forward slashes (*//*), *www.prenhall.com*, is the server address, or the domain name. The *domain name*, which is a unique name that identifies an Internet host site, will always have at least two parts, separated by dots (periods). This host/network identifier adheres to rules for the domain hierarchy. At the top of the domain hierarchy (the part on the right) is the country code for all countries except the United States. For example, the address for the Canadian Tourism Commission is *info.ic.gc.**ca***. Other common country codes are *au* (Australia), *dk* (Denmark), *fr* (France), and *jp* (Japan). The United States is implied when the country code is missing. The **top-level domains** or **TLDs,** such as *com*, denote affiliations. Colleges are in the *edu* TLD. Other TLDs are shown in Figure 3-6. The next level of the domain hierarchy identifies the host network or host provider, which might be the name of a business or college (*prenhall* or *stateuniv*). Large organizations might have networks within a network and need subordinate identifiers. The example Internet address *cis.stateuniv.edu* identifies the *cis* local area network at *stateuniv*. The Physics Department LAN at State University might be identified as *physics.stateuniv.edu*. An optional *www* prefaces most World Wide Web domain names.

- *Folder—http://www.prenhall.com/**long/11e**/main.html*. What follows the domain name is a folder or path containing the resources for a particular topic. The resource folder, */long* in this example, refers to the proposed Long and Long companion Internet site for all Prentice Hall books by Larry and Nancy Long. Several books are covered within this resource, so subordinate directories are needed to reference a specific book (*long/11e*, implying *Computers*, eleventh edition, folder within the */long* folder).

- *Filename—http://www.prenhall.com/long/11e/**main.html***. At the end of most URLs is the specific filename of the file that is retrieved from the server (the server named *www.prenhall.com* in this example) and sent to your PC over the Internet. The *html* (or *htm*) extension (after the dot) in the filename *main.html* indicates that this is an html file. **HTML (HyperText Markup Language)** is the language used to compose and format most of the content you see when cruising the Net. Some Web files have an *shtml* extension and refer to a type of html file that has nonstandard commands. Of course, the retrieved file can be an image file, an audio file, a video file, or some other type of file. Entering a URL domain name (*www.prenhall.com*) without the *http://* access method identifier or without a filename causes the site's home page to be displayed.

HTML: PUTTING THE PAGE TOGETHER

HTML is a **scripting language,** that is, the programmed tasks to be performed are described in script. A scripting language is interpreted within another program. An Internet browser such as Internet Explorer, the *client program* on your PC, interprets the HTML instructions and then interacts with the server program in accordance with those instructions to download the necessary elements (text, graphics, and so on) and display the Web page. Figure 3-7 shows an HTML source document and the resulting Web page. HTML documents are text (ASCII) files that can be created with any text editor or word processing package. In HTML, each element in the electronic

FIGURE 3–6

TOP-LEVEL DOMAINS The domain name that comes before these top-level domains can contain only letters, numbers, and hyphens (but not consecutive hyphens or hyphens at the beginning or end) and have at least 3 but no more than 63 characters (for example, www.3-to-63-letters-or-numbers.com).

U.S. Top-Level Domain Affiliation ID	Affiliation
aero	Airline groups
biz	Businesses
com	Commercial
coop	Business cooperatives
edu	Education
gov	Government
info	Purveyors of information
mil	Military
name	Personal Web sites
net	Network resources
org	Usually nonprofit organizations
museum	Museums
pro	Professional

FIGURE 3-7 A WEB PAGE AND ITS HTML SOURCE DOCUMENT

document is tagged and described (for example, justification). Elements include title, headings, tables, paragraphs, lists, and so on. In this example, the title and a paragraph are tagged.

<TITLE ALIGN=CENTER>A Centered Title of an Electronic Document</TITLE>

<P>This paragraph is displayed in standard paragraph format.</P>

Tags always come in pairs, with the last one including a forward slash (/). Tags can include attributes, which further describe the presentation of the element. For example, the title in the example is to be centered on the screen (ALIGN=CENTER). The HTML language also permits the identification of inline (inline with the text) graphic images to be inserted in the document. Inline images are retrieved from the server and inserted as per the HTML instructions (position and size).

For those people who are not used to programming, HTML can be rather cryptic. Fortunately, there are a number of good WYSIWYG development tools that allow you to generate HTML documents using drag-and-drop techniques along with fill-in-the-blank dialog boxes. The tags are inserted automatically for you. For example, you can create a word processing document in Microsoft Word, then save it as an html file, which can be posted to a Web server computer and made available over the Internet.

Over the last decade, billions of Web pages have been created with HTML. Recently, the World Wide Web Consortium announced that the more feature-rich **XHTML** would be the new standard. Effectively, this retires the now somewhat limited HTML. Although HTML is currently the official standard, it will take a while for XHTML to be accepted and used by Web developers.

3-1.1	The monthly service charge for Internet access for most commercial information services is set by law at $10 per month for unlimited usage. (T/F)
3-1.2	These communications channels are listed by capacity (from least to most): dialup, T-1, and T-3. (T/F)
3-1.3	In an Internet address, levels in the host/network identifier are separated by a(n): (a) period, (b) comma, (c) @ symbol, or (d) colon.
3-1.4	TCP/IP is the communications protocol for: (a) the Net, (b) sending faxes, (c) all internal e-mail, or (d) spherical LANs.
3-1.5	The Internet is short for (a) International Network, (b) interconnected networks, (c) internal net e-mail terminal, or (d) inner net.
3-1.6	Which of these communications services is distributed over POTS: (a) cable, (b) Wi-Fi, (c) 802.11b, or (d) DSL?
3-1.7	A dialup connection to the Internet is considered broadband access. (T/F)

3-2 Internet Browsers

The Internet browser, or *Web browser,* is a software tool that makes it possible for you to tap the information resources of the electronic world and to communicate with others frequenting the electronic world. All new PCs come with browser software already installed, usually Internet Explorer and/or Netscape. Browsers have several main functions.

- *Retrieve and view Internet-based information.* They enable us to retrieve and view information from World Wide Web and FTP server computers on the Internet, on internal (within an organization) intranets, and on any disk medium with HTML-based content (for example, some books, magazines, and company manuals are distributed as electronic versions in HTML format on CD-ROM).

- *Interact with servers.* They allow us to interact with server-based systems and to submit information to these systems.

- *View electronic documents.* They are the foundation tool for viewing electronic documents.

- *Download and upload information.* They let us download digital information, then view and/or hear the downloaded video, images, music, and so on. They let us upload information, as well.

- *E-mail.* They allow us to send and receive e-mail.

- *Newsgroups.* They allow us to participate with online newsgroups.

Here, we focus on the basic elements of browser software. E-mail and newsgroups are covered later.

The viewing area of a browser can be filled with documents containing any combination of text, images, motion video, and animation. The visual information can be enhanced with real-time audio. These various forms of communication are presented within HTML/XHTML documents. The browser opens an HTML/XHTML document and displays the information according to HTML/XHTML instructions embedded in the document. The HTML/XHTML document pulls together all the necessary elements, including image files, audio streams, and small programs. The browser accepts the program in the form of **applets** or **ActiveX controls,** then interprets and executes them. These applets or ActiveX controls give Web developers added flexibility to create imaginative animation sequences or interactive multimedia displays. Browsers can be used with or without an Internet connection; however, an Internet link is needed to access files other than those on your PC or your local area network. Here a few of the many things you can do with browsers:

- Visit the museums of the world.
- Listen to the very latest song from your favorite group.
- Do your grocery shopping.
- Track the progress of the space shuttle.
- Tune in to a radio station in Australia.
- Send and receive holiday greetings to/from friends and family.
- Make an inquiry regarding the status of an order.
- Study from an interactive book in preparation for an exam.
- Send digital business materials, such as contracts and portable documents.
- Participate in ongoing discussions about, and even with, your favorite celebrity.
- Learn more about Greek mythology, kangaroos, or almost anything else.

CONCEPTS AND FEATURES

We interact with word processing, desktop publishing, presentation, spreadsheet, and database software to create some kind of a document. Browser software is different in that there is no resulting document. Browsers let you retrieve and view information as well as interact with server computers. Compared to the other productivity tools, browsers are easy to use, almost intuitive. It's not unusual for non-IT-competent people, unfamiliar with browsers, to be cruising the Internet within minutes after their first exposure to the software.

To use browsers effectively, it helps to understand the basic makeup of the Internet and the browser's navigational tools.

Internet Organization

The vast majority of the Internet resources made available by millions of participating networks can be accessed by anyone, from anywhere. All that is needed is a browser and an Internet connection.

Most knowledge workers now have access to the Internet at work. Families and individuals get online by subscribing to an Internet service provider (ISP) or commercial information service.

The Web Site

At the top of the Internet's organization are the Internet servers, the computers that provide on-demand distribution of information. When you navigate to a particular Web site (perhaps that of your college), the first page you will normally view is the site's **home page.** Information on the Web, which may be graphics, audio, video, animation, and text, is viewed in **pages.** A Web page can contain text plus any or all of these multimedia elements.

Think of a Web page as a page in an alternative type of book, one with nonsequential linked documents at a Web site. The home page is the table of contents for the resources at a server site. A home page will have links to many other pages, some associated with the home page and located on the same server computer and others that may be elsewhere on the Internet. The home page for this book <*http://www.prenhall.com/long*> has hundreds of pages and links to other pages. The home page for Prentice Hall <*http://www.prenhall.com*>, the publisher of this book, has thousands of pages and links to other pages. A page has no set length and can be a few lines of text, or it can be thousands of lines with many graphic images. **Hyperlinks,** in a form of *hypertext* (usually a colored, underlined word or phrase), *hot images,* or *hot icons,* permit navigation between pages and between other resources on the Internet. Click on a hyperlink to jump (link) to another place in the same page or to another Web site on the Internet. All hyperlinks are hot; that is, when you click on one with your mouse, the linked page is retrieved for viewing. An image or icon is hot if the cursor pointer turns into a hand image when positioned over it. Hyperlinks make it easy to skip around within or between Web pages to find what you want.

Each Web page is actually a file with its own URL. Typically, you will start at a Web site's home page, but not always. A college's home page might be at URL http://stateuniv.edu, but each college or department might have a home page as well (for example, *http://stateuniv.edu/cis* for the Computer Information Systems Department's home page). A page is a scrollable file; that is, when it is too large for the viewing area, you can scroll up or down to view other parts of the page.

Internet Servers and Addresses

The World Wide Web (WWW), or Web server, with its multimedia capability, has emerged as the dominant server type on the Internet. The FTP server provides a storehouse for information (in downloadable files) and a convenient way to transfer files between computers. Browsers accommodate information retrieval for any type of Internet server.

We navigate to an address on the Internet just as we drive to a city street. These Internet addresses are called URLs. URLs must begin with *http://* (WWW site), *ftp://* (FTP site), *mail:,* or *news:.* The domain name is usually prefaced by *www* to designate a World Wide Web server (for example, *www.ford.com*).

The pages at a server site are set up within a hierarchy of URLs. At the top in the following example is the company URL, for example, Prentice Hall. Special-topic directories, such as home pages for various Prentice Hall authors (Kotler, Long, Macionis, and Morris in the following example), are subordinate to the company URL but have their own URLs. These directories have subdirectories, which may also have subdirectories, and so on, each of which has its own unique URL. This subset of some of the URLs at the Prentice Hall server site illustrates one hierarchy of URLs.

HOME PAGE *http://www.prenhall.com* (Prentice Hall home page URL)

■ *http://www.prenhall.com/kotler* (home page URL for Kotler books)

■ *http://www.prenhall.com/long* (the Internet Bridge, home page URL for all Long books)

   ● *http://www.prenhall.com/long/computers10e/index.html* (the opening page for a Long book)

      ▲ http:// . . . (other pages associated with the above book)

   ● *http://www.prenhall.com/long/computers11e/index.html* (the opening page for another Long book)

      ▲ http:// . . . (other pages associated with the above book)

■ *http://www.prenhall.com/macionis* (home page URL for Macionis books)

■ *http://www.prenhall.com/morris* (home page URL for Morris books)

Here's the good news. For most of your navigation around the Internet, you'll simply click on a named hyperlink to go to a URL. Occasionally, you will need to enter a URL, usually a home page. This hierarchy of URLs is illustrated in Figure 3-8.

Navigating the Internet

Microsoft Internet Explorer and Netscape, the dominant browsers, are shown in Figure 3-9. Internet Explorer is the Internet client of choice for four of every five users in the world.

The Menu Bar

The menu bar at the top of the user command interface is used to select File options (Print, Save, and so on), to select Edit options (including Copy, Cut, and Paste), and to set and change a variety of options (for example, how buttons are displayed, color options, font choices, and so on). As with most menu bars, the Help pull-down menu is the last option.

The Toolbar

In a typical browser session, most of your interaction is with the toolbar and the hot links in the Web pages. These are the navigation buttons on the Internet Explorer toolbar (Netscape's toolbar has similar functions).

- *Back*. During the course of a browser session you will normally view several pages, one after another. This button takes you back to the last site (or page) that you visited.

- *Forward*. Use this button if you clicked on the Back button and would like to go forward to the next site in the string of sites (or pages) you have viewed.

- *Stop*. Use the Stop button to abort any transfer of information to/from the server. The browser displays the last fully viewed site.

- *Refresh*. This button refreshes (reloads) the current document into the browser. Information on some pages is volatile and may need to be updated.

- *Home*. This button takes you to the URL that you have selected as your default home page, perhaps that of your college or company.

- *Search*. This button calls up the Internet portal that you have selected as your default search site. A **portal** is a Web site that offers a broad array of information and services, including a menu tree of categories, a tool that lets you search for specific information on the Internet, and a variety of services from up-to-the-minute stock quotes to horoscopes. Infoseek, Excite, and Yahoo! are portals.

- *Favorites*. Click on the Favorites button (in Internet Explorer) or Bookmarks button (Netscape) to view a list of sites that you placed in your Favorites or Bookmarks folder. Typically, these are the sites that you visit frequently.

    The browser logo symbol to the right of the toolbar is animated when your browser is transferring or waiting on the information from the server.

The URL/Search Bar

The URL/Search bar, sometimes called the location bar, serves several purposes.

- It allows you to key in (or paste in) the URL (the address or "location") of the desired Web site.

- It displays the URL of the page being displayed in the workspace.

- It includes a drop-down box with a list of previously visited URLs. To return to one of these sites, simply select it from the list.

- It permits keyword searches of Internet resources.

FIGURE 3–8

THE HIERARCHY OF URLS AT A SERVER SITE
This figure shows three levels of URLs at the United States Air Force site. In the background is the Air Force Link home page <www.af.mil>. Selecting the "Photos" option (in black menu bar) displays the photos page <www.af.mil/photos>. Selecting the "Fighters" hyperlink takes you to Photos-Fighters page <www.af.mil/photos/fighters.shtml>. Choosing a particular photo (each is a hyperlink) takes you to the next level that displays caption information and a larger image.

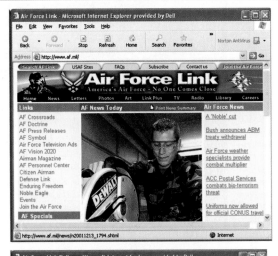

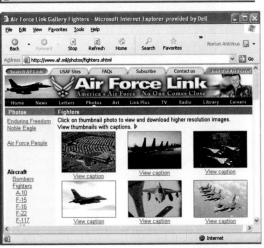

FIGURE 3–9

MICROSOFT INTERNET EXPLORER AND NETSCAPE BROWSERS
The functionality and appearance of these two browsers is similar and they have the same basic elements.

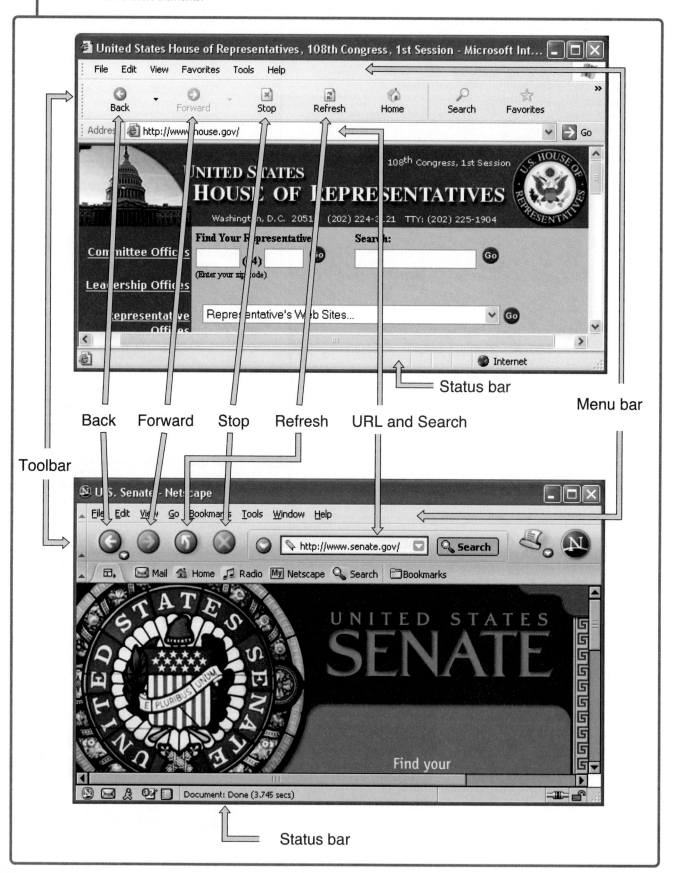

Status bar

Menu bar

Back   Forward   Stop   Refresh   URL and Search

Toolbar

Status bar

The Workspace

The workspace is that area in which the document is displayed. You can view documents by scrolling or by using the Page Up and Page Down keys. Left click on a hyperlink, a hot image, or a hot icon to navigate to and view another Web page. Right click to call up a menu that includes such options as adding the site to your Favorites list, saving the current document, downloading the image, and so on.

The Status Bar

The status bar is found below the workspace. This area displays the status of transmissions to and from Internet servers ("Finding site: *www.prenhall.com*," "Connecting to site," "Web site found. Waiting for reply," "Opening picture: logo.gif at *www.prenhall.com*," and so on). When transmission is complete, the status bar may display other information or instructions relating to the use of the browser. The transmission status box gives you a visual reference of transmission progress.

BROWSER PLUGINS

The function and use of Internet browsers are changing as quickly as the applications on the Internet. At this writing, there are a number of complementary applications, called **plugins**, which can enhance the functionality of browsers. Here are a few of the more popular plugins. Download sites are listed in parentheses.

- *Shockwave Player (www.macromedia.com)*. Macromedia Shockwave Player displays Web content created with Macromedia Shockwave software, such as interactive multimedia product demos, e-commerce presentations, animations, and multiuser games.

- *Flash Player (www.macromedia.com)*. Macromedia Flash Player lets Web surfers view content created with Macromedia Flash, including dynamic graphics and animations.

- *RealJukebox (www.real.com)*. The RealJukebox plugin gives you everything you need to play and record MP3 music.

- *Liquid Player (www.liquidaudio.com)*. The Liquid Player plugin lets you play and record MP3 music, plus you can read lyrics and liner notes, organize your music, view album art, and create your own CDs.

- *RealPlayer (www.real.com)*. RealPlayer lets you listen to streaming audio and view streaming video. **Streaming audio** and **streaming video** are different from downloading in that a file is not saved on your computer for replay.

- *QuickTime (www.apple.com)*. QuickTime lets you view QuickTime videos, listen to music, and view panoramas.

- *iPIX® Movies (www.ipix.com)*. This unique plugin lets you view an image from every direction. You can look up, down, and all around by simply pointing where you wish to view. The only way to understand fully this plugin is to view an iPIX movie (see Figure 3-10).

- *Acrobat Reader (www.adobe.com)*. Adobe Acrobat Reader reads and displays PDF-format electronic documents.

It may be inevitable that these and other capabilities will be integrated into future releases of major browsers. Browsers will continue to change with the technology, but most industry observers feel that browsers will remain intuitive and, perhaps, become even easier to use.

FIGURE 3–10

BROWSER PLUGINS: IPIX® MOVIES
The iPIX browser plugin is one of several Internet browser plugins. This one lets Net surfers view an image from every direction. Simply move a pointing hand to the edge of the image to look up, down, and all around. You can even zoom in for a closer look. Real estate companies can give prospective buyers a panoramic view of every room in a house. Colleges use these "bubble" or "360" images to make their Web sites stand out for students looking for a place to study.

3-2.1   The Internet browser is also called a Web browser. (T/F)
3-2.2   Small programs embedded in HTML documents are called: (a) apples, (b) applets, (c) applications, or (d) omelets.
3-2.3   Internet-based capabilities that help you find information on the Internet are: (a) seek portals, (b) find files, (c) search motors, or (d) search engines.
3-2.4   A URL that begins with http:// begins the address for what type of Internet server: (a) Web, (b) e-mail, (c) file transfer protocol, or (d) news?
3-2.5   To eliminate the spread of viruses, the uploading of files is no longer permitted on the Internet. (T/F)

3-3   Internet Resources and Applications

The Internet offers a broad spectrum of resources, applications, and capabilities. In this section, we'll discuss how to find what you need, the major Internet applications, and ways you can use the Internet to communicate with people.

FINDING RESOURCES AND INFORMATION ON THE NET

The Internet has thousands of databases, such as the *Congressional Record,* NIH clinical information, a list of job openings for the entire United States, and the lyrics to "Yesterday" by the Beatles. You name it and, if it can be digitized, there is a good chance that it is on the Net. The information on the Internet is out there, but getting to it can be challenging—and a lot of fun. We can search for it or just wander around the Internet until we find it. Or, we can be passive about it and let the information come to us.

There are three ways to search the Internet: *browse, search,* and *ask someone.* The function of a browser is to take you somewhere in the electronic world. Where you go and how you get there is entirely up to you. There are two basic approaches to using a browser: *browsing* and *searching.* The difference between browsing and searching is best explained through an analogy to a print book. When you leaf through a book, you're browsing. When you select a topic from the index and open the book to the indicated page, you're searching.

Browsing the Net

Browsers let you poke around the Internet with no particular destination in mind—this is browsing. Some people just get on the Internet and travel to wherever their heart leads them. All the popular portals on the Net offer a menu tree of categories. An Internet portal is always a good place to start. These portal sites divide the wealth of resources on the Internet into major categories. The categories for Yahoo!, one of the most popular portals, are representative.

Arts & Humanities	Entertainment	Recreation & Sports	Social Science
Business & Economy	Government	Reference	Society & Culture
Computers & Internet	Health	Regional	
Education	News & Media	Science	

Click on one of these main categories, each a hyperlink, to view subcategories. For example, clicking on Yahoo!'s "Arts & Humanities" displays subcategories: Art History, Artists, Arts Therapy, and so on. You may navigate through several levels of categories before reaching the pages you want. The typical portal will have a variety of service options as well, such as shopping, news and sports, new/used automobile research, job search, classified ads, games, horoscopes, people search, yellow pages, stock quotes, chat rooms, television listings, map search (maps and driving instructions), personals, and more.

Most of us have at least one general interest area in mind, even when browsing. For example, let's say you want to go shopping for holiday gifts. You can do this by going to the various "shop" categories, moving from virtual store to virtual store. Whether shopping or just surfing the Internet, browsing is always fun because you never know what you will find or where you will end up. Many pages have *banner ads* or *skyscraper ads* that entice us to click on them and travel to a totally unrelated site. With increasing frequency, Net surfers are experiencing *pop-under ads* (ads that open in a separate browser window "under" the requested page) and *floating ads* (an ad that "floats" over the requested pages for a few seconds). These ads often are context sensitive based on your preferences that may have been saved from previous sessions. For example, if you indicated an interest in skiing, a pop-under ad might present you with a special promotion package for a skiing vacation. Sometimes the ads appear based on your menu selection or search item. If you choose "skiing," up pops a related ad in a separate browser window. Such ads are becoming increasingly controversial.

Using Search Engines to Search the Net

You can browse the Net or you can search it. If you knew that you wanted to buy your parents sterling silver candlesticks for their twenty-fifth anniversary, then you would want to go directly to a site that sells them—the quicker the better.

The Net helps those who help themselves. Each major portal, such as Excite, provides a resource discovery tool, called a **search engine,** to help you find the information or service your need. Most of them let you find information by keyword(s) searches. You can search the Net by keying in one or more keywords, or perhaps a phrase, that best describes what you want (perhaps, information on "Julia Roberts" or who might offer a "masters degree biomedical engineering"). The rules by which you enter the keywords and phrases vary slightly between the search engines (see Figure 3-11). These hints may reduce your search time.

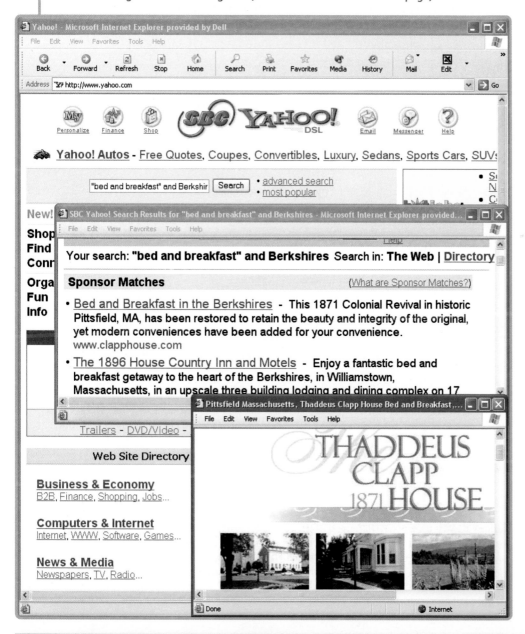

FIGURE 3–11

AN INTERNET SEARCH ENGINE
Yahoo!, shown here, is a popular Internet portal and search engine. Internet users can enter keywords or phrases (such as "bed and breakfast and Berkshires" in search box in the background window), and the search engine scans its database, and then lists applicable pages (see middle window). Clicking on the "Bed and Breakfast in the Berkshires" hyperlink took the user to the linked Web site (foreground window). Yahoo! also allows users to navigate to desired sites through a menu tree of categories and subcategories (see lower left of Yahoo! home page).

- *Read the search rules.* Each search engine has different rules for formulating the inquiry. Click on "help" and read the instructions first.

- *If you don't get results with one search engine, try another.* The results vary significantly between search engines, because their databases are compiled in completely different manners. For example, Yahoo!'s database is organized by category, encouraging topical searches such as "White House AND press room." Google's database is created from actual content on the Web, enabling searches for specific phrases, such as "Penn State Nitany Lions."

- *The results of the search are seldom exhaustive.* You may need to go to one of the listed sites, and then follow the hyperlinks to find the information you need.

- *Choose search words carefully.* The keywords and phrases you enter are critical to the success of your search. Try to be as specific as you can. You may wish to try the portal's advanced search options which enable you to narrow your search. For example, Yahoo! lets you limit your search to a particular language or country, or to a particular time frame (for example, past 3 months). You can identify words to be included or excluded.

- *Be persistent.* Many of your searches will result in something like "Search item not found." This doesn't mean that the information you need is not on the Internet. It means only that you need to extend your search to other search criteria and/or other search engines.

The Internet has hundreds of search tools, some of which focus on a particular area, such as technology or medicine. These are among the more popular search tools.

Yahoo! (www.yahoo.com)

Infoseek (www.infoseek.com)

Google (www.google.com)

AltaVista (www.altavista.com)

Search.com (www.search.com)

Excite (www.excite.com)

Northern Light (www.northernlight.com)

HotBot (www.hotbot.com)

Ask Jeeves (www.askjeeves.com)

MSN Internet Search (search.msn.com)

Netscape Search (search.netscape.com)

Metacrawler (www.metacrawler.com)

Dogpile (www.dogpile.com)

The last two, Metacrawler and Dogpile, search a number of search engines in parallel, then display the result for each search tool.

Search tools search only a fraction of Web content. Search engines index (include in their searches) only a small percentage of Web sites on the Internet. For most tools, searches cover no more than 20% of the Web. Most search less than 10%. Search engines tend to index the more popular sites, that is, those sites with the most **hits** and links to them. A hit is either when a Web page is retrieved for viewing or when a page is listed in results of a search.

Generally, portals with search engines are business ventures. Keep in mind that the companies sponsoring these widely used portals make money by selling advertising and by selling priority rights to a particular word or phrase. For example, if you enter the keywords "long-distance telephone," the company that purchased the rights to these words or this phrase would be listed in a priority position (first or possibly alone). It pays to tap into several portals to get the best deal or most impartial information.

Asking Someone

People on the Net are a family, ready to help those in need. Don't hesitate to post an inquiry to the people in the cyberworld via a topical newsgroup when you need help. Also, the Net is full of **FAQs (frequently asked questions)** pages and files that you can view or download. There is a good chance that your question has probably been asked and answered before.

INTERNET APPLICATIONS

World Wide Web servers have emerged as the choice for cruising the Internet; however, traditional not-as-user-friendly types of servers contain useful information still not available from World Wide Web sources. FTP, which predates the World Wide Web, is the most widely used resource for information outside of the Web. Critical resources on these servers are being reformatted and modernized for distribution via World Wide Web servers, but this may take a while. In the meantime, these resources remain available from these effective but old-fashioned servers.

Web Servers

The World Wide Web, affectionately called *the Web,* is an Internet system that permits linking of multimedia documents among servers on the Internet. By establishing a linked relationship between Web documents, related information becomes easily accessible. These linked relationships are completely independent of physical location. These attributes set Web servers apart from other Internet servers.

- *User-friendly.* Prior to the World Wide Web, most Internet users were techies and IT professionals. With Internet browsers, we can point-and-click our way around the Web.

- *Multimedia documents.* A Web page is much more than a page in a book. It can contain all of these multimedia elements: graphics, audio, video, animation, and text.

- *Hyperlinks.* Multimedia resources on the Web are linked via hyperlinks. Words, phrases, and graphics can be marked to create interactive links to related text or multimedia information.

- *Interactive.* The Web system, with its pages, enables interactivity between users and servers. There are many ways to interact with the Web. The most common form of interactivity is clicking on hyperlinks to navigate around the Internet. Some pages have input boxes into which you can enter textual information. You can click on option buttons to select desired options. **Option buttons** are circle bullets in front of user options that when selected include a dot in the middle of the circle. Each time you enter information in a text box or make selections, you will normally have to click on a submit button to transmit the information to the server computer. Also, the various browser plugins offer a variety of interactivity.

- *Frames.* Some Web sites present some or all of their information in **frames.** The frames feature enables the display of more than one independently controllable section on a single Web page (see Figure 3-12). When you link to a Web page that uses frames, the URL of that page is that of

FIGURE 3-12   **A WEB PAGE WITH FRAMES**
The home page for Slate, an e-zine (online magazine), uses frames to list the e-zine's departments (the vertical frame on the left) and the options for their affiliate MSN (the vertical frame on the right). A pop-out menu appears when the hand is positioned over a Slate department, showing hyperlinks to related articles. Slate articles (the Web site content) are displayed between the two always-available options frames.

a master HTML file that defines the size, position, and content of the frames. Ultimately, your request for a frames page results in multiple HTML files being returned from the Web server. The frames capability may be used to display the main site options in one small frame and the primary information page in another larger frame. Sometimes a third frame displays context-sensitive instructions.

FTP Servers

The **File Transfer Protocol** (**FTP**) allows you to download and upload files on the Internet, in much the same way you might manipulate files in folders on your PC. FTP has been around for a long time, so thousands of FTP sites offer millions of useful files—most are free for the asking. FTPing is a popular activity on the Net. You can download exciting games, colorful art, music from up-and-coming artists, statistics, published and unpublished books, maps, photos, utility and applications programs—basically anything that can be stored digitally. Many FTP sites invite users to contribute (upload) files of their own.

You must be an authorized user (know the password) to access protected FTP sites. Most, however, are anonymous FTP sites that maintain public archives. **Anonymous-FTP** sites allow anyone on the Net to transfer files without prior permission. If you are asked to enter a user ID and a password, don't panic. Just enter "anonymous" or "ftp" at the user ID prompt and enter your e-mail address (or just tap the Enter key) at the password prompt. Although most files on an FTP server might be restricted to the server computer and its users, often there is a public or "pub" directory that contains files accessible to all Internet users.

The trick to successful FTPing is knowing where to look. Fortunately, you can connect to FTP sites using a Web browser. Figure 3-13 demonstrates the hierarchical organization of FTP files.

WEBCASTING

Until recently, all Internet sites were more or less passive, waiting for Net surfers to find them. It's now apparent that the Internet can be a broadcast medium as well. For example, thousands of radio stations now **webcast** their audio signals over the Internet (see Figure 3-14). If you have an Internet con-

---

FIGURE 3–13

FTPING ON THE INTERNET
The browser image illustrates how you might navigate through the directories of an anonymous FTP site. The user proceeded from the /graphics/ directory to the /graphics/train/ directory to the /graphics/train/diesel/ directory to the 1189-1.GIF file (the train engine). The FTP site shown here, however, has been converted to a user-friendlier World Wide Web format (right). Other major FTP sites have undergone or are undergoing a similar transformation.

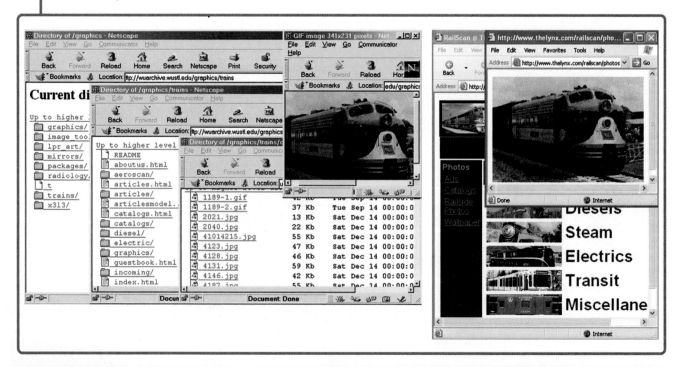

nection and a multimedia PC, there is no reason for you to miss the radio broadcast of any of your favorite team's games. To tune in to the game, simply use your browser to navigate to the webcasting radio station's Internet site, then request a *real-time audio stream* of the game. You may need a streaming audio browser plugin to receive and play the audio or video stream. The audio player plugins let you preset "stations" and scan them, much as you would in a car radio. Can TV broadcasting be far behind?

Generally, Internet applications are based on **pull technology** whereby the user requests information via a browser. Broadcast applications employ **push technology**, whereby information is sent automatically to a user. Several companies, including USA Today, broadcast news and other information in real time that can be customized to your information needs. For example, you can request news on a particular topic (personal computing, politics) or from a particular country, weather for a particular region, stock quotes for selected companies, business news for selected industries, sports news relating to a particular sport (even to your teams), and so on. The company periodically scans available Net sources then automatically delivers information to you via push technology for viewing (see Figure 3-15).

THE JUKEBOX

A major new Internet application is the **digital jukebox**. Now that virtually all music is digital, the Internet may be emerging as the primary delivery system for music in the near future. Jukebox software (see Figure 3-16), which is offered by Microsoft, Real Networks, and others records, stores, and plays music on the PC. The software can also download stored music to portable players. The Internet is truly alive with music, with lots of MP3 music files, and thousands of radio stations and other sites offering online music. The digital jukebox can help you gather MP3 and other audio files from Internet music resources. Use it to play stored music or real-time music from the Internet or CDs based on user-defined playlists. Jukebox software also has a capability to play popular videos along with the music. It also lets you visualize the music through abstract digital art that is constantly changing with the rhythm and sound of the music.

COMMUNICATING WITH PEOPLE OVER THE NET

The Internet is not just a resource for information and services; it is also an aid to better communication. There are several ways for people to communicate over the Internet, including e-mail, audio mail, newsgroups, mailing lists, chat rooms, instant messaging (IM), Internet telephone, and videophone.

E-mail

You can send e-mail to and receive it from anyone with an Internet e-mail address, which is just about everyone who uses the Internet. Each Internet user has an electronic mailbox to which e-mail is sent. E-mail sent to a particular person can be "opened" and read by that person. To send an e-mail message, the user simply enters the address (for example, *TroyBoy@mindspring.com*) of the recipient, keys in a message, adds a subject in the subject line, and clicks the send icon to place the message in the recipient's electronic mailbox. When you send an e-mail, it is routed over the Net to the destination server where it is stored on disk in the recipient's electronic mailbox. The e-mail remains there until the recipient logs on to the server and retrieves his or her e-mail. All e-mail to that address is then routed to the recipient's PC and e-mail client software for viewing.

You can send an e-mail message to anyone on the Net, even the President of the United States (*president@whitehouse.gov*). You can even use Internet e-mail to give your congressperson a few political hints.

FIGURE 3–15

PUSH TECHNOLOGY
The USA Today NewsTracker gathers news, weather, sports, and financial information according to preset user specifications and then delivers it in real-time via the Internet via push technology. The NewsTracker banner (top) can remain active at the top of the screen and other applications. The NewsTracker screen saver (bottom) presents current news on user-selected topics. Just click on a heading in the banner or screen saver to get the complete story or click on the "alerts" button to get personalized news, sports, and so on.

There are two ways to send/receive e-mail—via *e-mail client software* or via *Web-based e-mail*. E-mail client software, such as Microsoft Outlook, enables e-mail through a program running on your computer (see Figure 3-17). Web-based email is handled through interaction with a Web site, such as Yahoo! (see Figure 3-18). Each method has its advantages. The main advantages of the e-mail client approach are that e-mail can be integrated with other applications such as a calendar and task list, and all of these related applications can be incorporated with other e-mail client users on an organization's local area network. Web-based e-mail is easily accessible from any Internet-connected computer in the world—at a coffee house in Tokyo, a public library, a friend's house, and so on.

Your Internet e-mail address is your online identification. Once you get on the Internet, you will need to let other users and other computers know how to find you. All of your interaction will be done using your Internet address. Think of an Internet address as you would your mailing address. Each has several parts with the most encompassing part at the end. When you send mail outside the country, you note the country at the end of the address. The Internet address has two parts and is separated by an @ symbol. Consider this example Internet address for Kay Spencer at State University in CIS:

kay_spencer@cis.stateuniv.edu

- *Username*—***kay_spencer****@cis.stateuniv.edu*. On the left side of the @ separator is the username (usually all or part of the user's name). Organizations often standardize the format of the username so users don't have to memorize so many usernames. One of the most popular formats is simply the

FIGURE 3–16

DIGITAL JUKEBOXES

Millions of songs flow throughout the Internet everyday. Digital Jukeboxes, such as RealJukebox shown here in full and "skin" (not within a window) views, enable down-loading, cataloging, playing, and visualization of songs, along with artist information and Internet links to related sites.

FIGURE 3–17

E-MAIL VIA E-MAIL CLIENT SOFTWARE
Microsoft Outlook (shown here) is representative of e-mail client software and the presentation is representative of e-mail in general: to, cc (copy to), bcc (blind copy to), subject, text of message, and an attached file. The attached file is sent with the message. This e-mail client software (the software you use to receive and send e-mail) permits messages to be sent and viewed in rich text format, that is, with variations in font attributes and embedded graphics. The optional "personal information" placed automatically at the end of each message is called a signature. People usually include name, address, company (if appropriate), and communications information into the signature.

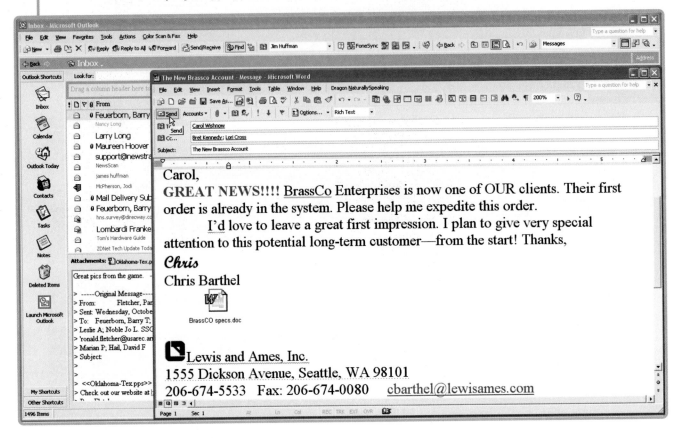

first and last name separated by an underscore (kay_spencer). Some organizations prefer an abbreviated format to help minimize keystrokes. For example, some have adopted a username format in which the first five letters of the last name are prefaced by the first letter of the first name (kspenc).

- *Domain name for the host/network*—*kay_spencer***@*cis.stateuniv.edu*.** That portion to the right of the @ identifies the host or network that services your e-mail, sometimes called the **e-mail server.** This is normally the Internet address for your Internet service provider (for example, sbcglobal.net), your information service (for example, aol.com), your college (for example, stateuniv.edu), or your company (for example, wal-mart.com).

The e-mail client software is the software that interacts with the e-mail server to enable sending and receiving of e-mail. Early e-mail client software packages limited messages to simple ASCII text. However, most modern e-mail client software and Web-based e-mail let you embed graphics and do fancy formatting as you might in a word processing document. Also, you can attach files to an e-mail message. For example, you might wish to send a program or a digitized image along with your message. The **attached file** is routed to the recipient's e-mail server computer along with the message. It and the message are downloaded to your PC when you ask for your e-mail.

The typical e-mail client software has some handy features. For example, you can send copies of your e-mail to interested persons. Or, you can forward to another person(s) e-mail messages that you received. Another feature lets you send a single e-mail to everyone on a particular distribution list (for example, workers in a particular department or players on a soccer team). You can even send your e-mail to a fax machine. E-mail features and services continue to grow (see Figure 3-19). One of the information services translates e-mail messages posted in French and German into English, and vice versa.

FIGURE 3–18

WEB-BASED E-MAIL
The interaction through Yahoo! Mail is via a Web site. Web-based e-mail is sent and delivered via a Web site versus an e-mail client. An advantage of this type of e-mail is that it provides seamless integration of your e-mail and the World Wide Web. With Web-based e-mail, folders containing your e-mail (inbox, sent, and so on) are maintained at the server site (for example, Yahoo!). This allows you to send and receive e-mail from any PC with an Internet connection and a browser.

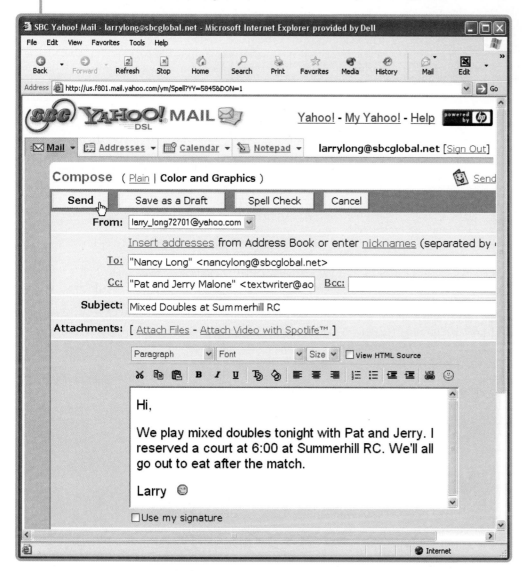

POP stands for both point-of-presence on the Internet (discussed earlier in this chapter) and **Post Office Protocol.** Post Office Protocol refers to the way your e-mail client software gets your e-mail from the server. When you get access from an Internet service provider, you also get a Post Office Protocol account. When you set up your e-mail client software, you will need to specify this account name to get your mail (usually your username).

The United States Postal Service is losing ground to electronic communications. As more people send birthday invitations and greeting cards via e-mail and business communications continues its trend away from "snail mail" to e-mail, look for substantial increases in e-mail volume and commensurate decreases in traditional mail. E-mail has resulted in tremendous changes in the business world, as did the invention of the telephone. The telephone, however, is essentially one-to-one communication, but e-mail can be one-to-one, one-to-many, or many-to-many—and it's written, documented information.

Audio Mail

E-mail is just text. But with audio mail software you speak your message instead of typing it. Users send sound files over the Internet (rather than e-mail), thus producing a form of worldwide audio

FIGURE 3-19 Wireless Inter-tainment Computer
With new Cybiko portable wireless inter-tainment system kids can chat with friends, play interactive games, send and receive emails, and enjoy hundreds of applications. The manufacturer has teamed with a number of shopping malls so that youth shoppers can receive and send your email wirelessly.

Courtesy of Cybiko, Inc.

messaging. Proponents of **audio mail** tout it as a faster and more effective way to communicate over the Internet. It eliminates the need to key in, edit, and spell-check text before sending a message, a time-consuming task for many of us. Also, audio mail conveys humor and other emotions that may be lost in e-mail messages. Audio mail is just evolving, but it's inevitable that this system of worldwide audio messaging will continue to grow and mature.

Newsgroups

A **newsgroup** is the cyberspace version of a bulletin board. A newsgroup can be hosted on Internet servers and on USENET servers. **USENET** is a worldwide network of servers that can be accessed over the Internet. "Newsgroups" is a misnomer in that you seldom find any real news. They are mostly electronic discussion groups. Tens of thousands of newsgroups entertain global discussions on thousands of topics, including your favorite celebrities or professional teams. If you're unable to reach celebrities via e-mail, you can talk about them on an Internet newsgroup. For example, *alt.fan.letterman* (the newsgroup's name) is one of the David Letterman newsgroups. Sometimes the talk show host joins the fun. If Letterman is not your cup of tea, you can join another newsgroup and talk about Madonna (*alt.fan.madonna*) or Elvis (*alt.fan.elvis-presley*). Real Elvis fans can learn about recent Elvis sightings on the *alt.elvis.sighting* newsgroup.

Newsgroups are organized by topic. The topic, and sometimes subtopics, is embedded in the newsgroup name. Several major topic areas include news, *rec* (recreation), *soc* (society), *sci* (science), and *comp* (computers). For example, *rec.music.folk* is the name of a music-oriented newsgroup in the recreation topic area whose focus is folk music. Another example is *rec.sport.tennis*.

You need *newsreader client software* or similar software that is built into most Internet browser clients. Generally, newsgroups are public, but if you wish to keep up with the latest posting in a particular newsgroup, you will want to subscribe to it (at no charge). The newsreader software lets you read previous postings (messages), add your own messages to the newsgroup, respond to previous postings, and even create new newsgroups. Figure 3-20 illustrates interaction with a newsgroup.

People who frequent newsgroups refer to the original message and any posted replies to that message as a **thread.** The newsreader sorts and groups threads according to the original title. For example, a thread that begins with a message titled "Pete Sampras' forehand" includes all of the replies titled "RE: Pete Sampras' forehand." If you post a message with an original title or reply to a message and change the title, you start a new thread. For example, posting a reply titled "Pete Sampras' backhand" begins a new thread.

FIGURE 3-20	**NEWSGROUPS ON THE INTERNET**

People frequenting the highlighted newsgroup (rec.music.fold) post messages related to aerobic fitness. This person has subscribed to this and eight other newsgroups (see list in folders window). In the example, a newsgroup subscriber was viewing a thread dealing with the subject "George—exceptionally talented, and Way under-credited and under-appreciated. . ." This user can reply as well and have his reply added to this thread for all subscribers to see.

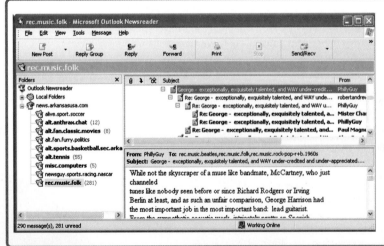

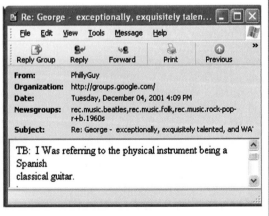

Mailing Lists: Listservs

The Internet **mailing list** is a cross between a newsgroup and e-mail. Mailing lists, which are also called *listserv's,* are like newsgroups in that they allow people to discuss issues of common interest. However, newsgroups are *pull technology* and mailing lists are *push technology;* that is, mailing list content is delivered automatically to your e-mail address.

There are mailing lists for most, if not all, of your personal interest areas. To find one of the interest areas, you scan or search available mailing lists from any of a number of sources. Portals, such as Infoseek, summarize and describe thousands of listserv's by description, name, and subject (just search on "mailing list"). When you find one you like, you simply send an e-mail message containing the word *subscribe* plus your name to the mailing list sponsor, and the sponsor puts you on the list. Mailing lists have two addresses, one to send instructions like subscribe (and unsubscribe) to the list, usually listserv@someplace.com. For example, you can subscribe to the Women's History mailing list at listserv@h-net.msu.edu. The other address is where you send e-mail messages to be distributed to others on the list. Most mailing lists are administered automatically at the server site.

Generally, there is no subscription fee. Once on the list, you receive every e-mail message sent out by the sponsor of the mailing list. Some mailing lists are one-way from the list's sponsor. Others accept and redistribute all e-mail received from subscribers. Sending mail to the list is as easy as sending an e-mail message to its mailing list address.

Subscribing to a mailing list can be stimulating and, possibly, overwhelming. Remember, each message posted is broadcast to all on the list. If you subscribe to a couple of active mailing lists, your Internet mailbox could be filled with dozens if not hundreds of messages—each day! So, if you can't get enough of David Letterman through a newsgroup, you can subscribe to a mailing list whose theme is Letterman.

Internet Relay Chat: IRC

At any given time, the Internet is filled with virtual chat sessions where people talk about anything from vintage muscle cars to yoga. They do this using the **Internet Relay Chat (IRC)** protocol, which allows users to join and participate in group chat sessions. A chat session is when two or more Internet users carry on a typed, real-time, online conversation. Chatting is a favorite pastime of million of cybernauts. They do this by establishing a link with a chat server; that is, an Internet server that runs the IRC protocol.

Chat servers let users join chat sessions called *channels.* A single chat server can have dozens, even thousands, of chat channels open at the same time. The name of the channel will usually reflect the general nature of the discussion. Usually channel names are unchanged, but topics on the channels are continuously changing. For example, in a channel called "Personal Computing," the topic might be "iMac tips" one day and "Windows XP troubleshooting" the next day.

The channel operator creates or moderates the channel and sets the topic. This way, chat participants can exchange ideas about common interests. Chats are ideal for group discussions. For example, many organizations schedule chat sessions as a way to exchange information between employees and customers. Universities schedule chat sessions to exchange technical information and advice. When you log into a chat session, you can "talk" by keying in messages that are immediately displayed on the screens of other chat participants (see Figure 3-21). Any number of people can join a channel discussion. The rate at which you communicate is, of course, limited by your keyboarding skills.

The natural evolution is from keyed-in chat to voice chat where the person's actual voice is heard in the chat room. Some people say that the inevitable emergence of voice chat signals the end of traditional chat. Others, however, cite the advantages of anonymity in text-based chat rooms and feel keyed-in chat will be around for some time to come.

Instant Messaging

Instant messaging (IM) is a logical outgrowth of e-mail. It is a convenient way for you to know when your friends, family, and colleagues are online so you can communicate with them in real-time. America Online popularized instant messaging, but now several Internet companies, including Yahoo! and Microsoft, provide instant messaging services.

To participate in instant messaging, you must first sign up with one of the instant messaging services and install its client software. Then you must create a contact list that contains the online identities of the people you wish to track for instant messaging. Typically, the people on your list will have you on their list. When you go online and sign in to the IM service, you are notified when your "buddies" are online and they are notified that you are online. You can then send instant messages, and even images, to those "buddies" currently online. Also, instant messaging software lets you initiate a telephone-type conversation with people on the contact list, if you wish to talk, rather than key in the words. Some instant messaging programs permit video conversations (see Figure 3-22).

THE CRYSTAL BALL:
Expanding Online Services Face-to-face services may dwindle as we find better ways to deliver services online. For example, many states let their citizens renew licenses (car, hunting, and so on) online without human intervention, thus saving states and their citizens time and money. To some extent, these services already are online: telemedicine, interactive artificial-intelligence-based technical support, elections and voting, religious confessionals, weddings, loan processing, college applications, the daily newspaper, most common legal services, courses at all levels of education, and remote participation in virtually any public meeting. Whether it is signing up for youth league soccer, ordering a pizza, or buying a house, our lives will be made less complex via this growing base of online services.

FIGURE 3–21

AN AOL CHAT SESSION
One of the most popular destinations on AOL is the thousands of chat rooms. AOL and other Chat programs let you "enter" a chat room and have real-time conversations with other people from all over the world.

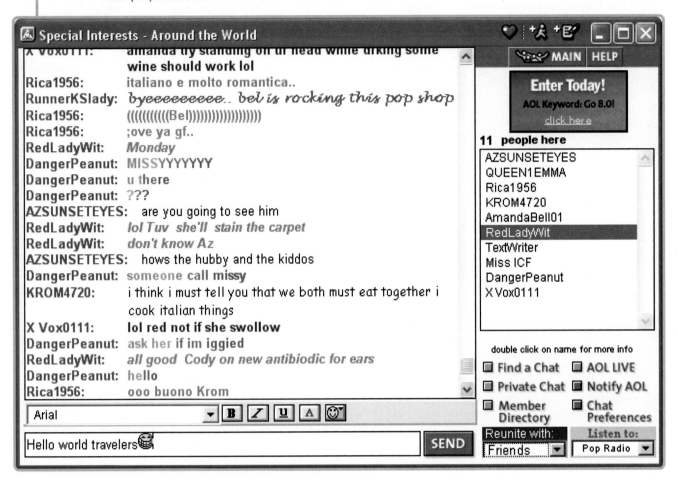

Originally designed to enable casual online interaction, instant messaging is rapidly becoming a viable business tool (see Figure 3-23). People in the business community have the same problem getting hold of their colleagues as the rest of us do communicating with our friends and neighbors. In fact, telephone tag may be the most played game in the corporate world. Instant messaging offers a new level of connectivity not available in e-mail or telephone exchanges. What instant messaging offers is a real-time link between people who routinely interact with one another in a business environment. IM immediately informs the others when one of their colleagues is available. Also, the most recent versions of instant messaging software permit sophisticated communication that includes file/application sharing, whiteboarding, and the ability to have audio and video conferencing. **Whiteboarding** enables participants to sketch and illustrate ideas. When one person runs the whiteboard option, it automatically appears on everyone's screen. Everything that is drawn on the whiteboard is displayed for all to see.

One side benefit that could have a major impact on how and where we work is that instant messaging provides managers with greater control over workers who may be telecommuting. The net effect is that companies are becoming more receptive to telecommuting arrangements.

The Internet Telephone

To make a traditional phone call we simply pick up a telephone, which is linked to a worldwide communications network, and speak into its microphone and listen through its speaker. Guess what? Millions of Internet users with multimedia PCs have these same capabilities: access to a worldwide network (the Internet), a mike, and a speaker. The Internet telephone application is becoming so popular that is being bundled with other popular Internet communications software, such as instant messaging (see Figure 3-22). Internet phone software capability lets you call people at other computers on

INSTANT MESSAGING: VIDEO CONVERSATION
The Windows Messenger instant messaging software permits text, audio, and video conversations (shown here).

FIGURE 3–23 Instant Messaging at the Office
The use of instant messaging is growing at the office. Employees "sign-in" and "sign-out" depending on their availability for electronic interaction.

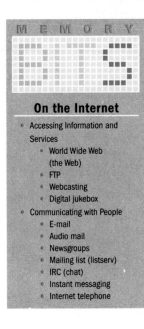

On the Internet

- Accessing Information and Services
  - World Wide Web (the Web)
  - FTP
  - Webcasting
  - Digital jukebox
- Communicating with People
  - E-mail
  - Audio mail
  - Newsgroups
  - Mailing list (listserv)
  - IRC (chat)
  - Instant messaging
  - Internet telephone

the Internet. These computers must have the same capabilities. By now, you are probably wondering about cost. There is no added cost over the cost of your PC and your Internet connection. People routinely use this capability to talk for hours on international calls!

Here is how the Internet telephones work. First, you establish a connection with the Internet, then open your Internet telephone software. The software automatically notifies the host server that you are available for calls. If you and your brother, who lives in Germany, wanted to talk via Internet telephone, you would both have to be online with Internet telephone software running and be registered with the same server. Internet telephone service is available that will let you call any traditional telephone in the world via your PC and the Internet, but there is a per-minute fee, which is usually less that the charges for traditional long-distance telephone service.

Cybertalk and Netiquette

Typically, we key in, rather than speak, our words and emotions when we communicate online. People who frequent chat rooms, do instant messaging, send e-mail, and participate in newsgroups have invented keyboard shortcuts and **emoticons** (emotion icons), which are sometimes called smileys, to speed up the written interaction and convey emotions. Some of the most frequently used keyboard shortcuts and smileys are illustrated in Figure 3-24.

In cyberspace there is no eye contact or voice inflection, so cybernauts use smileys to express emotions. They must be effective because many couples who meet on the information highway are eventually married. Their courtship may have involved some of the smileys in Figure 3-24.

There are some basic rules of **netiquette**, Internet etiquette.

- Avoid using all capital letters, unless you wish to shout.
- Never send spam, unsolicited e-mail, as this is the ultimate Internet faux pas.

FIGURE 3-24 CYBERTALK: KEYBOARD SHORTCUTS AND EMOTICONS

INTERNET SHORTHAND

AFJ	April fool's joke	LOL	Laughing out loud
<—AFK	Away from keyboard	ROFL	Rolling on the floor laughing
BRB	Be right back	TPTB	The powers that be
BTW	By the way...	TTYL	Talk to you later
F2F	Face-to-face	<VBG>	Very big grin
FAQs	Frequently asked questions	WAG	A guess
<GG>	Grin	Wizard	A gifted or experienced user
IMHO	In my humble opinion...	YKYBHTLW	You know you've been hacking too long when
IRL	In real life		

EMOTICONS: EMOTION ICONS

*	Kiss	:-~)	User with a cold
:-)	Smiling	:-@	Screaming
:'-(	Crying (sad)	:-&	Tongue tied
:'-)	Crying (happy)	:-Q	Smoker
:-(	Sad	:-D	Laughing
<:(	Dunce	:-/	Skeptical
:-o	Amazed	O :-)	Angel
:-|	Bored	;-)	Wink
:-I	Indifferent	:c)	Pigheaded
8-)	Wearing sunglasses	@—>—>—	A rose
::-)	Wearing glasses	[[[***]]]	Hugs and kisses

EMOTICONS: POP ART

+-(:-)	The Pope
==:-D	Don King
[8-]	Frankenstein
= =):-)=	Abe Lincoln
@@@@@@@:)	Marge Simpson
/:-)	Gumby
7:-)	Ronald Reagan
\	
8-]	FDR
*<(:')	Frosty the Snowman
(8-o	Mr. Bill
~8-)	Alfalfa
@;^D	Elvis

- Be sensitive to the moral compass of your recipients when forwarding Internet content, especially jokes.

- Never send e-mail containing the personal information of others without their permission.

- Use the "returned receipt requested" option sparingly.

- Be patient with newbies and recognize that they are working up the learning curve.

- Some people prefer a casual style of communication, so avoid making comments about keyboarding style, spelling, or grammar.

- Honor someone's private communication with you and keep it private.

- Think twice before attaching a large file to an e-mail going to someone with a slow dialup service.

- Never forward a virus warning without confirming it with reliable sources because most virus warnings are hoaxes.

- Use antivirus software to maintain a virus free environment, as most viruses are passed via e-mail.

CRUISING THE NET

Vast, enormous, huge, immense, massive—none of these words is adequate to describe the scope of the Internet. Perhaps *the Internet* may someday emerge as a euphemism for anything that is almost unlimited in size and potential. There are at least as many applications on the Internet as there are streets in Moscow. To truly appreciate Moscow, you would need to learn a little of the Russian language and the layout of the city. Navigating the Internet also requires a little bit of knowledge. Gaining this knowledge takes time and practice. In this brief space, we can hope to expose you to only some of the thoroughfares.

As you gain experience and confidence, you can veer off onto the Internet's side streets. For example, the Internet is a romance connection. Many married couples met and courted over the Net. Of course, where there is marriage there is divorce. Some couples prefer to negotiate their divorce settlement over Internet e-mail. This written approach to arbitration allows parties to choose their words more carefully and to keep records of exactly what has been said. In the religious arena, some people confess their sins over the Internet. To do so, they choose a sin from a menu, enter the date of their last confession, and then receive their penance.

As you can see, the Internet offers a vast treasure trove of information and services. Emotions of newbies (those new to the Internet) run high when they enter the Net for the first time. They simultaneously are shocked, amazed, overwhelmed, appalled, and enlightened. The Internet is so vast that seasoned users experience these same emotions. Figure 3-25 includes examples of a few of the millions of stops along the Internet.

FIGURE 3–25 **SURFING THE WORLD WIDE WEB**

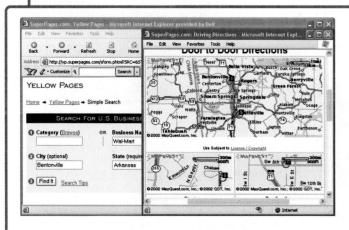

THE YELLOW PAGES
Use the "Yellow Pages" tab at SuperPages.com <www. SuperPages.com> on the Net to find quickly any business in the United States. A search for "Wal-Mart" in "Bentonville," "AR" listed the addresses and phones of area Wal-Mart stores and of the home office. The user can also request a map (inset) of a door-to-door or city-to-city street map from specific addresses. The SuperPage site lets you search for individuals, as well.

FIGURE 3–25 continued

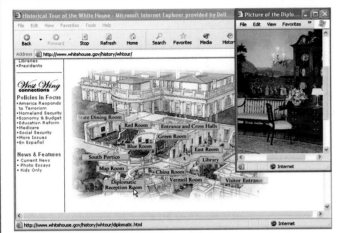

WHITE HOUSE TOUR
When you take your cybertour of the White House <www.whitehouse.gov> be sure to sign the guest book. During the tour, you can listen to the comments of President Bush and Vice President Cheney, meet the first family, and see the White House. In the breakout of the White House, you just click on a room to learn more about it. Shown here in the inset is the diplomatic reception room.

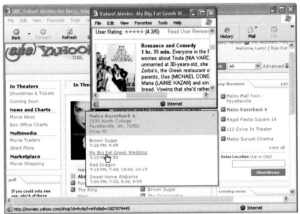

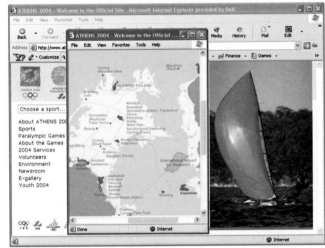

AT THE MOVIES
The Internet has just about everything but the movie (and that will change someday soon). You can even get show times at your local theaters (shown here). Click on a movie to read and view in-depth information about the movie, including reviews by professionals and people who just like movies.

THE ULTIMATE TRAVEL BROCHURE
The Internet has emerged as "the" source for travel information. It's easy to get information about any destination or event, including the 2004 Olympics in Athens, Greece.

SPECIAL-INTEREST PAGES
No matter what your interests or hobbies, whether whitewater rafting, bungee jumping, or ballooning, there is a wealth of information, including images, about it (or them) on the Internet.

STORY HOUR
There is something for children of all ages on the Net. The Wired for Books site offers many wonderful illustrated stories, in both text and audio formats, including *Alice's Adventures in Wonderland* by Lewis Carroll (shown here). Many stories at the site can be read from the Web pages or it can be viewed and heard as a streaming audio slide show, where the "pages" are turned automatically.

FIGURE 3–25 continued

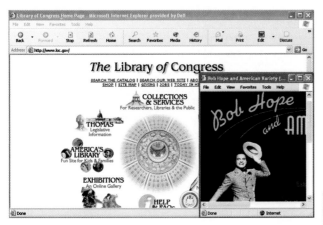

THE LIBRARY OF CONGRESS

Washington, D. C., has much to see, including the exhibits at the Library of Congress <www.loc.gov>. The electronic versions of many exhibits are posted to the Internet for people from all over the world to enjoy. Shown here in the inset is the Bob Hope and American Variety exhibit.

HEALTH INFORMATION ON THE INTERNET

More than half of all Internet users have sought out health-related information on the Internet, some from this Medem site <www.medem.com>.

STREAMING VIDEO

Internet surfers can view streaming video with audio at many Web sites. Here, CBS News has made an Osama bin Laden videotape available for viewing over the Internet. The U.S. Department of Defense released the tape that reveals bin Laden's role in the events of September 11, 2001. You can see thousands of live and taped videos of movies, sporting events, news broadcasts, speeches, interviews, walkthroughs of homes for sale, and so on.

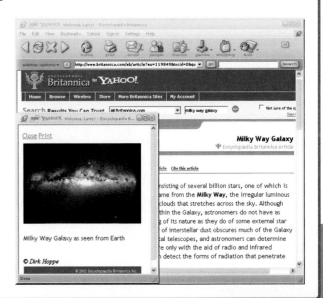

ENCYCLOPEDIA BRITANNICA

For decades, the 30-volume Encyclopedia Britannica <www.britannica.com> was a fixture in homes all over the world. Now it's online, available to anyone with Internet access. Just enter "Milky Way Galaxy" or any other topic to view Britannica content plus Web links to more related information.

FIGURE 3–25 continued

SHOPPER'S PARADISE

The Internet is becoming a shopper's paradise, whether for retail or the excitement of an auction. Online auctions at eBay <www.ebay.com> are going on 24 hours a day with thousands of items up for bid, including this pool table. Auctions take place over a few minutes or in as many as several days.

COMMERCIAL WEB PRESENCE

Most businesses, including the publisher of this book, Prentice Hall, have a presence on the Internet. Prentice Hall <www.prenhall.com> has a comprehensive Web site over which students and professors can communicate with one another and download important class materials. Users can thumb through the Prentice Hall College Division's catalog to obtain information about any book it offers. Many Prentice Hall books, including this one, have a companion Web site.

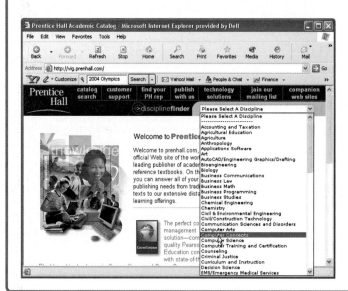

SECTION SELF-CHECK

3-3.1	The IRC protocol enables users to join and participate in group chat sessions. (T/F)
3-3.2	All Internet search engines have the same rules for formulating the inquiry. (T/F)
3-3.3	Which of these would not be considered an Internet portal: (a) Yahoo!, (b) Google, (c) Webcast, or (d) Excite?
3-3.4	What FTP feature allows anyone on the Net to use FTP sites without prior permission: (a) unsigned FTP, (b) secret FTP, (c) unnamed FTP, or (d) anonymous FTP?
3-3.5	Which of these applications is associated with text chat: (a) Internet telephone, (b) IRC, (c) e-mail, or (d) newsgroups?
3-3.6	The two ways e-mail is delivered are: (a) client and FTP, (b) Web-based and FTP, (c) Web-based and client, or (d) client and consumer.

3-1 THE INTERNET

The Internet (a worldwide collection of *inter*connected *networks*) is composed of thousands of independent networks in virtually every type of organization. The Department of Defense's ARPANET project was the genesis of the Internet. Volunteers from many nations coordinate the Internet. The Internet is transitioning to a privatization of the domain name registration process.

Communication channels are rated by their **bandwidth.** Channel capacities range from 56,000 **bits per second (bps)** for dialup service to high-speed **broadband access** at 622 M bps for commercial service. Narrowband dialup access is available to anyone with **POTS**—plain old telephone services. Common broadband options, which are up to 30 times faster than narrowband access, include cable, DSL, satellite, and wireless. A cable modem is required for cable access. **DSL (Digital Subscriber Line)** shares an existing telephone line and can provide access speed up to 9 M bps (the **downstream rate**) with an **upstream rate** (sending) of up to 1.5 M bps. The advantage of satellite service is that anyone in America with a southern exposure to the sky and the necessary equipment can have it. Wireless communication lets users take their PC anywhere within the range of a wireless signal and a link to a LAN via an **access point**, a wireless communications hub. The most popular standard used for short-range wireless communication is **Wi-Fi,** based on the **IEEE 802.11b** communications standard. The **IEEE 802.11a** communications standard permits a higher transmission rate but the effective range is less. Wireless devices must be equipped with a **wireless LAN PC card.**

The online world offers a vast network of resources, services, and capabilities. Most of us enter it simply by plugging the phone line into our PC's modem and running our communications software. **Newbies** are novice Internet users.

There are three levels at which you can connect your PC to the Internet. The easiest way to gain access is through a commercial information service's gateway. When you subscribe to a commercial information service such as America Online or CompuServe, you get communications software, a **user ID** (sometimes called a **screen name**), a **password** (required for **logon**), and a user's guide. Or you can make the connection via a **dialup connection** or a broadband connection through an *Internet service provider (ISP)*. At the third level, there is direct connection to the Internet whereby your PC is wired directly into the Internet. Such connections often use a DSL line (up to 9 M bps), a **T-1 line** (1.544 M bps), or a **T-3 line** (44.736 M bps).

The Transmission Control Protocol/Internet Protocol (TCP/IP) is the communications protocol that permits data transmission over the Internet. The *Transmission Control Protocol* sets the rules for the packaging of information into **packets.** The *Internet Protocol* handles the address, such that each packet is routed to its proper destination. When you dial up an ISP's local **POP (point-of-presence)**, each of which has a unique **IP address,** your dialup connection is made through a **PPP (Point-to-Point Protocol)** connection to an Internet host.

The typical **Internet appliance** integrates access to the Internet, e-mail, a built-in telephone, and home organization applications.

A **client program** runs on your PC and works in conjunction with a companion **server program** that runs on the Internet host computer. The client program contacts the server program, and they work together to give you access to the resources on the Internet server. An *Internet browser* is one kind of client. The dominant browsers are Microsoft Internet Explorer and Netscape.

The **URL (uniform resource locator)**, which is the Internet equivalent of an address, progresses from general to specific. That portion of the URL before the first colon (usually *http*) specifies the access method. The *http* tells the software to expect an **http (HyperText Transport Protocol)** file. That portion following the double forward slashes (*//*) is the server address, or the **domain name**. It has at least two parts, separated by dots (periods). The **top-level domains** or **TLDs,** such as *com* and *org*, denote affiliations. What follows the domain name is a folder or path containing the resources for a particular topic. At the end of the URL is the specific filename of the file that is retrieved from the server. **HTML (HyperText Markup Language)** is a **scripting language** used to compose and format most files on the Net. A more feature-rich **XHTML** is to become the new standard.

3-2 INTERNET BROWSERS

Internet browser, or Web browser, software lets us tap the information resources of the electronic world. It enables us to retrieve and view Internet-based information, interact with server-based systems, view electronic documents, pass digital information between computers, send and receive e-mail, and join newsgroups. The browser opens an HTML/XHTML document and displays the information according to HTML/XHTML instructions embedded in the document. The HTML/XHTML documents may reference **applets** or **ActiveX controls** which are small programs.

At the top of the Internet organization scheme are the Internet servers. Each World Wide Web server has one or more **home pages,** the first page you will normally view when traveling to a particular site. Web resources, which may be graphics, audio, video, animation, and text, are viewed in **pages.**

Each Web page is actually a file with its own URL. We navigate to an address on the Internet just as we drive to a street address. **Hyperlinks,** in a form of *hypertext, hot images,* or *hot icons,* permit navigation between pages and between other resources on the Internet. The pages at a server site are set up within a hierarchy of URLs.

The basic elements used for server navigation and viewing include the menu bar, the toolbar, the URL/search bar, the workspace, and the status bar. The toolbar has several navigational buttons, including the Search button. This button calls up the Internet portal that you have selected as your default search site. **Portals** are Web sites that offer a broad array of information and services, including a menu tree of categories and a capability that helps us find online resources.

There are a number of complementary applications, called **plugins,** that can enhance the functionality of browsers. Examples include *Shockwave Player, QuickTime,* and *RealPlayer,* which let you listen to **streaming audio** and view **streaming video.**

3-3 INTERNET RESOURCES AND APPLICATIONS

There are three ways to search the Internet: *browse*, *search*, and *ask someone*. You can browse through menu trees of *categories* or you can search using a variety of resource discovery tools, including **search engines**. People on the Net are ready to help those in need. There are also **FAQ (frequently asked questions)** pages and files.

The World Wide Web is an Internet application that permits linking of multimedia documents among Web servers on the Internet. By establishing a linked relationship between Web documents, related information becomes easily accessible. Web resources are designed to be accessed with easy-to-use browsers.

Web pages are linked via hyperlinks. The Web enables interactivity between users and servers. For example, you can click on **option buttons** to select desired options. Some Web sites present some or all of their information in **frames.**

The **File Transfer Protocol** (**FTP**) allows you to download and upload files on the Internet. Most are **anonymous FTP** sites. **Webcasting** (Internet broadcasting) has emerged as a popular Internet application. With **pull technology** the user requests information via a browser. With **push technology** information is sent automatically to a user.

Digital jukebox software records, stores, and plays music on the PC. It can help you gather MP3 and other audio files from Internet music resources.

The Internet is an aid to better communication. You can send e-mail to and receive it from anyone with an Internet e-mail address. The two ways to send/receive e-mail are via e-mail client software or via Web-based e-mail, which is handled through interaction with a Web site.

The Internet e-mail address has two parts, the username and the domain name, and is separated by an @ symbol. The domain name identifies the **e-mail server.** An **attached file** can be sent with an e-mail message. **Post Office Protocol** refers to the way your e-mail client software gets your e-mail from the server.

Audio mail lets you speak your Internet message instead of typing it.

A **newsgroup** can be hosted on Internet servers and on **USENET** servers. People who frequent newsgroups refer to the original message and any posted replies to that message as a **thread.** The Internet **mailing list** (listserv) is a cross between a newsgroup and e-mail.

The **Internet Relay Chat** (**IRC**) protocol allows users to participate in group chat sessions. A chat session is when two or more Internet users carry on a typed, real-time, online conversation.

Instant messaging is a convenient way for you to know when your friends are online so you can communicate with them in real time. Some versions of instant messaging software permit file/application sharing, **whiteboarding,** and the ability to have audio and video conferencing.

The Internet phone capability lets you call people at other computers on the Internet. Internet telephone service is available that will let you call any traditional telephone in the world via your PC and the Internet. People who communicate online have invented keyboard shortcuts and **emoticons** to speed up the written interaction and convey emotions. Rules of **netiquette,** Internet etiquette, demand sensitivity and concern for others in cyberspace.

The Internet offers a vast treasure trove of information and services.

KEY TERMS

access point (p. 134)
ActiveX controls (p. 141)
Anonymous FTP (p. 150)
applets (p. 141)
attached file (p. 154)
audio mail (p. 156)
bandwidth (p. 133)
bits per second (bps) (p. 133)
broadband access (p. 133)
broadband connection (p. 135)
client program (p. 138)
dialup connection (p. 135)
digital jukebox (p. 151)
domain name (p. 133)
downstream rate (p. 134)
DSL (Digital Subscriber Line) (p. 134)
dynamic IP address (p. 137)
e-mail server (p. 154)
emoticon (p. 160)
FAQ (frequently asked question)
  (p. 148)
frames (p. 149)
FTP (File Transfer Protocol) (p. 150)
hits (p. 148)

home page (p. 142)
HTML (HyperText Markup Language)
  (p. 139)
http (HyperText Transport Protocol)
  (p. 139)
hyperlink (p. 142)
IEEE 802.11a (p. 134)
IEEE 802.11b (p. 134)
Internet appliance (p. 138)
Internet Relay Chat (IRC) (p. 157)
IP address (p. 137)
logon (p. 135)
mailing list (p. 157)
netiquette (p. 160)
newbie (p. 135)
newsgroup (p. 156)
option button (p. 149)
packets (p. 137)
page (p. 142)
password (p. 135)
plugin (p. 145)
point-of-presence (POP) (p. 137)
portal (p. 143)
Post Office Protocol (p. 155)

POTS (p. 133)
PPP (Point-to-Point Protocol) (p. 137)
pull technology (p. 151)
push technology (p. 151)
screen name (p. 135)
scripting language (p. 139)
search engine (p. 147)
server program (p. 138)
streaming audio (p. 145)
streaming video (p. 145)
T-1 line (p. 136)
T-3 line (p. 136)
thread (p. 156)
top-level domain (TLD) (p. 139)
upstream rate (p. 134)
URL (uniform resource locator) (p. 138)
USENET (p. 156)
user ID (p. 135)
webcast (p. 150)
whiteboarding (p. 158)
Wi-Fi (p. 134)
wireless LAN PC card (p. 134)
XHTML (p. 140)

MATCHING

1. netiquette
2. newsgroup
3. broadband access
4. search engine
5. POP
6. TCP/IP
7. ARPANET
8. instant messaging
9. plugin
10. megabits
11. bandwidth
12. universally available Net access
13. dialup connection
14. HTML
15. Wi-Fi

a. Net resource discovery tool
b. high-speed Internet
c. enhances browser functionality
d. linking people in real-time
e. IEEE 802.11b
f. Internet etiquette
g. PPP
h. USENET
i. scripting language
j. satellite
k. rules for Internet packets
l. access point to the Net
m. channel capacity
n. millions of bits
o. early Internet

CHAPTER SELF-CHECK

3-1.1 One way to go online is to subscribe to a commercial information service. (T/F)

3-1.2 America Online has a self-contained network. (T/F)

3-1.3 The Internet is like AOL, a commercial information service. (T/F)

3-1.4 ARPANET was the first commercially available communications software package. (T/F)

3-1.5 A newbie is anyone with a fear of cyberspace. (T/F)

3-1.6 Which of the following is not a link to the Internet: (a) interstate bonds, (b) DSL, (c) cable, or (d) wireless satellite?

3-1.7 Which of the following is not included with a subscription to an information service: (a) communications software, (b) a user ID, (c) speech-recognition software, or (d) a password?

3-1.8 Which of the following is not an online commercial information service: (a) Dow Jones Business Information Service, (b) the Web, (c) AOL, or (d) CompuServe?

3-1.9 Which of these is not a U.S. top-level domain affiliation ID: (a) moc, (b) edu, (c) gov, or (d) org?

3-1.10 In the URL, *http://www.abccorp.com/pr/main.htm*, the domain is: (a) *http*, (b) *www.abccorp.com*, (c) *pr/main.htm*, or (d) *www*.

3-1.11 What type of company provides people with access to the Internet: (a) PSI, (b) ISP, (c) SPI, or (d) IPS?

3-1.12 In the e-mail address, *mickey_mouse@disney.com*, the user ID is: (a) *mickey_mouse*, (b) *mouse*, (c) *disney.com*, or (d) *@*.

3-1.13 A 56,000 bits-per-second channel is the same as a: (a) 56 kps pipe, (b) 56 K bps line, (c) dual 28000X2 K bps line, or (d) single-channel DSL.

3-1.14 A communication channel is rated by its: (a) channel aptitude, (b) bandwidth, (c) flow, or (d) datastream.

3-1.15 Narrowband has slightly more capacity than broadband. (T/F)

3-1.16 Which broadband service has a built-in lag in response time: (a) DSL, (b) satellite, (c) cable, or (d) Wi-Fi?

3-1.17 Which of these would not be associated with a wireless local area network: (a) access points, (b) Wi-Fi, (c) IEEE 802.11b, or (d) DSL?

3-1.18 Every home user is assigned a permanent IP address on the Internet. (T/F)

3-2.1 Internet portals are designed to permit searches by category or by keyword, but never both. (T/F)

3-2.2 On the Internet, only hypertext hyperlinks are hot. (T/F)

3-2.3 Which of the following labels might be included with an Internet address: (a) <bps>, (b) ULS, (c) http://, or (d) fpt://?

3-2.4 The opening page for a particular Web site normally is the: (a) opener page, (b) home page, (c) flip-flop page, or (d) master page.

3-2.5 Which of the following buttons is not one of the main buttons on a browser toolbar: (a) Back, (b) Forward, (c) Refresh, or (d) House?

3-2.6 Web pages can be tied together by: (a) cybertext links, (b) hydratext links, (c) hydrolinks, or (d) hyperlinks.

3-3.1 Yahoo! is a site on the Internet that can be used to browse the Net by content category. (T/F)

3-3.2 Subscribing to a popular mailing list would result in more Internet e-mail than posting a message to a newsgroup. (T/F)

3-3.3 A file attached to an e-mail is routed to the recipient's e-mail server computer along with the message. (T/F)

3-3.4 Which server on the Internet offers hypertext links: (a) QOQ, (b) Web, (c) Gopher, or (d) ftp?

3-3.5 All but which one of these would be a common way to search for information on the Internet: (a) browse, (b) search, (c) push/pull, or (d) ask someone on the Net?

3-3.6 What Web features enable the display of more than one page on a screen: (a) borders, (b) windows, (c) frames, or (d) structures?

3-3.7 Generally, today's Internet applications are based on what technology: (a) push, (b) pull, (c) place, or (d) draw?

3-3.8 On a newsgroup, the original message and any posted replies to that message are a: (a) needle, (b) thread, (c) pinpoint, or (d) tapestry?

E-MAIL ETIQUETTE

As a knowledge worker, you may spend an hour or more each day composing or responding to e-mail. E-mail is now as much a part of the business world as the paycheck. How we present ourselves in our e-mails can play a role in how effective we are in business and in what people think of us. You can leave a good or bad impression with your correspondents depending on your understanding of netiquette, a slang term for Internet etiquette, that is, *what* you say in your message and *how* you say it. During face-to-face conversations we use vocal inflections or body movements that clarify words or phrases. E-mail is just words, leaving the door open for misinterpretation of our intended message. Anyone composing e-mail should be aware that it's electronic and could be easily forwarded, printed, and even broadcast to others. Broadcasting sensitive information could be very embarrassing to you and to others. Every e-mailer should be careful what he or she writes and follow the basic tenets of e-mail etiquette. For example, you should inform senders when you forward their e-mail. A good e-mail message includes a subject, has a logical flow, and concludes with a signature (name, association, and contact information).

Discussion: *What would be considered good netiquette?*

Discussion: *Describe e-mails that you have received (or seen) that you feel are in poor taste and out of step with good e-mail etiquette. What could the sender have done to modify the e-mail while retaining the essential message?*

THE UNWANTED CHAT ROOM GUEST

The Internet and information services, such as America Online, sponsor hundreds of topical chat rooms where participants chat (via text input) with one another about a specific topic. Topics range from auto repair to Little League baseball to "over 60" to Harley-Davidson motorcycles. However, it's not unusual for at least one of the participants to be an unwanted guest. Unwanted guests make rude or obnoxious comments that have nothing to do with the focus of the chat room. Sometimes these comments become inappropriately profane and personal, causing well-meaning participants to leave the chat room.

Discussion: *Should those who enter a public chat room have the right to talk about whatever they wish, disregarding the stated topic of the chat rooms?*

Discussion: *What, if anything, should be done to stop these unwanted guests from wasting the time of the other participants and violating the purpose of the chat room?*

ADS IN PERSONAL E-MAIL

The search continues by marketing people for better ways to reach customers via Internet advertising. One company has introduced a technology that marketing people can use to advertise their products and services within your personal e-mail messages. It works like this: your e-mails are intercepted at the mail server and then wrapped with advertising content. In theory, the advertising will be tailored to the individual receiving the e-mail based on his/her demographic profile. Marketers are hoping that e-mail recipients will continue to open personal mail and, whether they like it or not, read the advertisements, as well.

Discussion: *Internet companies have found it necessary to integrate advertising within their services. Is this approach to Net advertising justified given the current economic climate of Internet commerce?*

Discussion: *Is this approach more or less palatable than spam to the e-mail community? Why?*

DISCUSSION AND PROBLEM SOLVING

3-1.1   Describe at least three things you do now without the aid of online communications that may be done in the online environment in the near future.

3-1.2   The federal government is calling for "universal service" such that everyone has access to the "information superhighway." Is this an achievable goal? Explain.

3-1.3   Discuss how you would justify spending $15 to $25 a month to subscribe to an ISP for dialup Internet access. How would you justify spending $40 to $60 a month for broadband Internet access?

3-1.4   Speculate on how Internet appliances might change your life during the next decade.

3-1.5   Which two America Online channels would be of most interest to you? Explain.

3-1.6   What is the organizational affiliation of these Internet addresses: smith_jo@mkt.bigco.com; politics@washington.senate.gov; and hugh_roman@anthropology.stuniv.edu?

3-1.7   Expand and discuss the meaning of the following acronyms: TCP/IP, ISP, http, and URL.

3-1.8   Briefly describe one of the three levels at which you can connect your PC to the Internet.

3-2.1   The Microsoft Internet Explorer browser is now the most used browser in the world. A few years ago, the Netscape browser was the dominant browser. Some will argue that Netscape still makes the best browser. Speculate on what might have caused the turnaround.

3-2.2   The Internet has over 2 billion pages of information, some of which are placed online and not updated for years. Should there an effort to purge inactive information on the Internet? Explain.

3-2.3   What is your favorite portal on the Internet and why?

3-2.4   Why are there so many plugins for Internet browsers and why are they not built into the original browser software?

3-3.1   In what ways is the World Wide Web different from other servers on the Internet?

3-3.2   Describe circumstances for which you would prefer browsing the Net to using a search engine.

3-3.3   Discuss the pros and cons of FTPing on the Internet.

3-3.4   Videophones are available on the Internet now. Is this innovation in personal communications something you are looking forward to or dreading? Explain.

3-3.5 Would you prefer to receive traditional e-mail or audio mail? Explain.

3-3.6 Discuss the advantages and disadvantages of e-mail and instant messaging in a domestic setting, and in a business setting.

3-3.7 What type of information would you like to be sent to you automatically via Internet push technology?

3-3.8 Describe five things you would like to do on the Internet.

3-3.9 What is your favorite Internet application and why?

FOCUS ON PERSONAL COMPUTING

1. If you have not already done so, spend a few minutes doing some serendipitous surfing on the Internet via a dialup, narrowband Internet link. Do the same on a system with a broadband connection. Briefly describe how your perspective, what you did, and where you went changed when you began the broadband session.

2. On an Internet-enabled PC, do at least two of the following tasks. Search for and play the signal from an Internet radio station based in a country other than your own. Find, download, and play a hit song. Find a long-lost friend (where they live or work). Plan your dream vacation (flight schedules and lodging). Describe your activities.

3. Send an e-mail. Find and visit a newsgroup of interest to you. Set up instant messaging with several of your friends. Be a participant in an Internet chat room. If possible, hold a voice conversation over the Internet. Which of these means of Internet communications is of the greatest interest to you? Explain.

INTERNET EXERCISES @ www.prenhall.com/long

1. The Online Study Guide (multiple choice, true/false, matching, and essay questions)

2. Internet Learning Activities
- The Internet
- Going Online

3. Serendipitous Internet Activities
- Magazines

Chapter 4

Learning Objectives

Once you have read and studied this chapter, you will have learned:

● How data are stored and represented in a computer system (Section 4-1).

● The function of and relationships between the internal components of a personal computer, including the motherboard, processor, random-access memory (RAM) and other memories, ports, buses, expansion boards, and PC cards (Section 4-2).

● How to distinguish processors by their word size, speed, and memory capacity (Section 4-3).

● Several approaches to processor design (Section 4-4).

INSIDE THE COMPUTER

Why this chapter is important to you

A PC card here, a DVD drive there, a few GHz, and all of a sudden you're talking big bucks. A modern midlevel, communications-ready PC configured with a "standard" set of peripheral devices will run you about two grand. Hang on a few extras and add more power and you're over $3,000. And that's just the hardware! With Mom, Dad, and the kids all wanting their own PC, it's not unusual for expenditures on hardware to top that of the family car. With a significant portion of your budget at stake, you want to make informed decisions when purchasing PCs.

When you purchase a car, you know that it will perform its basic function—to carry people over roadways from point to point. Not so with PCs. PCs have thousands of functions, and when you purchase one, you want to be sure that it will do what you want it to do. Most of us can easily grasp the variables involved in buying a house or a car. The average car buyer can assess functionality and style relative to his or her budget constraints and aesthetic tastes, then make a reasonably informed decision. However, to get what you want and need in a PC, and to get the most for your money, you need to have an overall understanding of the essential elements of a computer.

One desktop PC looks about like another, with perhaps a little variation in color, style, and size. The same can be said of notebooks. Look inside, however, and they can be vastly different. Similar-looking PC boxes can be mansions or efficiency apartments on the inside. One might have a 2.8-GHz processor and another a much slower 1.2-GHz processor. Differences in processor speed, cache and RAM capacity, type of RAM, speed of the modem, what's embedded on the motherboard, the type of bus, and so on, dictate overall system performance and ability to enhance the system. If you understand these essential elements, you'll be able to make informed decisions when purchasing PCs—and that may be as often as once or twice a year for work and family. Those people who depend on advice from the PC salesperson may end up spending far more than necessary and still not get what they need to do the job.

WHY THIS SECTION
IS IMPORTANT
TO YOU

Much of what we see, hear, and do is going digital: music, cell phones, photographs, books, movies, catalogues, and much more. This section will help prepare you for immersion into an increasingly digital world.

4-1 Going Digital

A computer is an entertainment center with hundreds of interactive games. It's a virtual university providing interactive instruction and testing. It's a painter's canvas. It's a video telephone. It's a CD player. It's a home or office library. It's a television. It's the biggest marketplace in the world. It's the family photo album. It's a print shop. It's a wind tunnel that can test experimental airplane designs. It's a recorder. It's an alarm clock that can remind you to keep an appointment. It's an encyclopedia. It can perform thousands of specialty functions that require specialized skills, such as preparing taxes, drafting legal documents, counseling suicidal patients, and much more.

In all of these applications, the computer deals with everything as electronic signals. Electronic signals come in two flavors—**analog** and **digital**. Analog signals are *continuous* waveforms in which variations in frequency and amplitude can be used to represent information from sound and numerical data. Traditionally, the sound of our voice has been carried by analog signals when we talk on the telephone. That, however, is changing. Just about everything in the world of electronics and communication is *going digital* because computers are digital. Computers use digital signals where everything is described in two states: The circuit is either *on* or *off*. Generally, the *on* state is expressed or represented by the number 1 and the *off* state by the number 0.

So how do you go digital? You simply need to **digitize** your material. To digitize means to convert data, analog signals, and images into the discrete format (1s and 0s) that can be interpreted by computers. For example, Figure 4-1 shows how music can be digitized. Once digitized, you can use a computer to work with (revise and copy, among other things) the music recording, data, image, shape, and so on. Old recordings of artists from Enrico Caruso to the Beatles have been digitized and then digitally reconstructed on computers to eliminate unwanted distortion and static. Some of these reconstructed CDs are actually better than the originals!

BINARY DIGITS: 1 AND 0

The electronic nature of the computer makes it possible to combine the two digital states—*on* and *off*—to represent letters, numbers, colors, sounds, images, shapes, and even odors. An "on" or "off" electronic state is represented by a *bit,* short for binary digit. In the **binary** numbering system (base 2), the *on-bit* is a 1 and the *off-bit* is a 0. Physically, these states are achieved in a variety of ways.

- In RAM (temporary storage), the two electronic states often are represented by the presence or absence of an electrical charge in an integrated circuit—a computer chip (see Figure 4-2).
- In disk storage (permanent storage), the two states are made possible by the magnetic arrangement of the surface coating on magnetic disks (see Figure 4-3).
- In CDs and CD-ROMs, digital data are stored permanently as microscopic pits.
- In fiber optic cable, binary data flow through as pulses of light.

Bits may be fine for computers, but human beings are more comfortable with letters and decimal numbers (the base-10 numerals 0 through 9). We like to see colors and hear sounds. Therefore, the letters, decimal numbers, colors, and sounds we input into a computer system while doing word pro-

FIGURE 4-1

GOING DIGITAL WITH COMPACT DISCS
The recording industry has gone digital. To create a master CD, analog signals are converted to digital signals that can be manipulated by a computer and written to a master CD. The master is duplicated and the copies are sold through retail channels.

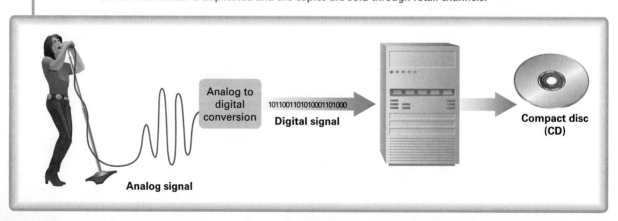

Analog signal

Analog to digital conversion

1011001101010001101000
Digital signal

Compact disc (CD)

cessing, graphics, and other applications must be translated into 1s and 0s for processing and storage. The computer translates the bits back into letters, decimal numbers, colors, and sounds for output on monitors, printers, speakers, and so on.

ENCODING SYSTEMS: BITS AND BYTES

Computers don't speak to one another in English, Spanish, or French. They have their own languages, which are better suited to electronic communication. In these languages, bits are combined according to an *encoding system* to represent letters, numbers, and special characters (such as *, $, +, and &), collectively referred to as *alphanumeric* characters.

ASCII and ANSI

ASCII (American Standard Code for Information Interchange—pronounced "*AS-key*") is the most popular encoding system for PCs and data communication. In ASCII, alphanumeric characters are *encoded* into a bit configuration on input so that the computer can interpret them. This coding equates a unique series of 1s and 0s with a specific character. Figure 4-4 shows the ASCII bit string of commonly used characters. Just as the words *mother* and *father* are arbitrary English-language character strings that refer to our parents, 01000010 is an arbitrary ASCII code that refers to the letter *B*. When you tap the letter *B* on a keyboard, the *B* is sent to the processor as a coded string of binary digits (01000010 in ASCII) as shown in Figure 4-5. The characters are *decoded* on output so we can interpret them. The combination of bits used to represent a character is called a *byte* (pronounced "*bite*").

FIGURE 4–2 Microminiaturization of the Chip's Bit
During the first generation of computers a bit was represented by a vacuum tube. This silicon wafer contains a number of thumbnail-sized Pentium 4 processor chips, each with the capability to process and store billions of bits.

Photo courtesy of Intel Corporation

FIGURE 4–3 Temporary and Permanent Storage
Digital video output is stored temporarily in the RAM chips on this circuit board (left), which enables displayed output from a PC. Video information can be stored permanently on magnetic disk (right). The time it takes to access information from this high-capacity Seagate disk drive is incredibly fast at around 5 milliseconds; however, accessing information stored in RAM is virtually instantaneous.

Courtesy of Sun Microsystems, Inc.
Courtesy of © Seagate Technology, Inc.

FIGURE 4-4

ASCII CODES

This figure shows the binary (base 2) ASCII codes, along with their decimal (base 10) and hexadecimal (hex, base 16) equivalents, for uppercase letters, numbers, and several special characters. The binary ASCII codes for uppercase and lowercase letters are similar. Replace the third binary digit with a 1 to get the lowercase equivalent of a capital letter (*B* is 01000010 and *b* is 01100010).

Character	ASCII Codes		
	Binary	**Decimal**	**Hex**
Space	00100000	32	20
!	00100001	33	21
"	00100010	34	22
#	00100011	35	23
$	00100100	36	24
%	00100101	37	25
&	00100110	38	26
'	00100111	39	27
(	00101000	40	28
)	00101001	41	29
*	00101010	42	2A
+	00101011	43	2B
,	00101100	44	2C
-	00101101	45	2D
.	00101110	46	2E
/	00101111	47	2F
0	00110000	48	30
1	00110001	49	31
2	00110010	50	32
3	00110011	51	33
4	00110100	52	34
5	00110101	53	35
6	00110110	54	36
7	00110111	55	37
8	00111000	56	38
9	00111001	57	39
A	01000001	65	41
B	01000010	66	42
C	01000011	67	43
D	01000100	68	44
E	01000101	69	45
F	01000110	70	46
G	01000111	71	47
H	01001000	72	48
I	01001001	73	49
J	01001010	74	4A
K	01001011	75	4B
L	01001100	76	4C
M	01001101	77	4D
N	01001110	78	4E
O	01001111	79	4F
P	01010000	80	50
Q	01010001	81	51
R	01010010	82	52
S	01010011	83	53
T	01010100	84	54
U	01010101	85	55
V	01010110	86	56
W	01010111	87	57
X	01011000	88	58
Y	01011001	89	59
Z	01011010	90	5A

The 7-bit ASCII code can represent up to 128 characters (2^7), but the PC byte is 8 bits. There are 256 (2^8) possible bit configurations in an 8-bit byte. Hardware and software vendors accept the 128 standard ASCII codes and use the extra 128 bit configurations to represent control characters (such as ringing a bell) or noncharacter images to complement their hardware or software product. Microsoft Windows uses the 8-bit **ANSI** encoding system (developed by the American National Standards Institute) to enable the sharing of text between Windows applications. The first 128 ANSI codes are the same as the ASCII codes, but the next 128 are defined to meet the specific needs of Windows applications.

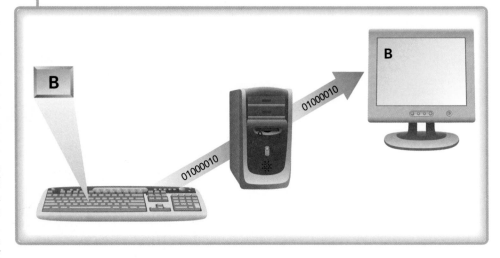

FIGURE 4–5 **ENCODING**
When you tap the B key on the keyboard, a binary representation of the letter *B* is sent to the processor. The processor sends the encoded *B* to the monitor, which interprets and displays a **B**.

Although the English language has considerably fewer than 128 printable characters, the extra bit configurations are needed to represent additional common and not-so-common special characters (such as - [hyphen]; @ [at]; | [a vertical bar]; and ~ [tilde]) and to signal a variety of activities to the computer (such as ringing a bell or telling the computer to accept a piece of datum).

Unicode

ASCII, with 128 character codes, is sufficient for the English language but we're now a global economy and ASCII falls far short of the Japanese language requirements (see Figure 4-6). The relatively new **Unicode**, a 16-bit encoding system, will enable computers and applications to talk to one another more easily and will handle most languages of the world (including Hebrew, Japanese, and Greek). Unicode's 16-bit code allows for 65,536 characters (2^{16}). Eventually, Unicode may be adopted as a standard for information interchange throughout the global computer community. Universal acceptance of the Unicode standard would make international communication in all areas easier, from monetary transfers between banks to e-mail.

FIGURE 4–6 **THE NEED FOR 16-BIT ENCODING**
An 8-bit encoding system, with its 256 unique bit configurations, is more than adequate to represent all of the alphanumeric characters used in the English language. The Japanese, however, need a 16-bit encoding system, like Unicode, to represent thousands of characters, some of which are shown on this Toyota Museum Web page. English has evolved as the language of the Internet, so many international sites give viewers an "English" option (see button at bottom).

Hexadecimal

Perhaps the biggest drawback to using the binary numbering system for computer operations is that we occasionally must deal with long and confusing strings of 1s and 0s. To reduce the confusion, the **hexadecimal**, or base-16, numbering system is used as shorthand to display the binary contents of RAM and disk storage.

Notice that the bases of the binary and hexadecimal numbering systems are multiples of 2—2 and 2^4, respectively. Because of this, there is a convenient relationship between these numbering systems. The table in Figure 4-7 illustrates that a single hexadecimal digit represents

FIGURE 4–7   NUMBERING SYSTEM EQUIVALENCE TABLE

Binary (Base 2)	Decinal (Base 10)	Hexadecimal (Base 16)
00	0	0
01	1	1
10	2	2
11	3	3
100	4	4
101	5	5
110	6	6
111	7	7
1000	8	8
1001	9	9
1010	10	A
1011	11	B
1100	12	C
1101	13	D
1110	14	E
1111	15	F
10000	16	10

four binary digits ($0111_2 = 7_{16}$, $1101_2 = D_{16}$, 1010_2, $= A_{16}$ where subscripts are used to indicate the base of the numbering system). Notice that in hexadecimal, or "hex," *letters* are used to represent the six higher-order digits.

Two hexadecimal digits can be used to represent an eight-bit byte. The binary and hex ASCII representations of the letter Z are 01011010_2 and $5A_{16}$, respectively. Figure 4-4 shows the binary, decimal, and "hex" equivalents for common characters.

SECTION SELF-CHECK

4-1.1   Data are stored permanently on magnetic storage devices, such as magnetic disk. (T/F)

4-1.2   Binary data flow through fiber optic cable as pulses of light. (T/F)

4-1.3   What are the two kinds of electronic signals: (a) analog and digital, (b) binary and octal, (c) alpha and numeric, or (d) bit and byte?

4-1.4   The combination of bits used to represent a character is called a: (a) bits on/off, (b) binary config, (c) 0-1 string, or (d) byte.

4-1.5   The 16-bit encoding system is called: (a) Unicorn, (b) Unicode, (c) Hexacode, or (d) 10 plus 6 code.

WHY THIS SECTION IS IMPORTANT TO YOU

If you want to take advantage of ever-advancing PC technology, get the most for your PC dollar, and allow your PC to grow with your capabilities, you need to know what's inside your PC. You need to know because personal computing is very personal. You are the decision maker. A little knowledge about what's inside can save you big bucks and make you a more effective user.

4-2   The PC System Unit

The processor, RAM, and a variety of other electronic components are housed in the *system unit,* usually a metal and plastic upright box (the tower), or inside the notebook's shell. As components get smaller, the system unit is being redefined with the integration of system unit components and the monitor into a single unit. In this section, we'll look inside the box at the major components of a computer system. Figure 4-8 gives you a peek inside the system unit of a PC.

Someday we won't have to worry about what's inside a PC. That day, however, will not be any time soon. So, let's start with the component that ties it all together, the *motherboard*.

THE MOTHERBOARD: THE CENTRAL NERVOUS SYSTEM

The *motherboard,* a single circuit board, provides the path through which the processor communicates with memory components and peripheral devices. Think of the processor as the PC's brain and the motherboard as the PC's central nervous system. Continuing the analogy, think of the motherboard's **chipset** as the heart of the system, controlling the flow of information between system components

FIGURE 4–8

SYSTEM UNIT AND MOTHERBOARD
The system unit is this box and its contents—the computer system's electronic circuitry, including the motherboard with the processor and various expansion boards (added capabilities discussed later in this chapter), and various storage devices.

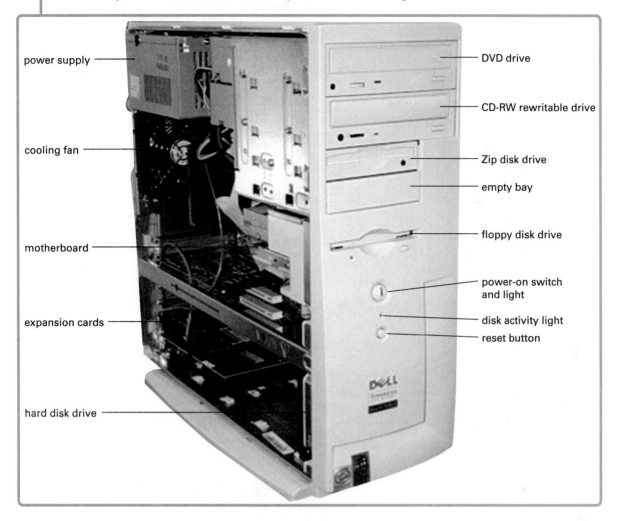

power supply

cooling fan

motherboard

expansion cards

hard disk drive

DVD drive

CD-RW rewritable drive

Zip disk drive

empty bay

floppy disk drive

power-on switch and light

disk activity light

reset button

connected to the board. The chipset is important because it determines what features are supported on the system (including types of processors and memory). In a personal computer, the following are attached to the motherboard (see Figure 4-9):

- Processor (main processor)
- Support electronic circuitry, such as the chipset
- Memory chips (for example, RAM and other types of memory)
- Expansion boards (optional circuit boards, such as a fax/modem)

The various chips have standard-sized pin connectors that allow them to be attached to the motherboard and, therefore, to a common electrical **bus** that permits data flow between the various system components.

Just as big cities have mass transit systems that move large numbers of people, the computer has a similar system that moves billions of bits a second. Both transit systems use buses, although the one in the computer doesn't have wheels. All electrical signals travel on a common electrical bus. The term *bus* was derived from its wheeled cousin because passengers on both buses (people and bits) can get off at any stop. In a computer, the bus stops are the processor's control unit and its arithmetic and logic unit, RAM and other types of internal memory, and the **device controllers** (small computers) that control the operation of the peripheral devices.

Ultimately, the type of processor and the amount of RAM placed on the motherboard define the PC's speed and capacity. The central component of the motherboard, the processor, is generally not made by the manufacturers of PCs. Companies that specialize in the development and manufacture of processors make it. A number of companies make PC processors, including Intel, Motorola, Advanced Micro Devices (AMD), and IBM.

FIGURE 4–9

MOTHERBOARD
Shown here is a motherboard ready to be installed to a PC (top) and the same motherboard installed in a system unit (bottom) and configured with a 2.8-GHz (gigahertz) Intel Pentium 4 processor (under the cooling fan) and 1 GB of RAM in two DIMMs.

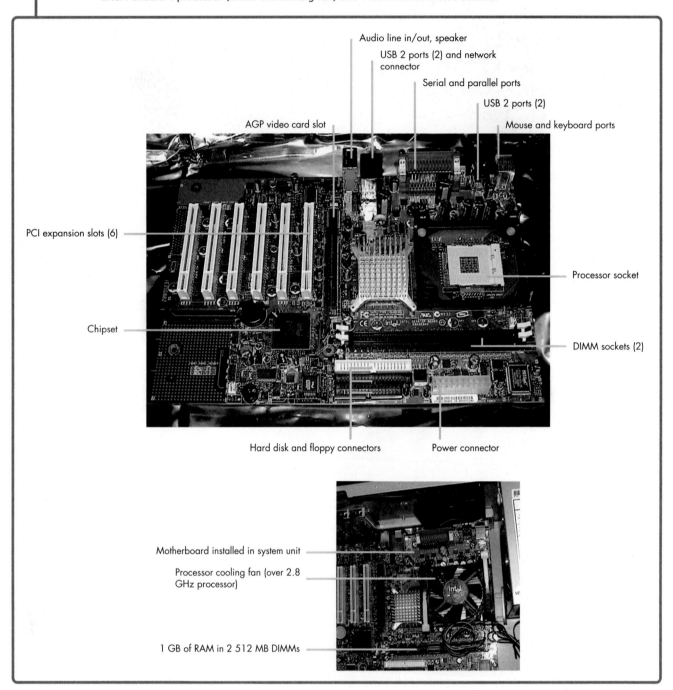

Audio line in/out, speaker

USB 2 ports (2) and network connector

Serial and parallel ports

USB 2 ports (2)

Mouse and keyboard ports

AGP video card slot

PCI expansion slots (6)

Processor socket

Chipset

DIMM sockets (2)

Hard disk and floppy connectors

Power connector

Motherboard installed in system unit

Processor cooling fan (over 2.8 GHz processor)

1 GB of RAM in 2 512 MB DIMMs

THE PROCESSOR: COMPUTER ON A CHIP

What is smaller than a postage stamp and found in wristwatches, sewing machines, and CD players? The answer is a *processor*. The processor is literally a "computer on a chip." We use the term *chip* to refer to any self-contained integrated circuit. The size of chips varies from fingernail size to postage-stamp size (about 1-inch square). Processors and small processors, called microprocessors, have been integrated into thousands of mechanical and electronic devices—even elevators, band saws, and ski-boot bindings. In a few years, virtually everything mechanical or electronic will incorporate processor technology into its design (see Figure 4-10).

The motherboard for the original (1981) and most of the *IBM PC-compatible* computers manufactured through 1984 used the Intel 8088 microprocessor chip. Since then, Intel has introduced a succession of increasingly more advanced processors to power the IBM PC-compatible PCs, called *PC compati-*

bles or, simply, *PCs*. The Intel "286" (Intel 80286), "386," and "486" processors took us into the 1990s followed by the Intel **Pentium®**, **Pentium® Pro, Pentium® II,** and **Pentium® III** series. Most new system units have an Intel **Pentium 4®** (see Figure 4-11), **Celeron®**, or **Itanium™** processor inside. The more expensive Pentium 4 or Itanium-based PCs offer the greatest performance, whereas the less expensive Celeron-based PCs offer good value with reduced performance.

Gordon Moore, cofounder of Intel Corporation, made a prediction in 1965 that has proven to be remarkably accurate. Moore's Law states that *the density of transistors on a chip doubles every 18 months.* Often Moore's Law is stated in terms of *processing power,* which is directly related to the density of a chip's transistors. Dr. Andy Grove, the other cofounder of Intel, has said that Moore's Law has become a self-fulfilling prophecy at Intel because no engineer wants to design a chip that would fall

FIGURE 4–10 Microprocessors Everywhere
Microprocessors are present in almost every aspect of our lives. The electrical and mechanical appliances plus a variety of personal computers are networked throughout this Portland, Oregon home. Microprocessors and structured wiring allows audio, video, computer and Internet signals to be routed anywhere in the home. Several wireless Tablet PCs allow home owners to surf the Web and control the connected products around their home from anywhere in the house.

Photo courtesy of Intel Corporation

below this implied standard. Some experts say that chip designers will begin to bump up against the laws of physics around 2005 and the pace of chip evolution may slow.

FIGURE 4–11 Intel Pentium 4 Processor
About the size of four keys on a keyboard, this 1.8-GHz Mobile Pentium 4 processor provides the processing capability for this notebook PC.

Photo courtesy of Intel Corporation

Inside the Processor

The processor runs the show and is the nucleus of any computer system. Regardless of the complexity of a processor, sometimes called the **central processing unit** or **CPU**, it has only two fundamental sections: the *control unit* and the *arithmetic and logic unit*. These units work together with RAM and other internal memories to make the processor, and the computer system, go. Figure 4-12 illustrates the interaction between computer system components.

The Control Unit

The **control unit** is the command center of the processor. It has three primary functions:

- To read and interpret program instructions
- To direct the operation of internal processor components
- To control the flow of programs and data in and out of RAM

During program execution, the first in a sequence of program instructions is moved from RAM to the control unit, where it is decoded and interpreted by the **decoder.** The control unit then directs other processor components to carry out the operations necessary to execute the instruction.

The processor contains high-speed working storage areas called **registers** that can store no more than a few bytes (see Figure 4-12). Because registers reside on the processor chip, they handle instructions and data at very high speeds and are used for a variety of processing functions. One register, called the **instruction register,** contains the instruction being executed. Other general-purpose registers store data needed for immediate processing. Registers also store status information. For example, the **program register** contains the location in RAM of the next instruction to be executed. Registers facilitate the processing and movement of data and instructions between RAM, the control unit, and the arithmetic and logic unit.

FIGURE 4–12

INTERACTION BETWEEN COMPUTER SYSTEM COMPONENTS
During processing, instructions and data are passed between the various types of internal memories, the processor's control unit and arithmetic and logic unit, and the peripheral devices over the common electrical bus. A system clock paces the speed of operation within the processor and ensures that everything takes place in timed intervals.

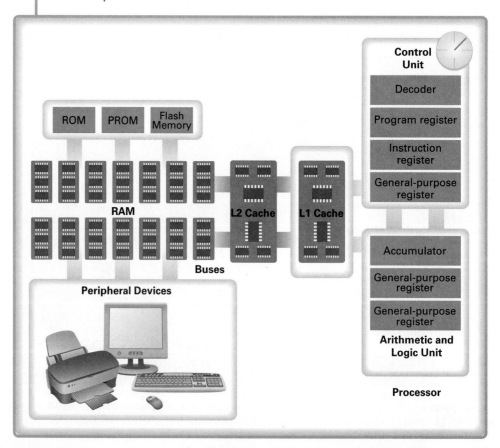

The Arithmetic and Logic Unit

The **arithmetic and logic unit** performs all computations (addition, subtraction, multiplication, and division) and all logic operations (comparisons). The results are placed in a register called the **accumulator.** Examples of *computations* include the payroll deduction for social security, the day-end inventory level, and the balance on a bank statement. A *logic* operation compares two pieces of data, either alphabetic or numeric. Based on the result of the comparison, the program "branches" to one of several alternative sets of program instructions. For example, in an inventory system each item in stock is compared to a reorder point at the end of each day. If the inventory level falls below the reorder point, a sequence of program instructions is executed that produces a purchase order.

RAM: Digital Warehouse

RAM enables data to be both read and written to *solid-state* memory. It is **volatile memory** because when the electrical current is turned off or interrupted, the data are lost. In contrast to permanent storage on disk, RAM provides the processor with only *temporary* storage for programs and data. All programs and data must be transferred to RAM from an input device (such as a keyboard) or from disk before programs can be executed and data can be processed. Once a program is no longer in use, the storage space it occupied is assigned to another program awaiting execution. Programs and data are loaded to RAM from disk storage because the time required to access a program instruction or piece of datum from RAM is significantly less than from disk storage. RAM is essentially a high-speed holding area for data and programs. In fact, *nothing really happens in a computer system until the program instructions and data are moved from RAM to the processor.*

The processor, according to program instructions, manipulates the data in RAM. A program instruction or a piece of datum is stored in a specific RAM location called an **address.** RAM is analogous to the rows of boxes you see in post offices. Just as each Post Office box has a number, each byte in RAM has an address. Addresses permit program instructions and data to be located, accessed, and processed. The content of each address changes frequently as different programs are executed and new data are processed.

The transfer of data to and from RAM is very fast because solid-state electronic circuitry has no moving parts. Electrically charged points in the RAM chips represent the bits (1s and 0s) that comprise the data and other information stored in RAM. RAM is attached to the motherboard, like the processor, and therefore to the electronic bus. Over the past two decades, researchers have given us a succession of RAM technologies, each designed to keep pace with ever-faster processors. Most new PCs are being equipped with **synchronous dynamic RAM (SDRAM), DDR SDRAM** (a newer "double data rate" SDRAM), or **Rambus DRAM (RDRAM).**

A state-of-the-art memory chip, smaller than a postage stamp, can store about 128,000,000 bits, or more than 12,000,000 characters of data! Physically, memory chips are installed on **single in-line memory modules,** or **SIMMs,** and on the newer **dual in-line memory modules,** or **DIMMs.** SIMMs are less expensive but have only a 32-bit data path to the processor, whereas DIMMs have a 64-bit data path. The RDRAM chips are installed on **rambus in-line memory modules (RIMMs).** The modules are about an inch high and four to six inches long (see Figure 4-9).

Cache and Other High-Speed Memories

Data and programs are being continually moved in and out of RAM at electronic speeds. But that's not fast enough. To achieve even faster transfer of instructions and data to the processor, computers are designed with **cache memory** (see Figure 4-12). Computer designers use cache memory to increase computer system throughput. **Throughput** refers to the rate at which work can be performed by a computer system.

Like RAM, cache is a high-speed holding area for program instructions and data. However, cache memory uses internal storage technologies that are much faster (and much more expensive) than conventional RAM. With only a fraction of the capacity of RAM, cache memory holds only those instructions and data that are *likely* to be needed next by the processor. Cache memory is effective because, in a typical session, the same data or instructions are accessed over and over. The processor first checks cache memory for needed data and instructions, thereby reducing the number of accesses to the slower RAM. When you purchase a PC, you will see references to level 1 (L1) and level 2 (L2) cache. *Level 1 cache* is built into the processor, whereas *level 2 cache* is on another chip, sitting between the processor and RAM (see Figure 4-12). L2 cache is ultra-fast memory that buffers the transfer of information between the processor and RAM, thereby accelerating internal data movement.

The user cannot alter another special type of internal memory, called *read-only memory (ROM)* (see Figure 4-7). The contents of **ROM** (rhymes with *"mom"*) are "hard-wired" (designed into the logic of the memory chip) by the manufacturer and can be "read only." When you turn on a microcomputer system, a program in ROM automatically readies the computer system for use and produces the initial display-screen prompt. A variation of ROM is **programmable read-only memory (PROM).** PROM is ROM into which you, the user, can load read-only programs and data.

THE CRYSTAL BALL:
Will Solid-State Memory Replace Rotating Memory? Many mainframe computers of the 1960s had only 512 KB of RAM. That amount of RAM was housed in refrigerator-size cabinets and could cost up to a million dollars. Today, digital cameras have thumbnail-size memory cards with 1,000 times that amount of RAM (512 MB of RAM) at a millionth the cost per byte. At an internal seminar in 1968, an IBM researcher told IBMers that all memory (RAM) in all the computers in the world at that time would fit into a brandy snifter by the turn of the century. Well, he was right. Indications are that we are in a transition from the relatively slow rotating disk storage to high-speed solid-state memory.

FIGURE 4–13 The Flash Memory Card
Nonvolatile flash memory cards are being used in many consumer products, such as digital cameras (shown here) and MP3 players. The flash cards hold images in the digital camera until the content can be uploaded to a personal computer. The memory card can be inserted directly into some PCs.

Photo courtesy of Intel Corporation

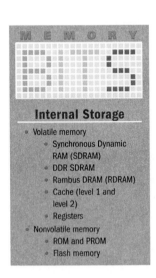

Flash memory (see Figure 4-13) is a type of PROM that can be altered easily by the user. Flash memory can be found on all new PCs, I/O devices, and storage devices. It is **nonvolatile memory** that retains its contents after an electrical interruption. The logic capabilities of these devices can be upgraded by simply downloading new software from the Internet or a vendor-supplied disk to flash memory. Upgrades to early PCs and peripheral devices required the user to replace the old circuit board or chip with a new one. The emergence of flash memory has eliminated this time-consuming and costly method of upgrade. The PC's **BIOS** (Basic Input Output System) is stored in flash memory. The built-in BIOS software contains the instructions needed to boot (start up) the PC and load the operating system. It also contains specific instructions on the operation of the keyboard, monitor, disk drives, and other devices. A PC's BIOS software should be periodically upgraded to the most recent version so that the PC can recognize new innovations in I/O and disk/disc storage.

What Happens Inside: Unraveling the Mystery

BASIC is a popular programming language. The simple BASIC program in Figure 4-14 computes and displays the sum of any two numbers (22 and 44 in the example). The instructions in this example program are intuitive; that is, you don't really need to know BASIC to understand what is happening. Figure 4-14 gives you insight into how a processor works by showing the interaction between RAM, the control unit, and the arithmetic and logic unit during the execution of this program. There is actually more going on in the processor, but this example captures the essence of what's happening. Figure 4-14 uses only 10 RAM locations and only for data. In practice, both programs and data would be stored in RAM, which usually has a minimum of 64 million storage locations.

The statement-by-statement walkthrough in Figure 4-14 illustrates generally what happens as each BASIC instruction is executed. More complex arithmetic and input/output tasks involve further repetitions of these fundamental operations. Logic operations (greater than, less than, equal to, and so on) are similar, with values being compared between RAM locations, the accumulator, and the various registers (see Figure 4-12).

The Instruction Cycle

We communicate with computers by telling them what to do in their native tongue—the machine language. You may have heard of computer programming languages such as BASIC (in Figure 4-14) and C++. Dozens of these languages are in common usage, but all need to be translated into the only language that a computer understands—its own **machine language.** Typically, each instruction in a human-oriented language, like BASIC, is translated into several machine language instructions. As you might expect, machine language instructions are represented inside the computer as strings of binary digits.

These instructions are executed within the framework of an **instruction cycle.** The speed of a processor is sometimes measured by how long it takes to complete an instruction cycle. The timed interval that comprises the instruction cycle is the total of the *instruction time,* or *I-time,* and the *execution time,* or *E-time.* The actions that take place during the instruction cycle are shown in Figure 4-15.

Most modern processors are capable of **pipelining;** that is, they can begin executing another instruction before the current instruction is completed. In fact, several instructions can be pipelined simultaneously, each at a different part of the instruction cycle. Pipelining improves system throughput significantly.

PUTTING IT ALL TOGETHER

The motherboard, with its processor and memory, is ready for work. Alone, though, a motherboard is like a college with no students. The motherboard must be linked to I/O, storage, and communication devices to receive data and return the results of processing.

A Fleet of Buses

The typical desktop motherboard includes several empty **expansion slots** (see Figure 4-9) that provide direct connections to the common electrical bus. These slots let you expand the capabilities of a PC by plugging in a wide variety of special-function **expansion boards,** also called **expansion cards.** These add-on circuit boards contain the electronic circuitry for many supplemental capabilities, such as extra ports, a modem, or video capture capability. Expansion boards are made to fit a particular type of bus. These are the more popular types of buses for PC compatibles:

- *PCI local bus.* The **PCI (Peripheral Component Interconnect) local bus** enables expansion boards to be linked directly to the system's common bus. Modern motherboards normally include several PCI local bus slots for expansion boards.

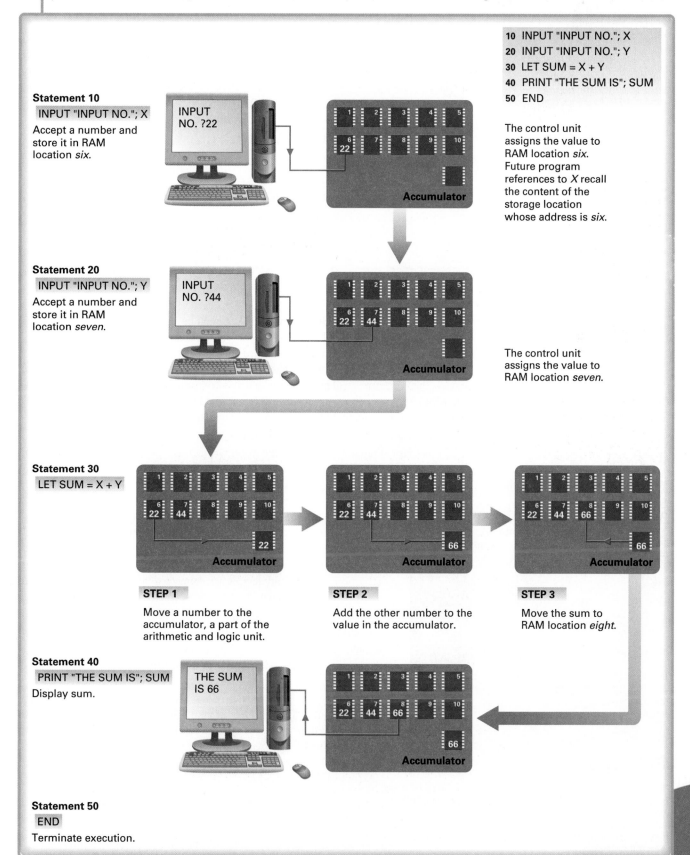

FIGURE 4–14   **WHAT HAPPENS INSIDE THE PROCESSOR**
Illustrated here is the essence of what happens inside a computer when the five-instruction BASIC program shown here is executed. The RAM in this example has 10 numbered storage locations. The accumulator is part of the arithmetic and logic unit.

10 INPUT "INPUT NO."; X
20 INPUT "INPUT NO."; Y
30 LET SUM = X + Y
40 PRINT "THE SUM IS"; SUM
50 END

Statement 10
INPUT "INPUT NO."; X
Accept a number and store it in RAM location *six*.

INPUT NO. ?22

The control unit assigns the value to RAM location *six*. Future program references to *X* recall the content of the storage location whose address is *six*.

Statement 20
INPUT "INPUT NO."; Y
Accept a number and store it in RAM location *seven*.

INPUT NO. ?44

The control unit assigns the value to RAM location *seven*.

Statement 30
LET SUM = X + Y

STEP 1
Move a number to the accumulator, a part of the arithmetic and logic unit.

STEP 2
Add the other number to the value in the accumulator.

STEP 3
Move the sum to RAM location *eight*.

Statement 40
PRINT "THE SUM IS"; SUM
Display sum.

THE SUM IS 66

Statement 50
END
Terminate execution.

FIGURE 4–15 THE INSTRUCTION CYCLE

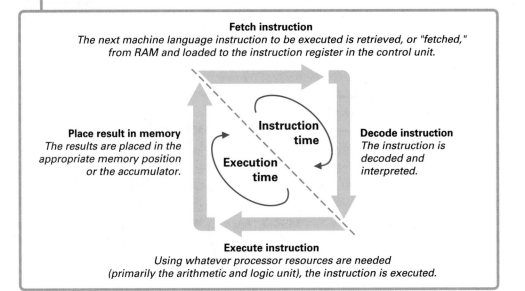

Fetch instruction
The next machine language instruction to be executed is retrieved, or "fetched," from RAM and loaded to the instruction register in the control unit.

Instruction time

Execution time

Place result in memory
The results are placed in the appropriate memory position or the accumulator.

Decode instruction
The instruction is decoded and interpreted.

Execute instruction
Using whatever processor resources are needed (primarily the arithmetic and logic unit), the instruction is executed.

PERSONAL COMPUTING:
Planning for USB USB (universal serial bus) 2.0 offers transmission speeds 40 times faster than the original USB standard. The new USB standard, which is available with new PCs, is backwards compatible, so you can continue to use early USB devices. When purchasing peripheral devices, look for the high-speed USB logo to ensure that they meet the emerging de facto standard, USB 2.0. Also, be aware that each USB port is considered an independent path which can transmit information no faster than the lowest performing element on the USB connection (USB devices can be daisy-chained). Avoid mixing and matching USB standards and either select a PC with plenty of USB 2.0 ports (six is usually sufficient) or choose a USB 2.0 hub.

- *Universal Serial Bus.* The **Universal Serial Bus** (**USB**) permits up to 127 peripheral devices to be connected to a single USB port (see Figure 4-16). The USB port eliminates the hassle of installing expansion cards. PC peripheral devices are designed to connect to the USB port on the motherboard. The USB **hot plug** feature allows peripheral devices to be connected to or removed from the USB port while the PC is running. This is especially helpful to gamers who like to switch game controllers when they begin a new game. Newer hardware is based on **USB 2.0,** a standard that permits data transfer at 480 M bps, about 40 times faster than the original USB standard.

- *1394 bus.* The **1394 bus** is a recent bus standard that supports data transfer rates of up to 400M bps, over 30 times faster than the USB bus. In the Apple world, this type of bus is called **FireWire.** The consumer electronics industry is very excited about the 1394 bus because it is ideal for devices that need to transfer data at very high speed in real time, such as audio/video (A/V) appliances. Up to 63 external devices can be daisy-chained to a 1394 port. Like USB, 1394 supports hot plugging.

- *SCSI bus.* The **SCSI** (**Small Computer System Interface**) **bus,** or "scuzzy" bus, provides an alternative to the expansion bus. Up to 15 SCSI peripheral devices can be daisy-chained to a SCSI interface expansion card via the SCSI port. That is, the devices are connected along a single cable, both internal and external, with multiple SCSI connectors (see Figure 4-17).

- *AGP bus.* The **AGP** (**Accelerated Graphics Port**) **bus** is a special-function bus designed to accommodate the throughput demands of high-resolution 3-D graphics. This special bus provides a direct link between the graphics adapter, which feeds video data to the monitor, and RAM.

In time, most of the peripheral devices will be designed for the easy-to-use USB and/or 1394 buses. Most new PCs come with at least one FireWire (1394) port and at least a couple of USB ports. FireWire is used mostly for devices that require high data transfer rates, such as digital video cameras and auxiliary hard disks.

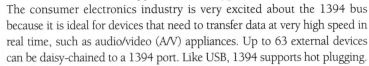

FIGURE 4–16 Peripherals World Record
Television personality Bill Nye, "The Science Guy," helped connect 111 peripheral devices to a single PC via a USB port, setting a new world record. Peripherals ranged from mice, joysticks, and keyboards to digital speakers and video conferencing systems.
Photo courtesy of Intel Corporation

Ports: Digital Entry/Exit Points on a PC

In a PC, external peripheral devices (such as a printer and a mouse) usually come with a cable and a multipin connector. To link a device to the PC, you plug its connector into a socket in much the same way you plug a lamp cord into an electrical outlet. The socket, called a *port*, provides a direct link to the PC's common electrical bus on the motherboard via a particular type of bus, such as the USB or PCI. Ports on a typical PC are shown in Figure 4-18.

External peripheral devices and other computers can be linked to the processor via cables or a wireless connection. The motherboard is designed with several port options, including at least one serial port and parallel port each, a keyboard port, a mouse port, plus a couple of USB ports.

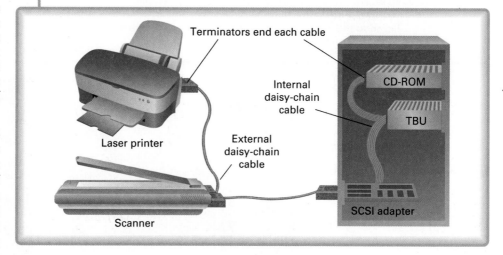

FIGURE 4–17 **SCSI BUS**
Two external devices, a printer and a scanner, are daisy-chained on the SCSI's external cable. Two internal devices, the CD-ROM and the tape backup unit, are daisy-chained on the SCSI's internal cable. Terminators are attached at the end of each cable to denote the end of the chain.

Terminators end each cable
Internal daisy-chain cable
CD-ROM
TBU
Laser printer
External daisy-chain cable
Scanner
SCSI adapter

- *Serial port.* The **serial port** allows the serial transmission of data, one bit at a time (see Figure 4-19). Imagine a line of fans going single-file through a turnstile at a high school football game. An external modem might be connected to a serial port. The standard for PC serial ports is the 9-pin or 25-pin (male or female) **RS-232C connector.** One of the 9 or 25 lines carries the serial signal to the peripheral device, and another line carries the signal from the device. The other lines carry control signals.

- *Parallel port.* The **parallel port** allows the parallel transmission of data; that is, several bits are transmitted simultaneously. Figure 4-19 illustrates how 8-bit bytes travel in parallel over 8 separate lines. Imagine 8 lines of fans going through 8 adjacent turnstiles at an NFL football game. Extra lines carry control signals. Parallel ports use the same 25-pin RS-232C connector or the 36-pin **Centronics connector.** These ports provide the interface for such devices as printers, external magnetic tape or disk backup units, and other computers.

- *SCSI port.* The **SCSI port** provides a parallel interface to the SCSI bus that enables faster data transmission than with serial and parallel ports. Also, up to 15 peripheral devices can be daisy-chained to a single SCSI port; that is, they are connected along a single cable. The typical off-the-shelf PC compatible may not come with a SCSI bus, the add-on circuitry needed for a SCSI port.

- *USB port.* The **USB port** is a relatively recent innovation in high-speed device interfaces. Most new PCs have up to six USB ports. Most new peripherals are set up to use USB ports; however, the USB cable may not be included with the new product. It is purchased as an accessory item.

- *1394 port.* The **1394 port** is the newest and fastest port. The 1394 bus is still a little pricey and is not included on all new PCs. Many people use their 1394 port to connect an external hard drive, a device that demands very fast data transfer rates.

- *Dedicated keyboard and mouse ports.* These two ports have a round 6-pin connector.

- *IrDA port.* The **IrDA port,** or **infrared port,** transmits data via infrared light waves. Many PCs and devices, such as printers, come with IrDA ports. As long as the devices are within a few feet, data can be transferred without the use of cables.

A variety of ports shown in Figure 4-18 enable system links with a joystick or MIDI music device (via the *game port*), cable television, a local area network, a telephone line, the monitor, and other devices.

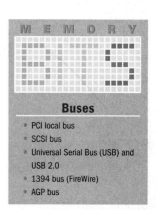

M E M O R Y

Buses
- PCI local bus
- SCSI bus
- Universal Serial Bus (USB) and USB 2.0
- 1394 bus (FireWire)
- AGP bus

PC GROWTH: ADDING CAPABILITIES

Today's PCs are designed such that they can grow with your personal computing needs. Initially you purchase what you need and/or can afford, then purchase and install optional capabilities as required.

Expansion Boards

The *expansion slots* associated with expansion buses (PCI, SCSI, AGP, etc.) let you add features to your PC by adding *expansion boards*. The number of available expansion slots varies from computer to computer (see Figure 4-9). Keep in mind that an expansion board and/or peripheral device is designed for use with

FIGURE 4-18

MAKING THE CONNECTION TO THE SYSTEM UNIT
Typically, external connections to the motherboard and expansion cards are made to the ports at the rear of the system unit. The various ports are labeled in the first illustration. Several of the many possible cables that can be connected to the ports are shown left to right (SCSI to scanner and parallel to printer in inset, SCSI to adapter, USB, coaxial network cable, keyboard, mouse, video, parallel, L and R speakers, microphone, headset, serial). Also shown is the hodgepodge of wires that result when devices are linked to the system unit. As you can see, a large number of devices using a variety of connectors and cables can be linked to a PC.

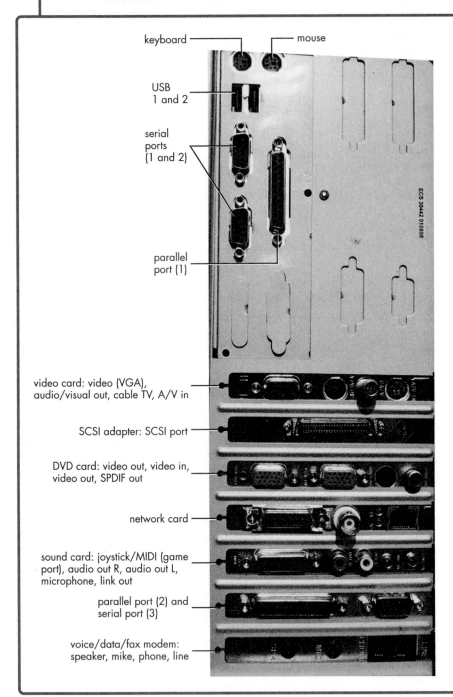

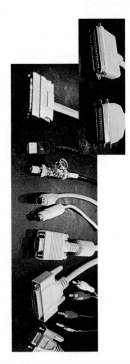

keyboard — mouse

USB 1 and 2

serial ports (1 and 2)

parallel port (1)

ECS 30442 010898

video card: video (VGA), audio/visual out, cable TV, A/V in

SCSI adapter: SCSI port

DVD card: video out, video in, video out, SPDIF out

network card

sound card: joystick/MIDI (game port), audio out R, audio out L, microphone, link out

parallel port (2) and serial port (3)

voice/data/fax modem: speaker, mike, phone, line

a particular type of expansion bus (PCI, SCSI, and so on). There are literally hundreds of expansion boards from which to choose. You will find these on most PCs:

- *Graphics adapter.* These adapters permit interfacing with video monitors. The VGA (video graphics array) board and the newer **AGP board** enable the interfacing of high-resolution monitors with the processor.

- *Sound.* The sound card, which is included on most new PCs, makes two basic functions possible. First, it enables sounds to be captured and stored on disk. Second, it enables sounds, including music and spoken words, to be played through external speakers. The sound card can add realism to computer games with stereo music and sound effects. It also allows us to speak commands and enter words to our PCs via speech recognition. The typical sound card will have receptacles for a microphone, a headset, an audio output, and a joystick. Basic sound card functionality is built into some motherboards; however, if you wish to have top-quality audio, you might want to upgrade to a sound card.

- *Data/voice/fax modem.* A *modem* permits communication with remote computers via a telephone-line link. The **data/voice/fax modem** performs the same function as a regular modem, plus it has added capability. It enables you to receive and make telephone calls, and it enables your PC to emulate a **fax** machine. Fax machines transfer images of documents via telephone lines to another location.

Depending on your applications needs, you might wish to enhance your system with some of these capabilities:

- *USB hub.* Plug a **USB hub** into a single USB port to expand the number of available USB ports (usually to either three, four, or five extra USB ports). The typical PC will need from 2 to 10 USB ports.

- *Network interface card.* The **network interface card** (**NIC**) enables and controls the exchange of data between the PCs in a local area network or a home network. Each PC in a network must be equipped with an NIC.

- *SCSI interface card.* The SCSI bus can be built into the motherboard or installed as an expansion board.

- *Video capture card.* This card enables full-motion color video with audio to be captured and played on a monitor or stored on disk. To capture video and convert it to digital format, simply plug the standard cable from the video camera or VCR into the video capture card and play the video. Once on disk storage, video information can be edited; that is, the content can be rearranged and integrated with text, graphics, special effects, and other forms of presentation, as desired. Some all-in-one AGP graphics cards include video capture card functionality, eliminating the need for a separate graphics card.

Personal computers are composed of components that are assembled in a case—the motherboard, the processor, several disks/discs, expansion boards as needed, and so on. Each year thousands of people order the components and build their own desktop PCs. Once you have the components in hand (see Figure 4-20), the assembly takes from one to three hours.

FIGURE 4–19 SERIAL AND PARALLEL DATA TRANSMISSION
In serial transmission, outgoing and incoming bits flow one-at-a-time through a single line. In parallel transmission, bytes flow together over eight separate lines.

To processor

0101001101010101010100100100100101000001101001100

From processor

0011001010000010100100100100101010101010101010011001010

Serial transmission

To processor

00000000 00000000 00000000
11111111 111111111 11111111
00000000 00000000 00000000
10100000 10100000 10100000
00001101 00001101 00001101
00001111 00001111 00001111
00100000 00100000 00100000
01010010 01010010 01010010

Parallel transmission

FIGURE 4–20 Build Your Own PC
Many people of all ages and backgrounds build their own desktop PCs. A junior high school student ordered these components and built his own high-end custom PC. All that is needed to assemble the components and load the operating system is a screwdriver. The components for this high-end PC include: (in the front) a 120-GB hard disk, a DVD drive, a PCI sound card, a 2.8-GHz Intel Pentium 4 processor and processor cooling fan, and two 512-MB DIMMs of DDR SDRAM; (in middle) a tower case with a 400-watt power supply and three cooling fans, a Zip disk drive, a DVD/CD read/write drive, and an Intel motherboard; and (on top) the Windows XP operating system and an AGP video card with 128 MB of video RAM. The PC was not configured with a modem because it would be linked to an Internet-enabled home network via the network interface card that is embedded in the motherboard.
Long and Associates

PC Cards: PCMCIA Technology

The **PCMCIA card**, sometimes called a **PC card**, is a credit card-sized removable expansion module that is plugged into an external PCMCIA expansion slot on a PC, usually a notebook (see Figure 4-21). The PC card functions like an expansion board in that it offers a wide variety of capabilities. PC cards can be expanded RAM, programmable nonvolatile flash memory, network interface cards (wireless and wired), data/voice/fax modems, hard-disk cards, and much more. For example, one PC card comes in the form of a mobile **GPS** (**global positioning system**). The mobile GPS card can be used to pinpoint the latitude and longitude of the user within a few feet, anywhere on or near earth. Business travelers use GPS cards in conjunction with computer-based road maps to help them get around in unfamiliar cities.

Notebook computers are equipped with at least one PCMCIA-compliant interface. PDAs (personal digital assistants) and notebook PCs do not have enough space for as many expansion slots as do their desktop cousins. Interchangeable PC cards let laptop users insert capabilities as they are needed. For example, a user can insert a data/voice/fax modem PC card to send e-mail, then do a *hot swap* (PC remains running) with a hard disk card to access corporate maintenance manuals.

FIGURE 4–21 PC Cards for Notebooks
Notebook PCs, because of their compact size, have fewer expansion slots than desktop PCs. For this reason, notebook PCs are designed with PCMCIA expansion slots. PC cards are plugged into PCMCIA expansion slots to give the system added capability. This PC Card, which is shown with its PCI card counterpart, serves as a wireless network interface card (NIC) or a wireless voice/data/fax modem.

Courtesy of Symbol Technologies, Inc.

SECTION SELF-CHECK

4-2.1	The arithmetic and logic unit controls the flow of programs and data in and out of main memory. (T/F)
4-2.2	The RS-232C connector provides the interface to a port. (T/F)
4-2.3	The rate at which work can be performed by a computer system is called: (a) system spray, (b) throughput, (c) push through, or (d) volume load.
4-2.4	The timed interval that comprises the instruction cycle is the total of the instruction time and: (a) execution time, (b) I-time, (c) X-time, or (d) delivery time.
4-2.5	PC components are linked via a common electrical: (a) train, (b) bus, (c) car, or (d) plane.

4-3 Describing the Processor and Its Performance

How do we distinguish one computer from the other? Much the same way we'd distinguish one person from the other. When describing someone we generally note gender, height, weight, and age. When describing computers or processors, we talk about *word size, core speed, bus speed,* and the *memory capacity* because it is these elements that make the biggest contribution to system performance. For example, a computer might be described as a 64-bit, 3.4-GHz, 1-GB PC with a 533 MHz bus. Let's see what this means.

WORD SIZE: BUS WIDTH

Just as the brain sends and receives signals through the central nervous system, the processor sends and receives electrical signals through its common electrical bus a word at a time. A **word**, or *bus width,* describes the number of bits that are handled as a unit within a particular computer system's bus or during internal processing. Internal processing involves the movement of data and commands between registers, the control unit, and the arithmetic and logic unit (see Figure 4-12). Many popular computers have 64-bit internal processing but only a 32-bit path through the bus. The word size for internal processing for most modern PCs is 64 bits (eight 8-bit bytes). Workstations, mainframes, and supercomputers have 64-bit word sizes and up.

CORE SPEED: GHZ, MIPS, AND FLOPS

A tractor can go 22 miles per hour (mph), a minivan can go 90 mph, and a slingshot drag racer can go 300 mph. These speeds, however, provide little insight into the relative capabilities of these vehicles. What good is a 300-mph tractor or a 22-mph minivan? Similarly, you have to place the speed of computers within the context of their design and application. Generally, PCs are measured in *GHz,* workstations and some server computers are measured in *MIPS,* and supercomputers are measured in *FLOPS.*

- *Gigahertz: GHz.* The PC's heart is its *crystal oscillator* and its heartbeat is the *clock cycle.* The crystal oscillator paces the execution of instructions within the processor. A PC's processor speed, or *core*

speed, is rated by its frequency of oscillation, or the number of clock cycles per second. Legacy PCs are rated in **megahertz**, or **MHz** (millions of clock cycles per second), but modern PCs are measured in **gigahertz**, or **GHz** (billions of clock cycles per second), with high-end PCs running in excess of 3 GHz. The elapsed time for one clock cycle is 1 divided by the frequency. For example, the time it takes to complete one cycle on an 4-GHz processor is 1/4,000,000,000, or 0.00000000025 seconds, or .25 nanoseconds (.25 billionths of a second). Normally several clock cycles are required to fetch, decode, and execute a single program instruction. The shorter the clock cycle, the faster the processor.

- *MIPS*. Processing speed may also be measured in **MIPS**, or millions of instructions per second. Although frequently associated with workstations and some server computers, MIPS is also applied to PCs. Computers can operate up to several thousand MIPS. Figure 4-22 illustrates relative performance (speed) of past and present Intel processors in MIPS. The MIPS measurement is not as accurate as MHz and FLOPS.

- *FLOPS*. Supercomputer speed is measured in **FLOPS**—floating point operations per second (see Figure 4-23). Supercomputer applications, which are often scientific, frequently involve floating point operations. Floating point operations accommodate very small or very large numbers. State-of-the-art supercomputers operate at speeds in excess of a trillion FLOPS.

BUS SPEED: THE PC BOTTLENECK

Modern processors are thousands of times faster than they were 25 years ago. The technology of the electronic bus which handles the movement of data between the various components on the motherboard has not kept pace with processor speed. This lag in speed has made the bus the chief bottleneck to processing efficiency within the PC. Like processors, bus speed is measured in cycles per second, but most processors operate at GHz speeds and buses operate at MHz speeds, usually around 250 to 600 MHz for modern PC processors.

FIGURE 4-22	**THE INTEL® FAMILY OF PROCESSORS**

The Intel family of processors has been installed in 9 of every 10 PCs in use today. This chart is an approximation of the relative speeds of popular Intel processors. The state-of-the-art processor has about 20,000 times the speed of the Intel 8088 (2000 MIPs to .2 MIPs), the processor that ushered in the age of personal computing. Note that this chart is logarithmic, so the MIP value increases by a factor of 10 at each labeled interval.

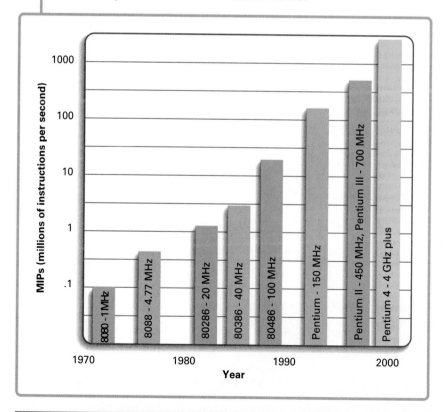

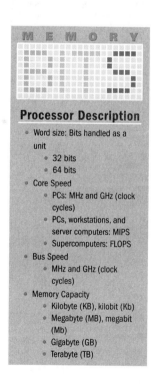

Processor Description
- Word size: Bits handled as a unit
  - 32 bits
  - 64 bits
- Core Speed
  - PCs: MHz and GHz (clock cycles)
  - PCs, workstations, and server computers: MIPS
  - Supercomputers: FLOPS
- Bus Speed
  - MHz and GHz (clock cycles)
- Memory Capacity
  - Kilobyte (KB), kilobit (Kb)
  - Megabyte (MB), megabit (Mb)
  - Gigabyte (GB)
  - Terabyte (TB)

FIGURE 4-24 HOW MUCH IS A KB, AN MB, A GB, AND A TB?

Gettysburg Address

Compare the number of characters in the Gettysburg Address to 1 KB (Kilobyte)

Compare the number of characters in this book to 1 MB (Megabyte)

Compare the number of people in China to 1 GB (Gigabyte)

Compare the number of gallons of water consumed each day in North America to 1 TB (Terabyte)

FIGURE 4–23 World Speed Record for Computers
This engineer at Sandia National Labs is inspecting a connection in one of the 86 cabinets that house the 9,200 processors. The collective power of thousands of processors enables this supercomputer to perform at more than one trillion operations-per-second (1 trillion FLOPS or TERAFLOPS). This record-setting supercomputer is used to ensure the safety, reliability, and effectiveness of the U.S. nuclear stockpile through computer simulation instead of nuclear testing.

Photo courtesy of Intel Corporation

MEMORY CAPACITY: MB, GB, AND TB

The capacities of RAM, cache, and other memories are stated in terms of the number of bytes they can store. Memory capacity for most computers is stated in terms of **megabytes** (**MB**) and **gigabytes** (**GB**). One megabyte equals 1,048,576 (2^{20}) bytes, about a million bytes. One gigabyte (2^{30} bytes) is about one billion bytes. Memory capacities of modern PCs range from 128 MB to 2 GB. High-speed cache memory capacities usually are measured in **kilobytes** (**KB**), the most common being 512 KB of cache. One kilobyte is 1024 (2^{10}) bytes of storage.

Some high-end server computers and supercomputers have more than 1000 GB of RAM. It's only a matter of time before we state RAM in terms of **terabytes** (**TB**), about one trillion bytes. GB and TB are frequently used in reference to high-capacity disk storage. Occasionally you will see memory capacities of individual chips stated in terms of **kilobits** (**Kb**) and **megabits** (**Mb**). Figure 4-24 should give you a feel for KBs, MBs, GBs, and TBs.

DIFFERENCES IN PROCESSOR PERSONALITY

Word size, *core and bus speed*, and *memory capacity* are the primary descriptors of processors and processor performance. However, computers, like people, have their own "personalities." That is, two similarly described computers might possess attributes that give one more capability than the other. For example, one 64-bit, 3.4-GHz, 1-GB PC with a 533-MHz bus might have 1 MB of cache memory and another with the same specs might have only 512 KB of cache. Remember this: When you buy a PC, the basic descriptors tell most but not the entire story.

4-3.1	*MIPS* is an acronym for "millions of instructions per second." (T/F)
4-3.2	A common bus width for modern PCs is 16 bits. (T/F)
4-3.3	Which has the most bytes: (a) a kilobyte, (b) a gigabyte, (c) a megabyte, or (d) a big byte?
4-3.4	The time it takes to complete one cycle on a 2-GHz processor is: (a) 1/2,000,000,000 second, (b) .000000005 second, (c).5 microseconds, or (d).5 thousandths of a second?
4-3.5	Word size is the same as: (a) bus speed, (b) bus width, (c) bus stop, or (d) bus capacity.

4-4 Processor Design

WHY THIS SECTION
IS IMPORTANT
TO YOU

Once you have read this section, you will be able to join in on office talk where your coworkers begin speculating about how computer systems can be made to run even faster.

Researchers in IT are continually working to create new technologies and processes that will make processors faster and better utilize resources, thereby improving system throughput. The design process extends to creating processors for use in different environments (see Figure 4-25).

PARALLEL PROCESSING: COMPUTERS WORKING TOGETHER

In a single processor environment, the processor addresses the programming problem sequentially, from beginning to end. Today, designers are building computers that break a programming problem into pieces. Work on each of these pieces is then executed simultaneously in separate processors, all of which are part of the same computer system. The concept of using multiple processors in the same computer system is known as **parallel processing.** In parallel processing, one main processor examines the programming problem and determines what portions, if any, of the problem can be solved in pieces (see Figure 4-26). Those pieces that can be addressed separately are routed to other processors and solved. The individual pieces are then reassembled in the main processor for further computation, output, or storage. The net result of parallel processing is better throughput.

Computer designers are creating server computers and supercomputers with thousands of integrated microprocessors. Parallel processing on such a large scale is referred to as **massively parallel processing (MPP).** These superfast supercomputers have sufficient computing capacity to attack applications that have been beyond that of computers with traditional computer designs. For example, researchers can now simulate global warming with these computers.

Neural Networks: Wave of the Future?

Most of us interact with digital computers. Digital computers are great at solving structured problems involving computations and logic operations. However, most of the challenges we face from day to day can't be solved with these capabilities. For example, several times each year we are confronted with this problem: to find a pair of shoes that fits. This is a very human problem, better suited to the workings

FIGURE 4–25

PC PROCESSOR DESIGN CONSIDERATIONS
Design considerations for processors used in desktop PCs, such as the Pentium 4 (the microscopic view), and notebook PCs are different. For example, the mobile Intel Celeron processor has a feature that drops the processor power consumption when the laptop is idle or inactive to preserve battery life. Laptop processors must also be designed to dissipate heat within smaller enclosures.

Photos courtesy of Intel Corporation

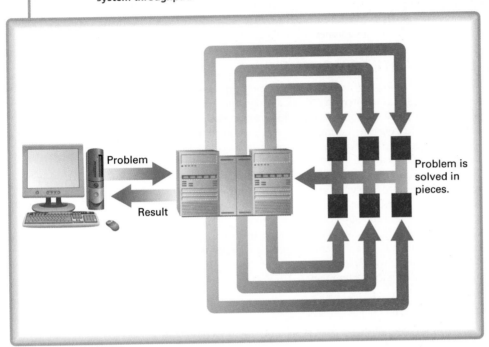

FIGURE 4–26

PARALLEL PROCESSING
In parallel processing, auxiliary processors solve pieces of a problem to enhance system throughput.

Problem

Result

Problem is solved in pieces.

of the human brain than for digital computers. Such problems involve unstructured input and outcomes that are unclear, so we use the best available processor—our brain. Scientists are studying the way the human brain works and are attempting to build computers that mimic the incredible human mind. The base technology for these computers is **neural networks**.

The neural network computer employs hundreds, even thousands, of small, interconnected processors, called *processing units*. The neural network works by creating connections and maintaining relationships between these processing units, the computer equivalent of neurons in the brain. Working within a specific sphere of knowledge (for example, worldwide agriculture strategies), the neural network computer can draw from its human-supplied knowledge base,

learn through experience, and make informed decisions in an unstructured environment. Here are but a few of an increasing number of neural network applications: playing chess, improving automobile engine efficiency, enabling improved vision technology, planning crop rotation strategies, and forecasting financial market fluctuations.

The primary difference between traditional digital computers and neural networks is that digital computers process *structured data sequentially* whereas neural networks process *unstructured information simultaneously*. Digital computers will always be able to outperform neural networked computers and the human brain when it comes to fast, accurate numeric computation. However, if neural networks live up to their potential, they will be able to handle tasks that are currently very time-consuming or impossible for conventional computers, such as recognizing a face in the crowd.

GRID COMPUTING: SHARING COMPUTING POWER

During the past few years, the potential of **grid computing** has been compared to that of the Internet. The basic premise of grid computing is to use available computing resources more effectively. The typical PC user has a computer that is more powerful than the behemoth mainframe computers of the 1960s and 1970s but these users use less than 1 percent of their PCs' processing capabilities. Now that the world is networked via the Internet and an increasing number of users are linked to the Net via broadband, it is now possible to share vast amounts of unused processing resources via grid computing. Grid computing takes advantage of the unused processing capabilities of hundreds, even thousands of personal computers, to address a single programming problem.

In terms of evolution, grid computing is about where the Internet was in the 1970s. It has devoted fans who expect it to define a new era in information technology; but grid computing may be several years away from widespread acceptance and use. Here is how it works. People who are willing to share unused computing capacity via a network to solve a large processor-oriented problem, perhaps the analysis of extraterrestrial data, download and install a program. The program enables an interface with the server computer that coordinates the grid computing effort. PCs in the grid system work on a piece of the problem, but only when the PC is not in use. In this way, grid systems can combine unused resources with processing potential greater than some supercomputers. Supercomputers can cost millions of dollars, but grid systems composed entirely of volunteer participants who willingly share their computing resources are routinely performing supercomputer-level processing for virtually nothing.

IBM, Oracle, and other major technology companies are beginning to employ grid computing. The word is out; grid computing works. It offers a way for companies to greatly expanding their computing capacity while saving significant amounts of money. If grid computing continues to grow at the same pace of acceptance and use, introductory information technology books will soon be devoting an entire chapter to this important new technology.

4-4.1 In a single processor environment, the processor addresses the programming problem sequentially. (T/F)

4-4.2 Parallel processing on a large scale is referred to as massively trapezoidal processing. (T/F)

4-4.3 The base technology for computers that mimic the human mind is called: (a) HAL, (b) neural network, (c) human brain focus, or (d) interconnected processing.

4-4.4 Which of the following would not be representative of a neural network application: (a) playing chess, (b) planning crop rotation strategies, (c) processing payroll, or (d) enabling improved vision technology?

4-1 GOING DIGITAL

The two kinds of electronic signals are **analog** and **digital.** To make the most effective use of computers and automation, the electronics world is going digital. The music industry **digitizes** the natural analog signals that result from recording sessions, then stores the digital version on CDs. Computers are digital and, therefore, work better with digital data.

The two digital states of the computer—on and off—are represented by a *bit,* short for binary digit. These electronic states are compatible with the **binary** numbering system. Letters and decimal numbers are translated into bits for storage and processing on computer systems.

Data are stored temporarily during processing in RAM and permanently on devices such as disk drives.

Alphanumeric (*alpha* and *numeric*) characters are represented in computer storage by unique bit configurations. Characters are translated into these bit configurations, also called *bytes,* according to a particular coding scheme, called an *encoding system.*

The 7-bit *ASCII* encoding system is the most popular encoding system for PCs and data communication. An extended version of ASCII, an 8-bit encoding system, offers 128 more codes. Microsoft Windows uses the 8-bit **ANSI** encoding system.

Unicode, a uniform 16-bit encoding system, will enable computers and applications to talk to one another more easily and will accommodate most of the world's languages.

The **hexadecimal,** or base-16, numbering system is used as shorthand to display the binary contents of RAM and disk storage.

4-2 THE PC SYSTEM UNIT

The processor, RAM, and other electronic components are housed in the *system unit.* The *processor* is literally a computer on a chip. This processor, the electronic circuitry for handling input/output signals from the peripheral devices, and the memory chips are mounted on a single circuit board called a *motherboard.* The motherboard's **chipset** controls the flow of information between system components.

The **bus** is the common pathway through which the processor sends/receives data and commands to/from RAM and disk storage and all I/O peripheral devices. Like the wheeled bus, the bus provides data transportation to all processor components, memory, and **device controllers.**

Most new system units have an Intel **Pentium® 4, Celeron®,** or **Itanium™** processor inside, but many older systems with **Pentium®, Pentium® Pro, Pentium® II,** and **Pentium® III** processors continue to be workhorses.

The processor is the nucleus of any computer system. A processor, which is also called the **central processing unit** or **CPU,** has only two fundamental sections, the **control unit** and the **arithmetic and logic unit,** which work together with RAM to execute programs. The control unit's **decoder** interprets

instructions, then the control unit directs the arithmetic and logic unit to perform computation and logic operations. During execution, instructions and data are passed between very high-speed **registers** (for example, the **instruction register,** the **program register,** and the **accumulator**) in the control unit and the arithmetic and logic unit.

RAM, or random-access memory, provides the processor with temporary storage for programs and data. Physically, memory chips are installed on **single in-line memory modules (SIMMs), dual in-line memory modules (DIMMs),** and **rambus in-line memory modules (RIMMs).** Most new PCs are being equipped with **synchronous dynamic RAM (SDRAM), DDR SDRAM,** or **Rambus DRAM (RDRAM).**

In RAM, each datum is stored at a specific **address.** RAM is **volatile memory** (contrast with **nonvolatile memory**); that is, the data are lost when the electrical current is turned off or interrupted. All input/output, including programs, must enter and exit RAM. Other variations of internal storage are **ROM, programmable read-only memory (PROM),** and **flash memory,** a nonvolatile memory. The **BIOS** software is stored in flash memory.

Some computers employ **cache memory** (level 1 and level 2) to increase **throughput** (the rate at which work can be performed by a computer system). Like RAM, cache is a high-speed holding area for program instructions and data. However, cache memory holds only those instructions and data likely to be needed next by the processor.

Every **machine language** has a predefined format for each type of instruction. During one **instruction cycle,** an instruction is "fetched" from RAM, decoded in the control unit, and executed, and the results are placed in memory. The instruction cycle time is the total of the instruction time (I-time) and the execution time (E-time). Most modern processors are capable of **pipelining** to speed up processing.

The motherboard includes several empty **expansion slots** so you can purchase and plug in optional capabilities in the form of **expansion boards** or **expansion cards.** The most common expansion boards plug into a **PCI local bus.** The **SCSI bus,** or "scuzzy" bus, allows up to 15 SCSI peripheral devices to be daisy-chained to a SCSI interface expansion card. The **Universal Serial Bus (USB)** permits up to 127 USB peripheral devices to be **hot plugged** to the PC. The **USB 2.0** standard is 40 times faster than the original USB standard. The **1394 bus (FireWire** in the Apple world) is a bus standard that supports data transfer rates of up to 400M bps. The **AGP bus** is a special-function bus for high-resolution 3-D graphics.

In a PC, external peripheral devices come with a cable and a multipin connector. A port provides a direct link to the PC's common electrical bus. External peripheral devices can be linked to the processor via cables through a **serial port, parallel port, SCSI port, USB port, 1394 port,** or **IrDA (infrared)**

port. The standard for PC serial ports is the **RS-232C connector.** The RS-232C and **Centronics connectors** are used with parallel ports.

Popular expansion boards include graphics adapters such as the **AGP** or **accelerated graphics port board,** sound, **data/voice/fax modem** (enables emulation of a **fax** machine), **network interface card (NIC),** and video capture card.

The **PCMCIA card,** sometimes called a **PC card,** provides a variety of interchangeable add-on capabilities in the form of credit-card-sized modules. The PC card is especially handy for the portable environment. A mobile **GPS (global positioning system)** can be a PC card.

4-3 DESCRIBING THE PROCESSOR AND ITS PERFORMANCE

A processor is described in terms of its word size (bus width), core speed, bus speed, and memory capacity.

A **word** is the number of bits handled as a unit within a particular computer system's common electrical bus or during internal processing.

Personal computer speed, called the core speed, is measured in **megahertz (MHz)** and **gigahertz (GHz).** High-end PC, workstation, and server computer speed is measured in **MIPS.** Supercomputer speed is measured in **FLOPS.**

Bus speed, which is less than core speed, is measured in cycles per second. Bus speed can be a bottleneck in processing performance.

Memory capacity is measured in **kilobytes (KB), megabytes (MB), gigabytes (GB),** and **terabytes (TB).** Chip capacity is sometimes stated in **kilobits (Kb)** and **megabits (Mb).**

4-4 PROCESSOR DESIGN

In **parallel processing,** one main processor examines the programming problem and determines what portions, if any, of the problem can be solved in pieces. Those pieces that can be addressed separately are routed to other processors, solved, then recombined in the main processor to produce the result. Parallel processing on a large scale is referred to as **massively parallel processing (MPP).**

Neural networks mimic the way the human brain works. The neural network computer uses many small, interconnected processors to address problems that involve *unstructured information.*

The basic premise of **grid computing** is to use available computing resources more effectively. Grid computing addresses a single programming problem by tapping the unused processing capabilities of many PCs via a network.

KEY TERMS

1394 bus (p. 184)
1394 port (p. 185)
accumulator (p. 181)
address (p. 181)
AGP board (p. 187)
AGP bus (p. 184)
analog (p. 172)
ANSI (p. 175)
arithmetic and logic unit (p. 181)
binary (p. 172)
BIOS (p. 182)
bus (p. 177)
cache memory (p. 181)
Celeron® (p. 179)
central processing unit (CPU) (p. 180)
Centronics connector (p. 185)
chipset (p. 176)
control unit (p. 180)
data/voice/fax modem (p. 187)
DDR SDRAM (p. 181)
decoder (p. 180)
device controller (p. 177)

digital (p. 172)
digitize (p. 172)
dual in-line memory module (DIMM) (p. 181)
expansion board (p. 182)
expansion card (p. 182)
expansion slot (p. 182)
fax (p. 187)
FireWire (p. 184)
flash memory (p. 182)
FLOPS (p. 189)
gigabyte (GB) (p. 190)
gigahertz (GHz) (p. 189)
GPS (global positioning system) (p. 188)
grid computing (p. 192)
hexadecimal (p. 175)
hot plug (p. 184)
infrared port (p. 185)
instruction cycle (p. 182)
instruction register (p. 180)
IrDA port (p. 185)
Itanium™ (p. 179)

kilobit (Kb) (p. 190)
kilobyte (KB) (p. 190)
machine language (p. 182)
massively parallel processing (MPP) (p. 191)
megabit (Mb) (p. 190)
megabyte (MB) (p. 190)
megahertz (MHz) (p. 189)
MIPS (p. 189)
network interface card (NIC) (p. 187)
neural network (p. 192)
nonvolatile memory (p. 182)
parallel port (p. 185)
parallel processing (p. 191)
PCI local bus (p. 182)
PCMCIA card (PC card) (p. 188)
Pentium 4® (p. 179)
Pentium® (p. 179)
Pentium® II (p. 179)
Pentium® III (p. 179)
Pentium® Pro (p. 179)
pipelining (p. 182)

MATCHING

1. 1394 bus
2. DDR SDRAM
3. pipelining
4. binary
5. Pentium 4
6. chipset
7. Moore's Law
8. BIOS
9. grid computing
10. registers
11. ASCII
12. machine language
13. throughput
14. hexadecimal
15. AGP

a. doubling of transistors each 1.5 years
b. graphics adapter
c. stored in flash
d. encoding
e. in processor control unit
f. rate of work by a CPU
g. language of computers
h. base 16
i. motherboard flow control
j. type of memory
k. 1, 0
l. networking of unused computing capacity
m. Intel processor
n. FireWire
o. overlapping instruction execution

CHAPTER SELF-CHECK

4-1.1 Bit is the singular of byte. (T/F)

4-1.2 The hexadecimal numbering system has 26 unique numbers. (T/F)

4-1.3 Stereo music cannot be digitized. (T/F)

4-1.4 The base of the binary number system is: (a) 2, (b) 8, (c) 16, or (d) 32.

4-1.5 How many ANSI bytes can be stored in a 32-bit word: (a) 2, (b) 4, (c) 6, or (d) 8?

4-1.6 What is the ASCII code for Q if the code for P is 01010000: (a) 01010011, (b) 01010010, (c) 01010001, or (d) 01011111?

4-1.7 A hexadecimal A3 is what in binary: (a) 10100011, (b) 01010011, (c) 00111010, or (d) 11110011?

4-2.1 The control unit is that part of the processor that reads and interprets program instructions. (T/F)

4-2.2 PC cards can be hot swapped while the PC is running. (T/F)

4-2.3 The 1394 bus transfers data at a slower rate than the USB bus. (T/F)

4-2.4 Which of the following memory groups are in order based on speed (slowest to fastest): (a) registers, cache, RAM, (b) cache, RAM, registers, (c) cache, registers, RAM, or (d) RAM, cache, registers?

4-2.5 BIOS software is stored permanently: (a) in flash memory, (b) in DDR SDRAM, (c) on hard disk, or (d) on DVD-ROM.

4-2.6 Which one of the following would not be attached to a motherboard: (a) RAM, (b) processor, (c) FLOP, or (d) expansion board?

4-2.7 Which port enables the parallel transmission of data within a computer system: (a) serial, (b) parallel, (c) Centronics, or (d) speaker?

4-2.8 Which two buses enable the daisy-chaining of peripheral devices: (a) USB and SCSI, (b) SCSI and infrared, (c) USB and PCI local bus, or (d) PCI local bus and ISA?

4-3.1 The word size of all PCs is 32 bits. (T/F)

4-3.2 Bus speed is always the same as core speed. (T/F)

4-3.3 A gigabyte of RAM has more storage capacity than a megabit of RAM. (T/F)

4-3.4 Which of these would not be a major factor in processor performance: (a) core speed, (b) bus width, (c) size of RAM, or (d) bus length?

4-3.5 A high-capacity hard disk would be measured in: (a) GB or TB, (b) KB or TB, (c) kilobits or megabits, or (d) MB or GB.

4-3.6 Supercomputer speed is measured in: (a) LOPS, (b) MOPS, (c) FLOPS, or (d) POPS.

4-4.1 In parallel processing, two main processors examine the programming problem and determine what portions, if any, of the problem can be solved in pieces. (T/F)

4-4.2 In grid computing, all PCs on the grid must commit their resources until processing is complete. (T/F)

4-4.3 Grid computing is well ahead of the Internet in technological evolution. (T/F)

4-4.4 The concept of using multiple processors in the same computer system is known as: (a) massive processing, (b) acute processing, (c) parallel processing, or (d) perpendicular processing.

4-4.5 Neural networks process unstructured information: (a) intermittently, (b) sequentially, (c) simultaneously, or (d) as time permits.

4-4.6 The neural network computer employs many small, interconnected processors, called: (a) brain units, (b) neural nets, (c) mini PCs, or (d) processing units.

4-4.7 Grid computing takes advantage of what capabilities in remote PCs: (a) printing, (b) Net search, (c) unused processing, or (d) lattice uploading?

IT ETHICS AND ISSUES

MONITORING OF E-MAIL

Many organizations monitor both e-mail and telephone conversations of their employees. These organizations cite productivity and quality control as justification. People who used to chat at the water cooler or snack counter do so now over office e-mail or instant messaging. Monitored e-mail is just as likely to surface "meet you at the gym after work" as "meet you in the conference room."

Realistically, e-mail is monitored to discourage nonbusiness messages and to keep employees focused on job-related activities. We now know that e-mail, when used responsibly, can boost productivity. We also know that, if abused, e-mail can be counterproductive.

Once an organization decides to monitor e-mail, it can do so in several ways. Individuals can scan e-mail archives for inappropriate transmissions, often a time-consuming process. In large organizations, computers scan e-mail archives for keywords (baseball, party, boss, and so on) and kick out messages with questionable content. Already many employees have been fired or disciplined for abusing e-mail.

Employees feel that monitoring of e-mail is an invasion of personal privacy. Many workers view e-mail as just another tool, such as a telephone, and that they should be allowed some reasonable personal use. The issue is being argued in the courts.

Discussion: *Does an employer's right to know outweigh the employee's right to privacy?*

Discussion: *What statements do you feel should be included in a corporate policy on e-mail usage?*

Discussion: *Which do you feel is more invasive, the monitoring of voice mail and inspection of lockers or the monitoring of e-mail? Why?*

Discussion: *The use of instant messaging is growing in the corporate world, but companies that monitor e-mail seldom monitor instant messaging. To be consistent, should they monitor instant messaging, too? Why or why not?*

TERM-PAPER FRAUD

Plagiarism, more specifically term-paper fraud, has been a problem in higher education throughout this century. However, only during the past few years have for-sale term papers on every common subject been showcased to the world and made readily available over the Internet. Students purchase these papers hoping to pass them off as originals. Typically, they will use a variety of software tools to add a personal touch to these recycled papers.

Many sites on the Internet offer "term-paper assistance" in a variety of topic areas. One site has both off-the-shelf and custom term-paper services, inviting students to "Get a brand-new paper written from scratch according to your exact specifications. Click here." Some states have passed laws prohibiting the sale of pre-fabricated term papers. However, term-paper mills circumvent these laws by stating that the intended purpose of their term papers is that they be used as models that students can use during the preparation of their own term papers.

Discussion: *Is plagiarism a problem on your campus? If so, how big a problem?*

Discussion: *What can students do to help deter plagiarism and encourage academic honesty? What can college administrators do? What can professors do? What can government do?*

Discussion: *Do students who plagiarize the work of others rob themselves of the knowledge and experience they gain from writing a well-developed paper? Explain.*

DISCUSSION AND PROBLEM SOLVING

4-1.1   Generally, computers are digital and human beings are analog, so what we say, hear, and see must be converted, or digitized, for processing on a computer. Speculate on how a family photograph might be digitized for storage and processing on a computer system.

4-1.2   Create a 5-bit encoding system to be used for storing uppercase alpha characters, punctuation symbols, and the apostrophe. Discuss the advantages and disadvantages of your encoding system in relation to the ASCII encoding system.

4-1.3   How many characters can be represented with a 12-bit encoding system?

4-1.4   Write your first name as an ASCII bit configuration.

4-2.1   List at least 10 products that are smaller than a toaster oven and use microprocessors. Select one and describe the function of its microprocessor.

4-2.2   Describe the advantages of a USB port over a parallel port. Also, describe the advantages of a parallel port over a serial port.

4-2.3   Distinguish between RAM and flash memory. Be specific.

4-2.4   Which two functions does the arithmetic and logic unit perform? Give a real-life example for each function.

4-2.5   Explain the relationship between a processor, a motherboard, and a PC.

4-2.6   Generally describe the interaction between the processor's control unit, registers, and RAM.

4-2.7   Give one example of where each of the memory technologies in question 4-2.6 might be used in a personal computer system.

4-2.8   Illustrate the interaction between the user RAM and the accumulator in the arithmetic and logic unit for the following basic program. Use the model shown in Figure 4-14.

```
INPUT "Enter ages for 3 children"; A, B, C
LET AVGAGE=(A+B+C)/3
PRINT "The average age is"; AVGAGE
END
```

4-2.9   List three expansion boards you would like to have on your own PC. How would you use these added capabilities?

4-2.10   Describe a hot swap as it relates to a PCMCIA-compliant interface.

4-2.11   Why do you suppose PC motherboards are designed to accommodate several types of buses?

4-2.12   Would you consider building your own computer? Why or why not?

4-3.1   Assume a move data instruction requires five clock cycles. Compute the time it takes, in nanoseconds, to execute a move data instruction on a 3-GHz processor.

4-3.2   Convert 5 MB to KB, Mb, and Kb. Assume a byte contains eight bits.

1. Explore the inside of a PC (yours or a lab computer made available to students for this exercise). Remove the cover on a tower PC to expose the motherboard. Usually, this is no more difficult than loosening a couple of thumbscrews and removing a side panel. Do not touch any electronic components since they are sensitive to static electricity. Identify as many of the motherboard components shown in Figure 4-9 as you can. Look inside and on the back of the computer to identify the number of PCI expansion slots and DIMM sockets on the motherboard. Also, count the number of USB ports.

2. Use available system monitoring software and/or system documentation to determine the following information for a particular PC (yours or a lab PC): processor speed, amount and type of RAM, and amount of L1 and L2 cache.

INTERNET EXERCISES @ www.prenhall.com/long

1. The Online Study Guide (multiple choice, true/false, matching, and essay questions)
2. Internet Learning Activities
   - Encoding
   - Processors, Chips, and RAM
3. Serendipitous Internet Activities
   - Popular Culture
   - Online Shopping

IT ILLUSTRATED

THE COMPUTER ON A CHIP

The invention of the light bulb in 1879 symbolized the beginning of electronics. Electronics then evolved into the use of vacuum tubes, then transistors, and now integrated circuits. Today's microminiaturization of electronic circuitry is continuing to have a profound effect on the way we live and work. The increased speed and capability of computers influence all the many services we may take for granted. Where would telecommunications, speech recognition, advanced software applications, and the Internet be without this technology?

Current chip technology permits the placement of hundreds of thousands of transistors and electronic switches on a single chip. Chips already fit into wristwatches and credit cards, but electrical and computer engineers want them even smaller. In electronics, smaller is better. The ENIAC, the first full-scale digital electronic computer, weighed 50 tons and occupied an entire room. Today, a computer far more powerful than the ENIAC can be fabricated within a single piece of silicon the size of a child's fingernail.

Chip designers think in terms of nanoseconds (one billionth of a second) and microns (one millionth of a meter). They want to pack as many circuit elements as they can into the structure of a chip. This is called *scaling,* or making the transistor, and the technology that connects it, smaller. High-density packing reduces the time required for an electrical signal to travel from one circuit element to the next—resulting in faster computers. Circuit lines on early 1980s PC processors were 10 microns wide. Today's circuit lines are .09 microns or 90 nanometers (one billionth of a meter). The reduced size of the circuit lines enables chips to hold over 100 million transistors and provide thousands of times the power of earlier processors.

As transistors become smaller, the chip becomes faster, conducts more electricity, and uses less power. Also, it costs less to produce as more transistors are packed on a chip.

The computer revolution will continue to grow rapidly into the twenty-first century as long as researchers find ways to make transistors faster and smaller, make wiring that links them less resistive to electrical current, and increase chip density. Each year, researchers have developed radically new techniques for manufacturing chips. For example, IBM recently began developing a logic chip and processor using silicon-on-insulator (SOI) technology, an innovative approach to the chip-making process. The process presented here provides a general overview that is representative of the various techniques used by chip manufacturers (see Figure 4-27).

Chips are designed and manufactured to perform a particular function. One chip might be a microprocessor, or the "brains," for a personal computer. Another, such as a memory chip, might be for temporary random-access storage (RAM). Logic chips are used in beverage vending machines, televisions, refrigerators, cell phones, and thousands more devices. Microprocessors, memory, and logic chips are three of the most common kinds of chips.

The development of integrated circuits starts with a project review team made up of representatives from design, manufacturing, and marketing. This group works together to design a product the customer needs. Next, they go through prototype wafer manufacturing to resolve potential manufacturing problems. Once a working prototype is produced, chips are manufactured in quantity and sent to computer, peripheral, telecommunications, and other customers.

The manufacturing of integrated circuits involves a multistep process using various photochemical etching and metallurgical techniques. This complex and interesting process is illustrated here with photos, from silicon to the finished product. The process is presented in five steps: design, fabrication, packaging, testing, and installation.

1. The width of circuit lines on today's integrated chip technology is measured in nanometers. (T/F)
2. Modern chip technology calls for at least 1000 layers of logic for each chip. (T/F)
3. Wafers are cut into individual chips with a diamond-edged saw. (T/F)
4. Which of the following is not a common type of chip: (a) memory, (b) microprocessor, (c) pulsar, or (d) logic?
5. Which substance is the basis for the ingots from which the wafers are made: (a) silicone, (b) uranium, (c) gold, or (d) silver?
6. Integrated circuits are fabricated in: (a) sparkling rooms, (b) semi-clean rooms, (c) semi-soiled rooms, or (d) clean rooms.

SECTION SELF-CHECK

Design

1. Using Cad For Chip Design

Chip designers use computer-aided design (CAD) systems to create the logic for individual circuits. Although a chip can contain up to 30 layers, typically there are 10 to 20 patterned layers of varying material, with each layer performing a different purpose. In this multilayer circuit design, each layer is color-coded so the designer can distinguish between the various layers. Some of the layers lie within the silicon wafer and others are stacked on top.

Courtesy of Micron Technology, Inc.

2. Creating a Mask

The product designer's computerized drawing of each circuit layer is transformed into a *mask,* or *reticle,* a glass or quartz plate with an opaque material (such as chrome) formed to create the pattern. The process used to transfer a pattern or image from the masks to a wafer is called *photolithography.* The number of layers depends on the complexity of the chip's logic. The Intel Pentium processor, for example, contains 20 layers. When all these unique layers are combined, they create the millions of transistors and circuits that make up the architecture of the processor. Needless to say, the manufacturing process forming this sequence of layers is a very precise one!

Courtesy of Micron Technology, Inc.

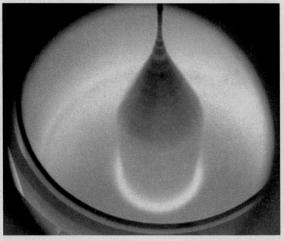

Fabrication

3. Creating Silicon Ingots

Molten silicon is spun into cylindrical ingots, usually from six to eight inches in diameter. Because silicon, the second most abundant substance, is used in the fabrication of integrated circuits, chips are sometimes referred to as "intelligent grains of sand."

M/A-COM, Inc.

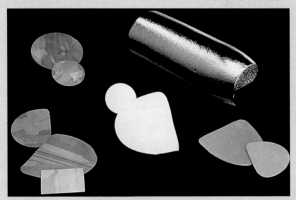

4. Cutting the Silicon Wafers

The ingot is shaped and prepared prior to being cut into silicon wafers. Once the wafers are cut to about the thickness of a credit card, they are polished to a perfect finish.

M/A-COM, Inc.

5. Wearing Bunny Suits

To help keep a clean environment, workers wear semi-custom-fitted Gortex® suits. They follow a 100-step procedure when putting the suits on.
Courtesy of Intel Corporation

6. Keeping a Clean House

Clean air continuously flows from every pore of the ceiling and through the holes in the floor into a filtering system at the manufacturing plant. A normal room contains some 15 million dust particles per cubic foot. A clean, modern hospital has about 10,000 dust particles per cubic foot. A class-1 clean room (the lower the rating, the cleaner the facility) contains less than one dust particle per cubic foot. All of the air in a "clean room" is replaced seven times every minute.

Portions of the microchip manufacturing process are performed in yellow light because the wafers are coated with a light-sensitive material called "photoresist" before the next chip pattern is imprinted onto the surface of the silicon wafer.

Courtesy of AMD

7. Coating the Wafers

Silicon wafers that eventually will contain several hundred chips are placed in an oxygen furnace at 1200 degrees Celsius. In the furnace, the wafer is coated with other minerals to create the physical properties needed to produce transistors and other electronic components on the surface of the wafer.

Photo courtesy of National Semiconductor Corporation

8. Etching the Wafers

A photoresist is deposited onto the wafer surface creating a film-like substance to accept the patterned image. The mask is placed over the wafer and both are exposed to ultraviolet light. In this way the circuit pattern is transferred onto the wafer. The photoresist is developed, washing away the unwanted resist and leaving the exact image of the transferred pattern. Plasma (superhot gases) technology is used to etch the circuit pattern permanently into the wafer. This is one of several techniques used in the etching process. The wafer is returned to the furnace and given another coating on which to etch another circuit layer. The procedure is repeated for each circuit layer until the wafer is complete.

Some of the layers include aluminum or copper interconnects, which leave a fine network of thin metal connections or wires for these semiconductor chips. The wires are used to link the transistors. Aluminum has long been the standard for semiconductor wiring, but recent innovations with the use of copper wiring, a better conductor of electricity, will help create the next generation of semiconductors.

Courtesy of Micron Technology, Inc.

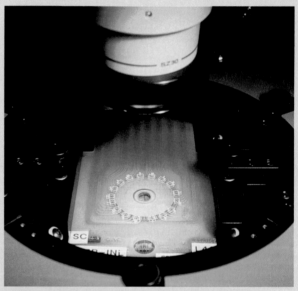

9. Tracking the Wafers

Fabrication production control tracks wafers through the fabricating process and measures layers at certain manufacturing stages to determine layer depth and chemical structure. These measurements assess process accuracy and facilitate real-time modifications.

Courtesy of Micron Technology, Inc.

10. Drilling the Wafers
It takes only a second for this instrument to drill 1440 tiny holes in a wafer. The holes enable the interconnection of the layers of circuits. Each layer must be perfectly aligned (within a millionth of a meter) with the others.

Courtesy of International Business Machines Corporation

13. Dicing the Wafers
A diamond-edged saw, with a thickness of a human hair, separates the wafer into individual processors, known as die, in a process called *dicing*. Water spray keeps the surface temperature low. After cutting, high-pressure water rinses the wafer clean. In some situations, special lasers are used to cut the wafers.

Courtesy of Micron Technology, Inc.

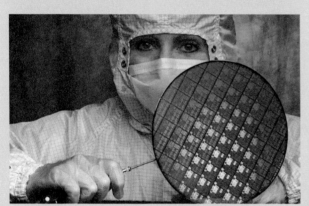

Packaging

11. Removing the Etched Wafers
The result of the coating/etching process is a silicon wafer that contains from 100 to 400 integrated circuits, each of which includes millions of transistors.

Courtesy of International Business Machines Corporation

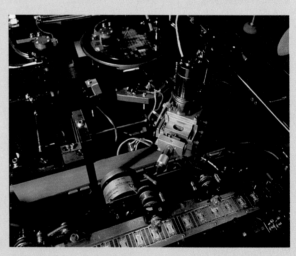

14. Attaching the Die
Individual die are attached to silver epoxy on the center area of a lead frame. Each die is removed from the tape with needles plunging up from underneath to push the die while a vacuum tip lifts the die from the tape. Lead frames are then heated in an oven to cure the epoxy. The wafer map created in probe tells the die-attach equipment which die to place on the lead frame.

Courtesy of Micron Technology, Inc.

12. Mounting the Wafer
Each wafer is vacuum mounted onto a metal-framed sticky film tape. The wafer and metal frame are placed near the tape, then all three pieces are loaded into a vacuum chamber. A vacuum forces the tape smoothly onto the back of the wafer and metal frame.

Courtesy of Micron Technology, Inc.

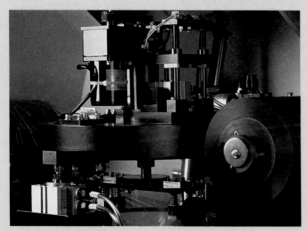

15. Packaging the Chips

The chips are packaged in protective ceramic or metal carriers. The carriers have standard-sized electrical pin connectors that allow the chip to be plugged conveniently into circuit boards. Because the pins tend to corrode, the pin connectors are the most vulnerable part of a computer system. To avoid corrosion and a bad connection, the pins on some carriers are made of gold.

Courtesy of International Business Machines Corporation

Testing

16. Testing the Chips

Each chip is tested to assess functionality and to see how fast it can store or retrieve information. Chip speed (or access time) is measured in nanoseconds (a billionth, 1/1,000,000,000th of a second). The precision demands are so great that as many as half the chips are found to be defective. A drop of ink is deposited on defective chips.

Courtesy of Micron Technology, Inc.

17. Burning In

This burn-in oven runs performance tests on every chip, simulating actual usage conditions. Each chip is tested by feeding information to the chip and querying for the information to ensure the chip is receiving, storing, and sending the correct data.

Courtesy of Micron Technology, Inc.

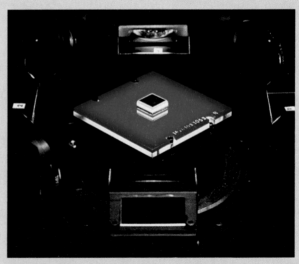

18. Scanning

All chips are scanned, using optics or lasers, to discover any bent, missing, or incorrectly formed leads.

Courtesy of Micron Technology, Inc.

Installation

19. Creating Circuit Boards

Pick and place equipment precisely positions various chips on the solder and contacts. Completed boards are then heated in the reflow ovens, allowing the lead coating and solder to melt together, affixing the chip to the printed circuit board.

20. Installing the Finished Chips

The completed circuit boards are installed in computers and thousands of other computer-controlled devices.

Chapter

5

Learning Objectives

Once you have read and studied this chapter, you will have learned:

● The relationship between mass storage and the various types of files (Section 5-1).

● The various types of magnetic disk devices and media, including organization, principles of operation, maintenance, performance considerations, and security concerns (Section 5-2).

● The operational capabilities and applications for the various types of optical laser disc storage (Section 5-3).

● The sources of computer viruses and approaches to protecting your system from these viruses (Section 5-4).

● Methods and procedures for backing up disk files (Section 5-5).

STORING AND RETRIEVING INFORMATION

Why this chapter is important to you

Not too long ago, we stored things in file drawers, hall closets, family photo albums, notebooks, recipe boxes, keepsake boxes, calendars, Rolodex name and address files, and many other places. We also had bookshelves filled with all kinds of reference books, from the phone books to encyclopedias. We had wire frame holders to store long-play record albums (LPs). Most of us still store things in these same places, but to a far lesser extent. The family photo album may be scanned and stored on a rewritable CD-ROM. Personal information software is rapidly replacing the Rolodex file. Young families are opting to buy an interactive encyclopedia on CD-ROM rather than an expensive, space-consuming 20-volume set. Music is now available from many electronic sources. You get the idea. Much of what used to be physical and tangible is now stored permanently in electronic form on various storage media.

This chapter gives you an overview of electronic storage media and devices. In a nutshell, media used for storage of data and various forms of information can be classified as disk, tape, or optical (such as a CD-ROM). Each has its advantages and disadvantages. For example, the functionality of the removable Zip disks and SuperDisks is similar, but speed and compatibility considerations may sway you toward one or the other. After studying this chapter, you'll be better prepared to answer the always popular question "How much hard disk space do I need?" Pointers throughout the chapter will help you protect your valuable data and information from electronic vandals and accidental loss.

The somewhat confusing array of storage options makes us all vulnerable to making big mistakes when purchasing and using computer systems. This chapter should help you sort out the options and give you some insight as to what (and how much) to buy. Plus, it will help you to know when and how to use the various storage alternatives.

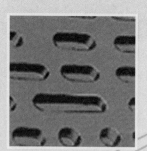

During the past few decades,
contents of our file cabinets,
photo albums, day planners,
calendars, and so on have been
slowly migrating to electronic
files on mass storage devices,
such as disk. Read on to better
prepare yourself to work with
scores, if not hundreds, of files
each day.

5-1 Mass Storage, Files, and File Management

Did you ever stop to think about what happens behind the scenes when you. . .

● Request a telephone number through directory assistance?

● Draw money from your checking account at an ATM?

● Check out at a supermarket?

● Download a file on the Internet?

Needed information—such as telephone numbers, account balances, item prices, or stock summary files on the Internet—is retrieved from rapidly rotating disk-storage media and loaded to random-access memory (RAM) for processing. Untold terabytes (trillions of bytes) of information, representing millions of applications, are stored *permanently* for periodic retrieval in magnetic (such as hard disk) and optical (such as DVD+RW) storage media. There they can be retrieved in milliseconds. For example, as soon as the directory assistance operator keys in the desired name, the full name and number are retrieved from disk storage and displayed. Moments later, a digitized version of voice recordings of numbers is accessed from disk storage and played in response to the caller's request: "The number is five, zero, one, five, five, five, two, two, four, nine."

STORAGE TECHNOLOGIES

Within a computer system, programs and information in all forms (text, image, audio, and video) are stored in both *RAM* and permanent **mass storage,** such as *magnetic disk and tape* (see Figure 5-1). Programs and information are retrieved from mass storage and stored *temporarily* in high-speed RAM for processing. In this section, we examine two common types of mass storage—magnetic disk and magnetic tape.

Over the years, manufacturers have developed a variety of permanent mass storage devices and media. Today the various types of **magnetic disk drives** and their respective storage media are the state of the art for permanent storage. **Optical laser disc** continues to emerge as an means of mass storage. Note that *disk* is spelled with a "k" for magnetic disk media and with a "c" for optical disc media. **Magnetic tape drives** complement magnetic disk storage by providing inexpensive *backup* capability and *archival* storage. First, let's take a look at the files stored on magnetic disk drives.

THE MANY FACES OF FILES

We have talked in general about the *file* in previous chapters. The file is simply a recording of information. It is the foundation of permanent storage on a computer system. To a computer, a file is a string of 0s and 1s (digitized data) that are stored and retrieved as a single unit. Each file has a user-supplied filename by which it is stored and retrieved.

Types of Files: ASCII to Video

There are many types of files (see Figure 5-2), most of which are defined by the software that created them (for example, a word processing document, graphics, or a spreadsheet). The following are among the more popular types of files.

● *ASCII file.* An **ASCII file** is a text-only file that can be read or created by any word processing program or text editor.

● *Data file.* A **data file** contains data in any format.

● *Document file.* All word processing and desktop publishing **document files** contain text and, often, embedded images.

● *Spreadsheet file.* A **spreadsheet file** contains rows and columns of data.

● *Web page file.* A **Web page file** is compatible with the World Wide Web and Internet browsers.

FIGURE 5–1

RAM AND MASS STORAGE
Programs and data are stored permanently in mass storage and temporarily in RAM.

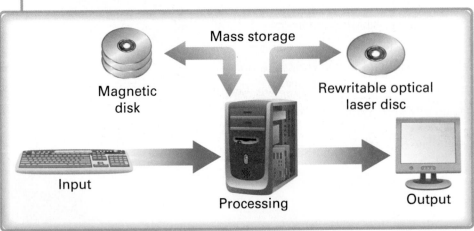

Mass storage

Magnetic disk

Rewritable optical laser disc

Input

Processing

Output

FIGURE 5–2

STORING DIGITIZED RESOURCES
Anything we digitize and store permanently takes up space on a disk or disc. This clip art (hot air balloon) is representative of thousands available for use in documents—the disk/disc storage requirement is 18 KB. A 4.88-second digital recording of an audio greeting (Sound Recorder software) can be attached to and sent with an e-mail message—the disk/disc storage requirement is 94 KB. This surreal art exhibit is all the more remarkable for the way the computer artist has used graphics techniques to model light, shadow, and reflections, mimicking a photograph's realism—the disk/disc storage requirement is 7.127 MB.

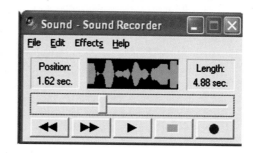

Photo courtesy of Intel Corporation

- *Source program file*. A **source program file** contains user-written instructions to the computer. These instructions must be translated to machine language prior to program execution.

- *Executable program file*. An **executable program file** contains executable machine language code.

- *Graphics file*. A **graphics file** contains digitized images.

- *Audio file*. An **audio file** contains digitized sound.

- *Video file*. A **video file** contains digitized video frames that when played rapidly (for example, 30 frames per second) produce motion video.

Files and Parking Lots

Mass storage is much like a parking lot for files. In a parking lot, a variety of vehicles—cars, buses, trucks, motorcycles, and so on—are put in parking places to be picked up later. Similarly, all sorts of files are "parked" in individual spots in mass storage, waiting to be retrieved later. To help you find your vehicle, large parking lots are organized with numbered parking places in lettered zones. The same is true with files and mass storage. Files are stored in numbered "parking places" on disk for retrieval. Fortunately, we do not have to remember the exact location of the file. The operating system does that for us. All we have to know is the name of the file. We assign user names to files, then recall or store them by name. Filenames in the Windows environment can include spaces, but some special characters, such as the slash (/) and colon (:), are not permitted. Your system will alert you if you include one of these special characters and give you an opportunity to rename the file. An optional three-character extension identifies the type of file and associates it with a program.

- *Readme.txt* is an ASCII file.

- *Student-Course.mdb* is a file containing a Microsoft Access database.

- *Letter.doc* is a Microsoft Word document file.

- *Income Statement.xls* is a Microsoft Excel spreadsheet file.

- *Adams School Home Page.htm* is a Web page file.

- *Module 1-1.vbp* is a Visual Basic source program file.

- *Play Game.exe* is an executable program file.

- *Family album.gif*, *Vacation Banff.bmp*, *Logo.jpg*, *Sarah.tif*, *Project A.pcx* are graphic files.

- *My_song.wav* is an audio file.

- *Introduction Sequence.mov* is a video file.

Figure 5-3 lists the common types of files and their associated programs. Many applications can work with a variety of file formats. For example, photo illustration programs can load *jpg, gif, tif,* and other graphics file formats. However, most popular applications programs have at least one **native file format** that is associated with that program—Microsoft Word is *doc*, Microsoft Excel is *xls*, and Adobe Acrobat is *pdf*.

What to Do with a File

Everything we do on a computer involves a file and, therefore, mass storage. But what do we do with files?

- *We create, name, and save files*. We create files when we name and save a letter, a drawing, a program, or some digital entity (an audio clip) to mass storage.

- *We copy files, move, and delete files*. We copy files from CD-ROMs to a hard disk to install software. We move files during routine file management activities. When we no longer need a file, we delete it.

- *We retrieve and update files*. We continuously retrieve and update our files (such as when we update the entries in a spreadsheet or revise a memo).

- *We display, print, or play files*. Most user files that involve text and graphics can be *displayed* and *printed*. Audio and video files are *played*.

- *We execute files*. We execute program files to run our software. In the Windows environment, executable filenames end in EXE, COM, BAT, and PIF.

- *We download and upload fZiles*. We download useful files from the Internet to our PCs. We sometimes work on, and then upload updated files to our company's server computer.

- We export/import files. The *file format,* or the manner in which a file is stored, is unique for each type of software package. When we import a file, we convert it from its foreign format (perhaps WordPerfect, a word processing program) to a format that is compatible with the current program (perhaps Microsoft Word, also a word processing program). We export files when we want to convert a file in the current program to a format needed by another program.

- *We compress files.* When the air is squeezed out of a sponge, it becomes much smaller. When you release it, the sponge returns to its original shape—nothing changes. **File compression** works in a similar fashion. File formats for most software packages are inefficient, resulting in wasted space on mass storage when you save files. Using file compression, a repeated pattern, such as the word *and* in text documents, might be replaced by a one-byte descriptor in a compressed file, saving two bytes for each occurrence of *and.* For example, "A band of sand stands grand in this land" might be compressed to "A bδ of sδ stδs grδ in this lδ," where the symbol "δ" replaces "and" in the stored file. One technique used when compressing graphics files replaces those portions of an image that are the same color with a brief descriptor that identifies the color only once and the area to be colored. Depending on the type and content of the file, file compression can create a compressed file that takes 10% to 90% less mass storage (the average is about 50%). The most popular file compression format is the zip format, which is supported by a variety of programs

FIGURE 5–3   COMMON FILE EXTENSIONS AND THEIR ASSOCIATED PROGRAMS

Word Processing and Text Documents

.DOC	Microsoft Word and WordPad
.WPD	WordPerfect
.WKS	Microsoft Works
.TXT	Plain ASCII text/unformatted
.PDF	Adobe Acrobat

Spreadsheets

.XLS	Microsoft Excel
.WQ1	Corel Quattro Pro
.WK1	Lotus 1-2-3
.WK3	
.WK4	

Database

.MDB	Microsoft Access

Presentation Graphics

.PPT	Microsoft PowerPoint

Graphics Formats (graphics programs typically open a variety of file types)

.GIF	CompuServe graphics interchange format
.JPG	JPEG compressed graphics format
.BMP	Windows bitmap
.PCT	PICT format
.TIF	Tagged image format (TIFF)
.PCX	PCX format
.WMF	Windows Meta File
.EPS	Encapsulated PostScript
.CGM	Computer Graphics MetaFile

Sound & Video Formats

.WAV	Windows WAV sound
.AIF	Macintosh AIFF sound
.RA	RealAudio sound
.AVI	Windows Video File
.MOV	Macintosh Quicktime video
.MPG	MPEG video format

Compressed Formats

.ZIP	PKzip/WinZIP compression
.HQX	BinHex compression (Macintosh)
.BHX	

System and Miscellaneous Files

.HTM	HTML code (Web pages)
.EXE	Executable file
.COM	
.BAT	MS-DOS batch file
.INI	Windows initialization file
.SYS	System file
.VBP	Visual Basic program file

and results in a **zip file.** A zipped file, which usually has a zip extension (such as longfile.zip), is compressed and must be unzipped before it can be used. A group of files can be compressed together as a single convenient zip file. When the zip file is unzipped, the individual files are restored. Zipped files take up less storage space and they take less time to download/upload on the Net. A special version of the zip file is the executable **self-extracting zip file.** These have an *exe* extension (longfile.exe) and must be executed (run) to unzip the file(s). The only relationship between zip files and Zip disks is that you can store a zip file on a Zip disk.

- *We protect files.* We can protect sensitive files by limiting access to authorized persons. For example, a human resources manager might want to limit access to the company's personnel file that might contain salary, health, and other sensitive information.

FILE MANAGEMENT

In the Windows environment, the *Windows Explorer* (the folder program icon) utility program is an integrated Web browser (Internet Explorer or the "e" program icon) and file management tool. The explorer becomes a Windows Explorer for file management when you enter or select a disk (for example, C:) in the address bar, or a Web browser if you enter a URL Internet address (for example, *http://www.wal-mart.com*). The Windows Explorer, which opens when you choose the *My Computer* icon on the desktop, lets you view files in several formats (see Figure 5-4). With the Explorer, you can do all of your file management tasks such as creating, copying, moving, and deleting folders and files, as well as other folder/file-related tasks. Folders are created for a specific disk drive. The PC used to capture the screen in Figure 5-4 has a hard disk (C:) and four interchangeable disk drives: a floppy drive (A:), a Zip disk drive (D:), a DVD/CD-ROM drive (E:), and a CD-RW drive (F:).

In Windows, a *folder* is a named grouping of related files and/or subordinate folders. We create folders to hold documents, programs, images, music, and other types of files. File types can be mixed within a folder; that is, the folder can hold any type of file. Some folders, such as the *Windows* and *Program Files* folders, are created by the Windows operating system during system installation; however, most folders are created by the user. Most people choose to create their folders in a hierarchical manner to provide a logical structure for their files. For example, the file structure on disk drive D: in Figure 5-5 has two main folders, *Family Photo Album* and *Personal*. In the *Family Photo Album* folder, photos are grouped in four subordinate folders: *Boy Scout Camp, Boys School Photos, Family Reunions,* and *Sports*. The *Sports* folder has four subordinate folders to enable sports images to be grouped by

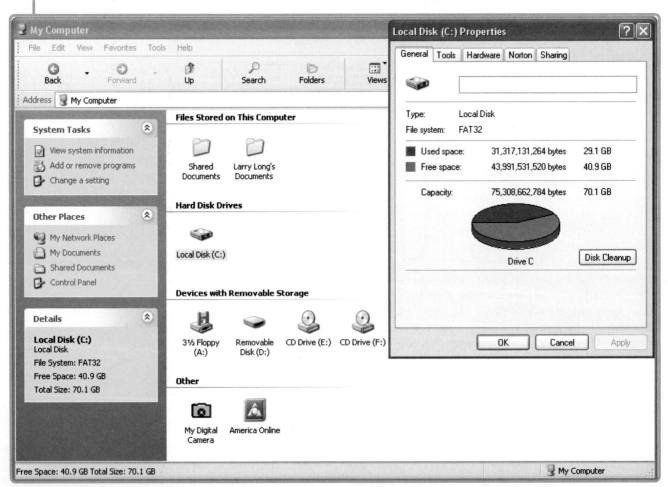

FIGURE 5–4

MY COMPUTER
Double-clicking on the *My Computer* icon on the desktop opens an Explorer window that shows active storage devices. As illustrated in the Icons view, this PC has a hard disk, referred to as Local Disk (C:), and four interchangeable disk drives: 3½ Floppy (A:), Removable Disk (D:), CD Drive (E:), and CD Drive (F:). Right-click on a disk icon and choose Properties to view disk usage information. The Properties dialog box for the hard disk (drive C:) shows 29.1 GB of used space and 40.9 GB of free space.

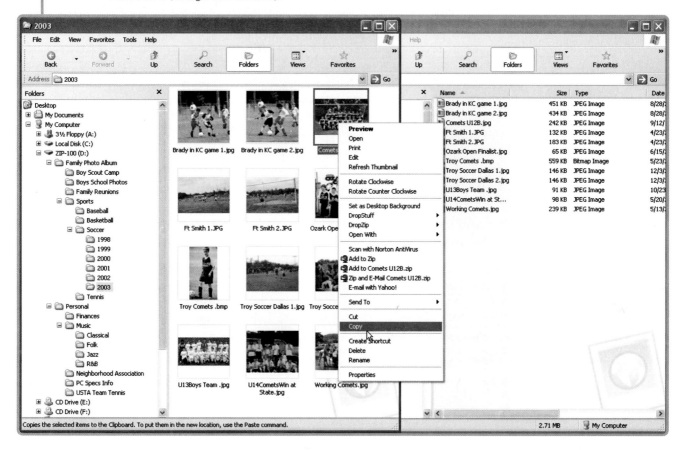

FIGURE 5–5

DISK DRIVES AND MEDIA
The Windows Explorer is a versatile utility program that lets you manipulate files and folders. Click on a disk or a folder in the Folders pane (left) and see the contents on the right. Click on the "+" to expand and list subordinate folders. Click on the "-" to hide subordinate folders. In this example, the files for the "Family Photo Album\Sports\ Soccer\2003" folder are displayed, both in Thumbnails view (foreground window) and Details view (background window).

sport. The *Soccer* folder has six subordinate folders so soccer photos can be organized by year. The *Personal* folder at the top of the hierarchy has five subordinate folders, one of which is *Music*. The *Music* folder has four subordinate folders: *Classical, Folk, Jazz,* and *R&B.*

You can store a specific file within a particular folder at any level in the hierarchy. For example, Sports photo images in Figure 5-5 are stored at the bottom of the hierarchy (for example, in the 2003 folder). Since files are stored within a hierarchical structure of folders, you must give the operating system the **path** to follow to store or retrieve a particular file. In Figure 5-5, for example, the image *Brady in KC game 1.jpg* has the following path:

Family Photo Album\Sports\Soccer\2003\Brady in KC game 1.jpg

The audio file for Beethoven's 5th Symphony (not shown in the figure) is stored in this path:

Personal\Music\Classical\Beethovens 5th.mp3

In the Mac OS X environment, a colon (:) is used in place of the backslash (\). In UNIX/Linux, it is a forward slash (/).

As mentioned previously, common file management activities include saving, opening, copying, moving, deleting, and renaming files. The commands used to perform these activities are described below.

● *Save/Save As.* Files are created and saved to a particular folder via the *Save* or *Save As* option in the *File* menu of an applications program. For an unsaved document, either save option lets you choose a disk, a folder, and a filename for the file. Choose *Save As* if you want to store the content of the current document, which has already been saved, in a new file with a new filename and/or a different disk/folder.

● *Open.* In the Explorer, navigate through the path to the filename, then double-click on the filename to open the file in the associated application program or to execute a program file. Or, you can choose *Open* in the *File* menu or the right-click shortcut menu (see Figure 5-5). For example, when you double-click on a Microsoft Word document, the Word application starts and the file is retrieved and displayed in the Word work area. Double-clicking a program file causes the program to open and run.

● *Copy.* The *Copy* command option in the Explorer lets you create a duplicate of one or more files or folders. Highlight what you want to duplicate and choose the *Copy* command from the *Edit* menu or from the shortcut menu. To highlight multiple files, press and hold the Ctrl key, and then click on each of the desired files or folders. To complete the copy operation, navigate to where you want to save the copy (the path), then choose the *Paste* option from the *Edit* menu or the shortcut menu. Or, if you prefer, you can press and hold the Ctrl key, and then use the mouse to drag the highlighted file(s)/folder(s) to their new location.

● *Cut (Move).* The *Cut* command option in the Explorer lets you move one or more files or folders. The *Cut* command (in the *Edit* menu or the shortcut menu) works like the *Copy* command, except that a cut operation deletes the highlight item(s) from its original folder. You also can use the mouse to drag item(s) to their new location (without pressing any additional keys).

● *Delete.* Tap the Delete key or choose *Delete* in the *Edit* menu or the shortcut menu to delete whatever files/folders are highlighted.

● *Rename.* To rename the file or folder, highlight the desired file or folder, then choose *Rename* from the shortcut menu.

Copy and cut operations place whatever has been copied or cut on the Clipboard; therefore, you can paste the Clipboard contents as many times as you want.

5-1.1	Data are retrieved from temporary mass storage and stored permanently in RAM. (T/F)
5-1.2	A file is to mass storage as a vehicle is to a parking lot. (T/F)
5-1.3	When we import a file, we convert a file in the current program to a format needed by another program. (T/F)
5-1.4	One way to reduce the size of a file is called file: (a) deflation, (b) compression, (c) downsizing, or (d) decreasing.
5-1.5	Magnetic tape storage provides inexpensive: (a) archival storage, (b) random-access storage, (c) direct-access storage, or (d) cache storage.

5-2 Magnetic Disks

Magnetic disks have *random-* or *direct-access* capabilities. You are quite familiar with these access concepts, but you may not realize it. Suppose you have Paul Simon's classic album, *The Rhythm of the Saints*, on CD. The first four songs on this CD are (1) "The Obvious Child," (2) "Can't Run But," (3) "The Coast," and (4) "Proof." Now suppose you also have this album on a cassette tape. To play the third song on the cassette, "The Coast," you would have to wind the tape forward and search for it sequentially. To play "The Coast" on the CD, all you would have to do is select track number 3. This simple analogy demonstrates the two fundamental methods of storing and accessing data—*sequential* and *random*.

For a mechanical device, magnetic disks are very fast, able to seek and retrieve information quicker than a blink of an eye (in milliseconds). This direct-access flexibility and speed have made magnetic disk storage the overwhelming choice of computer users, for all types of computers and all types of applications (see Figure 5-6). A variety of magnetic disk drives, the *hardware device,* and magnetic disks, the *medium* (the actual surface on which the information is stored), are manufactured for different business requirements.

HARDWARE AND STORAGE MEDIA

There are two fundamental types of magnetic disks: interchangeable and fixed.

● *Interchangeable magnetic disks.* **Interchangeable magnetic disks** can be stored offline and loaded to the magnetic disk drives as they are needed.

● *Fixed magnetic disks.* **Fixed magnetic disks,** also called hard disks, are permanently installed, or fixed. All hard disks are rigid and are usually made of aluminum with a surface coating of easily magnetized elements, such as iron, cobalt, chromium, and nickel. Today's integrated systems and databases are stored on hard disk, especially those used in workgroup computing. Such systems and databases require all data and programs to be online (accessible to the computer for processing) at all times.

Figure 5-7 shows some of the different types of interchangeable magnetic disks and fixed disks. As you can see, the drives for the various magnetic disk media are available in a wide variety of shapes and storage capacities. The type you (or a company) should use depends on the volume of data you have and the frequency with which those data are accessed.

MAGNETIC DISK DRIVES AND MEDIA

Virtually all PCs sold today are configured with at least one hard-disk drive and most have at least one interchangeable magnetic disk drive. The interchangeable disk drive provides a means for the distribution of data and software, and for backup and archival storage. The high-capacity hard-disk storage has made it possible for today's PC users to enjoy the convenience of having their data and software readily accessible at all times.

FIGURE 5–6 Information on Magnetic Disk
Today, most readily accessible information is stored on hard disk. The information provided by these interactive ATMs and kiosks is stored on disk and all transactions are recorded on disk.

Courtesy of Diebold, Incorporated

The Diskette

Four types of interchangeable disk drives are commonly used on PCs. These disk drives accept interchangeable magnetic disks, such as the traditional *diskette* and the newer high-capacity *SuperDisk, HiFD disk,* and *Zip disk.*

- *Diskette, SuperDisk, and HiFD disk.* The traditional 3.5-inch diskette, or *floppy disk,* is a thin, Mylar disk that is permanently enclosed in a rigid plastic jacket. The widely used standard for traditional diskettes permits only 1.44 MB of storage, not much in the modern era in which 4-MB images and 30-MB programs are commonplace. State-of-the-art versions, called **SuperDisk** and **HiFD disk,** can store 120 and 200 MB of information, respectively. The diskette, the SuperDisk, and the HiFD disk are the same size but have different disk densities. **Disk density** refers to the number of bits that can be stored per unit of area on the disk-face surface. In contrast to a hard disk, the diskette, the SuperDisk, and the HiFD disk are set in motion only when a command is issued to read from or write to the disk. The 120-MB SuperDisk and 200-MB HiFD disk combine floppy and hard disk technology to read from and write to specially formatted floppy-size disks. Both high-density drives read from and write to the traditional diskette as well.

- *Zip disk.* The original **Zip® drive** reads and writes to 100-MB **Zip® disks.** The most recent innovation, a 750-MB Zip drive, handles all versions of Zip disks (100, 250, and 750 MB). The SuperDisk, HiFD disk, and 750-MB Zip disk have storage capacities of 70, 139, and 521 floppy diskettes, respectively.

The diskette-based floppy disk drive is still standard equipment on most PCs; however, many PC buyers opt to upgrade to a SuperDisk or a HiFD disk, which can handle the floppy disk, too. Soon, the 3.5-inch floppy may become a historical artifact. The iMac™ from Apple Computer doesn't come with a floppy disk drive, relying instead on DVD-ROM/CD-RW combination drives, local area networks, and the Internet as vehicles for the transfer of information and programs.

FIGURE 5–7 DISK DRIVES AND MEDIA

SUPERDISK
This illustration compares the capacity of a 120-MB SuperDisk (right) to the traditional floppy disk. The SuperDisk drive is compatible with the traditional 1.44-MB diskette.

Courtesy of Imation Corporation

ZIP DISK
An alternative high-capacity inter-changeable disk is the 100-, 250-, or 750-MB Zip disk (shown here) with an external Zip drive.

Courtesy of Iomega Corporation

HARD DRIVE
This 50-GB hard drive is pictured as it is delivered to the manufacturer (in a sealed enclosure) and exposed to show its inner workings (12 platters with 24 read/write heads).

Courtesy of Seagate Technology

MICRODRIVE
IBM unveiled the world's smallest and lightest hard-disk drive with a disk platter that will fit into an egg. The IBM Microdrive weighs less than an AA battery and holds 340 MB. The device is designed for use in PDAs and palmtop PCs.

Courtesy of International Business Machines Corporation.
Unauthorized use not permitted.

PORTABLE HARD DISK
The external portable hard disk lets you take your files with you and access them on any PC with a USB port.

Courtesy of Iomega Corporation

A blank interchangeable disk has a very modest value. But once you save your files on it, its value, at least to you, increases greatly. Such a valuable piece of property should be handled with great care. Here are a few commonsense guidelines for handling interchangeable disks.

- Avoid temperature extremes.
- Store disks in a protected location, preferably in a storage tray away from direct sunlight and magnetic fields (for example, magnetic paperclip holders).
- Remove disks from disk drives before you turn off the computer, but only when the "drive active" light is off.
- Use an interchangeable drive cleaning kit periodically.
- Avoid force when inserting or removing a disk, as there should be little or no resistance.
- Don't touch the disk surface.

The Hard Disk

Hard disk manufacturers are working continuously to achieve two objectives: (1) to put more information in less disk space and (2) to enable a more rapid transfer of that information to/from RAM. Consequently, hard-disk storage technology is forever changing. There are three types of hard disks—those that are permanently installed, those that are portable, and those that are interchangeable between like systems.

- *Permanently installed hard disks.* Generally, the 1- to 5.25-inch (diameter of disk) permanent hard disks have storage capacities from about 20 GB (gigabytes) to over 200 GB. A 200-GB hard disk stores about the same amount of data as 42 DVDs or 308 CD-ROMs.

  A hard disk contains up to 12 disk platters stacked on a single rotating spindle. PC-based hard disks will normally have from one to four platters. Data are stored on all *recording surfaces.* For a disk with four platters, there are eight *recording surfaces* on which data can be stored (see Figure 5-8). The disks spin continuously at a high speed (from 7,200 to 15,000 revolutions per minute) within a sealed enclosure. The enclosure keeps the disk-face surfaces free from contaminants (see Figure 5-9), such as dust and cigarette smoke. This contaminant-free environment allows hard disks to have greater density of data storage than the interchangeable diskettes.

  The rotation of a magnetic disk passes all data under or over a **read/write head**, thereby making all data available for access on each revolution of the disk (see Figure 5-8). A fixed disk will have at least one read/write head for each recording surface. The heads are mounted on **access arms** that move together and literally float on a cushion of air over (or under) the spinning recording surfaces. The tolerance is so close that a particle of smoke from a cigarette will not fit between these "flying" heads and the recording surface!

- *Portable hard disk.* The **portable hard disk** is an external device that is easily connected to any personal computer via a USB port or FireWire port. All new PCs are configured with multiple high-speed USB 2.0 ports and many have at least one FireWire port. Port technology has finally caught up with portable hard disks enabling high-speed transfer of data (up to 480-M bps). Portable hard disks are popular in the business world where knowledge workers can take their user files with them to their home office or to a PowerPoint presentation in San Francisco. Portable hard disk capacities are similar to those of fixed hard disks and they weigh from .5 to 2 pounds.

- *Interchangeable hard disks.* Some systems are configured with interchangeable hard disks which are inserted and removed as easily as a CD-ROM disc. Systems that use interchangeable hard disks must be configured with the necessary disk drive hardware. Interchangeable hard disks are still in use, but customers now prefer portable hard disks because they can be connected to any PC.

FIGURE 5–8

FIXED HARD DISK WITH FOUR PLATTERS AND EIGHT RECORDING SURFACES
A cylinder refers to similarly numbered concentric tracks on the disk-face surfaces. In the illustration, the read/write heads are positioned over Cylinder 0012. At this position, the data on any one of the eight tracks numbered 0012 are accessible to the computer on each revolution of the disk. The read/write heads must be moved to access data on other tracks/cylinders.

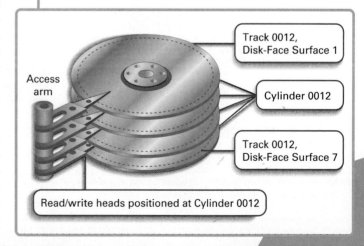

Access arm

Track 0012, Disk-Face Surface 1

Cylinder 0012

Track 0012, Disk-Face Surface 7

Read/write heads positioned at Cylinder 0012

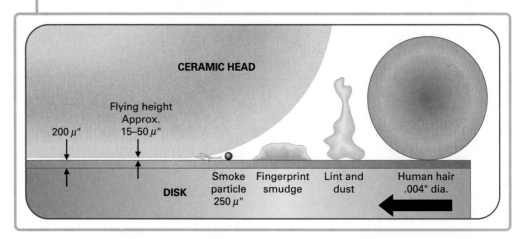

FIGURE 5–9 **DISK READ/WRITE HEAD FLYING DISTANCE**
When the disk is spinning at 7200 rpm, the surface of the disk travels across the read/write head at approximately 100 mph.

One of the most frequently asked questions is "How much hard drive capacity do I need?" The answer you hear most is "As much as you can afford." Disk space is like closet space—you never seem to have enough. If it's there, you tend to fill it with something. Software vendors are well aware of a rule of thumb that hard disk storage on new PCs doubles every year, so they keep building software to use our expanding hard drive space. For example, the original MS-DOS operating system was 160 KB, Windows 3.1 was 10 MB, and Windows XP is over 100 MB—over 600 times the size of DOS.

MAGNETIC DISK ORGANIZATION

The way in which data and programs are stored and accessed is similar for all hard disks. Conceptually, a floppy disk looks like a hard disk with a single platter. Both media have a thin film coating of one of the easily magnetized elements (cobalt, for example). The thin film coating on the disk can be magnetized electronically (see Figure 5-10) by the read/write head to represent the absence or presence of a bit (0 or 1).

Tracks, Sectors, and Clusters

Data are stored in concentric **tracks** by magnetizing the surface to represent bit configurations (see Figure 5-11). Bits are recorded using *serial representation;* that is, bits are aligned in a row in the track. The number of tracks varies greatly between disks, from as few as 80 on a diskette to thousands on high-capacity hard disks. The spacing of tracks is measured in **tracks per inch,** or **TPI.** The 3.5-inch diskettes are rated at 135 TPI. The TPI for hard disks can be in the thousands. The *track density* (TPI) tells only part of the story. The *recording density* tells the rest. Recording density, which is measured in *megabits per inch,* refers to the number of bits (1s and 0s) that can be stored per inch of track. High-density hard disks have densities in excess of 3 megabits per inch.

PC disks use **sector organization** to store and retrieve data. In sector organization, the recording surface is divided into pie-shaped **sectors** (see Figure 5-11). The number of sectors depends on the density of the disk. A hard disk may have hundreds of sectors. Typically, the storage capacity of each sector on a particular track is 512 bytes, regardless of the number of sectors per track. Adjacent sectors are combined to form **clusters,** the capacity of which is a multiple of 512. Typically, clusters range in size from 4,096 bytes up to 32,768 bytes (that's 8 up to 64 sectors). The cluster is the smallest unit of disk space that can be allocated to a file, so every file saved to disk takes up one or more clusters.

FIGURE 5–10 Bits on the Surface of a Magnetic Disk
This highly magnified area of a magnetic disk-face surface shows elongated information bits recorded serially along 8 of the disk's 1774 concentric tracks. One square inch of this disk's surface can hold 22 million bits of information.

Courtesy of International Business Machines Corporation. Unauthorized use not permitted.

Each disk cluster is numbered, and the number of the first cluster in a file comprises the **disk address** on a particular file. The disk address represents the physical location of a particular file or set of data on a disk. To read from or write to a disk, an access arm containing the read/write head is moved, under program control, to the appropriate *track* or *cylinder* (see

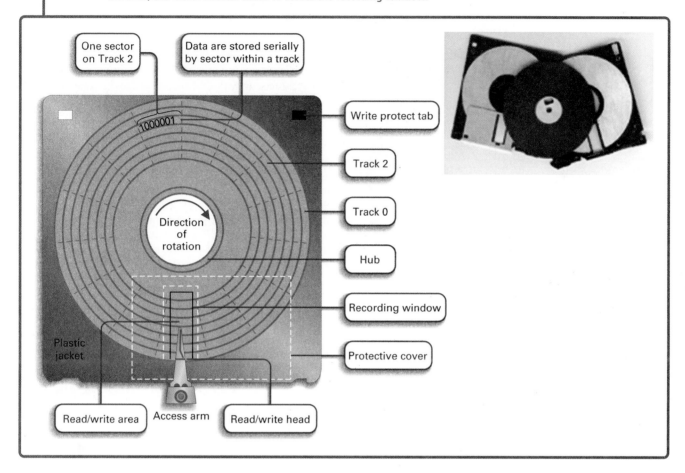

FIGURE 5-11
CUTAWAY OF A DISKETTE
The access arm on this 3.5-inch disk drive is positioned at a particular track (Track 2 in the example). Data are read or written serially in tracks within a given sector. On the right, the flexible 3.5-inch recording disk spins between two soft liners when accessed. The recording surface is sandwiched in a rigid plastic jacket for protection. When inserted, the metal shutter slides to reveal the recording window.

One sector on Track 2

Data are stored serially by sector within a track

1000001

Write protect tab

Track 2

Track 0

Direction of rotation

Hub

Recording window

Protective cover

Plastic jacket

Read/write area

Access arm

Read/write head

Figures 5-8 and 5-11). A particular **cylinder** refers to the same-numbered tracks on each recording surface (for example, Track 0012 on each recording surface; see Figure 5-8). When reading from or writing to a hard disk, all access arms are moved to the appropriate *cylinder.* For example, each recording surface has a track numbered 0012, so the disk has a cylinder numbered 0012. If the data to be accessed are on Recording Surface 01, Track 0012, then the access arms and the read/write heads for all eight recording surfaces are moved to Cylinder 0012. When the cluster containing the desired data passes under or over the read/write head, the data are read or written. Fortunately, software automatically monitors the location, or address, of our files and programs. We need only enter the name of the file to retrieve it for processing.

One of the major limitations of traditional sector organization is that recording space is wasted on the outer tracks. To overcome this limitation, some high-performance disk manufacturers employ a technique called **zoned recording.** In zoned recording, tracks are grouped into zones and all tracks in a particular zone have the same number of sectors (see Figure 5-12). A zone contains a greater number of sectors per track as you move from the innermost zone to the outermost zone. This approach to disk organization enables a more efficient use of available disk space.

The File Allocation Table

Each disk used in the Windows environment has a **Virtual File Allocation Table** (**VFAT**) in which information about the clusters is stored (it was a FAT in early operating systems). The table includes an entry for each cluster that describes where on the disk it can be found and how it is used (for example, whether the file is open or not). Clusters are *chained* together to store information larger than the capacity of a single cluster. Here's what happens when you or a program on your PC makes a request for a particular file.

FIGURE 5-12 ZONED RECORDING ON A HARD DISK
Zoned recording groups tracks into concentric zones such that the number of sectors in each track increases as the zones spread to the outer edge of the disk, thus enabling a more efficient use of storage space on the disk face surface.

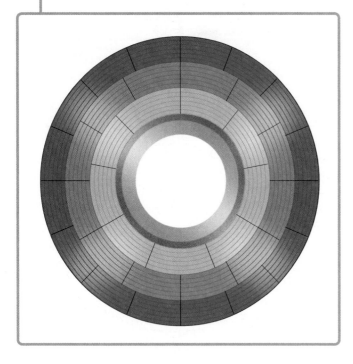

1. The operating system searches the VFAT to find the physical address of the first cluster of the file.

2. The read/write heads are moved over the track/cylinder containing the first cluster.

3. The rapidly rotating disk passes the cluster under/over the read/write head, and the information in the first cluster is read and transmitted to RAM for processing.

4. The operating system checks an entry within the initial cluster that indicates whether the file consists of further clusters, and if so, where on the disk they are located.

5. The operating system directs that clusters continue to be read and their information transmitted to RAM until the last cluster in the chain is read (no further chaining is indicated).

A 100-KB file being stored on a disk with 32,768 byte clusters would require four clusters (three clusters will store only 98,304 bytes). Most of the space in the fourth cluster is wasted disk space. Large clusters may improve overall system performance, but they tend to make more space inaccessible. The trade-off between system performance and efficient use of disk space is a major consideration during the disk design process.

Eventually your PC will give you a "lost clusters found" message, indicating that the hard disk has orphan clusters that don't belong to a file. Typically, lost clusters are the result of an unexpected interruption of file activity, perhaps a system crash or loss of power. Windows users should run the **ScanDisk** utility program periodically to "scan" the disk for lost clusters and, if any are found, let you return them to the available pool of usable clusters.

Defragmenting the Disk to Enhance Performance

The easiest and least expensive way to get a performance boost out of your PC (make it run faster) is to run a utility program called **Disk Defragmenter** in the Windows environment (see Figure 5-13). The program consolidates files into contiguous clusters; that is, the clusters for each file are chained together on the same or adjacent tracks (see Figure 5-14), thereby minimizing the movement of the read/write head. After running the program, each file stored on a disk is a single cluster or a chain of clusters. A 5-MB file may require hundreds of linked clusters. Ideally, all files would be stored on disk in contiguous clusters, but such is not the case with computing. Over time, files are added, deleted, and modified such that, eventually, files must be stored in noncontiguous clusters. When clusters are scattered, the read/write heads must move many times across the surface of a disk to access a single file. This excess mechanical movement slows down the PC because it takes longer to load a file to RAM for processing.

FIGURE 5-13 DEFRAG SUMMARY
The Speed Disk utility program within Symantec's Norton SystemWorks optimizes the disk by performing the defragmentation process. During the process, the Speed Disk program gives a visual overview of the status of each cluster on the hard drive. The colors indicate cluster status: used, bad, frequent access, applications, and so on.

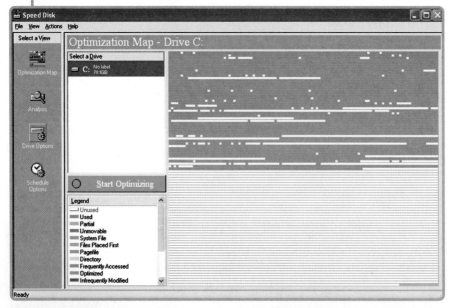

FIGURE 5–14

DISK DEFRAGMENTATION
(a) Initially, five files are stored ideally in contiguous clusters. (b) The user adds a few objects to a graphics file (blue), increasing its size and the number of clusters needed to store it. Note that file clusters are no longer contiguous. Then, a file (green) is deleted. (c) A new file (orange) is stored in noncontiguous clusters. (d) The disk is defragmented, resaving all files in contiguous clusters.

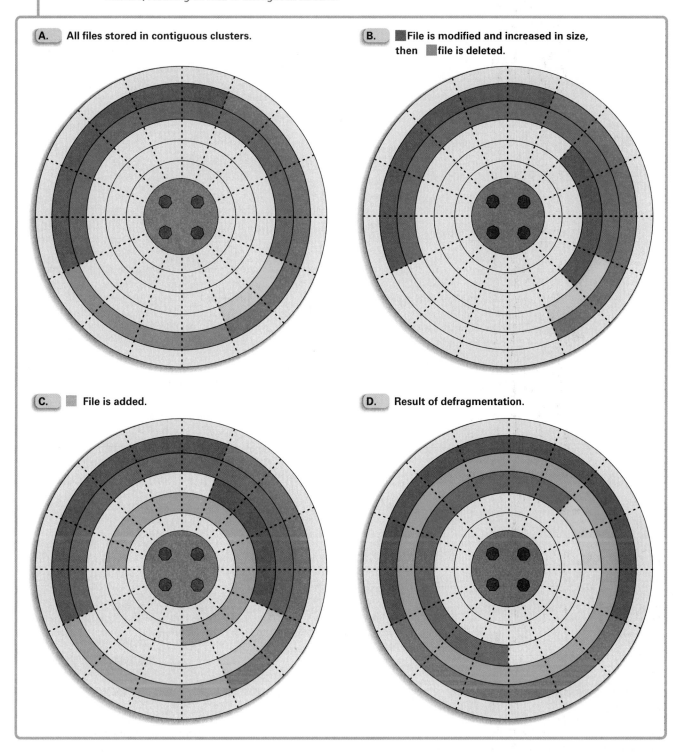

A. All files stored in contiguous clusters.

B. ■ File is modified and increased in size, then ■ file is deleted.

C. ■ File is added.

D. Result of defragmentation.

The mechanical movement of the disk read/write heads is the most vulnerable part of a PC system—the greater the fragmentation of files, the slower the PC. Fortunately, we can periodically reorganize the disk such that files are stored in contiguous clusters. This process, appropriately called **defragmentation**, is done with a handy utility program (see Figure 5-13). How often you run a "defrag" program depends on how much you use your PC. The fragmentation problem and the defragmentation solution are illustrated in Figure 5-14. In the example, five files are loaded to a disk,

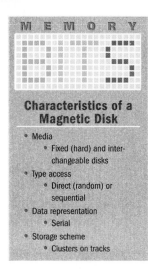

Characteristics of a Magnetic Disk

- Media
  - Fixed (hard) and inter-changeable disks
- Type access
  - Direct (random) or sequential
- Data representation
  - Serial
- Storage scheme
  - Clusters on tracks

each in contiguous clusters. A file is modified, another is deleted, and another is added, resulting in fragmentation of several files and a need for defragmentation. The defragmentation process rewrites fragmented files into contiguous clusters (see Figure 5-14).

Formatting: Preparing a Disk for Use

A new disk is coated with a surface that can be magnetized easily to represent data. However, before the disk can be used, it must be **formatted.** The formatting procedure causes the disk to be initialized with a recording format for your operating system. Specifically, it

- Creates sectors and tracks into which data are stored.
- Sets up an area for the virtual file allocation table.

If you purchased a PC today, the hard disk probably would be formatted and ready for use. However, if you added a hard disk or upgraded your existing hard disk, the new disk would need to be formatted.

DISK SPEED

Data access from RAM is performed at electronic speeds—approximately the speed of light. But the access of data from disk storage depends on the movement of mechanical apparatus (read/write heads and spinning disks) and can take from 4 to 8 milliseconds—still very slow when compared with the microsecond-to-nanosecond internal processing speeds of computers. Disk engineers want to reduce *access time* and increase the *data transfer rate*.

Access time is the interval between the instant a computer makes a request for the transfer of data from a disk-storage device to RAM and the instant this operation is completed. The read/write heads on the access arm in the illustration of Figure 5-8 move together. Some hard disks have multiple access arms, some with two read/write heads per disk-face surface. Having multiple access arms and read/write heads results in less mechanical movement and faster access times.

The **data transfer rate** is the rate at which data are read from mass storage to RAM or written to mass storage from RAM. Even though the data transfer rate from magnetic disk to RAM may be 400 million bytes per second, the rate of transfer from one part of RAM to another is much faster. **Disk caching** (pronounced *"cashing"*) is a technique that improves system speed by taking advantage of the greater transfer rate of data within RAM. With disk caching, programs and data that are *likely* to be called into use are moved from a disk into a separate disk caching area of RAM. When an application program calls for the data or programs in the disk cache area, the data are transferred directly from RAM rather than from the slower magnetic disk. Updated data or programs in the disk cache area eventually must be transferred to a disk for permanent storage. All modern PCs take full advantage of disk caching to improve overall system performance.

SECTION SELF-CHECK

5-2.1	Virtually all PCs sold today are configured with at least one DVD drive and one portable hard disk drive. (T/F)
5-2.2	The capacity of portable hard disks is about that of 100 floppy disks. (T/F)
5-2.3	Which has the greatest storage capacity: (a) the traditional floppy, (b) the latest Zip disk, (c) the SuperDisk, (d) or the HiFD disk?
5-2.4	The defragmentation process rewrites fragmented files into: (a) contiguous clusters, (b) continuous clusters, (c) circular clusters, or (d) Cretan clusters.
5-2.5	The rate at which data are read from disk to RAM is the: (a) TPI, (b) caching rate, (c) data transfer rate, or (d) streaming velocity.

5-3   Optical Laser Discs

Some industry analysts have predicted that *optical laser disc* technology eventually may make magnetic disk and tape storage obsolete. With this technology, two lasers replace the read/write head used in magnetic storage. One laser beam writes to the recording surface by scoring microscopic *pits* in the disc, and another laser reads the data from the light-sensitive recording surface. A light beam is easily deflected to the desired place on the optical disc, so a mechanical access arm is not needed.

Optical technology opens the door to new and exciting applications. Already this technology is leading the way to the library of the future. Because the world's output of knowledge is doubling every four years, the typical library is bursting at the seams with books and other printed materials. With library budgets declining, it may be impractical to continue to build structures to warehouse printed materials. Perhaps the only long-term solution for libraries is to move away from storing printed materials and toward storing information in electronic format—possibly some form of optical disc. Perhaps in the not-too-distant future we will check out electronic "books" by downloading them from a library's optical disc to our personal optical disc. In such a library of the future, knowledge will be more readily available and complete. In theory, the library of the future could have every book and periodical ever written. And, a "book" would never be out on loan.

Optical laser discs are becoming a very inviting option for users. These discs are less sensitive to environmental fluctuations, and they provide more direct-access storage at a much lower cost than does the magnetic disk alternative. Optical laser disc technology continues to emerge and has yet to stabilize. Common disc technologies are introduced in this section: *CD*, *CD-ROM*, *CD-R*, *CD-RW*, *DVD*, *DVD-ROM*, *DVD-R*, *DVD-RAM*, *DVD+RW*, *DVD-RW*, and *FMD-ROM*.

CD-ROM AND DVD-ROM

CD-ROM and DVD-ROM technologies have had a dramatic impact on personal computing and IT during the past decade because these technologies continue to provide ever-increasing storage capacity and ever-decreasing cost.

CD-ROM History

Introduced in 1980 for stereo buffs, the extraordinarily successful *CD*, or *compact disc*, is an optical laser disc designed to enhance the reproduction of recorded music. To make a CD recording, the analog sounds of music are digitized and stored on a 4.72-inch optical laser disc. Seventy-four minutes of music can be recorded on each disc in digital format in 2 billion bits. A bit is represented by the presence or absence of a pit on the optical disc. With its tremendous storage capacity per square inch, computer industry entrepreneurs immediately recognized the potential of optical laser disc technology. In effect, anything that can be digitized can be stored on optical laser disc: data, text, voice, still pictures, music, graphics, and motion video (see Figure 5-15).

CD-ROM and DVD-ROM Technology

CD-ROM, a spin off of audio CD technology, stands for *compact disc–read-only memory*. The name implies its application. Once inserted into the *CD-ROM drive*, the text, video images, and so on can be read into RAM for processing or display. However, the data on the disc are fixed—*they cannot be altered*. This is in contrast, of course, to the read/write capability of magnetic disks.

What makes CD-ROM so inviting is its vast capacity to store data and programs. The capacity of a single CD-ROM is up to 650 MB—about that of 450 diskettes. To put the density of CD-ROM into perspective, the words in every book ever written could be stored on a hypothetical CD-ROM that is 8 feet in diameter.

Magnetic disks store data in concentric tracks, each of which is divided into sectors (see Figure 5-11). The sectors on the inside tracks hold the same amount of information as those on the outside tracks, even though the sectors on the outside tracks take up more space. In contrast, CD-ROMs store data in a single track that spirals from the center to the outside edge (see Figure 5-16). The ultra thin track spirals around the disc thousands of times.

Data are recorded on the CD-ROM's reflective surface in the form of *pits* and *lands*. The pits are tiny reflective bumps that have been burned in with a laser. The lands are flat areas separating the pits. Together they record read-only binary (1s and 0s) information that can be interpreted by the computer as text, audio, images, and so on. Once the data have been recorded, a protective coating is applied to the reflective surface (the nonlabel side of a CD-ROM).

The pits and lands are more densely packed on the newer *DVD-ROM*, enabling 4.7 GB of storage. DVD-ROM comes in several versions. *Layering* the pits and lands increases the capacity to 8.5 GB. A *double-sided* DVD-ROM has either a 9.4 GB capacity (twice 4.7 GB) or 17 GB capacity (twice 8.5 GB or the capacity of 11,800 diskettes).

Popular CD-ROM drives are classified simply as 32X, 40X, or 75X. These spin at 32, 40, and 75 times the speed of the original CD standard. The faster the spin rate, the faster data are transferred to RAM for processing.

FIGURE 5–15 Sampling of CDs, CD-ROMs and DVDs
High-capacity CD-ROMs and DVDs, which evolved from the audio CD, have opened the door to exciting multi media applications with audio, video, graphics, and more. Also, they have become the standard for distribution of software and have replaced tape as the standard for the distribution of movies.

FIGURE 5–16

OPTICAL LASER DISC ORGANIZATION
A laser beam detector interprets pits and lands, which represent bits (1s and 0s), located within the sectors in the spiraling track on the CD-ROM reflective surface. Next to the illustration is a microscopic view of the pits and lands on the surface of a CD-ROM.

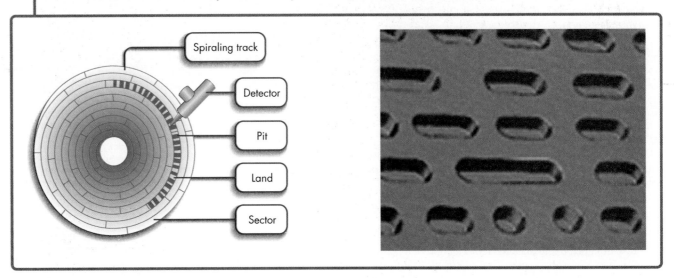

The slower speeds may cause program/image load delays and video to be choppy, especially when gaming. The original 1X CD-ROM data transfer rate was 150 KB per second, so the 75X CD-ROM data transfer rate is 75 times that, or 11.25 MB per second. The speed at which a given CD-ROM spins depends on the physical location of the data being read. The data pass over the movable laser detector at the same rate, no matter where the data are read. Therefore, the CD-ROM must spin more quickly when accessing data near the center.

Because data are more densely packed on a DVD-ROM, the data transfer rate is nine times that of a CD-ROM spinning at the same rate. For example, an 8X DVD-ROM drive transfers data at about the same rate as a 75X CD-ROM.

The laser detector is analogous to the magnetic disk's read/write head. The relatively slow spin rates make the CD-ROM access time much slower than that of its magnetic cousins. A CD-ROM drive may take 10 to 50 times longer to ready itself to read the information. Once ready to read, the transfer rate also is much slower.

The introduction of *multidisc CD-ROM player/changers* enables ready access to vast amounts of online data. This device is like a CD audio player/changer in that the desired CD-ROM can be loaded automatically to the CD-ROM disc drive under the control of a computer program. These CD-ROM player/changers, sometimes called **jukeboxes,** can hold from 6 to more than 500 CD-ROMs. The larger jukeboxes have multiple drives so that network users can have simultaneous access to different CD-ROM resources.

Just as CD-ROMs have become mainstream equipment, DVD-ROMs with much greater capacities are poised to replace them. The DVD-ROM has the same physical dimensions as the CD and the CD-ROM, but it can store from 7 to 25 times as much information. DVD-ROM drives are *backward compatible;* that is, they can play all of your CD-ROMs and CDs. They can read or play other DVD formats, too, including *DVD-video* and *DVD-audio.* DVD-video and DVD-audio are expected to replace videotapes and CDs in a few years. In 2002, the rental of DVD-video movies surpassed video tape rentals, signaling the inevitable replacement of VHS video tape with DVD-video format movies as the format of choice by video customers. This home entertainment version is usually shortened to simply DVD.

CD-ROM and DVD-ROM Applications

The tremendous amount of low-cost direct-access storage made possible by optical laser discs has opened the door to many new applications. The most visible application for CD-ROM is that it has emerged as the media-of-choice for the distribution of software. CD-ROM has the capacity to store massive sound, graphics, motion video, and animation files needed for multimedia applications. Many of the thousands of commercially produced CD-ROM discs contain reference material. The following is a sampling of available CD-ROM discs.

- Multimedia encyclopedias (including full text, thousands of still photos, motion video sequences, and sounds)

- Comprehensive reference materials (dictionary, thesaurus, almanac, atlas, book of facts, and more)
- The results of the 2000 U.S. Census at the county level
- The text of thousands of books, such as *Moby Dick*, the King James version of the *Bible*, *Beowulf*, *The Odyssey*, and many more
- Reviews and information on thousands of movies
- Street maps of the entire United States
- Games
- Sound effects (thousands of sound clips)
- Legal proceedings and cases for each state

The consumer cost of commercially produced CD-ROMs varies considerably from as little as a couple of dollars to several thousand dollars. All of these applications apply to DVD-ROM, too. DVD-ROM with its substantially greater capacities enables the distribution of bigger and better games on a single disc, larger databases (for example, huge clip-art libraries), feature-length movies, the telephone listings of everyone in the United States, and so on.

Creating CD-ROMs and DVD-ROMs for Mass Distribution

Most CD-ROMs and DVD-ROMs are created by commercial enterprises and sold to the public for multimedia applications and reference. Application developers gather and create source material, then write the programs needed to integrate the material into a meaningful application. The resulting files are then sent to a mastering facility. The master copy is duplicated, or "pressed," at the factory, and the copies are distributed with their prerecorded contents (for example, the complete works of Shakespeare or *Gone with the Wind*). Depending on the run quantity, the cost of producing and packaging a CD-ROM or DVD-ROM for sale can be less than a dollar apiece! These media provide a very inexpensive way to distribute applications and information.

REWRITABLE OPTICAL LASER DISC OPTIONS

Optical laser technologies are now in transition from write-only technologies, such as CD-ROM and DVD-ROM, to read and write technologies. This means that we, the end users, can make our own CD-ROMs and DVD-ROMs.

CD-R and CD-RW

Most of the world's PCs have CD-ROM or DVD-ROM drives. This rapid and universal acceptance of CD-ROM gave rise to another technology—**CD-R, compact disc-recordable.** A few years ago, the capability to record on CD-ROM media cost over $100,000. CD-R drives, at less than $100, brought that capability to any PC owner. While people were celebrating the arrival of CD-R, another more flexible CD technology was introduced—**CD-RW (CD-ReWritable).** This technology goes one step further, allowing users to rewrite to the CD-sized media, just as is done on magnetic disk media. With the cost of CD-R and CD-RW technologies converging, CD-R drives have disappeared from the optical drive landscape. CD-RW discs can be inserted and read on modern CD-ROM drives, but they will not work with the older models.

DVD+RW, DVD-RW, and DVD-RAM

As you might expect, DVD (digital video disc) technology is emerging like CD-ROM technology with recordable and read/write capabilities. **DVD-R** is like CD-R but with the recording density of DVD-ROM. **DVD+RW, DVD-RW,** and **DVD-RAM,** are like CD-RW, giving us rewritable capabilities for high-capacity DVD technology. DVD-RAM, DVD-RW, and DVD+RW are competing technologies, with the most recent technology, DVD+RW, appearing to emerge as the technology of choice for PC vendors. DVD rewritable alternatives are more costly than CD-RW, but as the price drops DVD rewritable drives might become a standard peripheral on new PCs. State-of-the-art DVD rewritable drives can read all DVD and CD-ROM formats. You can rewrite to rewritable discs thousands of times.

FIGURE 5–17 High-Capacity FMD-ROM
A single FMD-ROM disc can store printed documentation that, if stacked, would stretch almost two miles into the sky.
Courtesy of Constellation 3D

With **FMD-ROM** technology looming on the horizon, it won't be long before DVD technology is old hat. FMD-ROM, a very high-density, multilayer disc, holds up to 140 GB of data, 215 times that of CD-ROM and 30 times that of the 4.7 GB DVD-ROM (see Figure 5-17). FMD-ROM drives are backward compatible, able to read CD and DVD discs.

OPTICAL DISCS IN YOUR PC

The typical PC will have one or two optical drives. At a minimum, users want a PC with a DVD-ROM drive so they have full optical read capability and can enjoy all CD-ROM and DVD applications, including playing DVD movies. Increasingly, however, PC users are "burning" their own CDs and CD-ROMs, so they want rewritable capability, too. One of the most popular options is the *DVD-ROM/CD-RW combination drive* which gives users the flexibility to read CD-ROM and DVD-ROM format discs (including audio CDs and DVD movies) and to burn their own audio and video CDs, to burn discs for data transfer, and to provide read/write backup of user files. Some people choose to configure their PCs with both a DVD-ROM drive and a DVD-ROM/CD-RW combination drive to enable easy duplication of optical media.

Those users with a few extra dollars to spend and expanded application needs are choosing a *DVD+RW/CD-RW combination drive*. You can use it to store original videos on DVD disc or archive up to 4.7 GB of data to a DVD+RW disc. People who spend the money on this high-end rewritable disk combo drive will usually add a DVD-ROM drive, as well, to facilitate duplication tasks.

WHAT'S THE BEST MIX OF STORAGE OPTIONS?

The choice of which technologies to choose for a system or an application is often a trade-off between storage capacity, cost (dollars per megabyte), and speed (access time). You can never really compare apples to apples when comparing storage media because one might have an advantage in access time, portability, random access, nonvolatility, and so on. Solid-state storage (RAM) is the fastest and most expensive (about $0.20 per MB), but it's volatile. Hard disk offers fast, permanent storage for less than a half penny per MB. You can get 1 MB of interchangeable DVD-RW storage for about a quarter the cost of hard disk storage and about a hundredth the cost of RAM, but it is relatively slow. A well-designed system will have a mix of storage options. Each time you purchase a PC, you should spend a little extra time assessing your application and backup needs so you can configure your system with an optimum mix of storage options.

Storage is like money: No matter how much you have, you always want more. Each year, improvements are made in existing mass storage devices as the storage industry strives to meet our craving for more storage.

Rotating storage media may go the way of the steam engine when low-cost solid-state memory (RAM) can store as much in less space. Already, nonvolatile flash memory chips, such as the Mini USB drive, are being developed that will have many times more storage capacity than the largest flash chips currently available (see Figure 5-18). Flash memory already is the basis for e-book (electronic book) readers that hold many books, magazines, and so on (see Figure 5-19). Perhaps someday the only moving part on PCs will be the cooling fan.

What does being able to store more information in less space mean to you? It means videophones that can be worn like wristwatches. It means that you can carry a diskette-sized reader and all your college "textbooks" in your front pocket. Each new leap in storage technology seems to change much of what we do and how we do it.

FIGURE 5–18 The Mini USB Drive
About the size of a Car key, the solid-state, flash memory Iomega® Mini USB drive is a portable solution for transporting and sharing data. Plug it into any computer's USB port and it is immediately recognized as an active drive, enabling applications to be launched and run directly from the drive. The miniature drive requires no cables, adapters, or batteries.

Courtesy of Iomega Corporation

FIGURE 5–19 Solid-State Storage Applications
This RCA eBook uses solid state random access memory, rather than disk, to hold more than 5,000 pages of material. Popular magazines, novels, and periodicals are readily available for downloading and viewing on the eBook.

Photo courtesy of RCA Corporation

SECTION SELF-CHECK

5-3.1	CD-ROM is read-only. (T/F)
5-3.2	CD-RW technology is: (a) rewritable, (b) read-only, (c) write-only, or (d) nonwritable.
5-3.3	Which of these is poised to replace the CD-ROM: (a) VVV, (b) jukebox, (c) CD-R, or (d) DVD-ROM?
5-3.4	A double-sided DVD-ROM with layering has a capacity of 17 GB. (T/F)
5-3.5	Which disc drive offers the PC user the greatest flexibility: (a) DVD+RW/CD-RW, (b) DVD-ROM, (c) DVD-ROM/CD-RW, or (d) CD-R?

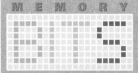

It was inevitable that the dark side would spread evil to the cyberworld. This evil comes in the form of computer viruses. Computers can get sick just like people. A variety of highly contagious viruses can spread from computer to computer, much the way biological viruses do among human beings. Just as a virus can infect human organs, a **computer virus** can infect programs, documents, and data-bases. It can also hide duplicates of itself within legitimate programs, such as an operating system or a word processing program. A computer virus is a man-made program or portion of a program that causes an unexpected event, usually a negative one, to occur. Viruses reside on and are passed between magnetic disks.

It is estimated that computer viruses cost businesses and individuals worldwide up to $20 billion a year. There are many viruses—over 50,000, to date. Some act quickly by erasing user programs and files on disk. Others grow like a cancer, destroying small parts of a file each day. Some act like a time bomb. They lay dormant for days or months but eventually are activated and wreak havoc on any software on the system. Several *denial of service* viruses cause the Internet to be flooded with e-mail, each with an attached program that causes more infected e-mail to be sent. These viruses place such heavy demands on e-mail server computer resources that they are unable to handle the volume, thus the denial of service. Some viruses attack the hardware and have been known to throw the mechanical components of a computer system, such as disk-access arms, into costly spasms. Many companies warn their PC users to back up all software prior to every Friday the thirteenth, a favorite date of those who write virus programs.

Some viruses are relatively benign, but can be annoying. For example, an error message might pop up that says, "This one's for you, Bosco." Another might insert the word "WAZZU" in the middle of your text. The Cookie Monster virus displays "I want a cookie" then locks up the system until you key in "Fig Newton."

TYPES OF COMPUTER VIRUSES

Two types of viruses—macro viruses and worms—have become alarmingly popular during the last few years. A **macro virus** is a program or portion of a program that is written in the macro language of a particular application, such as Microsoft Word or Microsoft Outlook. One well-publicized and hugely destructive macro virus was *Melissa,* which was distributed as an e-mail attachment. When opened, the macro program caused the virus to be sent to the first 50 people in the Outlook contact list. Melissa so overwhelmed millions of e-mail servers to the point they could no longer perform their function.

A **worm** is a computer program or portion of a program that makes copies of itself. Typically, the worm will interfere with the normal operation of a program or a computer. Worms exist as separate entities and do not attach themselves to files, programs, or documents. One of the most devastating incarnations of the worm was the *Love.bug* or *I Love You* worm that invaded millions of computers through e-mail and Internet Relay Chat (IRC) channels.

Though not officially a virus because it does not replicate itself, the **Trojan horse** can be equally damaging. Named after the wooden horse the Greeks used to capture Troy, the Trojan horse needs someone to e-mail it to you for it does not e-mail itself. Fortunately, most Trojan horses take the form of a practical joke, but some can be harmful. In a classic Trojan horse scenario, one claims to rid your PC of viruses but, instead, plants viruses in your system.

Most people who write and circulate virus programs fall into two groups. The first group, mostly young males from around the world, create viruses to impress each other with their cleverness. The second, and far more dangerous group, creates viruses with malicious intent. Some do not know the harm they do, but some do. These people are just plain mean and want their viruses to result in property damage and cause human suffering. Sadly, terrorists have embraced the virus as a weapon of war.

SOURCES OF COMPUTER VIRUSES

In the PC environment, there are three primary sources of computer viruses (see Figure 5-20).

- *The Internet.* The most common source of viral infection is the very public Internet, on which people download and exchange software and send e-mail. All too often, a user logs on to the Internet and downloads a game, a utility program, or some other enticing piece of freeware from an unsecured site, but gets the software with an embedded virus instead. Sometimes viruses are attached to e-mails. A good rule is to know the sender before opening anything sent with an e-mail.

- *Diskettes and DVDs/CD-ROMs.* Viruses also are spread from one system to another via common interchangeable disks. For example, a student with an infected application disk might unknow-

THE CRYSTAL BALL:
Cyber War We now live in a world in which we must be ever vigilant—there are those who want to harm us because of the color of our skin, our religious beliefs, our nationality, or for no particular reason at all. Traditionally, the efforts of terrorists have focused on the destruction of property and physical harm; however, terrorists now are researching ways to destroy one of our most valuable personal and commercial assets—the contents of our disks. They do this by seeking points of vulnerability in PCs and servers and by planting destructive viruses. Terrorists will also continue their denial-of-service attacks in an attempt to cripple server computers worldwide. Sadly, cyber terror is now part of the terrorist's arsenal of evil.

ingly infect several other laboratory computers with a virus, which, in turn, infects the applications software of other students. Software companies have unknowingly distributed viruses with their proprietary software products. Ouch!

● *Computer networks.* Viruses can spread from one computer network to another.

How serious a problem are viruses? They have the potential of affecting an individual's career and even destroying companies. For example, a financial adviser who inadvertently forwards a virus to his clients may lose credibility and clients. A company that loses its accounts receivables records—records of what the company is owed—could be a candidate for bankruptcy.

FIGURE 5-20   **HOW VIRUSES ARE SPREAD**

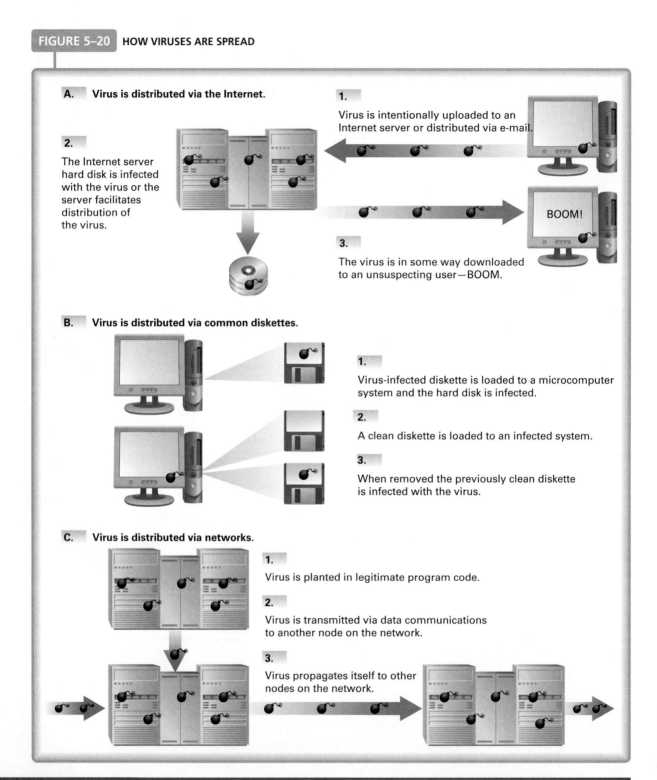

A.   **Virus is distributed via the Internet.**

1.
Virus is intentionally uploaded to an Internet server or distributed via e-mail.

2.
The Internet server hard disk is infected with the virus or the server facilitates distribution of the virus.

3.
The virus is in some way downloaded to an unsuspecting user—BOOM.

BOOM!

B.   **Virus is distributed via common diskettes.**

1.
Virus-infected diskette is loaded to a microcomputer system and the hard disk is infected.

2.
A clean diskette is loaded to an infected system.

3.
When removed the previously clean diskette is infected with the virus.

C.   **Virus is distributed via networks.**

1.
Virus is planted in legitimate program code.

2.
Virus is transmitted via data communications to another node on the network.

3.
Virus propagates itself to other nodes on the network.

VIRUS PROTECTION

The software package distributed with new PCs usually includes an **antivirus program** and a short-term subscription to a virus update service. The best way to cope with viruses is to recognize their existence and use an antivirus program. Your chances of living virus free are greatly improved if you periodically use this program to check for viruses and are careful about what you load to your system's hard disk. Computer viruses are introduced continuously into the cyberworld, so antivirus vendors, such as Symantec and McAfee, offer a subscription service that lets you download protection for new viruses.

Here are some tips that will help minimize your vulnerability to viruses.

- Delete e-mails from unknown, suspicious, or untrustworthy sources, especially those with files attached to an e-mail.

- Never open a file attached to an e-mail unless you know what it is, even if it appears to come from a friend.

- Download files from the Internet only from legitimate and reputable sources. If you feel comfortable with the source but want an extra level of protection, download the file to a floppy disk and test it with your own antivirus software.

- Update your antivirus software at least once a week as over 200 viruses are discovered each month.

- Back up your files periodically. If you catch a virus, your chances of surviving are pretty good if you maintain current backups of important data and programs.

Traditionally, virus protection has been at the PC or client level. However, this may change as companies look to network and Internet service providers for more services. New tools are being developed that can check for viruses at the server level before files reach the PC. An ISP's prescan of all files will protect subscribers from all known viruses at the time. This service is inviting for companies concerned about keeping current with protection from the never-ending stream of viruses circulating the Internet.

PERSONAL COMPUTING:
Virus Protection Don't leave home without protection from viruses and hackers. There is too much at stake, possibly your almost-completed term paper, your family photo album, the use of your PC for days or weeks, and so on. Typically, a new computer will have one of the popular virus protection programs installed; however, for continued protection from new viruses you will need to subscribe to the software vendor's online update service. Having antivirus software provides only partial protection (legacy viruses), so it is important to continually update the virus definitions database.

5-4.1	A computer virus is a computer-generated program that causes an unpleasant event on a computer. (T/F)
5-4.2	The number of computer viruses is in which range: (a) 25–50, (b) 100–500, (c) 20,000–30,000, or (d) 50,000 and up.
5-4.3	A denial of service virus place high demands on: (a) backup capabilities, (b) hackers, (c) server resources, or (d) vaccine research.
5-4.4	One way to fight computer viruses is to use what type of software: (a) antibug, (b) antivirus, (c) redo, or (d) backup?

SECTION SELF-CHECK

5-5 Backing Up Files: Better Safe Than Sorry

Safeguarding the content of your disks may be more important than safeguarding hardware. After all, you can always replace your computer, but you often cannot replace your lost files.

BACKUP FOR PERSONAL COMPUTING

The first commandment in computing, at any level, is *back up your files!*

The backup process serves two important functions.

- *Protection against loss of valuable files*. When you create a document, a spreadsheet, or a graph and you want to recall it at a later time, you *store* the file on disk. You can, of course, store many files on a single disk. If the disk is in some way destroyed (hard disk crash, demagnetized, burned, and so on), stolen, or lost, your files are gone unless you have a backup.

- *Archiving files*. Important files no longer needed for active processing can be archived to a backup medium. For example, banks archive old transactions (checks and deposits) for a number of years. PC users periodically archive their e-mail.

Backup Media

PC users employ a variety of backup media.

- *Rewritable optical media*. Rewritable optical discs—CD-RW or DVD+RW—have emerged as the backup medium of choice for the active PC user, offering 650-MB and 4.7 GB-capacities, respectively.

WHY THIS SECTION
IS IMPORTANT
TO YOU

At one time or another, just about everyone who works with computers loses work for which there is no backup. It's never a pleasant experience. This section helps you take that first step toward regularly backing up your valuable personal information and avoiding one of life's traumas.

- *Diskettes.* Backing up a complete hard disk to 1.44-MB floppies is impractical because it would require hundreds, perhaps thousands, of diskettes. However, if this is your only option, you should back up critical files to diskette.

- *High-capacity diskettes.* The Zip disk, SuperDisk, or HiFD disk drive provide a good backup medium for the casual PC user, offering disk backup capacities in the 100- to 750-MB range.

- *Backup to portable hard disks.* The cost of a portable hard disk continues to drop, making it an increasingly viable alternative for backup.

Backup Methods

You can choose from three common backup methods.

- *Full backup.* A full backup copies all files on a hard disk to backup media.

- *Selective backup.* Only user-selected files are backed up.

- *Incremental backup.* Only those files that have been modified since the last backup are backed up.

The frequency with which files are backed up depends on their *volatility,* or how often you update the files on the disk. If you spend time every day working with files, you should back them up each day. Others should be backed up no more often than they are used. Figure 5-21 illustrates a six-CD-RW or DVD+RW backup rotation.

Figure 5-22 illustrates and explains a backup procedure for only those critical files that are used daily. In the figure, two *generations* of backup are maintained on Backup Sets A and B. Critical disk

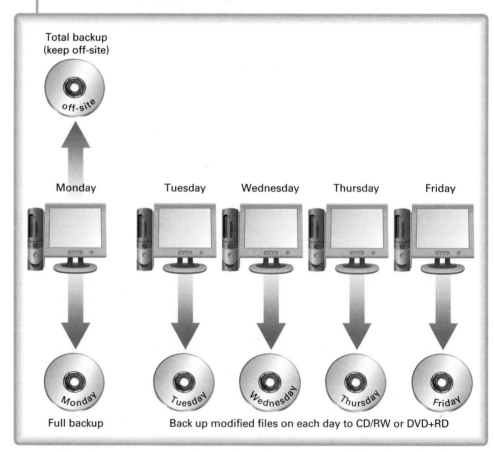

FIGURE 5–21

BACKUP ROTATION: SIX CD-RW OR DVD+RW DISCS
This six-CD-RW disc or six-DVD+RW disc backup rotation is common in small businesses and with individuals whose files have high volatility. Two total backups are done every Monday, one of which is taken to an offsite location. Only incremental backups (files that are modified on a given day) are made for each of the other weekdays. If all files are lost on Friday, the total backup from Monday is restored to the hard disk, then incremental backups are restored for Tuesday through Thursday.

Total backup
(keep off-site)

off-site

Monday   Tuesday   Wednesday   Thursday   Friday

Monday   Tuesday   Wednesday   Thursday   Friday

Full backup   Back up modified files on each day to CD/RW or DVD+RD

FIGURE 5–22

DISK/DISC BACKUP ROTATION: TWO BACKUP SETS
After each day's processing, critical disk files are copied alternately to Backup Sets A and B. In this manner, one backup set (possibly several interchangeable disks or a CD-RW or a DVD+RW) is always current within a day's processing. If the critical work files and the most recent backup are accidentally destroyed, a third backup is current within two days' processing. Backup Sets A and B are alternated as the most current backup.

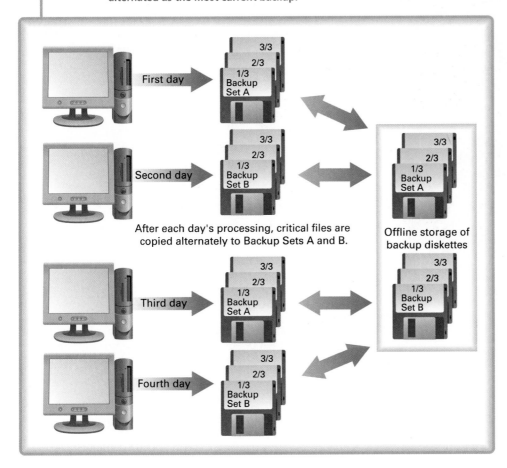

After each day's processing, critical files are copied alternately to Backup Sets A and B.

Offline storage of backup diskettes

files are copied alternately to Backup Sets A and B each day. This technique is popular with individual users whose main concern is the backup of their currently active files.

Restoring Files

If you lose your data or programs, you will need to restore the backed-up file to disk. If you use a backup system similar to the one shown in Figure 5-21, then some updating will occur between total backup runs. To re-create your files, you need to use the last total backup and then incorporate all subsequent incremental backups. For example, assume a virus wiped your hard drive clean at the end of the day on Thursday. To restore the backup files, you would restore the full backup from Monday, then the modified backup from Tuesday, and finally the modified backup tape from Wednesday. Then you would need to redo any processing that was done on Thursday prior to the virus striking.

Other Backup Options

In practice, the type of backup you employ depends on circumstances and available hardware. Here are a few more commonly used approaches to backup.

● *Backup to a server computer.* Users on a local area network can periodically upload user files to the server computer, whose files normally are backed up daily.

● *Backup to another PC on a home network.* Users on a home network can periodically upload their files to another PC on the network.

FIGURE 5–23 Automatic Retrieval Tape Storage
This robotic tape storage and retrieval unit holds hundreds of high-density tape cartridges, each with a capacity of 25 GB (gigabytes). The tape cartridges are automatically loaded and unloaded to a tape drive as they are needed for processing. Companies use tape storage and retrieval systems to back up massive master files on magnetic disk storage.

Courtesy of International Business Machines Corporation.

Unauthorized use not permitted.

- *Backup to a notebook/desktop PC.* Many people have both a desktop and a notebook PC, linking the PCs via USB or some other connector to transfer user files to whichever PC is in use. One system serves as backup to the other.

- *Magnetic tape.* The cost of rewritable optical disc drives has dropped so dramatically that the use of magnetic tape drives, called **tape backup units (TBUs)**, is all but eliminated for personal computing. TBUs, which are not applicable for routine information processing because they are sequential only, use a $1/4$-inch cartridge (QIC), also called a **data cartridge.** The self-contained data cartridge is inserted into and removed from the tape drive in much the same way you would load or remove a videotape from a VCR. TBUs are still common in the business environment. Some businesses use automatic retrieval tape storage (see Figure 5-23).

BACKUP FOR INTERNET AND NETWORK SERVERS

At the Skalny Basket Company in Springfield, Ohio, Cheryl Hart insisted on daily backups of the small family-owned company's accounts receivables files. The backups were inconvenient and took 30 minutes each day. Cheryl took the backup home each day in her briefcase, just in case. On December 23, she packed her briefcase and left for the Christmas holidays. Five days later, Skalny Basket Company burned to the ground, wiping out all inventory and its computer system. The company was up in smoke, all except for tape cartridges that contained records of its accounts receivables. Cheryl said, "We thought we were out of business. Without the tape, we couldn't have rebuilt."

Small companies like the Skalny Basket Company can use backup methods like those used in personal computers. However, larger companies that depend on online transaction processing and a shared database must be up and running at all times. When the system goes down, the company goes down. When downtime is simply unacceptable, the network server must be made **fault-tolerant.** That is, the network server must be designed to permit continuous operation even if important components of the network fail. To accomplish this goal, parts of the system must be redundant (for example, disk storage).

To minimize the impact of catastrophic disk failure, companies use **RAID (Redundant Array of Independent Disks)** to provide fault-tolerant backup of disk systems. RAID spreads data across several integrated disk drives such that a duplicate copy is maintained on a separate disk system at all times. When an online transaction is completed and logged on one disk, an exact entry is made to a duplicate disk. The disk system is considered fault-tolerant because it is highly unlikely that two disks will fail at the same time.

SECTION SELF-CHECK

5-5.1	The frequency with which work files are backed up depends on their volatility. (T/F)
5-5.2	Tape backup units store data on QIC tape cartridges. (T/F)
5-5.3	Which of these is a not a viable approach to backing up files: (a) backup to a server computer, (b) backup to another PC on a home network, (c) backup to RAM, or (d) backup to a notebook PC?

5-1 MASS STORAGE, FILES, AND FILE MANAGEMENT

Data and programs are stored in **mass storage** for permanent storage. **Magnetic disk drives** and **magnetic tape drives** are popular devices for mass storage. Tape is used mostly for backup capability and archival storage. **Optical laser disc** technology continues to emerge as a mass storage medium.

The file is the foundation of permanent storage on a computer system. Filenames in the Windows environment can include spaces, but some special characters are not permitted. An optional three-character extension identifies the type of file (for example, *myphoto.gif* is a graphics file). Popular file types include the **ASCII file** (txt), **data file** (mdb for Access), **document file** (doc for Word), **spreadsheet file** (xls for Excel), **Web page file** (htm), **source program file** (vbp for Visual Basic), **executable program file** (exe), **graphics file** (gif, bmp, jpg, tif, and pcx), **audio file** (wav), and **video file** (mov). Most popular applications programs have at least one **native file format.**

Everything we do on a computer has to do with a file and, therefore, mass storage. We can create, name, save, copy, move, delete, retrieve, update, display, print, play, execute, download, upload, export, import, compress, and protect files. **File compression** is used to economize on storage space. PC users routinely compress file to **zip files** for download/upload on the Net and unzip the compressed or "zipped" files for use in applications. The executable **self-extracting zip file** must be executed to unzip the file(s).

The Windows Explorer is a utility program that lets you view and manage folders/files. Folders are created for specific disk drives. You must give the operating system the **path** to follow to store or retrieve a particular file. Common file management activities include save/save as, open, copy, move, delete, and rename.

5-2 MAGNETIC DISKS

Data are retrieved and manipulated either sequentially or randomly. There are two types of magnetic disks: **interchangeable magnetic disks** and **fixed magnetic disks.** Magnetic disk drives enable random- and sequential-processing capabilities.

Popular types of interchangeable magnetic disks include the 3.5-inch diskette, also called a floppy disk, the 120-MB **SuperDisk,** the 200-MB **HiFD disk,** and the 100-, 250-, or 750-MB **Zip disk,** which is inserted into a **Zip drive.** The floppy disk, SuperDisk, and HiFD disk are the same size but have different **disk densities.**

There are three types of hard disks—those that are permanently installed, those that are portable, and those that are interchangeable between like systems. Hard disks contain at least one platter and usually several disk platters stacked on a single rotating spindle. The rotation of a magnetic disk passes all data under or over **read/write heads,** which are mounted on **access arms.** The **portable hard disk** is an external device that is easily connected to any personal computer via a USB port or FireWire port.

The way in which data and programs are stored and accessed is similar for both hard and interchangeable disks. Data are stored via serial representation in concentric **tracks** on each recording surface. The spacing of tracks is measured in **tracks per inch (TPI).** In **sector organization,** the recording surface is divided into pie-shaped **sectors,** and each sector is assigned a number. Adjacent sectors are combined to form **clusters.**

Each disk cluster is numbered, and the number of the first cluster in a file comprises the **disk address** on a particular file. The disk address designates a file's physical location on a disk. A particular **cylinder** refers to every track with the same number on all recording surfaces.

Some high-performance disk manufacturers employ **zoned recording** where zones contain a greater number of sectors per track as you move from the innermost zone to the outermost zone.

Each disk used in the Windows environment has a **Virtual File Allocation Table (VFAT)** in which information about the clusters is stored. Clusters are *chained* together to store file information larger than the capacity of a single cluster. The **ScanDisk** utility lets you return lost clusters to the available pool of usable clusters.

The **defragmentation** process rewrites fragmented files into contiguous clusters. A Windows utility program called **Disk Defragmenter** consolidates files into contiguous clusters.

Before a disk can be used, it must be **formatted.** Formatting creates *sectors* and *tracks* into which data are stored and establishes an area for the VFAT.

The **access time** for a magnetic disk is the interval between the instant a computer makes a request for transfer of data from a disk-storage device to RAM and the instant this operation is completed. The **data transfer rate** is the rate at which data are read from (written to) mass storage to (from) RAM. **Disk caching** improves system speed.

Apply the dictates of common sense to the care of diskettes (avoid excessive dust, avoid extremes in temperature and humidity, and so on).

5-3 OPTICAL LASER DISCS

Optical laser disc storage is capable of storing vast amounts of data. The main categories of optical laser discs are *CD, CD-ROM, CD-R, CD-RW, DVD, DVD-ROM, DVD-R, DVD+RW, DVD-RW, DVD-RAM,* and *FMD-ROM.*

A CD-ROM is inserted into the CD-ROM drive for processing. Most of the commercially produced read-only CD-ROM discs contain reference material or support multimedia applications. Multidisk player/changers are called **jukeboxes.**

A blank **compact disc-recordable (CD-R)** disc looks like a CD-ROM and once information is recorded on it, it works like a CD-ROM. **CD-RW (CD-ReWritable)** allows users to rewrite to the same CD media and "burn" discs, such as audio CDs.

The DVD (digital video disc) looks like the CD and the CD-ROM, but it can store up to about 17 GB. DVD drives can play CD-ROMs and CDs. **DVD-R** is like CD-R but with the recording density of DVD-ROM. **DVD-RAM, DVD+RW,** and **DVD-RW** are like CD-RW, giving us rewritable capabilities for high-capacity DVD technology. **FMD-ROM,** a very high density, multilayer disc, holds up to 140 GB of data.

The typical PC will have at least a DVD-ROM drive and possibly another read/write disc drive. Most people who want to burn discs and use optical media for backup and transfer purposes are installing a DVD-ROM/CD-RW combination drive or a DVD+RW/CD-RW combination drive.

The choice of which technologies to choose for a system or an application is often a trade-off between storage capacity, cost (dollars per megabyte), and speed (access time).

Each year, improvements are made in existing mass storage devices as the storage industry strives to meet our craving for more storage.

5-4 VIRUSES AND VIRUS PROTECTION

A **computer virus** is a program that "infects" other programs and databases upon contact. A **macro virus** is a program that is written in the macro language of a particular application. A **worm** is a computer program that exists as a separate entity and invades computers via e-mail and IRC. The **Trojan horse** does not replicate itself but depends on the cooperation of unsuspecting users to spread itself.

The primary sources of computer viruses are the Internet (e-mail and downloads), common interchangeable disks, and computer networks. **Antivirus programs** exist to help fight viruses.

5-5 BACKING UP FILES: BETTER SAFE THAN SORRY

You can replace your computer, but you often cannot replace your lost files, so back up your files. The backup process provides protection against loss of valuable files and enables archiving of files. Popular PC backup media includes rewritable optical media, diskettes/floppies, high-capacity diskettes, and portable hard disks.

Three common backup methods are full backup, selective backup of files, or incremental backup. When backing up only critical daily-use files, use at least two generations of backup.

Beside backup to a local disk/disc, you can also backup to a server computer, to another PC on a home network, to a notebook/desktop PC, or to magnetic tape drives, called **tape backup units** (**TBUs**), that use **data cartridges.** When downtime is unacceptable, the network server must be made **fault-tolerant.** **RAID** (**Redundant Array of Independent Disks**) minimizes the impact of catastrophic disk failure by spreading data across several integrated disk drives.

KEY TERMS

access arm (p. 217)
access time (p. 220)
antivirus program (p. 229)
ASCII file (p. 208)
audio file (p. 210)
CD-R (compact disc-recordable) (p. 225)
CD-RW (CD-ReWritable) (p. 225)
cluster (p. 218)
computer virus (p. 227)
cylinder (p. 219)
data cartridge (p. 232)
data file (p. 208)
data transfer rate (p. 220)
defragmentation (p. 221)
disk address (p. 218)
disk caching (p. 220)
Disk Defragmenter (p. 220)
disk density (p. 215)
document file (p. 208)
DVD+RW (p. 225)
DVD-R (p. 225)
DVD-RAM (p. 225)

DVD-RW (p. 225)
executable program file (p. 210)
fault-tolerant (p. 232)
file compression (p. 211)
fixed magnetic disk (p. 214)
FMD-ROM (p. 225)
formatted (p. 220)
graphics file (p. 210)
HiFD disk (p. 215)
interchangeable magnetic disk (p. 214)
jukebox (p. 224)
macro virus (p. 227)
magnetic disk drive (p. 208)
magnetic tape drive (p. 208)
mass storage (p. 208)
native file format (p. 210)
optical laser disc (p. 208)
path (p. 213)
portable hard disk (p. 217)
RAID (Redundant Array of Independent Disks) (p. 232)
read/write head (p. 217)

ScanDisk (p. 220)
sector (p. 218)
sector organization (p. 218)
self-extracting zip file (p. 211)
source program file (p. 210)
spreadsheet file (p. 208)
SuperDisk (p. 215)
tape backup unit (TBU) (p. 232)
track (p. 218)
tracks per inch (TPI) (p. 218)
Trojan horse (p. 227)
video file (p. 210)
Virtual File Allocation Table (VFAT) (p. 219)
Web page file (p. 208)
worm (p. 227)
Zip® disk (p. 215)
Zip® drive (p. 215)
zip file (p. 211)
zoned recording (p. 219)

MATCHING

1. fault-tolerant system
2. fixed disk
3. simgame.exe
4. TBU
5. zoned recording
6. virus type
7. disk clusters
8. DVD+RW
9. native file format
10. video file type
11. path
12. edit menu
13. zip file
14. cylinder
15. disk access time

a. chained together
b. tape backup
c. rewritable optical disc
d. hard disk
e. uses disk space efficiently
f. depends on read/write head movement
g. permits continuous server operation
h. worm
i. has multiple tracks
j. reference to file location
k. mov
l. associated with a program
m. compressed file
n. copy/cut/paste
o. executable file

5-1.1 An ASCII file is a text-only file that can be read or created by any word processing program or text editor. (T/F)

5-1.2 WINTER.SALES and .ADD are valid filenames in the Windows environment. (T/F)

5-1.3 The Windows Explorer is an integrated Web browser and file management tool. (T/F)

5-1.4 A move file operation results in two copies of the same file. (T/F)

5-1.5 We do all of the following to files except: (a) create files, (b) update files, (c) throw files, or (d) execute files.

5-1.6 Which of the following is not a type of file: (a) audio, (b) spreadsheet, (c) source program, or (d) book?

5-1.7 What must you give the operating system to retrieve a particular file: (a) its hierarchical position, (b) the file's path, (c) the outbound corridor, or (d) its directory name?

5-1.8 Which is not a path separator symbol in UNIX, Windows, or Mac OS X: (a) /, (b) \, (c) :, or (d) ;?

5-2.1 Magnetic disks have sequential-access capabilities only. (T/F)

5-2.2 Hard disks and fixed disks are one and the same. (T/F)

5-2.3 Both the diskette and the HiFD disk are the same size but have different disk densities. (T/F)

5-2.4 Information on interchangeable disks cannot be stored offline. (T/F)

5-2.5 The highest-capacity Zip disk has a greater capacity for storage than the HiFD disk. (T/F)

5-2.6 TPI stands for tracks per inch. (T/F)

5-2.7 The capacity of clusters is based on a multiple of 521 bytes. (T/F)

5-2.8 In a disk drive, the read/write heads are mounted on an access arm. (T/F)

5-2.9 Before a disk can be used, it must be formatted. (T/F)

5-2.10 The innermost zone has fewer sectors than the outermost zone in zoned recording. (T/F)

5-2.11 Which of these statements is *not* true: (a) the rotation of a magnetic disk passes all data under or over a read/write head; (b) the heads are mounted on access arms; (c) the standard size for PC hard disks (diameter) is 8 inches; (d) a hard disk contains several disk platters stacked on a single rotating spindle?

5-2.12 The standard size for common diskettes is: (a) 3.25 inches, (b) 3.5 inches, (c) 3.75 inches, or (d) 5.25 inches.

5-2.13 The VFAT is searched by the operating system to find the physical address of the (a) first cluster of the file, (b) read/write head, (c) microprocessor, (d) midsector of the file.

5-2.14 What denotes the physical location of a particular file or set of data on a magnetic disk: (a) cylinder, (b) data compression index, (c) CD-R, or (d) disk address?

5-2.15 TPI refers to: (a) sector density, (b) cylinder overload, (c) track density, or (d) bps thickness.

5-2.16 The disk caching area is: (a) on a floppy disk, (b) in RAM, (c) on a hard disk, or (d) on the monitor's expansion board.

5-2.17 In zoned recording, tracks are grouped into: (a) sectors, (b) regions, (c) zones, or (d) partitions.

5-3.1 CD-ROM is a spinoff of audio CD technology. (T/F)

5-3.2 A CD-ROM stores data in spiraling tracks. (T/F)

5-3.3 Jukebox refers to a player/changer that can handle multiple CD-ROMs. (T/F)

5-3.4 DVD+RW is like rewritable storage technology. (T/F)

5-3.5 The CD-ROM drive specifications 32X, 40X, or 75X refer to its: (a) speed, (b) diameter, (c) number of platters, or (d) sector groupings.

5-3.6 The data transfer rate for a 40X CD-ROM is how many MB per second: (a) 3, (b) 6, (c) 11.25, or (d) 12.

5-3.7 Which optical laser disc has the greatest storage capacity: (a) double-sided DVD-ROM, (b) FMD-ROM, (c) 75X CD-ROM, or (d) CD-RW?

5-4.1 Worms exist as separate entities and do not attach themselves to files. (T/F)

5-4.2 The Trojan horse e-mails itself. (T/F)

5-4.3 All downloaded files on the Internet are checked for viruses at the ISP level, eliminating the need for antivirus software at the PC level. (T/F)

5-4.4 The profile of one who writes viruses is an older female from southeast Asia. (T/F)

5-4.5 It is recommended to delete e-mails from unknown, suspicious, or untrustworthy sources. (T/F)

5-4.6 What can hide and duplicate itself within legitimate programs: (a) computer virus, (b) PC bug, (c) program germ, or (d) Trojan horse?

5-4.7 Which of these is not a virus: (a) Wooden Horse, (b) Melissa, (c) The Cookie Monster, or (d) Love.bug?

5-4.8 Which of these is not a source for computer viruses: (a) interchangeable disks, (b) the Net, (c) computer networks, or (d) antivirus programs?

5-4.9 Sometimes viruses are attached to: (a) e-mails, (b) chat notes, (c) hypertext, or (d) disk labels.

5-5.1 Any system with a weekly backup requirement from 100 MB to 1 GB is a candidate to use floppies as a backup medium. (T/F)

5-5.2 A fault-tolerant network is one designed to have continuous operation. (T/F)

5-5.3 Incremental backups play no role in restoring files. (T/F)

5-5.4 The backup process serves two important functions—protection against loss of valuable files and cache storage. (T/F)

5-5.5 Which of these would not be considered a backup medium: (a) CD-RW, (b) Zip disk, (c) DVD-ROM, or (d) portable hard disk?

5-5.6 Which of the following generally is not an application for magnetic tape storage: (a) routine information processing, (b) backup for disk storage, (c) archival storage, or (d) medium for transfer between computers?

5-5.7 In the full backup method: (a) only user-selected files are backed up, (b) only those files that have been modified since the last backup are backed up, (c) only volatile files are backed up, or (d) all files are backed up.

5-5.8 When performing critical files backup using interchangeable disks it is best to maintain at least: (a) one generation, (b) two generations, (c) four generations, or (d) eight generations.

ACCESSIBILITY TO E-MAIL ARCHIVES

E-mail may be the corporate Achilles heel when it comes to lawsuits. Attorneys can subpoena e-mail archives on disk or tape relative to pending lawsuits. Among the thousands of e-mail messages sent each day in a typical medium-sized company, attorneys are likely to find statements that support their cause. People tend to be conversational when writing e-mail messages. People don't write e-mail with the thought that it might be shown as evidence in a court of law. To avoid the potential for litigation, many companies routinely purge e-mail archives. Had the people at Microsoft Corporation been more diligent about purging their e-mail, U.S. government prosecutors would not have been able to subpoena the company's e-mail. The e-mail they eventually found was critical to the government's antitrust suit against Microsoft.

Discussion: *Should companies save e-mail? If so, for how long?*

Discussion: *Should attorneys be allowed to subpoena e-mail archives? Why or why not?*

MP3 FILE SHARING

MP3 is an abbreviation for a method of compressing audio files, usually music, into a digital format that can be downloaded easily and played on your PC or an MP3 player. Some MP3 players are as small as a watch and can hold several hours of music in their solid-state memory. The music industry, which has relied almost exclusively on CD and cassette tape media to market and distribute its products in recent years, is now confronted with millions of music-hungry people who routinely share MP3 files (via the Internet and diskettes), both commercially and noncommercially. In the same vein, netizens have begun to share movies, as well (over a half-million a day).

Discussion: *In the eyes of the music industry, if you receive an MP3 file containing copyrighted music, then you are receiving stolen goods. Do listeners share this view? Why or why not?*

Discussion: *Sometimes people attend concerts and tape parts of the concerts, make MP3 files of the music, then send these MP3 files to friends. Is this practice unethical or illegal, or both? Explain.*

Discussion: *People routinely use digital cameras and illegally tape first-run movies at theaters. They then post the movie file to the Internet. Would you download and view an illegal movie video? Why or why not?*

Discussion: *Violating copyright laws is punishable by up to five years in prison and a $250,000 fine. Describe what someone would have to do to get the maximum sentence for copyright violations.*

Discussion: *The upside to MP3 file sharing is that an aspiring artist can place his or her music on the Internet and make it available at little or no charge. Would it be ethical for an artist to change his or her mind and ask users to pay a fee for music that was previously offered for free?*

DISCUSSION AND PROBLEM SOLVING

5-1.1 Describe seven personal activities that might result in information being read from or written to magnetic disk (for example, buying a candy bar at Wal-Mart).

5-1.2 Name and briefly describe applications for four different types of files.

5-1.3 Describe file compression and why and how it might be used.

5-2.1 Traditionally, personal computers have had a floppy disk drive. However, some personal computers no longer come with a floppy drive. Is the floppy drive needed anymore? Explain.

5-2.2 A program issues a "read" command for data to be retrieved from hard disk. Describe the resulting mechanical movement and the movement of data.

5-2.3 What happens during formatting? Why must hard disks and diskettes be formatted?

5-2.4 A floppy disk does not move until a read or write command is issued. Once it is issued, the floppy begins to spin. It stops spinning after the command is executed. Why is a hard disk not set in motion in the same manner? Why is a floppy not made to spin continuously?

5-2.5 The SuperDisk and Zip disk serve similar purposes on a computer system. The SuperDisk drive is compatible with the traditional floppy diskette, but the Zip disk reads and writes data more rapidly. Costs are comparable. Which one would you choose and why?

5-2.6 What would determine the frequency with which you would need to defragment your hard drive? Explain.

5-3.1 List six content areas that are distributed commercially on CD-ROM (for example, electronic encyclopedias).

5-3.2 Describe the potential impact of optical laser disc technology on public and university libraries. On home libraries.

5-3.3 Describe at least two applications where CD-RW or DVD+RW would be preferred over a hard disk for storage.

5-3.4 The DVD+RW drive also has the capabilities of the CD-RW drive, the "CD burner." Currently the DVD+RW drive is more expensive than the CD-RW drive, but prices are converging. Speculate on when or if DVD+RW will replace CD-RW.

5-3.5 With the capability to store digital music, the audio CD has revolutionized the way we play and listen to recorded music. Now music can be downloaded over the Internet and played on PCs, solid-state MP3 players, and other electronic devices. Does this signal the beginning of the end of the audio CD? Explain.

5-3.6 The only internal mechanical movement in a typical notebook PC is associated with the disk and optical drives. Someday soon both may be replaced with solid-state nonvolatile memory. Speculate on how this might change the appearance of notebook PCs and on how we use and what we do with them.

5-4.1 What name is given to programs intended to damage the computer system of an unsuspecting victim? Describe three sources of these.

5-4.2 What would be appropriate punishment for the originator of a virus that destroyed the user files of thousands of people?

5-4.3 Several years ago, antivirus companies let owners of authorized copies of their software download updated virus protection at no cost. Now they charge an annual subscription of around $5. Is it worth it? Explain.

5-5.1 Describe a backup method, including backup medium, that might be used in a small company with a local area network serving 28 users.

5-5.2 Every Friday night a company makes backup copies of all master files and programs (over 30 GB). Why is this necessary? The company has a TBU (50-GB cartridges), a DVD+RW drive, and two 120-MB portable hard disk drives. Which storage medium would you suggest for the backup? Why?

5-5.3 How many 3.5-inch diskettes would you need to do a daily backup of the files (2 MB total) you created for a college course?

FOCUS ON PERSONAL COMPUTING

1. The typical PC user is somewhat lax when it comes to organizing folders and naming files; therefore, the typical PC's folder/file structure could use some cleanup. Set up a hierarchical file structure that includes specific folder categories within general areas of usage. For example, one major folder might be "State University" with subfolders for each semester. Each semester subfolder would have subfolders for your various classes and perhaps a miscellaneous folder with subfolders for your extracurricular activities. Rename folders/files as needed.

2. Set up a backup procedure within the context of available hardware that meets your ongoing backup needs. Label all interchangeable media, if applicable, and write up the backup procedure, including diagrams as needed. Backup your user files.

3. If you are an active user and have not defragmented your hard disk, use a disk defragmenter utility and "defrag" your hard disk. Defragmenting the hard disk can substantially improve system performance.

INTERNET EXERCISES @ www.prenhall.com/long

1. The Online Study Guide (multiple choice, true/false, matching, and essay questions)
2. Internet Learning Activities
  • Magnetic Disk
  • Optical Storage
3. Serendipitous Internet Activities
  • Travel

chapter

6

Learning Objectives

Once you have read and studied this chapter, you will have learned:

- **The operation and application of common input devices (Section 6-1).**

- **The operation and application of common output devices (Section 6-2).**

- **The scope of and technology for multimedia applications (Section 6-3).**

- **The breadth of assistive input/output technology for disabled people (Section 6-4).**

INFORMATION INPUT AND OUTPUT

Why this chapter is important to you

When PCs arrived as a viable consumer product in the late 1970s, choices for input were limited. Input was mostly via the standard QWERTY keyboard. Output was a small low-resolution monitor, a really slow printer, and a tinny little speaker that made annoying sounds when you tapped the wrong key. Now we have ergonomic keyboards, or, if you prefer, speech-recognition software that lets you talk to your PC. Monitors come in many different shapes, sizes, and qualities. All-in-one devices offer fast photo-quality color printing, along with copying, scanning, and faxing capabilities.

There is an endless array of input/output devices you can connect to a PC for what seems to be an infinite number of applications. You can scan in photographs. You can capture real-time video images from your camcorder. You can enter the TV signal directly to your PC for recording or viewing. An innovative input device can even give PCs a sense of smell. New and exciting I/O devices are being announced every month.

Today, you are the person who makes the decisions about which input/output devices you hang on your PC. If you have a good grasp of available input/output devices, you can take full advantage of your PC system. Did you know the mouse is but one of many options for point-and-draw devices? Did you know you could enjoy videophone conversations with your friends across town or around the world? Did you know that you could use your scanner to scan in text from printed documents? Did you know that carefully selected I/O options, such as ergonomic keyboards and speech-recognition software, could reduce neuromuscular problems associated with entering data to a computer? The knowledge you gain from this chapter should prove helpful when it comes time to configure and purchase a PC.

When it comes to buying a PC or related hardware, you are generally on your own. Realistically, you cannot depend on salespeople or friends to make these important monetary decisions for you. It takes personal knowledge and research. This and the previous two chapters should help you get the biggest bang for your PC buck.

6-1 Input Devices

We routinely communicate directly or indirectly with a computer. Even people who have never sat in front of a PC communicate with computers. Perhaps you have had one of these experiences.

● Have you ever been hungry and short of cash? No problem. Just stop at an automatic teller machine (ATM) and ask for some "lunch money." The ATM's keyboard and monitor enable you to hold an interactive conversation with the bank's computer. The ATM's printer provides you with a hard copy of your transactions when you leave. Some ATMs talk to you as well.

● Have you ever called a mail-order merchandiser and been greeted by a message like this: "Thank you for calling BrassCo Enterprises Customer Service. If you wish to place an order, press one. If you wish to inquire about the status of an order, press two. To speak to a particular person, enter that person's four-digit extension or hold, and an operator will process your call momentarily." The message is produced by a computer-based voice-response system, which responds to the buttons you press on your telephone keypad.

We communicate with these computers through input/output devices. *Input devices* translate our data and communications into a form that the computer can understand. The computer then processes these data, and an *output device* translates them back into a form we can understand. In our two examples, the ATM's keypad, touch screen monitor, and the telephone keypad serve as input devices, and the ATM's monitor, printer, and the voice-response system serve as output devices (see Figure 6-1).

Input/output devices are quietly playing an increasingly significant role in our lives. The number and variety of I/O devices are expanding even as you read this, and some of these devices are fairly exotic (see Figure 6-2). For example, there is an electronic nose that can measure and digitally record smells. It's used to analyze aroma in the food, drink, and perfume industries. Commuters enjoy another benefit of I/O as they drive through toll plazas at highway speeds. For each passing car, toll road computers grab the customer number from a credit card-sized transmitter mounted on the car windshield, then process the transaction and flash a "Thank You" message.

This chapter is about I/O devices. This first section is on input devices, and we will begin with the *keyboard* and the *mouse*, the most popular input devices.

FIGURE 6-1

TERMINALS FOR BANKING CUSTOMERS: AUTOMATIC TELLER MACHINES
The widely used automatic teller machine (ATM) supports a variety of input/output methods. The magnetic stripe on the ATM card contains identification and security information that, when read, is sent to the bank's computer system. The ATM responds with instructions via its monitor. The customer enters an identification number and data via a keypad. In the figure, the computer processes the customer's request and then provides instructions for the customer via the monitor and verbally with a voice-response unit.

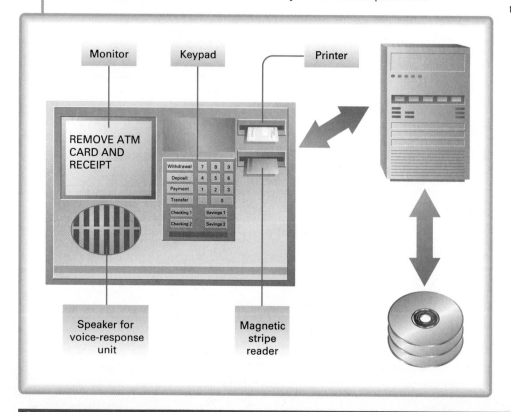

FIGURE 6-2 The Tablet PC
Innovations in input/output are happening all the time. This Acer PC is evolutionary in its approach to user interaction. The PC provides a variety of I/O options and easily converts from a tablet PC to a notebook PC by simply twisting the screen, which is closed with the screen on top when used as a tablet PC. The tablet PC offers full desktop PC functionality with the simplicity of a pen and paper.

Photo courtesy of Intel Corporation

THE KEYBOARD

Every notebook and desktop PC comes with a keyboard. There are two basic types of keyboards: alphanumeric keyboards and special-function keyboards.

Traditional Alphanumeric Keyboards

The typical keyboard has 101 keys with the traditional *QWERTY* (the first six letters on the third row) key layout, 12 function keys, a numeric keypad, a variety of special-function keys, and dedicated cursor-control keys (see Figure 6-3). PC, workstation, and terminal keyboards vary considerably in

---

FIGURE 6–3 **A REPRESENTATIVE PC KEYBOARD**

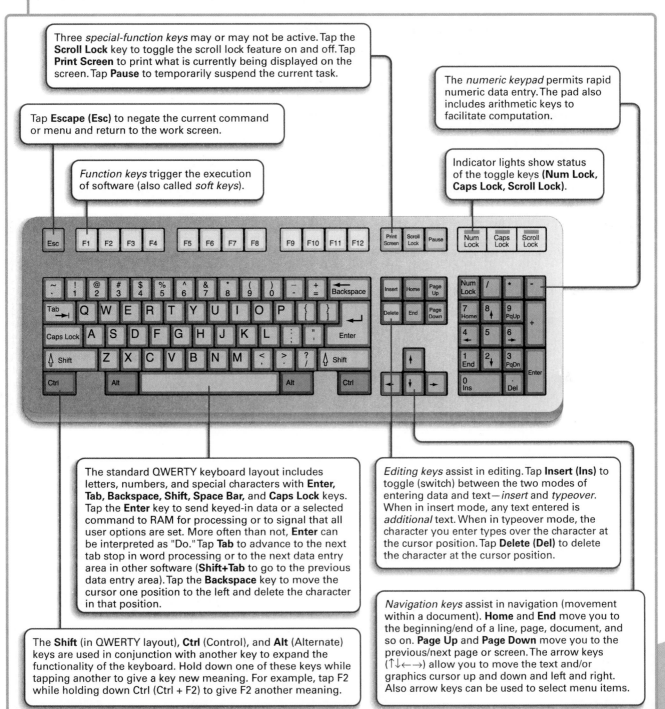

Three *special-function keys* may or may not be active. Tap the **Scroll Lock** key to toggle the scroll lock feature on and off. Tap **Print Screen** to print what is currently being displayed on the screen. Tap **Pause** to temporarily suspend the current task.

The *numeric keypad* permits rapid numeric data entry. The pad also includes arithmetic keys to facilitate computation.

Tap **Escape (Esc)** to negate the current command or menu and return to the work screen.

Function keys trigger the execution of software (also called *soft keys*).

Indicator lights show status of the toggle keys (**Num Lock, Caps Lock, Scroll Lock**).

The standard QWERTY keyboard layout includes letters, numbers, and special characters with **Enter, Tab, Backspace, Shift, Space Bar,** and **Caps Lock** keys. Tap the **Enter** key to send keyed-in data or a selected command to RAM for processing or to signal that all user options are set. More often than not, **Enter** can be interpreted as "Do." Tap **Tab** to advance to the next tab stop in word processing or to the next data entry area in other software (**Shift+Tab** to go to the previous data entry area). Tap the **Backspace** key to move the cursor one position to the left and delete the character in that position.

Editing keys assist in editing. Tap **Insert (Ins)** to toggle (switch) between the two modes of entering data and text—*insert* and *typeover*. When in insert mode, any text entered is *additional* text. When in typeover mode, the character you enter types over the character at the cursor position. Tap **Delete (Del)** to delete the character at the cursor position.

Navigation keys assist in navigation (movement within a document). **Home** and **End** move you to the beginning/end of a line, page, document, and so on. **Page Up** and **Page Down** move you to the previous/next page or screen. The arrow keys (↑↓←→) allow you to move the text and/or graphics cursor up and down and left and right. Also arrow keys can be used to select menu items.

The **Shift** (in QWERTY layout), **Ctrl** (Control), and **Alt** (Alternate) keys are used in conjunction with another key to expand the functionality of the keyboard. Hold down one of these keys while tapping another to give a key new meaning. For example, tap F2 while holding down Ctrl (Ctrl + F2) to give F2 another meaning.

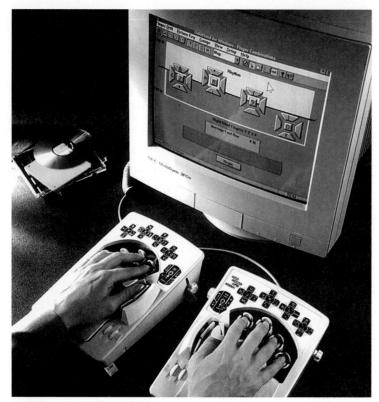

FIGURE 6–4 Keyboard Alternative
The DataHand System is ergonomically designed as two independent units molded to fit the shape of the human hand. The operator-friendly design incorporates the traditional key placement found on standard keyboards, allowing both beginners and experienced keyboard users to learn the DataHand System easily.

Courtesy of DataHand

appearance (see Figure 6-4). Some may have a few more special function keys (for example, retrieve mail or Windows "Start" buttons). Portable computers have a simple QWERTY keyboard with a minimum number of special-function keys. When tapped, the keyboard's **function keys** trigger the execution of some type of software activity. For example, HELP (context-sensitive user assistance) often is assigned to F1 (Function Key 1). Function keys are numbered and assigned different functions in different software packages.

The cursor-control keys, or arrow keys, can be used to select options from a menu. These keys also allow you to move the **text cursor** *up* (↑) and *down* (↓), usually a line at a time, and *left* (←) and *right* (→), usually a character at a time. The text cursor always shows the location of where the next keyed-in character will appear on the screen. The text cursor can appear as several shapes depending on the application, but frequently you will encounter a blinking vertical line (|). Other important keys common to most keyboards are illustrated and described in Figure 6-3.

Special-Function Keyboards

Some keyboards are designed for specific applications. For example, the cash-register-like terminals at most fast-food restaurants have special-purpose keyboards. Rather than key in the name and price of an order of French fries, attendants need only press the key marked "French fries" to record the sale. Such keyboards help shop supervisors, airline ticket agents, retail salesclerks, and many others interact more quickly with their computer systems.

POINT-AND-DRAW DEVICES

The keyboard is too cumbersome for some applications, especially those that rely on a *graphical user interface* (GUI) or require the user to point or draw. Of course, interaction with all Windows operating systems is via a GUI. The GUI lets you *point and click* with the mouse to navigate between and within programs and to issue commands. The effectiveness of GUIs depends on the user's ability to make a rapid selection from a screen full of menus or graphic icons (each of which represents a program or user option). In these instances, a point-and-draw device, such as a mouse, can be used to *point* to and select (click) a particular user option quickly and efficiently. Also, such devices can be used to *draw*. For example, computer artists use mice to create images.

The handheld mouse, or something like it, is a must-have item on any PC or workstation. When the mouse is moved across a desktop, the **mouse pointer** on the display moves accordingly. The mouse pointer can be positioned anywhere on the screen. It is displayed as an arrow, a crosshair, or a variety of other symbols, depending on the current application and its position on the screen. Figure 6-5 illustrates several of the many mouse pointer schemes available to users. The text cursor and mouse pointer may be displayed on the screen at the same time in some programs, such as word processing. The mouse is either attached to the computer by a cable (the mouse's "tail") or linked via a wireless connection (either infrared or radio wave as shown in Figure 6-6).

Mice and other point-and-draw devices have one or two buttons. Mice used with Wintel PCs typically will have a left and right button plus a wheel between the buttons to facilitate scrolling. Mouse operations are introduced in Chapter 2.

For the moment, the mouse remains the most popular point-and-draw device. However, a variety of devices are available that move the mouse pointer to point and draw, and each has its advantages and disadvantages. Here are a few of the more popular ones (see Figure 6-7).

● *Trackball.* The **trackball** is a ball inset in a small external box or adjacent to and in the same unit as the keyboard. The ball is rolled with the fingers to move the mouse pointer. Some people find it helpful to think of a trackball as an upside-down mouse with a bigger ball on the top.

- *Trackpad.* The **trackpad** has no moving parts and is common on notebook PCs. Simply move your finger about a small touch-sensitive pad to move the mouse pointer.
- *Joystick.* The **joystick** is a vertical stick that moves the mouse pointer in the direction the stick is pushed. Video arcade wizards are no doubt familiar with the joystick, which is used mostly for gaming.
- *Trackpoint.* A **trackpoint** is usually positioned in or near a notebook's keyboard. Trackpoints function like miniature joysticks but are operated with the tip of the finger.
- *Digitizer tablet and pen.* The **digitizer tablet and pen** is a pen and a pressure-sensitive tablet whose *X-Y* coordinates correspond with those on the computer's display screen. Some digitizing tablets also use a crosshair device instead of a pen. Digitizer tablets are used to enable drawing or sketching of images, such as X-rays, and for many other drawing and engineering applications.

SCANNERS

A variety of **scanners** read and interpret information on printed matter and convert it to a format that can be stored and/or interpreted by a computer (see Figure 6-8).

OCR and Bar Code Scanners

In **source-data automation,** data are entered directly to a computer system at the source without the need for key entry transcription. For example, scanners read preprinted **bar codes** on consumer products, eliminating the need for most key entry at checkout counters. **Bar code scanners** use laser technology to scan and interpret an image, printed text, or some kind of code, enabling source-data automation in many applications. Transactions at Wal-Mart stores throughout the world are recorded *automatically* at the *source* of the transaction (the cash register), keeping sales and inventory information up to the second.

Bar code scanners use **OCR (optical character recognition)** technology to read coded information and text information into a computer system. This ability includes reading your handwriting, as well. More commonly, scanners read bar codes. Bar codes represent alphanumeric data by varying the size of adjacent vertical lines. There is a variety of bar-coding systems. Compare the POSTNET bar codes on metered mail with those on packing labels and with those on consumer products. One of the most visible bar-coding systems is the Universal Product Code (UPC). The UPC, originally used for supermarket items, is now being printed on other consumer goods.

The United States Postal Service relies on both OCR and bar code scanning to sort most mail. At the Postal Service, light-sensitive scanners read and interpret the ZIP code and POSTNET bar code on billions of envelopes each day. The ZIP information is then sent to computer-based sorting machines that route the envelopes to appropriate bins for distribution.

Are there advantages to using OCR over bar codes or bar codes over OCR? The advantage of bar codes over OCR is that the position or orientation of the code being read is not as critical to the scanner. In a supermarket, for example, the UPC can be recorded even when a bottle of ketchup is rolled over the laser scanner.

Two types of OCR and bar code scanners—*contact* and *laser*—read information on labels and various types of documents. Both bounce a beam of light off an image, and then measure the reflected light to interpret the

FIGURE 6–5

MOUSE POINTER SCHEMES
This figure shows three of many predefined mouse pointer schemes available to Windows users. From left to right the schemes are the Windows system default scheme, ocean, and nature. Each mouse pointer shape provides a visual clue showing what Windows is doing or what you can do in various situations. The "normal select" pointer is highlighted in blue at the top of the figure.

Normal Select			
Help Select			
Working In Background			
Busy			
Precision Select			
Text Select			
Handwriting			
Unavailable			
Vertical Resize			
Horizontal Resize			
Diagonal Resize 1			
Diagonal Resize 2			
Move			
Alternate Select			
Link Select			

FIGURE 6–6 Wireless PC
This Intel concept PC gives us some insight as to what we might see in future PCs. Notice that the PC is wireless—the mouse, keyboard, and monitor are no longer tethered to the system unit by wires.

Photo courtesy of Intel Corporation

FIGURE 6–7   POINT-AND-DRAW DEVICES

TRACKPAD
This Dell Inspiron 8100 notebook PC is equipped with a trackpad that allows you to move the mouse pointer with the tip of your finger.

Photo courtesy of Dell Computer Corp.

JOYSTICK AND GAME PAD
This Microsoft Sidewinder Force Feedback Pro (joystick) and the Gravis Stinger (game pad) are designed specifically for PC action games and flight simulation programs. They move airplanes, aliens, and monsters, as well as the mouse pointers. The Sidewinder is both an input and output device. It provides tactile output in the form of force feedback (vibration and pressure) to add realism to the gaming experience.

Courtesy of Advanced Gravis Computer Technology Ltd.

PEN WITH TOUCH-SENSITIVE DISPLAY
These students are using a pen with a tablet PC's touch-sensitive display to interact remotely via a wireless link to the school's server computer and the Internet.

Courtesy of Xybernaut

TRACKPOINT
The trackpoint is conveniently located within the keyboard of this IBM ThinkPad i series notebook PC.

Courtesy of International Business Machines Corporation

DIGITIZER TABLET AND PEN
Infrared technology enables handwritten notes and drawings to be transferred to Palm organizers, such as the Palm VII shown here. As users write on the notepad with the SmartPen™, their notes and drawings are instantly transferred to the Palm. This digitizer tablet and pen gives users the best of both worlds.

Courtesy of Seiko Instruments USA Inc.

TRACKBALL
This Kensington Orbit Trackball is a mouse alternative that reduces wrist and elbow fatigue and, therefore, the risk of carpal tunnel syndrome.

Courtesy of Kensington Technology Group

CROSSHAIR AND DIGITIZER
This ALTEK digitizer uses a crosshair for medical imaging. The backlighting system enables the digitizing of x-rays for such applications as radiation treatment planning.

Courtesy of ALTEK Corporation

FIGURE 6–8   SCANNERS AND SCANNER APPLICATIONS

THE INTACTA.CODE™
The bar-code has taken on a new meaning with the recent invention of the INTACTA.CODE™. This print bar code is capable of storing photo images, MP3 music files, gaming software demos, or anything else that can be digitized. When newspaper or magazine readers scan the printed INTACTA.CODE™ into their computers, special software, working with standard scanners, decodes the dot pattern to the original electronic file.

Courtesy of Intacta Technologies

BAR CODES IN MANUFACTURING
Here at the Dell Computer Corporation manufacturing facility in Austin, Texas, bar codes on boxed parts are scanned as they are moved throughout the warehouse to ensure efficient inventory management, a goal of every manufacturing company.

Courtesy of Dell Computer Corp.

PERSONAL SCANNERS
Consumers are now using bar code scanners small enough to hang on a keychain to make purchases or gather information with one scan of a bar code. The tiny scanner allows consumers to scan products and services anywhere, anytime. Transactions such as purchases, inquiries, and payments can be made while commuting on a train or anywhere else. To retrieve the data contained in the scanner, the unit synchs up (synchronizes) with a PC, and uploads the data stored in its memory, enabling consumers to complete online transactions or locate additional information about the product or services of interest.

Courtesy of Symbol Technology, Inc.

FIGURE 6–8 continued

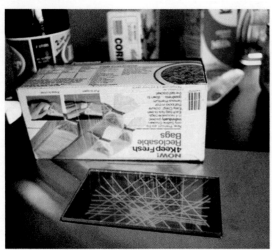 

SCANNERS IN THE SUPERMARKET: STATIONARY AND HANDHELD
Supermarket checkout systems are now an established cost-saving technology. The automated systems use stationary laser scanners to read the bar codes that identify each item (left). Price and product descriptions are retrieved from a database and recorded on the sales slip. Stockers use handheld scanners to order products and update the database (right).

Courtesy of International Business Machines Corporation

EXPEDITING THE 2000 U.S. CENSUS
One of the reasons the 2000 U.S. census went smoothly is that the millions of completed mark-sense census forms were read by page scanners enabling the data to be entered directly to the system for processing.

Courtesy of Lockheed Martin Corporation

image. Handheld contact scanners make contact as they are brushed over the printed matter to be read. Laser-based scanners are more versatile and can read data passed near the scanning area. Scanners of both technologies can recognize printed characters and various types of bar codes. Scanners used for OCR or bar code applications can be classified into three basic categories.

- *Handheld label scanners.* These devices read data on price tags, shipping labels, inventory part numbers, book ISBNs, and the like. Handheld label scanners, sometimes called **wand scanners,** use either contact or laser technology. You have probably seen both types used in libraries and various retail stores. Hoping to add value to its magazine, *Forbes* has distributed almost a million handheld scanners to its subscribers for free. Readers use the scanners to scan "cues" that take them directly to related Web sites for more information.

- *Stationary label scanners.* These devices, which rely exclusively on laser technology, are used in the same types of applications as wand scanners. Stationary scanners are common in grocery stores and discount stores.

- *Document scanners.* Document scanners are capable of scanning documents of varying sizes. Document scanners read envelopes at the U.S. Postal Service, and they also read turnaround documents for utility companies. A **turnaround document** is computer-produced output that we can read and is ultimately returned as computer-readable input to a computer system. For example, when you pay your utility bills, you return a check and a stub for the invoice (the turnaround document). The stub is scanned, and payment information is entered automatically to the utility company's system.

Most retail stores and distribution warehouses, and all overnight couriers, are seasoned users of scanner technology. Salespeople, inventory management personnel, and couriers would much prefer to wave their "magic" wands than enter data one character at a time.

Optical Mark Recognition

You are probably familiar with one of the oldest scanner technologies, *optical mark recognition (OMR)*. One of the most popular applications for these scanners is grading tests. All of us at one time or another has marked answers on a preprinted multiple-choice test answer form. The marked forms are scanned and corrected, comparing the position of the "sense marks" with those on a master to grade the test. The results of surveys and questionnaires often are tabulated with OMR technology.

Optical Scanners

Optical scanners can read written text and hard copy images then translate the information into an electronic format that can be interpreted by and stored on computers. The image to be scanned can be a photograph, a drawing, an insurance form, a medical record—anything that can be digitized. Once an image has been digitized and entered to the computer system, it can be retrieved, displayed, modified, merged with text, stored, sent via data communications to one or several remote computers, and even faxed. Manipulating and managing scanned images, known as **image processing**, is becoming increasingly important, especially with recent advances in optical storage technologies (for example, rewritable CD-ROM and DVD-RAM). Organizations everywhere are replacing space-consuming metal filing cabinets and millions of hard copy documents, from tax returns to warrantee cards, with their electronic equivalents. Image processing's space-saving incentive, along with its ease of document retrieval, is making the image scanner a must-have peripheral in most offices. The same is true of the home as people begin converting their family photo albums and other archives to electronic format.

Page and Hand Image Scanners

Image scanners are of two types: *page* and *hand.* Virtually all modern scanners can scan in both black and white images and color images. *Page image scanners* work like copy machines. That is, the image to be scanned is placed face down on the scanning surface, covered, then scanned. The result is a high-resolution digitized image. Inexpensive sheet-fed page scanners weighing less than two pounds accept the document to be scanned in a slot. The *hand image scanner* is rolled manually over the image to be scanned. About five inches in width, hand image scanners are appropriate for capturing small images or portions of large images.

In addition to scanning photos and other graphic images, image scanners can also scan and interpret the alphanumeric characters on regular printed pages. People use page scanners to translate printed hard copy to computer-readable format. For applications that demand this type of translation, page scanners can minimize or eliminate the need for key entry. Today's image scanners and the accompanying OCR software are very sophisticated. Together they can read and interpret the characters from most printed material, such as a printed letter or a page from this book.

Image Processing: Eliminating the Paper Pile

Companies and even individuals are becoming buried in paper, literally. In some organizations, paper files take up most of the floor space. Moreover, finding what you want may take several minutes to hours. Or, you may never find what you want. Image processing applications scan and index thousands, even millions, of documents (see Figure 6-9). Once these scanned documents are on the computer system, they can be easily retrieved and manipulated. For example, banks use image processing to archive canceled checks and to archive documents associated with mortgage loan servicing. Insurance companies use image processing in claims processing applications.

Images are scanned into a digital format that can be stored on disk, often optical laser disc because of its huge capacity. For example, a decade's worth of hospital medical records can be scanned and stored on a handful of optical laser discs that fit easily on a single shelf. The images are organized so they can be retrieved in seconds rather than minutes or hours. Medical personnel who need a hard copy can simply print one out in a matter of seconds.

The State of Louisiana Department of Public Safety routinely supplies driver information to other state agencies and to outside organizations, such as insurance companies, and is a perfect example of how image processing can reduce the need for paper while making records more accessible. The department has the dual problem of keeping up with thousands of documents received each week and with servicing thousands of requests for driver information, mostly for problem drivers. The amount of paperwork involved could be staggering. However, because this department has gone to image processing for driver information, other state agencies have direct access to the image bank over communication lines, and the department has no trouble handling outside requests for information. The department's long-range plan calls for using image processing to minimize or eliminate paper and microfilm in as many applications as possible.

The real beauty of image processing is that the digitized material can be easily manipulated. For example, any image can be easily faxed to another location (without being printed). A fax is sent and received as an image. The content on the fax or any electronic image can be manipulated in many ways. OCR software can be used to translate any printed text on the stored image to an electronic format (see Figure 6-9). For example, a doctor might wish to pull selected printed text from various patient images into a word processing document to compile a summary of a patient's condition. The doctor can even select specific graphic images (X-rays, photos, or drawings) from the patient's record for inclusion in the summary report.

MAGNETIC STRIPES AND SMART CARDS

The magnetic stripes on the back of charge cards and badges offer another means of data entry at the source. The magnetic stripes are encoded with data appropriate for specific applications. For example, your account number and personal identification number are encoded on a card for automatic teller machines.

Magnetic stripes contain much more data per unit of space than do printed characters or bar codes. Plus, because they cannot be read visually, they are perfect for storing confidential data, such as a personal identification number. Employee cards, security badges, and library cards (see Figure 6-10) often contain authorization data for access to physically secured areas, such as a computer center, or to protected resources, such as e-books in a library. To gain access, an employee or patron inserts a card or badge into a **badge reader.** This device reads and checks the authorization code before permitting the individual to enter a secured area. When badge readers are linked to a central computer, that computer can maintain a chronological log of people entering or leaving secured areas.

The **smart card** looks like any garden-variety charge card, but with a twist. It has an embedded microprocessor with up to 32 KB of nonvolatile memory (see Figure 6-11). Because the smart card can hold more information, has processing capability, and is almost impossible to duplicate, smart cards may soon replace cards with magnetic stripes. Already, smart cards are gaining widespread acceptance in Europe and in the United States, especially smart cards with *stored value*. The dual-function stored-value smart card serves as a credit card and as a replacement for cash. Customers with these cards can go to automatic teller machines to transfer electronic cash from their checking or savings account to the card's memory. They are used like cash at the growing number of stores that accept stored-value cards. Each time the card is used, the purchase amount is deducted from the card's stored value. To reload the card with more electronic cash, the card's owner must return to an automatic teller machine. The stored-value smart card is another big step toward the inevitable elimination of cash.

SPEECH RECOGNITION

Speech recognition was possible over 20 years ago, but only when the words were spoken in discrete speech (slowly, one word at a time) to an expensive, room-sized mainframe computer. The power of

FIGURE 6–9 IMAGE PROCESSING

PAGE SCANNER

Inexpensive image scanners have given rise to a variety of image processing applications. Here, a graphic artist scans an image into the system on a page scanner.

Photo courtesy of Hewlett-Packard Company

HAND SCANNER

A manager uses a hand scanner to convert text in a magazine into electronic text that can be inserted into a word processing document.

Courtesy of Caere Corporation

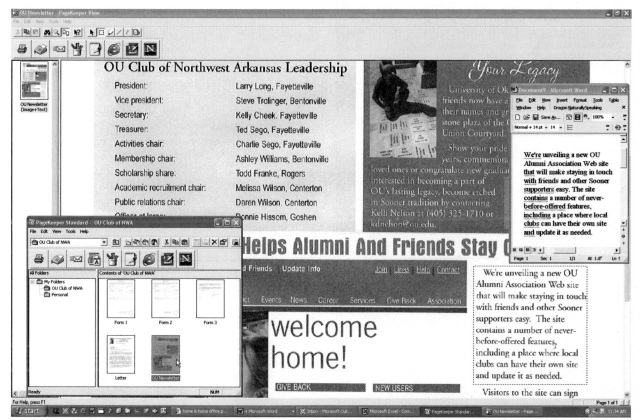

IMAGE PROCESSING SOFTWARE

PageKeeper image processor software helps you organize documents in your computer. The software lets you scan documents, such as this newsletter, into a folder system (bottom left). Once in the system, documents are retrieved and viewed easily (background). You also can make annotations on documents and copy contents to other documents (see the Word document on the right).

FIGURE 6–10 Intelligent Plastic
Smart cards and magnetic stripe cards have a variety of applications, including banking, medical records, security, and more. In the photo, a girl uses her card to gain access to the library's automated resources via a thin client workstation.
Courtesy of Sun Microsystems, Inc.

PCs has finally caught up with speech-recognition technology. With the modern speech-recognition software and a quality microphone, the typical off-the-shelf PC is able to accept spoken words in continuous speech (as you would normally talk) at speeds of up to 125 words a minute. Speech recognition has made hands-free interaction possible for surgeons during operations and for quality control personnel who use their hands to describe defects as they are detected. Many executives now dictate, rather than keyboard, their e-mail messages. Also, speech recognition is a tremendous enabling technology for the physically challenged.

Speech recognition has emerged as the newest *killer application*. In the PC world, a killer application has a profound impact on personal computing. The "killer app" handle places speech-recognition systems alongside some pretty good company: word processing, spreadsheet, database, and Internet browser applications. Speech recognition capability is now built into modern versions of the Microsoft Office suite. Software companies offer more sophisticated and/or application-specific speech recognition software (law, medicine, engineering, and so on).

Speaker-Dependent Speech Recognition

If you were to purchase a **speech-recognition system** for your PC, you would receive software, a generic vocabulary database, and a high-quality microphone with noise-canceling capabilities. Successful speech recognition depends on a strong, clear signal from the microphone. The microphone, which is mounted on a headset, filters out general office noise, including ringing phones and slamming doors. The size of the vocabulary database ranges from 30,000 words for general dictation to more than 300,000 words for technical, legal, or medical dictation.

Once you have installed the hardware and software, you are ready to speak to the computer. The basic steps involved in speech recognition are illustrated in Figure 6-12. The system will accept most of your spoken words (see Figure 6-13). However, you can *train* the system to accept virtually all of your words. It helps to train the system to recognize your unique speech patterns. We all sound different, even to a computer. To train the system, simply read to it for about an hour—the longer the better. Even if a word is said twice in succession, it will probably have a different inflection or nasal quality. The system uses artificial intelligence techniques to learn our speech patterns and update the vocabulary database accordingly. The typical speech-recognition system never stops learning, for it is always fine-tuning the vocabulary so it can recognize words with greater speed and accuracy. Each user on a given PC would need to customize his or her own vocabulary database. To further customize our personal vocabulary database, we can add words that are unique to our working environment, such as acronyms or product names (for example, QRCV or Xbox).

It is only a matter of time before we all will be communicating with our PCs in spoken English rather than through time-consuming keystrokes. Already, thousands of attorneys, doctors, journalists, and others who routinely rely on dictation and writing are enjoying the benefits of speech recognition.

Bill Gates of Microsoft has said that we will soon be able to operate our computers by verbally conversing with them. He also indicated that one of the options available to us, as users, would be to give our PCs a personality. What kind of personality would you give your computer: somber, serious, happy-go-lucky, polite, rude, frivolous, Valley girl, punk? The possibilities are endless.

Speaker-Independent Speech Recognition

Some speech-recognition systems are speaker-independent; that is, they can accept words spoken by anyone. Such systems are restricted to accepting only a limited number of words and tasks.

FIGURE 6–11 Smart Card Production
Each smart card has embedded nonvolatile memory and a processor (shown here) that can be loaded with information and programmed for a wide variety of applications.
Courtesy of Sun Microsystems, Inc.

However, speaker-independent speech-recognition systems are becoming more sophisticated, able to interpret more vocabulary from a wider audience with improved accuracy.

Today, speech-enabled applications are being implemented in all types of industries. For example, thousands of salespeople in the field can enter an order simply by calling in to the company's computer and stating the customer number, item number, and quantity. Several airline companies offer a speech-enabled airline reservation system. Telephone companies have introduced speech-enabled directory service. Modern speech-enabled systems speak to the users more like a human operator might. For example, rather than saying, "Would you like me to repeat the menu options?" it might say, "I did not understand you. Would you mind repeating that?" The system also allows people who are experienced with the system to "barge in" in the middle of a speech-response statement so that calls can be completed more quickly.

FIGURE 6–12

SPEECH RECOGNITION
The sound waves created by the spoken word *Move* are digitized by the computer. The digitized template is matched against templates of other words in the electronic dictionary. When the computer finds a match, it displays a written version of the word.

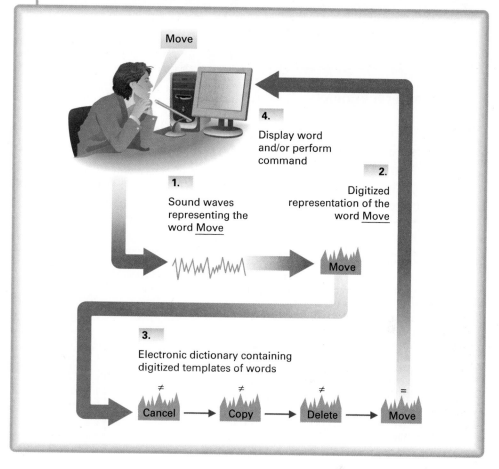

PATTERN RECOGNITION: "VISION" SYSTEMS

Some data are best entered and processed visually. However, the simulation of human senses, especially vision, is extremely complex. A computer does not actually see and interpret an image the way a human being does. Computers need cameras for their "eyesight." To create a visual database, a **pattern recognition system,** via a camera, digitizes the images of all objects to be identified, and then stores the digitized form of each image in the database. When the system is placed in operation, the camera enters each newly "seen" image into a digitizer. The system then compares the digitized image to be interpreted with the prerecorded digitized images in the computer's database, much like a speech-recognition system does with speech input. The computer identifies the image by matching the structure of the input image with those images in the database. This process is illustrated by the digital vision-inspection system in Figure 6-14.

As you can imagine, pattern recognition systems are best suited to very specialized tasks in which only a few images will be encountered. These tasks are usually simple, monotonous ones, such as inspection. For example, in Figure 6-14, a digital vision-inspection system on an assembly line rejects those parts that do not meet certain quality control specifications. The vision system performs rudimentary gauging inspections, and then signals the computer to take appropriate action. Security using biometric identification is another popular application for pattern recognition (see Figure 6-15).

Vision input offers great promise for the future. Can you imagine traveling by car from your hometown to Charleston, South Carolina, without the burden of actually driving? Sound far-fetched? Not really. DaimlerChrysler, the automobile maker, is actively developing a system that will allow you to do just that. The copilot system is a step up from cruise control, freeing the driver from both the accelerator pedal and the steering wheel. Like cruise control, the driver would remain behind the wheel, even when the system is operational. The foundation technology is vision input. When traveling down the German Autobahn, the system "sees" the lines on either side of the lane and makes minor adjustments in direction to keep the automobile centered in the lane. This part of the system works well; however,

FIGURE 6–13 TALKING TO COMPUTERS

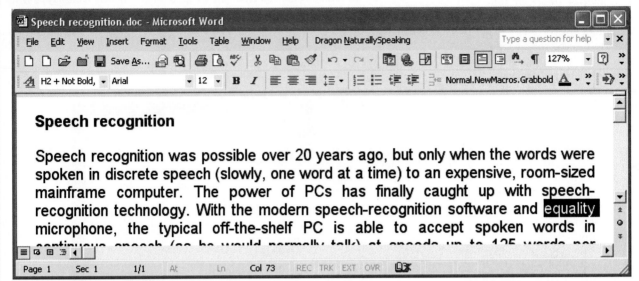

SPEECH RECOGNITION SOFTWARE
Dragon Systems® Dragon NaturallySpeaking™ is a flexible continuous speech-recognition system that allows users to input text and control applications by speaking naturally instead of typing. The software translates your spoken words into commands or dictated text. This caption and much of this book was dictated directly to the computer via Dragon NaturallySpeaking. The speech-recognition program displays a word or phrase that contains its best guesses when a spoken word or phrase has several interpretations. In this example, the only phrase not interpreted correctly was "a quality," which was interpreted as "equality." Over time, the program adapts to your voice; that is, its guesses get better as you use it. Words can be dictated directly into spreadsheet, database, presentation graphics, and any other type of software that accepts text.

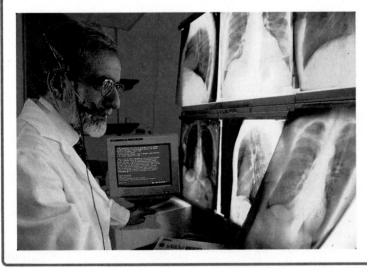

SPEECH RECOGNITION IN A MEDICAL CLINIC
This radiologist (right) is dictating his findings directly to the computer. He can also issue commands, such as "move left," "paste that," or "give me help."

Courtesy of Dragon Systems, Inc.

DaimlerChrysler engineers have many hurdles to overcome (exit ramps, pedestrians, and so on) before you see this feature in showroom automobiles. Someday the safest drivers on the road will not be driving at all.

DIGITAL CAMERAS: DIGICAMS

We all know that a picture is worth 1000 words, whether at home or the office. We now have the tools to capture still and video imagery, easily and economically. Personal computing and the Net have made it easy to share these images and video with our neighbors or with friends around the world.

Capturing Still Images

Most people still take photographs in the traditional manner—with a camera and film. We drop off our rolls of film for developing, and then we enjoy

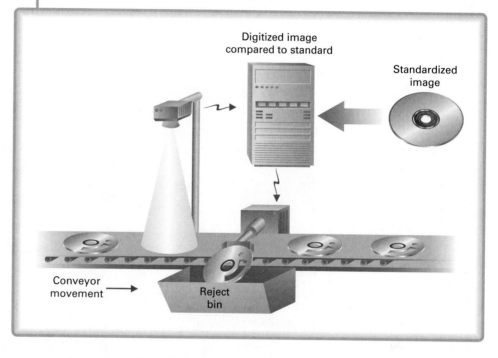

FIGURE 6–14

DIGITAL VISION-INSPECTION SYSTEM
In this digital vision-inspection system, the system examines parts for defects. If the digitized image of the part does not match a standard digital image, the defective part is placed in a reject bin.

Digitized image compared to standard

Standardized image

Conveyor movement

Reject bin

the results in the form of prints and slides. Some people use image scanners to digitize photos for use in newsletters, magazines, and so on. This process may change forever as the price of **digital cameras** continues to plummet. You can get a good digital camera for as little as $200 and a very good one for less than $500. Those used by professional photographers are considerably more expensive. When you take a picture with a modern **digicam**, a digitized image goes straight to onboard flash memory in the form of a memory stick. Once in the interchangeable memory cards or "stick," it can be uploaded to a PC and manipulated (viewed, printed, modified, and so on) as you would other graphic images (see Figure 6-16).

There are many applications for digital cameras. Customers from all over the world make special requests to a designer jewelry store. Store personnel take photos of available merchandise from various angles, and then they e-mail the photos to the customer. An automobile repair center takes photos of all major repair jobs to show customers exactly what the problem was and for training purposes. To help them to adjust braces better, orthodontists use digital cameras to track the migration of patients' teeth. Online retailers use digital cameras when preparing product Web pages, thereby skipping the film developing and scanning process altogether. One of the most popular applications is expanding the family photo album. Typically, photos are stored permanently on hard disk, optical laser discs, or high-density interchangeable disks, such as the Zip disk.

Photo images are an effective way to communicate. Now that the digital camera has become a popular consumer item, images are streaming through the Internet by the millions to grandmothers, parents, old friends, business colleagues, customers, clients, and just about everyone else. Most images are sent as attachments to e-mail. Here is a hint. To minimize upload/download time, send images in an efficient file format, such as JPG (or JPEG), and at a resolution that fits how the images are to be viewed/used. Choose high resolution only if the image is to be printed. The smaller the file, the more quickly it downloads.

Once you own a digital camera, the cost of photography plummets because the costly, time-consuming developing processing is

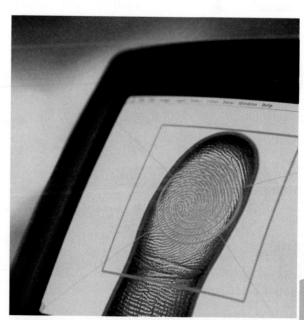

FIGURE 6–15 Pattern Recognition Applications
Security is an emerging application for pattern recognition, including fingerprint and facial identification.

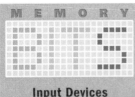

Input Devices

- Keyboard
- Point-and-draw devices
- Scanners
- Image scanners (*page and hand*)
- Badge reader (for magnetic stripes and smart cards)
- Speech-recognition systems
- Pattern recognition systems
- Digital cameras
- Digital video cameras
- Digital camcorders
- Handheld and wearable data entry devices

FIGURE 6–16

DIGITAL PHOTOGRAPHY
We may be entering an era of filmless photography. This image of Niagara Falls was taken with a digital camera, the one in the inset. You can capture, view, print, store, and transmit almost any image. Images are stored on interchangeable memory cards (see inset) or diskettes, then uploaded to a PC and used in countless applications, from the family photo album to training software.

Photo courtesy of Intel Corporation

Long and Associates

eliminated. With digital cameras, you can take all the photos you want and just keep the really good ones. With the cost of high-resolution digital cameras about that of a quality 35-mm camera, a lot more people are going digital for photography.

Desktop Video Cameras

Already the relative inexpensive digital video camera (around $70) is standard on some PCs. The desktop **digital video camera** lets you capture motion video in the area of the PC. Two popular uses for these cameras are to capture video for real-time Internet-based videophone conversations and as Webcams. If you have a PC, videophone software, an Internet connection, and a digital video camera, you are set to have videophone conversations, whereby you both see and hear the other party. Your digital video camera lets the other person see you and his or hers lets him or her see you. **Webcams** are digital video cameras that are continuously linked to the Internet, providing still and video imagery from thousands of sites, usually 24 hours a day. Webcams are located in zoos, classrooms, offices, living rooms, forests, on top of tall buildings, and just about any other place you can imagine beaming stills or video of whatever is happening into cyberspace.

Digital video cameras have many applications. They are used to create video content for Web pages. People use them to capture low-resolution still images. More and more companies are opting to save the airfare and have videoconferences instead. The emergence of low-cost rewritable optical disc storage means that you can use digital video cameras for the family video, too. Digital video imagery can really eat up the megabytes on a hard disk, so people often move captured video to optical laser discs. A CD-R will hold about 15 minutes of video.

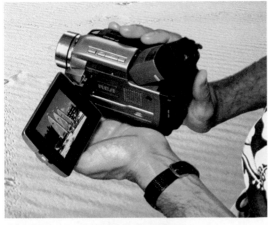

FIGURE 6–17 Digital Moviemaker
This RCA digital camcorder can capture favorite scenes that can be shared with your friends and relatives. The digital video can be viewed via TV or PC. Within a few years, most new camcorders will be digital.

Photo courtesy of RCA

Digital Camcorders

Handheld **digital camcorders** offer another way to capture video (see Figure 6-17). Digital camcorders offer greater portability and the quality of the video is higher than that of desktop cameras, but so is the price ($500 to $1000). Video is stored on digital tape, but it can be uploaded to a PC for digital video editing. Digital video is edited easily, that is, parts can be deleted, moved, or copied to meet application needs.

Another way to capture video is to use a standard analog camcorder or VCR in conjunction with a **video capture card**. Simply plug the cable from the camera or VCR into the expansion card and hit the record or play button. The analog signal is sent to the video capture card where it is digitized for viewing, editing, and storage.

HANDHELD AND WEARABLE DATA ENTRY DEVICES

Some close-to-the-source data entry tasks still require the use of some keystrokes and are best performed on handheld data entry devices. The typical *handheld data entry device,* which is actually a small computer, has the following:

- A limited external keyboard or a soft keyboard (displayed on a touch-sensitive screen)

- A small display that may be touch sensitive

- Some kind of storage capability for the data, usually solid-state nonvolatile flash memory

- A scanning device, capable of optical character recognition

After the data have been entered, the portable data entry device is linked with a central computer, and data are *uploaded* (transmitted from the data entry device to a central computer) for processing.

Stock clerks in department stores routinely use handheld devices to collect and enter reorder data. As clerks visually check the inventory level, they identify the items that need to be restocked. They first scan the price tag (which identifies the item), and then enter the number to be ordered on the keyboard.

Handheld and wearable computers, introduced in Chapter 1, frequently are used as data entry devices (see Figure 6-18). Some PCs have pressure-sensitive writing pads that recognize hand-printed alphanumeric characters. Also, they permit the entering of graphic information. For example, police officers use handheld PCs to document accidents, including recording the handwritten signatures of the participants.

FIGURE 6–18 Wearable Information Retrieval and Data Entry Hardware
This wearable PC is worn around the head and on the waist. This U.S. Army mechanic enters data and retrieves information in a hands-free environment, eliminating the need to carry maintenance manuals during field maneuvers.

Courtesy of Xybernaut

TOUCH SCREEN MONITORS

We usually think of monitors as output devices, but some enable input, as well. **Touch screen monitors** have pressure-sensitive overlays that can detect pressure and the exact location of that pressure. Users simply touch the desired icon or menu item with their finger. Educators realize that we are born with an ability to point and touch, and are beginning to use touch screen technology in the classroom to teach everything from reading to geography. Interactive touch screen systems are installed in shopping centers, zoos, airports, grocery stores, post offices, and many other public locations.

6-1.1	Input devices translate data into a form that can be interpreted by a computer. (T/F)
6-1.2	The wheel on the wheel mouse makes it easier to drag icons. (T/F)
6-1.3	The Universal Product Code (UPC) was originally used by which industry: (a) supermarket, (b) hardware, (c) mail-order merchandising, or (d) steel?
6-1.4	Which is not generally considered a source-data automation technology: (a) keyboard, (b) OCR, (c) speech recognition, or (d) UPC?
6-1.5	Memory on smart cards is: (a) volatile, (b) nonvolatile, (c) inert, or (d) never more than 1024 bits.
6-1.6	The Webcam is associated with all but which of the following: (a) digital video, (b) the World Wide Web, (c) touchpad input, or (d) The Internet?

SECTION SELF-CHECK

6-2 | Output Devices

Output devices translate bits and bytes into a form we can understand. There are many output devices, including monitors, printers, plotters, multimedia projectors, and voice-response systems, all presented in this section.

MONITORS AND GRAPHICS ADAPTERS

The output device we are most familiar with is the monitor, which displays system output. Monitors come in all shapes and sizes to meet a variety of application needs (see Figure 6-19). We describe monitors and their capabilities in terms of the following:

- Technology
- Graphics adapter (the electronic link between the processor and the monitor)
- Size (diagonal dimension of the display screen)
- Resolution (detail of the display)
- Refresh rate

Technology: CRT and Flat-Panel

The basic technology employed in the bulky, boxy **CRT monitors** that you see used with most desktop personal computers has been around since the 1940s. These monitors offer excellent resolution at a very competitive price. However, their footprint, the amount of space they take up on a desk, remains a user concern. The alternative, the **flat-panel monitor,** which is found on all notebook PCs, has a much smaller footprint. Some of the space-saving flat-panel monitors are less than 1/4-inch thick. The more expensive flat-panel monitor is becoming an increasingly viable option for the PC user as the price continues to drop toward that of the CRT. You must still pay a premium to save desk space and energy, as much as two to three times the cost per unit of viewing area. It is inevitable that the space-saving, energy-saving flat-panel displays will eventually displace the traditional CRT-type monitors for desktop PCs.

Flat-panel monitors use a variety of technologies, the most common being *LCD* (liquid crystal display). LCD monitors are *active matrix* or *passive matrix*. Active matrix monitors have higher refresh rates and better contrast, making for a more brilliant display. Active matrix LCD monitors are also known as TFT (thin film transistor) LCD monitors. Millions of transistors are needed for TFT LCD monitors. Color monitors need three transistors for each pixel: one each for red, green, and blue. Active matrix LCD displays are more expensive than passive matrix displays; therefore, active matrix LCD displays are usually associated with the better notebook PCs.

Graphics Adapters

The **graphics adapter** is the device controller for the monitor (see Figure 6-20). Some are built into the motherboard. On desktop PCs, graphics adapters usually are inserted into an *AGP bus* expansion slot on the motherboard. The monitor cable is plugged into the graphics adapter board to link the monitor with the processor. All display signals en route to the monitor pass through the graphics adapter, where the digital signals are converted to signals compatible with the monitor's display capabilities.

Most existing graphics adapters have their own RAM, called **video RAM** or **VRAM,** whereby they prepare monitor-bound images for display. The size of the video RAM is important in that it determines the number of possible colors and resolution of the display, as well as the speed at which signals can be sent to the monitor. Gamers, those who do video editing, and others who place extreme demands on graphics adapters will want to upgrade the standard graphics adapter to one with enough VRAM to handle heavy video demands. The newer AGP graphics adapters enjoy much better performance by using the PC system's RAM directly.

Monitor Size

Display screens vary in size from 5 to 60 inches (measured diagonally). The monitor size for newly purchased desktop PCs has inched up from 14 inches to 17 inches over the past 10 years and is now moving toward 19 inches. If your applications involve the heavy use of graphics, such as computer-aided design or commercial art, or you routinely switch between a variety of open programs, you might want to consider a 20-plus inch monitor. The larger displays, 30 inches and up, usually are designed for viewing by two or more people.

FIGURE 6–19 MONITORS

46-INCH TFT LCD PANEL DISPLAY
This 46-inch TFT LCD panel offers 1280 by 720 resolution and a 170° viewing angle in all directions.
Courtesy of Samsung Electronics Co., Ltd.

DURABLE MONITORS
In video arcades, the action takes place on large, durable monitors.
Photo courtesy of Intel Corporation

FLAT PANEL MONITORS
Flat-panel LCD monitors may be the wave of the future for desktop PCs.
Photo courtesy of Intel Corporation

MULTIPLE MONITOR ENVIRONMENTS
Monitors are an integral component of virtually all computer-based applications, including video editing. This one-person studio employs a variety of high-resolution CRT and flat panel monitors.
Photo courtesy of Hewlett-Packard Company

TOUCH SCREEN MONITORS
A growing number of ATMs (shown here) and public information kiosks use touch screen monitors with input/output capabilities.
Courtesy of Diebold, Incorporated

WORLD'S SMALLEST MONITOR
Kopin Corporation's CyberDisplay™ is the world's smallest high-performance, high-resolution, full-function information display. The microdisplays are especially designed for portable products, such as with cellular phone applications (videophone, e-mail, and so on), shown here, and also with wearable computers.
Courtesy of Kopin Corporation

FIGURE 6–20 High-Performance Graphics Adapter
This Sun Microsystems Elite3D graphics system enables real-time interactive 3D visualization, which is necessary for such applications as 3D design and modeling, dynamic simulation, and video effects.

Courtesy of Sun Microsystems, Inc.

Monitor Resolution

Monitors vary in their quality of output, or *resolution*. Resolution depends on the *number of pixels that can be displayed*, the *number of bits used to represent each pixel*, and the *dot pitch of the monitor*. A **pixel** is an addressable point on the screen, a point to which light can be directed under program control. The typical monitor is set to operate with a *screen area* of 786,432 addressable points in 1024 columns by 768 rows; however, most can have screen area settings ranging from 640 by 480 to 2000 by 1600. The 2000 by 1600 setting has over three million addressable points. The higher the number of pixels, the more information you can display on your screen.

Each pixel, short for *picture element* (see Figure 6-21), can be assigned a color or, for monochrome monitors, a shade of gray. **Gray scales** refer to the number of shades of a color that can be shown on a monochrome monitor's screen. Most color monitors mix red, green, and blue to achieve a spectrum of colors, and are called **RGB monitors.** One of the user options is the number of bits used to display each pixel, sometimes referred to as **color depth.** In 8-bit color mode, 256 colors are possible ($2^8 = 256$). The 16-bit mode *high-color* mode yields 65,536 colors. *True color* options, either 24-bit or 32-bit mode, provide photo-quality viewing with over 16 million to over 4 billion colors. There is a trade-off between resolution and system performance. Differences in color depth are illustrated in Figure 6-22. Greater resolutions demand more of the processor, leaving less capacity for other processing tasks.

Its **dot pitch,** or the distance between the centers of adjacent pixels, also affects a monitor's resolution—the lower the dot pitch number, the greater the number of pixels in the display. Any dot pitch equal to or less than .28 mm (millimeters) provides a sharp image. A dot pitch of .25 is even better. When you have an opportunity, use a magnifying glass to examine the pixels and observe the dot pitch on your computer's monitor.

Refresh Rate

The monitor's *refresh rate* also affects the quality of the display. The phosphor coating on a monitor's CRT (cathode-ray tube) must be repainted or refreshed 50 to over 100 times each second (Hz) to maintain clarity of the image. Generally, monitors with faster refresh rates have fewer flickers and are easier on the eyes.

FIGURE 6–21 Pixels
This photo of children enjoying a snow day off from school illustrates how computers use picture elements, or pixels, to portray digital images. Thousands (even millions) of pixels, each a single point on a graphics image, are arranged in rows and columns to create the image. In the inset image, the pixels are so close together they portray continuous color. The blowup highlights the individual pixels.

LCD PROJECTORS

Businesspeople have found that sophisticated and colorful graphics add an aura of professionalism to any report or presentation (see Figure 6-23). This demand for *presentation graphics* has created a need for corresponding output devices. Graphic images can be displayed on a monitor or they can be projected onto a large screen to be viewed by a group of people or an audience with the aid of a **multimedia projector.**

The need for overhead transparencies and 35-mm slides is beginning to fade as presenters discover the ease with which they can create dynamic multimedia presentations, then present them with multimedia projectors. These output devices fall into two categories: *LCD panels* and *LCD projectors*. The LCD panels, which are about the size of a notebook PC, are used with overhead projectors. The LCD panels are placed directly on the overhead projector as you would position a transparency acetate. The light from the overhead projector is directed through an LCD panel and whatever image is on its display is shown on a large screen for all to see. The LCD projectors use their own built-in lens and light source to project the image on the screen.

WEARABLE DISPLAYS

For those knowledge workers who are constantly in motion yet need access to critical information, there is the **wearable display.** Usually the wearable display is worn on a wireless headset, thus untethering us from our personal computer. Of course, the wearable display is standard with wearable PCs. A variety of technologies is emerging for wearable displays, one of which, RSD, eliminates any screen outside of the eye and addresses the retina with a stream of pixels.

There are many uses for wearable displays. For example, privacy-minded people use these displays in crowded areas, such as on an airplane. Mobile workers enjoy the convenience of being able to view needed information as they go about their jobs. For example, airplane quality control inspectors use wearable displays.

PRINTERS

Printers produce hard copy output, such as college term papers, management reports, cash register receipts, labels, memos, and payroll checks. Dozens of manufacturers produce hundreds of printers. There is a printer manufactured to meet the hard copy output requirements of any individual or company, and almost any combination of features can be obtained (see Figure 6-24). You can specify its size (some weigh less than a pound), speed, quality of output, color requirements, and even noise level. PC printers sell for as little as a pair of shoes or for as much as a wardrobe full of clothes. High-speed, high-volume enterprise printers that produce utility bills, credit-card charge summaries, and the like can cost as much as a house.

Any person or company about to purchase a printer must consider:

- What's the budget?
- Is color needed or will black and white do?
- What will be the volume of output (pages per hour, day, or week)?
- How important is the quality of the output?
- What special features are needed (ability to print envelopes, on legal size paper, on multipart forms, on both sides of the paper, and so on)?
- Can printing needs be met with an all-in-one printer/copier/scanner/fax device?
- If the printer is to be shared on a network, what do the other users want?

Think about these considerations as you read about various printer options. Keep in mind that color, additional features, and each increment in speed and quality of output add to the cost of the printer.

Printer technology is ever changing. Three basic technologies dominate the PC printer arena: page (laser), ink-jet, and dot-matrix. The advantages and disadvantages of these technologies are summarized in Figure 6-25. All PC printers have the capability of printing graphs and charts and offer considerable flexibility in the size and style of print. All printers also can print in portrait or landscape format. **Portrait** and **landscape** refer to the orientation of the print on the page. Portrait format is like the page of this book—the lines run parallel to the shorter sides of the page. In contrast, landscape output runs parallel to the longer sides of the page. Landscape is frequently the orientation of choice for spreadsheet outputs with many columns (see Figure 6-26).

FIGURE 6–22 **COLOR DEPTH**
The same Niagara Falls image is shown at three levels of color depth: 8 bit with 256 (2^8) possible colors, 16-bit *high color* with 65,536 (2^{16}) possible colors, and 32-bit *true color* with over 4 billion (2^{32}) possible colors.

8-bit

16-bit high color

32-bit true color

FIGURE 6–23 LCD Projectors
LCD projectors are used in conjunction with presentation software, such as Microsoft PowerPoint, and notebook PCs.

Photo courtesy of Hewlett-Packard Company

Page Printers

Nonimpact **page printers** use laser, LED (*light-emitting diode*), LCS (*liquid crystal shutter*), and other laser-like technologies to achieve high-speed hard copy output by printing *a page at a time*. Page printers are also referred to simply as **laser printers**. The operation of a laser-based page printer is illustrated in Figure 6-27. Most of the laser printers in use print shades of gray; however, color laser printers are becoming increasingly popular as their price continues to drop.

Economically priced desktop page printers have become the standard for office printing. These printers, which print at speeds of 4 to 32 pages per minute (ppm) for text-only printing, can run through up to six feet of paper during a business day. Printing in color (when available) and/or printing graphic images may slow down output to about 25% the rated monochrome text-only output speed. Most page printers print on standard letter and legal paper.

FIGURE 6–24 PRINTERS

COLOR PRINTERS
Color printers let users add color to their everyday business (memos, reports, spreadsheets, graphs) and home (banners, invitations, photos) printing needs. The Hewlett-Packard color ink-jet (left) and color laser (right) printers provide high-quality color output. The ink-jet printer can print photo-quality images directly from a digital camera or via a PC.

Photos courtesy of Hewlett-Packard Company

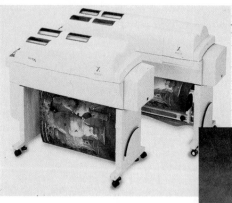

LARGE-FORMAT PRINTERS
Typical applications for this large-format ink-jet printer include point-of-sale displays, billboards, banners, backlit signs, backdrops for photography or video, and trade show graphics. Large-format prints are typically 22 inches and larger.

Courtesy of Xerox Corporation

IT'S A FAX, A PRINTER, A COPIER, AND A SCANNER
This compact and lightweight four-in-one RCA Docuport lets road warriors take the office with them.

Photo courtesy of RCA

SPECIAL-FUNCTION PRINTERS
There is a printer for every job. This printer prints wristbands for hospital patients. The wristbands include bar-coded patient information that can be read with wand scanners.

Courtesy of Diebold, Incorporated

ENTERPRISE PRINTERS
Enterprise printers are designed for high-volume printing (telephone bills, financial statements, insurance coverage summaries, and so on). This IBM printer can print over 400 miles of cut sheet paper per month at 600 dpi resolution.

Courtesy of International Business Machines Corporation.
Unauthorized use not permitted.

FIGURE 6–25 PRINTER SUMMARY

	Pros	Cons	Outlook
Page/laser printers	• High-resolution output • Fast (up to 32 ppm) • Quiet • Low cost per page	• High purchase price • Cut sheet only	• High-speed, high-quality page printers will remain the mainstay of office printing for the foreseeable future.
Ink-jet printers	• High-resolution output (but less than that of page) • Quiet • Small footprint • Energy-efficient	• Higher cost per page than laser • Slower than laser (up to 20 ppm) • Cut sheet only • High cost of print cartridges	• Ink-jet printers will remain the choice for any environment, home or office, with low-volume printing needs.
Dot-matrix printers	• Inexpensive • Can print multipart paper • Can print on fanfold paper • Low cost per page • Energy efficient	• Noisy • Low resolution • Poor quality graphics output • Limited font selection	• Dot-matrix printers are used only in those situations that require printing on multipart forms and/or fan-fold paper.
All-in-one (multifunction) printers	• Can function as a printer, a scanner, a copier, and a fax machine • Get four functions for the price of 1 or 2 • Functional specifications close to separate devices (output quality, speed, and so on)	• Can handle only one function at a time • Larger footprint than a comparable printer	• The all-in-one printer has emerged as the choice in the home or home office with copier, scanner, and fax needs, too

FIGURE 6–26

PORTRAIT AND LANDSCAPE ORIENTATION
Shown here are print previews—for a word
processing document to be printed in portrait orientation, and a spreadsheet document to be printed in landscape orientation.

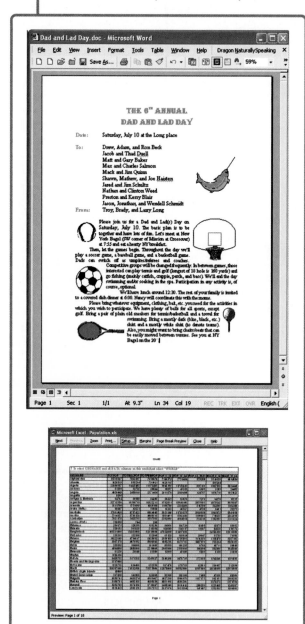

All desktop page printers are capable of producing *near-typeset-quality* (*NTQ*) text and graphics. The resolution (quality of output) of the low-end desktop page printer is 600 *dpi* (dots per inch). High-end desktop page printers are capable of at least 1200 dpi. The dpi qualifier refers to the number of dots that can be printed per linear inch, horizontally or vertically. That is, a 600-dpi printer is capable of printing 360,000 (600 times 600) dots per square inch. Commercial typesetting quality is a minimum of 1200 dpi and is usually in excess of 2000 dpi. Desktop page printers are also quiet (an important consideration in an office setting). Other pros and cons of page printers are summarized in Figure 6-25.

Ink-Jet Printers

To the naked eye, there is little difference between the print quality of nonimpact **ink-jet printers** and page printers. Although the output quality of ink-jet printers is more in line with page printers, their mechanical operation is more like that of the dot-matrix printer because they have a print head that moves back and forth across the paper to write text and create the image (see Figure 6-28). Several independently controlled injection chambers squirt ink droplets on the paper. The droplets, which dry instantly as dots, form the letters and images. Resolutions for the typical ink-jet printer are about that of page printers, 1200 dpi for regular black and white printing and up to 4800 dpi for color printing on premium photo paper. Print speeds for high-quality color output (photos) range from 1 to 2 ppm and print speeds for normal black-and white-only printing are 4 to 8 ppm. Print speeds for draft (low-resolution) output are significantly higher, up to 15 ppm for draft color output and 20 ppm for draft black and white output.

The color ink-jet printer is emerging as the choice for budget-minded consumers. SOHO (small office/home office) buyers also are opting for color ink-jet printers by the millions. The cost of color ink-jet printers ranges from about $100 to about $500. The pros and cons of home/office ink-jet printers are summarized in Figure 6-25.

Large-Format Ink-Jet Printers

Page, ink-jet, and dot-matrix printers are capable of producing page-size graphic output, but are limited in their ability to generate large-scale, high-quality, perfectly proportioned graphic output. For example, on a blueprint, the sides of a 12-foot-square room must be exactly the same length. Architects, engineers, graphics artists, city planners, and others who routinely generate high-precision, hard copy graphic output of widely varying sizes use another hard copy alternative—**large-format ink-jet printers**, also called **plotters.** Plotters use ink-jet technology to print on roll-feed paper up to 4 feet wide and 50 feet in length. Plotters can be used for large printing needs, such as commercial posters or blueprints, or they can be used to produce continuous output, such as plotting earthquake activity or a five-year project activity chart.

Dot-Matrix Printers

The **dot-matrix printer** forms images *one character at a time* as the print head moves across the paper. The dot-matrix printer is an *impact printer;* that is, it uses from 9 to 24 tiny *pins* to hit an ink ribbon and the paper. The dot-matrix printer arranges printed dots to form characters and all kinds of images in much the same way as lights display time and temperature on bank signs. Dot-matrix printers print up to 450 cps (characters per second).

Most dot-matrix printers can accommodate both *cut-sheet paper* and *fanfold paper* (a continuous length of paper that is folded at perforations). The *tractor-feed* that handles fanfold paper is standard with most dot-matrix printers. Impact printers, as opposed to nonimpact printers, touch the paper and can produce carbon copies along with the original. Other pros and cons of dot-matrix printers are summarized in Figure 6-25.

The All-in-One: Print, Fax, Scan, and Copy

Traditionally, businesses have purchased separate machines to handle these paper-related tasks: computer-based printing, facsimile (fax), scanning, and copying (duplicating). The considerable overlap in the technologies used in these machines has enabled manufacturers to create **all-in-one peripheral devices**. These multifunction devices are popular in the small office/home office environments and in other settings where the volume for any of their functions is relatively low. The laser all-in-one peripheral is more expensive than the ink-jet all-in-one.

You can easily pay in excess of $1000 for a printer, a scanner, a copier, and a fax machine. Many people with low volume needs are choosing the all-in-one device for 20 to 40% of the cost of separate peripherals. It's an easy choice when you consider that there is relatively little loss of functionality when compared to separate devices. The popularity of the all-in-one device has exploded since the print/scan/copy quality and the speeds of the all-in-one are now comparable to that of the separate devices.

FIGURE 6–27 **LASER-BASED PAGE PRINTER OPERATION**
The enclosure of a desktop page printer is removed to expose its inner workings. (A) Prior to printing, an electrostatic charge is applied to a drum. Then laser beam paths to the drum are altered by a spinning multisided mirror. The reflected beams selectively remove the electrostatic charge from the drum. (B) Toner is deposited on those portions of the drum that were affected by the laser beams. The drum is rotated and the toner is fused to the paper to create the image.

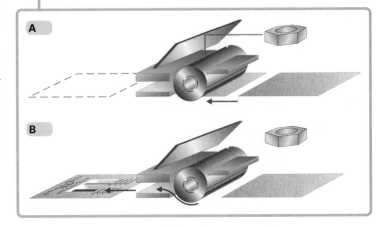

FIGURE 6–28 **INK-JET PRINTERS**
Ink-jet printers are miniature technological marvels. Tiny droplets of ink, about one millionth the volume of a drop of water, in either blue, red, yellow, or black, are positioned with great precision on the paper to form characters and images. The droplets, which are mixed to form a wide range of possible colors, are squirted from a nozzle less than the width of a human hair. Ink-jet printers use interchangeable cartridges with up to 100 nozzles for each of the four colors. Frequently, black has its own cartridge, whereas the other colors share a separate cartridge. Movement of the print heads and paper are coordinated under program control to squirt the dots to form the text and images. Several methods are used to squirt the droplets onto the paper. One method involves superheating ink in a tiny chamber such that it boils and the pressure forces droplets out the nozzle. The chamber cools, ink flows into the chamber, and a process is repeated every few millionths of a second. The dots of color are overlapped to increase the density and, therefore, the quality of the image.

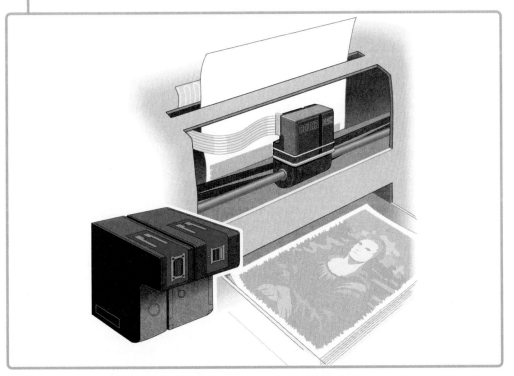

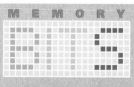

Output Devices

- Monitors
  - CRT
  - Flat-panel
  - Touch screen (input and output)
  - Wearable display
- Printers
  - Page (laser) printers (color option)
  - Ink-jet printers
  - Large-format ink-jet printers (color option)
  - Dot-matrix printers
  - All-in-one multifunction peripherals (print, fax, scan, and copy)
- Multimedia projectors (screen image projection for groups)
- Sound systems
- Voice-response systems
  - Recorded voice
  - Speech synthesis

SOUND SYSTEMS

For the first decade of personal computing small, tinny-sounding speakers came with PCs, primarily to "beep" users when an operation was completed or interaction was needed. PC sound systems have come a long way since then. Today we watch surround sound DVD movies and we listen to CDs and MP3 music recordings on our PCs. We also use our PCs for gaming and multimedia presentations. Simple speakers can no longer meet today's audio output requirements for PCs.

PC sound systems vary from a couple of small speakers embedded in notebook PCs to sophisticated sound systems that provide surround sound with subwoofers, thunderous Dolby Digital audio, and up to 100 watts of power. As with any quality sound system, audio can be adjusted to fit the user's tastes.

VOICE-RESPONSE SYSTEMS

Anyone who has used a telephone has heard "If you're dialing from a touch-tone phone, press 1." You may have driven a car that advised you to "fasten your seat belt." These are examples of talking computers that use output from a voice-response system. There are two types of **voice-response systems**: One uses a *reproduction* of a human voice and other sounds, and the other uses **speech synthesis**. Like monitors, voice-response systems provide temporary, soft-copy output.

The first type of voice-response system selects output from a digitized audio recording of words, phrases, music, alarms, or anything you might record, just as a printer would select characters. In these recorded voice-response systems, the actual analog recordings of sounds are converted into digital data, then permanently stored on disk or in a memory chip. When output occurs, a particular sound is routed to a speaker. Sound chips are mass-produced for specific applications, such as output for automatic teller machines, microwave ovens, smoke detectors, elevators, alarm clocks, automobile warning systems, video games, and vending machines, to mention only a few. When sounds are stored on disk, the user has the flexibility to update them to meet changing application needs.

Speech synthesis systems, which convert raw data into electronically produced speech, are popular in the PC environment. All you need to produce speech on a PC are a sound expansion card, speakers (or headset), and appropriate software. Such **text-to-speech software** often is packaged with speech recognition software. Text-to-speech technology produces speech by combining phonemes (from 50 to 60 basic sound units) to create and output words.

The existing technology produces synthesized speech with only limited vocal inflections and phrasing, however. Despite the limitations, the number of speech synthesizer applications is growing. For example, a visually impaired person can use the speech synthesizer to translate printed words into spoken words. Some people use their notebook PCs to "read" their e-books to them. Translation systems offer one of the most interesting applications for speech synthesizers and speech-recognition devices. Researchers are making progress toward enabling conversations among people who are speaking different languages. A prototype system has already demonstrated that three people, each speaking a different language (English, German, and Japanese), can carry on a computer-aided conversation. Each person speaks in and listens to his or her native language.

SECTION SELF-CHECK

6-2.1	Ink-jet printers are nonimpact printers. (T/F)
6-2.2	You would be more likely to print a spreadsheet in landscape format than in portrait format. (T/F)
6-2.3	The tractor-feed on dot-matrix printers enables printing on what kind of paper: (a) cut-sheet paper, (b) fanfold paper, (c) landscape paper, or (d) portrait paper?
6-2.4	What technology converts raw data into electronically produced speech: (a) voice response, (b) reproduction analysis, (c) speech synthesis, or (d) sound duping?
6-2.5	All other things being equal on a monitor, which dot pitch would yield the best resolution: (a) .24 dot pitch, (b) .26 dot pitch, (c) .28 dot pitch, or (d) .31 dot pitch?

6-3 The Multimedia Experience

The quality, sophistication, and diversity of input/output devices continue to grow. Dolby sound, colorful digital imagery, tactile feedback, and many other devices that tickle our senses have transformed personal computing into a multimedia experience. That experience could be anything from colorful illustrations for a cyber greeting card to full multimedia class presentations involving sound, animation, and motion video.

MULTIMEDIA: SHOW TIME

Multimedia is an umbrella term that refers to the capability that enables the integration of computer-based text, still graphics, motion visuals, animation, and sound. In the mid-1990s, multimedia was relatively new and multimedia PCs, still a bit pricey, were atypical. Today, all PCs are multimedia-ready; that is, they have peripheral devices, including storage, and software that can deliver the multimedia experience. Most software packages and the Net take advantage of a PC's multimedia capabilities. Consider the *show biz* appeal of the applications in Figure 6-29 and in these examples.

- *The Internet.* You can go on the Web and listen to live broadcasts from hundreds of radio stations, view animated visuals of how things work, visit pages for vacation spots and view videos of the local attractions, and much more.

- *Video Editing.* **Video editing** is the process of manipulating **video** images. Not too long ago, video editing was the exclusive purview of video editing specialists working with hardware that cost in excess of $100,000. Now, you can do sophisticated video editing on your home PC. The hardware and software needed over and above a typical PC—a video capture card and video editing software—can be purchased for under $100. Video editing software lets you pick the video segments you want, sequence the clips, add background music, add scene transitions, place text over video, and employ many other special effects. You can even do fast and slow motion to create exciting "movie" sequences.

- *Presentations.* Knowledge workers prepare convincing presentations by blending colorful charts with animation and attention-getting audio.

- *Kiosks.* Interactive kiosks with touch-sensitive screens provide public users with detailed information about a city, a company, a product, events, and so on.

- *Tutorials.* Multimedia is rapidly becoming the foundation of computer-based training. For example, companies prepare interactive tutorials to introduce newcomers to company procedures. Thousands of workers are now learning Word, Excel, and other popular applications via interactive multimedia tutorials that are enlivened with music, graphics, and motion. A Department of Defense study concluded that such tutorials take about a third less time, cost about a third less, and are more effective than traditional training methods.

- *Online reference.* CD-ROM-based and Web-based multimedia alternatives are beginning to replace encyclopedias, technical reference manuals, product information booklets, and the like. Electronic versions of reference materials are easier to use and much, much lighter to carry.

- *Interactive publications.* Books, magazines, and newspapers are already being distributed as multimedia publications on CD-ROM and online via the Internet. The printed page will never be able to share moving visuals and sounds.

- *The family photo album.* The PC has emerged as the modern photo album. We use digital cameras to take pictures, then, if needed, we do touch-ups with photo illustration software. Photos in an electronic photo album are easily accessible and viewed. CD and DVD burners have made it possible for us to select video clips and images from the family archives and burn custom CDs and DVDs.

- *Entertainment center.* Our notebooks are portable movie theaters, capable of showing DVD movies or streaming video over the Internet. They can play any of millions of songs now available for download over the Internet or they can play the music from thousands of Internet radio stations from around the world. With a video capture card, your PC is easily transformed into a television with a remote channel changer.

With multimedia, the combined use of text, sound, images, motion video, and animation transforms a PC into an exciting center for learning, work, or play.

Growing with Multimedia

The next stage of multimedia growth comes when you decide to *develop* sophisticated multimedia applications—either your own multimedia title on CD-ROM or DVD, an interactive tutorial, a Web site, or an information kiosk. At this point, you or your company may need to invest in some or all of the following hardware and software.

- *Video camera, videocassette recorder/player, audiocassette player, and television.* These electronic devices are emerging as staples in many households and companies. The video camera (digital or analog) lets you capture motion video source material that can be integrated with multimedia applications. The videocassette recorder/player and audiocassette player are handy, but not a requirement. The television provides an alternative output device.

FIGURE 6–29   MULTIMEDIA APPLICATIONS

3-D IMAGES THAT INCLUDE YOU

Virtual reality may be the ultimate multimedia experience. The virtual reality (VR) theater at Iowa State University lets you interact with 3D images, including a tornado. The VR theater presents computer-generated images on the walls, floor, and ceiling and the view changes based on the viewer's perspective.

Courtesy of Iowa State University Photo Service

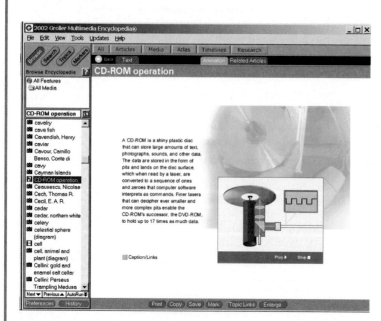

THE MULTIMEDIA ENCYCLOPEDIA

Far more people are choosing multimedia encyclopedias, such as the *2001 Grolier Multimedia Encyclopedia* shown here, than traditional print encyclopedias. They cost considerably less, are about 100 pounds lighter, and offer the advantages of multimedia. With electronic encyclopedias you can enjoy animation presentations, such as the audio-supported animation of how a CD-ROM works (shown here), and video that are not possible in print encyclopedias.

Grolier Multimedia Encyclopedia © 2001 by Grolier Interactive Inc.

FIGURE 6–29 continued

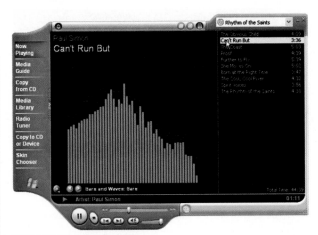

WINDOWS MEDIA PLAYER

The Windows Media Player software that comes with any Windows operating system lets you play your digital media, including music, videos, DVDs, Internet radio, and audio CDs. The software lets you hear and "see" the music on Paul Simon's classic CD, *Rhythm of the Saints*.

SIMULATION IN EDUCATION

People retain 10% of the information they see; 20% of what they hear; 50% of what they see and hear; and 80% of what they see, hear, and do. These facts make a good case for increased use of computer-based simulation in education and training. Commercial airline pilots use flight simulators, such as this one, to learn normal flight operations and to practice emergency procedures.

Courtesy of Lockheed Martin Corporation

MULTIMEDIA IN THE HOME AND OFFICE

Multimedia capability opens the door for a broad range of applications. This telecommuter uses his PC to do video editing for a film production studio.

Courtesy of Autodesk, Inc.

INFORMATIVE KIOSKS

The manner in which we obtain information is changing rapidly. Virgin Entertainment Group provides kiosks that enable customers to preview hundreds of thousands of CDs, DVDs, and Console Games.

Courtesy of International Business Machines Corporation. Unauthorized use not permitted.

FIGURE 6-29 continued

LCD PROJECTORS
Dr. C. Everett Koop, former U.S. Surgeon General, uses an LCD projector and multimedia displays during his speeches to make his points and illustrate concepts.

Photo courtesy of Intel Corporation

PERSONAL COMPUTING AND PHOTOGRAPHY
Miss America photographer Bruce Boyajian prints a photo on a high-resolution ink jet printer for Miss Texas, Stacy James, along the runway between rehearsals during the 81st annual Miss America Pageant being held in Atlantic City, N.J. Digital photos can be easily enhanced with special effects or lightened/darkened as needed.

Courtesy of Epson America, Inc. Photo by Thomas P. Costello.

THE CRYSTAL BALL:
The E-Book Books haven't changed much since Johann Gutenberg invented the printing press. The printed page is limited for any book or document that contains an index, including all varieties of reference books, encyclopedias, "how to" books, and, of course, textbooks. By 2010, virtually all of these books will be electronic books. Many are now. E-books will continue to evolve with greater flexibility in that they can be formatted for any device with a display and memory, even cell phones and automobile dashboard displays. E-books offer many advantages over traditional books: animation, motion video, drill-down capability, "active words" (for related information), hyperlinks, and margin notes.

● *Synthesizer.* A good keyboard synthesizer can reproduce a variety of special effects and sounds, including those of almost any musical instrument. A synthesizer can be played to create original source music for inclusion in a multimedia application.

● *Video capture card.* This expansion card lets you capture and digitize full-motion color video with audio. The digitized motion video can then be used as source material for a CD-ROM-based multimedia application.

● *Scanner.* A scanner lets you capture black/white and color images from hard copy source material.

● *Digital camera.* A digital camera captures high-resolution digital images that can be integrated into multimedia applications.

● *CD-RW or DVD+RW.* Optical laser rewritable technology lets you write and rewrite to high-capacity optical media. Multimedia applications generally have huge storage requirements and usually are distributed on CD-ROM or DVD.

● *Applications development software.* If you plan to develop sophisticated multimedia applications, you will need to upgrade to application development tools and authoring systems. **Authoring systems** let you create multimedia applications that integrate sound, motion, text, animation, and images.

● *PC source library.* The source library contains digitized "clips" of art, video, and audio that you can use as needed to complement a multimedia application.

Multimedia File Resources

Multimedia applications draw content material from a number of sources, such as text and database files, sound files, image files, animation files, and motion video files.

Text and Database Files

A little over a decade ago, most computer-based applications were designed strictly around text and numbers. However, this has changed. An animation of how the human heart works is far more effective than is a textual description of how it works.

Many CD-ROM titles and Web sites involve the use of databases. For example, one CD-ROM title contains information on every city in the United States (name, population, major industries, and so on) stored and sorted in a database. Retail Web sites maintain databases of the products they sell in their online stores.

Sound Files

Sound files are of two types: *waveform* and *nonwaveform*. The waveform files, or **wave files**, contain the digital information needed to reconstruct the analog waveform of the sound so it can be played through speakers. The primary Windows waveform files are identified with the WAV extension (for example, SOUNDFIL.WAV).

Another popular sound file format is MP3, which enables CD-quality music to be compressed to about 8% of its original size while retaining CD sound quality. For example, a three-minute song on CD takes 33 MB of disk space, but it can be compressed to 3 MB in MP3 format. That is a compression ratio of 11 to 1. The compression to MP3 format causes no noticeable loss of the quality of the sound because the compression process simply removes sounds outside of the audible range of the human ear, both low and high.

The nonwaveform file contains instructions as to how to create the sound, rather than a digitized version of the actual sound. For example, an instruction might tell the computer the pitch, duration, and sound quality of a particular musical note. The most common nonwaveform file, which is primarily for recording and playing music, is known as the **MIDI file**. MIDI files are identified with the MID extension (for example, MUSICFIL.MID). MIDI stands for Musical Instrument Digital Interface. MIDI provides an interface between PCs and electronic musical instruments, such as the synthesizer. A typical application involving MIDI files has the PC recording notes played by a musician on a synthesizer. The musician then adds additional instruments to the original track (layering) to create a full orchestral sound (see Figure 6-30). MIDI files occupy much less file space than comparable waveform audio files.

Image Files

Multimedia is visual, so it involves plenty of images. These are the most common sources of images.

- *You.* You can create your own images using the graphics software and techniques discussed in Chapter 2, "Software," and in this chapter.

- *Clip art.* Anyone serious about creating multimedia material will have a hefty clip art library of up to 100,000 images. Copyright-free clip art is readily available on the Web.

- *Scanned images.* If you have a scanner, you can scan and digitize any hard copy image (photographs, drawings, and so on).

- *Photo images.* Commercial photo image libraries make vast photo image resources available to the public, for a fee. Photo illustration software is often packaged with a variety of copyright-free images. Also, you can create your own images with a digital camera and/or a scanner.

Photo illustration software enables you to create original images as well as to dress up existing digitized images, such as photographs, scanned images, and electronic paintings. Images can be retouched with special effects to alter dramatically the way they appear (see Figure 6-31). Photo illustration software is to an image as word processing software is to text. A word processing package allows you to edit, sort, copy, and generally do whatever can be done to electronic text. Photo illustration software allows you to do just about anything imaginable to digitized photos or drawings. The result of a photo illustrator's effort is a composite image with stunning special effects.

FIGURE 6–30

DIGITAL AUDIO SEQUENCER AND MIDI
Digital Orchestrator Pro™ (a software product from Voyetra Turtle Beach, Inc.) is one of the most popular digital audio sequencers. The program lets you create multitrack recordings from external audio sources, such as the output from a keyboard synthesizer or an audio CD. Digital audio and MIDI tracks exist side by side in perfect sync, making song editing a snap. This image is one of the many views in the intuitive user interface that allows users to edit virtually any facet of a song.

ans	S	M	Pan	Reverb	Chorus		
			<0>	..	..	1	
			<0>	..	..	2	
			<0>	..	..	3	
			<0>	..	..	4	
			<11			5	
			32>			6	
			<0>			7	
			<0>			8	
			<0>			9	
			16>	66	..	10	
			<18	62	6	11	
			<0>	123	..	12	
			<0>	..	83	13	
			<0>	62	6	14	
			<30	40	90	15	
			<27	22	33	16	
			<0>	46	..	17	
			7>	..	32	18	
			<5	..	40	19	

FIGURE 6–31

PHOTO ILLUSTRATION SOFTWARE
Photo illustration software, such as *Microsoft® PhotoDraw®* (shown here), lets you work with digital images, such as those resulting from a digital photograph and scan of an image. With photo illustration software you can touch up your photographs and apply a wide variety of special effects to all or portions of your images. Once you're satisfied with your artistic work, you can post them to the Internet or print them on greeting cards, T-shirts, calendars, and so on.

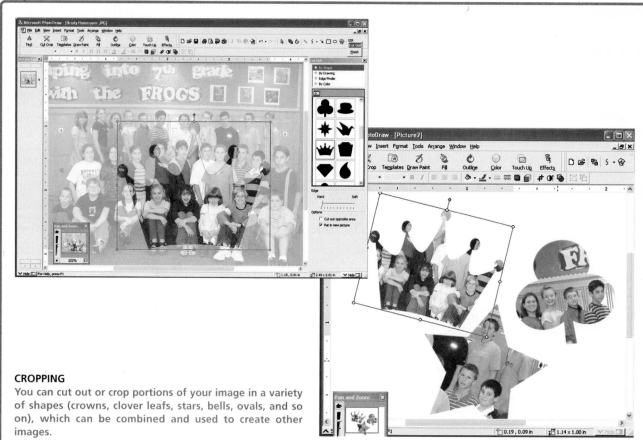

CROPPING
You can cut out or crop portions of your image in a variety of shapes (crowns, clover leafs, stars, bells, ovals, and so on), which can be combined and used to create other images.

CONTRAST AND BRIGHTNESS
The contrast and brightness feature can be used to save photographs that may otherwise be too dark (or light) in spots. Here, the contrast and brightness are adjusted to enhance the quality of the photo.

SPECIAL EFFECTS
The special effects shown here are but a few of the many that can be applied to give your digital images an artistic touch. Clockwise from the original image at the top left, they are the mosaic (image is flipped horizontally), *glowing edges, neon glow,* and *grayscale* effects.

For example, you can show the changes that take place as one image is modified to become an entirely different image. This process is called **morphing,** a term derived from the word *metamorphosis*. You also can feather images to blend with their surroundings, enter artistic text over the image, change colors, include freehand drawings, isolate objects for special treatment, distort specific objects (for example, *glass blocking*), and much more.

An interesting application of what photo illustration software can do is the electronic aging of missing children. Artists combine a child's snapshot with a database of measurements showing how human facial dimensions change in a fairly predictable way over time. Such retouched snapshots have helped find hundreds of children since the mid-1980s.

Animation Files

The next step up from a static display of images is a dynamic display—that is, one that features movement within the display. **Animation,** or movement, is accomplished by the rapid repositioning (moving) of objects on the display screen. For example, animation techniques give life to video-game characters. You can create your own animation using software, such as Macromedia® Director®, or you can purchase a commercial animation library. The latter contains animation templates that can be applied to different presentation needs.

Animation involves the rapid movement of an object, perhaps the image of a dollar sign, from one part of the screen to another (see Figure 6-32). The animation is accomplished by moving the object in small increments in rapid succession, giving the illusion of movement. The object may gradually change shape, as well. Most presentation software packages, which are discussed in Chapter 2, have several built-in animation features that help you include simple animation in the slides used in a presentation. For example, the *animated bullet build* feature can be applied to a simple text chart to integrate animation into the presentation of the bullet points on the chart. Also, the *animated charting* feature can be applied to bar and pie graphs to animate the presentation of the important aspects of the graph.

The judicious use of animation can enliven any presentation. Some of the most important presentations take place in courtrooms. How can a lawyer best present evidence to help the judge and jury understand the case? An increasing number of lawyers are illustrating expert testimony with animated computer graphics. In re-creating a plane crash, for example, data from the plane's data recorder can be used to prepare an animated graphic showing the exact flight path, while the cockpit voice recorder plays in the background.

Motion Video Files

Obtaining relevant motion video for a particular multimedia application can be a challenge. You will need a video camera and a video capture board to produce original motion video for inclusion in a multimedia application. Depending on your presentation, you may need actors, props, and a set, as well. For example, you will frequently see video clips of on-screen narrators in multimedia presentations and tutorials. Videos are produced as you would any video product (set, actor, and so on), then digitized for storage on optical media or hard disk.

Motion video files are disk hogs; that is, they take up lots of space, up to a gigabyte per minute of video unless files are compressed. Just as we can compress text (zip files) and audio (MP3 and MIDI files), we can also compress video files. Digital video is functionally like motion picture film, whereby still images are displayed rapidly, from 15 to 60 frames per second, to create the illusion of motion. Video can be compressed up to 20 to 1 by recording and storing that portion of the image that changes from

FIGURE 6–32

ANIMATION
Macromedia®, a software company, practices what it preaches. Here, the movie feature found in *Director*® is used to create an animated example that demonstrates the software's "Ink Effects" (window in lower right corner).

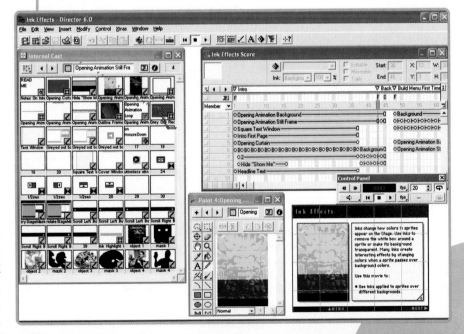

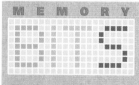
frame to frame. Video compression is greater when motion is minimal (for example, a talking head). These are popular video compression formats in use today (filename extensions are in parentheses).

- **Video for Windows** (avi) from Microsoft Corporation
- **QuickTime** (mov) from Apple Computer Company
- **MPEG** (mpg) is an ISO (International Standards Organization) standard developed by MPEG (Moving Picture Experts Group)

Each of these formats is being continually redefined and upgraded to new standards to take advantage of continually improving technologies (computing capacity, Internet bandwidth, monitor resolution, and so on). Once video is encoded and compressed, the resulting files can be stored locally or at Internet server sites for playback.

CREATING A MULTIMEDIA APPLICATION: PUTTING THE RESOURCES TOGETHER

Once you have prepared and/or identified the desired sight and sound resource material, you are ready to put it together. A variety of software packages is available to help you accomplish this task.

- *Presentation software.* As we have already seen in Chapter 2, presentation software such as PowerPoint can help you prepare and create stimulating multimedia presentations.
- *Authoring systems.* To create interactive multimedia tutorials and titles, you will need an authoring system, such as ToolBook or Macromedia Director.
- *Multimedia programming.* The creation of sophisticated commercial multimedia titles, such as the multimedia encyclopedia, may require the use of several multimedia development tools, including high-end authoring systems and programming languages, such as Visual Basic and C++.

Multimedia possibilities stretch the human imagination to its limits. Already we see that multimedia will change the face of publishing. Many feel that interactive e-books based on multimedia technology have the potential to be more accessible and effective than traditional books, especially as learning tools. Early indications are that passive entertainment, such as TV and movies, may have to move aside to make way for interactive multimedia entertainment that involves the viewer in the action.

SECTION SELF-CHECK

6-3.1 Animation is accomplished by the slow, but gradual, repositioning of objects on the display screen. (T/F)

6-3.2 Video can be compressed up to 20 to 1 by recording and storing that portion of the image that changes from frame to frame. (T/F)

6-3.3 What photo illustration process takes place as one image is modified to become an entirely different image: (a) morphing, (b) transforming, (c) morphic, or (d) transformer?

6-3.4 The process of manipulating video images is: (a) movie handling, (b) video capturing, (c) tape processing, or (d) video editing.

6-4 Technology for the Disabled

The Americans with Disabilities Act of 1990 prohibits discrimination that might limit employment or access to public buildings and facilities. Under the law, employers cannot discriminate against any employee who can perform a job's "essential" responsibilities with "reasonable accommodations." Increasingly, these "accommodations" take the form of a personal computer with special input/output peripherals and software, called **assistive technology.** Almost 20,000 assistive technology-based products are available for the disabled (see Figure 6-33). Assistive technology in its many forms has enabled people with disabilities greater freedom to work and live independently.

For example, getting a complete impression of the contents of a computer screen is a problem for the visually impaired, as is the ability to maneuver around such features as pull-down windows and click-on icons. The partially sighted can benefit from adaptive software packages that create magnified screen displays, while voice synthesizers can let the blind "read" memos, books, and computer screens.

For the hearing impaired, voice mail and a computer's beeps can be translated into visual cues, such as a screen display of text or flashing icons. Advances in communications and video technologies have made it possible for users to sit in front of their respective computer screens and have sign language conversations.

FIGURE 6–33 | ASSISTIVE TECHNOLOGY FOR DISABLED PEOPLE

KEYBOARD INPUT AND BRAILLE OUTPUT

This personal computer is configured with a traditional keyboard for input and an electronic Braille display, enabling this blind man real-time two-way interaction with his PC. Electronic Braille displays have from 20 to 80 cells, the Braille equivalent to a character. The electronic Braille display processes eight dots per cell, rather than the six used for Braille embossing. The dots convey certain attributes, such as capitalization, cursor location, and so on.

MAGNIFIER UTILITY PROGRAM

This visually impaired person uses a seeing eye dog for navigation around town and a magnifier utility program for navigation around Windows and applications programs.

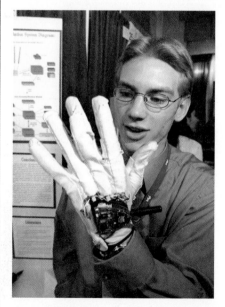

SIGN LANGUAGE TO TEXT CONVERSION

At 18, Ryan Patterson won the Intel Science Talent Search and a $100,000 prize. His winning entry was a glove that converts American Sign Language to text. Those people with speech can use speech recognition software for rapid text entry and, now, those without speech can enjoy rapid text entry, too. To do so, they use their sign language while wearing Ryan's invention, a device that is sure to improve the quality of life for many people.

Virtually any type of physical movement can be used to input commands and data to a computer. This is good news for people with limited use of their arms and hands. Alternative input devices can range from a standard trackball (instead of a mouse) to the relatively slow sip-and-puff devices to speech-recognition systems. There are even software programs that allow keystroke combinations to be entered one key at a time.

Surveys show that employers who provide "assistive technologies" to their employees gain highly motivated and productive workers.

SECTION SELF-CHECK

6-4.1 The Americans with Disadvantages Act of 2002 prohibits discrimination that might limit employment or access to public buildings and facilities. (T/F)

6-4.2 Under the law, employers must make what kind of accommodation for disabled people: (a) reasonable, (b) sensible, (c) rational, or (d) logical?

CHAPTER SUMMARY

6-1 INPUT DEVICES

A variety of input/output (I/O) peripheral devices provides the interface between the computer and us. There are two basic types of keyboards: traditional alphanumeric keyboards and special-function keyboards. A widely used keyboard layout is the 101-key keyboard with the traditional *QWERTY* key layout, 12 **function keys,** a numeric keypad, a variety of special-function keys, and dedicated cursor-control keys. The cursor-control keys can be used to select menu options or to move the **text cursor.** Some special-function keyboards are designed for specific applications. The mouse and its cousins enable interaction with the operating system's graphical user interface (GUI) and they help us to draw. These include the **trackball, trackpad, joystick, trackpoint,** and **digitizer tablet and pen.** When these point-and-draw devices are moved, the **mouse pointer** on the display moves accordingly. Along with buttons, the wheel mouse also has a wheel for scrolling.

The trend in data entry has been toward **source-data automation.** A variety of **scanners** read and interpret information on printed matter and convert it to a format that can be interpreted directly by a computer. **OCR (optical character recognition)** is the ability to read printed information into a computer system. **Bar codes** represent alphanumeric data by varying the size of adjacent vertical lines. Two types of OCR or **bar code scanners**—*contact* and *laser*—read information on labels and various types of documents. Scanners used for OCR or bar code applications can be classified into three basic categories—handheld label scanners (called **wand scanners**), stationary label scanners, and document scanners (which are often used with **turnaround documents**).

The most popular application for *optical mark recognition* (*OMR*) is for grading sense-mark tests.

An **optical scanner** uses laser technology to scan and digitize an image. Image scanners provide input for **image processing.** Image scanners are of two types: *page* and *hand.*

Magnetic stripes, **smart cards,** and badges provide input to **badge readers.**

Speech-recognition systems can be used to enter spoken words in continuous speech at speeds of up to 125 words a minute by comparing digitized representations of words to similarly formed templates in the computer system's electronic dictionary. Some speech-recognition systems are speaker-independent; that is, they can accept words spoken by anyone.

Pattern recognition systems are best suited to very specialized tasks in which only a few images will be encountered.

Digital cameras (digicams) are used to take photos that are represented digitally (already digitized). The desktop **digital video camera** lets you capture motion video in the area of the PC. The **Webcam** is a popular application for these cameras. Handheld **digital camcorders** offer another way to capture video. Use a **video capture card** to capture video from a standard analog video camera or VCR.

Handheld and wearable data entry devices have a limited external keyboard or a soft keyboard, a small display that may be touch-sensitive, nonvolatile RAM, and often a scanning device.

Touch screen monitors permit input as well as output. They have pressure-sensitive overlays that can detect pressure and the exact location of that pressure.

6-2 OUTPUT DEVICES

Output devices translate bits and bytes into a form we can understand. The most common "output only" devices include monitors, printers, plotters, **multimedia projectors,** sound systems, and voice-response systems.

Monitors are defined in terms of their technology (**CRT monitor** or **flat-panel monitor**), **graphics adapter** (which has **video RAM** or **VRAM**), size, resolution (number of **pixels,** number of bits used to represent each pixel, and **dot pitch**), and *refresh rate.*

Gray scales are used to refer to the number of shades of a color that can be shown on a monochrome monitor's screen. **RGB monitors** mix red, green, and blue to achieve a spectrum of colors. One user option is the number of bits used to display each pixel, sometimes referred to as **color depth.**

Flat-panel monitors are used with notebook PCs and some desktop PCs, many of which use LCD technology. **Wearable displays** give us freedom of movement.

Three basic PC printer technologies include page, ink-jet, and dot-matrix. Printers can print in **portrait** or **landscape** format. Nonimpact **page printers** (**laser printers**) use several technologies to achieve high-speed hard copy output by printing a page at a time. The color option is available for laser and ink-jet printers.

Nonimpact **ink-jet printers** have print heads that move back and forth across the paper, squirting ink droplets to write text and create images. The color ink-jet printer is emerging as the choice for home and small office consumers.

Large-format ink-jet printers, also called **plotters,** use ink-jet technology to print on roll-feed paper up to four feet wide.

The **dot-matrix printer,** an impact printer, forms images one character at a time as the print head moves across the paper.

Multifunction **all-in-one peripheral devices** are available that handle several paper-related tasks: computer-based printing, facsimile (fax), scanning, and copying.

PC sound systems vary from a couple of small speakers embedded in notebook PCs to sophisticated sound systems that provide surround sound.

Voice-response systems provide recorded or synthesized audio output (via **speech synthesis**). **Text-to-speech software** enables you to produce speech on a PC.

6-3 THE MULTIMEDIA EXPERIENCE

Multimedia refers to the capability that enables the integration of computer-based text, still graphics, motion visuals, animation, and sound. A good example of multimedia is **video editing,** the process of manipulating *video* images. Three elements in particular distinguish multimedia: sound, motion, and the opportunity for interaction.

The next stage of multimedia growth would include some or all of the following hardware and software: a video camera, a videocassette recorder/player, an audiocassette player, a television, a synthesizer, a video capture card, a scanner, a digital camera, CD-RW or DVD+RW, professional applications development software, and a source library.

Multimedia applications draw content material from a number of sources, including text files, database files, sound files, image files, animation files, and motion video files. Sound files are of two types: *waveform* (or **wave file**) and *nonwaveform* (or

MIDI file). Sources for image files include those the user creates, clip art, scanned images, and photo images.

Photo illustration software enables you to create original images as well as to dress up existing digitized images. Images can be retouched with special effects, such as **morphing**. **Animation** is accomplished by the rapid repositioning of objects on the display screen.

Motion video files can be compressed up to 20 to 1. The most popular video compression formats in use today are **Video for Windows** (avi), **QuickTime** (mov), and **MPEG** (mpg).

Popular tools for creating multimedia applications include presentation software, **authoring systems**, and multimedia programming (for example, Visual Basic and C++).

6-4 TECHNOLOGY FOR THE DISABLED

Personal computers with special input/output peripherals and software, called **assistive technology**, have enabled people with disabilities greater freedom to work and live independently. These include magnified screen displays and voice synthesizers for people with visual impairment. Some paraplegics use sip-and-puff devices. Hiring disabled people and equipping them with assistive technologies has proven to be a good business strategy.

KEY TERMS

all-in-one peripheral device (p. 263)
animation (p. 271)
assistive technology (p. 272)
authoring system (p. 268)
badge reader (p. 248)
bar code (p. 243)
bar code scanner (p. 243)
color depth (p. 258)
CRT monitor (p. 256)
digital camcorder (p. 254)
digital camera (digicam) (p. 253)
digital video camera (p. 254)
digitizer tablet and pen (p. 243)
dot pitch (p. 258)
dot-matrix printer (p. 262)
flat-panel monitor (p. 256)
function key (p. 242)
graphics adapter (p. 256)
gray scales (p. 258)
image processing (p. 247)
ink-jet printer (p. 262)

joystick (p. 243)
landscape (p. 259)
large-format ink-jet printer (p. 262)
laser printer (p. 260)
MIDI file (p. 269)
morphing (p. 271)
mouse pointer (p. 242)
MPEG (p. 272)
multimedia (p. 265)
multimedia projector (p. 258)
OCR (optical character recognition) (p. 243)
optical scanner (p. 247)
page printer (p. 260)
pattern recognition system (p. 251)
photo illustration software (p. 269)
pixel (p. 258)
plotter (p. 262)
portrait (p. 259)
QuickTime (p. 272)
RGB monitor (p. 258)

scanner (p. 243)
smart card (p. 248)
source-data automation (p. 243)
speech-recognition system (p. 250)
speech synthesis (p. 264)
text cursor (p. 242)
text-to-speech software (p. 264)
touch screen monitor (p. 255)
trackball (p. 242)
trackpad (p. 243)
trackpoint (p. 243)
turnaround document (p. 247)
video capture card (p. 255)
video editing (p. 265)
Video for Windows (p. 272)
video RAM (VRAM) (p. 256)
voice-response system (p. 264)
wand scanner (p. 247)
wave file (p. 269)
wearable display (p. 259)
Webcam (p. 254)

MATCHING

1. smart card
2. assistive technology
3. MPEG
4. color depth
5. landscape
6. photo illustration software
7. all-in-one peripheral device
8. video RAM
9. dot-matrix printer
10. animation
11. pattern recognition system
12. mouse pointer
13. multimedia projector
14. video editing
15. joystick

a. page orientation for spreadsheets
b. moved with a point-and-draw device
c. rapid repositioning of objects
d. gives freedom to disabled people
e. fax, copy, print, and scan
f. video format
g. printing multipart forms
h. gaming control
i. "vision" capability
j. number of colors
k. morphing
l. VRAM
m. provides screen image display for groups
n. embedded processor
o. sequencing video clips

6-1.1 The primary function of I/O peripherals is to facilitate computer-to-computer data transmission. (T/F)

6-1.2 An ATM's input/output capabilities are: (a) input only, (b) output only, (c) both input and output, or (d) customer input only.

6-1.3 Use the keyboard's numeric keypad for rapid numeric data entry. (T/F)

6-1.4 Only those keyboards configured for notebook PCs have function keys. (T/F)

6-1.5 Which of the following is not a point-and-draw device: (a) joystick, (b) document scanner, (c) trackpad, or (c) trackpoint?

6-1.6 User interaction with the Windows XP operating systems is via a(n): (a) GUI, (b) Gooie, (c) mouse interface, or (d) user-friendly menu.

6-1.7 Pattern recognition systems are best suited to generalized tasks in which a wide variety of images will be encountered. (T/F)

6-1.8 Optical character recognition is a means of source-data automation. (T/F)

6-1.9 The preprinted bar codes on consumer products have actually increased the number of keystrokes at supermarket checkout counters. (T/F)

6-1.10 The United States Postal Service uses OCR to sort mail. (T/F)

6-1.11 Speech-recognition systems can be trained to accept words not in the system's original dictionary. (T/F)

6-1.12 The enhanced version of cards with a magnetic stripe is a(n): (a) badge card, (b) intelligent badge, (c) smart card, or (d) debit card.

6-1.13 Which of these is not a type of scanner: (a) document scanner, (b) stationary label scanner, (c) wand scanner, or (d) magnetic scanner?

6-1.14 Manipulating and managing scanned images would be considered: (a) image processing, (b) parallel processing, (c) scanner management, or (d) image administration.

6-1.15 Which of the following is not true of digital cameras: (a) uses the same film as 35-mm cameras, (b) digitized images are uploaded from the camera, (c) uses flash memory to store photos, or (d) can be purchased for as little as $200?

6-2.1 Dot-matrix printers generate graphs with greater precision than plotters. (T/F)

6-2.2 The graphics adapter is the device controller for a high-resolution speech synthesizer. (T/F)

6-2.3 The passive matrix LCD monitor provides a more brilliant display than those with active matrix technology. (T/F)

6-2.4 What type of printer would you be most likely to find in a busy office: (a) laser printer, (b) ink-jet printer, (c) multifunction duplicator system, or (d) glove box printer?

6-2.5 Which of these is not one of the capabilities of all-in-one multifunction peripheral devices: (a) duplicating, (b) faxing, (c) scanning, or (d) vision input?

6-2.6 Which of these does not play a part in determining a monitor's resolution: (a) number of colors mixed within a pixel, (b) number of pixels, (c) number of bits that represent a pixel, or (d) dot pitch?

6-2.7 Which of these would not be a pixel density option for monitors: (a) 1024 by 768, (b) 640 by 480, (c) 123 by 84, or (d) 1600 by 1200?

6-2.8 Most flat-panel monitors are used in conjunction with: (a) server computers, (b) tower PCs, (c) notebook PCs, or (d) desktop PCs.

6-2.9 Which of these I/O devices produces hard copy output: (a) monitor, (b) printer, (c) multimedia projector, or (d) voice-response system?

6-2.10 Which kind of printer is used to print originals with carbon copies: (a) ink-jet, (b) large-format ink-jet, (c) dot-matrix, or (d) laser?

6-2.11 In text-to-speech technology, speech is produced by combining: (a) firmware, (b) synonyms, (c) phonemes, or (d) digitized templates.

6-2.12 Gamers looking to purchase a new PC would pay special attention to the amount of what: (a) gray scales, (b) VRAM, (c) image RAM, or (d) ppm of output.

6-3.1 Books and newspapers are not yet available as multimedia publications. (T/F)

6-3.2 Which is the following would not normally be associated with multimedia hardware: (a) scanner, (b) digital camera, (c) modem, or (d) video capture card?

6-3.3 Which of the following would not be considered one of the major elements of multimedia: (a) sound, (b) sequential access, (c) the opportunity for interaction, or (d) animation?

6-3.4 What type of program lets you create multimedia applications that integrate sound, motion, text, animation, and images: (a) authoring, (b) writer, (c) integrator, or (d) direction?

6-3.5 MIDI files are: (a) waveform files, (b) nonwaveform files, (c) minidigital files, or (d) minifiles.

6-3.6 Which of these is out of place: (a) avi, (b) gif, (c) mpeg, or (d) mov?

6-4.1 One input device used by disabled people is the sip-and-puff device. (T/F)

6-4.2 Assistive technology for the disabled includes what piece of electronically-wired clothing that converts sign language to text: (a) a set of rings, (b) two bracelets, (c) a pair of shoes, or (d) a glove?

IS WHAT WE SEE AND HEAR REAL OR NOT?

There was a time when photographs could be used as evidence in a court of law. Powerful computers and photo illustration software have changed that. Most image professionals now deal with digital images that can be electronically modified to achieve the desired result. Magazines routinely alter fashion covers to hide the "flaws" of supermodels. For example, a graphics artist might take a little off the thigh or add a little shadow to highlight the cheekbone. Advertisers "fix" deficiencies in product presentations and, generally, enhance the image whenever possible. It is impossible to distinguish the reality from "special effects" in TV commercials and at the movies. All commercial music is digitally recorded and, if needed, digitally enhanced to remove mistakes or to get the right sound.

Discussion: *Has information technology taken away our ability to perceive what is artificial and what is natural? Explain.*

Discussion: *Is it ethical to present a digitally enhanced still image, video, or song without warning those who might otherwise assume that what they see and hear is real?*

PREDICTING ELECTION RETURNS

Prior to 1951, people had to wait until the votes were counted to find out who won an election. That changed when a "giant brain," the Univac I computer, predicted Dwight Eisenhower the winner over Adlai Stevenson in the 1951 presidential election with only 5% of the votes counted. Today, computers are as much a part of Election Day as political rhetoric and flag waving. In presidential elections, the major television networks predict the state results for most states shortly after polls are closed. In the 2000 election, all major television networks gave Florida to Democratic candidate Al Gore early in the evening, only to withdraw their prediction later. Then several major networks predicted Republican candidate George W. Bush the Florida winner in the middle of the night. The Vice President conceded the election because Florida gave Bush a majority of the electoral votes. Again, the networks admitted they were premature, so Gore

withdrew his concession. During all the television hoopla of the 2000 election, the Internet pollsters were using exit interviews to predict races and post results online before the polls closed.

Critics contend that these computer predictions may not be accurate and can keep people who have not voted away from the polls. Voters confess, "Why vote when the winner is already known?" The news media contend that it's the public's right to know.

Discussion: *Should the media be allowed to report predicted election results on the day of the election before all polls across the various time zones are closed?*

Discussion: *Would you go to the polls and vote if you knew that several major news services have already picked your candidate to win? How about if they predicted your candidate's opponent to win?*

Discussion: *The major TV networks have agreed to wait until the polls close in a particular state before predicting the winner for the state. The Internet media have no such agreement. Should they?*

THE SPYCAM

Wireless technology for peripheral devices and the proliferation of small, inexpensive, wireless video cameras has created many new applications for personal computing—some good and many bad. The video cameras can be placed within 100 feet of the host unit and can send back clear streaming video images. Moreover, the camera is tiny and is hidden easily from view. You can imagine where pranksters and the lower elements of our society might have placed these cameras. Restrooms, college communal showers, conference rooms, the doctor's office, every room in the house, and so on, are now vulnerable to the spycam.

Discussion: *Should those who purchase wireless video cameras be warned of the legal consequences of using this technology to "spy" on people, perhaps by a cigarette-like label? Explain why or why not.*

Discussion: *What would you do if you had a wireless video camera that could be placed discretely anywhere within 100 feet of your PC?*

DISCUSSION AND PROBLEM SOLVING

6-1.1 Describe two instances during the past 24 hours in which you had indirect communication with a computer; that is, something you did resulted in computer activity.

6-1.2 Describe an automated telephone system with which you are familiar that asks you to select options from a series of menus. Discuss the advantages and disadvantages of this system.

6-1.3 Name four types of point-and-draw devices. Which one do you think you would prefer? Explain your reasoning.

6-1.4 What is the relationship between a trackpad and a mouse pointer? Between a trackpad and a text cursor?

6-1.5 The QWERTY keyboard, which has been the standard on typewriters and keyboards for decades, was actually designed to keep people from typing so rapidly. Speculate on why built-in inefficiency was a design objective.

6-1.6 Today's continuous speech-recognition systems are able to interpret spoken words more accurately when the user talks in phrases. Why would this approach be more accurate than discrete speech where the user speaks one word at a time with a slight separation between words?

6-1.7 In the next generation of credit cards, the familiar magnetic stripe probably will be replaced by embedded microprocessors in smart cards. Suggest applications for this capability.

6-1.8 Some department stores use handheld label scanners, and others use stationary label scanners to interpret the bar codes printed on the price tags of merchandise. What advantages does one scanner have over the other?

6-1.9 Compare today's pattern recognition systems with the vision capability portrayed in such films as 2001 and 2010. Do you believe we will have a comparable vision technology by the year 2010?

6-1.10 Today, literally billions of pages of documentation are maintained in government and corporate file cabinets. Next year, the contents of millions of file cabinets will be digitized via image processing. Briefly describe at least one situation with which you are familiar that is a candidate for image processing. Explain how image processing can improve efficiency at this organization.

6-1.11 Describe how your photographic habits might change (or have changed) if you owned a digital camera.

6-2.1 Four PCs at a police precinct are networked and currently share a 5 ppm ink-jet printer. The captain has budgeted enough money to purchase one page printer (20 ppm) or two more 5 ppm ink-jet printers. Which option would you suggest the precinct choose and why?

6-2.2 Describe the input/output characteristics of a workstation/PC that would be desirable for engineers doing computer-aided design (CAD).

6-2.3 By purchasing 17-inch low-quality monitors rather than 19-inch high-quality monitors, a large company can save up to $200 per employee on the cost of new PCs. In the long run, however, health and overall efficiency implications of this decision may result in costs that far exceed any savings. Explain.

6-2.4 In five years, forecasters are predicting flat-panel monitors less than .25-inch thick may be placed everywhere around the home and office. Speculate on how these ultrathin monitors might be used in the home. In the office.

6-2.5 Would an all-in-one multifunction peripheral be appropriate in your home or would you prefer purchasing separate devices for the various document-handling functions (duplicating, faxing, printing, and scanning)? Explain your reasoning.

6-2.6 Describe the benefits of using a notebook PC in conjunction with a multimedia projector during a formal business presentation as opposed to the traditional alternative (transparency acetates and an overhead projector).

6-2.7 People are calling PC-based speech-recognition software a "killer app." Why?

6-3.1 Multimedia was the buzzword of the mid-1990s, but its glitter is wearing off. Why?

6-3.2 Describe two scenarios for which information kiosks would be applicable.

6-3.3 Identify and briefly describe at least three situations where you have witnessed the use of computer animation.

6-3.4 Would a music composer work with a wave file or a MIDI file? Explain.

6-4.1 Employers can easily spend from $20,000 to $50,000 on assistive technology for a single disabled employee. What is the payback to the employer?

6-4.2 Discuss possible applications for an assistive device (the electronic glove) that enables conversion of American Sign Language to text.

FOCUS ON PERSONAL COMPUTING

1. It seems as if we are always in a hurry to do something specific when we do personal computing and we don't take time to assess and, if needed, adjust I/O features to meet our needs more effectively. Take time to explore these features. Open your Control Panel and open the settings for any I/O device. Familiarize yourself with the device's features and settings and customize them as you see fit. For example, you might prefer the "nature" scheme for the mouse pointer or you might opt for a higher resolution on your display. Examine and customize all input/output devices on your system, including sound and audio devices.

2. Modern operating systems provide a minimum level of functionality for people with disabilities. For example, one utility provides visual warnings for system-produced sounds. Another enables the keyboard to perform mouse functions. Search for "accessibility" in the Windows Help and Support Center and learn more about these capabilities. Open and experiment with the Magnifier utility and/or use your system's text-to-speech capabilities. These may not be available with all operating systems or they may need to be installed.

INTERNET EXERCISES @ www.prenhall.com/long

1. The Online Study Guide (multiple choice, true/false, matching, and essay questions)

2. Internet Learning Activities
- Input
- Output
- Printers
- Multimedia

Chapter 7

Learning Objectives

Once you have read and studied this chapter, you will have learned:

● How the application of the concept of connectivity is affecting your life (Section 7-1).

● Alternatives and sources of data transmission services that have enabled the networking of our world (Section 7-2).

● The function and operation of data communications hardware (Section 7-3).

● The various kinds of network topologies, essential local area network concepts and terminology, and the scope and potential of home networking (Section 7-4).

NETWORKS AND NETWORKING

Why this chapter is important to you

Ten years ago, the number-one reason people purchased a PC was for word processing. Now people buy PCs for many reasons, but frequently they do so to get on the Internet. Everyone wants to logon and travel through cyberspace, soaking up all it has to offer. Each day our world is becoming increasingly connected—electronically. If you are not already online, you, too, will eventually want to be connected. When you are, you can save yourself both time and money by knowing the basics of data communications and networking.

Data communications was relatively new in the mid-1960s. During the first 25 years of the communications era, data communications experts purchased, installed, and maintained multimillion-dollar communications hardware and channels. Now, most of the connected computer systems are personal computers owned by people like you. Relatively few of us are blessed with a technical support staff at our beck-and-call, so we, the users, are the people who purchase, install, and maintain our own communications hardware and channels—not the experts. Usually the hardware is no more involved than a modem and a telephone line. However, this is beginning to change as homes and small offices begin to network multiple PCs and upgrade to broadband (high-speed) Internet connections.

This chapter introduces you to data communications and networking concepts that will prove helpful at home and make you a more informed employee at work. You'll learn about communications-related hardware and be introduced to various delivery alternatives, including transmission options over traditional voice-grade telephone lines, cable TV lines, and wireless alternatives. Many people have literally thrown up their hands in frustration when dealing with communications tasks and issues. Hopefully, what you learn from this chapter will help eliminate some of that frustration.

WHY THIS SECTION
IS IMPORTANT
TO YOU

People who understand information technology trends, such as digital convergence and global connectivity, are better prepared to cope with our increasingly wired society.

7-1 Our Wired World

Millions of people are knowledge workers by day and Internet surfers by night. As knowledge workers, we need ready access to information. In the present competitive environment, we cannot rely solely on verbal communication to get that information. Corporate presidents cannot wait until the Monday morning staff meeting to find out whether production is meeting demand. Field sales representatives can no longer afford to play telephone tag with headquarters personnel to get answers for impatient customers. The president, the field rep, and the rest of us now rely on *computer networks* to retrieve and share information quickly. Of course, we will continue to interact with our coworkers, but computer networks simply enhance the efficiency and effectiveness of that interaction.

As surfers, we surf the Internet, America Online, CompuServe, or other commercial information services. Once logged on to one of these networks, cybersurfers can chat with friends, strangers, and even celebrities. We can go shopping, peruse electronic magazines, download interesting photos and songs, plan a vacation, play games, buy and sell stock, send e-mail, and generally hang out. It's official: We now live in a weird, wild, wired world where computer networks are networked to one another and we are never far from a computer network (see Figure 7-1). This chapter is devoted to concepts relating to computer networks and communications technology. Once you have a grasp of this technology, you will find it easier to understand the different uses and applications of networks.

DIGITAL CONVERGENCE

We are going through a period of **digital convergence.** That is, TVs, PCs, telephones, movies, college textbooks, newspapers, and much, much more are converging toward digital compatibility. For example, movies that are now frames of cellulose are in the process of digital convergence. The 200,000

FIGURE 7–1

YESTERDAY AND TODAY
When you contrast businesses of today with those of yesterday, one thing sticks out—communications and networking. The main links between filling stations of the 1950s and their suppliers were the telephone and the postal service. Today, customers can pay at the pump via credit card or via a wireless "billfold." Point-of-sale terminals inside the convenience stores record each sale and change inventory directly on corporate server computers.

Photo courtesy of Phillips Petroleum Company

frames required for a full-length movie will converge to 16 billion bits. Major components of this book's learning system are on CD-ROM and the Internet. Future editions will follow the trend toward digital convergence with an increasing portion of the material being distributed digitally. You can even go online and purchase the digital equivalent of United States Postal Service postage stamps. Millions of printed pages in the file cabinets of thousands of companies are being converted to more easily accessible digital images via image processing.

Digital convergence, combined with an ever-expanding worldwide network of computers, is enabling our society to take one giant leap into the future. Already the TV, PC, video game, stereo system, answering device, and telephone are on a collision course that will meld them into communications/information centers. We'll have video-on-demand such that we can view all or any part of any movie ever produced at any time, even in a window on our office PC. Instead of carrying a billfold, we might carry a credit-card-sized device that would contain all the typical billfold items such as money, credit cards, pictures, driver's license, and other forms of identification. These items will all be digital. When we buy a pizza in the future, we might simply enter a code into our electronic billfold to order and pay for the pizza automatically. The possibilities are endless.

Digital convergence is more than a convergence of technologies. Information technology is the enabling technology for the convergence of industries, as well. For example, the financial industries—banking, insurance, and securities—are rapidly converging. Health care establishments—clinics, hospitals, medical insurers, medical schools—are converging. Government agencies, including the air traffic control agencies (see Figure 7-2), are consolidating their efforts through digital convergence.

With half the industrial world (and many governments) racing toward digital convergence, there is no question that we are going digital over the next few years. Our photo album will be digital. Our money will be digital. Already, digitized movies are being transmitted to theaters where they are shown via high-definition projection units.

CONNECTIVITY

All of this convergence is happening so that information will be more easily accessible to more people. To realize the potential of a universe of digital information, the business and computer communities are continually seeking ways to interface, or connect, a diverse set of hardware, software, and databases. This increased level of **connectivity** brings people from as close as the next room and as far as the other side of the world closer together.

- Connectivity means that a marketing manager can use a PC to access information in the finance department's database.

- Connectivity means that a network of PCs can route output to a shared page printer.

- Connectivity means that a manufacturer's server computer can communicate with a supplier's server computer.

- Connectivity means that you can send your holiday newsletter via e-mail.

- Connectivity means that the appliances, including PCs, in your home can be networked.

Connectivity is implemented in degrees. We can expect to become increasingly connected to computers and information both at work and at home during the coming years. Thirty years ago, there were tens of thousands of computers. Today, there are hundreds of *millions* of them! Plus, we have the Internet! Computers and information are everywhere. Our challenge is to connect them.

THE ERA OF COOPERATIVE PROCESSING

We are living in an era of *cooperative processing*. Companies have recognized that they must cooperate internally to take full advantage of company resources, and that they must cooperate externally with one another to compete effectively in a world market. To promote internal cooperation, businesses are setting up **intracompany networking** (see Figure 7-3). These networks allow people in, say, the sales department to know the latest information from the production department. Companies cooperate externally (with customers and other companies) via **intercompany networking** (see Figure 7-3) or, more specifically, via **business-to-business (B2B)** e-commerce. **E-commerce**, electronic commerce, is the term used to describe business conducted online. B2B relies on computer networks and the Internet to transmit data electronically between companies.

FIGURE 7–2 Air-to-Ground Connectivity
At any given time, thousands of commercial airplanes are airborne. Each, however, is connected to the ground in that it is continuously updating the database for Air Route Traffic Control Centers around the country, such as this one in Seattle, Washington.

Courtesy of Lockheed Martin Corporation

FIGURE 7–3   INTRACOMPANY AND INTERCOMPANY NETWORKING

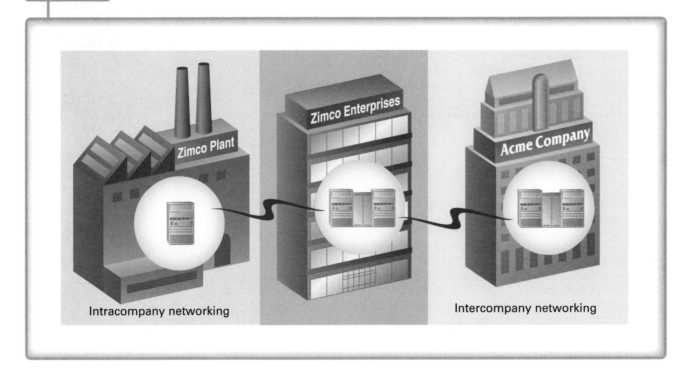

Intracompany networking   Intercompany networking

Increasingly, business between companies is being moved to the Internet. More specifically, it will be moved to a company's *intranet* with actual B2B interactions taking place over their *extranets*. An **intranet** is essentially a closed or private version of the Internet that is based on TCP/IP protocols (see Figure 7-4). Employees use the same browser that they use for the Internet, so an intranet looks and feels like the Internet. In fact, employees can browse seamlessly between their intranet and the Internet. However, it is accessible only by those people within the company. For most organizations, building an intranet is relatively easy because the typical organization provides Internet service and, therefore, has everything in place for the intranet—servers, support for TCP/IP, browser software, local area networks (LANs), and so on. A wealth of company information is made available on intranets, including daily announcements, the sales/marketing database, the menu for the company cafeteria, human resources information (benefits, job openings, and so on), corporate policies, and so on.

An **extranet** is simply an extension of an intranet such that it is partially accessible to authorized outsiders, such as customers and suppliers (see Figure 7-4). In practice, an extranet is two or more overlapping intranets. Invoices, orders, and many other intercompany transactions can be transmitted via an extranet. For example, at major retail chains, such as Wal-Mart, over 90% of all orders are processed directly—business to business—often via an extranet.

For decades, companies have leased communications lines from telecommunications companies to create their own private networks that link offices in remote locations, suppliers, and, sometimes, customers. This type of private network, however, is an expensive proposition, primarily because of the line cost. An alternative is the **virtual private network,** or **VPN,** which has evolved as a less expensive alternative to the private network. The cost savings for VPNs is realized because its channels for communications are over a public infrastructure—the Internet (see Figure 7-4). The VPN employs encryption and other security measures to ensure that communications are not intercepted and that only authorized users are

FIGURE 7–4   **THE INTERNET, INTRANETS, EXTRANETS, AND VPNS**
This figure illustrates how VPNs use tunneling technology and the Internet. The graphical communications overview also shows the relationships between TCP/IP-based intranets and extranets, both with and without Internet access.

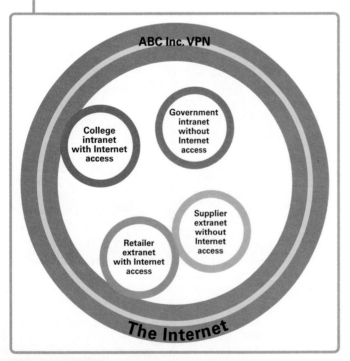

FIGURE 7–5

BUSINESS-TO-BUSINESS E-COMMERCE
In the figure, the traditional interaction between a customer company and a supplier company are contrasted with similar interactions via business-to-business (B2B) e-commerce. Enabling technologies for B2B include extranets and VPNs.

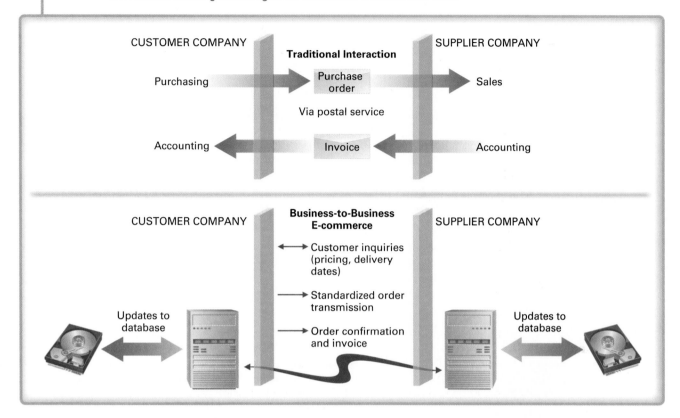

allowed access to the network. VPN uses **tunneling** technology. In tunneling, one network uses the channels of another network to send its data. In the case of VPNs, transmissions are "tunneled" through the Internet. VPNs have been a boon to companies whose policies encourage telecommuting and want knowledge workers on the go to stay connected.

In time, B2B e-commerce will be entirely over the Internet, an extranet, or a VPN. Figure 7-5 contrasts the traditional interactions between a customer and supplier company with interactions via B2B and extranets. Business-to-business commerce is expected to grow to a whopping $1.6 trillion by 2005, almost 10% of all U.S. business trade!

The phenomenal growth of the use of PCs in the home is causing companies to expand their information system capabilities to allow linkages with home and portable PCs, primarily via the Internet. This form of cooperative processing increases system efficiency while lowering costs. For example, in many banks, services have been extended to home PC owners in the form of home banking systems. Subscribers to a home banking service use their personal computers as terminals linked to the bank's server computer system, either directly or via the Internet, to pay bills, transfer funds, and ask about account status.

7-1.1	We are going through a period of digital convergence. (T/F)
7-1.2	B2B is the same as intracompany networking. (T/F)
7-1.3	VPN uses what type of technology for its channels: (a) conduit, (b) tunneling, (c) canals, or (d) subway?
7-1.4	One approach to using computers to transmit data electronically between companies is called: (a) 3CPO, (b) 2B or -2B, (c) B2B, or (d) DIT.

SECTION SELF-CHECK

7-2 The Data Communications Channel

A **communications channel** is the medium through which digital information must pass to get from one location in a computer network to the next. People often use slang terms for communications channel, such as *line, link,* or *pipe.* Communications channels link PCs, servers, and other devices in a network. They provide links between networks, whether between rooms at home or between remote offices. And, they enable you, other individuals, and companies to access the Internet, which, itself, is made up of a variety of communications links.

TRANSMISSION MEDIA

Some communication channels involve a physical link (wire or cable) and others are wireless. Channels are rated by their capacity to transmit information, which is cited in terms of *bits per second (bps).*

Twisted-Pair Wire

Twisted-pair wire is just what we think of as regular telephone wire. Each twisted-pair wire is actually two insulated copper wires twisted around each other. At least one twisted-pair line provides **POTS** (plain old telephone services) to just about every home and business in the United States. Telephone companies offer two different levels of twisted-pair service. All companies offer voice-grade service. The other service may or may not be available in your area.

● *POTS.* When you call the telephone company and request a telephone line, it installs POTS. This analog line permits voice conversations and digital transmissions with the aid of a modem. Traditional modem technology permits data transmission up to 56 K bps.

● *DSL. Digital Subscriber Line (DSL)* is delivered over a POTS line. Data can stream along the same line while you talk. DSL, one of the broadband options, is introduced in Getting Started and discussed further in Chapter 1.

Coaxial Cable

Most people know coaxial cable as the cable in "cable television." **Coaxial cable**, or "coax," contains electrical wire (usually copper wire) and is constructed to permit high-speed data transmission with a minimum of signal distortion. It is laid along the ocean floor for intercontinental voice and data transmission; it's used to connect terminals and computers in a "local" area (from a few feet to a few miles); and it delivers TV signals to close to 100 million homes in America alone. Coaxial cable has a very "wide pipe." That is, it is a high-capacity channel that can carry digital data at up to 10 M bps, as well as more than 100 analog TV signals. Internet access via cable TV coax cable is hundreds of times faster than POTS. Cable modem broadband access, introduced in Getting Started and Chapter 1, is comparable to DSL.

Wireless Communication

High-speed communications channels do not have to be wires or fibers. Data can also be transmitted via **microwave signals** or **radio signals** in much the same way that signals travel from a remote control to a TV or VCR or between a cellular telephone tower and a cell phone. Transmission of these signals is line-of-sight; that is, the signal travels in a straight line from source to destination.

Microwave signals are transmitted between transceivers. Because microwave signals do not bend around the curvature of the earth, signals may need to be relayed several times by microwave repeater stations before reaching their destination. Repeater stations are placed on the tops of mountains, tall buildings, and towers, usually about 30 miles apart.

Satellites: Sky High Repeater Stations

Satellites eliminate the line-of-sight limitation because microwave signals are bounced off satellites, avoiding buildings, mountains, and other signal obstructions. One of the advantages of satellites is that data can be transmitted from one location to any number of other locations anywhere on (or near) our planet. Satellites are routinely launched into orbit for the sole purpose of relaying data communications signals to and from earth stations (see Figure 7-6). A satellite, which uses microwave signals and is essentially a repeater station, is launched and set in a **geosynchronous orbit** 22,300 miles above the earth. A geosynchronous orbit permits the communications satellite to maintain a fixed position relative to the earth's surface. Each satellite can receive and retransmit signals to slightly less than half of the earth's surface; therefore, three satellites are required to cover the earth effectively (see Figure 7-7). Internet access via satellite is available to companies and to individuals at speeds up to 48 M bps. Broadband digital satellite Internet access, which is introduced in Getting Started and Chapter 1, is comparable to cable modem and DSL access speeds.

PCs Communicating without Wires

PCs in the office and on the road can be linked via wireless connections often using *Wi-Fi* (the *IEEE 802.11b* standard) technology introduced in Chapter 3. One of the greatest challenges and biggest

FIGURE 7–6 WIRELESS COMMUNICATION

INTERNET ACCESS VIA DIGITAL SATELLITE
This digital satellite dish enables two-way high-speed access to the Internet. All that is needed for this type of wireless link is a southern exposure to the satellite, a satellite modem, a dish, and a coaxial cable to transmit the signal to the PC.

Long and Associates

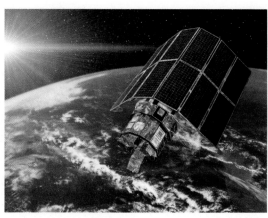

SATELLITE COMMUNICATIONS
Common carriers rely heavily on communications satellites and a network of earth stations to help them offer high-speed data communications to customers. This Orbital Seastar satellite enables wireless data transmissions via satellite.

Courtesy of Lockheed Martin Corporation

Courtesy of Orbital Sciences Corporation

expenses in a computer network is the installation of the physical links between its components. The **wireless transceiver** provides an alternative to running a permanent physical line (twisted-pair wire, coaxial cable, or fiber optic cable). A wireless LAN PC card about the size of a thick credit card replaces a physical line to the data source. For example, wireless communication is routinely used to link these devices:

● Desktop PC and notebook PC

● PC (desktop, laptop, or palm/pocket) and local area network (LAN)

● PC and server computer

● PCs in a home network

The wireless LAN PC card hooks into a USB, PCI, or PCMCIA slot. Transceivers, which have a limited range (about 50 feet), link computers via omnidirectional (traveling in all directions at once) radio waves. Access points, which are hardwired to a central server computer, are positioned throughout a building, a neighborhood, or a college campus to extend the reach of the wireless LAN. When using transceivers, the source computer transmits digital signals to its transceiver, which, in turn, retransmits the signals over radio waves to the other transceiver. Transceivers provide users with

FIGURE 7-7

SATELLITE DATA TRANSMISSION
Three satellites in geosynchronous orbit (staying over the same point on earth) provide worldwide data transmission service.

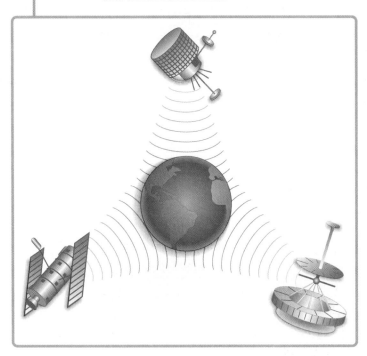

tremendous flexibility in the location of PCs and terminals in a network.

The 2002 Winter Olympics in Salt Lake City, USA, was the perfect venue for widespread use of wireless networks. Many sites at the games were temporary or difficult to wire and were thus made-to-order situations for wireless networks. Wireless networks allowed judges, statisticians, and journalists to move with the action within and between venues.

The Future of Wireless

Very high speed wireless Internet service may be headed to our doorstep. Line-of-sight wireless technologies **MMDS** (Multichannel Multipoint Distribution Service) and **LMDS** (Local Multipoint Distribution Service) provide for network access at fiber optic-level speeds. Industry forecasters are predicting that MMDS will provide Internet services at 1 G bps (gigabits per second) for 70% of the residential and small office market within 5 years. That is about 1000 times faster than current domestic broadband options. ISPs are very interested in MMDS because it can offer high-speed Internet service within a 35-mile radius with minimal investment in equipment. LMDS is a wireless solution to bringing very high bandwidth to homes and offices on the last mile of connectivity.

Fiber Optic Cable: Light Pulse

Twisted-pair wire and coaxial cable carry data as electrical signals. **Fiber optic cable** carries data as laser-generated pulses of light (see Figure 7-8). Made up of bundles of very thin, transparent, almost hair-like fibers, fiber optic cables transmit data more inexpensively and much more quickly than do copper wire transmission media. The Internet backbone, the primary channels for Internet transmissions, is mostly fiber optic cable. In the time it takes to transmit a single page of *Webster's Unabridged Dictionary* over twisted-pair copper wire (about 3 seconds) over a regular modem, the entire dictionary could be transmitted over a single optic fiber! Businesses that demand very high-speed B2B communications have fiber optic cable linked directly to their server computers.

Each time a communications company lays a new fiber optic cable, the world is made a little smaller. In 1956, the first transatlantic cable carried 50 voice circuits. Then, talking to someone in Europe was a rare and expensive experience. Today, a single fiber can carry over 32,000 voice and data transmissions, the equivalent of 2.5 billion bits per second. Nowadays, people call colleagues in other countries or link up with international computers as readily as they call home.

Another of the many advantages of fiber optic cable is its contribution to data security. It is much more difficult for a computer criminal to intercept a signal sent over fiber optic cable (via a beam of light) than it is over copper wire (an electrical signal).

Fiber optic technology is taking giant leaps. Already scientists are able to transmit data over a special fiber optic cable at 3.28 terabits per second (trillion bps), but only over a distance of a city block. At that rate, the new high-tech fiber can transmit the equivalent of three days' worth of Internet traffic (worldwide) in a single second! This technology is still in the laboratory, but this new technology may give us a very big "pipe" through which to receive information in the near future.

M E M O R Y

Transmission Media

- Twisted-pair wire
  - POTS
  - DSL
- Coaxial cable
- Wireless
  - Microwave
  - Radio signals
- Fiber optic cable

COMMON CARRIERS

It is impractical for individuals and companies to string their own fiber optic cable between distant locations, such as Hong Kong and New York City. It is also impractical for them to set their own satellites in orbit, although some companies have. Therefore, most people and companies turn to communications **common carriers,** such as AT&T, MCI, and Sprint, to provide communications channels for data transmission. Organizations pay communications common carriers, which are regulated by the Federal Communications Commission (FCC), for *private* or *switched* data communications service.

A **private line** (or **leased line**) provides a dedicated data communications channel between any two points in a computer network. The charge for a private line is based on channel capacity (bps) and distance. Some companies have private lines that link remote offices, primarily with fiber optic cable.

FIGURE 7–8

FIBER OPTIC CABLE
For the better part of the 20th century, our country was being laced with the twisted-pair copper wire extending between telephone poles. Today, wherever possible, telephone poles and twisted-pair wire are being replaced by the more versatile fiber optic cable. More than 90% of long-distance telephone and Internet traffic in the United States is carried over 15 million miles of optical fiber, the hair-thin strands of glass that make up fiber optic cable. Fiber optic cable is capable of transmitting voice, video, and computer data as laser-generated pulses of light. Two optical fibers can handle the equivalent of 625,000 telephone calls or Internet dialup connections at once.

Courtesy of International Business Machines Corporation. Unauthorized use not permitted.

Courtesy of Corning, Inc.

A **switched line** (or **dialup line**) is available strictly on a time-and-distance charge, similar to a long-distance telephone call. You (or your computer) make a connection by "dialing up" a computer, then a modem sends and receives data. Switched lines offer greater flexibility than do private lines because they allow you to link up with any communications-ready computer. A regular POTS telephone line is a switched line.

The number and variety of common carriers is expanding. For decades, it was just the telephone companies. Now cable TV and satellite companies provide common carrier services. Data rates offered by common carriers range from voice-grade POTS (up to about 56 K bps with a modem) to the widest of all pipes, the massive 622 M bps channel.

The emergence of Internet-connected intranets, extranets, and VPNs has changed the way companies link with remote locations and other companies. Although the leased line is still the corporate choice when very high-speed communication is required, most companies opt for cost-saving Internet-based alternatives for all other communication needs.

CONTROLLING TRANSMISSIONS OVER COMMUNICATIONS CHANNELS

Computers must adhere to strict rules when transmitting information between computers.

Communications Protocols

Communications protocols are rules established to govern the way data are transmitted in a computer network. A protocol describes how these data are transmitted. Communications protocols are defined in *layers,* the first of which is the physical layer. The physical layer defines the manner in which nodes in a network are connected to one another. Subsequent layers, the number of which vary between protocols, describe how messages are packaged for transmission, how messages are routed through the network, security procedures, and the manner in which messages are displayed. A number of different protocols are in common use. The protocol you hear about most often is TCP/IP (Transmission Control Protocol/Internet Protocol), which actually is a collective reference to the protocols that link computers on the Internet (TCP and IP). These protocols are discussed in Chapter 3, "Going Online."

Asynchronous and Synchronous Transmission

Protocols fall into two general classifications: *asynchronous* and *synchronous* (see Figure 7-9). In **asynchronous transmission,** data are transmitted at irregular intervals on an as-needed basis. Most communication between computers and devices is asynchronous, occurring as needed at irregular intervals. Internet interaction is asynchronous. *Start/stop bits* are appended to the beginning and end of each message. The start/stop bits signal the receiving terminal/computer at the beginning and end of the message. In PC data communications, the message is a single byte or character. Asynchronous transmission, sometimes called *start/stop transmission,* is best suited for low-speed data communications, such as that between the Internet and a PC with a standard 56 K bps modem.

In **synchronous transmission,** the source and destination operate in timed synchronization to enable high-speed data transfer. Start/stop bits are not required in synchronous transmission. Data transmission between computers and hardware that facilitates high-speed data communications is normally synchronous.

DATA TRANSMISSION IN PRACTICE

A communications channel from Computer A in Seattle, Washington, to Computer B in Orlando, Florida (see Figure 7-10), usually would consist of several different transmission media and, perhaps, multiple protocols. The connection between Computer A and a terminal in the same building is probably coaxial cable or twisted-pair wire. The Seattle company might use a common carrier company such as AT&T to transmit the data via a leased line. AT&T would then send the data through a combination of transmission facilities that might include copper wire, microwave signals, radio signals, and fiber optic cable.

FIGURE 7–9 | **ASYNCHRONOUS AND SYNCHRONOUS TRANSMISSION OF DATA**
Asynchronous data transmission takes place at irregular intervals. In asynchronous transmission, the message is typically a single character with parity bits added to ensure transmission accuracy. Synchronous data transmission requires timed synchronization between sending and receiving devices. The message is typically a block of characters.

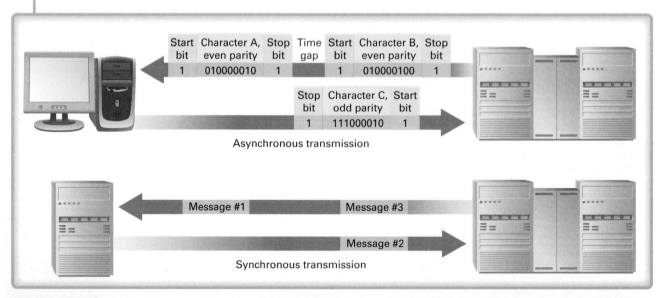

FIGURE 7–10

DATA TRANSMISSION PATH
It's more the rule than the exception that data are carried over several transmission media between source and destination.

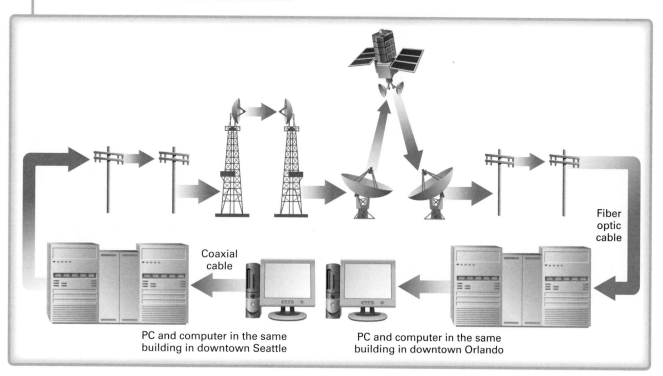

PC and computer in the same building in downtown Seattle

PC and computer in the same building in downtown Orlando

Coaxial cable

Fiber optic cable

7-2.1 It is more difficult for a computer criminal to tap into a fiber optic cable than a copper telephone line. (T/F)

7-2.2 The wireless transceiver will never replace the physical link between the source and the destination in a network. (T/F)

7-2.3 Synchronous transmission is best suited for data communications involving low-speed I/O devices. (T/F)

7-2.4 Communications satellites in geosynchronous orbit are how many miles above the earth: (a) 200, (b) 2,200, (c) 22,300, or (d) 100,000?

SECTION SELF-CHECK

7-3 Data Communications Hardware

WHY THIS SECTION IS IMPORTANT TO YOU

Data may be entered in St. Paul, processed in St. Petersburg, and the results displayed in St. Croix, but how? Read on to learn about the hardware that makes data communications possible, as you will surely use these capabilities in the home and at the office.

Data communications, or **telecommunications,** is the electronic collection and distribution of information between two points. Information can appear in a variety of formats—numeric data, text, voice, still pictures, graphics, and video. As we have already seen, raw information must be digitized before we can input it into a computer. For example, numerical data and text might be translated into their corresponding ASCII codes. Once the digitized information has been entered into a computer, that computer can then transfer the information to other computers connected over a network. Ultimately, all forms of digitized information are transmitted over the transmission media (for example, fiber optic cable) as a series of binary bits (1s and 0s).

Data communications hardware is used to transmit digital information between terminals and computers or between computers and other computers. There is a vast array of communications and networking hardware. Figure 7-11, which shows the integration of some of these devices with terminals and computer systems, is a representative computer network. With so much networking hardware, networks are a lot like snowflakes—no two are alike. Unlike snowflakes, however, networks never melt. Once created, networks seem to have a life of their own, growing with the changing needs of the organization.

With the trend toward digital convergence, the number and variety of network hardware components that enable data communications continue to evolve, with new devices being introduced almost monthly. There are *concentrators, switching hubs, bridges, routers, brouters* (combination bridges and routers), *network interface cards, front-end processors, multiplexors,* various types of *modems,* and

FIGURE 7–11 THE EVOLUTION OF TERMINALS

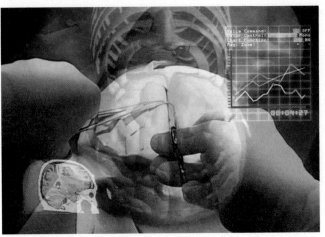

WEARABLE DISPLAY TERMINAL
The terminal is the visual link to a computer system for many knowledge workers; however, it is being redefined with recent technological innovations. This Microvision wearable display is integrated into eyeglasses, goggles, or helmets. The system enables the display of an image that doesn't block the user's (a surgeon in this example) view but will, instead, superimpose a color image on top of it.

Photo courtesy of Microvision Incorporated

AIRLINE CHECK-IN KIOSK
For decades, the terminal has been behind the airline check-in counter. Now, many airlines are making a terminal available to their customers in the form of a self-service check-in kiosk. This airline check-in kiosk has a touch screen monitor, allowing the passenger to interact with the airline's central computer system.

Courtesy of International Business Machines Corporation. Unauthorized use not permitted.

many more special-function devices that route, pass along, convert, package and repackage, and format and reformat bits and bytes traveling along communications links. Most of these are beyond the scope of an introductory study of IT. We will, however, talk about a couple of the more personal devices: the modem, a device that comes with most new PCs, and the network interface card, a device found on most corporate PCs and an increasing percentage of home PCs. Also, we will talk about a few other devices to help you better understand the fundamental terminology of data communications.

THE STANDARD TELEPHONE-LINK MODEM

Even if your PC is not connected to a corporate local area network with a digital line to cyberspace, you can establish a communications link between it and any remote computer system in the world, assuming you have the authorization to do so. However, you must first have ready access to a *telephone line,* and your PC must be equipped with a *modem.*

Telephone lines were designed to carry *analog signals* for voice communication, not the binary *digital signals* (1s and 0s) needed for computer-based data communication. The modem (modulator-demodulator) converts *digital* signals into *analog* signals so data can be transmitted over telephone lines (see Figure 7-12). The digital electrical signals are modulated to make sounds similar to those you hear on a touch-tone telephone. Upon reaching their destination, these analog tone signals are demodulated into computer-compatible digital signals for processing. A modem is always required for two computers to communicate over a telephone line. It is not needed when the PC is wired directly to a computer network (for example, cabling between embedded network interface cards) or another PC (for example, via USB cables).

FIGURE 7–12

HARDWARE COMPONENTS IN DATA COMMUNICATIONS
Devices that handle the movement of data in a computer network are the modem, the multiplexor, the front-end processor, the router, network interface cards (expansion cards in the local area network-based PCs), and the host computer. Also in the figure, electrical digital signals are modulated (via a modem) into analog signals for transmission over telephone lines and then demodulated for processing at the destination. The lightning bolts indicate transmission between remote locations.

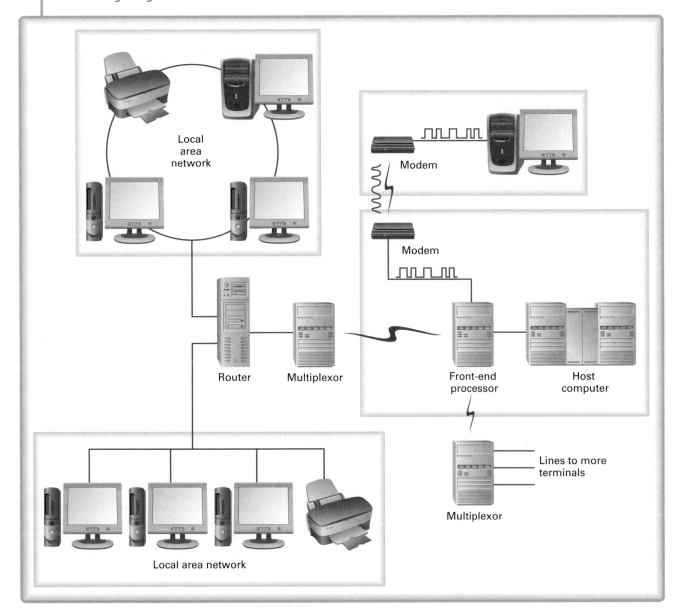

Modems for PCs and terminals are *internal* and *external*. Most PCs have internal modems; that is, the modem is on an optional add-on circuit board that is simply plugged into an empty expansion PCI slot in the PC's motherboard. On notebooks, modems are on interchangeable PC cards or built into the motherboard. The external modem is a separate component, as illustrated in Figure 7-12, and is connected via a serial interface or USB port. To make the connection with a telephone line and either type of modem, you simply plug the telephone line into the modem just as you would when connecting the line to a telephone.

The typical modem is a voice/data/fax modem. Besides the data communications capabilities, it allows you to make telephone calls through your PC and modem hookup (using a microphone, speakers, and/or a headset). The fax feature enables a PC to simulate a *fax* machine. Instead of sending a document to a printer, you simply send it to the fax modem along with a destination fax number. With people routinely using e-mail (with attachments as needed) you might think that the fax machine might be gathering dust, but this is not the case. A survey indicated that the number of faxes sent in large companies almost doubled in the first year of this millennium to about 2000 per day.

OTHER MODEMS

Traditional modems are largely unused by those people with broadband Internet access. Instead, they use a cable modem, a DSL modem, or a satellite modem. Typically, these broadband modems are external and connect to the PC via a USB port; however, they may be installed in an expansion slot or linked via a network interface card, too.

The *cable modem* that supports cable Internet access (over cable TV lines) is similar to the telephone modem, but instead of modulating the PC's digital signals to analog tone signals, it modulates the digital signals to RF (radio frequency) carrier signals. The RF carrier signals are demodulated by another cable modem to digital information upon arrival at their destination.

The *DSL modem* isn't actually a modem. It is a DSL transceiver, but tradition calls for the "modem" moniker. Regardless of what it is called, it provides the connection between the user's computer or network and the DSL line. All DSL signals are routed to a telephone company's **DSLAM** (**Digital Subscriber Line Access Multiplexor**), where they are combined into a very-high speed Internet connection, usually a fiber-optic cable.

The modem name tag also is attached to the device that enables uplink and downlink from satellite—the *satellite modem*. The satellite modem is actually two modems, one for the uplink signal conversion and one for the downlink signal conversion.

NETWORK INTERFACE CARDS

The *network interface card* (*NIC*), which we introduced in Chapter 4, "Inside the Computer," is an add-on board or PC card (for notebooks) that enables and controls the exchange of data between the PCs in a LAN. Each PC in the LANs in Figure 7-12 must be equipped with an NIC. The cables or wireless transceivers that link the PCs are connected physically to the NICs. Whether as an add-on board or a PC card, the NIC is connected directly to the PC's internal bus. With the Ethernet standard for LAN architecture a de facto standard, the NIC is often called an **Ethernet Card.**

ROUTERS

Computer networks are everywhere—in banks, in law offices, in the classroom, and in the home. In keeping with the trend toward greater connectivity, computer networks are themselves being networked and interconnected to give users access to a greater variety of applications and to more information. For example, the typical medium-to-large company links several PC-based networks to the company's enterprise-wide network. This enables end users on all networks to share information and resources.

Because networks use a variety of communications protocols and operating systems, incompatible networks cannot "talk" directly to one another. The primary hardware/software technology used to alleviate the problems of linking incompatible computer networks is the **router.** Routers help to bridge the gap between incompatible networks by performing the necessary protocol conversions to route messages to their proper destinations.

Organizations that are set up to interconnect computer networks do so over a **backbone.** The backbone is a collective term that refers to a system of routers and other communications hardware and the associated transmission media (cables, wires, and wireless links) that link the computers in an organization.

Routers, once limited to the business environment, are becoming popular in the home, too. Broadband ISPs often sell routers to their customers to enable sharing of the Internet signal on a home network. If you wish to share an Internet signal among several PCs in your home network, ask your ISP if you will need a router or if you can share the Internet through your PCs peer-to-peer networking capability.

TERMINALS

A variety of terminals enables both *input to* and *output from* a remote computer system. Interactions via a terminal form the foundation for a wide variety of applications, from airline reservations to point-of-sale systems in retail outlets.

Dumb and Smart Terminals

Terminals come in all shapes and sizes and have a variety of input/output capabilities (see Figure 7-11). The most popular general-purpose terminal is the traditional **video display terminal** (**VDT**) that you

THE CRYSTAL BALL:
Fax on the Brink of Extinction
Facsimile or fax was invented in 1842, by the Scotsman Alexander Bain; however, the first wire photo was sent from Cleveland to New York in 1924. By the mid-1950s, the fax had become a mainstream business tool and its use has increased steadily until now. Everything the fax does can be done more quickly, more efficiently, and at less cost within the context of online systems, image processing, networking, and the Internet. As people familiarize themselves with the alternatives, look for fax machines to take their place alongside the typewriter and other obsolete off line business equipment.

see in hospitals and airports. The primary input mechanism on the *VDT*, or simply the *terminal*, is a *keyboard*. Output is displayed on a *monitor*. Most of these terminals are dumb; that is, they have little or no intelligence (processing capability).

Some terminals, called **Windows terminals**, have some processing capabilities and RAM; however, they are not designed for stand-alone operation. The Windows terminal is so named because the user interacts with a Windows graphical user interface (GUI). All Windows terminals are configured with some type of point-and-draw device, such as a mouse, to permit efficient interaction with the GUI.

Telephone Terminals and Telephony

The telephone's widespread availability is causing greater use of it as a terminal. You can enter alphanumeric data on the touch-tone keypad of a telephone or by speaking into the receiver (voice input via speech recognition). You would then receive computer-generated voice output from a voice-response system. Salespeople use telephones as terminals for entering orders and inquiries about the availability of certain products into their company's server computer. Brokerage firms allow their clients to tap into the firm's computers via telephone.

The telephone by itself has little built-in intelligence; however, when linked to a computer, potential applications abound. **Telephony** is the integration of computers and telephones, the two most essential instruments of business. In telephony, the computer, often a PC, acts in concert with the telephone. For example, a PC can analyze incoming telephone calls and take appropriate action (take a message, route the call to the appropriate extension, and so on).

Special-Function Terminals: ATMs and POSs

The number and variety of special-function terminals are growing rapidly. Special-function terminals are designed for a specific application, such as convenience banking. You probably are familiar with the *automatic teller machine* (*ATM*) and its input/output capabilities.

The ATM idea has caught on for other applications. A consortium of companies is installing thousands of ATM-like terminals that will let you order and receive a wide variety of documents on the spot. For example, you can now obtain an airline ticket, your college transcript, and an IRS form electronically, and many more applications are on the way.

Another widely used special-function terminal is the *point-of-sale* (*POS*) terminal. Clerks and salespeople in retail stores, restaurants, and other establishments that sell goods and services use POS terminals. POS terminals have a keypad for input, at least one small monitor, and a printer to print the receipt. Some have other input/output devices, such as a badge reader for credit cards, a wand or stationary scanner to read price and inventory data, and/or a printer to preprint checks for customers.

SPECIAL-FUNCTION COMMUNICATIONS DEVICES IN THE BUSINESS COMMUNITY

In Figure 7-12, there is a *host computer*, or server computer, that is responsible for the overall control of the network and for the execution of applications (for example, a hotel reservation system). To improve the efficiency of a business computer system, the *processing load* is sometimes *distributed* among several other special-function processors. The two communications-related processors in the network of Figure 7-12, the front-end processor and the multiplexor, are under the control of and subordinate to the host. In Figure 7-12, the host computer is a large server computer; however, the host could just as well be a PC or a supercomputer, depending on the size and complexity of the network.

The terminal or computer sending a **message** is the *source*. The terminal or computer receiving the message is the *destination*. The **front-end processor** establishes the link between the source and destination in a process called **handshaking**. The term *front-end processor* has evolved to a generic reference for a computer-based device that relieves the host computer of a variety of communications-related processing duties. These duties include the transmission of data to and from remote terminals and other computers. The host can instead concentrate on overall system control and the execution of applications software.

If you think of messages as mail to be delivered to various points in a computer network, the front-end processor is the post office. Each computer system and terminal/PC in a computer network is assigned a **network address.** The front-end processor uses these addresses to route messages to their destinations. The content of a message could be a prompt to the user, a user inquiry, a program instruction, an "electronic memo," or any type of information that can be transmitted electronically—even the image of a handwritten report.

The **multiplexor** is an extension of the front-end processor. It is located down line from the host computer—at or near a remote site. The multiplexor collects data from several low-speed devices, such as terminals and printers. It then "concentrates" the data and sends them over a single communications channel (see Figure 7-13) to the front-end processor. The multiplexor also receives and

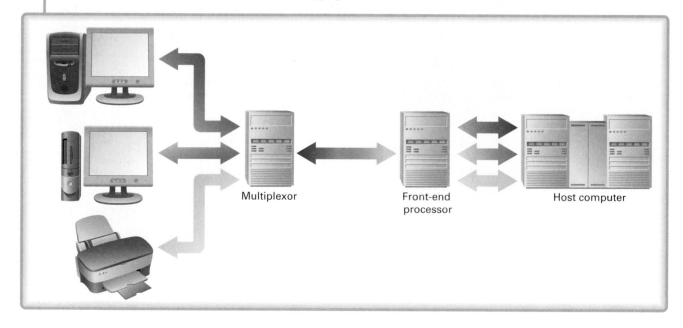

FIGURE 7–13 CONCENTRATING DATA FOR REMOTE TRANSMISSION
The multiplexor concentrates the data from several low-speed devices for transmission over a single high-speed line. At the host site, the front-end processor separates the data for processing. Data received from a front-end processor are interpreted by the multiplexor processor and routed to the appropriate device.

Multiplexor   Front-end   Host computer
                   processor

distributes host output to the appropriate remote terminals. Using one high-speed line to connect the multiplexor to the host is considerably less expensive than is using several low-speed lines to connect each terminal to the host. For example, an airline reservation counter might have 10 terminals, and it would be very slow and very expensive to connect each directly to the host computer. Instead, each terminal would be connected to a common multiplexor, which in turn would be connected to the central host computer.

SECTION SELF-CHECK

7-3.1	The electronic collection and distribution of information between two points is referred to as telecommunications. (T/F)
7-3.2	Another name for a server is a multiplexor. (T/F)
7-3.3	The communications device that facilitates the interconnection of dissimilar networks is: (a) a server, (b) a client, (c) a DSL line, or (d) a router.
7-3.4	Each computer system and PC in a computer network is assigned: (a) a network address, (b) a mailbox, (c) a P.O. address, or (d) an alphabetic identifier?
7-3.5	The integration of computers and telephones is known as: (a) telecommunications, (b) telephony, (c) autophony, or (d) IT phoning.

7-4 Networks

Networks are about sharing and communication. Networks facilitate the sharing of hardware (from printers to backup disk storage to server computers), software, data, and Internet access. They also make it easier for us to share ideas and communicate all kinds of information, from meeting schedules to product design data. The telephone system is the world's largest computer network, so you have been sharing and communicating on a network for most of your life. A telephone is an endpoint, or a **node**, connected to a network of computers that routes your voice signals to any one of the 500 million telephones (other nodes) in the world.

In a computer network the node can be a terminal, a computer, or any destination/source device (for example, a printer, an automatic teller machine, or even a telephone). Within an organization, computer networks are set up to meet the specific requirements of that organization. Some have 5 nodes; others have 10,000 nodes. Each network is one of a kind (see Figure 7-14). We have already seen the hardware and transmission media used to link nodes in a network. In this section, we intro-

FIGURE 7–14 NETWORKS IN PRACTICE

VISUAL AREA NETWORKING

Using a wireless tablet PC, Dr. Eng Lim Goh of SGI demonstrates Visual Area Networking. Visual Area Networking allows users to interact with visualization supercomputers anywhere they are, with any client device. It removes the requirement to have either the data or the advanced visualization capability local to the user.

Courtesy of SGI. Tablet image courtesy of SONICblue, Inc. Screen images courtesy of Landmark Graphics Corporation.

NETWORK CONTROL CENTER

This Global Network Control Center controls the entire ORBCOMM satellite constellation. ORBCOMM's mission is to revolutionize the way companies and individuals use wireless data communications. The satellites envelop the earth in low-altitude orbits, which allows messages to be sent and received by small, low-power access devices.

Courtesy of Orbital Sciences Corporation

HOSPITALS LINK UP

The workstations and PCs at this hospital are on a network and linked to a server computer. A computerized patient records system allows physicians to easily access up-to-date patient chart information from workstations throughout the hospital.

Courtesy of Harris Corporation

WIRELESS LOCAL AREA NETWORK

From anywhere within the hospital, this doctor can insert a wireless local area network PC Card into his notebook to enable a link to the hospital's LAN. Wireless links permit mobile users to create networks in minutes, without restrictive, conventional wire connections.

Courtesy of Raytheon Company

duce network topologies and the various types of networks. LANs, the most popular type of network, are discussed in more detail.

NETWORK TOPOLOGIES

A **network topology** is a description of the possible physical connections within a network. The topology is the configuration of the hardware and shows which pairs of nodes can communicate. The basic computer network topologies—star, ring, and bus—are illustrated in Figure 7-15. However, a pure form of any of these three basic topologies is rare in practice. Most computer networks are *hybrids*—combinations of these topologies.

Star Topology

The **star topology** involves a centralized host computer connected to several other computer systems, which are usually smaller than the host. The smaller computer systems communicate with one another through the host and usually share the host computer's database. The host could be anything from a PC to a supercomputer. Any computer can communicate with any other computer in the network. Banks often have a large home-office computer system with a star network of smaller server computer systems in the branch banks.

Ring Topology

The **ring topology** involves computer systems of approximately the same size, with no one computer system as the focal point of the network. When one system routes a message to another system, it is passed around the ring until it reaches its destination address.

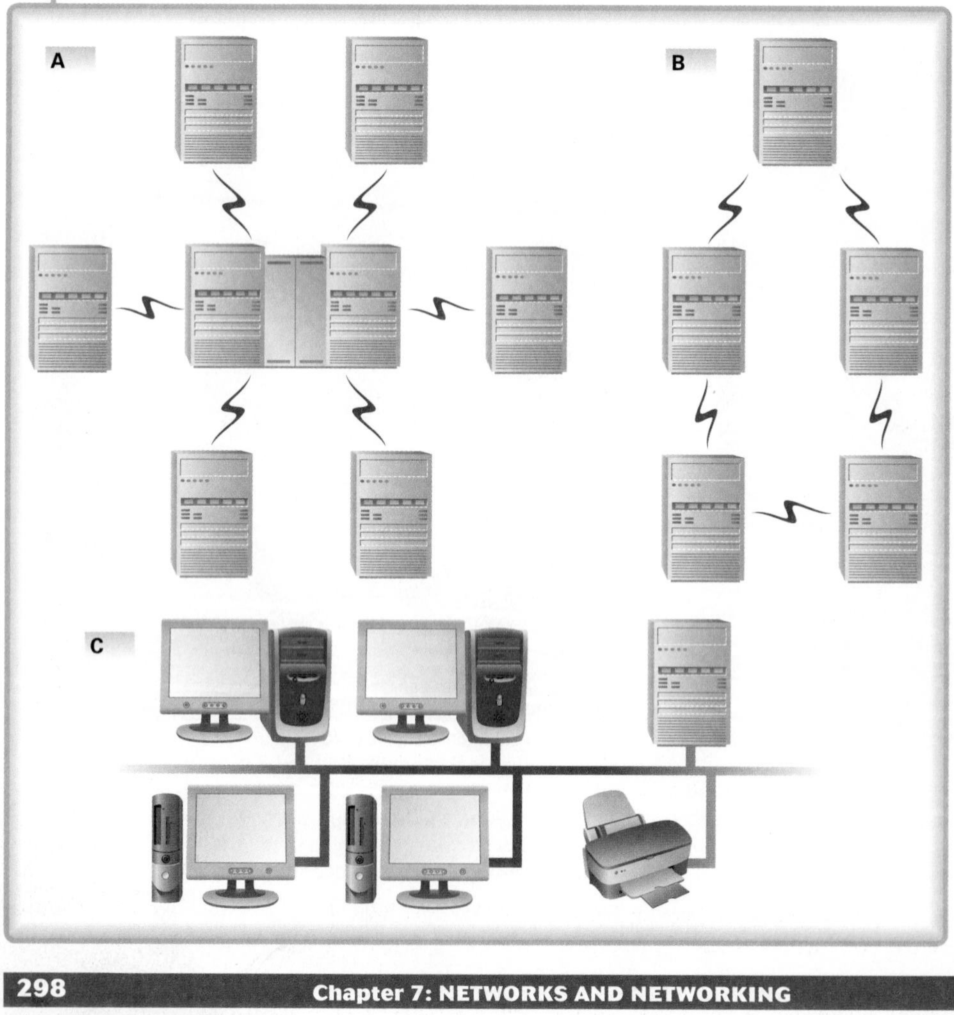

Bus Topology

The **bus topology** permits the connection of terminals, peripheral devices, and PCs along a common cable called a **network bus**. The term *bus* is used because people on a bus can get off at any stop along the route. In a bus topology a signal is broadcast to all nodes, but only the destination node responds to the signal. It is easy to add devices or delete them from the network, as devices are simply daisy-chained along the network bus. Bus topologies are most appropriate when the linked devices are physically close to one another.

TYPES OF NETWORKS

Networks tend to be classified by the proximity of their nodes.

- *The LAN.* The *local area network* (*LAN*), or **local net**, connects nodes in close proximity, such as in a suite of offices or a building. The local net, including all data communications channels, is owned by the organization using it. Because of the proximity of nodes in local nets, a company can install its own communications channels (such as coaxial cable, twisted

FIGURE 7–15 **NETWORK TOPOLOGIES**
Network topologies include (A) star, (B) ring, and (C) bus.

pair wire, fiber optic cable, wireless transceivers, and so on). Therefore, LANs do not need common carriers. LANs, the most popular type of network, are more fully explained later in this section.

- *The WAN.* A **WAN,** or **wide area network,** connects nodes, usually local area networks (LANs), in widely dispersed geographic areas, such as cities, states, and even countries. Wal-Mart, the largest retailer in the world, links the LANs in over 2000 stores and warehouses. The WAN often depends on the transmission services of a common carrier to transmit signals between nodes in the network. The emergence of virtual private networks (VPNs) and the potential for cost savings has resulted in many WANs being setup as VPNs over the world's grandest WAN, the Internet.

- *The MAN.* The **MAN,** or **metropolitan area network,** is a network designed for a city. MANs are more encompassing than local area networks (LANs) but smaller than wide area networks (WANs).

When we refer to LANs, WANs, and MANs, we refer to all hardware, software, and communications channels associated with them.

The focus of this section is the LAN, the most common network. Strictly speaking, any type of computer can be part of a LAN, but, in practice, PCs, thin clients, and workstations provide the foundation for local area networks. PCs in a typical LAN are linked to each other and share resources such as printers and disk storage. The distance separating devices in the local net may vary from a few feet to a few miles. As few as two and as many as several hundred PCs can be linked on a single local area network.

Most corporate PCs are linked to a LAN to aid in communication among knowledge workers. LANs make good business sense because these and other valuable resources can be shared.

- *Applications software.* The cost of a LAN-based word processing program (for example, Microsoft Word) is far less than the cost of a word processing program for each PC in the LAN.

- *Links to other LAN servers.* Other LANs become an accessible resource. It is easier to link one or more LANs to a single LAN than to many individual PCs.

- *Communications capabilities.* Many users can share a dedicated communications line or broadband Internet access.

- *I/O devices.* With a little planning, a single page printer, plotter, or scanner can support many users on a LAN with little loss of office efficiency. In a normal office setting, a single page printer can service the printing needs of up to 20 LAN users.

- *Storage devices.* Databases on a LAN can be shared. For example, some offices make a national telephone directory available to all LAN users.

- *Add-on boards.* Add-on boards, such as video capture boards, can be shared by many PCs.

Like computers, automobiles, and just about everything else, local nets can be built at various levels of sophistication. At the most basic level, they permit the interconnection of PCs in a department so that users can send messages to one another and share files and printers. The more sophisticated local nets permit the interconnection of server computers, PCs, and the spectrum of peripheral devices throughout a large but geographically constrained area, such as a cluster of buildings.

In some offices, you plug a terminal or PC into a network just as you would plug a telephone line into a telephone jack. This type of data communications capability is being installed in the new "smart" office buildings.

LAN OVERVIEW

Local nets, or LANs, are found in just about any office building. The basic hardware components in a PC-based LAN are the network interface cards, or NICs, in the PCs; the transmission media that connect the nodes in the network; and the servers. LANs may also have routers, modems, and other previously mentioned network hardware.

LAN Access Methods

Only one node on a LAN can send information at any given time. The other nodes must wait their turn. The transfer of data and programs between nodes is controlled by the access method embedded in the network interface card's ROM. The two most popular access methods are *token* and *Ethernet*.

Token Access Method

When a LAN with a *ring* topology uses the **token access method,** an electronic *token* travels around a ring of nodes in the form of a header. Figure 7-16 demonstrates the token-passing process for this type

FIGURE 7–16   THE TOKEN ACCESS METHOD IN A LAN WITH A RING TOPOLOGY

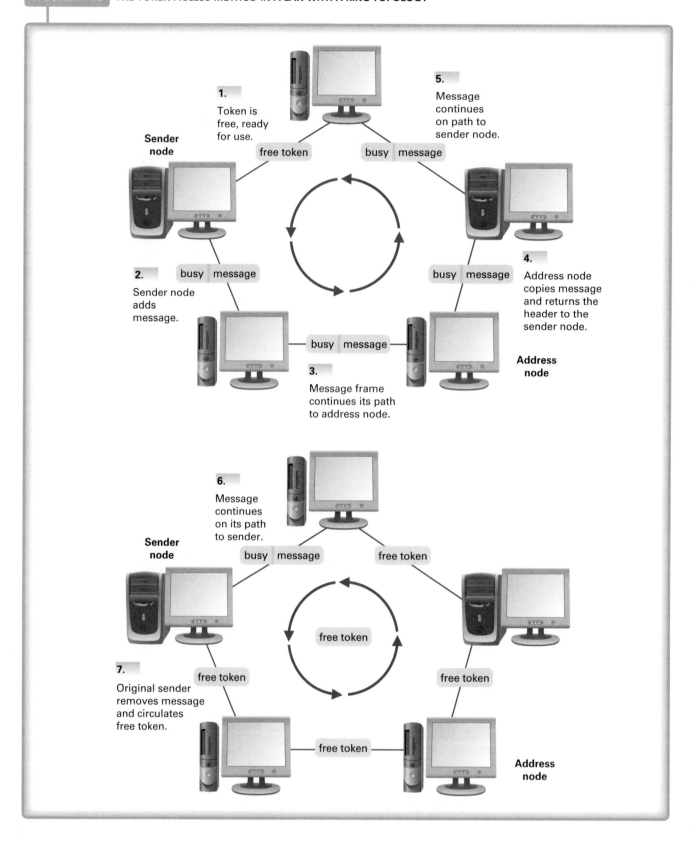

of LAN. The header contains control signals, including one specifying whether the token is "free" or carrying a message. A sender node captures a free token as it travels from node to node, changes it to "busy," and adds the message. The resulting *message frame* travels around the ring to the addressee's NIC, which copies the message and returns the message frame to the sender. The sender's NIC removes the message frame from the ring and circulates a new free token. When a LAN with a *bus* topology uses the token access method, the token is broadcast to the nodes along the network bus. Think of the token as a benevolent dictator who, when captured, bestows the privilege of sending a transmission.

Ethernet

In the popular **Ethernet** access method, nodes on the LAN must contend for the right to send a message. To gain access to the network, a node with a message to be sent automatically requests network service from the network software. The request might result in a "line busy" signal. In this case the node waits a fraction of a second and tries again, and again, until the line is free. Upon assuming control of the line, the node sends the message and then relinquishes control of the line to another node. Ethernet LANs operate like a conversation between polite people. When two people begin talking at the same time, one must wait until the other is finished. This all happens very quickly as Ethernet LANs can transmit information at up to 1 GB (one billion bits) per second.

LAN Transmission Media and Servers

Three kinds of transmission media can be connected to the network interface cards: twisted-pair wire, coaxial cable, and fiber optic cable. In wireless transmission, the cable runs from the transceiver to the NIC. Figure 7-17 illustrates how nodes in a LAN are connected in a bus topology with a wiring hub at the end that allows several more nodes to be connected to the bus.

In a LAN, a *server* is a component that can be shared by users on the LAN. The three most popular servers are the file server, the print server, and the communications server.

- *File server.* The **file server** normally is a dedicated computer, sometimes a high-performance PC or a workstation, with a high-capacity hard disk for storing the data and programs shared by the network users. For example, the master customer file, word processing software, spreadsheet software, and so on would be stored on the server disk. When a user wants to begin a spreadsheet session, the spreadsheet software is downloaded from the file server to the user's RAM.

- *Print server.* The **print server** typically is housed in the same dedicated PC as the file server. The print server handles user print jobs and controls at least one printer. If needed, the server *spools* print jobs; that is, it saves print jobs to disk until the requested printer is available, then routes the print file to the printer.

- *Communications server.* The **communications server** provides communication links external to the LAN—that is, links to other networks. To accomplish this service, the communications server controls one or more modems, or perhaps access to a DSL line.

These server functions may reside in a single PC or can be distributed among the PCs that make up the LAN. When the server functions are consolidated, the server PC usually is *dedicated* to servicing the LAN. Some PCs are designed specifically to be dedicated **LAN servers.** Until recently, you would purchase a traditional single-user PC and make it a dedicated server. Using a single-user PC continues to be an option with small- to medium-sized LANs, but not in large LANs with 100 or more users. Now, PC vendors manufacture powerful computers designed, often with multiple processors, specifically as LAN servers. LAN servers are configured with enough RAM, storage capacity, and backup capability to handle the resource needs of hundreds of PCs.

LAN SOFTWARE

In this section, we explore LAN-based software, including LAN operating systems alternatives and a variety of applications software.

Network Operating Systems

LAN operating systems, the nucleus of a local net, come in two formats: *peer-to-peer,* sometimes called *P2P,* and *dedicated server.* In both cases, the LAN operating system is actually several pieces of software. Each processing component in the LAN has a piece of the LAN operating system resident in its RAM. The pieces interact with one another to enable the nodes to share resources and communication.

The individual user in a LAN might appear to be interacting with an operating system, such as Windows XP. However, the RAM-resident LAN software *redirects* certain requests to the appropriate LAN component. For example, a print request would be redirected to the print server.

FIGURE 7–17

LAN LINKS
In this figure, nodes in a LAN are linked via a bus topology. One of the nodes is linked to a wiring hub that enables several PCs to be connected to the network bus. The wiring hub acts like a multiplexor, concentrating transmissions from several nodes. The LAN is linked to other LANs with fiber optic cable.

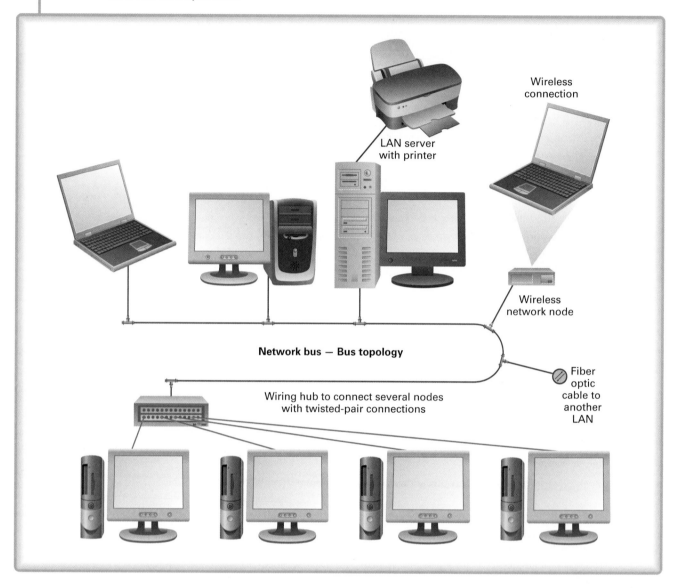

Peer-to-Peer LANs

In a **peer-to-peer LAN**, all PCs are peers, or equals. Any PC can be a client to another peer PC or any PC can share its resources with its peers. Peer-to-peer LANs are less sophisticated than those that have one or more dedicated servers in support of client/server networking. Because they are relatively easy to install and maintain, peer-to-peer LANs are popular when small numbers of PCs are involved (for example, from 2 to 20). PCs running the Windows operating system can be linked together in a peer-to-peer LAN.

Client/Server LANs

In LANs with dedicated servers, the controlling software resides in the file server's RAM. LANs with dedicated servers can link hundreds of clients (PCs and thin clients) in a LAN while providing a level of system security that is not possible in a peer-to-peer LAN. Control is distributed among the clients in the LAN. Novell, IBM, and Microsoft are major providers of LAN software. Each offers a family of LAN operating system, or "server," software to meet a variety of networking and Internet-based processing needs.

Applications Software for LANs

LAN-based PCs can run all applications that stand-alone PCs can run, plus those that involve electronic interaction with groups of people.

Shared Applications Software

LANs enable the sharing of general-purpose software, such as CBT (computer-based training), word processing, spreadsheet, and so on. LAN-based applications software is licensed for sharing. The PCs on the LAN with a dedicated central server interact with a file server to load various applications programs. When a LAN-based PC is booted, software that enables the use of the network interface card, communication with the file server, and interaction with the operating system are loaded from the PC's hard disk to RAM. Depending on how the LAN system administrator configured the LAN, you may see a graphical user interface that lists software options or you may see a prompt from the operating system. When you select a software package, it is downloaded from the LAN's file server to your PC's RAM for processing. You can then work with shared files on the file server or with your own local files (those stored on your PC).

Groupware: Software for the Group

LANs have opened the door to applications that are not possible in the one-person, one-computer environment. For example, users linked together via a LAN can send electronic mail to one another. Scheduling meetings with other users on the LAN is a snap. This type of multi-user software designed to benefit a group of people is called *groupware*. Local area networks and groupware provide the foundation for *workgroup computing*. The breadth of workgroup computing encompasses any application that involves groups of people linked by a computer network. The following is a sampling of workgroup computing applications.

- *Electronic mail (e-mail).* E-mail enables people on a LAN to route messages to one another's electronic mailbox.

- *Instant messaging.* Instant messaging allows messages to be sent and displayed in real-time.

- *Calendar and scheduling.* People can keep online calendars and schedule meetings automatically. The scheduling software automatically checks appropriate users' electronic calendars for possible meeting times, schedules the meeting, and informs the participants via electronic mail.

- *Brainstorming and problem solving.* A LAN enables collaborative brainstorming and problem solving.

- *Shared whiteboarding.* Shared whiteboards permit a document or image to be viewed simultaneously by several people on the network. All people involved can draw or make text annotations directly on the shared whiteboard. The annotations appear in the color associated with a particular participant.

- *Setting priorities.* Groupware is available that enables LAN users to establish priorities for projects through collective reasoning.

- *Electronic conferencing.* Conferencing groupware lets LAN users meet electronically.

- *Electronic forms.* American businesses and government spend over $400 billion each year to distribute, store, and update paper forms. Electronic forms groupware lets LAN users create forms for gathering information from other LAN users.

Networks on the Fly

The number and variety of workgroup computing applications can only increase. Already, notebook PC users are creating networks on the fly. That is, they bring their computers to the meeting and attach them to a common cable or activate their wireless transceivers to create a peer-to-peer LAN. In effect, we have progressed from the *portable computer* to the *portable network*. Once part of a LAN, users can enjoy the advantages of networking and groupware. Many colleges now have classes in which students bring notebook PCs to class, then create a wireless LAN with each other and with the professor's PC.

THE HOME NETWORK

A few years ago it was unthinkable to maintain a local area network in a home. The cost of hardware, software, and professional technical support was simply prohibitive. Today, people routinely link their computers in a *home network* (see Figure 7-18). The home network is a term coined to refer to small LANs in the home—perhaps two, three, or four nodes.

FIGURE 7-18 Wireless Home Network
This notebook PC is link to the Internet via a wireless home network.
Courtesy of International Business Machines Corporation. Unauthorized use not permitted.

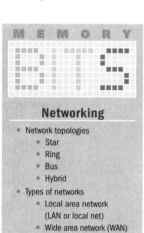

Networking

- Network topologies
  - Star
  - Ring
  - Bus
  - Hybrid
- Types of networks
  - Local area network (LAN or local net)
  - Wide area network (WAN)
  - Metropolitan area network (MAN)
- LAN operating systems
  - Peer-to-peer
  - Client/server
- LAN applications software
  - Shared
  - Groupware for workgroup computing
- The home network
  - HPNA networking standard
  - Peripheral and file sharing
  - Internet connection sharing
  - Multiplayer gaming

Homes with one or more kids' PCs, a parents' PC, and perhaps a parent's notebook PC from the office are becoming more the norm than the exception in the United States. Most families subscribing to broadband Internet access are multiple PC homes and over 80% of them have opted to set up a home network. About 20 million American families have home networks. And, why not? They are inexpensive, easy to install, and provide tremendous value to the family. Enabling broadband access to all PCs in the household is a tremendous value. Plus, the home network permits the sharing of all kinds of resources—the printer, the scanner, the DVD burner, files, and more. Not to be overlooked is the gaming aspect of home networking: at home, the whole family can join in a multiplayer game.

Most home networks are built around the **HPNA** networking standard developed by the Home Phoneline Networking Alliance. HPNA, also called **HomePNA**, allows the elements of the network to communicate over the home's existing telephone wiring. A home's phonelines can support voice/fax/data, broadband internet access, and HPNA networking—simultaneously. This is possible because each service occupies a different frequency band. Most home networks use phone lines, but they can be set up as wireless LANs, as well. The wireless option is slightly more expensive; however, wireless offers the ultimate mobility to the notebook user, who can work as easily in the backyard under a shade tree as in the home office.

To set up a home network you will need to purchase and install HPNA network interface cards (adapters) in all PCs planned for the network. The HPNA adapters are installed in an expansion slot in desktop PCs or inserted in a PC card slot in notebook PCs. HPNA USB external adapters can be used, as well. The relatively inexpensive HPNA cards (about $30 to $50 per PC) may be all you need for the home network. However, the type of broadband service (DSL, cable modem, or satellite) and/or ISP selected may require the use of specific software or hardware (for example, a router or Ethernet card).

The Windows environment makes it easy for you to set up a peer-to-peer local area network for Internet, peripheral, and file sharing. When you turn on the PCs for the first time, the Windows network wizard leads you through the setup procedure. For example, you will be given the option to share your files and/or printer with others.

Internet sharing can be accomplished via software or hardware. When using the software approach, one of the PCs is designated as a "gateway" to the Internet. The gateway and all other PCs on the network run Internet connection sharing (ICS) software. In this method, the broadband Internet access signal is fed into the gateway PC and the ICS software coordinates Internet access among the networked PCs. The downside of the ICS approach is that the gateway computer must be turned on for the other computers to access the Internet.

The hardware approach to Internet sharing involves the use of a router. The router was price prohibitive for home networking until recently, but the explosion of home networks has resulted in a dramatic reduction in router prices, to the point that it is a viable option for home networking. The router, which connects to a broadband modem, is the gateway to the Internet and shares access directly with the other PCs on the network. The router handles all Internet sharing processing duties, so a PC need not be dedicated to these tasks.

SECTION SELF-CHECK

7-4.1	An endpoint in a network of computers is called a: (a) break point, (b) stop bit, (c) node, or (d) PC.
7-4.2	Twisted-pair wire, coaxial cable, and fiber optic cable can be used to connect nodes on a LAN via network interface cards. (T/F)
7-4.3	Which of the following doesn't fit: (a) WAN, (b) LAN, (c) DAN, or (d) MAN?
7-4.4	Which would not be a type of LAN server: (a) communications server, (b) file server, (c) print server, or (d) scan server?
7-4.5	Which of the following devices would be an unlikely component in a home network: (a) router, (b) notebook PC, (c) dedicated Internet server, or (d) NIC?

7-1 OUR WIRED WORLD

We rely on *computer networks* to retrieve and share information quickly; thus the current direction of **digital convergence.** **Connectivity** facilitates the electronic communication between companies and the free flow of information within an enterprise.

This is the era of cooperative processing. To obtain meaningful, accurate, and timely information, businesses have decided that they must cooperate internally and externally to take full advantage of available information. To promote internal cooperation, businesses are promoting both **intracompany** and **intercompany networking.** Intercompany networking can also be called **business-to-business (B2B) e-commerce.** More business between companies is being moved to the Internet. More specifically, it will be moved to a company's *intranet* with actual B2B interactions taking place over their *extranets.* An **extranet** is an extension of an **intranet,** a closed or private version of the Internet.

A **virtual private network** uses **tunneling** technology to enable a private network over the Internet. A **VPN** employs encryption and other security measures to ensure that communications are not intercepted.

7-2 THE DATA COMMUNICATIONS CHANNEL

A **communications channel** is the facility through which digital information must pass to get from one location in a computer network to the next.

A channel may be composed of one or more of the following transmission media: telephone lines of copper **twisted-pair wire, coaxial cable, microwave signals, radio signals, fiber optic cable,** and **wireless transceivers.** Satellites are essentially microwave repeater stations that maintain a **geosynchronous orbit** around the earth. Two services are made available over twisted-pair wire: **POTS** (plain old telephone services) and Digital Subscriber Line (DSL). Some cable television systems offer high-speed Internet access over coaxial cable (cable modem). Line-of-sight wireless technologies **MMDS** (Multichannel Multipoint Distribution Service) and **LMDS** (Local Multipoint Distribution Service) provide for network access at fiber optic-level speeds.

Communications **common carriers** provide communications channels to the public, and lines can be arranged to suit the application. A **private** or **leased line** provides a dedicated communications channel. A **switched** or **dialup line** is available on a time-and-distance charge basis.

Communications protocols are rules established to govern the way data are transmitted in a computer network. The protocol you hear about most often is **TCP/IP (Transmission Control Protocol/Internet Protocol),** the foundation protocol for the Internet.

Asynchronous transmission begins and ends each message with start/stop bits and is used primarily for low-speed data transmission. **Synchronous transmission** permits the source and destination to communicate in timed synchronization for high-speed data transmission.

7-3 DATA COMMUNICATIONS HARDWARE

Data communications (also called **telecommunications**) is the electronic collection and distribution of information from and to remote facilities. Data communications hardware is used to transmit digital information between terminals and computers or between computers. These hardware components include the modem, the *network interface card* (*NIC*), the **front-end processor,** the **multiplexor,** and the **router.** The NIC often is called an **Ethernet Card.**

Voice/data/fax modems, both internal and external, modulate and demodulate signals so that data can be transmitted over telephone lines. Besides the data communications capabilities, they let you make telephone calls via your PC and simulate a fax machine. The cable modem, a DSL modem, or a satellite modem enables broadband Internet access. The **DSLAM (Digital Subscriber Line Access Multiplexor)** routes DSL signals to telephone companies for processing.

The front-end processor establishes the link between the source and destination in a process called **handshaking,** then sends the **message** to a **network address.** The front-end processor relieves the host computer of communications-related tasks. The multiplexor concentrates data from several sources and sends them over a single communications channel.

The primary hardware/software technology used to enable the interconnection of incompatible computer networks is the **router.** A **backbone** is composed of one or more routers and the associated transmission media.

Terminals enable interaction with a remote computer system. The general-purpose terminals are the **video display terminal (VDT)** and the *telephone.* Terminals come in all shapes and sizes and have a variety of input/output capabilities.

Windows terminals with processing capabilities enable the user to interact via a graphical user interface. **Telephony** is the integration of computers and telephones.

An assortment of special-function terminals, such as automatic teller machines (ATMs) and point-of-sale (POS) terminals, are designed for a specific application.

7-4 NETWORKS

Computer systems are linked together to form a computer network. In a computer network, the **node** can be a terminal, a computer, or any other destination/source device. The basic patterns for configuring computer systems within a computer network are **star topology, ring topology,** and **bus topology.** The bus topology permits the connection of nodes along a **network bus.** In practice, most networks are actually hybrids of these **network topologies.**

The local area network (LAN), or **local net,** connects nodes in close proximity and does not need a common carrier. A **WAN,** or **wide area network,** connects nodes, usually LANs, in widely dispersed geographic areas. The **MAN,** or **metropolitan area network,** is a network designed for a city.

The physical transfer of data and programs between LAN nodes is controlled by the access method embedded in the network interface card's ROM, usually the **token access method** or **Ethernet.** The three most popular servers are the **file server,** the **print server,** and the **communications server.** These server functions may reside in a dedicated **LAN server.**

The **LAN operating system** is actually several pieces of software, a part of which resides in each LAN component's RAM. In a **peer-to-peer LAN,** all PCs are equals. Any PC can share its resources with its peers. In LANs with dedicated servers, the controlling software resides in the file server's RAM.

LANs and *groupware* provide the foundation for *workgroup computing.* The breadth of workgroup computing encompasses any application that involves groups of people linked by a computer network. Workgroup computing applications include electronic mail, instant messaging, calendar and scheduling, brainstorming and problem solving, shared whiteboarding, and others.

The home network is a term coined to refer to small LANs in the home. Home networks enables Internet connection sharing, peripherals sharing, and multiplayer gaming. Most home networks are built around the **HPNA (HomePNA)** networking standard. Internet sharing can be accomplished via software where one of the PCs is designated as a "gateway" to the Internet, or it can be done via hardware with a router handling the Internet sharing duties.

KEY TERMS

asynchronous transmission (p. 290)
backbone (p. 294)
bus topology (p. 298)
business-to-business (B2B) (p. 283)
coaxial cable (p. 286)
common carrier (p. 288)
communications channel (p. 285)
communications protocol (p. 290)
communications server (p. 301)
connectivity (p. 283)
data communications (p. 291)
digital convergence (p. 282)
DSLAM (Digital Subscriber Line Access Multiplexor) (p. 294)
e-commerce (p. 283)
Ethernet (p. 301)
Ethernet Card (p. 294)
extranet (p. 284)
fiber optic cable (p. 288)
file server (p. 301)
front-end processor (p. 295)

geosynchronous orbit (p. 286)
handshaking (p. 295)
HPNA (HomePNA) (p. 304)
intercompany networking (p. 283)
intracompany networking (p. 283)
intranet (p. 284)
LAN operating system (p. 301)
LAN server (p. 301)
LMDS (p. 288)
local net (LAN) (p. 298)
MAN (metropolitan area network) (p. 299)
message (p. 295)
microwave signal (p. 286)
MMDS (p. 288)
multiplexor (p. 295)
network address (p. 295)
network bus (p. 298)
network topology (p. 298)
node (p. 296)

peer-to-peer LAN (p. 302)
POTS (p. 286)
print server (p. 301)
private line (leased line) (p. 288)
radio signal (p. 286)
ring topology (p. 298)
router (p. 294)
star topology (p. 298)
switched line (dialup line) (p. 289)
synchronous transmission (p. 290)
telecommunications (p. 291)
telephony (p. 295)
token access method (p. 299)
tunneling (p. 285)
twisted-pair wire (p. 286)
video display terminal (VDT) (p. 294)
virtual private network (VPN) (p. 284)
WAN (wide area network) (p. 299)
Windows terminal (p. 295)
wireless transceiver (p. 287)

MATCHING

1. VPN
2. node
3. digital convergence
4. B2B
5. WAN
6. intranet
7. fiber optic cable
8. twisted-pair wire
9. front-end processor
10. Ethernet
11. MAN
12. asynchronous transmission
13. POS system
14. switched line
15. DSLAM

a. combines DSL signals
b. network access method
c. e-commerce
d. transmitted at irregular intervals
e. PC in a home network
f. network in metropolitan area
g. POTS media
h. dialup line
i. retail store terminals
j. relieves host of communications duties
k. more encompassing than a LAN
l. pulses of light
m. tunnels on Net
n. internal Internet
o. moving toward digital compatibility

CHAPTER SELF-CHECK

7-1.1   Either a company has connectivity or it does not, with no in-between. (T/F)

7-1.2   Electronic commerce is the term used to describe business conducted online. (T/F)

7-1.3   An intranet uses the TCP/IP protocol. (T/F)

7-1.4   Connectivity is implemented: (a) all at once, (b) after the Internet option has failed, (c) in degrees, or (d) to thwart B2B.

7-1.5   VPN stands for: (a) virtual private network, (b) very personal network, (c) virtual POTS net, or (d) vat pat nat.

7-1.6   A closed or private version of the Internet is called: (a) a fishnet, (b) an intranet, (c) an overnet, or (d) an addnet.

7-2.1 The two basic types of service offered by common carriers are a private line and a switched line. (T/F)

7-2.2 Microwave relay stations are located approximately 500 miles apart. (T/F)

7-2.3 The channel capacity for DSL service is about 10 times that of cable TV digital service. (T/F)

7-2.4 Communications protocols describe how data are transmitted in a computer network. (T/F)

7-2.5 The unit of measure for the capacity of a data communications channel is: (a) bps, (b) bytes per second, (c) RAM units, or (d) megabits.

7-2.6 Which of these terms is not used to refer to a communications channel: (a) link, (b) pipe, (c) passageway, or (d) line?

7-2.7 DSL service is delivered to homes over what kind of line: (a) POTS, (b) satellite, (c) cable, or (d) fiber?

7-2.8 Which transmission media offers the greatest capacity: (a) fiber optic cable, (b) twisted-pair wire, (c) coax, or (d) microwave signal?

7-3.1 The typical modem is a voice/data/fax modem. (T/F)

7-3.2 The DSLAM facilitates satellite broadband communications. (T/F)

7-3.3 A communications device establishes the link between the source and destination in a process called: (a) handshaking, (b) greeting, (c) hello good-bye, or (d) messaging.

7-3.4 What device converts digital signals into analog signals for transmission over telephone lines: (a) router, (b) brouter, (c) modem, or (d) client/server?

7-3.5 Which of these is not used for broadband communications: (a) cable modem, (b) DSL modem, (c) twisted-pair modem, or (d) satellite modem?

7-3.6 Special-function terminals can be found in most department stores. (T/F)

7-3.7 ATMs are now available in some areas of the country that will let you order and receive Internal Revenue Service (IRS) forms and airline tickets. (T/F)

7-3.8 The telephone is considered a terminal. (T/F)

7-3.9 Which terminal permits system interaction via a GUI: (a) a dumb terminal, (b) a Windows terminal, (c) a text-based terminal, or (d) a traditional VDT?

7-3.10 The primary input/output on the VDT is: (a) the mouse and microphone, (b) the keyboard and speaker, (c) a hard disk and monitor, or (d) the keyboard and monitor.

7-4.1 In a LAN with a dedicated server, the operating system for the entire LAN resides in the server processor's RAM. (T/F)

7-4.2 In a peer-to-peer LAN, the less powerful PCs are clients to the more powerful PCs. (T/F)

7-4.3 A router is required for any home network doing Internet sharing. (T/F)

7-4.4 A LAN is designed for "long-haul" data communications. (T/F)

7-4.5 The central cable called a network bus is most closely associated with which network topology: (a) ring, (b) star, (c) bus, or (d) train?

7-4.6 Which LAN access method passes a token from node to node: (a) token, (b) Ethernet, (c) contention, or (d) parity checking?

7-4.7 Which of these applications permits a document or image to be viewed simultaneously by several people on the network: (a) scheduling, (b) whiteboarding, (c) electronic forms, or (d) brainstorming?

7-4.8 Most home networks are built around what networking standard: (a) phoneline PD, (b) HPNA, (c) home networking, or (d) Ethernet?

IT ETHICS AND ISSUES

THE DIGITAL DIVIDE: IS IT RACIAL OR ECONOMIC?

Much has been made in the news about an ever-growing digital divide that heretofore has been described primarily along racial lines. The divide refers to the disparity between groups of people who have computers and access to the Internet and those who do not. Politicians have presented the digital divide as a disparity between races, generally white and African American. A comprehensive study, however, reveals that the digital divide is not so much an issue of race, but of economics. A very high percentage of those with the money to buy PCs and be online make the cyber investment. Those without funds do not have that option.

Discussion: *What can be done about the digital divide?*

Discussion: *Universal access to the Internet is a stated goal of many U.S. politicians. Discuss approaches to achieving this universal access given that only 70% of the population can afford PCs or Internet appliances in their homes.*

THE INTERNET'S IMPACT ON THE FAMILY UNIT

According to the results of an Internet usage survey at Stanford University's Institute for the Quantitative Study in Society, Americans report they spend less time with friends and family,

shopping in stores, and watching television. Also, Americans spend more time working for their employers at home—without cutting back their hours in the office. Another result indicated that time on the Internet increased with Internet experience (number of years using the Internet).

Discussion: *Is the Internet having a negative impact on the family unit? Explain.*

Discussion: *The survey showed that regular Internet users (5 or more hours per week) choose to work more at home than others in the general population. Why do you think they do this?*

Discussion: *A key finding of the study was that "the more hours people use the Internet, the less time they spend in contact with real human beings." Should society make an effort to educate people to this trend? Why or why not?*

SHARING INTERNET ACCESS VIA WI-FI

The price structure for broadband Internet service, such as cable modem and GSL, is based on the statistical reality that the average consumer will use less than 1% of the line's potential capacity to carry information. Many consumers have picked up on the fact that they have a lot of excess capacity and are willingly to share this capacity through wireless "home networking," which, in fact, may involve PCs in a dozen apartments and a dozen families. Broadband providers claim that their fee structure is designed for single-family usage. Broadband consumers claim that they are paying for always-on Internet access and how they use it is up to them.

Discussion: *Businesses pay significantly more for broadband capacity, primarily because businesses can be expected to use a signifi-* cantly higher percentage of the lines capacity than a family. Should individuals be allowed to share Internet capacity, even if they do it for free?

Discussion: *In many cases, a broadband line is installed and billed to a particular address, but users in nearby apartments on a wireless LAN share the Internet and the bill. Discuss the legal ramifications of this arrangement from the account owner's perspective. From the perspective of those who share the line. From the Internet provider's perspective.*

DISCUSSION AND PROBLEM SOLVING

7-1.1 Discuss ways that the trend toward digital conversion has changed your life over the last two years. Speculate on ways that it might change your life during the next five years.

7-1.2 Select a type of company and give an example of what information the company might make available over its Internet, its intranet, and its extranet.

7-2.1 It's getting crowded in space with so many companies and countries launching communications satellites into geosynchronous orbit. Is there a danger of having too many satellites hovering above the earth? If so, what can be done about it?

7-2.2 Describe circumstances in which a leased line would be preferred to a dialup line.

7-2.3 The cost of a normal 56 K bps dialup connection with unlimited access to the Internet costs anywhere from $15 to $25. How much more would you pay to get Internet access via cable TV, satellite, or DSL that is 10 to 50 times faster than that provided by a 56 K modem? Explain.

7-2.4 Speculate on the different types of transmission media that might be used to transmit data for a one-hour Internet session.

7-3.1 Explain why you must use a modem to send data over a plain old telephone line.

7-3.2 Describe how a multiplexor can be used to save money.

7-3.3 Over the years, Internet access speeds have moved gradually higher. Do you expect to see a significant jump in consumer-oriented Internet access speeds, perhaps a doubling of capacity, over the next few years? Why or why not?

7-4.1 Identify the type and location of at least five different types of nodes in your college's network.

7-4.2 A variety of communications hardware, including a router, is needed to link local area networks that use different communications protocols. Why are not all LANs designed to use the same standards for communication so that communications hardware tasks can be simplified?

7-4.3 Describe how information can be made readily accessible to many people in a company, but only on a need-to-know basis.

7-4.4 The five PCs in the purchasing department of a large consumer-goods manufacturer are used primarily for word processing and database applications. What would be the benefits associated with connecting the PCs in a local area network?

7-4.5 The mere fact that PCs on a LAN are networked poses a threat to security. Why?

7-4.6 Some metropolitan area networks are completely private; that is, communications common carrier services are not used. Network nodes can be distributed throughout large cities. How do companies link the nodes on the network without common carrier data communications facilities?

7-4.7 Describe at least one situation in academia or the business world where creating a portable network would be inappropriate. That is, a situation where people with notebook PCs link them in a network by attaching them to a common cable or by using wireless transceivers. Briefly describe what the network might do.

7-4.8 Do you have a home network? If so, describe it in detail, listing all related communications hardware and software. If not, speculate on when and why you might consider installing a home network.

FOCUS ON PERSONAL COMPUTING

1. On your Windows desktop, click *Start* on the taskbar, then choose *Help and Support*. Enter "home networking" and then open appropriate descriptions in the results list and learn more about home networking in the Windows environment. Click on hypertext links to expand your knowledge of the topic, as needed. Now, do the same for "HPNA," the technology used in most home networks, and "ICS," the type of software that enables Internet connection sharing. Briefly describe at least one newfound piece of knowledge for each topic that you feel will help you in the creation of a home network.

2. Do the preliminary design for a phone-line-based home or small office network, preferably for a home or office with which you are familiar. Draw a diagram of the house or office including the location of each PC, shared resource (printer, scanner, DVD burner, and so on), and telephone jack. Create a table and label the columns "PCs," "Modems," "Network adapters," "Peripherals," and "To be purchased," then fill in the table. The last column would list the extra hardware you will need to implement your home/small office network (HPNA adapters, ethernet cards, router, and so on). Go online and price out the hardware needed to create the network.

1. The Online Study Guide (multiple choice, true/false, matching, and essay questions)
2. Internet Learning Activities
   - Online Books
   - Transmission Media
   - Terminals
   - Networks
3. Serendipitous Activities
   - Government

PERSONAL COMPUTING BUYER'S GUIDE

From the time you purchase and plug in your first PC, you are committed to a lifetime of buying newer and better PCs, PC upgrades, PC peripherals, and PC software. Also, you subscribe to PC services and are caught up in an endless loop of PC supplies and accessories. The personal computing adventure is great fun, but it isn't cheap. But neither is Disneyworld.

The emphasis in this buyer's guide is on the actual buying and decision processes. Other sections of the book cover hardware, software, and Internet concepts.

BEFORE YOU BUY: ANSWER THESE QUESTIONS

A sleek new PC is like a shiny new car; it invites impulse buying. Resist this urge and get a system that fits your budget and meets your personal computing needs. Before you purchase anything, answer these important questions.

How Much to Spend?

You can purchase a new personal computer for under $500. However, if you choose an array of performance features and opt for the latest technology in peripheral and storage devices, the cost of a personal computer could easily exceed $5000. Ultimately, the amount you spend on a personal computer depends on your financial circumstances and your spending priorities. If personal computing is one of your priorities, here is a good rule to follow: *purchase as much power and functionality in a personal computer system as your budget will permit.* You'll need it more quickly than you think.

Desktop PC or Notebook PC?

The choice between a *desktop PC* and a *notebook PC* (see Figure 7-19) usually hinges on two considerations: *need for portability* and *cost*.

- *Portability.* If your lifestyle demands portability in personal computing and you are willing to pay considerably more for approximately the same computing capability as a comparable desktop PC, then you should seriously consider a notebook PC.
- *Cost.* If cost is a concern and portability isn't, the desktop PC is for you.

Notebook PC owners sacrifice some conveniences to achieve portability. For instance, input devices, such as the keyboard and point-and-draw devices, are given less space in portable PCs and may be more cumbersome to use. These inconveniences, however, are offset by the convenience of having your PC and its capabilities with you wherever you are.

Desktop PCs outsell notebook PCs two to one; however, each year notebooks are gaining significant ground and should surpass desktops in sales in the near future.

Figure 7–19 — DESKTOP OR NOTEBOOK PC?
The desktop PC offers more power for your personal computing dollar, but the notebook PC offers portability.

Which Platform?

The Wintel PC (Windows o.perating system, Intel or equivalent processor) represents the dominant PC platform with over 90% of the PC pie. The Apple Computer Company line of personal computers represent about 5% of the PC market, and the remainder of the market is comprised mostly of Linux-based systems and those with legacy Microsoft operating systems.

When making the platform decision, consider compatibility with the other PCs in your life: your existing PC (if you have one), the one at work/home, and/or the one in your college lab. Also, consider your career interests. Apple computers have it all and do it all; some would argue that they do it better than Wintel machines. Nevertheless, the Apple line of computers, especially at the high end, have been tabbed as niche machines because they are so pervasive in certain types of industries, including publishing, video/film editing, graphics, animation, illustration, and music.

Companies, whether software or automobile, tend to build products for the largest markets, in the case of software—Wintel. Therefore, Wintel PCs have a substantial advantage in the range of available software and, because of volume sales, software prices. Apple computer users also have access to a wide range of software; however, the Apple selection pales when you compare it to available Wintel software.

Who Will Use the PC and How Will It be Used?

Plan not only for yourself, but also for others in your home that might use the system. Get their input and consider their needs along with yours. The typical off-the-shelf entry-level notebook or desktop personal computer has amazing capabilities and will do most anything within the boundaries of the digital world. Nevertheless, depending on how you plan to use the system (for example, video editing, gaming, multimedia viewing), you may need to supplement the basic system with additional hardware and software.

What Input/Output Peripheral Devices Do You Need?

A good mix of input/output peripheral devices can spice up your computing experience. I/O devices come in a variety of speeds, capacities, and qualities. Generally, the more you pay the more you get. However, there is no reason to pay for extra speed, capacity, or quality if you do not need it.

Several suggestions for I/O devices are listed below for the "typical" user. *Priority suggestions are listed first.* Of course, priorities will vary, but these should give you a benchmark for decision making. Normally, the printer (or possibly an all-in-one peripheral: print, scan, fax, and copy) is the only additional peripheral input/output device that you would get at or near the time of purchase; however, you should consider upgrading the monitor, mouse, and keyboard. All other optional I/O devices you might want can be purchased as the need arises at the best prices.

1. Printer or All-in-One Peripheral
No PC system is complete without access to a printer. The keyword here is "access." If you already have a PC system in your home with an acceptable printer, you probably don't need two printers. This resource is easily shared via walk-net or a home network. Walk-net is just transferring print files via interchangeable discs or diskettes.

The ink-jet printer has emerged as the overwhelming choice of budget-minded people buying home/home office PC systems. The quality of any of today's mainline ink-jet printers is remarkable, so your decision boils down to how much you are willing to pay for additional print quality, faster print speeds, and special features (for example, printing on both sides of the paper).

You might wish to consider getting an all-in-one multifunction peripheral, that is, a device that prints, faxes, scans, and copies (duplicates). The considerable overlap in the technologies used in these machines has enabled manufacturers to create a reasonably priced machine that does it all.

2. PC Headset
Desktop PCs are sold with a basic microphone and speakers. You'll need to purchase a quality headset with a mike (from $25 to $50) if you wish to take advantage of the speech recognition capability made available with the newer Microsoft Office suites (see Figure 7-20). If you purchase speech recognition software separately, the headset comes with the product.

Figure 7–20 — THE PC HEADSET
If you plan to use speech recognition technology, you will need a high-quality headset with a directional microphone that picks up the user's voice, but not the ever-present noises around the office and home.

3. Scanner
If you choose an all-in-one peripheral (see priority peripheral #1), you will not need a stand-alone scanner. The scanner is a good investment in your personal computing adventure. With a scanner, you can convert any color hardcopy document and even small 3D images (jewelry, heirlooms, and so on) to an electronic image that can be integrated into anything from a newsletter to a greeting card. The scanner can read text and speak the words with the help of text-to-speech software. The scanner doubles as a copy machine for small volume copying (scanner to printer) and as a fax machine (used in conjunction with the fax software that comes with all PCs and a dial-up modem). Any name-brand flatbed scanner with an 8.5-inch by 11.7-inch scanning area that scans at 1200 X 2400 dpi (dots per inch) or better should be all you need unless you are doing professional image editing.

4. Internet or Web Camera
The Internet or Web camera certainly is not a PC system necessity, but for as little as $50, it can add some serious spice to your personal computing experience. These versatile little cameras, which can capture both still and video images, plug into your computer like any other peripheral. You can use them for many tasks, including videophone conversations, setting up a Webcam (streaming images over the Internet), maintaining security, or for monitoring your baby.

5. Game Controllers

If you have gamers in the house, game controllers are must-have items. The game controller is very much a matter of personal preference, so be sure and invite input from your gamers before buying. Many computer games are multi-player games, so you may wish to purchase two of these relatively inexpensive devices.

6. Digital Camera/Digital Camcorder

If you enjoy taking and sharing pictures, then you will want to consider owning a digital camera. With a digital camera, the cost of photography plummets because the costly, time-consuming developing processing is eliminated. With digital cameras, you can take all the photos you want and just keep the good ones. Once the images are downloaded to your PC, you can enhance, edit, send, or view them at your leisure.

If you are in the market for a *digital camcorder,* you may not need to spend the extra money for a separate digital camera for still photography. Most modern digital camcorders let you take excellent megapixel still images, as well as digital video.

7. USB Multiport Hub

The most popular way to connect input/output devices to a PC is via a USB port. Typically, a personal computer will have two or six USB ports. Those ports, however, can be filled quickly. Fortunately, USB technology allows you to daisy-chain multiple devices to a single port. It's quite possible that you'll need more ports than are made available on the system unit, and, if you do, you will need to purchase a USB 2.0 multiport hub.

ENTRY LEVEL, SWEET SPOT, AND PERFORMANCE PERSONAL COMPUTERS

New desktop or notebook PCs can be grouped into three general categories based on cost and performance—*entry-level systems, sweet spot systems,* and *performance systems.* Soon after their introduction, these systems begin their slow slide into a lower category or obsolescence—for example, the performance system moves into the sweet spot category and, eventually, into the entry-level category.

Technological innovation continues its relentless march toward defining a new level of across-the-board performance each year. This means that what was a performance system a couple of years ago can look very much like today's entry-level system.

Buying an Entry-Level Personal Computer

If your financial circumstances and spending priorities dictate that you purchase an entry-level system, you have no choice but to go with a minimal system or, perhaps, a used PC system. In most circumstances, this system will do the job. Today's entry-level PCs can be five times as fast as a performance PC that was purchased five years ago for $5000. All modern PCs are amazingly capable machines.

Entry-level or "affordable" personal computers offer good value, but, typically, they do not give the buyer as much flexibility to customize the PC at the time of the sale. For example, you may have only one or two choices for the monitor. Often, affordable personal computers are sold off-the-shelf, as is.

Generally, fewer, slower, less, and older are terms used to describe the system components for entry-level PCs. For example, an affordable PC system might have fewer USB ports, a slower CD-RW disc drive, less RAM, and a processor with older technology. But you have to put these descriptors into perspective. An affordable PC may have a processor that is 40% slower than a performance machine processor, but it still is very, very fast.

The downside of purchasing an entry-level system is that a new affordable PC may be at least one year, and as much as two years, closer to technological obsolescence than one of the more expensive intermediate or high-end PCs. To be sure, if you purchase an entry-level PC you will lose out on technology bragging rights, but you can always brag about saving enough money to purchase a big-screen TV.

Hitting the Sweet Spot PC

In sports, the "sweet spot" is the area on a baseball bat, a tennis racket, or head of a golf club that is the most effective part with which to hit a ball. Every consumer market has a sweet spot, too. The PC market's sweet spot offers the greatest value. When you purchase a sweet spot PC, you're not paying a premium for state-of-the-art technology, but you still are getting near leading-edge performance. Most people looking to buy their first PC or another PC will want a good, solid PC that will run virtually all current and future applications over the next two or three years. For these people, a good place to look is the sweet spot in the personal computing market.

Typically, the PC sweet spot is a desktop PC that is about 6 to 12 months off the technology; that is, the major components in the system, such as the processor and hard disk, were introduced up to a year earlier. State-of-the-art performance systems might be 30% faster and capable of storing twice the information, but they may cost twice, even three times, as much as a sweet spot PC.

Finding the Sweet Spot PC

Generally, the sweet spot is relatively easy to find. To find it, go to the Web site for any major PC vendor that markets directly to the public (for example, Dell, Hewlett Packard, IBM, or Gateway), then navigate to the page that features their home/small office desktop PC options. The system in the middle represents the current "sweet spot." Once you have perused the system specifications at several vendor Web sites, you should have a good read on the current PC sweet spot. Be advised, however, that the sweet spot is continuously changing and what you see today as the high-end system may be featured as a sweet spot system in a few days.

If you don't have access to the Internet, the sweet spot is fairly obvious at any major PC retailer, such as Best Buy, Office Depot, and so on. The sweet spot is represented by those similarly priced PC systems in the middle price range.

Customizing the PC Sweet Spot System

You may not have the flexibility to customize a sweet spot system. Those sold in retail outlets and, sometimes, online via direct marketers may be offered as a package deal—what you see is what you get. However, most vendors that market directly to customers, via the Internet or telephone sales, give the consumer plenty of flexibility to customize their orders.

It is likely that the come-on price of a sweet spot system will not include some needed and important upgrades. Depending on your budget and personal computing needs, consider the following recommendations. *The recommendations are listed by value, with the biggest payout for your PC dollar listed first.*

- *Buy a surge suppressor.* Inexpensive surge protectors provide essential protection from lightning hits and other electrical aberrations. An uninterruptible power source (UPS) offers superior protection to a surge suppressor but adds $60 to $80 to the system price.
- *Upgrade memory.* The easiest and most effective way to improve performance of a personal computer is to increase RAM. Modern PCs operate reasonably well at 256 MB; however, increasing RAM to 512 MB or more has a tremendous impact on overall performance, as much as 50%, depending on your mix of applications.
- *Buy the three-year warranty.* This is the best deal of all the manufacturers' options at the time of purchase, especially for notebooks. It gives you piece of mind that you have somewhere to go when something goes wrong or you need some answers—and, there is a good chance that it will and you will.
- *Upgrade the size/type of the monitor.* The standard off-the-shelf PC system normally comes with a manufacturers-grade CRT monitor (15 to 17 inches). These are of acceptable quality for home use and should outlast the other PC components. However, with so much of what we do being presented as multimedia, a 19-inch or bigger monitor will enhance your personal computing adventure. Expect to pay about $100 per extra inch for a CRT-style monitor. An alternative to the CRT monitor is the space-saving, flat-panel LCD monitor. Although the price of flat-panel LCD monitors is dropping, you can expect to pay a premium for LCD monitors— especially the larger ones (19 inches and up).
- *Upgrade the speaker system.* For $30 to $90 extra, you can have a speaker system with surround sound and a floor-shaking subwoofer that will make those DVD movies, MP3 downloads, and games come alive with sound. If you choose top-of-the-line speakers, you may need to upgrade the *sound card,* as well.
- *Upgrade the keyboard and mouse.* For about $30 to $60 extra, you can get an enhanced keyboard and an ergonomically designed mouse that will last the useful life of the system (which may not be the case with the standard devices). Wireless versions of these devices let you interact with your computer from anywhere near the PC.
- *Upgrade the hard disk capacity.* You can never have enough hard disk space, especially if you have gamers in the house and/or you plan to store digital images and videos on the PC. Generally, choose a hard disk that is at least one step above the hard disk bundled with the standard sweet spot system.
- *Choose the de facto standard office suite.* Given a choice between Microsoft Office and some other office suite, choose the home or small business version of Microsoft Office. The applications in the Microsoft Office suite are taught in virtually all schools at all levels and this suite is the de facto standard in business and government. If you work at home, consider the professional version.
- *Upgrade the CD-ROM/DVD option.* If the sweet spot system is not configured with a rewritable option, CD-RW and/or DVD+RW, you should consider choosing a combination drive (DVD/CD-RW) or choosing one of the rewritable options for the second drive bay, which is normally empty. If you plan on creating and copying custom CDs, having a CD-ROM drive and a separate drive for rewritable media is handy. Also, having a rewritable disc drive facilitates important backup duties.
- *Upgrade the video card.* The interface between the processor and the monitor is the video card. Any modern video card will handle the display tasks for a typical user; however, if you expect to be involved with sophisticated multimedia applications and/or serious gaming, you should consider upgrading to a high-quality video card with at least 64 MB of VRAM.
- *All-in-one multifunction peripheral: print, scan, fax, and copy.* An all-in-one multifunction peripheral (see Figure 7-21) capable of handling all print, scan, fax, and copy functions rounds out any PC system. Purchasing individual devices to achieve this level of functionality could cost up to $1000. A quality multifunction peripheral can be purchased for 25% of that amount. You can live a long and healthy life without sending/receiving another fax, but we now live in a multimedia world where printing and scanning high-resolution images is commonplace. Plus, the duplication capability comes in handy.
- *HPNA adapter.* For an extra $20 or so, you can add a home networking HPNA adapter PCI card to your system. This relatively inexpensive upgrade makes your new PC ready for phoneline home networking if and when you need it.

Figure 7-21 — THE ALL-IN-ONE MULTIFUNCTION PERIPHERAL
This telecommuter configured his tower PC with a multifunction peripheral that is a printer, fax machine, a copier, and a scanner—all in one device. Multifunction printers are ideal for the home or small offices where volume for any single function is low.

Photo courtesy of Hewlett-Packard Company

These are the essential upgrades and/or choices you might wish to consider. Everything else, such as game pads, digital cameras, extra USB ports, software, and so on can be purchased later as your personal computing needs come into focus.

The Performance PC

If you are in the market for a performance PC, you are flushed with a surplus of discretionary funds or you are a power user with special processing needs. Those special needs might include, but are not limited to, video editing, computer-aided design (CAD), Web design, software development, IT writing/publishing, and graphics/illustration.

The performance PC represents leading-edge technology and, in contrast to the entry-level system, the key descriptors are more, faster, greater, and newer. The performance PC will have every kind of port, and plenty of them. It will have a DVD+RW drive and, perhaps, 1 to 2 GB of RAM. It will have at least one state-of-the-art processor. The performance PC is feature rich, with high-end video and sound cards that could add as much as $700 to the price of the system. The system might be configured with a video editing package that would include a video capture card and related software. The system unit would include an enhanced power unit and extra fans for cooling the many heat-producing components.

People who buy performance PCs are veteran PC users who have collaborated on the purchase of many PCs in the past. They already are aware of the considerations presented in this buyer's guide.

WHAT SPECIAL HARDWARE DO YOU NEED FOR INTERNET ACCESS AND HOME NETWORKING?

Your personal computer can be linked to the rest of the world through the Internet or to the other PCs at your house via home networking.

Internet Access

Internet access falls into two categories, *dialup access* and *broadband access*. You pay a little more for broadband, which can be up to 50 times faster than the traditional dialup access.

Dialup Internet Access
The dialup, 56 K bps data/voice/fax modem is installed in virtually all new PCs. Keep this relatively inexpensive (about $20) option because, eventually, you may need it for data, voice, or fax communications.

Broadband Internet Access
The difference between dialup and broadband access is stark: dial-up is a lot of click and wait where broadband displays Web pages in seconds or fractions of seconds. *Cable* (via cable modems), *DSL*, and *satellite* are the leading broadband technologies for home Internet access.

Depending on which service you choose, you will need a cable modem, a DSL modem, or a satellite modem, but, normally, you purchase the broadband modem when you subscribe to the service, not when you purchase your PC. Sometimes the modem is included with the subscription fee and, sometimes, you must buy it. In any case, it's always a good idea to use the modem suggested by the broadband service provider.

Home Networking

The spread of PCs throughout the house has prompted the growth of home networking (see Figure 7-22). Two special types of network interface cards (NICs) allow families to link all their PCs using ordinary phone lines or wireless communications for simultaneous Internet access, printer and file sharing, and multiplayer gaming.

Figure 7–22 — HOME NETWORKING
These two teenager PCs are on a phone-line home network with mom's PC, which has the printer, and dad's PC, which has the scanner. The router (on top of the system unit in the inset) enables sharing of the DSL broadband signal via the phone-line network. All PCs have HPNA phone-line adapters, two external (to the left of the monitor) and two internal.

To set up a home network you need the software, which is built into all Windows operating systems, and you need a home networking NIC, an *HPNA adapter*, installed on each PC on the network (about $20 each). The adapter can be installed internally or be connected via USB externally. HPNA adapters can be selected as an option at the time you purchase your PC or they can be purchased and easily installed at a later date.

FACTORS TO CONSIDER WHEN BUYING A PC

It's easy to overlook important considerations that could influence your decisions. This summary offers insight that can help you avoid some of the problems incurred by other PC buyers.

What Software is Preinstalled on the PC?

Arguably, the most challenging aspect of choosing between alternative PCs is appraising the worth of the software preinstalled with the system and integrating that assessment into the overall evaluation of the PC system. And, that's the way PC vendors meant it to be. They want the quality or variety of their software bundle(s) to either confuse the buyer or be the difference maker, depending on the quality of their offerings.

If the PC purchase decision was based solely on hardware, we could compare oranges with oranges—but it's not. When you bundle software into the PC purchase price, and all vendors do this, it's more like comparing oranges to grapefruit.

The bundled software frequently is the biggest variable in the PC purchase decision process. What software PC vendors choose to offer with their systems can be substantially different between competitors and even within their own line of PCs.

The Operating System

Every new PC is sold with an operating system, typically the latest version of *Microsoft Windows,* either the *Home Edition* or the *Professional Edition.* The Home Edition is sufficient for 95% of the home computers. The Professional Edition has a few security and networking features that might be reason enough for the telecommuter to pay extra for this advanced version of Windows.

The Software Suite

A software suite is bundled with all but the very low-end PCs and some promotional PCs. Most new personal computers are bundled with *Microsoft Office XP Standard* (also called *Office XP Small Business*), *Microsoft Office XP Professional,* or *Microsoft Works Suite.* Occasionally, a vendor will offer an alternative suite, such as the *WordPerfect Suite,* which continues to be popular in the legal field.

If Microsoft Works is the default software bundle for a particular system, you can expect to pay about $100 to upgrade to the industry standard Microsoft Office suite. If you are buying an off-the-shelf PC with Works already installed, the upgrade to Office XP may not be an option.

These software suites may or may not be accompanied by other software or service incentives. For example, additional software preinstalled with Microsoft Office XP might include antivirus software, a personal finance package, or perhaps an online encyclopedia.

Optional Software Bundles

When you purchase a PC online or via mail order, major direct marketer manufacturers will give you an opportunity to order additional software. These offerings are in two main categories: *individual software packages* and *optional bundles* (topical groups of three or four software packages).

Generally, any of the individual software packages can be purchased online or at retail outlets at the PC vendor's offering price or for a few dollars less. Don't feel as if you need to make a decision now on these individual software packages, unless antivirus software is not included with the price of the PC. If this is the case and the vendor offers a quality antivirus package, you should purchase it with the system.

Quality of Hardware/Software Support Services

PC hardware is very reliable and routinely operates continuously without incident for years. Even with a history of reliability, the possibility exists that one or several of the components eventually will fail and have to be repaired. Most retailers or direct-marketer vendors will offer a variety of hardware service contracts from same-day, on-site repairs that cover all parts and service to a carry-in (or mail-in) service that does not include parts and can take several weeks.

Since hardware support services vary within and between vendors, you should look over the options carefully and choose the one right for your circumstances. It's important that you understand *exactly* what you must do to get your system repaired. As a rule of thumb, choose at least some level of repair service for the effective life of your system (about 3 years).

WHERE TO BUY HARDWARE/SOFTWARE?

PCs and associated hardware and software can be purchased at thousands of convenient bricks-and-mortar locations and from hundreds of retail sites on the Internet.

Bricks-and-Mortar Computer Retailers with Authorized Service Centers

Several national retail chains and many regional chains specialize in the sale of PC hardware and/or software. Also, there are thousands of computer stores with no chain affiliation. Most market and service a variety of PC systems. Some make their own line of computers and are happy to custom-build one for you. Find these dealers under "Computer and Equipment Dealers" in the Yellow Pages.

Bricks-and-Mortar Computer Retailers without Authorized Service Centers

Computer/electronics departments of most department stores, discount warehouse stores, and office supply stores sell PCs and PC software. For the most part, these stores treat computers as they would any consumer item. When you walk out the door, you are covered by the manufacturer's warranty. For this category of retailers, what you see on the shelf is what you get. Any further technical support comes from the hardware and software manufacturers within the limits of their warranties. These are prepackaged systems and the retailer has relatively little flexibility in system configuration because they do not have a service center.

Direct Marketers

Most major manufacturers of PC hardware (Dell, Gateway, Hewlett-Packard, IBM, and so on) and most major software companies (Microsoft, Symantec, Broderbund, and so on) are direct marketers; that is, they sell directly to the customer. The direct marketer's "store window" is a site on the Internet (see Figure 7-23). Orders can be entered via the Internet, telephone, fax, or mail. The trend is toward entering orders interactively via the Internet. The direct marketer makes and sends the requested product(s) to the customer within a few days. Direct marketers offer an array of popular PC software and accessories.

The strength of the direct marketer's sales program is online sales via the Internet. Once you decide which PC system you want, you can *customize,* or *configure,* it to pick exactly the options you want on your PC system.

Buying directly from the manufacturer via the Internet has many advantages. The manufacturers' Web sites are comprehensive in that they present all conceivable options, plus they provide enough information to answer any questions you might have.

Retailers of Preowned and Refurbished Computers

The used-computer retailer was as inevitable as the used-car dealer was. A computer that is no longer powerful enough for one user may have more than enough power for

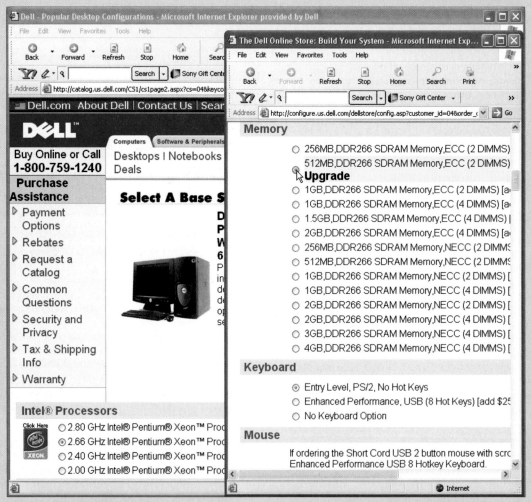

Figure 7–23 — BUYING DIRECT
Dell Computer Corporation is a direct marketer with a Web site that provides detailed information about any available system. The customer can go to the Dell Web site to customize and purchase a system entirely online. In this example, the customer is given an opportunity to choose from 14 RAM options up to 4 GB and from two keyboards.

another. Used-computer retailers are easy to find: just look under "Computer and Equipment Dealers—Used" in the Yellow Pages.

Most major computer manufacturers also sell used computers, called *refurbished* or *remanufactured computers*. Typically, such systems are current models and were used only for a few days or weeks. For whatever reason, these systems were returned to the manufacturer. The problem components were replaced, probably with refurbished components, and the system was offered for sale via the company's Web site at a 10 to 15% discount off the price of the new system. The warranty remains the same.

Online Auctions

A great source for anything used is an online auction. PCs and electronics are among the most popular items up for auction on the Internet. Online auctions go on 24 hours a day with people all over the world registering bids on millions of items. The typical PC system put up for auction on eBay at *www.ebay.com* is 3 to 5 years off the technology and goes for $50 to $250. Avoid bidding on any system that is deinstalled because it offers no software.

WHICH PC MANUFACTURER IS BEST FOR YOU?

All big-name manufacturers, such as Dell, Hewlett-Packard, Compaq (now part of Hewlett-Packard), Gateway, IBM, and Apple, produce quality personal computers that can be expected to last well beyond their useful life. Surprisingly, however, these big-name manufacturers account for a less than half of personal computer sales.

The bulk of PC sales are by small "white box" PC vendors. Many small PC companies have emerged that custom-build and sell "no-name" PCs to school districts, city governments, small companies, and individuals. Some of these small players are excellent and have a solid record of providing good service, price, and flexibility. White box vendors typically sell for less than mainstream manufacturers. To do so, however, they may use components of lesser quality, reduced motherboard features, and/or components that may be off the technology.

Ultimately, the answer to the question "Which PC manufacturer is best for you?" is the manufacturer that offers systems that provide the best match for your personal computing needs and your personal bank account.

THE TOTAL COST OF OWNERSHIP

The spending on personal computing continues once you have paid for and installed the hardware and software. As soon as you get your PC system, you will want to stock up on supplies, subscribe to vital services, and purchase important accessories. Invariably, you will want to build your software portfolio (see Figure 7-24). Most personal computing consumables are associated with the printer and interchangeable disk drives (Zip disks, CD-R, DVD+RW discs, and other storage media). These considerations bring us to an important concept in personal computing—the *total cost of ownership.*

Figure 7–24 — THE SOFTWARE PORTFOLIO This mix of software, which includes a smattering of utility, applications, and games software, might be considered typical for a home office software portfolio. The retail cost of the software shown here is over $2000.

The amount shown on the price tag for a PC system is in no way representative of what you must pay to get into the personal computing business. That price tag doesn't include a printer. The cost of a printer seldom includes a cable, another expense. Of course, you will want paper on which to print, probably two or three different qualities and in several shades. Printer cartridges can cost $40 or more.

It's easy for a teenager to spend $500 a year on gaming hardware and software. You'll need a place to put the PC and a comfortable chair. Access to the Internet will cost you from $20 to $60 a month. And the costs go on and on. If you have a spending limit, consider the estimated incidental costs shown in Figure 7-25.

FIGURE 7–25 ONE-TIME AND ANNUAL INCIDENTAL EXPENSES FOR PERSONAL COMPUTING
The personal computing cost ranges listed are for a first-time user. The low end of
the ranges is representative for casual home users and the high end of the ranges is
applicable to sophisticated users with home offices.

	One-Time Cost	Annual Cost
Software	$100–$1500	$100–$800
Cables	$0–$50	
Supplies (printer cartridges, plain paper, photo paper, diskettes, Zip disks, CD-RW and/or DVD+RW discs, and DVD/CD-R blanks, and so on)	$100–$200	$100–$500
Internet service provider (ISP) and/or Information service	$0–$500 (one-time ISP costs are setup and installation fees plus equipment cost [modem, router, satellite dish, and so on] for broadband service)	$250–$800 (includes basic Internet service; the high-side expense is for broadband service)
Subscriptions (technology magazines, virus protection service, online databases, and so on)		$0–$200
UPS (uninterruptible power source) or Surge Protector	$40–$300	$0–$100 (UPS battery replacement)
Additional data telephone line (optional)	$0–$50	$0–$350
Furniture and Accessories (desk, chair, lights, mouse pad, and so on)	$30–$500	$50–$150
System Maintenance (this amount is nothing until the warranty runs out)		$0–$300
Insurance		$0–$100
Miscellaneous, including accessories (USB 2.0 hub, new game pad, and so on)		$0–$300
TOTAL ESTIMATED INCIDENTAL EXPENSES	$270–$3100	$500–$3600

SECTION SELF-CHECK

1. As a rule, you should purchase as much power and functionality in a PC system as your budget will permit. (T/F)

2. The choice between a desktop PC and a notebook PC usually hinges between the need for portability and styling. (T/F)

3. An entry-level PC has components that are no more than six months off the technology. (T/F)

4. The surge protector is designed to provide protection from lightning hits. (T/F)

5. Hardware upgrades are not advised for sweet spot PC systems. (T/F)

6. As a rule of thumb, choose at least some level of repair service for the effective life of your new PC system. (T/F)

7. The all-in-one peripheral device does all but which of the following document tasks: (a) fax, (b) print, (c) scan, or (d) shred?

8. Which device would you expect to be the most costly: (a) game pad, (b) scanner, (c) Web camera, or (d) headset with a mike?

9. Which of these devices is required for phoneline home networking: (a) multifunction peripheral device, (b) 1394 ports, (c) surge protector, or (d) HPNA adapters?

10. Although direct marketers offer customers a variety of ways to enter their PC orders, the trend is toward entering orders via: (a) telephone, (b) the Internet, (c) fax, or (d) snail mail.

11. The total cost of ownership of a PC encompasses all but which of the following: (a) opportunity costs, (b) PC purchase price, (c) ISP charges, or (d) printer supplies?

chapter 8

Learning Objectives

Once you have read and studied this chapter, you will have learned:

- To place society's dependence on computers in its proper perspective (Section 8-1).

- Key ergonomic and environmental concerns that should be considered in the design of your workplace (Section 8-2).

- Considerations critical to evaluating important ethical questions in the use of information technology (Section 8-3).

- The types and scope of computer and IT crime (Section 8-4).

- The points of security vulnerability for a computer center, an information system, and a PC (Section 8-5).

IT ETHICS AND HEALTHY COMPUTING

Why this chapter is important to you

Information technology is not all bits, bytes, and procedures. The IT revolution continually raises difficult questions that beg for answers and serious issues that must be resolved.

How we fare as a society depends on how we cope with a continuous stream of information technology issues. Just about any IT issue is fuzzy, and there are few historical individual, corporate, or national perspectives from which to derive a solution. Frequently, we must address these issues as they surface to determine what course of action to take. This chapter should help you make better decisions on the critical IT issues of the day and make you more sensitive to ethical concerns.

Eventually, we probably will wear our computer systems, but until then, you will spend much of your day an arm's length from your PC. Reading this chapter will give you a better understanding of the ergonomics (human-machine interaction) of computing and help you build a healthy workplace and avoid some of the health problems associated with the computing environment.

Trillions of bytes of information travel over millions of miles of wires and through the air from computer to computer. This information, which often is sensitive in nature, eventually resides on magnetic storage devices. Whether traveling at the speed of light or spinning on a disk, this information is vulnerable to theft and/or abuse. This chapter will help you to understand better what can be done to minimize the exposure of information and computer systems to the criminal elements of our society.

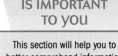
8-1 The Information Technology Paradox

We as a society are caught in an information technology paradox: Information technology is thriving in a society that may not be ready for it.

ARE WE READY FOR INFORMATION TECHNOLOGY?

One in every seven VCRs blinks "12:00" because its owner is unable to set the clock. Less than 20% of the working population can claim information technology competency. Many college curricula do not require courses on computers or IT. Corporate executives are seriously concerned that the skill level of workers is not keeping pace with the technology. Worse, millions of workers may not have the foundational skills needed for retraining. Executives throughout the country are concerned about spending money on remedial training just to get their employees to the point that they can give them information technology-related job training. To better prepare the workforce for the explosion of information technology applications (see Figure 8-1), we may need to revise curricula and raise standards at all levels of education.

DO WE REALLY WANT INFORMATION TECHNOLOGY?

Some of us want to wrap ourselves in information technology. Some of us want nothing to do with it. Most of us want it, but in moderation. This reluctant acceptance of information technology has resulted in many IT-based opportunities being overlooked or ignored. For whatever reasons, business, government, and education have elected not to implement computer applications that are well within the state of the art of computer technology. Literally thousands of money-saving IT-based systems are working in the laboratory and, on a small scale, in practice. However, society's pace of IT acceptance has placed such applications on the back burner. A few examples follow.

Smart houses feature computer-controlled lighting, temperature, and security systems. Such systems start the coffeemaker so we can awaken to the aroma of freshly brewed coffee. They even help with paying the utility bills and provide perimeter security. This technology is available today and is relatively inexpensive if properly designed and installed during construction. In any case, such a system would pay for itself in a few years through energy savings alone. Generally, neither those in the construction industry nor potential buyers are ready for smart houses, even though they offer tremendous benefits and are cost effective.

Although sophisticated computer-controlled medical equipment is used routinely in health care, relatively few physicians take advantage of the information-producing potential of the computer to improve patient care. There are expert systems that can help them diagnose diseases, drug-interaction databases that can help them prescribe the right drug, computer-assisted searches that can call up literature pertinent to a particular patient's illness, and online forums through which they can solve health problems and share ideas. Large groups of physicians are not ready for the age of information, even though these applications have the potential for saving lives.

On a larger scale, society continues to rebuke the concept of a cashless society. A cashless society is technologically and economically possible. In a cashless society, the amount of a purchase is transferred automatically from the purchaser's bank account to the vendor's bank account. Thus, billing, payment, and collection problems are eliminated, along with the need to write checks and to remember to mail them. Properly implemented, a cashless society will result in substantial savings for all concerned—government, business, and individuals. We are on a journey to a cashless society and already are 90% there. The remainder of the journey will take a few years because too many of us still like the jingle in our pockets.

Why have these cost-effective and potentially beneficial computer applications not been implemented? Among the reasons are historical momentum, resistance to change, limited education, and lack of available resources. In the case of domestic-control systems, it is probably a matter of education, both of the builder and the homeowner. In the case of computer diagnosis of illness, some physicians are reluctant to admit that the computer is a valuable diagnostic aid, and IT is a void in medical school curricula. In the case of the cashless society, concerns about invasion of privacy are yet to be resolved.

These and thousands of other "oversights" will not be implemented until enough people have enough knowledge to appreciate their potential. This is where you come in!

REACHING THE POINT OF NO RETURN

Albert Einstein said that "concern for man himself and his fate must always form the chief interest of all technical endeavors." Some people believe that a rapidly advancing information technology exhibits little regard for "man himself and his fate." They contend that computers are overused, mis-

THE CRYSTAL BALL:
Centralized Online Placement Services for College Graduates For decades, face-to-face on-campus interviews have defined the student recruitment process. Many students still find jobs through this traditional approach to placement services; however, within a few years we can expect a single, mature one-stop Web site to emerge that will be sensitive to the privacy of student information. Today, students may send hundreds of printed resumes only to be filtered by employers with a one-criterion glance. The one-stop site offers a more efficient approach. It will allow students to post comprehensive resumes that would allow interested employers to drill down for more information. Employers would have a new level of filter options.

FIGURE 8–1   OUR DEPENDENCE ON COMPUTERS

HERTZ'S NEVERLOST® SYSTEM

Many travelers are beginning to depend on Hertz's NeverLost® onboard navigation system. The system gives drivers turn-by-turn driving directions to almost any destination via an in-car, video screen and/or voice prompts. At the heart of the NeverLost system is a GPS receiver, used to calculate the exact location of the car based upon signals from orbiting satellites, a computer map, and a database that directs the traveler to his or her designated destination.

©2000 Hertz System, Inc. Hertz is a registered service mark and trademark of Hertz Systems, Inc.

PERSONAL COMPUTING AND HOME NETWORKING

The spread of personal computing and home networking has prompted further dependence on our computers for many of life's little chores, including help with homework, real-time stock quotes, personal finances, shopping, personal interactions around town and around the world, and a thousand other tasks.

Photo courtesy of Intel Corporation

CRUISE SHIP SYSTEMS

Professionals in all endeavors continue to include greater use of technology in their jobs. Crew members on-board the "Radiance of the Seas" of the Royal Caribbean Cruise Lines have in-cabin access on to the Internet and productivity applications, including the CrewNection service which links the ship's crew and integrates the services database and processing.

Courtesy of International Business Machines Corporation. Unauthorized use not permitted.

used, and generally detrimental to society. This group argues that the computer is dehumanizing and is slowly forcing society into a pattern of mass conformity. To be sure, the age of information is presenting society with difficult and complex problems; but they can be overcome.

Information technology (IT) has enhanced our lifestyles to the point that most of us take it for granted. There is nothing wrong with this attitude, but we must recognize that society has made a real commitment to computers. Whether it is good or bad, society has reached the point of no return in its dependence on IT, including a growing dependence on the Internet. Competition demands a continued and growing use of IT. On the more personal level, we are reluctant to forfeit the everyday conveniences made possible by IT. For example, our PCs and the conveniences of the Internet are now an integral part of our daily activities.

Society's dependence on computers is not always apparent. For example, today's automobile assembly line is as computer dependent as it is people dependent: An inventory-management system makes sure that parts are delivered to the right assembly point at the right time; computer-controlled robots do the welding and painting; and a process-control computer controls the movement of the assembly line.

Turn off the computer system for a day in almost any company and observe the consequences. Most companies would cease to function. Within minutes, we would be without gas, electricity, water, radio, TV, or any modern means of communication. The world's financial institutions would fall into disarray.

Turn off a computer system in a business for several days and there is a good chance that the company would cease to exist. It is estimated that a large bank would be out of business in two days if its computer systems were down. A distribution company would last three days, a manufacturing company would last five days, and an insurance company would last six days. In fact, the probability of a victim company's long-term survival would be low if it were unable to recover critical operations within 30 hours. Recognizing their dependence on computers, most companies have made their systems fault-tolerant or have made contingency plans to follow in case of disaster.

Dependence on IT is not necessarily bad as long as we keep it in perspective. However, we can't passively assume that information technology will continue to enhance the quality of our lives. It is our obligation to learn to understand computers so that we can better direct their application for society's benefit. Only through understanding can we control the misuse of information technology. As a society we have a responsibility to weigh the benefits, burdens, and consequences of each successive level of automation.

WHY THIS SECTION IS IMPORTANT TO YOU

The information in this section should help you to be comfortable in and to remain healthy at your workplace.

8-2 The Workplace

Our workplace is changing because we are attuned more to considerations involving human safety and comfort, and we are more sensitive to the growing importance of *green computing*.

ERGONOMICS AND WORKPLACE DESIGN

For close to a hundred years, the design of automobiles was driven by two basic considerations: appearance and functionality. Engineers were asked to design cars that were visually appealing and could go from point A to point B. Surprisingly little attention was given to the human factor. That is, no one considered the connection between the driver and passengers and the automobile. About 25 years ago, automobile executives discovered that they could boost sales and enhance functionality by improving this human connection. Thus began the era of ergonomically designed automobiles. Today, human factors engineers apply the principles of ergonomic design to ensure that the interface between people and cars is *safe, comfortable, effective,* and *efficient.*

Ergonomics is the study of the relationships between people and the things we use. The emergence of ergonomics is beginning to have an impact on the relationship between knowledge workers and their workplaces. Computers are still relatively new in the workplace, and ergonomics has only recently emerged as an important consideration in fitting computers into workplace design (see Figure 8-2).

FIGURE 8–2 HARDWARE FOR THE ERGONOMICALLY DESIGNED WORKPLACE

THE IN-AIR MOUSE

Ultra Mouse is a wireless mouse that employs gyroscopic, motion-sensing technology such that it can be used on and away from the desktop. The Ultra Mouse's gyroscope lets you use intuitive in-air gestures to control the movement of the mouse pointer. With the in-air mouse, you can have frequent changes in postures, thus reducing some of the uncomfortable symptoms associated with repetitive motion.

Courtesy of Gyration, Inc.

HANDS FREE MOUSE

NaturalPoint™ Smart-Nav™ mouse alternative products give you hands free control of a computer cursor. The ergonomic Smart-Nav™ provides precise cursor control through simple head movement allowing your hands to remain on your keyboard, or at your side. The user positions a reflective dot on his/her forehead, glasses, or microphone and an infrared camera tracks its motion to move the cursor.

Courtesy of Natural Point

FACTORY MICE

This ITAC Systems Mouse-Track is a mouse alternative, ergonomically designed for use in extremely harsh environments. The dust-resistant dome encoder lets you point with your index finger, not your elbow or thumb, thus reducing the risk of carpal tunnel syndrome.

Courtesy of ITAC Systems, Inc.

STRESS RELIEVER

The repetitive-stress injuries (RSIs) associated with the keyboard may be eliminated at some time in the future as more people move to speech-recognition technology to interact with their PCs. This executive dictates directly to a computer system using speech-recognition software.

Courtesy of International Business Machines Corporation. Unauthorized use not permitted.

USING THE FEET FOR INPUT

Give your hands a rest with a programmable Foot Switch. This Foot Switch adds input versatility with a three-button keyboard for your feet.

Use Courtesy Kinesis® Corporation, Bothell, WA

CONTOURED KEYBOARD

This contoured keyboard is designed to fit the shape and movements of the human body. The design puts less stress and strain on muscles, reducing the user's risk for fatigue in hands, wrists, and arms.

Courtesy of Kinesis Corporation

REASONS FOR CONCERN

During the 1980s, the knowledge worker's workplace gained attention when workers began to blame headaches, depression, anxiety, nausea, fatigue, and irritability on prolonged interaction with a terminal or PC. These and other problems often associated with extended use of a terminal or PC are called **video operator's distress syndrome**, or **VODS.** Although there was little evidence to link these problems directly with using terminals or PCs (the same problems occurred in other work environments), VODS caused people to take a closer look at the workplace and the types of injuries being reported. As the number of *repetitive-stress injuries* (*RSIs*) increased for knowledge workers, workstation ergonomics became an increasingly important issue for corporate productivity.

A poorly designed workplace has the potential to cause **cumulative trauma disorder** (**CTD**), a condition that can lead to a permanent disability of motor skills. CTD now accounts for more than half of all work-related problems. It typically occurs when people ignore human factors considerations while spending significant time at the keyboard. Other workstation-related injuries include mental stress, eyestrain, headaches, muscular injuries, and skeletal injuries. Hand and wrist problems associated with keyboarding have always been the main complaint, with the repetitive-stress injury called **carpal tunnel syndrome** (**CTS**) being the most common. A few years ago, the options for reducing keystrokes were few. Today, we speak to our computers via speech-recognition software with accuracy rates in excess of 95%, thus substantially reducing keystrokes and, in some situations, eliminating keystrokes altogether.

Talk about the radiation emitted by CRT-type monitors has unduly frightened office workers. A controversial, and apparently flawed, study in the late 1980s concluded that women who are exposed to the radiation emitted from terminals and PCs may have a higher rate of miscarriage than those who are not. A comprehensive four-year federal government study concluded that women who work with terminals and PCs and those who do not have the same rate of miscarriage.

WORKPLACE DESIGN

Proper workplace design, whether on the factory floor or in the office, is good business. Any good manager knows that a healthy, happy worker is a more productive worker. A good manager also knows that the leading causes of lost work time are back/shoulder/neck pain and CTD.

The key to designing a proper workplace for the knowledge worker is *flexibility*. The knowledge worker's workplace should be designed with enough flexibility to enable it to be custom-fitted to its worker. Figure 8-3 highlights important considerations in workplace design. Ergonomic problems in the workplace are being addressed in legislation and in proposed regulations from the Occupational Safety and Health Administration (OSHA).

Attention to the overall environment can reduce stress and increase worker performance. For example, indirect lighting can reduce glare. Proper ventilation eliminates health concerns caused by the ozone emitted by laser printers. Excessive exposure to ozone can cause headaches and nausea.

One of the most important factors in ergonomic programs is employee training. Workers should be shown how to analyze their workstations and make necessary adjustments (such as lowering monitor contrast and brightness or increasing chair lumbar support). Each knowledge worker can then contribute to the quality of his or her workplace by following a couple of simple rules. First, make the adjustments necessary to custom-fit your workplace. Second, take periodic minibreaks. These minibreaks should involve looking away from your monitor and/or generally altering your body orientation for a few seconds (make a fist, turn your head from side to side, roll your shoulders, walk around your desk, wiggle your toes, wrinkle your nose, twirl your arms, and so on).

WORKING SMART

Information technology has proven many times over that it can play a role in improving personal productivity and overall office efficiency. If abused, however, information technology, especially relating to the PC and the Internet, can have the opposite effect. These are common abuses that, if eliminated, can make a positive contribution to workplace efficiency.

- *Sending and receiving frivolous e-mail.* Most organizations tolerate an appropriate amount of personal e-mail, just as they do personal telephone calls. But, there is a limit. Nonessential e-mail, live chat, and instant messaging cause breaks in work momentum resulting in reductions in efficiency of as much as 50%. Of course, knowledge workers should resist the urge to subscribe to nonbusiness-related mailing lists (joke of the day, bizarre news, and so on).

FIGURE 8–3

ERGONOMIC CONSIDERATIONS IN WORKPLACE DESIGN
Knowledge workers often spend four or more hours each day at a PC or terminal. Today workers are more sensitive to the impact of workplace design on their health and effectiveness, so they are paying more attention to the ergonomics (efficiency of the person-machine interface) of the hardware, including chairs and desks.

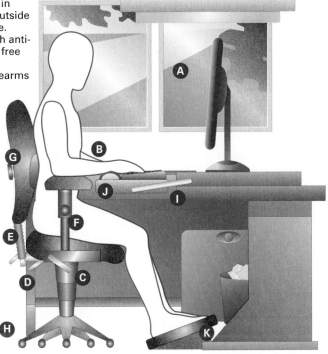

The Hardware
Monitor location (A). The monitor should be located directly in front of you at arm's length with the top at forehand level. Outside windows should be to the side of the monitor to reduce glare. *Monitor features.* The monitor should be high-resolution with anti-glare screens. *Monitor maintenance.* The monitor should be free from smudges or dust buildup. *Keyboard location (B).* The keyboard should be located such that the upper arm and forearms are at a 90-degree angle. *Keyboard features.* The keyboard should be ergonomically designed to accommodate better the movements of the fingers, hands, and arms.

The Chair
The chair should be fully adjustable to the size and contour of the body. Features should include: *Pneumatic seat height adjustment (C); Seat and back angle adjustment (D); Back-rest height adjustment (E); Recessed armrests with height adjustment (F); Lumbar support adjustment (for lower back support) (G); Five-leg pedestal on casters (H).*

The Desk
The swing space. Use wraparound workspace to keep the PC, important office materials, and files within 18 inches of the chair. *Adjustable tray for keyboard and mouse (I):* The tray should have height and swivel adjustments.

The Room
Freedom of movement. The work area should permit freedom of movement and ample leg room. *Lighting.* Lighting should be positioned to minimize glare on the monitor and printed materials.

Other Equipment
Wrist rest (J). The wrist rest is used in conjunction with adjustable armrests to keep arms in a neutral straight position at the keyboard. *Footrest (K).* The adjustable footrest takes pressure off the lower back while encouraging proper posture.

- *Engaging in nonbusiness Internet browsing.* With all the resources of the Internet at our fingertips it is easy to seek out reviews of the latest movies, determine the book value of your old car, or check out the statistics from last night's game. Some companies have adopted zero-tolerance policies while others are struggling with ways to control nonbusiness cybersurfing.

- *Gaming on company time.* Personal computing offers plenty of opportunities to play games. Operating systems are even distributed with games. Hundreds of games are available for download. It is easy to join a multiplayer game on the Internet. You can play games of chance. Most corporations frown on employees doing gaming on company time.

- *Toying with the technology.* The typical user exploits less than 20% of a software package's features. Some people view software as a toy and are carried away with all of the interesting features. They learn about and integrate sophisticated features into their projects even though all of the extra effort does little or nothing to enhance the end result. This type of technological overkill wastes time.

The PC can be an invaluable tool in the workplace or it can be a serious diversion. Those who make good use of IT and do not abuse information technology tend to realize career goals more quickly.

GREEN COMPUTING

The dawning of the age of green computing is upon us. **Green computing** is merely environmentally sensible computing. Computers drain critical resources such as electricity and paper. They also produce unwanted electrical, chemical, and bulk-waste side effects. As a society, we finally are adopting a more environmentally sound position with respect to the use and manufacture of computing hardware.

Saving Energy and Trees

United States government agencies and many businesses have adopted policies that require that all new PCs, monitors, and printers must comply with the Environmental Protection Agency's *Energy Star* guidelines. To comply with Energy Star requirements, monitors and processors in standby mode (not in use) can consume no more than 30 watts of power. Printers are permitted a range of 30 to 45 watts. Computer manufacturers have been moving toward more energy-efficient products in hopes of reducing manufacturing costs and increasing product competitiveness.

It costs about $250 a year to keep a PC and laser page printer running 24 hours a day. We could save a lot of money and fossil fuel if we turn off our PCs and peripheral devices or place them in energy-saving standby mode when not in use. Judicious computing can even save trees—why print a letter or send a fax when e-mail is faster and better for the environment? Green computing means printing only what needs to be printed, saving the paper for more meaningful applications.

Other recommendations by green computing proponents include buying equipment from vendors who are manufacturing environmentally safe products, purchasing recycled paper, recycling paper and toner printer cartridges (which would probably end up in landfills), buying reconditioned components rather than new ones, recycling old PCs and printers, shopping electronically to save gas, and telecommuting at least once or twice a week.

What to Do with Old PCs?

Eventually every PC wears out or simply becomes obsolete. No level of maintenance, upgrading, or troubleshooting can save them. Within the next year, over 300 million computers will outlive their usefulness and have no market value. If these PCs were simply thrown out with the trash, they would contribute over 8 million tons of very unfriendly waste to landfills. A typical PC and its peripherals will contain mercury, cadmium, lead, and other toxic and bioaccumulative compounds. Any environmentalist can tell you that these elements and compounds can have a dramatic impact on ground, water, and air quality.

The average useful life is about three years for a business PC and about four years for a home PC. Currently, only about 20% of PCs and peripherals are recycled (see Figure 8-4), compared to 70% for major appliances, such as dishwashers and refrigerators. Clearly, we need to act more responsibly with PCs at the end of their lives.

At present, there is little or no economic incentive to recycle hardware. For most companies, it is less expensive and easier to throw old hardware in the dumpster (but only where it is legal to do so). Adopting a **product stewardship policy** is often the difference between practicing environmentally responsible recycling and having a dumpster full of potentially harmful electrical components. Consider this: a CRT monitor contains 2-plus pounds of lead to protect users from radiation.

The throwaway option, however, may disappear over the next few years as more states place PCs and their peripheral devices on their lists of hazardous materials. In some states, dumping old hardware already is illegal. Many states are requiring or will be requiring consumers to pay a disposal fee in advance when they purchase their PC systems. It is only a matter of time before each of us will have "cradle-to-grave" responsibility for PCs and computer hardware.

If you feel your system still has some useful life, consider giving it to an individual or to an organization, such as a nursery school, that needs it. However, keep this in mind: about 70% of all hardware donations are discarded. Literally, millions of people are looking for individuals and organizations that might want their old PCs and peripherals, so only give away systems that are no more than four or five years off the technology, fully functional, have a good mix of software, and are Internet ready. Realistically, the rest have little or no value.

A number of recycling companies and several major computer vendors, such as Intel and IBM, provide PC recycling services both to consumers and to businesses of all sizes. If your old PC system is a candidate for recycling, send your old system away for proper disposal. Expect to pay between $30 and $40 (including shipping) for this service.

FIGURE 8–4 Recycling Obsolete PCs
Most of the components in obsolete PCs can be recycled, including these plastic cases from old computers.

8-2.1 Attention to the overall workplace design can reduce stress and increase worker performance. (T/F)

8-2.2 Hardware manufacturers that comply with the Environmental Protection Agency's Energy Star guidelines sell only recycled PCs. (T/F)

8-2.3 Problems associated with extended use of a PC are collectively called: (a) VODS, (b) CTS, (c) CTD, or (d) SOV.

8-2.4 Environmentally sensible computing is called: (a) blue computing, (b) green computing, (c) yellow computing, or (d) red computing.

8-2.5 A typical PC contains all but which of the following: (a) potassium hydroxide, (b) cadmium, (c) mercury, or (d) lead?

8-3 Ethics in Information Technology

WHY THIS SECTION IS IMPORTANT TO YOU

IT ethics-conscientious people are more likely to protect personal privacy, honor copyright laws, report unethical activity, and generally do what is right when confronted with controversial situations relating to technology. The material in this section will prepare you to make good decisions regarding IT ethics and issues.

The computer revolution has generated intense controversy about IT ethics. Society continues to raise questions about what is and is not ethical with regard to IT activities. These ethics issues are so important to our society that IT ethics are being integrated into college curricula. Educators believe that if people are made aware of the consequences of their actions, then fewer people will be motivated to plant dangerous computer viruses, contaminate information systems with false information, post pornographic material to the Internet, or abuse the sanctity of intellectual property. Educators warn us of dire consequences should we fail to instill a sense of ethics in future generations. If ethical abuses are left unabated, all roads on the information superhighway will be toll roads for encrypted data; that is, only those who pay for the key to the encrypted information can view it. If this were to happen, we would become a more secretive society, far less willing to share accumulated knowledge.

AN IT CODE OF ETHICS

Most major IT professional societies have adopted a code of ethics. Their codes warn the members, who are mostly professionals in the information technology fields, that they can be expelled or censured if they violate them. Rarely, however, has any action been taken against delinquent members. Does this mean there are no violations? Of course not. A carefully drafted code of ethics provides some guidelines for conduct, but professional societies cannot be expected to police the misdeeds of their members. In many instances, however, a code violation is also a violation of the law.

A code of ethics provides direction for IT professionals and users so that they act responsibly in their application of information technology. The recently updated Association for Computing Machinery (ACM) Code of Conduct summarized in Figure 8-5 provides excellent guidelines for both knowledge workers and for computing and IT professionals. ACM is the largest professional society for computing and IT professionals.

If you follow the ACM code shown in Figure 8-5, it is unlikely that anyone will question your ethics. Nevertheless, well-meaning people routinely violate this simple code because they are unaware of the tremendous detrimental impact of their actions. With the speed and power of computers, a minor code infraction easily can be magnified to a costly catastrophe. For this reason, the use of computers in this electronic age is raising new ethical questions, the most visible of which are discussed in the following sections (see Figure 8-6).

THE PRIVACY OF PERSONAL INFORMATION

The issue with the greatest ethical overtones is the privacy of personal information. Some people fear that computer-based record keeping offers too much of an opportunity for the invasion of an individual's privacy.

Who Knows What about You?

Each day your name and personal information are passed from computer to computer. Depending on your level of activity, this could happen 100 or more times a day. Thousands of public- and private-sector organizations maintain data on individuals. The data collection begins before you are born and does not end until all your affairs are settled and those maintaining records on you are informed of your parting. Much of this personal data is collected without your consent and then is passed freely between organizations, again, without your consent.

THE CRYSTAL BALL:
Online Voting on the Horizon After the Florida election debacle, we are acutely aware that United States voting machines are antiquated. Similar punched-card technology was used in 1890 for taking the national census. It is now apparent that U.S. cities, counties, states, and the nation need a better way to elect candidates. Several major companies and consortiums claim that the U.S. could implement a standardized, federally supported online voting system that would be easier to use, more accessible, more accurate, far more reliable, verifiable, and more secure. Plus, the results would be posted internationally in real time. Other countries, including Brazil, and even states, including Arizona, have conducted online elections. You should be able to vote from your PC within this decade.

FIGURE 8–5

A CODE OF CONDUCT FOR KNOWLEDGE WORKERS AND IT PROFESSIONALS
The first two sections (shown here) of the Association for Computing Machinery (ACM) Code of Conduct are applicable to all knowledge workers and IT professionals. The full code and detailed explanations can be found at the ACM Web site at <http://acm.org>. The last two sections (not shown) deal with organizational leadership and code compliance.

---

1. General Moral Imperatives

1.1 Contribute to society and human well-being

1.2 Avoid harm to others

1.3 Be honest and trustworthy

1.4 Be fair and take action not to discriminate

1.5 Honor property rights including copyrights and patents

1.6 Give proper credit for intellectual property

1.7 Respect the privacy of others

1.8 Honor confidentiality

2. More Specific Professional Responsibilities

2.1 Strive to achieve the highest quality, effectiveness, and dignity in both the process and products of professional work

2.2 Acquire and maintain professional competence

2.3 Know and respect existing laws pertaining to professional work

2.4 Accept and provide appropriate professional review

2.5 Give comprehensive and thorough evaluations of computer systems and their impacts, including analysis of possible risks

2.6 Honor contracts, agreements, and assigned responsibilities

2.7 Improve public understanding of computing and its consequences

2.8 Access computing and communication resources only when authorized to do so

---

- *Tax data.* The Internal Revenue Service maintains the most visible stockpile of personal information. It, of course, keeps records of our whereabouts, earnings, taxes, deductions, employment, and so on. Now the IRS is supplementing basic tax information with external information to create personal profiles to tell if a person's tax return is consistent with his or her lifestyle. By law, all IRS data must be made available to about 40 different government agencies.

- *Education data.* What you have accomplished during your years in school, such as grades and awards, is recorded in computer-based databases. Included in these databases is a variety of information such as your scores on college entrance exams, data on loan applications that include details of your family's financial status, roommate preferences, disciplinary actions, and so on. In one instance, a Chicago woman was turned down for several government jobs because of a note her third-grade teacher had entered in her file. In the note, the teacher stated that in her view the girl's mother was crazy.

- *Medical data.* Medical files, which contain a mountain of sensitive personal data, are not always treated with the respect they deserve. In many hospitals, hundreds of employees, most of whom do not have a need-to-know, have ready access to patient information. Your medical records list all your visits to clinics and hospitals, your medical history (and often that of your family), allergies, and diseases you (and often members of your extended family) have or have had. They also may include assessments of your mental and physical health.

- *Driver and crime data.* State motor vehicle bureaus maintain detailed records on over 150 million licensed drivers. This information includes personal descriptive data (sex, age, height, weight, color of eyes and hair) as well as records of arrests, fines, traffic offenses, and whether your license has been revoked. Some states sell descriptive information to retailers on the open market. The FBI's National Crime Information Center (NCIC) and local police forces maintain databases that contain rap sheet information on 20 million people. This information is readily available to hundreds of thousands of law-enforcement personnel.

- *Census data.* With the 2000 census still fresh in our minds, we are reminded that the U.S. Bureau of the Census maintains some very personal data: names, racial heritage, income, the number of bathrooms in our home, and persons of the opposite sex who share our living quarters. Individual files are confidential. Statistics, however, are released without names.

- *Insurance data.* Insurance companies have formed a cooperative to maintain a single database containing medical information on millions of people. This revealing database includes claims, doc-

FIGURE 8–6 **IT ISSUES**

ETHICS AND COMPUTERS
We all have an obligation to adopt a code of ethics when working with computers. The focus of this CAD designer's work is a closely held corporate secret until the first newly designed automobile hits the showroom.

Courtesy of Sun Microsystems, Inc.

PERSONAL INFORMATION
Many times each day, even as you sleep, businesses, government agencies, or other institutions are creating or updating your personal information on their databases. Here, the Municipal Services Department uses image processing to maintain records on parking violations. Anymore, most of the events in our lives become a matter of someone's record (purchases at a department store, electronic payment of a highway toll, the results of a test, surfing to a particular Web page, a cell phone call, a traffic violation, and so on).

Courtesy of Lockheed Martin Corporation

tors' reports, whether you have been refused insurance, how risky you would be as an insuree, and so on.

- *Lifestyle data.* A number of cities are installing two-way cable TV that allows the accumulation of information on people's personal viewing habits. When you watch an X-rated movie, or any other movie, your choice is recorded in the family's viewing database. As interactive cable TV matures, you will be able to use it to pay bills, respond to opinion polls, and make dinner reservations. This, of course, will add a greater variety of information to your personal file.

- *Credit data.* Credit bureaus routinely release intimate details of our financial well-being. About one third of those who ask to review their records (you have the right to do this at any time) challenge their accuracy. Credit bureaus are bound by law to correct inaccuracies within two weeks of being notified of them.

- *World Wide Web data.* When you visit a Web site, your e-mail address may be recorded in a user database on the Web site's server computer. If you interact with a site, your selections and preferences may be noted and placed on the database. Any personal information you enter goes in the database, too. Some Web sites share information for the same e-mail address enabling them to build a more comprehensive personal profile of their visitors/customers. Frequent cybersurfers may have records in hundreds or even thousands of Web site databases.

- *Employment data.* Even before you report to work, your employer has gathered a significant body of data on you. Job-related information is maintained at current and past employers, including the results of performance reports, disciplinary actions, and other sensitive data.

- *Financial institutions.* Banks and various financial institutions not only keep track of your money, they also monitor the volume and type of transactions you make. Their records include how much money you have or owe and how you choose to invest your money.

- *Miscellaneous data.* Every time you make a long-distance telephone call, the number is recorded. Many Web sites not only record your visit but they also record your activities at the site, as well. When you make a credit card purchase, your location at the time and the type of item you buy are recorded. Local and state governments maintain records of property transactions that involve homes, automobiles, boats, guns, and so on.

The social security number, now assigned to all U.S. citizens, is the link that ties all our personal information together. It doubles as a military serial number, and in many states, it serves as your driver's license number. It is the one item, along with your name, that appears on almost all personal forms. For example, your social security number is a permanent entry in hospital, tax, insurance, bank, employment, school, and scores of other types of records.

The few organizations discussed here represent the tip of the personal information iceberg. Political organizations, magazines, telemarketers, charities, and hundreds of other organizations maintain and often share personal information. For the most part, these and thousands of other organizations are making a genuine attempt to handle personal data in a responsible manner. However, instances of abuse are widespread and give us cause for concern.

Information technology is now the basis for processing and storing personal information, and the storage of personal information will increase in the future. However, it's not IT or computers that abuse the privacy of our personal information; it's the people who manage them. We as a society must be prepared to meet the challenge with a system of laws that deals realistically with the problem. At present, Federal laws give individuals little protection. We are not told when data are being gathered about us. We are not allowed to choose who sees this information. In most cases, we are not allowed to view, remove, or correct personal information contained on some database. The good news is that laws are being put in place that will, though slowly, provide better protection for our personal information. For example, a new law limits what data-gathering companies can do with "personally identifiable financial information." The law dictates that these companies must get your permission before they can sell your credit report data, including your name, address, telephone number, and social security number. This means that those in the data gathering business and direct marketers will need to work harder and spend more money to get targeted personal information.

Sources of Personal Data

There is indeed reason for concern regarding the privacy of personal information. For example, credit card users unknowingly leave a "trail" of activities and interests that, when examined and evaluated, can provide a surprisingly comprehensive personal profile.

The date and location of all credit card transactions are recorded. In effect, when you charge lunch, gasoline, or clothing, you are creating a chronological record of where you have been and your spending habits. From this information, a good analyst could compile a very accurate profile of your lifestyle. For example, the analyst could predict how you dress by knowing the type of clothing stores you patronize. On a more personal level, records are kept that detail the duration, time, and numbers of all your telephone calls. With computers, these numbers easily can be matched to people, businesses, institutions, and telephone services. So each time you make a phone call, you also leave a record of whom or where you call. The IRS, colleges, employers, creditors, hospitals, insurance companies, brokers, and so on maintain enormous amounts of personal data on everyone. A person with access to this information could create quite a detailed profile of almost anyone, including you. The profile could be fine-tuned further by examining your Internet activity, such as what messages you posted to the Internet, what sites you visited, and the kinds of software you downloaded.

We, of course, hope that the information about us is up-to-date and accurate. However, this is not always the case. You can't just write to the federal government and ask to see your files. To be completely sure you examine all your federal records for completeness and accuracy, you would have to write and probably visit more than 5000 agencies, each of which maintains databases on individuals. The same is true of personal data maintained in the private sector.

Computer experts feel that, whatever the source, the integrity of personal data can be more secure in computer databases than it is in file cabinets. They contend that we can continue to be masters and not victims if we implement proper safeguards for the maintenance and release of this information and enact effective legislation to cope with the abuse of it.

Violating the Privacy of Personal Information

Now you know that a lot of your personal information exists on computers, but is this information being misused? Some say yes, and most will agree that the potential exists for abuse. Consider the states that sell lists of the addresses and data on their licensed drivers. At the request of a manager of several petite women's clothing stores, a state provided the manager with a list of all its licensed drivers who were women between the ages of 21 and 40, less than 5 feet 3 inches tall, and under 120 pounds. Is the sale of such a list an abuse of personal information? Does the state cross the line of what is considered ethical practice? You be the judge.

When you visit a Web site, the server may gather and store information about you, both on its system and on your system. Frequently, Web sites will leave a cookie on your hard disk. The **cookie** is a message given to your Web browser by the Web server being accessed. The information in the cookie, which is in the form of a text file, then is sent back to the server each time the browser requests a page from the server. The cookie may contain information about you, including your name, e-mail address, interests, and personal preferences. Anytime you enter personal information at a Web site, chances are your browser is storing it in a cookie. The main purpose of the cookie is to personalize your interaction with the Web site and to enable the server to present you with a customized Web page, perhaps with your name at the top of the page. A cookie is not necessarily bad because it contains your personal preferences and basic personal information. A good cookie can make your interaction with an often-visited Web site more efficient and effective.

A recent study found that none of the 100 most popular shopping Web sites was in compliance with Fair Information Practices, a set of principles that provides basic privacy protection. Personal information has become the product of a growing industry. Companies have been formed that do nothing but sell information about people, including their e-mail addresses. Not only are the people involved not asked for permission to use their data, they seldom are told that their personal information is being sold! A great deal of personal data can be extracted from public records, both manual and computer-based. For example, one company sends people to county courthouses all over the United States to gather publicly accessible data about people who have recently filed papers to purchase a home. Computer-based databases then are sold to insurance companies, landscape companies, members of Congress seeking new votes, lawyers seeking new clients, and so on. Such information even is sold and distributed over the Net. Those placed on these electronic databases eventually become targets of commerce and special-interest groups.

The use of personal information for profit and other purposes is growing so rapidly that the government has not been able to keep up with abuses. Antiquated laws, combined with judicial unfamiliarity with information technology, make policing and prosecuting abuses of the privacy of personal information difficult and, in many cases, impossible.

Computer Matching

In **computer matching,** separate databases are examined and individuals common to both are identified. The focus of most computer-matching applications is to identify people engaged in wrongdoing. For example, federal employees are being matched with those having delinquent student loans. Then, wages are garnished to repay the loans. In another computer-matching case, a $30-million fraud was uncovered when questionable financial transactions were traced to common participants.

The Internal Revenue Service also uses computer matching to identify tax cheaters. The IRS gathers descriptive data, such as neighborhood and automobile type, then uses sophisticated models to create lifestyle profiles. These profiles are matched against reported income on tax returns to predict whether people seem to be underpaying taxes. When the income and projected lifestyle do not match, the return is audited.

Proponents of computer matching cite the potential to reduce criminal activity. Opponents of computer matching consider it an unethical invasion of privacy.

Creating New Applications for Personal Information

The mere fact that personal information is so readily available has opened the door for many new applications of information technology. Some people will praise their merits and others will adamantly oppose them. For example, one Federal proposal is to have computer-based background checks done on all airline passengers. The results of the checks would be used to identify which passengers' luggage to search. The proposed system would examine names, addresses, telephone numbers, travel histories, and billing records to search for irregularities that might indicate possible terrorist or smuggler activity. This application, like many others that involve the use of personal information, has the potential to have a positive impact on society. Protectors of the rights of individuals will argue that the benefits derived may not be great enough to offset this invasion into personal information.

Each new application involving the use of personal information will be scrutinized carefully; but it is inevitable that our personal information will be used for a variety of applications. These may include systems that locate compatible mates, assign schoolchildren to classes, track sex offenders, identify employees who do not meet company character standards, target sales to likely customers, and so on.

No Easy Answers to the Privacy Question

The ethical questions surrounding the privacy of personal information are extremely complex and difficult to resolve. For example, consider the position of the American Civil Liberties Union. On one hand, the ACLU is fighting to curb abuses of personal information and on the other, it is lobbying the government for greater access to government information, which may include personal information. Are these goals in conflict?

On one side of the fence, consumer organizations and privacy advocates are lobbying for privacy legislation that can protect the interests and rights of online users. The e-commerce sector is pulling legislatures in the other direction. Online businesses want voluntary controls and industry self-regulation instead of new privacy legislation. New laws probably will reflect a compromise between the two views on the privacy of personal information.

As automation continues to enrich our lives, it also opens the door for abuses of personal information. Research is currently being done that may show that people with certain genetic and/or personality makeups have a statistical predisposition to a physical problem or a mental disorder, such as early heart failure or depression. Will employers use such information to screen potential employees?

By now, it should be apparent to you that we may never resolve all of the ethical questions associated with the privacy of personal information. Just as the answer to one question becomes clearer, a growing number of applications that deal with personal information raises another.

COMPUTER MONITORING

One of the most controversial applications of information technology is **computer monitoring**. In computer monitoring, computers continuously gather and assimilate data on job activities to measure worker performance, often without the workers' knowledge (see Figure 8-7). Today, computers monitor the job performance of millions of American workers and millions more worldwide. Most of these workers are online and routinely interact with a server computer system via a terminal or PC. Others work with electronic or mechanical equipment linked to a computer system.

Many clerical workers are evaluated by the number of documents they process per unit of time. At insurance companies, computer-monitoring systems provide supervisors with information on the rate at which clerks process claims. Supervisors can request other information, such as time spent at the PC or terminal and the keying-error rate.

Computers also monitor the activities of many jobs that demand frequent use of the telephone. A computer logs the number of inquiries handled by directory-assistance operators. Some companies employ computers to monitor the use of telephones by all employees.

Although most computer monitoring is done at the clerical level, it also is being applied to persons in higher-level positions, such as commodities brokers, programmers, loan officers, and plant managers. For example, CIM (computer-integrated manufacturing) enables corporate executives to monitor the effectiveness of a plant manager on a real-time basis. At any given time, executives can tap the system for productivity information, such as the rate of production for a particular assembly.

Not all computer monitoring is aimed at assessing ongoing job performance. About two-thirds of all U.S. companies monitor employee Internet browsing activities, too. Companies would prefer that their employees not view pornography, play games, gamble, or engage in nonwork browsing while at work. In fact, one in every four companies has fired at least one employee based on the results of Web monitoring information.

Many organizations encourage management scrutiny of employee electronic mail. In this form of monitoring, a robotic scanner "reads" employee e-mail searching for key words and phrases ("party," "skiing," "have a drink," and so on). Questionable e-mail messages are sent to management for review. The purpose of this type of monitoring is to ensure that internal communications are work-related and of a certain level of quality. Companies justify e-mail monitoring by citing their need to protect intellectual property and to provide documentation that can protect the company in case of litigation. Many organized worker groups have complained that this form of monitoring is an unnecessary invasion of privacy and can actually be counterproductive.

Workers complain that being constantly observed and analyzed by a computer adds unnecessary stress to their jobs. However, management is reluctant to give up computer monitoring because it has proved itself to be a tool for increasing worker productivity. In general, affected workers are opposing any further intrusion into their professional privacy. Conversely, management is equally vigilant in its quest for better information on worker performance and Internet activities.

FIGURE 8–7 **COMPUTER MONITORING**

MONITORING MOBILE WORKERS
With a portable terminal, this trucker is expected to communicate with headquarters. He can send sales information, transaction records, and progress reports quickly, accurately, and wirelessly to the host computer. The host computer can also dispatch instructions, updates, and work orders back out to its workforce. Anyone who records transactions on a computer system is a candidate for computer monitoring.

Courtesy of Symbol Technologies, Inc.

MONITORING OFFICE KNOWLEDGE WORKERS
The scope and extent of computer monitoring is on the rise in companies throughout the world, especially among knowledge workers who perform transactions. Companies that do not use computer monitoring are the exception.

Courtesy of Sun Microsystems, Inc.

8-3.1 Personal information has become the product of a growing industry. (T/F)

8-3.2 Your personal data cannot be passed from one organization to another without your consent. (T/F)

8-3.3 A message given to your Web browser by the Web server being accessed is a: (a) cake, (b) pie, (c) cookie, or (d) tart.

8-3.4 The term used to describe the computer-based collection of data on worker activities is called: (a) computer matching, (b) computer monitoring, (c) footprinting, or (d) pilferage.

SECTION
SELF-CHECK

8-4 | Computer and IT Crime

The ethical spectrum for computer issues runs from that which is ethical, to that which is unethical, to that which is against the law—a computer crime. There are many types of computer and IT crimes, ranging from the use of an unauthorized password by a student in a college computer lab to a billion-dollar insurance fraud. The first case of computer crime was reported in 1958. Since then, all types of computer-related crimes have been reported: fraud, theft, larceny, embezzlement, burglary, sabotage, espionage, and forgery. We know computer crime is a serious problem, but we don't know how serious. Some studies estimate that each year the total money lost from computer crime is greater than the sum total of that taken in all other robberies. In fact, no one really knows the extent of computer crime because much of it is either undetected or unreported. In those cases involving banks, officers may elect to write off the loss rather than announce the crime and risk losing the goodwill of their customers. Computer crimes involving the greatest amount of money have to do with banking, insurance, product inventories, and securities.

A record number of computer crime cases are being reported each year; however, the federal government is opting not to prosecute many of them. The increase in computer crime combined with the

WHY THIS SECTION IS IMPORTANT TO YOU

Everything associated with computers is growing rapidly—the number of computer professionals, robotics, the Internet, and *computer crime*. Understanding the material in this section will reduce the chances of you becoming a victim of a computer-related crime and will help you understand what you can do to prevent it.

reluctance to prosecute gives us some insight into the progress of the government's war on computer crime. In recent years, prosecutors filed charges in only 25% of the hundreds of computer crime cases given to federal prosecutors. This percentage of referrals being prosecuted is considerably lower than the average of all referrals. The FBI has noted that computer crime is very difficult to prove. Also, prosecutors may be ill-prepared from a technical perspective to prosecute such cases. Most of those who are convicted receive relatively light sentences or are released on probation with no jail time.

Fortunately, only a small percentage of the people with an inclination toward crime are capable of committing high-tech crimes. Unfortunately, the criminal element in our society, like everyone else, is moving toward information technology competency. Thanks to the improved controls made possible through automation, though, business-related crime, in general, is decreasing. Computers have simply made it more difficult for people to commit business crimes. For the most part, stereotypical criminals and undesirables do not commit computer crimes. Instead, trusted computer users commit them with authorized access to sensitive information.

COMPUTERS AND THE LAW

Companies try to employ information technology within the boundaries of any applicable laws. Unfortunately, the laws are not always clear because many legal questions involving the use of information technology are being debated for the first time. For example, is e-mail like a letter or a memo, subject to freedom-of-information laws? Or, is it private, like telephone calls? This question is yet to be resolved. To no one's surprise, IT law is the fastest growing type of law practice.

Laws governing information technology are beginning to take shape (see Figure 8-8). Prior to 1994, federal laws that addressed computer crime were limited because they applied only to those computer systems that in some way reflected a "federal interest." The Computer Abuse Amendments Act of 1994 expanded the scope of computer crimes to computers "used in interstate commerce." Effectively, this applies to any computer, including home PCs, with a link to the Internet. These laws make it a felony to gain unauthorized access to a computer system with the intent to obtain anything of value, to defraud the system, or to cause more than $1000 in damage. Although most states have adopted computer crime laws, current laws are only the skeleton of what is needed to direct an orderly and controlled growth of information technology applications.

The Children's Online Privacy Protection Act (COPPA) went into effect in 2000. There was a two-year transition period giving Internet organizations an opportunity to gear up for conforming to the new law. It is the first law governing online privacy. The new law requires that Internet Web sites obtain verifiable consent from parents before collecting, using, or disclosing personal information from children under the age of 13. The law offers a variety of methods for parental consent, including e-mail, snail mail, fax, and so on. Parents are overwhelmingly in favor of this law; however, critics say that it may limit the variety of activities that children will have on the Internet.

Existing federal and state laws concerning the privacy of personal information are being updated every year. At the same time, new laws are being written. Current federal laws outline the handling of credit information, restrict what information the IRS can obtain, restrict government access to financial information, permit individuals to view records maintained by federal agencies, restrict the use of education-related data, and regulate the matching of computer files. States have or are considering laws to deal with the

FIGURE 8–8

IT LEGISLATION
Information technology-related legislation is being revised in the House of Representatives as quickly as it is being proposed. The background screen shows the most recent version of a proposed bill—the Networking and Information Technology Research Advancement Act. The House and Senate Web sites make the full text of proposed legislation and other pertinent information available online, including pages dedicated to providing current information for the press (see inset).

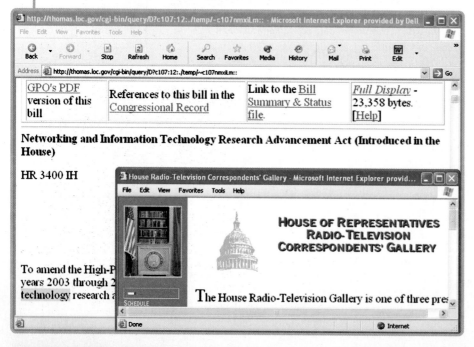

handling of social security numbers, criminal records, telephone numbers, financial information, medical records, and other sensitive personal information.

Computer crime is a relatively recent phenomenon. As a result, legislation, the criminal justice system, and industry are not yet adequately prepared to cope with it. Only a handful of police and FBI agents in the entire country have been trained to handle cases involving computer crime. And when a case comes to court, few judges and even fewer jurors have the background necessary to understand the testimony.

AREAS OF COMPUTER AND IT CRIMINAL ACTIVITY

Computer and IT crimes can be grouped into several categories, described in the following sections.

Crimes That Create Havoc Inside a Computer

Computer viruses and *Trojan horses* (discussed in Chapter 5) fall into this category. A computer virus is a program that takes control of the victim's system, with results that range from exasperating (the display of a harmless political message) to tragic (the loss of all programs and data). Furthermore, computer viruses can copy themselves from system to system when unsuspecting users exchange infected disks. A Trojan horse is any seemingly useful program that hides a computer virus or a logic bomb. A **logic bomb**, in contrast, is a set of instructions that is executed when a certain set of conditions are met. For example, a disgruntled employee might plant a logic bomb to be "exploded" on the first Friday the thirteenth after his or her record is deleted from the personnel database.

Crimes That Involve Fraud and Embezzlement

Most computer crimes fall under the umbrella of fraud and embezzlement. Fraud involves obtaining illegal access to a computer system for the purpose of personal gain. Embezzlement concerns the misappropriation of funds.

- A 17-year old high school student tapped into an AT&T computer and stole more than $1 million worth of software. (Fraud)

- One person hacked his way into a system and illegally transferred $10,200,000 from a U.S. bank to a Swiss bank. He probably would have gotten away with this electronic heist if he had not felt compelled to brag about it. (Fraud)

- A U.S. Customs official modified a program to print $160,000 worth of unauthorized federal payroll checks payable to himself and his co-conspirators. (Embezzlement)

- Three data entry clerks in a large metropolitan city conspired with welfare recipients to write over $2 million of fraudulent checks. (Embezzlement)

Computers can be both an invitation to fraud and a tool to thwart fraud. For example, at one time, the automated system in place in the pits at the Chicago Board of Trade and the Chicago Mercantile Exchange made it possible for traders to fill personal orders either simultaneously or ahead of their customers to get better prices. A system, involving handheld computer trading devices, could be implemented that would electronically record every trade in sequence, preventing such abuses.

The *salami technique* for embezzlement requires that a Trojan horse (unauthorized code hidden in a legitimate program) be planted in the program code of a financial system that processes a large number of accounts. These covert instructions cause a small amount of money, usually less than a penny, to be debited periodically from each account and credited to one or more dummy accounts. A number of less sophisticated computer-manipulation crimes are the result of data diddling. *Data diddling* is changing the data, perhaps the "ship to" address, on manually prepared source documents or during online entry to the system.

Attempts to defraud a computer system require the cooperation of an experienced IT specialist. A common street thug does not have the knowledge or the opportunity to be successful at this type of computer crime. Over 50% of all computer frauds are internal, that is, employees of the organization being defrauded commit them. About 30% of those defrauding employees are IT specialists.

Crimes That Involve Negligence or Incompetence

Not all computer crime is premeditated. Negligence or incompetence can be just as bad for an organization as a premeditated crime. Such crimes usually are a result of poor input/output control. For example, after she paid in full, a woman was sent follow-up notices continually and was visited by collection agencies for not making payments on her automobile. Although the records and procedures were in error, the company forcibly repossessed the automobile without thoroughly checking its procedures and the legal implications. The woman had to sue the company for the return of her automobile. The court ordered the automobile returned and the company to pay her a substantial sum as a penalty.

Companies that employ computers to process data must do so in a responsible manner. Irresponsible actions that result in the deletion of a bank account or the premature discontinuation of electrical service would fall into this category. Lax controls and the availability of sensitive information invite scavenging. *Scavenging* is searching for discarded information that may be of some value on the black market, such as a printout containing credit card numbers.

Crimes That Involve Unauthorized Access to the Internet and Networking

Security on the Internet and computer networks is an ongoing problem. Internet-related intrusions number in the thousands each month. The Internet is so vulnerable that computer science professors have been known to ask their students to break into files at a particular site on the Internet. Successful students bring back proof of system penetration to show they understand the protocols involved.

Any computer enthusiast who enjoys the lawful excesses of personal computing (programming, building PCs, and so on) would qualify as a **hacker.** Hackers created the term **cracker** to distinguish themselves from overzealous hackers, who "crack" through network/Internet security and tap into everything from local credit agencies to top-secret defense systems. These "electronic vandals" often leave evidence of unlawful entry, perhaps a revised record or access during nonoperating hours, called a **footprint.**

Many of the millions of Internet sites are vulnerable to attacks by vandals. Vandals have substituted images on home pages with ones that are embarrassing to the organization. Others have bombarded sites with thousands of randomly generated requests for service to preclude their use by legitimate users. These are called *denial of service* attacks. Each day hackers and crackers are finding new ways to wreak havoc on the Internet.

One of the major motivators for unauthorized access is **industrial espionage.** Companies representing most of the world's countries have attempted a shortcut to success and have attempted to steal product design specifications, product development schedules, trade secrets, software code, strategic plans, sales strategies, customer information, or anything else that would give them a competitive advantage. The typical corporate computer has everything corporate spies would want, so their objective is to circumvent security measures and gain access to a target company's system, look around, and extract whatever pertinent information they can.

The Computer Abuse Amendments Act of 1994 changed the standard for criminal prosecution from "intent" to "reckless disregard," thus increasing the chances of successful prosecution of crackers. Two computer crackers were sentenced to federal prison for their roles in defrauding long-distance carriers of more than $28 million. The crackers stole credit card numbers from MCI. The cracker who worked at MCI was sentenced to three years and two months, and the other cracker was sentenced to a one-year prison term. Countries throughout the world are struggling to define just punishment for cybercrimes. Some countries have adopted a zero tolerance policy in their cyber laws. For example, two brothers in China were executed for a $30,000 electronic heist. There is a concern that the media glorifies criminally oriented hackers, creating heroes for a new generation of computer criminals. This glorification may begin to fade as we read about more and more crackers serving hard time.

The Internet's cybercops on the Computer Emergency Response Team (CERT) often work around the clock to thwart electronic vandalism and crime on the Internet. CERT concentrates its efforts on battling major threats to the global Internet. Lesser problems are left to the Internet service providers and to police. A few years ago, the cybercops tracked hackers who were out to prove their ingenuity by breaking into systems just to prove they could. These hackers were mostly harmless, more out to prove their hacking abilities than to act maliciously. Now cyberthiefs are after more than self-esteem: They want to steal something. They intercept credit card numbers, reroute valuable inventory, download copyrighted software, or make illegal monetary transactions. Fortunately, CERT has found that security incidents generally are decreasing relative to the size of the Internet. Unfortunately, as soon as CERT people plug a hole in the Internet, another is found. The problem will not go away and may become more difficult to cope with as perpetrators gain sophistication.

Security experts say that the best way to deal effectively with crime on the Internet is the universal adoption and use of an international encryption standard. At present, some people and companies are reluctant to adopt such a standard because it would effectively end open worldwide communication. However, if abuse continues, universal encryption may be the only solution.

Unauthorized entry to a computer network is achieved in a variety of ways. The most common approach is *masquerading.* People acquire passwords and personal information that will enable them to masquerade as an authorized user. The *tailgating* technique is used by company outsiders to gain access to sensitive information. The perpetrator simply begins using the terminal or computer of an authorized user who has left the room without terminating his or her session. The more sophisticated user might prefer building a trap door, scanning, or superzapping. A *trap door* is a Trojan horse that permits unauthorized and undetected access to a computer system. Trap doors usually are implemented by an insider during system development, usually a programmer. *Scanning* involves the use of a computer to test different combinations of access information until access is permitted (for example, by stepping through a four-digit access code from 0000 to 9999). *Superzapping* involves using a program that enables someone to bypass the security controls.

Crimes in Which the Internet Becomes a Tool for Crime

To thousands of con artists, the Internet offers a quicker, more efficient vehicle for dozens of old-fashioned scams: pyramid schemes, chain letters, offers of free government money, debt-elimination schemes, rip and tear (the big prize—for a fee), and a wealth of get-rich-quick rip-offs. The Internet, also, has opened the door for more sophisticated, technology-based scams, such as **pumping and dumping,** which is illegal. In this scam, seemingly legitimate sources flood the Internet with bogus information about the successes of a particular company. The Internet blitz travels via e-mail, news-groups, instant messaging, and other means of Internet communication. If the fraud works, the net effect is to artificially "pump" up the price of the company's stock. The con artists then "dump" their stock at peak value to realize big gains.

Online auction sites, such as eBay, expand the con artist's reach to millions of people. Scammers are delighted to have this opportunity to sell things they do not have and will never deliver. With over 100,000 bids being posted every hour on millions of items up for auction, this type of scam is difficult to prevent.

Cyberstalking has emerging as one of the fastest-growing areas of Internet crime. Cyberstalking is technology-based stalking where the Internet becomes a vehicle by which the stalker directs threatening behavior and unwanted advances to another netizen (citizen of the Internet). Cyberstalkers find their victims in chat rooms, in newsgroups, in discussion forums, and through e-mail. Most cyberstalkers are men and target women and children. Cyberstalking can be in the form of a threatening or obscene communication (real-time or e-mail), flaming (verbal abuse), mountains of junk e-mail, sexually explicit images, inappropriate messages left at various online locations, viruses, and identity theft. When cyberstalking goes offline, it can become a terrifying experience that elevates electronic harassment to the potential for physical harm.

Crimes That Involve the Abuse of Personal Information

With so much personal information floating around cyberspace, **identity theft** has emerged as one of the fastest growing criminal activities. Identity theft occurs when someone is able to gather enough personal information on you (without your knowledge) to assume your identity. The objective of identity theft is fraud or theft. Identity thieves open new credit card accounts using your name, address, date of birth, and social security numbers. Then, they spend away, sticking you with the bill. Identity thieves have become very imaginative, setting up cellular phone accounts and bank accounts in your name.

Any willful release or distribution of inaccurate personal information would fall into this category, as well. For example, it is a crime to post false information about an individual to the Internet with intent to defame.

Crimes That Support Criminal Enterprises

Money laundering and databases that support drug distribution would fall into this category. Technology has tremendous potential to improve the plight of humanity. Sadly, it has just as much potential for evil. The criminal elements of our society have ingeniously used information technology to support hundreds of criminal ventures from illegal gambling to complex multi-country money laundering schemes.

Crimes That Involve the Theft of Software or Intellectual Property

Federal copyright law automatically protects software from the moment of its creation. This law is the same one that protects other intellectual property (books, audio recordings, films, and so on). The Copyright Law of 1974 gives the owner of the copyright "the exclusive rights" to "reproduce the copyrighted word." Unless specifically stated in the license agreement, the purchasers can install the software to only one computer. The general rule is: one software package per computer. Any other duplication, whether for sale or for the owner's personal use, is an infringement of copyright law.

It is copyright infringement to allow simultaneous use of a single-user version on a LAN by more than one person. LAN versions of software packages are sold with a *site license* that permits use by a specific number of users. Also, the Software Rental Amendments Act of 1990 prohibits the rental, leasing, or lending of copyright software.

The unlawful duplication of proprietary software, called **software piracy,** is making companies vulnerable to legal action by the affected vendors (see Figure 8-9). The term **pilferage** is used to

FIGURE 8–9 **PROTECTION FOR INTELLECTUAL PROPERTY**

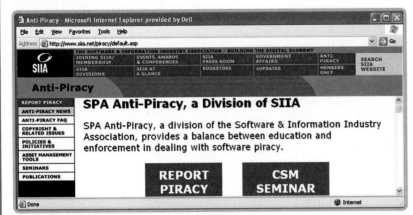

SOFTWARE PIRACY

The Software & Information Industry Association (SIIA) sponsors a vigorous ongoing anti-piracy campaign to protect copyrighted software. Anti-piracy information and support are available from its Web site at http://www.siia.net. The task of catching pirates who sell illegal copies of popular computer programs has become more challenging with the advent of the Internet. The site makes it easy for people to report copyright abuses. Almost 1 million Web sites offer illegal software, resulting in a loss of revenue to software vendors of about $15 billion per year.

COPYRIGHT LAW

Copyright laws protect literature, music, the design of a silicon chip, and software, to name a few. The law protects Intel's innovative bumpless technology chip design.

Photo courtesy of Intel Corporation

describe the situation in which a company purchases a software product without a site-usage license agreement, then copies and distributes the software throughout the company. If such piracy is done "willfully and for the purpose of commercial advantage or private financial gain," perpetrators are subject to fines up to $250,000 and 5 years in jail. Software piracy doesn't pay. Two pirates in Canada were forced to walk the plank with a $22,500 fine. This and similar rulings have sent the message loud and clear: Software piracy will not be tolerated.

Vendors of software for personal computers estimate that for every software product sold, two more are illegally copied. Software piracy is a serious problem, and software vendors are acting vigorously to prosecute people and companies who violate their copyrights. Worldwide, the software industry loses billions of dollars a year to software piracy. According to figures compiled by the Business Software Alliance (BSA), virtually all of the software in Vietnam (97%) is illegal (without a license). China is close behind at 94%, followed by Indonesia (89%) and Russia (88%). It is estimated that the software industry loses about $11 billion a year through software piracy.

The Net poses big problems for software vendors, especially with the widespread use of broadband access, which permits downloads in minutes rather than hours. How do you keep people from distributing copies of software over the Internet? In all likelihood, software eventually will be encrypted such that the purchaser receives a cryptographic key to decode the program and data files. The key would exist in the program, identifying the owner and the buyer. If the buyer illegally distributes the program over an electronic highway, cybercops will be able to trace the action back to the source of the crime.

Some company managers confront the issue head-on and state bluntly that software piracy is a crime and offenders will be dismissed. This method has proven effective. Some, who are actually accomplices, look the other way as subordinates copy software for office and personal use.

Intellectual property rights issues have been front-page news since recording companies began actively suing file sharing enterprises to get them to stop promoting the sharing of copyrighted MP3 songs. The sharing of songs has been attractive to netizens, even to those with slow dialup Internet access. Now, with the rapid expansion of broadband access, netizens are beginning to share pirated versions of feature length movie files. Industry analysts are estimating that up to 400,000 first-run movies are downloaded illegally each day. Films on DVD-ROM are copied and posted to the Net. Digital camcorders are taken to movie theaters where they are used to capture films illegally for Net distribution. The abuse of intellectual property rights in the film industry is nowhere near that of the music recording industry, however, we can look for aggressive litigation as movie moguls move to protect their intellectual property rights.

The penalties for copyright infringements are now more severe. In the United States, crimes involving copyright and identity theft violations result in increased punishment. The creation of counterfeit intellectual material, such as software, music, and books, can result in prison sentences up to 16 months, no matter what the motivation of the perpetrator. The greater the market value of the counterfeit copies is, the stiffer the punishment.

8-4.1	Many legal questions involving computers and information processing are yet to be incorporated into the federal laws. (T/F)
8-4.2	What law is violated when an organization duplicates proprietary software without permission: (a) civil rights, (b) antitrust, (c) copyright, or (d) patent?
8-4.3	The first law governing online privacy is: (a) COPPA, (b) Cabana, (c) adult-oriented, or (d) temporary.
8-4.4	A set of instructions that is executed when a certain set of conditions are met is called a: (a) logic virus, (b) scavenger, (c) data diddler, or (d) logic bomb.

SECTION SELF-CHECK

8-5   Computer, Internet, and System Security

Computer security has been breached and financial losses were incurred in about 80% of the organizations responding to a recent survey, almost half of them within the past year. Losses often are in the millions. The problem is serious and will not go away anytime soon. To minimize unethical abuses of information technology and computer crime, individuals and organizations must build an envelope of security around hardware and embed safeguards into the information systems. Security concerns take on added importance now that millions of businesses have a presence on the Internet and/or are actively involved in e-commerce. In either case, their computer systems are connected via the Internet and, therefore, are vulnerable. Their link to the Net is just one of many points of vulnerability, and too much is at stake to overlook the threats to the security of any computer system. These threats take many forms—white-collar crime, computer viruses, natural disasters (such as earthquakes and floods), vandalism, and carelessness.

In this section, we discuss commonly applied measures that can help to neutralize security threats to a computer center, an information system, and a PC.

COMPUTER-CENTER SECURITY

Enterprise-wide information systems provide information and processing capabilities to workers throughout a given organization. Some systems extend to customers, suppliers, and others outside the organization. Generally, network server computers located in centralized computer centers handle such systems. The center can be anything from a secure room for the LAN server to an entire building for the organization's server computers and the information services staff. Whether a room or a building, the computer center has a number of points of vulnerability: *hardware, software, files/databases, data communications (including the Internet),* and *personnel.* We discuss each separately in this section and illustrate them in Figure 8-10.

Hardware

If the hardware fails, the information system fails. The threat of failure can be minimized by implementing security precautions that prevent access by unauthorized personnel and by taking steps to keep all hardware operational.

Common approaches to securing the premises from unauthorized entry include the use of closed-circuit TV and monitors, alarm systems, as well as computer-controlled devices that check employee badges, fingerprints, or voice prints before unlocking doors at access points. Computer centers also should be isolated from pedestrian traffic. Computer-room fires should be extinguished by a special chemical that douses the fire but does not destroy the files or equipment.

Any complex system is subject to failure. However, for many organizations, network failure is simply unacceptable. For example, if the network supporting the Hilton Hotel reservation system went down for a couple of hours, thousands of reservations and, perhaps, millions of dollars would be lost. Such systems must be made *fault-tolerant.* Fault-tolerant networks are designed to permit continuous operation even if important components of the network fail. To accomplish this goal, parts of the system, such as the server computer or hard disks, must be duplicated. For example, a LAN might have an alternate LAN server. RAID systems, discussed in Chapter 5, "Storing and Retrieving Information," provide fault-tolerant backup of disk systems. Fault-tolerant networks are designed to enable alternate routing of messages. Of course, no network can be made totally fault-tolerant. The degree to which a network is made fault-tolerant depends on the amount of money an organization is willing to spend.

FIGURE 8-10

SECURITY PRECAUTIONS
Some or all of the security measures noted in the figure are in force in most organizations. Each precaution helps minimize the risk of a computer center's, an information system's, or a PC's vulnerability to crime, disasters, and failure.

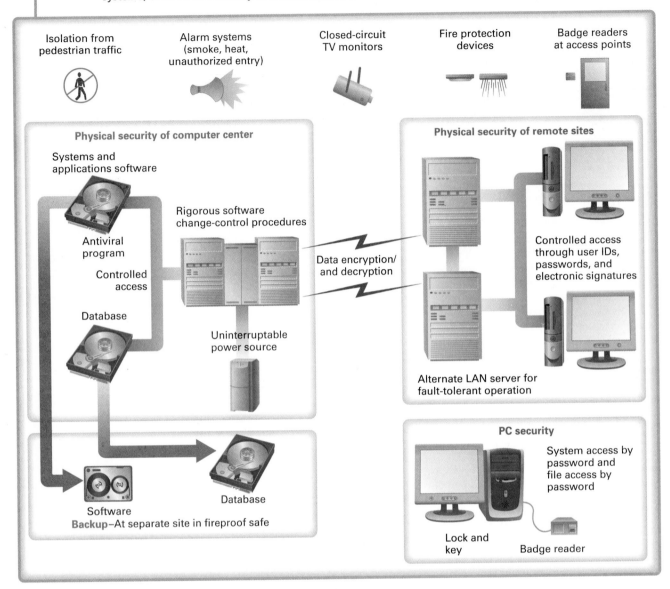

Computers must have a "clean," continuous source of power. To minimize the effects of "dirty" power or power outages, each critical computer should draw its power from an **uninterruptible power source (UPS)**. Dirty power, with sags and surges in power output or brownouts (low power), causes data transmission errors and program execution errors. A UPS system serves as a buffer between the external power source and the computer system. In a UPS system, batteries deliver clean power to the computer and are regenerated continuously by an external power source. If the external power source fails, the UPS system permits operation to continue for a period of time after an outage. This time cushion allows operators to either "power down" normally or switch to a backup power source, usually a diesel-powered generator. UPS systems are considered essential equipment in the business world where server computers must be operational 24/7. Each year, the UPS system is becoming more widely accepted as a critical component of a home or small office PC.

Software

Unless properly controlled, the software for an information system can either be modified for personal gain or vandalized and rendered useless. Close control of software development and the documentation of an information system are needed to minimize the opportunity for computer crime and vandalism.

Unlawful Modification of Software

Bank programmers certainly have opportunities to modify software for personal gain. In one case, a couple of programmers used the salami embezzlement technique and modified a savings system to make small deposits from other accounts to their own accounts. Here's how it worked: The interest for each savings account was compounded and credited daily, with the calculated interest rounded to the nearest penny before being credited to the savings account. Programs were modified to round down all interest calculations and put the "extra" penny in one of the programmers' savings accounts. It may not seem like much, but a penny a day from thousands of accounts adds up to a lot of money. The "beauty" of the system was that the books balanced and depositors did not miss the 15 cents (an average of 1/2 cent per day for 30 days) that judiciously was taken from each account each month. Even auditors had difficulty detecting this crime because the total interest paid on all accounts was correct. However, the culprits got greedy and were apprehended when someone noticed that they repeatedly withdrew inordinately large sums of money from their own accounts. Unfortunately, other enterprising programmers in other industries have been equally imaginative.

Operational control procedures built into the design of an information system will constantly monitor processing accuracy. Unfortunately, cagey programmers have been known to get around some of them. Perhaps the best way to safeguard programs from unlawful tampering is to use rigorous change-control procedures. Such procedures require programmers to obtain authorization before modifying an operational program. Change-control procedures make it difficult to modify a program for purposes of personal gain.

Viruses

Melissa, Chernobyl, Michelangelo, Friday the 13th, Stoned, Jerusalem, and *Love Bug* are phrases that strike fear in PC users. They're names of computer viruses. The infamous *Michelangelo* virus hits on March 6, the artist's birthday, destroying stored data. *Friday the 13th* causes its damage on those days. Even though computer viruses have no metabolism of their own, some people are convinced that they fit the definition of a living system because they use the metabolism of a host computer for their parasitic existence.

The growing threat of viruses has resulted in tightening software controls. *Virus software,* which has been found at all levels of computing, "infects" other programs and databases. The virus is so named because it can spread from one system to another like a biological virus. Viruses are written by outlaw programmers to cause harm to the computer systems of unsuspecting victims. Left undetected a virus can result in loss of data and/or programs and even physical damage to the hardware. Viruses are discussed in detail in Chapter 5, "Storing and Retrieving Information."

Individuals and companies routinely run antivirus programs on both client and server computers, to search for and destroy viruses before they can do their dirty work. Many organizations encourage employees to run antivirus programs prior to March 6th and any Friday the 13th. IBM researchers are working on an electronic *immune system* that would automatically detect viruses and neutralize them with digital antibodies. The immune system would inoculate other computers on the network, stopping the spread of the virus.

Files/Databases

A database contains the raw material for information. Often the files/databases of a company are its lifeblood. For example, how many companies can afford to lose their accounts receivable file, which documents who owes what? Having several *generations of backups* (backups to backups) to all files is not sufficient insurance against loss of files/databases. The backup and master files should be stored in fireproof safes in separate rooms, preferably in separate buildings. Approaches to system backup are covered in Chapter 5.

Data Communications

The mere existence of data communications/Internet capabilities poses a threat to security. A knowledgeable criminal can tap into the system from a remote location and use it for personal gain. In a well-designed system, such hacking is not an easy task. The typical company experiences over 30 hacker attacks each week, but rarely is an attack successful. But it can be and has been done! When one criminal broke a company's security code and tapped into the network of computers, he was able to order certain products without being billed. He filled a warehouse before he eventually was caught. Another tapped into an international banking exchange system to reroute funds to an account of his own in a Swiss bank. In another case, an oil company consistently was able to outbid a competitor by "listening in" on the latter's data transmissions. On several occasions, overzealous hackers have tapped into sensitive defense computer systems. Fortunately, no harm was done.

How do companies protect themselves from these criminal activities? Most companies use the science of **cryptography** to scramble sensitive communications sent over computer networks or the Internet. Cryptography is analogous to the code book used by intelligence people during the "cloak-and-dagger" days of the post–World War II era. Instead of a code book, however, a key is used in conjunction with **encryption/decryption** techniques to unscramble the message. Here is how it works. Before a message is sent, it is *encrypted* such that the bit structure of the message is rearranged according to some mathematical algorithm. Both sender and receiver (people and/or computers) must have the *key,* which may be a number or phrase. The key is the basis for both encryption and decryption. Once encrypted according to an algorithm and its key, the message becomes a meaningless string of bits to anyone who might unlawfully intercept it. The receiver, a person or a computer, uses a key to decrypt and read the message.

Two types of encryption systems are in common use, symmetric-key encryption and public-key encryption. **Symmetric-key encryption** requires that each computer in a communications loop have the key needed to encrypt/decrypt the message. **Public-key encryption** requires both a private key, known only to a particular person/computer, and a public key.

With the rapid growth of e-commerce, Internet security is beginning to mature. A few years ago, people were reluctant to send their credit card number over the Internet. Today, people routinely purchase items with their credit cards. The difference is that Web site security has been beefed up with protocols for transmitting data securely over the World Wide Web. One protocol, **Secure Sockets Layer** (SSL) uses public-key encryption technology to encrypt data that are transferred over the SSL link. Many Web sites use this protocol to transmit sensitive information, such as credit card numbers, between Web client and Web server. There are a couple of ways to tell if you are using a secure Internet protocol. The "http" in the browser's URL bar becomes "https" and/or a padlock icon appears in the status bar at the bottom of the browser.

Most personal transmissions over the Internet are e-mail. Some who send sensitive information are opting to use a digital ID. The **digital ID** serves as an electronic substitute for a sealed envelope. The digital ID becomes part of the browser or e-mail software and allows you to encrypt your e-mail. The digital ID ensures that messages and attachments are protected from tampering, impersonation, and eavesdropping.

Recently a new federal law legalized online signatures. In effect, the **e-signature** has the same legal status as a personalized signature on many documents. However, it does not apply to family law documents, such as wills, trusts, adoptions, or divorce. It is not legal for several other situations, including cancellation of utility services or insurance, rental agreements, or product recall notifications. An e-signature is the ability to e-sign an electronic document. The e-signature has one or more electronic symbol(s) and an embedded security procedure that verifies that the e-signature is from a specific individual and any changes to the electronic document must be detectable. The legalization of the e-signature should have a positive impact on e-commerce. It is expected to reduce administrative costs and it should expedite online transactions.

Personnel

Possibly the biggest threat to a company's security system is the dishonesty and/or negligence of its own employees. Managers should pay close attention to who is hired for positions with access to computer-based information systems and sensitive data. Many companies flash a message on each networked PC or terminal such as: "All information on this system is confidential and proprietary." It's not very user-friendly, but it gets the message across to employees that they may be fired if they abuse the system. Someone who is grossly negligent can cause just as much harm as someone who is inherently dishonest.

INFORMATION SYSTEMS SECURITY

Information systems security is classified as physical or logical. **Physical security** refers to hardware, facilities, magnetic disks, and other items that could be illegally accessed, stolen, or destroyed. For example, restricted access to the server computer room is a form of physical security (see Figure 8-11).

Logical security is built into the software by permitting only authorized persons to access and use the system. Logical security for online systems, including Internet-based systems, is achieved primarily by using *user IDs* and *passwords.* Only those people with a need to know are given user IDs and told the password. On occasion, however, these security codes fall into the wrong hands. When this happens, an unauthorized person can gain access to programs and sensitive files simply by dialing up the computer and entering the codes.

User IDs and passwords remain the foundation of logical security. Users of LAN-based PCs must enter IDs and passwords before being allowed access to LAN resources. The user ID is your electronic

FIGURE 8–11 COMPUTER AND IT SECURITY

LOCK IT UP

The Kensington MemoryLock™ effectively blocks access to the inside of your computer. The hard drive, memory, and all your important information are protected when you lock it up.

Courtesy of Kensington
Technology Group

HIGH-TECH SECURITY SYSTEMS

Physical security is serious business in many companies, especially in areas that house sensitive information and access to computer systems. Shown here is the security control center where computers monitor access to secure areas throughout the company. In the inset, an employee swipes a smart card to gain access to a controlled area. The security system generates an ongoing log of personnel movement in and out of secure areas. Also, the system can monitor the whereabouts of individual employees.

Courtesy of Diebold, Incorporated

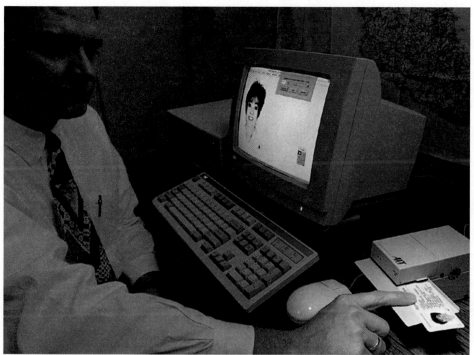

THE PC ID CARD

This Secure ID Document System provides instant access to sensitive real-time information for such applications as border monitoring, health care, and voter registration. A virtually tamper-proof identification card includes information on the bearer that can easily be verified using scanner technology.

Courtesy of E-Systems, Inc.

identifier and may be known by your friends and colleagues. The password, however, is yours alone to protect and use.

- Never tell anyone your password.
- Never write down your password.
- Change your password frequently.

Keeping user IDs and passwords from the computer criminal is not easy. One approach companies use is to educate employees about techniques used to obtain user IDs and passwords, such as tailgating. The tailgater simply continues a session begun by an authorized user when the user leaves the room. Some companies have added another layer of security with the *electronic signature*. The electronic signature, which is built into hardware or software, can be a number or even a digitized signature of an individual. The host or server computer checks the electronic signature against an approved list before permitting access to the system. This measure thwarts the tailgater who attempts to use illegally obtained passwords on unauthorized PCs or software.

Biometric identification systems, once considered revolutionary, are now in common use all around us. With biometric identification systems, we don't need to enter a user ID and password. Biometric identification systems detect unique personal characteristics that can be matched against a database containing the characteristics of authorized users. Several biometric methods are illustrated in Figure 8-12, including fingerprint, palm print (hand geometry), iris scans, and facial recognition. The voiceprint is another common means of biometric identification. Biometric devices are considered superior to traditional methods because they detect personal characteristics that can't be duplicated. All of these biometric technologies are being used for IT security and for other types of security, as well.

In the aftermath of the September 11, 2001, terrorist attack on America, it has become apparent that Americans may be willing to make greater personal privacy sacrifices than in the past in return for safety. **Face recognition technology,** which has been implemented at a number of major airports, enables the identification of known criminals and terrorists. The system creates a digital map of a person's face, called a *faceprint,* which is matched against a database of digital maps to see if there is a match. The system can scan faces in the crowd or a line at an airport ticket counter. In all likelihood, your face will be matched against a database of criminals and terrorists at some time in the future at airports and other public venues that might be vulnerable to attack.

PC SECURITY

Twenty-five years ago, the security problem was solved by wrapping the mainframe-based computer center in an envelope of physical security. Today the security issue is far more complex. PCs more powerful than the mainframes of 25 years ago pepper the corporate landscape. We even carry them with us. It's impractical to apply mainframe standards of security to PCs. If we did, we would all be working in concrete buildings under heavy security, and mobile computing would end.

Server computer security is planned and controlled carefully by security professionals. In contrast, PC security frequently is the responsibility of the individual users who may or may not have security training. As PC users, we have an ongoing obligation to be ever aware of security concerns. Generally, our PCs are readily accessible to other people in the area.

The conscientious PC user has several physical and logical security measures that can be used to safeguard valuable and/or sensitive information. The most frequently used physical tools include the *lock and key* and the *badge reader.* The lock and key, which come standard on most modern PCs, work like an automobile ignition switch. That is, the PC functions only when the lock is turned to the enable position. The badge reader is an optional peripheral device that reads magnetic stripes on badges, such as credit cards. The PC is disabled until an authorized card is inserted and read by the badge reader.

Often the content of your PC's screen bares your soul or perhaps sensitive corporate data. Some people place a special filter over the screen that permits only straight-on viewing. People use it in the office, airplane, or wherever they need to feel secure about their display.

Individual files on a PC can be secured by assigning them unique passwords. For example, if you were using a word processing package to prepare personnel performance evaluations, you could secure these files by assigning each a password. To recall a file at a later session, you or any other user would have to enter the name of the file and the associated password to gain access to it.

LEVEL OF RISK

No combination of security measures will completely remove the vulnerability of a computer center, an information system, a PC, or a file. Security systems are implemented in degrees. That is, an information system can be made marginally secure or very secure, but never totally secure. Each company

FIGURE 8–12

BIOMETRIC ACCESS METHODS
Biometrics is a method of measuring unique physical traits or behavioral characteristics. Shown here are four techniques. Your fingerprint, palm print, retina, or face can be used to verify your identity. The security industry has looked to biometric identification technologies to help consumers protect themselves against theft and fraud. Soon we may no longer have passwords or user IDs that can be stolen or forgotten.

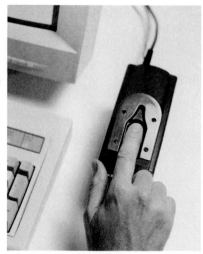

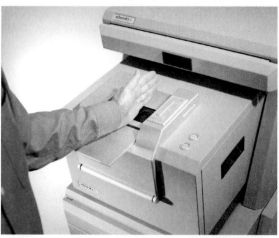

FULL HAND PALM SCANNER
The full hand palm scanner captures a digital image of the entire hand from the carpal crease to the fingertips. Over 30% of the latent prints at a crime scene are from the palm, not the fingers, so forensic examiners have more information they can use to find criminals.

Courtesy of Identix Corporation

FINGERPRINT SCANNER
In a fraction of a second, this biometric sensor can verify, compare, and store a user's fingerprint template. This fingerprint recognition system can be used to secure a computer system from unauthorized use and/or limit access to specific data or files.

Courtesy of Identix Corporation

IRIS SCANNER
Biometric iris scanning technology, which scans the eye's retina through the pupil, provides a quick security access system in businesses and public facilities around the world.

Courtesy of International Business Machines Corporation. Unauthorized use not permitted.

FACE RECOGNITION SYSTEM
Face recognition software (left) uses a neural-based pattern-recognition technology that can extract local features unique to each face to eliminate the need for passwords or user IDs. Although face recognition systems do their job automatically, security control room operators have the flexibility to home in on specific subjects and do manual scans, as well (right).

Courtesy of Identix Corporation

must determine the level of risk that it is willing to accept. Unfortunately, some corporations are willing to accept an enormous risk and hope that those rare instances of crime and disaster do not occur. Some of them have found out too late that *rarely* is not the same as *never*!

SECTION SELF-CHECK

8-5.1	Virusology is the study of the assignment of security codes. (T/F)
8-5.2	Public-key encryption requires both a private key and a public key. (T/F)
8-5.3	Logical security for online systems is achieved primarily by user IDs and: (a) passwords, (b) secret codes, (c) numerical IDs, or (d) social security numbers.
8-5.4	What letter is added to "http" in the URL bar to indicate a secure Internet protocol: (a) i, (b) p, (c) s, or (d) t?
8-5.5	Data can be transmitted securely over the World Wide Web with which protocol: (a) Secure Sockets Layer, (b) ATM, (c) ASCII, or (d) security sheet protocol?

8-1 THE INFORMATION TECHNOLOGY PARADOX

We as a society are caught in an information technology paradox: Information technology is thriving in a society that may not be ready for it.

A reluctant acceptance of information technology has resulted in many information technology-based opportunities being overlooked or ignored. Among the reasons they are not implemented are historical momentum, resistance to change, limited education, and lack of available resources.

Society has reached a point of no return with regard to dependence on computers. Only through understanding can we control the misuse or abuse of computer technology.

8-2 THE WORKPLACE

Human factors engineers are applying the principles of **ergonomic** design to ensure that the interface between knowledge worker and workplace is safe, comfortable, effective, and efficient. The knowledge worker's workplace should be designed with enough flexibility to enable it to be custom-fitted to its worker. Attention to the overall environment (lighting, noise, and ventilation) can reduce stress and increase worker performance.

Problems associated with extended use of a terminal or PC are referred to as **video operator's distress syndrome**, or **VODS**. As the number of **repetitive-stress injuries** (**RSIs**) increased for knowledge workers, workstation ergonomics became an increasingly important issue for corporate productivity. A poorly designed workplace has the potential to cause **cumulative trauma disorder** (**CTD**), a condition that can lead to a permanent disability of motor skills.

The PC can be an invaluable tool in the workplace or it can be a serious diversion. These diversions may include sending and receiving frivolous e-mail, engaging in nonbusiness Internet browsing, gaming on company time, and toying with the technology.

Green computing adopts a more environmentally sound position with respect to the use and manufacture of computing hardware. The EPA's *Energy Star* guidelines are being used to standardize energy usage for monitors and processors. Good green computing includes sending e-mail (rather than paper), purchasing recycled paper, buying reconditioned components, and telecommuting once or twice a week.

Individuals and companies should adopt a **product stewardship policy** that encourages recycling and the proper handling of obsolete PCs and computer hardware.

8-3 ETHICS IN INFORMATION TECHNOLOGY

A code of ethics provides direction for IT professionals and users so they can apply computer technology responsibly.

Thousands of public- and private-sector organizations maintain data on individuals, including tax, education, medical, driver and crime, census, insurance, lifestyle, credit, Web, employment, financial, and other data.

The dominant ethical issue is the privacy of personal information. As automation continues to enrich our lives, it also opens the door for abuses of personal information. Personal information has become the product of a growing industry. Not only are the people involved not asked for permission to use their data, they seldom are told that their personal information is

being sold. The mere fact that personal information is so readily available has opened the door for many new applications of information technology. For example, **cookies** containing personal information are passed freely around the Internet. **Computer matching** involves the examination of separate databases to identify individuals common to both. **Computer monitoring** is used to measure worker performance.

8-4 COMPUTER AND IT CRIME

Computer and IT crime is a relatively recent phenomenon. Therefore, laws governing information technology are few, and those that do exist are subject to a variety of interpretations.

Crimes that create havoc inside a computer include computer viruses and Trojan horses. A **logic bomb** is a set of instructions that is executed when a certain set of conditions are met.

Most computer crimes fall under the umbrella of fraud and embezzlement. Fraud involves obtaining illegal access to a computer system for the purpose of personal gain. Embezzlement concerns the misappropriation of funds. The salami technique and data diddling are used for fraud and embezzlement.

Negligence or incompetence can be just as bad for an organization as a premeditated crime. Such crimes usually are a result of poor input/output control.

Many computer and IT crimes involve unauthorized access to the Internet and networking. Overzealous **hackers** and **crackers** often leave evidence of unlawful entry called a **footprint**. One of the major motivators for unauthorized access is **industrial espionage.** The Internet's cybercops on the Computer Emergency Response Team are ever vigilant in the fight against Internet crimes. Unauthorized entry to a computer network is achieved in several ways, including masquerading, tailgating, a trap door, scanning, and superzapping.

The Internet has become a tool for crime where con artists have updated traditional scams for use in the cyberworld and have created new technology-based crimes such as **pumping and dumping** and **cyberstalking.**

Identity theft, one of the fastest growing criminal activities, is a crime that involves the abuse of personal information.

Computers and IT are used in support of many criminal enterprises, including money laundering.

Crimes that involve the theft of software or intellectual property often leave evidence of the unlawful duplication of proprietary software, called **software piracy,** and **pilferage.** The sharing of copyrighted MP3 and movie files over the Internet is a crime.

8-5 COMPUTER, INTERNET, AND SYSTEM SECURITY

The threats to the security of computer centers and information systems call for precautionary measures. A computer center can be vulnerable in its hardware, software, files/databases, data communications (including the Internet), and personnel.

Organizations use a variety of approaches to secure the computer center, including the installation of an **uninterruptible power source** (**UPS**) and the use of **cryptography** to scramble messages sent over data communications channels. A key is used in conjunction with **encryption/decryption** techniques to scramble/unscramble the message. Two types of encryption systems are in common use, **symmetric-key encryption** and **public-key encryption.**

The **Secure Sockets Layer** (SSL) protocol enables the transmission of data securely over the World Wide Web. The **digital ID** is the equivalent of a sealed envelope for our e-mail.

A new federal law legalized **e-signatures**, giving them the same legal status as a personalized signature on many documents.

The growing threat of viruses has resulted in the tightening of software controls. Virus software "infects" other programs and databases. Antivirus programs search for and destroy viruses.

To protect your work, maintain several generations of backups, storing them in fireproof safes in separate rooms or buildings.

Information systems security is classified as **physical security** or **logical security.** Logical security for online systems is achieved primarily by using user IDs and passwords. Another security measure is the electronic signature.

In the PC environment, people use several methods to control accessibility, including the *lock and key* and the *badge reader.* Properly equipped PCs can add an extra layer of security by incorporating biometric security methods, such as fingerprints, voice prints, retinal scans, and so on.

Security systems are implemented in degrees, and no computer center, LAN server, PC, or system can be made totally secure.

KEY TERMS

biometric identification system (p. 346)
carpal tunnel syndrome (CTS) (p. 326)
computer matching (p. 333)
computer monitoring (p. 334)
cookie (p. 333)
cracker (p. 338)
cryptography (p. 344)
cumulative trauma disorder (CTD) (p. 326)
cyberstalking (p. 339)
digital ID (p. 344)

encryption/decryption (p. 344)
ergonomics (p. 324)
e-signature (p. 344)
face recognition technology (p. 346)
footprint (p. 338)
green computing (p. 327)
hacker (p. 338)
identity theft (p. 339)
industrial espionage (p. 338)
logic bomb (p. 337)
logical security (p. 344)

physical security (p. 344)
pilferage (p. 339)
product stewardship policy (p. 328)
public-key encryption (p. 344)
pumping and dumping (p. 339)
Secure Sockets Layer (SSL) (p. 344)
software piracy (p. 339)
symmetric-key encryption (p. 344)
uninterruptible power source (UPS) (p. 342)
video operator's distress syndrome (VODS) (p. 326)

MATCHING

1. pilferage
2. green computing
3. public-key encryption
4. ergonomics
5. scavenging
6. https
7. logic bomb
8. cracker
9. computer monitoring
10. cyberstalking
11. CTD
12. ACM
13. cookie
14. pumping and dumping
15. COPPA

a. contains information sent to a Web site
b. can result in motor skill disability
c. overzealous hacker
d. has IT code of conduct
e. stock scam
f. indicates a secure Net link
g. causes damage to computers
h. measurement of worker performance
i. online privacy law
j. low-tech way to get sensitive information
k. engineering for humans
l. environmentally sensible computing
m. requires private and public key
n. corporate theft of copyright software
o. targets women and children

CHAPTER SELF-CHECK

8-1.1 The expert diagnosis system is as much a part of the doctor's medical kit as the stethoscope. (T/F)

8-1.2 Society now embraces the concept of a cashless society. (T/F)

8-1.3 Which of these is not a reason potentially beneficial computer applications have not been implemented: (a) historical momentum, (b) resistance to change, (c) too much education, or (d) lack of available resources?

8-1.4 Which of these is not an emphasis in medical school curricula: (a) the use of IT, (b) internal medicine, (c) SDTs, or (d) human anatomy?

8-2.1 A monitor emits radiation. (T/F)

8-2.2 The typical user takes advantage of 95% of a software package's features. (T/F)

8-2.3 Personal e-mail is never tolerated in a business environment. (T/F)

8-2.4 A greater percentage of home appliances are recycled than PCs. (T/F)

8-2.5 All states now require that PCs be recycled. (T/F)

8-2.6 What is the approximate cost of running a PC and a laser printer 24 hours a day for a year: (a) $10, (b) $50, (c) $250, or (d) $2250?

8-2.7 The study of the relationships between people and their machines is called: (a) humanology, (b) human economics, (c) ergology, or (d) ergonomics.

8-2.8 Hand and wrist problems are associated with: (a) ACL, (b) carpal tunnel syndrome, (c) CLA, or (d) SC syndrome.

8-2.9 Laser printers can emit: (a) lead, (b) a harmless water-based compound, (c) sulfur dioxin, or (d) ozone.

8-3.1 The ACM Code of Conduct was recently adopted by the U.S. Senate and is now the law of the land. (T/F)

8-3.2 Over 90% of all knowledge workers embrace new technology and seek to incorporate it in their jobs. (T/F)

8-3.3 Credit bureaus are bound by law to correct inaccuracies in their personal data. (T/F)

8-3.4 All Internet Web sites must be in compliance with Fair Information Practices. (T/F)

8-3.5 About what percentage of all U.S. companies monitor employee Internet browsing activities: (a) 1%, (b) 15%, (c) 67%, or (d) 100%?

8-3.6 When separate databases are examined and individuals common to both are identified, this is: (a) computer matching, (b) footprinting, (c) computer monitoring, or (d) pilferage.

8-3.7 The number of federal government agencies that maintain computer-based files on individuals is between: (a) 50 and 100, (b) 500 and 1000, (c) 5000 and 10,000, or (d) 50,000 and 100,000.

8-4.1 Over 50% of all computer frauds are internal. (T/F)

8-4.2 Crackers created the term hacker to distinguish themselves from overzealous crackers. (T/F)

8-4.3 A trap door is a Trojan horse that permits unauthorized and undetected access to a computer system. (T/F)

8-4.4 In the United States, gaining unauthorized access to any computer system with the intent of defrauding the system is a: (a) violation of public ethics, (b) misdemeanor, (c) high crime, or (d) felony.

8-4.5 Which term is used to describe the situation in which a company copies and distributes software without a site-usage license agreement: (a) pilferage, (b) thieving, (c) pinching, or (d) filching?

8-4.6 The evidence of unlawful entry to a computer system is called a: (a) bitprint, (b) footprint, (c) handprint, or (d) fingerprint.

8-5.1 Although expensive, some companies implement the security measures needed to be totally secure. (T/F)

8-5.2 Normal ceiling-mounted water sprays are installed in all computer centers for fire protection. (T/F)

8-5.3 What name is given to a program intended to damage the computer system of an unsuspecting victim: (a) virus, (b) bug, (c) germ, or (d) fever?

8-5.4 When network downtime is unacceptable, the network must be made: (a) earthquake ready, (b) faultless, (c) uptime tolerant, or (d) fault-tolerant.

8-5.5 What can be used to scramble messages sent over data communications channels: (a) public keys, (b) encoding, (c) cryptography, or (d) ASCII plus?

8-5.6 An e-signature is the ability to e-sign: (a) an encrypted SSL Layer 1 packet, (b) an OCR label, (c) a system unit, or (d) an electronic document.

IT ETHICS AND ISSUES

RECYCLING OLD COMPUTERS

They say a dog year is equal to 7 human years. One computer year is about the same as 20 human years, so computers get "old" very quickly. Old cars of ages 20 or older still get people from point A to point B and some become desirable antiques. But what do you do with an old computer whose components are worth virtually nothing? About 80% of those computers, about 300 million worldwide, are sent to landfills and only 20% are recycled. Electronic components in computers are generally not biodegradable and they can contain many toxic substances.

Discussion: Should the government regulate the disposal of obsolete computers? Justify your response.

Discussion: What did you do with your obsolete computer? What will you do with your current PC once it becomes obsolete?

Discussion: Should corporations police themselves and adopt a PC product stewardship policy? If not, why? If so, write a proposed policy.

COOKIES AND PERSONAL PRIVACY

Some Internet Web sites create and store a file on the user's PC called a *cookie*. Each time the user accesses that Web site the personal information in the cookie is sent to the Web server. The cookie may contain your name and other personal information, perhaps your password to access that Web site, and personal preferences. Most Web sites use cookies to personalize the user's interaction with the Web site. For example, some online retailers have "one-click" ordering where all the personal information needed to complete an order is extracted from your cookie. Over 95% of the top e-commerce sites use cookies.

Discussion: Discuss the advantages and disadvantages of cookies from the perspective of the Web site sponsor. From the perspective of the user.

Discussion: E-commerce companies are using the information in cookies to give preferential services, performance, and pricing to high-priority customers. Is it ethical for companies to treat visitors to their Web site differently? Explain.

Discussion: Would you be for or against legislation that would require all telecommunications companies, including online information services and companies with a presence on the Web, to tell people what information is being collected on them and how it's being used?

VIOLATING THE COPYRIGHT OF INTELLECTUAL PROPERTY

Educators report that they are having difficulty instilling respect for the copyrights on intellectual property. The statistics confirm their concerns. It is estimated that for every legitimate copy of a software package there are two pirated versions installed on other PCs. In some countries, virtually all software is counterfeit. The original developers receive no royalties for sales.

Discussion: The capabilities for copying CDs, CD-ROMs, and DVDs are now commonplace in the home and office. People routinely use these capabilities to duplicate copyrighted music and software for friends and, occasionally, for corporate use. If you knew of someone who routinely violated copyright laws, would you report him or her? Why or why not?

Discussion: *Your boss asked you to install your graphics program on three other PCs in the office. The license permits only one installation. What would be your response to your boss's request?*

Discussion: *A neighbor of yours who lives paycheck to paycheck has asked if he can borrow your copy of Quicken (financial management software). He installs the software on his computer and returns the Quicken CD-ROM to you within an hour. Was anyone guilty of violating copyright laws? Explain.*

Discussion: *How would you respond to a teenager arrested for shoplifting who downplayed the crime saying, "Everybody does it and nobody ever gets caught"? How would you respond to a manager charged with duplicating copyrighted software who downplayed the incident saying, "Everybody does it and nobody ever gets caught"?*

Discussion: *What can each of us do to help guard against the pirating of copyrighted software?*

SCANNING FOR SHOPLIFTERS

A high-tech surveillance technology that has been used in the past to trap pedophiles, terrorists, and, at European soccer games, hooligans, is being employed by some retailers to identify shoplifters. The face-recognition technology matches a digital facial scan against a database of known shoplifters. The technology can scan people's faces within a crowd using 80 facial features and identify people with 99% accuracy. There are, of course, concerns about invasion of personal privacy; however, individual scans are deleted after they had been matched against the database. Also, this technology offers great promise for apprehending criminals; the governments of many countries are using it or evaluating it.

Discussion: *Do you consider this application of face-recognition technology an invasion of privacy? If so, do the benefits justify the means?*

Discussion: *Identify and describe at least two other applications (not mention above) for face-recognition technology.*

DISCUSSION AND PROBLEM SOLVING

8-1.1 Describe what yesterday would have been like if you had not used the capabilities of computers. Keep in mind that businesses with which you deal rely on computers and that many of your appliances are computer-based.

8-1.2 Two lawyers used the Internet to broadcast thousands of e-mail messages advertising their services. They were subsequently flamed (sent angry e-mail messages) and vilified by Internet users for what they believed to be an inappropriate use of the Net. The attorneys broke no laws. Was the reaction of the Internet users justified? Explain.

8-2.1 Why is green computing important to society?

8-2.2 Expand these abbreviations and briefly describe what they mean: VODS, RSI, and CTD.

8-2.3 Evaluate your workplace at home, school, or work from an ergonomic perspective. Consider the concepts presented in Section 8-2 and the guidelines illustrated in Figure 8-3.

8-2.4 What can you do, which you are not doing now, that would be a move toward green computing?

8-3.1 Give an example of how computer monitoring might be applied at the clerical level of activity. Give another example for the operational, tactical, or strategic level.

8-3.2 The Internal Revenue Service also uses computer matching to identify those who might be underpaying taxes. Is this an invasion of privacy or a legitimate approach to tax collection?

8-3.3 In the past, bank officers have been reluctant to report computer crimes. If you were a customer of a bank that made such a decision, how would you react?

8-3.4 Who knows what about you? List as many nongovernment organizations (specific names or generic) as you can that collect and maintain personal information about you. Do the same for government organizations.

8-3.5 Discuss the kinds of personal information that can be obtained by analyzing a person's credit card transactions during the past year.

8-4.1 Why would a judge sentence one person to 10 years in jail for an unarmed robbery of $25 from a convenience store and another to 18 months for computer fraud involving millions of dollars?

8-4.2 Discuss what you can do at your college or place of employment to minimize the possibility of computer crime.

8-4.3 Generally, society has an erroneous perception of hackers. What is this perception and why is it erroneous?

8-4.4 Internet cybercops at CERT are no longer concerned with minor intrusions to Net security. Why is this?

8-5.1 What should be done at your college to improve computer security?

8-5.2 What should be done at your place of work to improve computer security?

8-5.3 Which scenario offers the greatest security for your credit card: paying for a meal at a restaurant, buying a pair of shoes over the Internet, or purchasing a PC via telephone mail order? Explain.

8-5.4 What precautions can be taken to minimize the effects of hardware failure?

8-5.5 The use of a digital ID provides secure passage for your e-mail and its attachments. How much would you pay for the use of a digital ID per e-mail?

8-5.6 The e-signature does not apply to family law documents, such as wills, trusts, adoptions, or divorce. Should it? Explain.

FOCUS ON PERSONAL COMPUTING

1. With green computing now a societal imperative, if not law, we have cradle-to-grave responsibility for our PCs. Survey five people who have discarded obsolete PCs. Assess each with regard to proper product stewardship. Find an organization that will accept and probably dispose of computer hardware. Describe the process by which you transfer your obsolete hardware to the organization and note the cost to you.

2. Write a personal computing code of ethics that relates to your specific computing environment and can serve as your guide during personal computing activities, including your interaction with the cyberworld.

3. Assess your workplace. Describe what you can do to make it more ergonomically compatible with personal computing, that is, minimize health concerns and maximize effective interaction.

INTERNET EXERCISES @ www.prenhall.com/long

1. The Online Study Guide (multiple choice, true/false, matching, and essay questions)
2. Internet Learning Activities
- Ergonomics
- Ethics in Computing
3. Serendipitous Internet Activities
- Music

chapter

9

Learning Objectives

Once you have read and studied this chapter, you will have learned:

- The crux of critical Internet issues that must be confronted by our information society (Section 9-1).

- The scope and concepts associated with e-commerce (Section 9-2).

- The concepts and potential of electronic publishing (Section 9-3).

- The pros and cons of telecommuting (Section 9-4).

- Approaches, considerations, and techniques associated with the design and publishing of Web sites (Section 9-5).

EXPLORING THE CYBERWORLD

Why this chapter is important to you

Someday in the near future all of us may be online—all the time. We will use a variety of devices, including cell phones, wearable PCs, handhelds, e-book readers, Internet appliances, and other devices not yet imagined. These devices will be in our home, office, car, pocket, or just about any place. If you are not now immersed into the cyberworld, you surely will be in the near future.

To function effectively in the cyberworld, you need to be sensitive to critical Internet issues because eventually you may need to resolve, or at least confront, these issues personally, with your family, and at work. The downside to issues associated with cyberspace, such as the accessibility of sexually explicit material, gambling, and other controversial issues, are addressed in this chapter.

Life at school, at home, and at work is easier if you understand the directions in which our information society is headed. This chapter presents several major trends that have, or surely will have, a major impact on your personal and professional life. These include electronic commerce (e-commerce), electronic publishing, and telecommuting. Electronic commerce has emerged as a major strategic priority in most corporations. The discussion herein should help you get on board. The shift has begun from print publishing to electronic (Web) publishing. In this chapter, you'll learn about electronic publishing and why it is rapidly changing the way information is distributed. Throughout most of the past century, people traveled to the workplace then returned home in the evening. For millions, that model is changing now that communication technology allows people to telecommute to work. The material in this chapter will help you learn more about this important career alternative.

One of the best ways to explore the cyberworld is to become a part of it and create your own presence on the Internet. In this section, you'll learn the concepts associated with creating and publishing a Web site.

For most of us, the cyberworld is largely unexplored. After completing this chapter, it is likely that you will have discovered some areas of the cyberworld that may have a lasting impact on your life and, possibly, the lives of those around you.

Prior to 1989 and the introduction of the World Wide Web and its user-friendly interface (see Figure 9-1), the Internet was used mostly by technical people who were willing to learn its cryptic text interface. The Web opened the Internet to the masses and to inevitable abuse. The Internet remains a digital Wild West, largely without law and order. Nevertheless, the lure of this new frontier has an endless stream of wagon trains "heading west." Like the Wild West, anyone can come along.

THE SHADY SIDE OF THE INTERNET

The Internet is public land; therefore, accessibility is one of the inherent problems on the Internet. With unlimited accessibility come mischievous hackers, hate mongers, and pornography.

Hackers

Misguided hackers and crackers are continually doing what they can to disrupt the flow of information. Often these electronic assaults are on Internet servers and the other communications devices that route data from node to node on the Net. These actions are like changing the road signs along the interstate highway system. Unfortunately, overzealous hackers and crackers don't stop at changing the road signs. They also plant computer viruses on the Internet disguised as enticing downloadable files or distributed as e-mail. Once downloaded or opened as an e-mail attachment, the virus infects the PC and creates havoc, often destroying files and sometimes even entire hard disks. Crackers have stolen valuable software, traded corporate and country secrets, hijacked telephone credit card numbers, distributed copyrighted photos and songs, and run online securities scams.

Hate Mongers

The Internet is filled with hate mongers—those who would spew venom designed to divide further the world by race, gender, color, politics, ideology, nationality, or religion. Their objective is to foster hate, discrimination, prejudice, bigotry, and/or intolerance. Before the Internet, these extremists would march on courthouses, distribute leaflets, rent space on roadside signs, speak to whomever would listen on street corners, or do whatever they could to get media attention. Typically, they would reach a few dozen or, maybe, a few thousand people. In this new Internet era, they can create hate sites espousing their messages to millions throughout the world.

Hate and lies can be spread over cyberspace with anonymity. However, according to our courts and the sentiments of most people, anonymous speech is part of the price we pay for a democracy. Unfortunately, the privilege of anonymity on the Net is abused routinely.

Hate is easy to find on the Internet. To put Internet hate into perspective, these are just a few of the themes you might find on the Internet: antiwhite, antiblack, anti-Semitic, Anti-Judeo-Christian, anti-Muslim, antigay, antiwomen, antimen, anti-AOL, anti-Spice Girls, anti-Beatles, anti-Star Trek, anti-Survivor (the TV show), anti-Olympics, anti-Ford, and anti-Chevy. There are even "I hate you" sites. Hate also is promoted through newsgroups, mailing lists, and aggressive spam campaigns.

By definition, these hate sites represent extremist views. Some, however, get very personal, often attacking public figures in politics, sports, and the film industry. Some hate sites simply attack individuals who have differing views, often to the point of libel. Clearly, some sites have ignored legal and moral authority in inviting readers to harm selected people or to destroy their property.

FIGURE 9–1 The First Web Server Computer
The World Wide Web originated here in 1989 at the CERN computer center. CERN is the European Organization for Nuclear Research. Did Web inventor Tim Berners-Lee envision the many serious issues that would result from millions of interconnected Web servers?

Courtesy of CERN

Some hate sites are parodies that are meant to be "funny," but at the expense of those people, ideas, institutions, and so on being attacked. Typically, the small groups of people who help sling the mud see the humor, but most people are repulsed.

What can or should be done to thwart the efforts of hate mongers? Some say nothing should be done. After all, the Internet is free and generally unrestricted regarding content. Others cannot understand why these users would be allowed to maintain a presence on the Internet. Under pressure, several major Internet portals have decided not to include such sites in their indices (the sites they categorize for their menus and search engines). This action doesn't make them go away; it just makes them harder to find. Also, the United States government is beginning to crack down on hate mongers who threaten physical harm or damage. Several people have been imprisoned for the words and/or images they included on their hate sites.

Pornography

It's possible to get hundreds of thousands, if not millions, of hits when you enter sex-related keywords, such as "XXX," into a major Internet portal's search engine. Sexually explicit material comprises 1.5% of all Internet content—that's a lot when you consider that the Internet has billions of pages.

Any conceivable type of sexually explicit content that can be digitized is on the Internet. Much of this is available to whomever wishes to explore the sites, but mostly, sexually explicit sites require users to subscribe to their fee-based services. The services might include adult language, links to nudity, still images, live video, and interactive sessions where users have a video and voice/text link with the site. Sadly, the online sale of pornography is one of e-commerce's biggest success stories.

The controversy about whether sexually explicit material on the Internet should be banned or controlled has been debated by local library boards and in the highest courts of the land. The debate will rage on because controlling Net content is difficult, if not impossible, in the current environment. Therefore, parents with children who go online and facilities that make the Internet available to the public, such as libraries, can opt to use **filtering programs** that deny access to certain types of "undesirable" content (sexually explicit material, those that foster terrorism, gambling, and so on). Because Internet pornography has become an international issue, these sites are at least making an effort to discourage viewing by minors (young people). They do this by asking visitors to confirm that they are adults and that they understand exactly what is contained at the Web site. As you might imagine, many ignore the warnings and just click through to the content pages.

GAMBLING

Internet gambling, also called online gambling, is simply placing bets on sports contests or the playing of casino-type games (roulette, slot machines, lotteries, bingo, Keno, video poker, and so on) over the Internet (see Figure 9-2). The betting, playing, and passing of money is done through Internet technology. All Internet casinos are located offshore, outside the United States. These casinos are licensed in countries that promote gambling as an opportunity to improve their economy.

Several hundred sites offer Internet gambling, but all require that you deposit money before gambling with them. Winnings are deposited to your account and losses are deducted.

Gambling is illegal in most areas of the United States, but Internet technology has rendered state and country boundaries to be nothing more than lines on a map. Nevertheless, the legal and moral issues surrounding online gambling are being addressed at all levels of government. Internet gambling is one of those issues whose growth is much faster than the legal system can accommodate. Already, it is clear that controversy is sure to surround Internet gambling indefinitely.

INTERNET SECURITY

Security on the Internet is a serious issue, especially with the recent explosion of *e-commerce*. E-commerce means the electronic transfer of money and plenty of opportunity for fraud and theft. Organizations have been forced to return to the days of walled forts and castles to protect themselves from cyberthieves. One approach is to set up *intranets* within enterprises that permit access to the Internet through a firewall. A **firewall** is software that is designed to restrict unwanted access to an organization's network or its intranet. Virtually all Internet server computers are protected by firewall software, which sets up a communications filter between the computer and the Internet. The firewall screens electronic traffic in both directions so that organizational security is maintained. The screening process can be adjusted to various levels of security. For example, an organization can set restrictions on the size and/or number of e-mail attachments permitted to enter the system.

Always-on broadband Internet access via DSL, cable modem, and satellite poses greater risks of unauthorized access for home networks and individual computers. Fortunately, firewalls are available for home networks and individual PCs, as well, through either the operating system or a router.

The security of individual transactions on the Internet is protected by a variety of technologies, including *encryption* techniques, which are discussed in Chapter 8, and digital certificates. A **digital**

THE CRYSTAL BALL:
The Trend Toward Internet-Based Personal Communications The telephone has been the foundation of remote personal communication for almost 100 years and it remains so, today. That, however, is changing. Over the next few years, we can expect costly electronic telephone switching networks and their limited audio communications capability to give way to sophisticated Internet telephony that includes videoconferencing. Although at its embryonic stage of development, Internet telephony is on target to provide a wide range of communications capabilities for considerably less cost because it is delivered over a computer network. Each year a greater percentage of our personal communications will shift to the Internet and the telephone as we know it will begin to fade away.

FIGURE 9–2 NET CONCERNS AND ISSUES

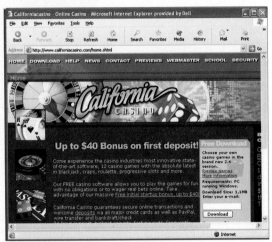

ONLINE GAMBLING

Gambling is one of the more established e-commerce applications and is readily available for those who wish to gamble. An online gambling casino gives you up to $50 in chips to get you started.

ATMs EVERYWHERE

Many cyberworld issues are not apparent. The existence and/or location of an ATM are issues for some people. While most of us see ATMs as a convenience, others see them as unsafe and a threat to their money or as a future crime site.

Courtesy of Diebold, Incorporated

TYPICAL SPAM

Anybody with an e-mail address gets it—spam, or unsolicited e-mail. This spam, which is in html format (versus text), is representative. The html format enables formatting and embedded images, making the files larger and your wait to view your legitimate mail longer. Several spam items invite you to apply for very inexpensive life insurance. "John" gives us an opportunity to earn $50,000 with only a $20 investment. How about getting a university diploma without studying or going to class? You are invited to become a "legally ordained minister within 48 hours." One spammer asks us to buy four million e-mail addresses so we can become spammers.

certificate is an attachment to an electronic message that verifies that the sender is who he or she claims to be. Such devices minimize the possibility that a credit card number, a legal document, financial information, or a private communication can be intercepted or passed off as something that it is not. It is far more likely that your credit card would be stolen by a thief with roving eyes at a checkout counter than as a result of an Internet transaction. Web sites that give you the option to pay by credit card provide detailed explanations of their security policies and what they do to protect the integrity of your information.

SPAM

And then there's spam, what we used to think of as junk mail, except that now it's in the cyberworld as well (see Figure 9-2). *Spam* is unsolicited junk e-mail, mostly advertising for commercial products or services. Occasionally **spammers,** or those who send spam, spam unsuspecting people with political messages. Though most of us would prefer not to be spammed, it's as difficult to rid the public Internet of spam as it is to rid our mail boxes of junk mail. Just like at home, we must sort through the spam to find our legitimate e-mail. Also, people are concerned that spam is taking up valuable bandwidth on the Internet, stressing the information capacity of the Net.

Let's dispel the myth that the term, spam, was derived from the SPAM luncheon meat made by Hormel Foods. Actually, the derivation of spam can be traced back to an old Monty Python comedy routine where Vikings howled "spam spam spam spam" to drown out other conversations. Similarly, spam tends to overwhelm people's e-mail inboxes, making important messages difficult to find. Hormel Foods is no longer concerned about the unfortunate association with their lunchmeat, but the company has asked that people show a little respect for their SPAM by spelling it with capital letters.

Spammers get your e-mail address through a variety of sources. It is difficult to track how you turn up on somebody's spam list. One thing is for sure, spam costs you more to receive than it does for it to be sent. Consider the fact that millions of spam messages are sent each day to AOL users. The result is that these users must spend up to 10 cumulative person-years simply deleting these unwanted messages. Generally, we perceive spam to be advertisements for worthless, deceptive, and/or partly or entirely fraudulent products or services. Commercial information services, such as AOL, and ISPs use sophisticated filters, which are continually updated, to minimize the amount of spam that reaches their customers. Most e-mail client software, such as Microsoft Outlook, has filters capable of deleting much of the pornography-related spam. The client filter also routes spam to a junk e-mail folder for review if user-specified keywords or phrases are in the subject and/or message ("100%," "guaranteed," "best mortgage," "refinance," "FREE," "!!!," and so on).

Regrettably, spammers are very imaginative and do what they can to stay one step ahead of efforts to stop them. For example, often spammers use the "hit and run" approach where they open an account with an ISP, send thousands of unsolicited e-mail messages, then leave town and do it again somewhere else. Spammers don't stay put long enough to be **flamed**, although recipients sometimes try. Flaming results in a barrage of scathing messages from irate Internet users. More often, flaming is for people who post something outlandish, inappropriate, or out of phase with the societal norms to a newsgroup or mailing list.

Others who might be outraged at happenings on the Internet are fighting back through the legal system and with their pocketbooks. They're placing pressure on legislatures, often through e-mail campaigns, to make laws more in line with societal norms. Others are simply choosing not to frequent sites or to shop at sites they believe offer inappropriate content. A store without customers soon folds.

To date, there is no central clearinghouse to which you can write to get your name taken off a direct e-mail advertiser's mailing list. However, a number of spammers advertise such a service as a way of adding names to their spam database. Information services and ISPs are doing what they can to thwart spam, but options are limited for the individual user. Some of the more ethical online advertisers give users a legitimate option to be removed from their mailing lists. At the other end of the spectrum are those spammers who ask you to call them to be removed. What they don't tell you is that you are being charged $2 per minute for the call.

As we change, the Internet changes. The Internet is a worldwide work-in-progress. It is our duty to promote positive change, but we must at all times recognize that it will continue to shape us as individuals and as a society. In time, this information medium, like its predecessors, newspapers, radio, and television, will be taken for granted like the air we breathe. It's incumbent upon us to ensure that we continue to breathe clean air, both in the real world and in cyberspace.

9-1.1 The Internet is now secure and no longer vulnerable to malicious hackers. (T/F)

9-1.2 Internet law and order is refined and explicit. (T/F)

9-1.3 Conducting business online is called: (a) electronic business, (b) cyber commerce, (c) e-commerce, or (d) cyber business.

9-1.4 Unsolicited junk e-mail is called: (a) spam, (b) pam, (c) weanies, or (d) flames.

SECTION **SELF-CHECK**

9-2   E-Commerce

In time, whatever can go online probably will—in business, in academia, and in government. The trend in the business world is to encourage people to go online via *electronic commerce*.

WHAT IS E-COMMERCE?

E-commerce is simply business conducted online or via some form of data communications. The scope of electronic commerce includes a variety of activities related to the buying and selling of goods or services over the Internet (see Figure 9-3). Some of the major activities often associated with e-commerce include the following.

- **Virtual marketplaces** that provide **e-tailing** (online retailing)
- Internet-based marketing or advertising

WHY THIS SECTION IS IMPORTANT TO YOU

As businesses and educational institutions strive for the competitive advantage and government organizations strive for improved service, implementation of electronic commerce (e-commerce) has emerged as a strategic planning priority. This section will give you the understanding you need to become a full partner in the inevitable shift to e-commerce.

- Online market research and surveys designed to gather product use, demographic, and other appropriate market research data
- *Business-to-business* (or *B2B*), the computer-to-computer exchange of data and information between businesses
- **Business-to-consumer** (**B2C**), the electronic interactions between businesses and consumers via Internet server computers
- The use of a variety of technology-based approaches aiding interactions among businesses and between businesses and consumers (e-mail, fax, intranets, extranets, Internet telephoning, and so on)

The scope of e-commerce is illustrated in Figure 9-4. E-commerce makes good economic sense.

FIGURE 9–3   **E-COMMERCE ON THE ROAD**

HIGH SPEED TOLL BOOTHS
Electronic commerce takes on many forms. For example, scanners along many toll roads read driver information sent from windshield-mounted transponders (see inset) as cars pass through at highway speeds. The electronic tollbooths transmit the data directly to a central computer system, often over the Internet, and the toll is deducted from the driver's account.

Courtesy of Lockheed Martin Corporation

GAMING IS BIG BUSINESS
This young man is on vacation in a car, enjoying the scenery, and playing a video game with a friend back home via a wireless Internet link. He is viewing the game via a wearable display. Rather than purchase gaming software, some gamers pay a monthly fee to a gaming service, then download and play any of hundreds of games.

Photo courtesy of Microvision Incorporated

- *Customers/patrons can go online to obtain information.* It's much less expensive than having to mail expensive brochures, newsletters, or manuals.

- *Customers/patrons can complete transactions and submit information online.* A growing number of taxpayers file their tax returns online. The tax returns are checked and processed electronically, saving time and money for the taxpayer and the government.

- *Customers can shop online.* E-tailers (online retailers) can sell and process orders entirely online, and then ship goods directly from the manufacturer/supplier, thus eliminating the need for hand processing and for bricks-and-mortar storefronts.

- *Businesses can communicate computer to computer.* Business-to-business (B2B) falls under the umbrella of e-commerce. In B2B, computers from one company can talk directly to computers of another company on many applications, such as payment and billing, thus eliminating the need for time-consuming paper

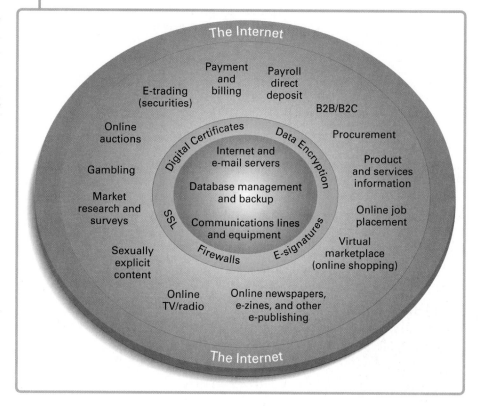

FIGURE 9–4

SCOPE OF E-COMMERCE
The Internet with its Internet servers, databases, and communications facilities enables a wide array of e-commerce applications. These tools of e-commerce are protected by a variety of security measures, such as encryption and firewalls.

transaction processing and the delays associated with postal delivery. Also, automated processing of transactions results in far fewer errors.

- *Students can learn online.* Universities and other providers of education are leveraging intellectual content previously designed for the classroom into online courses that no longer require a classroom space.

ELECTRONIC COMMERCE LEVELS THE PLAYING FIELD

The business model of the twentieth century made it very difficult for small companies to go head-to-head with larger companies. Electronic commerce appears to be emerging as the business model for the twenty-first century. E-commerce, which evolved from the Internet, has leveled the playing field. Companies no longer need large, geographically dispersed sales staffs or experienced international trade specialists to operate on a global scale. Judicious use of e-commerce enables people to reach potential customers without dedicating huge amounts to sales staff, advertising, and public relations campaigns. In the e-commerce world, small and large businesses compete side-by-side. The same is true for start-up and established businesses. Once a business gets a customer's attention, it can establish a close relationship with the consumer by offering a variety of real-time Net-based services, such as online buying, online training sessions, access to databases, continuously updated product catalogs, and so on.

E-MONEY AND E-COMMERCE

Over the past few millenniums, people have used many different types of personal assets to make business transactions. We've bartered (traded) with animals, goods (precious stones, corn, and so on), and personal services. In modern times, we've used money (paper and coin) and written checks. We've used charge cards, debit cards, and various electronic banking systems, such as automatic withdrawal. Today, relatively seldom do we pay for items with actual money. We are drawing closer to a cashless society and e-commerce is giving us a push to move even closer to a cashless society (see Figure 9-4). This is because e-commerce revolves around systems where money changes hands over the Internet or through other electronic means.

THE CRYSTAL BALL:
Shopping in 2010 The electronic storefront is slowly changing the way we shop and purchase products. Each year, online sales comprise a bigger piece of total sales. By 2010, online sales may rival storefront sales. The driving forces behind this shift in shopping habits will be *convenience, customization, selection,* and *price.* You can shop the world in front of your PC. You can customize products to meet your needs, from pants to automobiles. The selection is comprehensive. Competition is fierce because price comparison is a one-click process in the virtual marketplace.

E-commerce deals in digital money where withdrawals and deposits of any size and complexity are done at the speed of light. Standards for the manner in which money is exchanged are continuing to evolve. Standards are further along for B2B, but several proprietary payment schemes are available for B2C. For example, several companies offer online purchasing systems that enable consumers to create and use an **electronic wallet** that stores their billing and shipping information in controlled server facilities. Credit card numbers are encrypted in a database that is not connected to the Internet. The consumer simply clicks on a "Pay" button to send all billing and shipping information already stored in the electronic wallet to the merchant and makes a credit card transaction via a secure Internet server.

E-COMMERCE SECURITY

Mention e-commerce and people immediately share their concerns about security. Among the masses, Internet security is still viewed as suspect, even though experts argue that e-commerce transactions done in cyberspace are more secure than those in the physical world. When you pay with a credit card at a hotel or over the phone to a mail order retailer, your credit card number is exposed directly to several people. That exposure and the often lax procedures for handling records of your number, such as the store's copy, make such transactions vulnerable to fraud. Retail sales employees, outside of the cyberworld, are responsible for most credit card fraud.

In the cyberworld, e-commerce transactions are safer for both merchant and consumer because they are encrypted using Secure Sockets Layer (SSL), a communications protocol that provides a secure connection to a particular server, thus protecting information transmitted over the Internet to and from the server.

Certainly, there is no 100% guarantee that Internet-based credit card or transaction information will not be compromised. However, those who deal in cyber security assure us that such information is safer running through the Internet via SSL than it is working its way through a manual paper flow system. On the business side, an e-commerce site may be safer than a bricks-and-mortar store that can be robbed, flooded, burned, or blown away.

BUSINESS-TO-BUSINESS APPLICATIONS

Business-to-business applications have the potential to save companies substantial amounts of money. For example, companies are estimating that B2B via the Internet can reduce purchasing costs by up to 20%. Companies are buying direct and using just-in-time strategies to minimize third-party involvement and reduce inventories.

B2B also is being explored in many other areas, including the matching of unused patents to companies that might benefit from them, thus slashing R&D expenses. Now, almost everything is on the Internet auction block. That is, any excess in services (extra seats at a seminar) or in inventory (too many perishable apples) that might otherwise be wasted can be made available to the highest bidder.

The most popular and easily implemented B2B applications involve buying and selling between companies. However, the applications for B2B are limitless, so we can expect increasing electronic cooperation between companies in what are usually win-win and even win-win-win situations. At present, those industries enjoying the greatest growth in business-to-business e-commerce are in hardware and software, automobile parts, health care, electronics, chemicals, and transportation. Other industries, however, are moving as quickly as possible into e-commerce and B2B.

BUSINESS-TO-CONSUMER APPLICATIONS

Whenever businesses can reach and interact with consumers more efficiently online and/or via a computer, they turn that opportunity into a B2C application. Government agencies, places of learning, and companies are encouraging each other and us to do more business online with an ever-increasing number of B2C applications. It simply costs less money when activities are moved online and paper, people, and other expenses are minimized. Also, the level of service may be better. For example, why do people in the United States who file their taxes electronically via PC receive a tax credit? It's both economics and service. The cost of manually handling a return is much higher than the cost of the $10 tax credit. Because the return is processed faster, the taxpayer receives his or her refund more quickly. The IRS is on target to get 80% participation by 2007.

B2C applications let you do all of these things and more (see Figure 9-5).

- Do a week's worth of grocery shopping in 10 minutes.
- Purchase gourmet chocolates without being tempted by the goodies at the candycounter.
- Book your airline and motel reservations without making a dozen calls.
- Check out job openings in your area of the country.

FIGURE 9–5 BUSINESS-TO-CONSUMER (B2C) APPLICATIONS

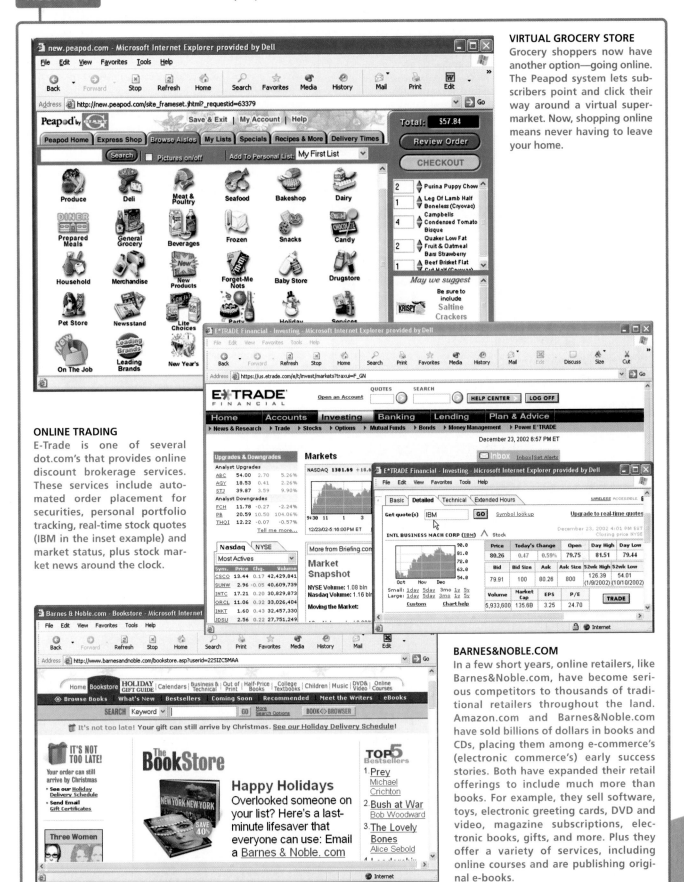

VIRTUAL GROCERY STORE
Grocery shoppers now have another option—going online. The Peapod system lets subscribers point and click their way around a virtual supermarket. Now, shopping online means never having to leave your home.

ONLINE TRADING
E-Trade is one of several dot.com's that provides online discount brokerage services. These services include automated order placement for securities, personal portfolio tracking, real-time stock quotes (IBM in the inset example) and market status, plus stock market news around the clock.

BARNES&NOBLE.COM
In a few short years, online retailers, like Barnes&Noble.com, have become serious competitors to thousands of traditional retailers throughout the land. Amazon.com and Barnes&Noble.com have sold billions of dollars in books and CDs, placing them among e-commerce's (electronic commerce's) early success stories. Both have expanded their retail offerings to include much more than books. For example, they sell software, toys, electronic greeting cards, DVD and video, magazine subscriptions, electronic books, gifts, and more. Plus they offer a variety of services, including online courses and are publishing original e-books.

FIGURE 9–5 continued

E-TAILING

The world's largest retailer may someday be the world's largest e-tailer. Forecasters are predicting that by 2005 those people who use the Internet for shopping will account for three fourths of all retail dollars spent. Currently, 68% of all online shoppers say they researched products online before purchasing them from traditional retailers.

FLOWERS FAST

One of the most frequently purchased items on the Net is flowers. At this FTD site, click on the type of occasion, select a floral arrangement, then enter the desired delivery date, a gift card message, billing information, and a send-to address. It's as simple as that.

ONLINE AUCTIONS

Online auction Web sites, such as eBay Motors, let you bid on automobiles, trucks, and other vehicles that people from all over the world are willing to put up for auction. eBay Motors, an eBay spinoff dedicated to motor vehicles, lists thousands of vehicles. In the example, "Porsche 911" was selected and 239 related items were being auctioned off, including many Porsche 911 cars. You can bid on an item until the end of the bidding period. The winner is notified by e-mail and the seller and buyer communicate to complete the deal.

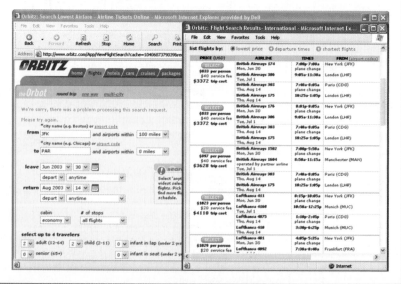

AIRLINE TRAVEL PLANNING

The Orbitz Web site enables you to make airline reservations and purchase tickets. Simply tell the system how many are traveling, where you will depart from and where you want to go, the dates of travel, the type of tickets you want, and any airline preferences. The system returns the best-priced itineraries for your travel dates, then gives you an opportunity to select and purchase the tickets. This area of B2C is causing concern among travel agents in that more and more people are choosing to go online to buy their tickets.

- Send flowers (virtual and real).
- Trade stocks online.
- Do your banking transactions from home.

Rather than loading the kids into the SUV or minivan on shopping day, you can send them out to play and do your shopping and other business from the comfort of your home. Millions of busy people have traded their shopping carts for keyboards to take advantage of the emergence of e-commerce.

In a few years, according to projections, e-commerce in cyberspace will be just as significant as in-person, mail, and telephone sales. If businesses are not planning for this real-time economy, they may not be doing business to the fullest (if at all) in a few years. Any business that hopes to stay in business in this new millennium is offering or planning to offer its products and/or services online. These few examples should give you some insight into what we have and can expect in the near future.

E-Tailing: Internet Retailing

Some people mistakenly think e-commerce means online shopping. It is that and much, much more, but online shopping via e-tailers that sell consumer goods remains the foundation of B2C. Online shoppers can purchase toys, electronics, greeting cards, automobiles, securities, houses, U.S. stamps, just about anything that Wal-Mart sells, and a lot more (see Figure 9-5). Currently, the most popular consumer items purchased over the Internet are books, CDs, and all computer products. However, action is rapidly increasing on everything from groceries to pickup trucks.

People go online to shop for many reasons. The reason cited most often is that the stores are always open. People love the convenience of shopping anytime—day or night—and in whatever they happen to be wearing. People also go online to save time. They avoid traffic, crowds, lines, and the never-ending search for a parking place. Another reason is product availability. You may need to go to a dozen different shoe stores to find a particular style and size of sneaker. In contrast, an e-tailer would offer every style in every size for one-stop shopping. Increasingly, shoppers are noting price and service as reasons to shop electronically. Many e-tailers can sell for less, sometimes a lot less. They can keep a low inventory (or no inventory when items are shipped directly from the manufacturer). Plus, they avoid the real estate and personnel expenses associated with a traditional storefront. E-tailers can offer a variety of services that might not be available in a traditional store. For example, an online bookstore might notify you via e-mail when a particular book is available in paperback.

E-tailers can offer these benefits to online shoppers.

- Electronic databases and catalogs let shoppers find products easily and quickly.
- You can compare prices more easily. Some Web sites, such as mySimon.com and PriceGrabber.com, do it for you, giving you prices from and hyperlinks to several e-tailers.
- Online e-tailers make detailed product information readily available to consumers.
- Online shoppers can configure customizable products, such as personal computers, and see how changes to the configuration affects the price.

Of course, the traditional storefront has its advantages as well. Shoppers can interact with a real, live salesperson and they can take their purchases home on the same day. You can try on clothes and drive cars before you buy them. Eventually, however, forecasters predict that these advantages may not be enough as e-tailers begin to find ways to satisfy customer demands. Already, online shoppers can create three-dimensional models of themselves for when they wish to "try on" clothes. This may not be the same, but will it be enough when combined with the other conveniences of online shopping?

The one big advantage that the traditional storefront has over cyberbusinesses is *fulfillment;* that is, the process of actually delivering the product or service to the customer. In the traditional store, the customer takes the item off-the-shelf, pays for it, and walks out the door. In the cyberworld, money is exchanged and the e-tailer sends the customer a shipping order via e-mail stating when the order is to be shipped. It is not unusual for merchandise to be delivered within a day or two. Most online stores shoot for fulfillment within five business days. Fulfillment, however, has been the biggest problem for the so-called "dot.com" businesses. Many that have failed to deliver in a timely manner have folded. We can expect to see a variety of imaginative solutions to the fulfillment problem over the next few years.

The future of online retailing and selling is very bright, but what about traditional approaches to sales? What will become of our department stores, specialty stores, bookstores, and so on? It is unlikely that any of these would disappear anytime soon; however, it's apparent that people are shopping and buying more at the virtual store and less at the bricks-and-mortar store. Each approach has its advantages. It looks like we'll still have the option to shop downtown or online for the foreseeable future.

Groceries Online

"Smart Shopping for Busy People"® is Peapod's® slogan. Peapod, an e-tail grocer on the Internet, has made life easier for a great many people in many large cities throughout the United States. Peapod and other online grocers are giving us a glimpse into the future of retailing—the *virtual grocery store*. Grocery subscribers go shopping at the virtual grocery store by logging onto the store's Web site. Once online, they can shop interactively for grocery items, including fresh produce, deli, bakery, meat, and frozen products (see Figure 9-5). Rather than running from aisle to aisle, they simply point and click around the screen for the items they want.

Online grocery stores, such as Peapod and Wal-Mart, are linked directly to their partner stores' computer systems (for example, Safeway, Jewel, and Wal-Mart Supercenter). When you send your shopping list to an online grocer, an order is transmitted to the nearest partner store. A professionally trained shopper takes your order, grabs a shopping cart, and does your shopping for you. The professional shopper takes a fraction of the time you would take because the list is ordered by aisle and the shopper knows exactly what to get. You can redeem your coupons when the shopper/delivery person arrives with your food. Food is delivered in temperature-controlled containers.

Books and CDs Online

If you've traveled in the World Wide Web at all, you've probably run across Amazon.com and Barnes&Noble.com, two of the most well-known online stores (see Figure 9-5). These virtual stores are more than just bookstores. They offer thousands of books, CDs, audiobooks, DVDs, computer games, toys, and more, including customer reviews, personal recommendations, best-seller lists, musical chart toppers, and gift suggestions. From Alternative to Zydeco, Hip-hop to Bebop, their online customers will find everything from the latest releases to hard-to-find gems in nearly 300 musical genres.

E-Trading: Internet Brokerage Services

Why would you want to make online investments electronically through an online brokerage service instead of through a full-service broker? Those who do, cite price and the ability to make their own trading decisions as the main reasons they go online. To date, online companies that provide **e-trading** services have been very competitive on price, a serious motivator to savvy investors. Generally, an e-trading charge is much less than that of a traditional broker. Frequent users of online brokerage services enjoy the autonomy of having the information resources they need to do their own research.

Currently, less than 10% of U.S. households are involved in online finance. This includes securities trading and online banking. However, online trading companies are experiencing tremendous growth in trading volume as more and more investors switch to online trading.

Online trading companies, such as E-Trade Group Inc., Charles Schwab & Co. Inc., and Datek Online Brokerage Services Corporation, are providing online discount brokerage services, including automated order placement, portfolio tracking and related market information, news, and other information services 24 hours a day, 7 days a week (see Figure 9-5). Online services offer essentially the same order options as their full-service cousins, including limit, stop, and stop limit orders for all securities trading on U.S. exchanges. And, the services usually are free. The investor pays only a relatively small fee to place the order.

Online Auctions

You can be part of a live auction 24 hours a day when you visit the eBay (see Figure 9-5) or ONSALE site. Just enter "online auctions" into an Internet search engine and you'll be amazed at what can be traded, bought, and sold.

Every day you can experience a new set of auctions where you will find thousands of items on which to bid. eBay boasts itself as the world's largest personal online trading community with millions of registered users. Individuals can use eBay to buy and sell items in more than 1000 categories, including collectibles, antiques, sports memorabilia, computers, toys, Beanie Babies, dolls, figures, coins, stamps, books, magazines, music, pottery, glass, photography, electronics, jewelry, gemstones, and much more. Users can find the unique and the interesting on eBay—everything from china to chintz chairs, teddy bears to trains, and furniture to figurines. Even Universal Studios has online auctions of exclusive celebrity memorabilia and collectibles direct from popular movies and television shows.

To make a bid, registered users simply select the item they want and enter the amount they wish to bid. At the end of the bidding period, which can be hours, a week, or more, the highest bid wins. Buyer and seller communicate directly to complete the deal.

Big Business B2C

Businesses not associated with selling consumer products are moving toward B2C whenever possible, as well. For example, most major airlines are committed to **electronic ticketing** (**e-ticketing**) and have begun to phase out traditional paper tickets. Several online ticketing companies, such as Orbitz.com and Travelocity.com, provide comprehensive, up-to-the-minute schedules and pricing. Once you have selected your flight(s), your e-ticket confirmation is e-mailed, faxed, or mailed directly to you. The e-ticket offers a number of advantages, one of which is reduced cost to airlines and passengers. E-tickets cannot be lost; they make it easy to change your flight itinerary; they offer same-day ticketing; and they offer faster refunds. Also, most major airports offer time-saving self-service check-in kiosks that let you check in, obtain a boarding pass, check your luggage, and, if you wish, change your seat assignment. The boarding pass, along with a picture ID, is shown at the departure gate, resulting in one less line on your trip.

General Motors executives are hoping that B2C will enable them to offer what customers say they want most—efficiently delivered, customized vehicles. They expect that the majority of all vehicles will be customized in the near future. GM has hundreds of e-commerce experts dedicated to creating B2C applications. Already over a million customers subscribe to GM's OnStar, a wireless emergency communications service that provides security, location and navigation guides, among other conveniences. GM and other automakers are developing a B2B and B2C system that will enable large-scale online trading of auto parts among automotive businesses and between businesses and consumers.

BUILDING A WEB SITE FOR E-COMMERCE

The system design and programming work that go into creating an e-commerce Web site to support a worldwide online auction site, such as eBay, or a large commercial e-tail site, such as Wal-Mart online, could take many millions of dollars and even a year or more to complete. However, a small company can get into the e-commerce business within a week for as little as $100 a month—as long as only a few products are to be sold. A number of **e-commerce hosting services** are available that enable customers with little or no experience in e-commerce to build their own e-commerce site. The e-commerce hosting service offers a customer everything needed to create an e-commerce site that will let customers shop and then "place" products in an *online shopping cart*. Customers simply click "check out" and the e-commerce hosting service processes the orders, all for a small monthly fee. Now that the construction of e-commerce sites is relatively quick, easy, and inexpensive, we can look for an explosion of B2C applications as small businesses come online to sell their goods and services.

E-COMMERCE'S RETURN ON INVESTMENT

The consensus in the industrial world is that e-commerce eventually will save businesses trillions of dollars, perhaps within a few years. Every company would like a piece of the action; however, successful e-commerce sites are the exception rather than the rule. It is not unusual for a company to spend millions of dollars in anticipation of tremendous returns only to find out that it was too late or used the wrong approach. Nevertheless, the corporate world has no option but to make a commitment to e-commerce, as there is too much at stake to be left behind. Top executives are concerned that standing still on e-commerce will allow the competition to gain an insurmountable lead. Competitive pressures to build e-commerce infrastructures within the companies are causing executives to reevaluate corporate and information technology priorities.

During the past few years, business has become much more aggressive about implementing the latest innovations in information technology. Management is increasingly motivated to implement information technology because of its potential for increasing profitability and its return on investment (estimated at 50%). Also, innovative use of information technology has a history of being the fastest and most economical way to give an organization a competitive advantage.

9-2.1	E-commerce takes place when businesses use copper wire to network company PCs. (T/F)
9-2.2	B2B is the computer-to-computer exchange of data and information between businesses. (T/F)
9-2.3	Which of the following is not true of Secure Sockets Layer: (a) provides a secure connection to a particular Internet server, (b) is abbreviated as SSL, (c) is a communications protocol, or (d) secures all peripheral cables to a PC's system unit?
9-2.4	What stores individual billing and shipping information to facilitate consumer e-commerce: (a) e-billfold, (b) handheld purse, (c) digital folder, or (d) electronic wallet?

SECTION SELF-CHECK

WHY THIS SECTION IS IMPORTANT TO YOU

For centuries, the words and images of the world were written/published and viewed on paper. That's changing. Much of what used to be printed is now in electronic format. An awareness of how it is done and what is available will help you take full advantage of this trend in publishing.

9-3 | Electronic Publishing

The ability to store and retrieve massive amounts of information from online storage (various types of disks) and the ability to make that information available through the Internet and networking have resulted in enthusiastic acceptance and use of electronic publishing. Indeed, we are seeing a dramatic shift in the way we get information, both for simple documents, such as internal project reports, and electronic magazines, called **e-zines.** The cyberworld already enables you to click your way to literally millions of online documents. Your microwave's users' guide is available online in case you lose it. College and universities post their general catalogs to the Net. State and federal tax forms and instructions are online. Brochures for cities, national parks, and thousands of tourist destinations are available online. Annual reports for many companies can be accessed on the Internet. All of these and millions more online documents can be viewed online or printed.

Consider those glossy brochures you get in your mailbox almost daily. These could cost the sender as much as five dollars or more. This is a very expensive way to introduce your product or service. These advertising dollars are, of course, built into the cost of the product or service. Organizations in government, education, and the private sector are looking to the Internet and electronic publishing to reduce or minimize this cost by making this information available online. For example, approximately one-third of the colleges in the United States now offer virtual tours of their campuses to prospective students. The virtual tours are much more than can be offered in a print brochure. The student has access to interactive maps, still and even motion video scenes from all over campus as well as campus life, interactive answers to many common questions, and much more.

ELECTRONIC DOCUMENTS

Historically, word processing and desktop publishing software have been used to produce documents that can be physically distributed in hard copy—letters, periodicals, magazines, books, reports, manuals, and many other forms of written communication and documentation. However, more and more of what we write never makes it to paper. Look at written correspondence. A few years ago, we wrote and sent letters and memos, but today e-mail outnumbers print correspondence 300 to 1.

An alternative to producing hard copy documents is **electronic publishing.** In electronic publishing, *electronic documents* are created that can be retrieved from disk storage—locally on a PC, on a public kiosk, on a portable device (palm PC, wearable PC, e-book, cellular phone, and so on), or from a remote server computer (see Figure 9-6). Electronic documents, also called *online documents*, are normally stored on a hard disk (the PC's, the network server's, the kiosk's, or an Internet server's) or in flash memory on a portable device. Electronic documents also are distributed on interchangeable disks, such as read-only CD-ROM or DVD, and on diskettes, such as Zip disks. All such documents are designed to be viewed on a monitor and most are interactive with hyperlinks to other parts of the same document or to other local or Net-based documents.

The business world is now linked via the Internet, intranets (an Internet within an organization), extranets (an intranet that is partially accessible to authorized outsiders, such as suppliers and customers), and VPNs (a virtual private network that works within the Internet's infrastructure). This electronic linking of the world has revolutionized the way we enter, retrieve, send, maintain, and view information. This worldwide networking has made it possible for business to move toward greater use of electronic publishing, which also is called **e-publishing.**

PERSONAL COMPUTING:
Shifting to Electronic Documents You may never take full advantage of your PC until you adopt an attitude that emphasizes electronic documents over printed hardcopy. Even though we work with electronic documents in Word and Excel, and we surf the Internet's Web pages, many of us still feel compelled to print electronic documents and Web pages, often for no reason. The next time you prepare to print a document ask yourself if you really need a hardcopy. You may be surprised to find that in many cases, a hardcopy is not needed and the best approach would be simply to recall the electronic document as needed. The shift to e-documents requires a shift in attitude, too. If you organize your folders to enable ready access to your electronic documents, you can save a lot of paper.

THE ADVANTAGES OF ELECTRONIC PUBLISHING

When compared to print publishing, the advantages of e-publishing become overwhelming for many publishing needs. Just about every printing need is a candidate for electronic publishing. Restaurant menus, college textbooks, magazines, romance novels, corporate sales manuals, civic club newsletters, annual reports, travel brochures, IRS forms, and many more traditional print documents are being published electronically.

Electronic Publishing Is Good for the Environment

Electronic publishing has eliminated the need to use trees to produce billions of printed pages. Electronic documents are being composed and distributed as bits. The availability of electronic publishing raises an important question: Can the fossil fuel, as well as the human effort, required to distribute millions of pounds of personnel manuals, reports, policy statements, newsletters, and many other types of printed material be put to better use?

FIGURE 9–6 READING THE ELECTRONIC DOCUMENT

EARLY CHILDHOOD LEARNING STATION

For these preschool children using IBM's KidSmart Early Learning Program, it is likely that interactive electronic documents, from e-books to quizzes, will be the norm throughout their years of formal and continued education.

Courtesy of International Business Machines Corporation. Unauthorized use not permitted.

THE ELECTRONIC BOOK

The main advantage of a traditional paper book over an electronic book is that you can take it anywhere and read it anywhere. That advantage is disappearing as people move to small, mobile notebook PCs, handheld PCs, and special-function e-books, such as this RCA eBook. The eBook can be taken anywhere and read anywhere, plus, it can store a dozen full-color books.

Photo courtesy of RCA

DISPLAYING E-DOCUMENTS IN A SQUARE INCH

An entire set of user manuals and corporate procedures can be placed on a memory card in a wearable PC. This knowledge worker can view any of thousands of "pages" of electronic documents on his high resolution Kopin CyberDisplay.

Courtesy of Kopin Corporation

ELECTRONIC INK

E Ink has created a technology that will enable us to read electronic documents, even books, that have the same look and feel as paper (shown here by Paul Drzaic). A special type of electronic ink is applied to flexible paper or almost any surface. Each one of the many millions of tiny microcapsules contains white particles suspended in a dark dye. Electronic signals cause the particles to move within the microcapsules, thus enabling the presentation of information. The company expects that e-books using this technology will be possible in five years.

Courtesy of E Ink Corporation

Electronic Documents Are Easily Updated

A company may print thousands of sales manuals. But when the company changes product prices, a routine occurrence in many industries, the printed sales manuals become out of date. The federal government routinely prints large quantities of informational documents. However, printed government documents are often inaccurate because of frequent changes in regulations and laws. In a world that is in constant change, print documents have become simply too difficult to maintain. In contrast, companies, the government, and anyone else can produce online documents that can be easily updated to reflect current circumstances. There is only one copy of an electronic document to change, and it is available electronically on demand. For decades, IBM sales and systems personnel spent several hours each month inserting updated pages in three-ring binders containing their product manuals. Now these documents are easily accessible, continuously updated online documents. Also, the oversized attaché case and its 30-pound load are no longer needed.

Electronic Documents Offer a Much Richer Form of Communication

An electronic format enables the integration of audio clips, video clips, and even animation, within the text and graphics. Print documents include only text and graphics. Electronic travel advertisements frequently include video clips that take you on visual tours of the local sites. The illustrations in online technical manuals are brought to life via an added dimension—animation. Animation can also be used to simplify complex diagrams.

Electronic Documents Can Be Interactive

Electronic documents permit interactivity. Electronic documents can include forms, pop-up boxes, and buttons that allow the user to enter information to a system. For example, the exercises associated with the companion Internet site for this book are interactive. A response box that allows the student to enter an answer to the exercise follows each exercise. Student answers to the exercises are sent via e-mail to the instructors.

Electronic Documents Facilitate Navigation

In the electronic environment, it is easy to move between areas of the documents. In a print document, you go to the table of contents or the index to obtain a page number for the topic of interest. Then you physically flip through the pages to find the topic. In an electronic document, the user simply clicks on the desired topic and the topic is immediately displayed for viewing.

Electronic Documents Are Searchable

Electronic documents are electronically searchable. An automobile parts sales representative can use the *find* feature to locate all references to a particular part in an online sales manual. The representative does this by entering a part name, a part number, or, possibly, the characteristics of the part (for example, water pump, Mercedes 380SL, or 1985).

Electronic Documents Are Tied Together by Hyperlinks

The hyperlink feature enables electronic links between different sections of an electronic document, or to other related electronic documents. In the print world, documents stand alone. In the electronic world, documents are "networked." A viewer has only to click on a hyperlink (usually highlighted text, an image, or a graphic icon) to navigate to and view related material. These hyperlinks enable a single electronic document to reach far beyond what you see on the screen.

CREATING ELECTRONIC DOCUMENTS

The three most popular formats for electronic documents are *word processing, HTML,* and *portable document.* Figure 9-7 shows how the material can be presented in each of these three formats.

Word Processing Documents

During the early 1990s, word processing was used extensively to create both print and online documents. The online documents, however, were created for use within the confines of a particular organization. This is because the viewer for such documents is the word processing software used to create them. This type of online document works well as long as all users have the same word processing program. This lack of portability, though, limits the effectiveness of word processing-based electronic

FIGURE 9–7   FORMATS FOR ELECTRONIC DOCUMENTS

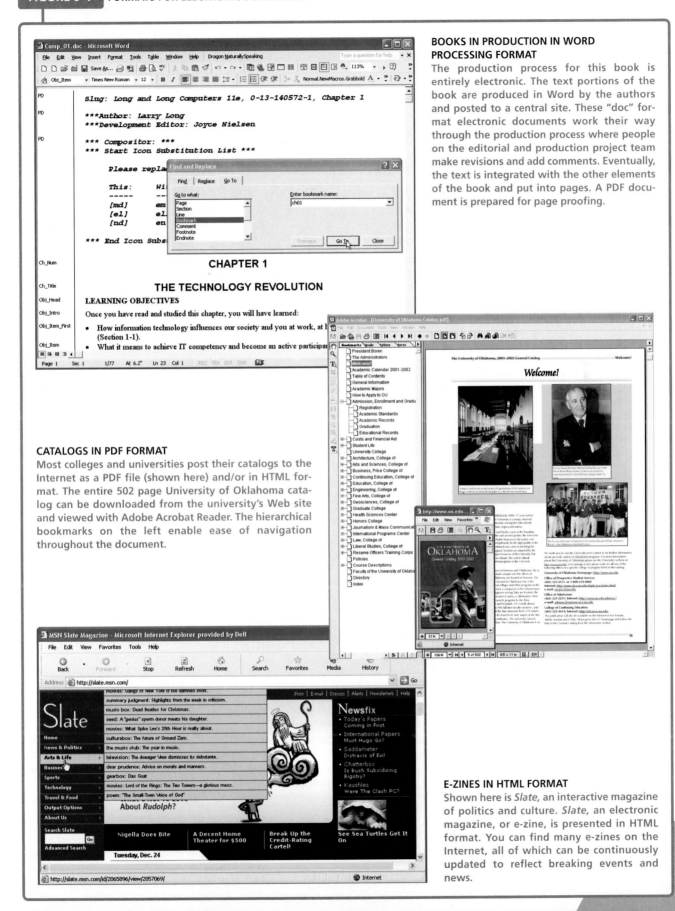

BOOKS IN PRODUCTION IN WORD PROCESSING FORMAT
The production process for this book is entirely electronic. The text portions of the book are produced in Word by the authors and posted to a central site. These "doc" format electronic documents work their way through the production process where people on the editorial and production project team make revisions and add comments. Eventually, the text is integrated with the other elements of the book and put into pages. A PDF document is prepared for page proofing.

CATALOGS IN PDF FORMAT
Most colleges and universities post their catalogs to the Internet as a PDF file (shown here) and/or in HTML format. The entire 502 page University of Oklahoma catalog can be downloaded from the university's Web site and viewed with Adobe Acrobat Reader. The hierarchical bookmarks on the left enable ease of navigation throughout the document.

E-ZINES IN HTML FORMAT
Shown here is *Slate*, an interactive magazine of politics and culture. *Slate*, an electronic magazine, or e-zine, is presented in HTML format. You can find many e-zines on the Internet, all of which can be continuously updated to reflect breaking events and news.

documents. The de facto standard for word processing is the Microsoft Word document (doc format). The trend is to online documents that are platform-independent. In short, that means Internet technologies.

HTML Documents

The most popular format for electronic documents is *HTML* (HyperText Markup Language). HTML provides a description of how the information is to be presented on the screen. All Internet browsers, including Netscape browsers and Microsoft Internet Explorer, can retrieve HTML documents from their servers and display them for viewing. Companies and individuals who wish to make publications available via World Wide Web Internet servers must create HTML-compliant documents. A number of Web design programs are available; however, one of the easiest ways to create HTML documents is to use a word processing program such as Microsoft Word or Corel WordPerfect. Once the word processing document is complete, simply save it as an HTML document (with the file extension *htm* or *html*). The result is an HTML folder, which contains the elements that make up the Web page, that is ready to be posted to the Internet.

Portable Documents

You can pass a **portable document** around the electronic world as you would a print document in the physical world. It can be embedded in HTML-based World Wide Web pages on the Internet, attached to e-mail messages, distributed on a CD-ROM, and generally made available in any computing environment. The most popular format is the *portable document format,* or **PDF** (created by Adobe Corporation) **file.** The PDF file has emerged as the de facto standard for portable documents, including contracts, financial reports, advertising brochures, personnel forms, and many other publishing needs. Millions of Internet users have downloaded the Adobe Acrobat Reader (for free), the software needed to view PDF documents. PDF documents are created with a variety of proprietary products from Adobe Corporation, including Acrobat and Acrobat Capture. These Adobe software products can automatically convert a document in any popular file format, such as Word (doc) or HTML, to a PDF file.

The PDF format is ideal for Internet publishing because it integrates the viewing of PDF files directly into Web browsers. PDF files can be highly compressed (more information in smaller files), thereby reducing the time required to send them to the end user. Also, a PDF file looks the same on all platforms. In contrast, similar HTML-based content can take longer to transmit, and its appearance may vary depending on the platform on which it is viewed.

DISTRIBUTION OF ELECTRONIC DOCUMENTS

Most electronic documents are distributed over the Internet, intranets, extranets, or VPNs. Online documents meant for public consumption are placed on the Internet. Those designed for internal use, such as employee benefits manuals, are made available over intranets. Portable documents are frequently uploaded, downloaded, and attached to e-mail. Some applications call for distribution of documents via CD-ROM or DVD. For example, many companies now distribute their annual reports via print and/or CD-ROM.

CONVERTING PRINT DOCUMENTS TO ELECTRONIC DOCUMENTS

Software vendors are aware of the trend to electronic publishing and are working diligently to create products that make it easier for us to produce online documents from existing print-oriented documents. Software products are available that can automatically convert a document in any popular file format, such as Word or HTML, to a PDF file.

We can export word processing documents directly to HTML or PDF format. Some software products enable scanned hard copy documents to be converted to fully searchable PDF documents that look just like the original. That means that a flashy marketing brochure, a census form, or any other hard copy document can be easily converted for online distribution. Having these tools means that the countless existing documents can be easily converted for use in the electronic environment.

THE TREND TOWARD ELECTRONIC PUBLISHING

During this transition from print to electronic publishing, the debate continues as to when, if ever, traditional print publishing will fade away. It will be many years before we know whether the transition will ever be complete. However, the trend is undeniable. Already, one-third of the population cites the Internet as their primary source of news. Every important newspaper and magazine maintains a major presence on the Internet, often offering a significant amount of content for free. Some e-zines and other publishers require a paid subscription.

Both publishers and readers are continually evaluating the benefits of electronic publishing. For example, many new and established professional journals, which publish scholarly findings, are going electronic to enable these time-sensitive journals to be made available to the academic and scientific communities more quickly and at a reduced cost. It will be interesting to follow this transition as comic book, college textbook, and other publishers assess the advisability of making the jump to purely electronic publishing.

9-4   Working at Home

People who work at home have accounted for more than half of all new jobs since 1987. In 1990, 2 million Americans telecommuted to work. Telecommuting is "commuting" to work via data communications. In this new millennium, over 30 million telecommute to work at least part time. Analysts predict that over 40% of all American workers will telecommute at least part time by 2005 and that over 50 million American workers will be telecommuting by 2030. Even if the soothsayers are half right, the telecommuting movement is on course to turn office tradition upside down.

For many knowledge workers, work is really at a PC or over the telephone, whether at the office or at home. PCs and communications technology make it possible for these people to access needed information, communicate with their colleagues and clients, and even deliver their work (programs, stories, reports, or recommendations) in electronic or hard copy format. Interaction with colleagues often is electronic via e-mail, instant messaging, and videoconferencing. More and more people are asking: "Why travel to the office when I can telecommute?" Powerful PCs, broadband Internet access, home networks, VPNs, personal and corporate economics, concerns about the environment, and other factors serve to fuel the growth of *cottage industries* where people work exclusively from their home offices.

THE TREND TOWARD TELECOMMUTING

The most significant workplace trend is toward more telecommuting (see Figure 9-8). Millions of people are working at home full time: stockbrokers, financial planners, writers, programmers, buyers, teachers (yes, some teachers and professors work exclusively with online students), salespeople, editors, manufacturer's representatives, project managers, and graphic artists, to mention a few. A larger group is working at home at least one day a week: engineers, lawyers, certified public accountants, company presidents, mayors, physicians, and plant managers, to mention some. Anyone who needs a few hours, or perhaps a few days, of uninterrupted time to accomplish tasks that do not require direct personal interaction is a candidate for telecommuting.

Through the early 1990s, telecommuting was discouraged. Management was reluctant to relinquish direct control of workers. Managers were concerned that workers would give priority to personal, not business, objectives. Now we know that telecommuters are not only more productive, but they tend to work more hours. A Gartner Group study reported increases in productivity between 10% and 40% per telecommuter (as measured by employers). Various studies show that on average a telecommuter experiences a 2-hour increase in work time per day and saves the company about $6000 in annual facilities costs. Perhaps it is only a matter of time before all self-motivated knowledge workers at all levels and in a variety of disciplines are given the option of telecommuting at least part of the time. Look at what companies and governments are already doing.

- The United States Department of Transportation (DOT) has announced a pilot program that is designed to reduce traffic and pollution by encouraging commuters to "e-commute." They're doing this by offering significant incentives in the form of redeemable cash, pollution credits, or reduced taxes to companies that let their employees work at home. Los Angeles, Houston, Philadelphia, Denver, and Washington were chosen as the pilot cities.

FIGURE 9–8   THE TREND TO TELECOMMUTING

TELECOMMUTING OFFERS FLEXIBILITY

Because of her wireless link to a home network and broadband Internet access, this telecommuter is able to stay online no matter where she is around the house. The familiar surroundings of home inspire some people to do their best work. Others, however, are more comfortable working in a traditional office setting.

Photo courtesy of Intel Corporation

TELECOMMUTING FOR THOSE WITH DISABILITIES

Telecommuting may be a solution for people who are blind, deaf, or have other disabilities that impede their mobility. John Gardner (shown here), a professor of physics at Oregon State University, is working to improve the Internet interface to make Net access easier for these groups of people.

Copyright 2001 Oregon State University

THE ULTIMATE IN MOBILITY

This telecommuter can carry his IBM 10.5-ounce Wearable PC with him wherever he goes. It fits in his pocket, yet offers enough power to run the Windows operating system and speech recognition software. This hands-free computer's headset provides audio output and a miniature eye-level display for viewing.

Courtesy of International Business Machines Corporation

- AT&T is encouraging its employees to telecommute on Tuesdays. Among other reasons, AT&T management is trying to support the lifestyle people think is desirable. About 25% of the AT&T workforce telecommutes to work and, each week, they average five more hours of work at home than at the office.

- The Canadian government hopes to save taxpayers hundreds of millions of dollars by encouraging telecommuting for public servants. Those who participated in a government-sponsored telecommuting pilot project reported a 73% increase in productivity.

- Telecommuters at American Express handled 26% more calls and produced 43% more business than their office-based counterparts.

- Blue Cross and Blue Shield of South Carolina reported 50% gains in the productivity for telecommuters.

TOOLS OF TELECOMMUTING

The typical PC-ready, Internet-connected home can be easily set up for telecommuting. The big difference between a telecommuter's home office and a traditional on-site office is that it is in a home. Each office will need the essential furniture, a PC, and a link to the Internet and corporate network. The home office, however, may need a few pieces of equipment that might be shared via a LAN in a normal office setting. These are the essential elements of a telecommuter's office.

- Ergonomically designed workspace (see Chapter 8, Section 8-2, "The Workplace," for detailed recommendations), preferably isolated from the main corridors of the home.
- Business PC, either a desktop PC or a notebook with a port replicator, as needed.
- All-in-one multifunction peripheral (print, scan, fax, and copy) or these peripherals as separate devices (printer, fax machine, and copy machine with the scanner being an optional device depending on job requirements).
- Backup storage device and media (rewritable optical disc drive—CD-RW or DVD+RW, or Zip disk drive).
- Other peripheral devices to meet application needs, such as a digital video camera for videoconferencing.
- Uninterruptible power supply (UPS) unit to protect the PC and its data from electrical surges.
- Software to meet application needs.
- Telephone (dedicated line for voice conversations).
- Full-time Internet access (preferably via a broadband line, such as cable modem, DSL, or satellite).
- Security system to protect the physical premises and the integrity of the telecommuter's work.
- The usual office supplies (three-hole punch, stapler, paper clips, and so on).

HOTELING

Even telecommuters like to know that they can go to the office on occasion and have a place to work. Maintaining office space for telecommuters can be expensive and may offset savings resulting from telecommuting. However, companies recognize that these mobile and remote workers need their own space when they come to the office. They use **hoteling**, an office space management concept, to provide on-site office space for these workers. Generally, telecommuters and mobile workers do not require that office space be assigned to them on a full-time basis. In hoteling, a pool of offices is designated for these people. Telecommuters and mobile workers reserve these offices as they would a room in a hotel. Depending on the type of business, companies are able to provide convenient office space with a ratio of as much as 10 employees per desk.

THE PROS AND CONS OF WORKING AT HOME

Telecommuting has it proponents and opponents. Many managers see telecommuting as a win-win situation in which both employee and company benefit. Others feel that telecommuting causes resentment among office-bound colleagues and weakens corporate loyalty.

Why Work at Home?

Everyone has a different reason for wanting to telecommute. A programmer with two school-age children says, "I want to say goodbye when the kids leave for school and greet them when they return." A writer goes into the office once a week, the day before the magazine goes to press. She says, "I write all of my stories from the comfort of my home. An office that puts out a weekly magazine is not conducive to creative thinking." A company president states emphatically, "I got sick and tired of spending nights up in my office. By telecommuting, I'm at least within earshot of my wife and kids." A Florida database administrator says, "Working twice a week from home has substantially improved my quality of life."

These are the most frequently cited reasons for working at home.

- *Increased productivity*. Telecommuters get more done at home than at the office.
- *Better retention of employees*. Having the telecommuting option attracts and helps to retain top talent. Not having to hire and train people continuously can result in substantial savings.
- *Improve employee morale*. Telecommuters cite improved morale and job satisfaction.
- *Greater flexibility*. Telecommuters can optimize the scheduling of their activities. For example, they can work late on Monday and take off for a few hours to exercise on Tuesday.

- *Money savings on office space.* Companies can reduce required office space.
- *Money savings on commuting expenses.* Employees can save from $25 to $250 a week in fares, tolls, parking, gasoline, and automobile wear-and-tear costs.
- *Improved relations with family.* Telecommuters spend more time with or around their family.
- *No commute.* The average commuter in a major metropolitan area spends the equivalent of one working day a week traveling to and from work. The telecommuter eliminates transportation expenses associated with the commute and gains valuable time that can be used more productively.
- *More comfortable and less expensive clothes.* Men willingly trade ties for T-shirts and women prefer sneakers to heels.
- *Reduction of sick time.* Telecommuters miss fewer days of work as a result of sickness, thus lowering overall health-care-related costs (an average of five sick days per year in the city of Los Angeles).
- *Fuel savings.* Eliminating the commute saves precious nonrenewable fossil fuel and helps solve pollution problems.

Arguments Against Working at Home

Working at home is not the answer for all workers or companies. Some people are easily distracted and need the ready access to management and the routine of the office to maintain a business focus. The culture, function, and/or tradition at some companies may be incompatible with telecommuting. Telecommuting is not possible when job requirements demand daily face-to-face meetings (for example, bank tellers and elementary school teachers). Telecommuters routinely interact with clients and colleagues over the telephone, by e-mail, instant messaging, and videoconferencing. However, those arguing against telecommuting say that this type of interaction does not permit "pressing of the flesh" and the transmittal of the nonverbal cues that are essential to personal interaction.

A Silicon Valley dot.com executive says, "We're creating new things and building new solutions and we need people working side by side, in the office, sharing ideas." A CEO of a consulting firm is concerned that "You just miss out on the value of hallway conversations and the quickly scheduled five-minute meetings." These views, though valid, have done little to hamper the emergence of telecommuting as a mainstream business strategy.

TELECOMMUTING AND DEMOGRAPHICS

Several years ago telecommuting, though desirable by many, was cumbersome for some. Generally, telecommuter access to the Internet and enterprise computers was at a relatively slow 56 K bps or less. Also, corporate information systems were designed for use on internal networks, not by remote workers linked by dialup lines. Today, broadband access to the Internet is widely available, plus enterprise-wide systems are being designed with a built-in flexibility to accommodate e-commerce, B2B, and telecommuters. Now, telecommuters can logon and interact with enterprise systems and databases as if they were on the fourth floor of the headquarters building. Also, the growth of wireless technologies untethers people further, giving them e-mail on their belt or purse and the flexibility to watch a kid's soccer game and still be connected.

This capability to support a remote office that is compatible with an on-site office, combined with the inherent benefits of telecommuting, has made telecommuting a truly viable career option. Some say that it will grow to the point that it may change the demographics of developed countries. Already millions of people telecommute. Many of these people are big-city dwellers who formerly worked in office buildings. They now realize that they could just as well live in the city of their choice. Because they are no longer tied to a physical office, literally millions of telecommuters are migrating to wherever their lifestyle criteria takes them—to smaller towns, warmer weather, their roots, nearer water, or the Rocky Mountains. The net result is that telecommuting has emerged as a major contributor to the changing demographics throughout the United States and other countries.

SECTION SELF-CHECK

9-4.1	Telecommuting has shown increases in productivity between 2 and 5% per telecommuter. (T/F)
9-4.2	All companies must offer candidates for employment an opportunity for telecommuting. (T/F)
9-4.3	Which of these is not an argument for telecommuting: (a) increased productivity, (b) increased sick time off from work, (c) less on-site office space required, or (d) reduced clothing expense?
9-4.4	Which is not a reason for increased telecommuting: (a) B2B, (b) slow Internet lines, (c) e-commerce, or (d) remote communications?

One of the best ways to explore cyberspace is to be a part of it; that is, become a Web author so you can create and maintain your own Web site. It sounds complicated, but it's no more difficult to create an informative Web site than it is to create a newsletter with word processing software. A simple Web site can be created and published in minutes. A variety of tools is available to help you become a Web author. The tools vary in complexity from straightforward fill-in-the-blank wizards to sophisticated programming. There are three common approaches to establishing a Web site presence on the Internet.

- *The "free" Web site.* A number of major portals and services, such as Yahoo and AOL, provide a user-friendly service through which you can build a simple Web site. They provide the service at no extra cost to you in exchange for the right to present Internet advertising (usually banners and pop-up ads) along with your Web pages. The ads offset the cost of providing this free service. To design and create a straightforward Web site, you select a template that is closely aligned with your presentation needs then work through a page-building wizard that walks you through the interactive, step-by-step process. During the walkthrough, you customize the design of the pages and provide personal or business content for the site (see Figure 9-9).

- *The minimal fee-based Web site.* If you would prefer that those visiting your Web site not be bombarded with Internet advertising, you might wish to consider paying a small fee (from $5 to $50 per month) to a Web-hosting service, such as Microsoft bCentral or Angelfire. Several popular portals offer this service. These services also provide Web site templates and a page-builder Wizard for your convenience. If you would prefer a more sophisticated presence, you might wish to create your Web site using **Web page design software**, such as Microsoft FrontPage or Adobe GoLive. Most people, including the professionals, use this type of WYSIWYG ("what-you-see-is-what-you-get") development software. These user-friendly menu-driven packages are used routinely in schools by students, in CPA offices by accountants, in doctors' clinics by doctors, and, of course, in major corporations by professional Web developers and Webmasters. A **Webmaster** is a person who manages a Web site.

- *The domain name Web site.* If you would prefer a uniquely identifiable presence on the Internet, you should consider purchasing your own Internet domain name and contracting with a **Web hosting company** to host the site. The Web hosting company maintains a network of interconnected Web servers that store information and program files for the Web sites. This approach is oriented to businesses willing to pay for a domain name, professional Web site design, the hosting service, and, possibly, an onsite Webmaster.

WHY BUILD A WEB SITE?

Web sites give the Bentonville High School Drama Club, a local True Value hardware store, or the Green Country Rotary Club, a *presence on the Internet.* So why might you want a presence on the Internet? One reason might be to create a **personal home page.** A personal home page can be made relatively obscure, known only to family and friends, or it can be placed on any of a number of searchable home page directories. Each home page is different, reflecting the personality of the site's namesake. A home page might include personal and family history, an ancestral tree, historical and current photos, vacation summaries (with photos, of course), a holiday newsletter, personal news and/or commentary, links to areas of personal interest, a résumé, and so on. Or, perhaps you might wish to create a presence on the Internet for your child's Boy/Girl scout troop or basketball team, your fraternity/sorority, or your civic service club. Some people use the Net to showcase their artistic work (paintings, e-art, original music, and so on). College students often create Web sites to collect data and post survey results or to publish findings of research projects. Professors create Web sites in support of their classes—posting the class syllabus, assignments, and links to class resources. Also, you can create a Web site for your employer's company, giving it a very important presence on the global Internet.

BUILDING A WEB SITE

The complexity of the Web sites ranges from a personal home page to a simple one-page résumé to a comprehensive e-trading Web site, such as the Morgan Stanley site. The latter offers real-time portfolio valuation to clients along with real-time stock quotes and an online buying service. The content for a single page can be created easily with a word processing program, such as Microsoft Word, and then saved as an HTML page that can be downloaded and viewed in browsers. Other office suite programs, such as spreadsheet and presentation software, can export directly to HTML as well. More sophisticated Web sites involving interactivity, dynamic updating, and so on, require the use of Web development tools and, possibly, original programming.

WHY THIS SECTION IS IMPORTANT TO YOU

Every day hundreds of thousands of people and companies create and publish new Web sites that make text and visual information on the sites readily accessible to billions of people around the world. The material in this section will help you to better understand how you, too, can create you own Web site for your office or your home.

FIGURE 9–9

THE "FREE" WEB SITE
America Online offers subscribers a free home page where they can share their interests and/or highlight their businesses. The service offers almost 100 Web site templates in several categories including, "All about You," "Your Thoughts," and "Your Hobbies." For example, templates in the "Your Hobbies" category include "My Photography Page" (shown here), "My Poetry," and "My Art Gallery."

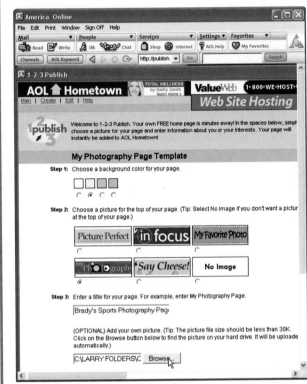

THE PAGE-BUILDING WIZARD
The AOL page-building wizard walks you step by step through the Web page authoring process. In Step 1, you choose a background color. In Step 2, you choose a picture for the top of the page. In Step 3, you title the page and choose an image for the home page. These and the remaining steps vary depending on the template selected.

PUBLISHING THE WEB PAGE
Once you have completed the wizard and saved the Web page information to the AOL Web site hosting computer, you have a home page and become a presence on the Internet. The entire process, from concept to a home page, can be completed in a few minutes.

An Internet Web site is actually a group of files pulled together and presented as Web pages, which are interconnected by hyperlinks. We learned in Chapter 3 that the basic document on the World Wide Web is a text file containing HTML commands, or *tags*, that supply information about the Web page's structure, appearance, and content. Internet browsers interpret the HTML instructions and display the page accordingly. The process of displaying a single Web page typically will involve the pulling together of several files (for example, a GIF or JPG file of the company logo must be downloaded and inserted in the displayed page).

Programming in HTML can be confusing to some. However, you do not need to know HTML to use Web design software such as Microsoft FrontPage®. FrontPage is WYSIWYG software that lets you create Web documents as you would a word processing document. Simply enter text in text boxes, then drag-and-drop images and other elements as needed into the WYSIWYG display (see Figure 9-10). The HTML code that eventually will be interpreted by browsers is generated automatically. This process is transparent to you unless you wish to edit the HTML code directly. FrontPage

FIGURE 9–10

MICROSOFT FRONTPAGE: WEB DESIGN SOFTWARE
Microsoft FrontPage, illustrated here, offers a variety of templates to help you get started. For example, there are templates available to help you prepare a corporate presence on the Web (in the example), a customer support Web site, a discussion Web site, and a personal home page. Using templates helps give your Web site a consistent appearance, an important design consideration.

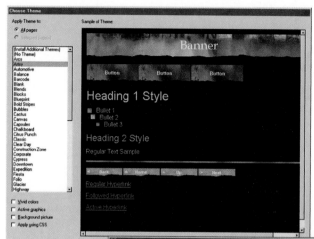

WEB PAGE THEMES
FrontPage offers you a variety of preset *themes* from which to choose. A theme is an integrated set of design elements and color schemes that can be applied to each page on your Web site. The colors and font styles are defined by the theme. Preset themes are easily customized to meet individual taste.

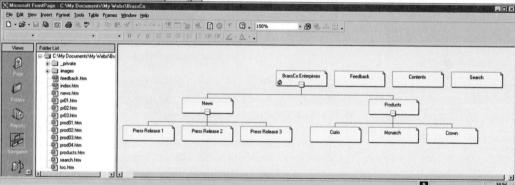

THE NAVIGATION STRUCTURE
In FrontPage, the pages in a Web site are interconnected in a hierarchy called the *navigation structure*. The structure shows how Web pages are related to each other. The home page is always the first page in the navigation structure. Others at the top of the hierarchy are these top-level pages: Feedback, Contents, and Search. Under the top level are parent pages (News and Products) and child-level pages (Curio, Monarch, and Crown are the children of the Products page).

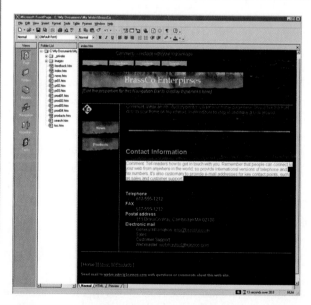

PAGE VIEW (NORMAL)
It is in page view that you integrate content into a Web document in a WYSIWYG manner. It is here that elements (text boxes, banner images, and so on) are added, deleted, and modified. The FrontPage page view allows both WYSIWYG and HTML editing. The menu-driven program lets you easily insert text, graphics, page banners, tables, forms, hyperlinks, banner ads, marquees, buttons, hit counters, and so on. You can apply a variety of text formats as you would in other office suite software. Elements on the page can be animated to enliven the presentation.

FIGURE 9–10 continued

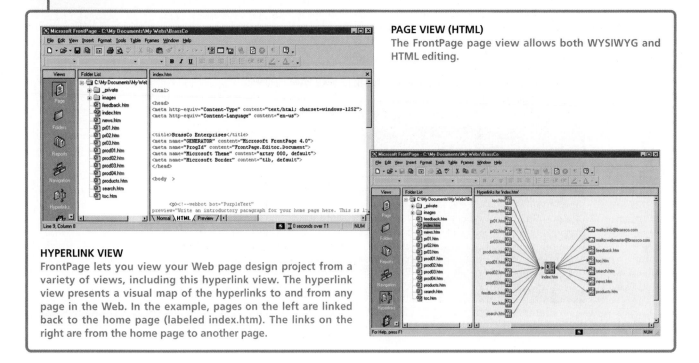

PAGE VIEW (HTML)
The FrontPage page view allows both WYSIWYG and HTML editing.

HYPERLINK VIEW
FrontPage lets you view your Web page design project from a variety of views, including this hyperlink view. The hyperlink view presents a visual map of the hyperlinks to and from any page in the Web. In the example, pages on the left are linked back to the home page (labeled index.htm). The links on the right are from the home page to another page.

lets you create simple Web pages or professional-looking Web pages with advanced features such as hit counters (counts the number of times a page is accessed).

Web design software features usually are sufficient for most Web design tasks; however, programming may be required for those sites that require sophisticated interactivity with database and multimedia. Some pages have *applets* or **script** file references embedded in the HTML code. These are small programs that are downloaded with the Web page and run on the client PC. Often, applets and scripts are run to show such things as animated ad banners and animated graphics. A variety of programming languages are used to create these small programs.

WEB AUTHORING TIPS

Within minutes, you can have a presence on the Internet with personal content that is available to billions of people. The difference between having a convoluted, mediocre Web site and an attractive, informative Web site is a little up-front planning. Follow these tips and you will enjoy the latter.

- *Have a purpose for your Web site.* Rambling and pointless Web sites can be a turnoff. Netizens tend to navigate to and view topical Web sites that have a clear and meaningful reason to exist.

- *Know your audience.* Who do you think will be visiting your site? Talk to these people in the language and imagery that they will appreciate and understand.

- *Keep it simple.* Resist the urge to overload pages with Web page features and information. The most effective Web pages are clean, carefully-planned presentations that can be visually comprehended with ease.

- *Minimize download time.* The vast majority of netizens access the Internet at relatively slow dialup speeds. People cruising the Internet at these speeds tend to click through slow-building pages. The critical factor in page download time is the size and number of images on the page. If you have several images, present thumbnail image hyperlinks to larger versions of the images.

- *Be yourself.* Your personal Web site is about you, no matter what the topic. Be honest with yourself and those who might visit your site.

- *Maintain your Web site.* Web site content is dynamic, ever-changing. If you post something to the Internet, you have an obligation to yourself and to your fellow netizens to keep it current.

- *Invite feedback.* Frequently, netizens are moved to interact with Web authors. Give them that opportunity by providing contact information.

PUBLISHING A WEB SITE ON THE NET

When a book is printed and distributed to bookstores, it is said to have been published. When content is placed online for public viewing via Internet browsers, the Web site is said to have been published. Most HTML content is published on the Internet for public viewing; however, Web sites also are developed for *intranets* where access is limited to those people on a company's network, and *extranets,* which are essentially intranets that are expanded to permit limited access outside the organization (perhaps to suppliers). Web-type content also is developed for CD-ROM and DVD. For example, a number of college textbooks have been reformatted as Web pages with hyperlinks and interactivity, and then distributed on CD-ROM.

If you're developing a Web site for your company and your company has an Internet presence, publishing your Web site may be as easy as sending your Webmaster a copy of the Web site folder generated as a result of your Web design activity. The Webmaster then posts the Web site content to the company's Internet (Web) server. If it is not password protected, it is then available for public viewing on the worldwide Internet. The Internet server file structure is much like that on your PC—a hierarchy of folders and subfolders containing files. Unlike your PC, however, each folder is a URL destination and the property of a different owner.

If you want to publish a personal home page or create a Web site for an organization that does not have a Web presence, then you'll need to make arrangements with an organization that might be willing to host your Web site on its Internet server. A number of Web hosting providers would be delighted to host your Web site for a fee. The amount charged varies significantly based on expected activity, disk space required, and quality of service needed. You probably will not need a Web presence provider unless you wish to establish a business presence on the Net. Most Internet service providers (ISPs), including America Online, will allow you to post a personal home page of limited size as part of your usage fee. Many universities let students and professors create their personal home pages on the colleges' Net servers. Each of these host sites will have specific directions as to where and to whom you would send your Web content for publishing.

9-5.1	Web page design software is WYSIWYG. (T/F)
9-5.2	HTML knowledge is a requirement for those wishing to create a Web site. (T/F)
9-5.3	A Web site is not appropriate for which of the following: (a) the Internet (b) an extranet, (c) an intranet, or (d) an alternet?
9-5.4	A person who manages a Web site is a(n): (a) www guru, (b) Webmaster, (c) Webruler, or (d) omnipotent one.

SECTION SELF-CHECK

9-1 INTERNET ISSUES

The Internet is a digital Wild West. Hackers and crackers are continually doing what they can to disrupt the flow of information on the Net. In addition, the Internet is filled with hate mongers, whose objective is to foster hate, discrimination, prejudice, bigotry, and/or intolerance.

The controversy about whether sexually explicit material on the Internet should be banned or controlled is debated, but the use of **filtering programs** can deny access to certain types of "undesirable" content. Internet gambling is one of those issues whose growth is much faster than the legal system can accommodate.

With e-commerce growing so rapidly, security is an important issue on the Internet. **Firewalls** are being implemented to restrict unwanted access to an organization's network or its intranet. Encryption techniques are just one of the ways the security of individual transactions on the Internet is protected. A **digital certificate** is an attachment to an electronic message that verifies that the sender is who he or she claims to be.

People who send discourteous communications over the Net are frequently **flamed. Spammers** send spam, the electronic equivalent of junk mail and, at present, there is no foolproof way for netizens to keep spam out of the received e-mail list.

9-2 E-COMMERCE

E-commerce is simply business conducted online or via some form of data communications. Activities often associated with e-commerce include **virtual marketplaces** that provide **e-tailing** (online retailing), **e-trading** (online brokerage services), Internet-based marketing or advertising, online market research and surveys, business-to-business (B2B), **business-to-consumer** (B2C), and other technology-based approaches to doing business.

E-commerce makes good economic sense and appears to be emerging as the business model for the twenty-first century. Standards for the way in which digital money is exchanged continue to evolve. Several companies offer online purchasing systems that enable consumers to create and use an **electronic wallet** that stores their billing and shipping information in controlled server facilities.

Security is a problem whether in an online or offline situation. Most e-commerce transactions use encryption. Specifically, the Secure Sockets Layer (SSL) communications protocol provides a secure connection to a particular server, thus protecting information transmitted over the Internet.

There are many applications for business-to-business, but the most popular and easily implemented B2B applications involve buying and selling between companies. Whenever businesses can reach and interact with consumers more efficiently online, they turn that opportunity into a B2C application. For example, most major airlines are committed to **electronic ticketing** (**e-ticketing**). Other B2C applications include buying groceries, books, and CDs; online investment management; live auctions; e-tailing; and much, much more.

Creating an e-commerce Web site can be done by the businesses themselves or through an **e-commerce hosting service** which offers a customer everything needed to create an e-commerce site. The high potential of return on investment is motivating executives to implement e-commerce and other information technology solutions. Innovative use of information technology has a history of giving organizations the competitive advantage.

9-3 ELECTRONIC PUBLISHING

The ability to make stored information available through the Internet and networking has resulted in a greater and more varied use of **electronic publishing** (**e-publishing**). Electronically published documents, such as **e-zines,** have many advantages: Paper is eliminated (no sacrificing of trees); they are updated easily; they can integrate audio clips, video clips, and animation within the text and graphics; they more readily permit interactivity and navigation; they are easily searchable; and they can be tied together by hyperlinks.

The three most popular formats for electronic documents are *word processing, HTML,* and **portable document.** One of the easiest ways to create HTML documents is to use a word processing program. Once the word processing document is complete, simply save it as an HTML document and the resulting HTML folder is ready to be posted to the Internet. The **PDF file** has emerged as the standard for portable documents, including contracts, financial reports, and many other publishing needs.

Most electronic documents are distributed over the Internet, intranets, extranets, or VPNs. Because of the increase in the use of electronic publishing, software vendors are working to create products that make it easier for us to produce electronic documents from existing printed documents.

9-4 WORKING AT HOME

Telecommuting is "commuting" to work via data communications. The trend toward PCs and networks has also fueled the growth of *cottage industries* where people work exclusively from their home offices. A telecommuter's workplace is much like that of on-site workers, but it is located in (or near) the home. In **hoteling,** an office space management concept, mobile and remote workers use on-site office space. There are arguments for and against working at home. With broadband access to the Internet widely available, enterprise-wide systems are being designed with built-in flexibility to accommodate e-commerce, B2B, and telecommuters. Telecommuting is a major contributor to the changing demographics throughout the United States and other countries.

9-5 CREATING A WEB SITE

A variety of tools are available to help you become a Web author. The tools vary in complexity from straightforward fill-in-the-blank wizards to sophisticated programming applications. Common approaches to establishing a Web site presence on the Internet include the "free" Web site (which may come with banners and pop-up ads), the minimal fee-based Web site, and the domain name Web site.

To design and create a straightforward Web site, you select a template, then work through a user-friendly page-building wizard. If you would prefer a more sophisticated presence, you might wish to create your Web site using **Web page design software.** A **Webmaster** is a person who manages a Web site. To have a uniquely identifiable Net presence, you may need to purchase an Internet domain name and contract with a **Web hosting company.** Some individuals post **personal home pages** on the Internet.

An Internet Web site is a group of files that are pulled together and presented as Web pages, which are interconnected by hyperlinks. The process of displaying a single HTML Web page typically will involve the pulling together of several files.

Web page design software automatically generates the HTML code from the Web design. Browsers eventually interpret the code and the Web page is displayed.

Some Web pages have *applets* or **script** file references embedded in the HTML code. These are small programs run on the client PC.

Follow these Web site design principles: have a purpose for your Web site, know your audience, keep it simple, minimize download time, be yourself, maintain your Web site, and invite feedback.

Most HTML content is published on the Internet for public viewing; however, Web sites also are developed for *intranets* and *extranets*. Web-type content is developed also for CD-ROM and DVD.

To publish a Web site you may need a Web hosting provider or you might be able to do so through your ISP.

KEY TERMS

business-to-consumer (B2C) (p. 360)
digital certificate (pp. 357–358)
e-commerce hosting service (p. 367)
electronic publishing (e-publishing) (p. 368)
electronic ticketing (e-ticketing) (p. 367)
electronic wallet (p. 362)
e-tailing (p. 359)

e-trading (p. 366)
e-zine (p. 368)
filtering program (p. 357)
firewall (p. 357)
flame (p. 359)
hoteling (p. 375)
PDF file (p. 372)
personal home page (p. 377)

portable document (p. 372)
script (p. 380)
spammer (p. 358)
virtual marketplace (p. 359)
Web hosting company (p. 377)
Web page design software (p. 377)
Webmaster (p. 377)

MATCHING

1. firewall
2. hoteling
3. Web hosting company
4. Webmaster
5. eBay
6. spammer
7. electronic document
8. script
9. hyperlink
10. HTML
11. telecommuting
12. PDF file
13. flame
14. e-zine
15. business-to-consumer

a. provides Net presence for a fee
b. links online documents
c. small program
d. B2C
e. online magazine
f. describes Web page makeup
g. office space management
h. online document
i. manages a Web site
j. one who sends spam
k. to barrage with messages
l. portable document
m. working at home
n. restricts unwanted access
o. online auction site

CHAPTER SELF-CHECK

9-1.1   A firewall provides unrestricted access to an organization's intranet. (T/F)

9-1.2   All hackers are crackers, too. (T/F)

9-1.3   Hate can be spread over the Internet with anonymity. (T/F)

9-1.4   An attachment to an electronic message that verifies that the sender is who he or she claims to be is a: (a) flame identifier, (b) cyber signature, (c) digital signature, or (d) digital certificate.

9-1.5   Some organizations use what type of software to deny access to "undesirable" Internet content: (a) sifting, (b) filtering, (c) screening, or (d) straining.

9-2.1   An Internet server computer is an integral part of B2C. (T/F)

9-2.2   E-money and debit cards are the same. (T/F)

9-2.3   Online courses at a university would be considered e-commerce. (T/F)

9-2.4   Which of the following is an online auction site: (a) eBay, (b) BayWatch, (c) Datek Online, or (d) CyberCash?

9-2.5   Virtual marketplaces: (a) are oriented to B2B, (b) offer online reference services, (c) provide e-tailing, or (d) are ISPs.

9-2.6   Which of the following does not fall under the e-commerce umbrella: (a) B2B, (b) online shopping, (c) B2C, or (d) Net etiquette?

9-2.7   Which of these would not be considered among the more popular consumer items purchased over the Internet: (a) shop tools, (b) computer products, (c) CDs, or (d) books?

9-3.1   The file extension hmtl is associated with an HTML document. (T/F)

9-3.2   A disadvantage of electronic documents is that they are not electronically searchable. (T/F)

9-3.3   Which corporation created the PDF format: (a) Adobe, (b) IBM, (c) Apple, or (d) Microsoft?

9-3.4   An electronic magazine is an: (a) e-periodical, (b) e-zine, (c) e-mag, or (d) e-pub.

9-3.5   Electronic documents are stored permanently in all but which of the following: (a) CD-ROM, (b) cache memory, (c) flash memory, or (d) hard disk?

9-4.1   Telecommuting contributes to the changing demographics throughout the United States and other countries. (T/F)

9-4.2 Telecommuters cite improved morale and job satisfaction as justification for telecommuting. (T/F)

9-4.3 Telecommuters miss more days of work as a result of sickness than their in-office counterparts. (T/F)

9-4.4 The culture, function, and/or tradition at some companies may be incompatible with telecommuting. (T/F)

9-4.5 An office space management concept intended to provide on-site office space for telecommuters and mobile workers is: (a) hosteling, (b) internetting, (c) intranetting, or (d) hoteling.

9-4.6 Which of these would not be a factor that fuels the trend to telecommuting: (a) powerful PCs, (b) fax machines, (c) VPNs, (d) broadband access?

9-5.1 A well-designed Web site provides contact information. (T/F)

9-5.2 In the file structure on an Internet server, all folders have the same "owner." (T/F)

9-5.3 Which of these is not a common approach to establishing a Web site: (a) minimal fee-based Web site, (b) the "free" Web site, (c) the gopher Web site, or (d) the domain name Web site?

9-5.4 Which of these is a small program that is embedded in HTML code: (a) script, (b) smallcode, (c) HTML program, or (d) G-code?

9-5.5 The basic Web document is a text file containing HTML commands called: (a) tags, (b) marks, (c) labels, or (d) stickers.

IT ETHICS AND ISSUES

ADDICTION TO THE INTERNET

The Internet has emerged as the centerpiece in the lives of many people, but is it addictive? People who study this issue believe that Internet addiction is as real as alcoholism. People will spend time on anything that is fun to do, but many in the medical community have observed that some people have moved past fun to clinical addiction.

These people are said to have Internet addiction disorder (IAD). People with this disorder often lose control and crave surfing the Internet, much as a smoker craves a cigarette. Like others who are addicted to something, whether gambling, cocaine, or exercise, they suffer withdrawal symptoms when they are forced to forego the Internet.

Millions of Internet users routinely go online without any detrimental effects, but the Internet still takes its toll on a small, but growing, sector of the online community. These people spend from 4 to 10 hours a day on the Internet and will occasionally "binge" for up to 24 hours at a time.

Numerous cases have been reported where the Internet was blamed for broken marriages, for students dropping out of school, and even for illnesses that result in hospital stays. Although most are addicted to the Internet in general, many are addicted to a particular facet of the Net, such as multi-player gaming, pornography, Internet Relay Chats, instant messaging, or e-mail.

It's ironic, but people with IAD often use the Internet to help them cope with their disorder. Some seek out online IAD support groups. Addicts routinely confess their addiction on the Internet. Susie says, "I don't eat. . .I have lost weight. . .I don't sleep. . .I have been sucked into the Internet, hook, line and sinker." Tracey says, "My addiction is so bad I'm flunking most of my classes." John says, "It's ruining my marriage!" Gordon says, "I'm insanely addicted to the Internet and the sad thing about it is that I don't even want to do anything about it."

Discussion: *Have you seen any evidence of Internet addiction disorder (IAD)? If so, describe what you perceive to be the symptoms.*

Discussion: *Is it possible for someone to become addicted to the Internet in a clinical sense? If so, what, if anything, can you do to help someone who has IAD? How can a college help? An employer?*

WHO GETS PERMISSION TO TELECOMMUTE?

Ten years ago companies would set aside one day each year when workers could come to work in casual clothes. That day was so well received by employees that some companies decided to do it once each month, then once a week. Now, casual professional dress is the norm at many companies. The same thing is happening with telecommuting. Ten years ago, a few people with special

circumstances were allowed to telecommute. Others said, "I want to do it too." Now, the telecommuting option must be in place in some industries to get qualified people to interview. Still, very few companies offer the telecommuting option to all employees. Typically, only people at certain levels of management or in certain jobs, especially high-tech jobs and some PC-based clerical jobs, can telecommute and work at home at least part time. Those not permitted that option often are upset with management.

Discussion: *Would you like to telecommute, at least part time, to work? Why or why not?*

Discussion: *Is it ethical for companies to let some people telecommute while asking others to continue the traditional commute?*

Discussion: *Does telecommuting increase or decrease corporate productivity? How about worker productivity?*

Discussion: *Allowing employees to telecommute to work can reduce overall expenses. What corporate expenses are reduced? How about employee expenses?*

CYBERSQUATTING

Legislation has been passed that is aimed at curtailing "cybersquatting." This is when people register Internet domain names that are similar to well-known trademarks, such as Ford, Sony, or Microsoft. In the past, many companies have had to purchase registered domain names from someone who had the foresight to register enticing names that imply affiliation with an organization and/or include a company or product's name within the domain name (for example, Microsoft-technology.com). The practice of cybersquatting has made many people millionaires.

Discussion: *Some would argue that cybersquatting plays on a company's trademark name or that it is unethical. Others say that cybersquatters are simply imaginative entrepreneurs taking full advantage of business opportunities. Where do you stand on this issue and why?*

Discussion: *Most common words in the dictionary are registered as Internet domain names. Cybersquatters are not interested in creating Web sites with these names. They simply register the names, then hope that someday, some company will pay them for the right to use its name. Discuss the ethics of wholesale domain name registration of common words.*

MOUSE TRAPPING

Have you ever been surfing the Web and suddenly your *Back* button is dimmed, thus locking you into the current page? This is called mouse trapping. Some Web sites automatically add scripts to pages that cause the display of more of their pages when you click the *Back* or *Close* buttons. When this happens, you're in their "mousetrap" and are kept from leaving the Web site. A couple of years ago this mouse trapping practice was limited to the sleazy sites on the Web. Now, many mainstream sites use this practice.

Discussion: Should laws be passed to stop attempts by Web sites to control a visitor's online behavior? Why or why not?

Discussion: Have you been a victim of mouse trapping? Did the "trap" change your attitude toward the organization supporting the Web site? If so, in what way?

DISCUSSION AND PROBLEM SOLVING

9-1.1 The Internet is a digital Wild West. Should presence on the Internet be more tightly controlled to help bring law and order to the Internet?

9-1.2 Gambling could be one of the most profitable computer applications ever. Americans spent 70 times as much on gambling last year as they spent on movies. Internet gambling is currently hosted offshore. Argue for or against legalizing Internet gambling within the U.S.

9-1.3 The Internet is public and much of the readily accessible content on the Internet is considered inappropriate for viewing by young people. Should legislation be enacted to control Internet content?

9-1.4 Dissatisfied customers routinely create Web sites devoted to criticizing a company's product or services. The company's name usually is embedded in the domain name in a derogatory manner. Companies being attacked are seeking legislative relief. Should the government get involved?

9-2.1 Many traditional bricks-and-mortar companies have failed to turn a profit with B2C e-commerce solutions. Speculate on why. What do you think are the keys to successful implementation of e-commerce?

9-2.2 Why would buying online be less risky than buying face-to-face in a regular storefront? Via telephone mail order?

9-2.3 Name two types of companies that might benefit from B2B. Describe the B2B interactions between the two companies.

9-2.4 Identify and describe at least three B2C applications that you have used or with which you are familiar.

9-2.5 Discuss the advantages, if any, of buying online. Of selling online.

9-3.1 Given your current computing situation, how convenient would it be to check the daily news online versus that of a daily newspaper or television? Explain.

9-3.2 What types of electronic publishing documents have you used in the last month? Relate your experiences.

9-3.3 Many of our federal tax documents (forms and instructions) are online. What types of problems do you think officials must consider when deciding to put these online?

9-3.4 Speculate on what year, if ever, the sale of e-books will surpass the sale of print books.

9-4.1 What kind of work would you like to be doing in five years? Explain how you might telecommute to accomplish part or all of your work.

9-4.2 How does telecommuting affect demographics? Speculate on the impact telecommuting has had in your community.

9-5.1 Describe why and for what reason you might want to design and publish a Web site.

9-5.2 Describe content that you would like to put on your personal home page.

9-5.3 Describe circumstances for which a company might create a Web site for an extranet.

FOCUS ON PERSONAL COMPUTING

1. Create and build a personal Web site. Enter "free Web site hosting" in any Internet search engine and select one of the free hosting services. Refer to the Web authoring tips in Section 9-5 and plan your Web site. Use the hosting site's page-building wizard to create and publish your site to the Internet.

2. Explore the breadth of e-commerce on the Internet. Visit at least three e-commerce Web sites (for example, online shopping, e-trading, and travel). You may be asked to register as a user. Familiarize yourself with the services provided at each site and

work through an e-commerce process but do not complete the transaction (for example, scheduling a flight between Chicago and Seattle). Briefly, contrast these e-commerce transactions with traditional off-line transactions.

3. Go online and find at least five electronic documents (at least one PDF document and at least one HTML document) that relate to your personal circumstances (for example, a college catalog or the user's manual for your cellular phone). List and indicate the format for each document.

INTERNET EXERCISES @ www.prenhall.com/long

1. The Online Study Guide (multiple choice, true/false, matching, and essay questions)

2. Internet Learning Activities
  • Internet Issues
  • E-commerce
  • Telecommuting
  • Web Page Development

chapter 10

Learning Objectives

Once you have read and studied this chapter, you will have learned:

● How the use of computers and information technology can result in a competitive advantage (Section 10-1).

● The qualities of information and how information needs and decision making vary at each level of an organization (Section 10-2).

● The elements, scope, and capabilities of an information system (Section 10-3).

● The capabilities of a data processing system and a management information system (MIS) (Section 10-4).

● The tools and capabilities of a decision support system (DSS) (Section 10-5).

● The concepts and applications of an expert system (Section 10-6).

● The concepts and applications of intelligent agents (Section 10-7).

INFORMATION SYSTEMS

Why this chapter is important to you

In the world of computers, systems are everywhere. There are enterprise systems, real-time systems, information systems, expert systems, computer systems, operating systems, and these are just the beginning. Many computer terms and concepts begin with the word *system(s)*. There's a *system this* or a *system that* in just about every office conversation. We've got the *system operator,* the *system board,* the *system administrator,* the *system check,* the *system life cycle,* and on and on. At times, you'll be convinced that everything is some kind of system. Generally, that's true in information technology (IT).

Most systems involve and/or affect people and that's where you come in. Every day of your life you will be a part of a system, a direct or indirect target of a system, or a user of a system. On most days, we are all of these.

In any office there are curious people standing around the perimeter of information technology discussions wondering what is going on. Unfortunately, about all these people can be is curious. They may lack a depth of system understanding to be an active participant. After you read and study this chapter, you'll be more willing to step into the conversation. You will be more confident about making meaningful contributions at company meetings that revolve around e-commerce, business-to-business (B2B), and enterprise systems. The material in this chapter will help you sort out common systems terminology so you can understand your role within a system better, be more effective as a target of a system, and know when and what kind of system to use.

Managers and knowledge workers are seeking strategies that
can give their companies the
competitive advantage, especially in the area of computers
and information technology.
Often, having effective IT strategies can mean the difference
between profitability and failure.

10-1 Information Technology as a Competitive Strategy

The increased competition of the world market is pressuring corporate managers and knowledge workers into making better decisions. Those with a genuine desire to make their businesses survive and flourish are doing everything they can to improve profitability. Unions are accepting wage concessions. Executives are flying coach rather than first class. The days are gone when good management and hard work were considered competitive advantages that would invariably result in success and profits. Today, these corporate qualities are the standard for mere survival. Managers are seeking any strategies that can give their companies the competitive advantage. These strategies often involve computers and information technology.

Every company has plenty of opportunities to use technology to achieve a competitive edge. Information technology can give a company ready access to a world market, improve product and service quality, reduce costs, increase productivity, aid communication between employees, and even improve company morale. What's more, new and innovative uses of information technology are being discovered and implemented every day. We know now that money invested in IT responses to competition and in solutions to business problems yields tremendous returns, often 50% or more.

Not only are computers and information technology changing the way we do things, they are changing the function and purpose of major companies. We can expect companies to merge and provide vertical integration of information technology-based products and services. For example, look for banks, brokerage firms, insurance companies, and other financial services companies to begin offering similar products and services. It only makes sense for companies to leverage their capabilities, and companies in all industries are doing it. In this B2B era, companies are looking to use IT to leverage their information resources into better decision making.

COST, RISK, AND CHANGE

The obvious question becomes, "If information technology is so clearly the solution to establishing a competitive advantage, why isn't everybody doing it?" There are three primary reasons.

- *IT solutions often are expensive and time consuming.* The implementation of information technology to achieve a competitive advantage is a perfect example of a situation in which you have to spend money to make money.

- *There is usually an element of risk in the implementation of information technology.* Traditionalist managers would opt to maintain the status quo rather than subject themselves to the risk of failure, even at the expense of losing market share. Of course, if achieving the competitive advantage were inexpensive and easy, everybody's advantage would be nobody's advantage.

- *The implementation of information technology inevitably means change.* People inherently resist change.

The economic environment and fierce competition have focused attention on the computer and information resources. Those enterprises that challenge their managers and executives to tap the potential of these resources are gaining the competitive advantage.

LEVERAGING INFORMATION TECHNOLOGY

If corporations had instincts, their first instinct would be to survive. To survive, a company must make a profit. Once profitability is established, the corporate instinct is to do whatever is needed within the bounds of business ethics to continue to improve profitability. Improved profitability can be achieved in many ways, such as expanding the product line, work force reduction, adjusting pricing, and leveraging information technology (see Figure 10-1).

Increasing Sales

IT technology can be leveraged to increase sales in a number of ways, including increasing market share and creating new business.

Increasing Market Share

Even junkyards have gone high tech. Traditionally, dealers in recycled auto parts have been local businesses that catered to customers in the immediate vicinity of the yard. If they did not have what the customer needed, they would call a competitor at the other end of town or in a nearby city. If none of them had the part, the customer would be out of luck. Today, hundreds of "local" auto salvage dealers have banded together via an Internet database of recycled parts to create a national market for their products. The net effect of this system is to increase each of the participating salvage dealer's share of the recycled auto parts market. Without the system, a dealer is limited to selling what he or she has in stock or to what he or she can find by making a few telephone calls. With the system, the online salvage dealer has a distinct competitive advantage over nonnetworked dealers in the local area.

Creating New Business

One way to gain a competitive advantage is to be there first with information about a product, and at timely intervals thereafter. The key to the successful implementation of this strategy is knowing when to arrive with the information and when to return with more information. Several manufacturers that specialize in baby products have employed this strategy and used information systems to establish a competitive advantage. One manufacturer gives an ample supply of sampler

Computer and information technology

Corporate performance

Increased sales
Increased productivity and reduced cost
Improved customer service
Better resource management

kits to hospitals so that these kits can be distributed to expectant mothers. The kits include samples of products, informative literature, and, most importantly, a return card and a reference to their Web site. The mother-to-be completes the card or Web page form that requests critical marketing information, such as name, address, and expected date of birth. The information is all the company needs to be there first and at timely intervals thereafter. For example, the information system automatically triggers the delivery of prenatal promotional literature (coupons) and samples (shampoo) just prior to the expected delivery date. Thereafter, the company sends the consumer a monthly newsletter (both hardcopy and via e-mail) that focuses on the needs and expectations of mother and baby during the coming month. The newborn newsletter arrives just before the expected date of delivery. The company provides a valuable service to potential consumers of its products while keeping its name and products in the forefront of the consumer's mind. Competing companies must use the more costly shotgun approach to reach the consumer.

Increasing Productivity and Reducing Cost

Increased productivity and cost reduction go hand in hand. Having exhausted virtually all the traditional approaches to cost reduction, executives are looking to IT for more opportunities.

Collecting Data at the Source

In recent years, health care has become a competitive industry. Overcapacity and the emergence of for-profit hospitals have forced hospital administrators to pursue the competitive advantage, usually via implementation of information technology. A cost reduction program involving information systems would normally encompass several facets of hospital operation. A study at one hospital revealed that nurses devoted over 40% of their time to recording what they do. For example, nurses must log every prescription that they deliver and every time they respond to a patient call. At that hospital a computer-based data collection system was developed and installed that enables data to be captured in machine-readable format (for example, bar codes) from bedside terminals at the point of care. The system not only reduces the time that nurses spend recording data about their activities from 40 to 5%, but the system also frees up time that can be devoted to direct patient care.

Eliminating the Intermediary

One of the best ways to reduce the cost of a product or service is to eliminate the intermediary, usually the person or people who sell the products or services to the consumers. Companies that sell directly to the consumer can offer products or services at a substantially reduced cost. For example, some insurance companies have been able to keep premiums low by handling all transactions (sales and service) over the Internet or telephone, thereby eliminating field agents and the cost of commissions. A few offer extended Internet-based services that let customers view and update their policies, pay premiums, get quotes, file claims, and so on, all without interaction with an agent (see Figure 10-2). By eliminating the intermediary and providing direct online service, these companies can enjoy significant savings and a competitive advantage.

FIGURE 10–2   **LEVERAGING IT IN INDUSTRY**

USING IT IN THE INSURANCE INDUSTRY
The USAA insurance company has a high-tech relationship with USAA members. The company does not have field agents, so members interact with the company via the member services Web site and, if needed, by telephone. USAA members can log in to a secure Web site for access to a variety of insurance and banking services. You might expect that the impersonal nature the technology-oriented Internet/telephone service offered by USAA would be a concern to policyholders, but this is not the case. *Consumer Reports* consistently ranks USAA at or near the top of all insurance companies in customer satisfaction.

TECHNOLOGY AS A COMPETITIVE TOOL
In today's competitive environment, there is no such thing as business as usual. The smart company is dynamic, doing everything possible to ensure that knowledge workers have the information and tools they need to stay competitive in a world market. Some companies have introduced wearable PCs, which allow knowledge workers to perform a wide range of mobile tasks, thus enabling them to realize substantial gains in productivity. This man at a bicycle manufacturing company uses his arm-mounted PC along with a scanner to select assembly components and update inventory.

Courtesy of Symbol Technologies, Inc.

Improving Customer Service

All things being equal, customers tend to take their business to the companies that can provide the best service. For example, financial institutions, especially banks, have been among the most progressive users of IT. Deregulation of the banking industry has sent bank executives scurrying for strategic advantages, especially in the area of customer convenience. Today, most banks offer 24-hour ATMs, so they must implement some other IT strategy to gain a competitive advantage. Many now offer the next level of banking convenience—*home banking*. The bank that gives their customers the freedom to go online and view their accounts, open an account, apply for a loan, get a credit/debit card, pay bills, and transfer funds has a distinct competitive advantage over the bank that does not offer this service. IT has become such a strategic weapon in the banking industry that second-tier banks are merging to be able to justify expensive technological solutions to competitive situations.

SECTION SELF-CHECK

10-1.1   Managers are seeking the competitive advantage through IT strategies. (T/F)

10-1.2   One way to increase sales is to increase market share. (T/F)

10-1.3   Which of these is not a way to improve corporate profitability: (a) adjusting prices, (b) work force reduction, (c) expanding the product line, or (d) limiting the use of IT?

To be successful, managers and knowledge workers must fully understand and use the four major resources: money, materials, people, and information. Managers have become skilled at taking full advantage of the resources of *money, materials,* and *people;* but only recently have they begun to tap the potential of the *information* resource.

QUALITIES OF INFORMATION

Just as we describe automobiles in terms of features, color, and size, we describe information in terms of its *accuracy, verifiability, completeness, timeliness, relevance,* and *accessibility.*

Accuracy and Verifiability of Information

The *accuracy* quality of information refers to the degree to which information is free from error. Information usually is assumed to be accurate unless it is presented otherwise. Sometimes it is not economically feasible to collect information that is 100% accurate. For example, a market analyst may poll only a fraction of the potential consumers for a proposed product, and then extrapolate the results to all potential consumers. Also, manual data entry introduces the possibility of human error and, ultimately, those errors affect the accuracy of the data.

Accuracy and *verifiability* go hand in hand. A decision maker is reluctant to assume that information is accurate unless it is verifiable. For example, managers usually are comfortable with the accuracy of financial information. Financial information can be verified (usually by auditors) because records are kept of all financial transactions (for example, payments and receipts). Decision makers accept and use unverifiable information, but they do so with caution and skepticism.

Too often managers at all levels are quick to accept computer-generated information as gospel. This can be a mistake. Information is only as good as the data from which it is derived. As the saying goes, "garbage in, garbage out" or **GIGO** (pronounced "*GUY go*").

Completeness of Information

Information can be totally accurate and verifiable, but it may not tell the whole story. The *completeness* quality of information refers to the degree to which it is free from omissions. There is, of course, no relationship between the amount of information supplied to a decision maker and its completeness. Benefit/cost analysis offers a good example of the importance of considering the completeness of information in the decision-making process. If the benefit information is complete and the cost information is incomplete, the omission of the rest of the costs may result in an unprofitable project being approved. Unfortunately, this very situation is a common occurrence in the business world.

Timeliness of Information

The *timeliness* quality of information refers to the time sensitivity of information. Up-to-the-minute information on today's market trends may be of significant value to an executive. The same information will have less value in a month and probably no value in six months. IT has contributed more toward improving the timeliness quality of information than any of the other information qualities. IT has made it possible for managers and knowledge workers to have not only the right information, but the *right information* at the *right time* (see Figure 10-3). Fifteen years ago, managers were conditioned to waiting as much as two weeks for IT professionals to handle relatively simple requests for information. Today, the person desiring the information can handle similar requests in just minutes.

FIGURE 10–3 Access to Quality Information
A sales assistant is helping this couple make an informed decision about which appliance to put into their new kitchen. With his wireless handheld PC and access to a database, he can respond quickly to customer inquiries relating to the product, stock status, and delivery schedules. The information he provides has all the qualities of good information (accuracy, verifiability, completeness, relevance, timeliness, and accessibility).

Relevance of Information

The *relevance* quality of information refers to the appropriateness of the information as input for a particular decision. *Information overload* continues to be a problem for decision makers. Information overload occurs when the volume of available information is so great that the decision maker can't determine which information is relevant and which is not. One of the primary causes of information overload is the accumulation of information that is not relevant to a particular decision.

Accessibility of Information

Information technology has redefined the *accessibility* quality of information. Information in a well-organized database can be made easily accessible via the Internet and computer networks to all with a need to know. A considerable body of information remains untapped because it is poorly organized and buried in manual file cabinets. For all practical purposes, this information is inaccessible.

MAKING DECISIONS TO PRODUCE PRODUCTS AND SERVICES

The four levels of information activity within a company are *strategic, tactical, operational,* and *clerical.* IT-based information systems *process data* at the clerical level and *provide information* for managerial decision making at the strategic, tactical, and operational levels.

- *Strategic.* Strategic-level managers determine long-term strategies and set corporate objectives and policies to be consistent with these objectives. The information available for a strategic-level decision is almost never conclusive. To be sure, information is critical to strategic-level decision making, but virtually all decision makers at this level rely heavily on personal judgment and intuition.

- *Tactical.* Tactical-level managers must implement the objectives and policies made at the strategic level of management by identifying specific tasks that need to be accomplished. The information available for a tactical-level decision is seldom conclusive. That is, the most acceptable alternative cannot be identified from information alone. At this level, personal judgment and intuition used in conjunction with available information provide the foundation for most decisions.

- *Operational.* Operational-level managers complete the specific tasks as directed by tactical-level managers. The information available for an operational-level decision is often conclusive. That is, the most acceptable alternative can be clearly identified based on information available to the decision maker. At this level, personal judgment and intuition play a reduced role in the decision-making process.

The business system model shown in Figure 10-4 helps place the decision-making environment in its proper perspective. Managers (the top three levels) must use all the resources at their disposal to meet corporate objectives and perform the management functions of *planning, organizing, leading,* and *controlling.*

Figure 10-4 illustrates how the corporate resources of *money, materials* (including facilities and equipment), *people,* and *information* become "input" to the various functional units, such as operations, sales, and accounting. Employees use their talent and knowledge, together with these resources, to produce products and services.

The business system acts together with several *entities,* such as employees, customers, and suppliers (see Figure 10-4). An entity is the source or destination of information flow. An entity also can be the source or destination of materials or product flow. For example, suppliers are a source of both information and materials. They are also the destination of payments for materials. The customer entity is the destination of products and the source of orders.

FILTERING INFORMATION

The quality of an information system is judged by its output. A system that generates the same report for personnel at both the clerical and strategic levels defeats the purpose of an information system. The information needs at these two levels of activity are different. For example, an administrative assistant might need names, dates of employment, and other data to enroll employees in a pension plan. The president of the company doesn't need that level of detail but might need information on overall employee pension contributions.

Different employees in a company need different types of information to do their jobs. The key to using information effectively is to *filter* it. This way, employees receive just the information they need to accomplish their job functions—no more, no less. **Filtering** information results in the *right information* reaching the *right decision maker* at the *right time* in the *right form.* There are four basic levels of knowledge workers in every company, and each level has its own information needs.

FIGURE 10–4   A BUSINESS SYSTEM MODEL

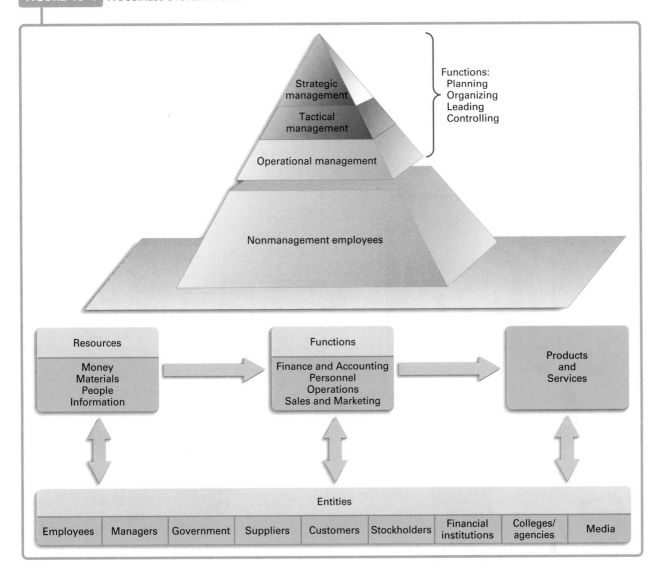

Clerical Level

Clerical-level personnel, those involved in repetitive tasks, are concerned primarily with *transaction handling*. You might say that these employees process data. For example, a sales clerk might key in customer orders on his or her terminal, and an airline ticket agent might confirm and make flight reservations.

Operational Level

Personnel at the operational level have well-defined short-term tasks that might span as long as three months. Their information requirements often consist of *operational feedback*. For example, the manager of the Eastern Regional Sales Department for Bravo International, a small high-tech firm, might want an end-of-quarter sales summary report (see Figure 10-5).

Managers and knowledge workers at the operational, tactical, and strategic levels often request **exception reports** that highlight critical information. They can make such inquiries directly to the system (see the example in Figure 10-5).

Tactical Level

At the tactical level, managers and knowledge workers concentrate on achieving a series of goals required to meet the objectives set at the strategic level. The information requirements at this level are usually *periodic*, but on occasion workers require one-time and what-if reports. *"What-if" reports*

FIGURE 10-5 FILTERING OF INFORMATION

FOUR-YEAR SALES TREND BY PRODUCT($1000)

PRODUCT	2001	2002	2003	2004	4-YEAR AVERAGE
ALPHAS	3,604	3,866	4,001	4,640	4,028
BETAS	1,106	2,240	2,855	3,590	2,448
GAMMAS	2,543	2,587	2,610	2,613	2,588
DELTAS	0	450	2,573	5,846	2,217
TOTALS	7,253	9,143	12,039	16,689	

A strategic-level sales-trend-by-product report shown in tabular and graphic formats. The sales-trend report and bar graph are prepared in response to inquiries from Bravo International's president, a strategic-level manager. Knowing that it is easier to detect trends in a graphic format than in a tabular one, the president requests that the trends be summarized in a bar graph. From the bar graph, the president easily can see that the sales of Alphas and Gammas are experiencing modest growth while the sales of Betas and Deltas are better.

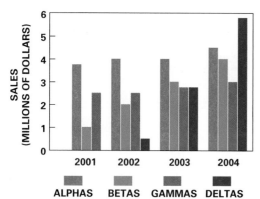

FOUR-YEAR SALES TREND BY PRODUCT

CORPORATE SALES REGIONAL SUMMARY($1000)-1ST QUARTER

REGION	ALPHAS	BETAS	GAMMAS	DELTAS	TOTAL
EASTERN	321	233	224	367	1145
SOUTHERN	180	202	196	308	886
WESTERN	369	250	150	472	1241
NORTHERN	250	170	162	254	836
TOTALS	1120	855	732	1401	4108

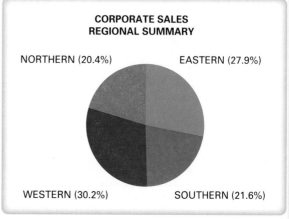

CORPORATE SALES
REGIONAL SUMMARY

NORTHERN (20.4%)   EASTERN (27.9%)

WESTERN (30.2%)   SOUTHERN (21.6%)

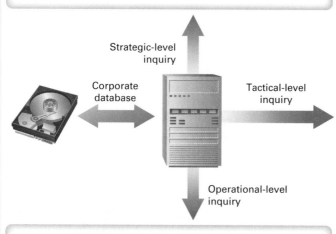

Strategic-level inquiry

Corporate database

Tactical-level inquiry

Operational-level inquiry

A tactical-level sales summary report shown in tabular and graphic formats. The sales summary report and pie graph are prepared in response to inquiries from Bravo International's national sales manager, a tactical-level manager. The report presents dollar-volume sales by sales region for each of the company's four products. To get a better sense of the relative sales contribution of each of the four regional offices during the first quarter, the national sales manager requested that the total sales for each region be presented graphically in a pie graph.

An operational-level sales summary and exception report. These sales reports are prepared in response to inquiries from an operational-level manager. The top report shows dollar-volume sales by salesperson for each of Bravo International's four products: Alphas, Betas, Gammas, and Deltas. In the report, the sales records of the top (Cook) and bottom (Ritter) performers are highlighted so that managers can use this range as a basis for comparing the performance of the other salespeople.

The eastern regional sales manager used a fourth-generation language to produce the exception report (bottom). The manager's request was: "Display a list of all eastern region salespeople who had sales of less than $15,000 for any product in this quarter." The report highlights the subpar performances of Baker and Ritter.

SALES DEPARTMENT - EASTERN REGION
SALES SUMMARY ($1000) - 1ST QUARTER

SALESPERSON	ALPHAS	BETAS	GAMMAS	DELTAS	TOTAL
BAKER	70	10	14	65	159
COOK	60	40	37	77	214
JONES	55	28	40	57	180
LUCAS	20	50	48	68	186
MILLER	45	34	28	48	155
OTT	39	47	29	42	157
RITTER	32	24	28	10	94
TOTALS	321	233	224	367	1145

SALES DEPARTMENT - EASTERN REGION
SALES SUMMARY ($1000) - 1ST QUARTER
SALESPERSONS WITH SALES<$15,000 FOR ANY PRODUCT

SALESPERSON	ALPHAS	BETAS	GAMMAS	DELTAS	TOTAL
BAKER	70	10	14	65	159
RITTER	32	24	28	10	94

are generated in response to inquiries that depict what-if scenarios ("What if sales increase by 15% next quarter?"). Tactical-level personnel are concerned primarily with operations and budgets from year to year. In the sales information system, the national sales manager, who is at the tactical level, might want the "Corporate Sales" report shown in Figure 10-5.

Strategic Level

Strategic-level managers are objective-oriented. Their information system requirements are often *one-time reports, what-if reports,* and *trend analyses.*

FIGURE 10–6 TYPES OF DECISIONS

Decision Characteristic	Programmed Decisions	Nonprogrammed Decisions (information-based decisions)
Difficulty	Easy	Tough
Horizon	Short-term	Long-term
Decision-maker level	Clerical	All management levels
Decision problem	Well-defined and structured	Ill-defined and unstructured
Confidence in making the right decision	High	Low to medium
Information requirement	Primarily applicable policies, standards, or procedures	Relevant information in meaningful format

For example, the president of the company might ask for a report that shows the four-year sales trend for each of the company's four products and overall (see Figure 10-5).

TYPES OF DECISIONS

Two basic types of decisions are the relatively easy **programmed decisions** and the tough **information-based decisions** (see Figure 10-6). Purely programmed decisions address well-defined problems. The decision maker cannot use his or her judgment because the actual decision is determined by existing policies or procedures (see Figure 10-7). A computer alone can make many such decisions. For example, the decision required to restock inventory levels of raw materials is often a programmed decision. This decision can be made by an individual or by a computer using predefined rules. When the inventory level of a particular item drops below the reorder point, perhaps a two months' supply, a decision to replenish the inventory by submitting an order to the supplier can be automatic.

FIGURE 10–7 JOHN GLENN'S RETURN TO SPACE
Shown here is the liftoff for John Glenn's historic flight to space to investigate the effects of weightlessness on senior citizens. NASA's computer systems at the space flight center and onboard the space shuttle make routine programmed decisions, leaving the operators and astronauts more time to make the more difficult information-based decisions.

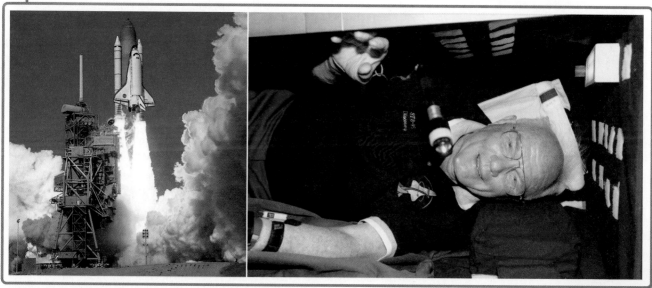

NASA

With information-based decisions, the decision maker needs information to make a rational decision. Such decisions involve unstructured problems; that is, the problems are hard-to-define and the rules are unclear. The information requirement implies the need for managers to use judgment and intuition in the decision-making process. Corporate policies, procedures, standards, and guidelines provide direction for information-based decisions made at the operational level, less direction at the tactical level, and little or no direction at the strategic level. The greater the programmability of a decision, the greater the confidence of the decision maker that the best choice was made.

WHY THIS SECTION IS IMPORTANT TO YOU

Every day, most of us are directly or indirectly affected by several information systems. This section gives you the information system basics you need to understand all this activity.

10-3 | All about Information Systems

During a typical day, you will probably interact with several information systems, perhaps your college's online registration system, a retailer's POS system, a bank's customer service system (at an ATM), or a Web-based system with a music lyrics database. Also, unbeknownst to you, many more information systems will be processing your personal information, perhaps the system at your state's revenue office, the system at your cellular phone company, or a system evaluating you as a candidate for employment. This section describes an information system and what it can do.

WHAT IS AN INFORMATION SYSTEM?

Hardware, software, people, procedures, and *data* are combined to create an *information system* (see Figure 10-8). The term *information system* is a generic reference to a technology-based system that does two things:

FIGURE 10-8 **CREATING AN INFORMATION SYSTEM**

- Provides *information processing capabilities* for an individual or, perhaps, an entire company. The processing capability refers to the system's ability to handle and process information (for example, order processing).

- Provides *information people need to make better, more informed decisions.* Information systems provide decision makers with on-demand reports and inquiry capabilities as well as routine periodic reports (daily, weekly, and so on). Information systems routinely make programmed decisions without people being involved.

An information system can service a portion of an organization (perhaps a department), an entire organization (perhaps a company), the extended organization (perhaps a company and all business-to-business partners), or the world (an Internet-based e-commerce system). The information system concepts in this chapter apply to all types of information systems (see Figure 10-9): PC-based systems, LAN-based systems, enterprise-wide systems, and Internet-based systems.

WHAT CAN AN INFORMATION SYSTEM DO?

Not surprisingly, an information system has the same four capabilities as a computer system: *input, processing, storage,* and *output* (see Figure 10-10).

Input

The information system has the capability to accept various forms of input.

- *Source data.* Source data result from the recording of a transaction or an event (for example, a bank deposit or the receipt of an online order).

- *An inquiry.* An inquiry is any request for information.

- *A response to a prompt.* When prompted, you might click the "add to shopping cart" button while cybershopping.

FIGURE 10–9 INFORMATION SYSTEMS

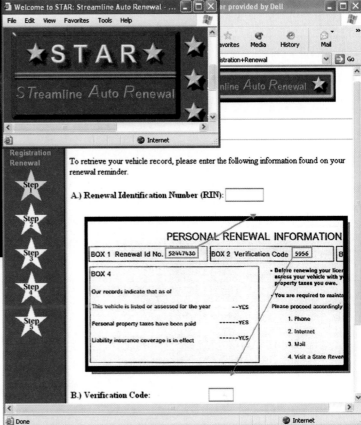

AN INFORMATION SYSTEM FOR AIR TRAFFIC CONTROL
This Air Traffic Management center has an information system that handles the air traffic over England and Wales. It is the world's largest facility dedicated to air traffic control.
Courtesy of Lockheed Martin Corporation

ONLINE MOTOR VEHICLE REGISTRATION
The STAR system is an extension of Arkansas Department of Finance and Administration's information system that enables Arkansas residents to go online to renew motor vehicle registrations. Residents logon to the Internet-based information system, any time of the day or night, from the comfort of their home or office, and then enter data directly to the state's system. The registration is sent automatically by return mail.

- *An instruction.* "Store file" or "Print invoice" could be instructions.
- *A message to another user on the system.* This could be via e-mail or some other messaging capability.
- *A change.* When you edit a word processing document, you are entering change data.

Processing

The information system has the capability to perform various types of processing.

- *Retrieving, recording, and updating data in storage.* You can retrieve a customer's record from a database for processing, enter expense data into an accounting system's database, and change a customer's address on a marketing database, respectively.
- *Summarizing.* You can present information in a condensed format to show totals and subtotals.
- *Selecting.* You can select records by criteria (for example, "Select all employees with 25 or more years of service in the company").
- *Manipulating.* You can perform arithmetic operations (addition, multiplication, and so on) and logic operations (comparing an employee's years of service to 25 to determine if they are greater than, equal to, or less than 25).

FIGURE 10–10 **INFORMATION SYSTEM CAPABILITIES**

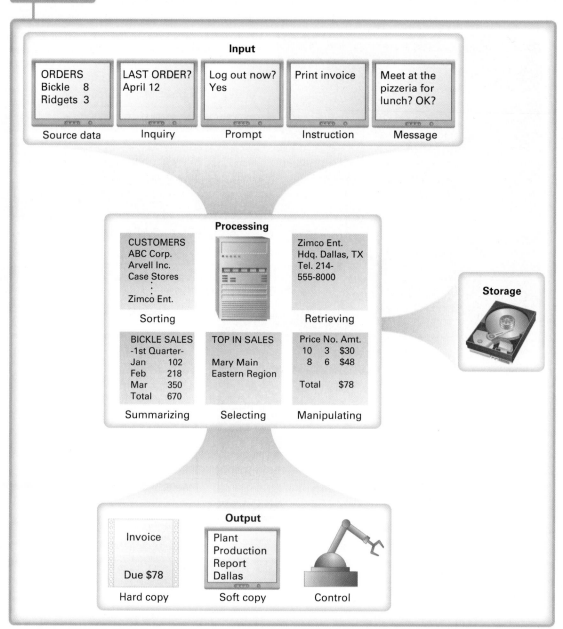

Storage

The information system has the capability to store *data, text, images* (graphs, pictures), and *other digital information* (voice messages) so that they can be recalled easily for output or further processing.

Output

The information system is capable of producing output in a variety of formats.

- *Hard copy.* Printed reports, documents, and messages are hard copy.
- *Soft copy.* Temporary displays on monitors and voice-mail messages are soft copy.
- *Control.* Instructions to industrial robots or automated processes are also output.

LOTS OF OPPORTUNITIES FOR AUTOMATION

When we speak of an information system today, we usually mean an automated system. In a *manual system,* the automated elements of an information system (the hardware and software) aren't there. Manual systems consist of people, procedures, and data only. Many information systems in industry, government, and education are still manual, from large organizations with hundreds of computers to two-person companies. Tens of thousands of manual systems have been targeted to be upgraded to IT-based information systems. Ten times that many are awaiting tomorrow's creative users and IT professionals to identify their potential for automation.

Both manual systems and computer-based information systems have an established pattern for work flow and information flow. In a manual payroll system, for example, a payroll clerk receives time sheets from supervisors. The clerk then retrieves each employee's records from folders stored alphabetically in a file cabinet. Next, the clerk uses a calculator to compute gross and net pay, then manually writes (or types) the payroll check and stub. Finally, the payroll clerk compiles the payroll register, which is a listing of the amount paid and the deductions for each employee, on a tally sheet with column totals. About the only way to find and extract information in a manual payroll system is to thumb through employee folders—a painstaking process in an organization of any size.

Today most payroll systems have been automated. But look in any office in almost any company and you will find rooms full of filing cabinets, tabbed three-ring binders, circular address files, or drawers filled with 3 by 5 inventory cards. These manual information systems are opportunities to improve a company's profitability and productivity through the application of computer and information technologies.

THE ONGOING INTEGRATION OF INFORMATION SYSTEMS

An information system can be either function-based or integrated. A **function-based information system** is designed for the exclusive support of a specific application area, such as inventory management or accounting. Its database and procedures are, for the most part, independent of any other system. The databases of function-based information systems probably contain data that are maintained in other function-based systems within the same company. For example, much of the data needed for an accounting system would be duplicated in an inventory management system. It is not unusual for companies with a number of autonomous function-based systems to maintain customer data in 5 to 10 different databases. When a customer moves, the address must be updated in several databases (accounting, sales, distribution, and so on). This kind of data redundancy is an unnecessary financial burden to a company.

During the past 25 years, great strides have been made in the integration of function-based systems. The resulting **integrated information systems** share a common database. The common database helps minimize data redundancy and allows departments to coordinate their activities more efficiently. This integration is being extended between businesses as more and more business-to-business systems are implemented. In B2B, businesses empower their information systems to interact with one another directly, thus eliminating much of the manual transaction handling of the past (printed orders, checks, status reports, and so on).

GETTING DATA INTO THE SYSTEM

In a computer system, the input, output, and data storage components receive data from and transmit data to RAM and, eventually, the processor. These hardware components are said to be *online* to the processor. Hardware devices that are not accessible to a processor are said to be *offline*. The concepts of online and offline also apply to data. Data are said to be *online* if they can be accessed and manipulated by the processor. All other data are considered *offline*. For example, when you are logged in to a LAN from a PC, the data on a LAN file server are said to be online. When you log off you are offline.

Often, data do not exist in a form that can be "read" by the computer. For example, supervisors may record manually the hours worked by the staff on a time sheet. Before the payroll checks can be computed and printed, the data on these time sheets must be entered to the computer. Someone does this in an online operation at a PC or terminal. The time sheet is the **source document**, and, as you might expect, the data on the time sheet are the **source data.** Whenever possible, data are entered via source data automation, such as with point-of-sale UPC scanners in grocery stores.

The term *data entry* describes the process of entering data into an information system. Information systems are designed to provide users with display-screen prompts to make online data entry easier. The display on the user's screen, for example, may be the image of the source document (such as a time sheet). A *prompt* is a brief message to the user that describes what should be entered (for example, "Enter hours worked").

Data entry generally falls into one of these categories.

- *Batch processing.* In **batch processing,** transactions are grouped, or batched, and entered consecutively, one after the other.

- *Transaction-oriented processing.* In **transaction-oriented processing,** transactions are entered directly to the system as they occur.

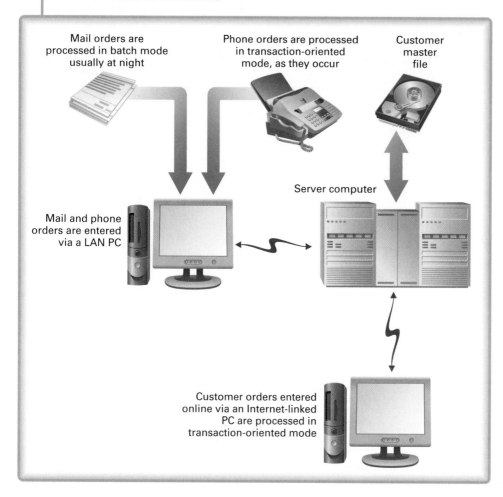

FIGURE 10–11

BATCH AND TRANSACTION-ORIENTED PROCESSING
This typical order entry system accepts orders by mail, by phone, and online via the Internet.

Mail orders are processed in batch mode usually at night

Phone orders are processed in transaction-oriented mode, as they occur

Customer master file

Server computer

Mail and phone orders are entered via a LAN PC

Customer orders entered online via an Internet-linked PC are processed in transaction-oriented mode

To illustrate the difference between batch and transaction-oriented processing, consider the order processing system illustrated in Figure 10-11. The system accepts orders by both mail and phone. The orders received by mail are accumulated, or batched, for data entry—usually at night. Phone orders do not need to accumulate. People taking the phone orders interact with the company information system via PCs or terminals and enter the order data online while talking with the customer. Batch processing is appropriate mainly when information on source documents needs to be transcribed.

The primary advantage of transaction-oriented data entry is that records on the database are updated immediately, as the transaction occurs. With batch data entry, records are batched periodically. In a transaction-oriented environment, the database remains continuously up-to-date and can be queried at any time. Most data entry into enterprise-wide systems or into local area network-based systems is done online, regardless of whether the processing being done is batch or transaction-oriented.

SECTION SELF-CHECK

10-3.1 Hardware, software, people, places, and information are combined to create an information system. (T/F)

10-3.2 An information system can provide information processing capabilities for an individual or an entire company. (T/F)

10-3.3 The summarizing activity would be associated with which capability of an information system: (a) input, (b) output, (c) processing, or (d) storage?

10-3.4 In which type of processing are transactions grouped together for processing: (a) transaction-oriented, (b) bin, (c) batch, or (d) group-driven?

10-4 The DP System and the MIS

Information technology is constantly redefining itself and so it is with information systems. For example, data processing systems evolved into management information systems. This section describes these systems and the differences between them.

DATA PROCESSING SYSTEM

Let's begin with the most basic forms of automated information system, the **data processing systems,** or **DP systems,** and then progress to more sophisticated information systems. DP systems are concerned with *transaction handling* and *record keeping,* usually for a particular functional area and, sometimes, for an entire enterprise. Data are entered and stored in a file format, and stored files are updated during routine processing. Periodic outputs include *action documents* (invoices) and *scheduled reports,* primarily for clerical personnel and operational-level managers. The major drawback of data processing systems is that they are inflexible and cannot accommodate data processing or information needs that are not already built into the system. In fact, DP systems are little more than electronic filing cabinets. Most companies have moved beyond the scope of DP systems and now have systems with the flexibility of providing management with information in support of an ever-changing decision-making environment.

MANAGEMENT INFORMATION SYSTEMS

In the not-too-distant past, most payroll systems were data processing systems that did little more than process time sheets, print payroll checks, and keep running totals of annual wages and deductions. As managers began to demand more and better information about their personnel, payroll *data processing systems* evolved into human resource **management information systems.** A human resource management information system is capable of predicting the average number of worker sick days, monitoring salary equality between minority groups, making more effective use of available personnel skills, and providing other information needed at all three levels of management—operational, tactical, and strategic.

What Is a Management Information System?

If you were to ask any five executives or IT professionals to define a management information system, or **MIS,** the only agreement you would find in their responses is that there is no agreement on its definition. An MIS has been called a method, a function, an approach, a process, an organization, a system, and a subsystem. The following definition is a mouthful, but it captures the essence of the MIS: *An MIS is a computer-based system that optimizes the collection, transfer, and presentation of information throughout an organization by using an integrated structure of databases and information flow.*

The MIS versus the Data Processing System

Here are a few differences between an MIS and a DP system.

- The integrated database of an MIS enables greater flexibility in meeting the information needs of management.
- An MIS integrates the information flow between functional areas (accounting, marketing, inventory management, and so on), whereas DP systems tend to support a single functional area (see Figure 10-12).
- An MIS caters to the information needs of all levels of management, whereas DP systems focus on the clerical and operational levels.
- Management's information needs are supported on a timelier basis with an MIS than they are with a DP system. An MIS, for example, has online inquiry capability for the immediate generation of reports, whereas a DP system usually produces only scheduled reports.

Characteristics of Management Information Systems

These are *desirable* characteristics of an MIS.

- An MIS supports transaction handling and record keeping.
- An MIS uses an integrated database and supports a variety of functional areas.
- An MIS provides operational-, tactical-, and strategic-level managers with easy access to timely but, for the most part, structured information.
- An MIS is somewhat flexible and can be adapted to meet the changing information needs of the organization.
- An MIS can boost system security by limiting access to authorized personnel.

The MIS in Action

All major airlines rely on management information systems to assist in day-to-day operations and provide valuable information for short- and long-term planning. At the core of such an MIS is the airline reservation subsystem. Airline reservation agents and individuals scheduling their own flights interact with the MIS's integrated database via computer networks and/or the Internet to update the database the moment a seat on any flight is filled or becomes available.

An airline MIS does much more than keep track of flight reservations. It also closely monitors departure and arrival times so that ground crew activities can be coordinated. The system even

FIGURE 10–12 MANAGEMENT INFORMATION SYSTEMS

GOLF COURSE MANAGEMENT SYSTEM
Golf courses throughout the world use the ProLink golf course management system to facilitate play on the golf course and course administration in the office. The system is driven by a GPS (global positioning system) navigation system to deliver a real-time information flow to golfers on the course and to course managers. The monitor in each golf cart presents a graphic of each hole such that, at a glance, golfers can see the entire hole (or course), the obstacles, and their exact distance to the green and the pin. After the game, the system helps golfers analyze their game, identifying strengths and weaknesses. Wireless communication between the remote cart-based systems allows course managers to tap the status of the golf course at any time.

Courtesy of ProLink

THE FEDEX INFORMATION SYSTEM
Federal Express has one of the world's most sophisticated information systems, providing up-to-the-minute information for its 150,000 employees. The system uses advanced telecommunications to monitor the status of millions of shipments as they move through key handling points in the system. The FedEx system handles more than 60 million online data transmissions each day.

compiles and produces many kinds of information needed by management: the number of passenger miles flown, profit per passenger on a particular flight, percentage of arrivals on time, average number of empty seats on each flight for each day of the week, and so on.

You may be interested to know that airlines routinely overbook flights. That is, they book seats they do not have. The number of extra seats sold is based on historical "no-show" statistics compiled by the MIS from data in the integrated database. Although these statistics provide good guidelines, occasionally everyone does show up!

The influence of the MIS is just as pervasive in hospitals (patient accounting, point-of-care processing, and so on), insurance (claims-processing systems, policy administration, actuarial statistics, and so on), colleges (student registration, placement, and so on), and other organizations that use computers both for information processing and to gather information for decision making.

10-5 Decision Support Systems

The decision support system and its many tools enable managers and knowledge workers to make better and timelier decisions. This section describes the decision support system and compares it to the MIS.

WHAT IS A DECISION SUPPORT SYSTEM?

Decision support systems (DSS) are *interactive* information systems that rely on an integrated set of user-friendly decision support tools (both hardware and software) to produce and present information to support management in the decision-making process. Decision makers can often rely on their experience to make a quality decision. When they cannot, the information that is readily available from the integrated corporate MIS is usually enough to help them through. However, decision makers, especially at the tactical and strategic levels, are sometimes confronted with complex decisions whose factors are beyond their human abilities to synthesize properly. These types of decisions are "made to order" for decision support systems.

A decision support system can help close the gap between the information they have and the information they need to make quality decisions. By using the latest technological innovations, planning and forecasting models, user-oriented query languages, and even artificial intelligence, DSS hardware and software provide managers with an unparalleled decision-making tool.

Generally, the DSS helps decision makers choose between alternatives. Some DSSs can even automatically rank alternatives based on the decision maker's criteria. Decision support systems also can be used merely to help remove the tedium of gathering and analyzing data. For example, managers no longer have to be burdened with such laborious tasks as manually entering and totaling rows and columns of numbers. They no longer have to be bothered with problems presenting or outputting reports or decision materials because graphics software in the DSS helps managers generate illustrative bar and pie graphs in a matter of seconds. And, with the availability of a variety of user-oriented DSSs, managers can get the information they need without having to depend on direct technical assistance from an IT professional.

At Johns Hopkins University, a decision support system helps administrators predict enrollment. The admissions officers are adapting various DSS techniques to predict which accepted applicants will ultimately select Johns Hopkins. The system examines trends and patterns in student data, past and present, looking for common personal characteristics among university enrollees. This system has proven to be twice as accurate as traditional decision models. This type of system is extremely important to universities that limit admissions in that small errors can have a dramatic impact on the university. For example, accepting too many students can result in some students not having university-guaranteed housing. Accepting too few might cause budget problems.

THE DSS VERSUS THE MIS

Management information systems are best at supporting decisions that involve *structured* problems, such as when to replenish raw materials inventory and how much of an inventory item to order. This type of routine operational-level decision is based on production demands, the cost of holding the inventory, and other variables that depend on the use of the inventory item. The MIS integrates these variables into an inventory model and presents specific order information (for example, order quantity and order date) to the manager in charge of inventory management.

In contrast to the MIS, decision support systems are designed to support decision-making processes involving *semistructured* and *unstructured* problems. A semistructured problem might be the need to improve the delivery performance of suppliers. The problem is structured partially in that information comparing the on-time delivery performance of suppliers can be obtained directly from the integrated database supporting the MIS. The unstructured facets of the problem, such as extenuating circumstances, rush-order policy and pricing, and so on, make this problem a candidate for a DSS.

An example of an entirely unstructured problem would be the evaluation and selection of an alternative to a raw material currently being used. A decision maker might enlist the aid of a DSS to provide information on whether it would be advisable to replace a steel component with a plastic or aluminum one. The information requirements for such a decision are diverse and typically beyond the scope of an MIS.

Another distinction we can make between an MIS and a DSS is that an MIS is designed and created to support a set of applications. A DSS is a set of decision support tools that can be adapted to any decision environment.

CHARACTERISTICS OF DECISION SUPPORT SYSTEMS

These are *desirable* characteristics of a DSS.

- A DSS helps the decision maker in the decision-making process.
- A DSS is designed to address semistructured and unstructured problems.
- A DSS supports decision makers at all levels, but it is most effective at the tactical and strategic levels.
- A DSS is an interactive, user-friendly system that can be used by the decision maker with little or no assistance from an IT professional.
- A DSS makes general-purpose models, simulation capabilities, and other analytical tools available to the decision maker.
- A DSS can be readily adapted to meet the information requirements of any decision environment.
- A DSS can interact with the corporate database.
- A DSS is not executed in accordance with a preestablished production schedule (for example, weekly production reports).

FIGURE 10–13

THE DECISION SUPPORT SYSTEM
A decision support system is a set of software and hardware tools that can be adapted to any decision environment.

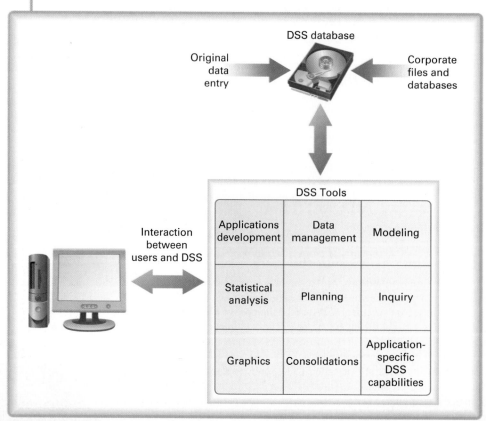

THE DSS TOOL BOX

A DSS consists of a set of decision support tools that can be adapted to any decision environment (see Figure 10-13). Together, these tools help managers address decision-making tasks in specific application areas (the evaluation and promotion of personnel, the acquisition of companies, and so on). DSS includes the following tools.

Applications Development

Some decision support systems provide users with the capability of developing computer-based systems to support the decision-making process. These applications typically involve the input, processing, and storing of data and the output of information. The ease with which DSS applications can be created has spawned a new term—**throwaway systems.** Often DSS applications are developed to support a one-time decision and are then discarded.

Data Management

DSS software packages have many approaches to database management—that is, the software mechanisms for the storage, maintenance, and retrieval of data. Perhaps the most popular DSS data management tool is **data warehousing.** Data warehousing involves moving existing operational files and integrated databases to a **data warehouse.** The data warehouse is a relational database created specifically to help managers get the information they need to make informed decisions (see Figure 10-14).

In many organizations, mountains of mission-critical data are compiled during routine transaction processing, but the data are in cumbersome function-based files and databases. Such data, which are not integrated and may include redundant data, are not easily accessible by management. The DSS data management tool enables scattered data from existing operational corporate files and databases to be collected and copied to a data warehouse. The data in the data warehouse are reorganized into a format that gives decision makers ready access to valuable, time-sensitive information. The operational files and databases may include data about customer buying patterns, inventory supply, seasonal manufacturing trends, and so on, and they must be constantly updated. This constant change of the operational data means that the data warehouse must be reconstructed periodically, perhaps each day or each week, depending on the volatility of the data.

Once data are consolidated in a data warehouse, managers can make complex queries and do analysis not possible with data spread all over the organization. For example, **data mining,** one of many analytical techniques, involves the analysis of large databases, such as data warehouses. Data mining essentially is getting answers to unasked questions and detecting unanticipated trends from databases. Data mining software is composed of very sophisticated algorithms that examine large amounts of data for elusive relations or correlations. Data mining has resulted in information that led to increased sales per customer, getting new customers, reducing marketing expenses, identifying cross-selling opportunities, creating customer loyalty, and reducing exposure to fraud. At Coca-Cola, data mining revealed that Diet Coke drinkers buy seven or more books a year, whereas Classic Coke drinkers buy only one or two. This unexpected piece of information resulted in changes to Coca-Cola's marketing campaigns. Telecommunications companies such as MCI use data mining to detect fraud as early as possible. For example, data mining might highlight an account whose pattern of calls has changed dramatically, such as infrequent calls to Colorado becoming frequent calls to Colombia.

FIGURE 10–14

TAPPING THE DATA WAREHOUSE
SAS Institute has long been a leader in the creation of DSS and EIS software. The SAS® Enterprise Reporter™ provides decision support by helping nontechnical users tap the resources of a data warehouse and create formatted reports (shown here) that can be distributed on paper or via the Internet.

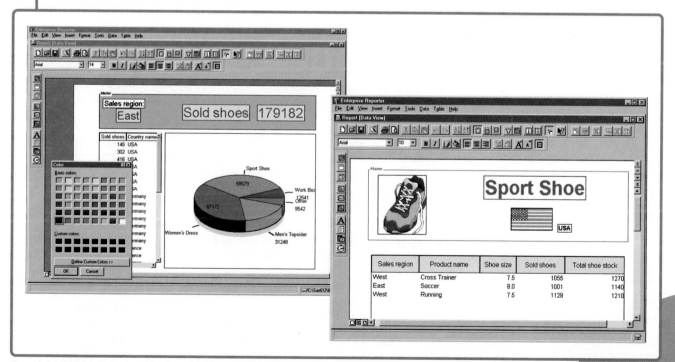

This DSS data management tool may be needed to ensure compatibility between a DSS database and an integrated set of DSS tools. Typically, this DSS tool enables access to a wide variety of databases. For example, the DSS data management tool can *import* and use data from a server-based database or a PC-based spreadsheet. The DSS data management tool also can do the reverse; that is, *export* DSS data for use by another program.

Modeling

Decision support systems enable managers to use mathematical modeling techniques to re-create the functional aspects of a system within the confines of a computer. These simulation models are appropriate when decisions involve a number of factors. For example, models often are used when uncertainty and risk are introduced, when several decision makers are involved, and when multiple outcomes are anticipated. In these cases, each decision needs to be evaluated on its own merit.

In the business community, managers use modeling DSS software to simulate sales, production, demand, and much more. Simulation techniques are being applied to other aspects of life as well. Simulations have proven effective in predicting social, environmental, and biological trends.

Statistical Analysis

The DSS statistical analysis capability can handle everything from simple statistics, such as average, median, and standard deviation; to more analytical techniques, such as regression analysis and exponential smoothing; to complex procedures, such as multivariate analysis. Risk analysis and trend analysis are common applications of DSS statistical tools.

Planning

Managers often are faced with making decisions that will be implemented at some time in the future. To help them get a glimpse into the future, they rely on DSS software that permits forecasting, what-if analysis, and goal seeking. In *what-if analysis,* managers make inquiries such as "What would be the impact on sales if we boosted the advertising budget by 30%?" In *goal seeking,* managers make inquiries such as "How much do we need to increase the advertising budget to achieve a goal of $120 million in sales for next year?"

Inquiry

DSS software helps managers to make online inquiries to the DSS database using English-like commands. For example, a personnel manager may enter this request: "What percentage of employee compensation goes to retirement benefits?" With DSS query capability, users are able to query corporate databases in much the same language that they would use to communicate with their colleagues.

Graphics

With the graphics DSS tool, managers can create a variety of presentation graphics based on data in the DSS database, including bar graphs, pie graphs, and line graphs. The graphics tool allows you to "drill down" into a graph to uncover additional information. For example, a user viewing a monthly sales bar graph can "drill down" and display a weekly sales bar graph for any given month.

Consolidations

DSS tools are available that enable the consolidation of like data from different sources. A sample use of this DSS tool is the consolidation of financial statements from subsidiary companies into a single corporate financial statement.

Application-Specific DSS Capabilities

DSS tools that support a particular decision environment, such as financial analysis and quality control, are being introduced routinely into the marketplace.

EXECUTIVE INFORMATION SYSTEMS

Just when we start to get used to decision support systems, the IT community introduces us to an even more intricate information system: the **executive information system.** As with the terms *MIS* and *DSS,* the term *executive information system,* or **EIS,** has been introduced with fanfare and anticipation but without a common understanding of what it is. The EIS offers the same decision support tools as the DSS, but each tool is designed specifically to support decision making at the executive levels of management, primarily the tactical and strategic levels. The EIS is easy to use, yet offers powerful information gathering and presentation tools. Like the MIS and the DSS, the EIS may eventually gain an identity of its own, but today's commercially available executive information systems look suspiciously like what most managers know as decision support systems.

10-5.1 Decision support systems are designed to support decision-making processes involving totally structured problems. (T/F)

10-5.2 What-if analysis and goal seeking are addressed with the DSS planning tool. (T/F)

10-5.3 Which of the following types of information systems is designed specifically for decision support at the tactical and strategic levels of management: (a) expert systems, (b) executive information systems, (c) DP systems, or (d) management information systems?

SECTION SELF-CHECK

10-6 | Expert Systems

WHY THIS SECTION IS IMPORTANT TO YOU

Terms like *expert system* and *artificial intelligence* sound futuristic and, to some, a bit threatening to humanity. After reading this section you will be able to sort out myth from reality.

The kinds of problems that can be solved by computers extend well past those usually associated with computation and information retrieval. Today's computers can simulate many human capabilities, such as reaching, grasping, calculating, speaking, remembering, comparing numbers, and drawing. Researchers are working to expand these capabilities and, therefore, the power of computers, by developing hardware and software that can imitate intelligent human behavior. For example, researchers are working on systems that have the ability to reason, to learn or accumulate knowledge, to strive for self-improvement, and to simulate human sensory and mechanical capabilities. This general area of research is known as **artificial intelligence (AI)**.

Artificial intelligence? To some, the mere mention of artificial intelligence creates visions of electromechanical automatons replacing human beings. But as anyone involved in the area of artificial intelligence will tell you, there is a distinct difference between human beings and machines. Computers will never be capable of simulating the distinctly human qualities of creativity, humor, and emotions! However, computers can drive machines that mimic human movements (such as picking up objects and placing them at a prescribed location), enable us to talk to our computers, and provide the "brains" for systems that simulate the human thought process within the domain of a particular area of expertise (tax preparation, medical diagnosis, and so on). For example, computers have proven to be effective marriage counselors and wise corporate colleagues. The software that gives the computer these human-like capabilities is the expert system.

WHAT IS AN EXPERT SYSTEM?

The **expert system** is a relatively recent addition to the circle of information systems. Like the DSS, expert systems are computer-based systems that help managers resolve problems or make better decisions. However, expert systems do so with a decidedly different twist. An expert system is an interactive system that responds to questions, asks for clarification, makes recommendations, and generally helps the user in the decision-making process (see Figure 10-15). In effect, working with an expert system is much like working directly with a human expert to solve a problem because the system mirrors the human thought process. It even uses information supplied by real experts in a particular field such as medicine, taxes, astronomy, or geology. Expert systems are particularly good at making critical decisions that we might not be making because of lack of time, interest, resources, knowledge, and so on. In many ways, expert systems re-create the decision process better than humans do. We tend to miss important considerations or alternatives—expert systems don't.

An expert system applies IF-THEN rules to solve a particular problem, such as determining a patient's illness. Like the MIS and DSS, an expert system relies on factual knowledge, but an expert system also relies on *heuristic knowledge* such as intuition, judgment, and inferences. Both the factual knowledge and the heuristic rules of thumb used in an expert system are acquired from one or more real live *domain experts*, human experts in a particular field, such as jet engine repair, life insurance, oceanography, or property assessment. The expert system uses this human-supplied knowledge to model the human thought process within a particular area of expertise. Once completed, an expert system can approximate the logic of a well-informed human decision maker.

Technically speaking, an *expert system* is the highest form of a **knowledge-based system**. The less sophisticated knowledge-based systems are called **assistant systems**. An assistant system helps users make relatively straightforward decisions. Assistant systems are usually implemented to reduce the possibility that the end user will make an error in judgment rather than to resolve a particular problem. For example, assistant systems are used to help people make online charge-card approvals and quote rates for life insurance.

THE CRYSTAL BALL:
Expert System in Your Future The potential of expert systems is virtually untapped. The time is ripe for the acceptance and applications for expert systems to explode. Within a few years, expert systems will be conceived and implemented in every situation that calls for IF-THEN logic and consistent decision making. In the near future, each of us will have "expert" help and guidance at home and in our respective professions. Expert systems will be a part of our everyday life: they will diagnose our illnesses and tell us what to do; they will help us troubleshoot PC problems; they will provide assistance at tax time; they will help us choose a college or an employer; and they will provide marriage counseling (if needed).

FIGURE 10–15 EXPERT SYSTEMS IN PRACTICE

EXPERT SYSTEMS IN THE OIL BUSINESS
Phillips Petroleum Company was one of the first companies to create and employ widespread use of expert systems. As many as 75 expert systems have given knowledge workers guidance in the oil refinery (shown here), research and development, administration, and other areas throughout the company.

Photo courtesy of Phillips Petroleum Company

EXPERT SYSTEMS IN ECOSYSTEMS
Here, an Oak Ridge National Laboratory scientist gathers data on the effect of greenhouse gases on a forested ecosystem. The data goes into a knowledge base for an expert system that provides insight into how changes in climate affect plant photosynthesis and, by extension, food production.

Courtesy of Lockheed Martin Corporation

THE CRYSTAL BALL:
Computers with Common Sense
Research in the field of artificial intelligence is slowly coming to fruition in the form of practical applications such as speech recognition and robotics. One effort to give computers common sense has resulted in a knowledge base of three million rules of thumb and about 300,000 terms and concepts. This "common sense" knowledge base is the result of 600 person-years of effort, yet it only scratches the surface of the 100 million things the typical person knows about the world. Nevertheless, this knowledge base will continue to grow and, by 2010, should provide the framework that will allow us to talk with reasonably "intelligent" computers on a variety of topics.

In effect, expert systems simulate the human thought process. To varying degrees, they can *reason, draw inferences,* and *make judgments.* Let's use medical diagnosis expert systems, which have proven themselves remarkably accurate, for an example. Upon examining a patient, a physician might use an expert diagnosis system to get help in diagnosing the patient's illness or, perhaps, to get a second opinion. First, the doctor would relate the symptoms to the expert system: male, age 10, temperature of 103°, and swollen glands about the neck. Needing more information, the expert system might ask the doctor to examine the parotid gland for swelling. Upon receiving an affirmative answer, the system might ask a few more questions and even ask for lab reports before giving a diagnosis. A final question for the physician might be whether the patient had been previously afflicted with or immunized for parotitis. Based on the information, the expert system would diagnose the illness as parotitis, otherwise known as mumps.

In recent years, expert systems have been developed to support decision makers in a broad range of disciplines, including medical diagnosis, oil exploration, financial planning, tax preparation, chemical analysis, surgery, locomotive repair, weather prediction, computer repair, troubleshooting satellites, computer systems configuration, nuclear power plant operation, newspaper layout, interpreting government regulations, and many others.

AN EXPERT SYSTEM EXAMPLE

Anyone who has owned a printer for any length of time has had it act up or, worse, refuse to act at all. You do not have many alternatives when this happens. You can try to decipher an often-incomplete manual, call a knowledgeable friend, or bite the bullet and call an expensive professional. Now, several printer companies offer a more palatable alternative—an expert system. These expert systems do what call-in technical service people used to do—guide users through the problem to a solution. These expert systems have a knowledge base derived from the knowledge of technical service personnel who have handled thousands of such calls. The knowledge base contains:

- A means of identifying the problem(s) to be solved

- Possible solutions to the problem(s)

- How to progress from problem to solution (primarily through facts and rules of inference)

All of this knowledge is integrated in an interactive online expert system that can help users solve most problems in a matter of minutes.

This expert system is probably the beginning of a new trend in technical support. Because technical support tends to be very expensive, hardware and software vendors can't afford very many calls from a customer before their profit from the sale of a product has eroded. Major vendors have hundreds (a few have thousands) of people doing nothing but handling calls for technical support. In some companies, 25% of their employees staff the tech support lines. In a very few years, look for vendors to integrate more and more expert systems into their tech support strategies. The trend to this alternative form of customer service is gathering momentum as more and more people gain access to the Internet.

ARE EXPERT SYSTEMS IN YOUR FUTURE?

The number and variety of expert system applications have increased dramatically with the advent of powerful, cost-effective PCs. Expert systems advise financial analysts on the best mix of investments; help taxpayers interpret the tax laws; help computer repairpersons diagnose the problems of a malfunctioning computer; and help independent insurance agents select the best overall coverage for their business clients.

In the short period of their existence, expert systems have operated impressively, and they continue to improve. Decision makers in every environment are developing or contemplating developing an expert system. Attorneys will hold mock trials with expert systems to "pre-try" their cases. Doctors routinely will ask a second opinion. Architects will "discuss" the structural design of a building with an expert system. Military officers will "talk" with the "expert" to plan battlefield strategy. City planners will "ask" an expert system to suggest optimal locations for recreational facilities.

One of the myths surrounding expert systems, though, is that they will actually replace human experts. Although expert systems augment the capabilities of humans and make them more productive, expert systems will never replace people. Expert systems and humans complement one another in the decision-making process. The computer-based expert system can handle routine situations with great accuracy, thereby relieving someone of the burden of a detailed manual analysis. However, humans can combine the insight of an expert system with their flexible intuitive abilities to resolve complex problems.

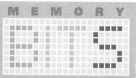

Information Systems

- Data processing (DP) system
  - Functional area support
  - Transaction handling and record keeping
- Management information system (MIS)
  - Integrated database
  - DP functions plus management information
- Decision support system (DSS)
  - Interactive system
  - Various tools that support decision making
- Executive information system (EIS)
  - Subset of DSS
  - Decision support at tactical and strategic levels
- Expert system
  - Interactive knowledge-based system
  - Simulates human thought process
- Intelligent agent (bot)
  - Has the authority to act on our behalf
  - Performs a variety of tasks

10-6.1 Artificial intelligence refers to an area of research that uses computers to simulate human capabilities. (T/F)

10-6.2 An assistant system is the highest form of a knowledge-based system. (T/F)

10-6.3 Which type of information system has the greatest potential to reduce dependencies on critical personnel: (a) MIS, (b) expert system, (c) DP system, or (d) EIS?

SECTION SELF-CHECK

10-7 Intelligent Agents and Bots

In days of yore, well-to-do people had butlers and maids to do their bidding, day and night (and some still do). A recent innovation in information technology may enable a return to the days of yore—sort of. In cyberland, **intelligent agents** will "live" in our computer systems and assist us with the chores of life, both at home and at work. Intelligent agents, like expert systems, are a type of artificial intelligence. An intelligent agent also is called a **bot,** which is short for software robot.

Like all information systems, intelligent agents provide information that can help us make decisions, but they do it in a very different way. An intelligent agent has the authority to act on our behalf, just as a human agent does. We set the information or processing goals for our agents, and the agents act to reach those goals. The agent reacts to meet the demands of a specified goal in several different ways.

- The agent may remain in continuous motion working toward an ongoing goal.

- The agent performs an action when a specified event occurs.

- The agent performs actions needed to accomplish a one-time goal.

For example, you might ask an agent to alert you one week prior to birthdays of selected friends and relatives (an ongoing goal). A week before a birthday, the agent will alert you (an action triggered by an event):

WHY THIS SECTION IS IMPORTANT TO YOU

Other people are using intelligent agents to help them with many of life's chores. Read on so that you, too, are aware of what these agents can do for you.

FIGURE 10–16 The Future of Information Systems
Shell Oil Company's automated SMART Pump may give us a glimpse at the future of artificial intelligence-based information systems. The SMART pump being tested at a site in Sacramento, California, will offer consumers the ability to refuel their car without leaving the driver's seat. The Shell SMART Pump identifies the car model and the robotic filler locates and opens the fuel door and refuels the car. All transactions are recorded automatically, as well. The customer's account is debited, inventory is adjusted, and the sale amount is logged. Other information is recorded for statistical purposes, such as type of car refueled, time of day, and location.

Courtesy of Shell Oil Company

Linda's 25th birthday is Monday, June 3. Last year you sent a humorous Internet birthday greeting and two dozen red roses from Higdon Floral.

The agent can then be set up to send an e-mail or postal greeting, send flowers (you specify price range), or arrange a party and send out announcements, whichever you tell it to do. If you wish, you can instruct the agent to purchase and deliver a present to Linda (a one-time goal). The agent's response is based on the information contained in Linda's profile (friends, preferences, and so on). If you give an agent the authority to handle all birthdays, you may never have to worry about birthdays again. Of course, if the agent plans a party, you should attend.

The number and variety of intelligent agents is growing steadily, especially those focusing on the Internet or intranets. Today, uses for intelligent agents include the following.

- Intelligent agents can sort through e-mail. The agent scans each message and routes junk e-mail to the electronic equivalent of the trash can. E-mail from designated correspondents is given priority treatment.
- Intelligent agents scan online newspapers and magazines for articles in our interest areas (for example, your favorite college basketball team, folk music, environmental issues).
- Intelligent agents, called *shop bots*, can search the Internet for the best price on specified products.

  In a few years, intelligent agents will be helping us do many more jobs.

- A sailor might instruct an intelligent agent to alert her to favorable wind conditions at the local lake. To achieve this goal, the agent must tap weather information on a regular basis.
- We can tell the intelligent agent the type of vacation we want to take, and it will comb through online databases, looking for the best combination of price and luxury. When the bot reports back, we can make our selection, and the bot will make the reservations.

As you can see, the possibilities for agents are endless. Agents are already at work doing hundreds of tasks and their applications are expected to grow. A number of major companies are developing products and services that will accommodate these agents.

It won't be long before our computers and we are online 24 hours a day to our office, home, college, and the information superhighway. As we evolve to an environment in which we are always online, look for intelligent agents and other artificial intelligence applications to take on an ever-increasing workload (see Figure 10-16). Unlike butlers and maids who have a few days off, intelligent agents never stop working for us.

SECTION SELF-CHECK

10-7.1 Intelligent agent software has the authority to act on our behalf. (T/F)
10-7.2 An intelligent agent reacts to meet the demands of a: (a) working relationship, (b) personal wish, (c) system objective, or (d) specified goal.

10-1 INFORMATION TECHNOLOGY AS A COMPETITIVE STRATEGY

New and innovative uses of information technology are being implemented every day. Each company has a seemingly endless number of opportunities to use technology to achieve a competitive edge. Money spent on information technology yields tremendous returns.

The increased competition of the world market is pressuring corporate managers and knowledge workers into leveraging computer and information technology to gain a competitive advantage. IT technology can be leveraged to increase sales, increase productivity and reduce cost, and improve customer service.

10-2 INFORMATION AND DECISION MAKING

Traditionally managers and knowledge workers have been adept at taking full advantage of the resources of money, materials, and people, but only recently have they begun to make effective use of information. The quality of information can be described in terms of its *accuracy, verifiability, completeness, timeliness, relevance,* and *accessibility.* Information is only as good as the data from which it is derived ("garbage in, garbage out," or **GIGO**). By **filtering** information, the right information reaches the right decision maker at the right time in the right form.

Information systems help process data at the clerical level and provide information for managerial decision making at the operational, tactical, and strategic levels. Managers at the operational, tactical, and strategic levels often request **exception reports** that highlight critical information. For decisions made at the tactical and strategic levels, information is often inconclusive, and managers also must rely on their experience, intuition, and common sense to make the right decision.

The two basic types of decisions are **programmed decisions** and **information-based decisions.** Purely programmed decisions address well-defined problems. Information-based decisions involve ill-defined and unstructured problems.

10-3 ALL ABOUT INFORMATION SYSTEMS

Hardware, software, people, procedures, and data are combined to create an information system. An information system provides companies with data processing capabilities and the company's people with information.

An information system has the same four capabilities as a computer system: input, processing, storage, and output. The processing capabilities include sorting; retrieving, recording, and updating data in storage; summarizing; selecting; and manipulating.

An information system can be either function-based or integrated. A **function-based information system** is designed for the exclusive support of a specific application area. **Integrated information systems** share a common database.

Source data on **source documents** must be transcribed into a machine-readable format before a computer can interpret them. Data entry describes the process of entering data into an information system.

When transactions are grouped together for processing, it is called **batch processing.** In **transaction-oriented processing,** transactions are entered as they occur.

10-4 THE DP SYSTEM AND THE MIS

Data processing (DP) systems are file-oriented systems that focus on transaction handling and record keeping and provide periodic output aimed primarily at operational-level management.

A **management information system,** or **MIS,** is a computer-based system that optimizes the collection, transfer, and presentation of information throughout an organization by using an integrated structure of databases and information flow.

An MIS not only supports the traditional data processing functions but also relies on an integrated database to provide managers at all levels with easy access to timely but structured information. An MIS is flexible and can provide system security.

An MIS is oriented to supporting decisions that involve structured problems.

10-5 DECISION SUPPORT SYSTEMS

Decision support systems are interactive information systems that rely on an integrated set of user-friendly hardware and software tools to produce and present information targeted to support management in the decision-making process.

A **DSS** supports decision making at all levels by making general-purpose models, simulation capabilities, and other analytical tools available to the decision maker. A DSS can be readily adapted to meet the information requirements of any decision environment.

In contrast to the MIS, decision support systems are designed to support decision-making processes involving semi-structured and unstructured problems.

A decision support system is made up of a set of software tools and hardware tools. The categories of DSS software tools include applications development (frequently resulting in **throwaway systems**), data management (including the ability to import and export data), modeling, statistical analysis, planning, inquiry, graphics, consolidations, and application-specific DSS capabilities.

Data warehousing involves moving existing operational files and databases from multiple applications to a **data warehouse.** The data warehouse is a relational database created specifically to help managers get the information they need to make informed decisions. **Data mining** in data warehouses is used to identify unanticipated trends and problems.

We use the term *import* to describe the process of converting data in one format to a format that is compatible with the calling program, in this case the data management tool. The DSS data management tool also can do the reverse, that is, *export* DSS data for use by another program, or, perhaps, a database package.

The **executive information system** (EIS) is designed specifically to support decision making at the tactical and strategic levels of management.

10-6 EXPERT SYSTEMS

Artificial intelligence (AI) is an area of research concerned with giving computer systems an ability to reason, to learn or accumulate knowledge, to strive for self-improvement, and to simulate human sensory and mechanical capabilities. **Expert systems,** an area of AI, help managers resolve problems or make better decisions. They are interactive systems that respond to questions, ask for clarification, make recommendations, and generally help in the decision-making process. An expert system is the highest form of a **knowledge-based system**, but in practice, the two terms are used interchangeably. The less sophisticated knowledge-based systems are called **assistant systems.**

The user interface component of an expert system enables the interaction between end user and expert system needed for heuristic processing. Some computer industry observers believe that expert systems are the wave of the future and that each of us will have "expert" help and guidance at home and in our respective professions.

10-7 INTELLIGENT AGENTS AND BOTS

Intelligent agents have the authority to act on our behalf, just as human agents do. We set the goals for our intelligent agents, also called **bots,** and they act to reach those goals.

KEY TERMS

artificial intelligence (AI) (p. 407)
assistant system (p. 407)
batch processing (p. 399)
bot (p. 409)
data mining (p. 405)
data processing system (DP system)
  (p. 400)
data warehouse (p. 405)
data warehousing (p. 405)
decision support system (DSS) (p. 403)

exception report (p. 393)
executive information system (EIS)
  (p. 406)
expert system (p. 407)
filtering (p. 392)
function-based information system
  (p. 399)
GIGO (p. 391)
information-based decision (p. 395)
integrated information system (p. 399)

intelligent agent (p. 409)
knowledge-based system (p. 407)
management information system (MIS)
  (p. 401)
programmed decision (p. 395)
source data (p. 399)
source document (p. 399)
throwaway system (p. 404)
transaction-oriented processing (p. 399)

MATCHING

1. information-based decision
2. decision support system
3. data mining
4. source data
5. transaction-oriented processing
6. AI
7. filtering
8. expert system
9. exception report
10. GIGO
11. programmed decision
12. throwaway system
13. executive information system
14. data warehouse
15. intelligent agent

a. simulation of human sensory capabilities
b. system supporting a one-time decision
c. results from recording a transaction
d. has the authority to act on our behalf
e. the right information at the right time
f. transactions entered as they occur
g. addresses unstructured problems
h. highlights critical information
i. answers to unasked questions
j. relies on heuristic knowledge
k. garbage in garbage out
l. EIS
m. analytical tools for managers
n. addresses well-defined problems
o. DSS tool that holds files and databases

CHAPTER SELF-CHECK

10-1.1 The traditional shotgun approach to creating new business is still more effective than IT-based targeting. (T/F)

10-1.2 IT-driven cost reduction programs in hospitals are not compatible with quality patient care. (T/F)

10-1.3 Home banking includes all of the following services except: (a) bill paying, (b) brokerage, (c) loan application, or (d) funds transfer.

10-2.1 Money spent on information technology yields positive returns. (T/F)

10-2.2 It is easier for a manager to detect trends presented in a tabular format than in a graphic format. (T/F)

10-2.3 Exception reports highlight critical information. (T/F)

10-2.4 Which of these would not be considered a quality of information: (a) verifiability, (b) relevance, (c) weight, or (d) timeliness?

10-2.5 Common corporate resources would include all but which of the following: (a) prestige, (b) money, (c) materials, or (d) information?

10-3.1 An integrated information system is designed for the exclusive support of a specific application area. (T/F)

10-3.2 Source data result from the recording of a transaction or an event. (T/F)

10-3.3 A CD-ROM sitting on a shelf is said to be: (a) offline, (b) online, (c) system-oriented, or (d) sealed.

10-3.4 The information system processing capability that does not encompass logic operations is: (a) selecting, (b) manipulating, (c) recording, or (d) sorting.

10-3.5 A brief message to a user entering data would be called: (a) a question, (b) a prompt, (c) an answer, or (d) a user query.

10-4.1 The focus of data processing systems is: (a) transaction handling only, (b) record keeping only, (c) transaction handling and record keeping, or (d) strategic reporting.

10-4.2 An MIS has the capability to limit access to authorized personnel. (T/F)

10-4.3 An MIS can be a computer-based system or a manual system. (T/F)

10-4.4 MIS is an abbreviation for what term: (a) management information system, (b) mega information system, (c) managing Internet system, or (d) metropolitan IT system?

10-4.5 Which of these is not a characteristic of an MIS: (a) is flexible, (b) provides security, (c) uses an integrated database, or (d) does not support transaction handling?

10-5.1 An MIS is a subset of an EIS. (T/F)

10-5.2 Which DSS tool is used to analyze data warehouses to identify possible trends and problems: (a) planning, (b) inquiry, (c) modeling, or (d) data management?

10-5.3 A DSS is most effective at which two levels of management: (a) clerical and operational, (b) operational and tactical, (c) tactical and strategic, or (d) clerical and strategic?

10-5.4 DSS applications that are discarded after providing information support for a one-time decision are called: (a) throwaway systems, (b) toss-out programs, (c) junk systems, or (d) legacy systems.

10-6.1 Computers already are capable of simulating human humor and emotions. (T/F)

10-6.2 An expert system relies on factual knowledge and on heuristic knowledge. (T/F)

10-6.3 Expert systems are designed to replace human experts. (T/F)

10-6.4 An expert system is the highest form of: (a) assistant system, (b) specialist system, (c) factoid, or (d) knowledge-based system.

10-7.1 Intelligent agents already are dated technology and are disappearing from the corporate landscape. (T/F)

10-7.2 Intelligent agents fall under which of these software umbrellas: (a) operating systems, (b) IT, (c) artificial intelligence, or (d) data management?

10-7.3 Which of these types of information systems reacts automatically to meet the demands of a user-specified goal: (a) DSS, (b) smart manager systems, (c) intelligent agent, or (d) EIS?

IT ETHICS AND ISSUES

E-MAIL, PRODUCTIVITY, AND THE BOTTOM LINE

Most would argue that e-mail has a positive impact on productivity and the bottom line within an organization. However, a comprehensive study indicated that employees waste an average of 115 hours a year interacting via e-mail on non-job-related communications. That is about a half hour each day. The estimated annual loss to the organization is approximately $4000 per employee.

 Discussion: *If you were asked to present an argument to emphasize the positive contributions of e-mail, what would you say?*

 Discussion: *What kind of information would you need in order to calculate the estimated annual savings to an organization that result from the judicious use of e-mail?*

DOES THE INTERNET REALLY CHANGE EVERYTHING?

It has been said many times in the media, the home, and in small group conversations at work that "the Internet changes everything." To be sure, it has changed the way we communicate with one another. Internet-based information systems are changing the way we plan vacations and the way we buy and sell merchandise. It is emerging as the source of preference for news and other information for the majority of Americans.

 Discussion: *The Internet has changed much of what we do, but is it an exaggeration to say "the Internet has changed everything"? If so, what is unaffected by the Internet? If there are elements of our society untouched by the Internet, will they remain so in the future?*

 Discussion: *Are we developing a healthy or unhealthy dependency on the Internet? Explain.*

E-COMMERCE AND PROFILING

Many companies involved in e-commerce build and maintain user profiles so they can use their information systems to better target their marketing efforts. They gather information about you through your interaction with their site and, often, from other sources. A recent report concluded that profiling is becoming more extensive and marketing techniques are becoming more intrusive. Most major Web sites post their "Privacy Policy" but if you read it closely, it doesn't necessarily mean that your personal information is safe; it just means that they have a policy.

 Discussion: *Enter "privacy policy" on any search engine to find sites with written privacy policies. Read one of these policies in detail. Evaluate the policy relative to what you perceive to be good policy regarding the privacy of personal information.*

 Discussion: *Generally, these privacy policy statements place no limit on the amount of information that can be gathered and maintained on you or anyone else. Should there be limitations? If so, describe these limitations.*

 Discussion: *Some sites gather and sell information about you. If you have surfed pornography sites, done some online gambling, spent time at the Alcoholics Anonymous site, or requested information on HIV, then that interest may have been added to someone's profile on you. Someone might even sell that information to others. Discuss the ethical considerations of selling personal information gathered over the Internet.*

 Discussion: *The potential exists for profiles to be leaked or subpoenaed for custody or divorce cases, employment decisions, insurance coverage, and so on. Is this ethical? If not, what can be done about it?*

10-1.1 What is meant when someone says that a company is on the bleeding edge of technology?

10-1.2 What is the major difference between improving profitability through traditional approaches and through those that involve computer and information technology?

10-1.3 Describe IT strategies that any specific federal agency or body (FBI, CIA, the Senate, IRS, White House, and so on) could employ to reduce the burden on the taxpayer and/or provide better service.

10-1.4 Describe IT strategies that universities could employ to achieve a competitive advantage in their efforts to attract the better students.

10-1.5 The insurance company featured in the chapter has no field insurance agents, yet it is ranked consistently at or near the top of all insurance companies in customer satisfaction. How can this be?

10-2.1 It is often said that "time is money." Would you say that "information is money"? Discuss.

10-2.2 In general, top executives have always treated money, materials, and people as valuable resources, but only recently have they recognized that information is also a valuable resource. Why do you think they waited so long?

10-2.3 Pick a type of business (for example, automobile manufacturing, hotels, or city government) and give an example how information may be filtered for use by management.

10-2.4 Select an article in the newspaper on a current event and evaluate the information relative to its accuracy, verifiability, completeness, timeliness, relevance, and accessibility.

10-2.5 For each of the three levels of management illustrated in the business system model in Figure 10-4, what would the horizon (time span) be for planning decisions? Explain.

10-3.1 Give examples within the context of a corporate information system for these information system processing capabilities: retrieving, summarizing, and manipulating.

10-3.2 Reflect on your activities of the past week and identify those activities that generated source data for information systems.

10-3.3 A company has five function-based information systems. What would you say to convince management to spend the money necessary to consolidate these systems into a single integrated information system?

10-4.1 Describe transactions that might be processed by an insurance company's DP system.

10-4.2 Describe reports that might be requested by an operational-level manager at a large bank. By a tactical-level manager. By a strategic-level manager.

10-4.3 Suppose the company you work for batches all sales data for data entry each night. You have been asked to present a convincing argument to top management about why funds should be allocated to convert the current system to an MIS with transaction-oriented data entry. What would you say?

10-5.1 Is it possible for an organization to have both a DSS and an MIS? Explain.

10-5.2 How often would the data warehouse need to be updated (reconstructed) in a university? Justify your answer.

10-5.3 The upside of data mining is that a company can identify trends early, then make adjustments to corporate operations. Is there a downside to data mining? Explain.

10-5.4 Give examples of what-if inquiries that the mayor of a large city might make to a DSS.

10-5.5 The IT community regularly introduces buzzwords, especially for tools designed to provide information for management. Frequently, these terms are not clearly defined when introduced (for example, DSS and EIS). Would having definitions that are more concrete help or hinder IT progress? Explain.

10-6.1 Describe at least three ways in which artificial intelligence applications can help disabled persons cope with the routine of everyday living.

10-6.2 AI researchers have spent more time creating a chess-playing computer than on any other project. Why?

10-6.3 To varying degrees, computers can see, hear, speak, feel, and smell. Some people think we should continue to pursue this area of AI research with vigor. Some feel that machines should not be given human qualities. Where do you stand and why?

10-6.4 Describe a specific decision environment that would be appropriate for the implementation of an expert system.

10-6.5 Describe a specific decision environment that would be appropriate for the implementation of an assistant system.

10-7.1 Give an example of how an intelligent agent might be able to help you at home.

10-7.2 Give an example of how an intelligent agent might be able to help you at work.

1. A decade ago, the only people interacting with information systems were knowledge workers logged on to their company's computer network. Today, individuals (customers, citizens, and so on) have access to a variety of Internet-based information systems. Go online, and then seek out and explore at least one such system (for example, the student system at your college, the state license tag renewal system, an employee system, an employment system, and so on). You may need to become a registered user. Describe your experience.

2. The first decision support tool was the spreadsheet. If you are not familiar with spreadsheet software, open a worksheet and learn about spreadsheet capabilities. Briefly describe ways in which spreadsheet software can support decision making. Give an example.

1. The Online Study Guide (multiple choice, true/false, matching, and essay questions)
2. Internet Learning Activities
   - Internet Issues MIS/DSS/EIS
   - E-commerce Artificial Intelligence
3. Serendipitous Internet Activities
   - Politics
   - Distance Learning

Chapter 11

Learning Objectives

Once you have read and studied this chapter, you will have learned:

- The four stages of the system life cycle (Section 11-1).

- The basic system development techniques and the concepts associated with these techniques (Section 11-2).

- The scope and capabilities of CASE (Computer-Aided Software Engineering) tools (Section 11-3).

- The concepts and phases of prototyping, including the general activities that take place during system analysis and design (Section 11-4).

- Approaches to converting an existing information system to a new one (Section 11-5).

- Basic programming concepts and the programming process, as well as an overview of popular programming languages (Section 11-6).

DEVELOPING BUSINESS INFORMATION SYSTEMS

Why this chapter is important to you

Throughout the day we interact with information systems. Information systems let us deposit and withdraw money from an ATM. Each month information systems calculate what we are owed for wages and what we owe to our creditors. Everywhere we go, we run into an information system—at the point-of-sale terminal in a department store, when making an online airline reservation, or while enrolling at college.

Information systems don't just happen. They might be purchased, leased, or developed from scratch. In any case, those who will use the system frequently are involved in development and/or implementation of the system. If you are part of the system, and there is a good chance you will be, it is to your advantage to provide input into the development process. Ultimately, the quality of an information system depends on the input and ongoing feedback from you and other users. Too often, life at work is a joy or a pain depending on the quality and effectiveness of the information system being used.

Information systems are dynamic, ever changing, and must be constantly upgraded to meet changing information and processing needs of your organization. You will be the user of an information system, and as such, it's your responsibility and duty to provide feedback on its operation and effectiveness.

This chapter acquaints you with the system development life cycle so you can be an effective contributor to any IT project team, whether for a new development project or during a system upgrade. A good effort on a high-profile information system project team is a great way to gain corporate visibility and earn points for an early promotion.

11-1 | The System Life Cycle

During the early years of automation, information systems were built to handle the basic flow of information within an organization: general accounting data and reports, inventory management, and human resource applications. Typically, they were custom systems built in-house to meet specific organization needs. Most were batch systems where transactions were accumulated or batched prior to processing. Data entry, reporting, and computation were done in or near a central computer center. After a couple of decades in this mode, technology specialists began to seek out new ways to improve existing information systems. First, they integrated separate function-based information systems, eliminating system redundancy. Second, they began to incorporate wide area and local area networks into system design, thus moving information processing activities closer to the action (for example, in the accounting office or on the shop floor).

Today, information systems are being implemented at a fever pitch. Corporate executives, users, and IT specialists are continually seeking new ways to employ technology to improve productivity and product quality. For example, for 30 years, trucking companies knew when their trucks departed and when they arrived (assuming the driver called the dispatcher upon arrival). Modern trucking companies use global positioning systems (GPS) to track trucks wherever they go. This GPS information system constantly feeds dispatchers the exact geographic location (and speed) of company trucks. This and all other information systems have a well-defined system life cycle.

STAGES OF THE LIFE CYCLE

Information systems, like human beings, have life cycles. Information systems are born from an idea and grow to become ready-to-use systems, complete with hardware, software, procedures, data, and the people who use them. Once operational, information systems contribute to organizations by processing data, providing information, or providing Internet-based services. As in life, information systems grow old and pass on. This life cycle for information systems is called the **system life cycle.** The four stages of this life cycle (birth, development, production, and end-of-life) are illustrated in Figure 11-1. The emphasis in this chapter is on the *development stage* of the life cycle.

APPLICATIONS SOFTWARE

An organization can progress through the development stage of the system life cycle and satisfy its information processing needs in three basic ways. Organizations can *buy it, rent it,* or *make it.*

● *Purchase an information system.* An organization can purchase and install a **proprietary software package.** The proprietary software industry thrives because similar types of organizations have similar information processing needs. A particular proprietary software package is developed by a software vendor to sell to a specific audience, perhaps large universities. Software vendors have created thousands of software packages that can fit in millions of organizations, from billing systems

FIGURE 11-1   THE SYSTEM LIFE CYCLE

Birth stage.

In the *birth* stage of the system life cycle, someone has an idea about how the computer can help provide better and more timely information.

Development stage.

The idea becomes a reality during the *development* stage of the system life cycle. During this stage, computer professionals and users work together to analyze an organization's information processing needs and design an information system. The design specifications are then translated into programs and the system is implemented.

End-of-life stage.

The accumulation of system modifications to a dynamic information system eventually takes its toll on system efficiency. The *end-of-life* stage arrives when an information system becomes so cumbersome to maintain that it is no longer economically or operationally effective. At this time it is discarded and the system life cycle is repeated.

Production stage.

Upon implementation, the information system enters the *production* stage and becomes operational, serving the information needs of an organization. The production stage is the longest of the four stages and will normally last from four to seven years. During this stage, information systems are continuously modified to keep up with the changing needs of the organization.

The System
Life Cycle

End-of-life   Birth   Development   Production

for veterinarians to general-ledger accounting systems for billion-dollar multinational companies. There are proprietary information systems to handle the processing and information needs for small public accounting firms, for Rotary clubs, for cities that offer several types of public utilities, for banks of all sizes, for dermatology clinics, for department stores, for Boy Scout troops, and for hundreds of other types of organizations.

- *Use an application service provider.* There is a growing trend to outsource support for all or part of an organization's information services needs to an **applications service provider** (**ASP**). An ASP is a company that provides software-based services and solutions to customers either through a wide area network (WAN) or the Internet, both from a central server computer (see Figure 11-2). Companies pay the third-party ASP to use its applications software, server computer, and storage capabilities. By "renting" a system from an ASP, a company can have information systems without having to maintain hardware, software, or an in-house staff. ASPs are thriving because they help organizations overcome some of today's serious challenges, such as hiring and retaining scarce information technology professionals. There is a perennial shortage of qualified IT people. Another challenge is the need to continually upgrade personnel skills, software, and hardware to keep pace with the technology. Although ASPs are frequently thought of as solutions for small to medium-sized businesses that might not be able to afford the full range of information technology services, ASPs are beginning to provide enterprise-wide systems for large companies as well. For example, many large school districts are opting to use ASP services via the Internet. At present the most commonly outsourced application is payroll. In the near future we can expect to have many vertically oriented ASPs that can offer a full range of information services to specific industries, such as health care.

- *Develop a custom information system.* Most organizations maintain IT professionals who can develop custom information systems, sometimes referred to simply as *applications*. Often outside consultants are retained to augment the in-house IT staff during the development projects. As a rule of thumb, organizations choose in-house development when the operational characteristics of the proposed system are unique to that particular organization (see Figure 11-2). In these cases, there is no proprietary software available for the task anyway.

FIGURE 11–2 APPLICATIONS SOFTWARE DEVELOPMENT OPTIONS

APPLICATIONS SERVICE PROVIDER
This ASP partners with customers to provide systems integration, IT training and outsourcing services to clients, including data center operations.

Courtesy of Lockheed
Martin Corporation

CUSTOM INFORMATION SYSTEM
Hertz's Instant Return information system was developed in-house by Hertz and offers credit-card customers a speedy return service. During peak hours, at over 100 airport locations in the US, a Hertz service representative meets the customer at carside in the car return lot. Using handheld computers, which are linked to a server by radio-frequency, the representative processes the return and issues an itemized receipt for the rental in under a minute. This information system makes rental return easier for customers by bringing the service to them.

©2000 Hertz System, Inc. Hertz is a registered service mark and trademark of Hertz Systems, Inc.

These three options pose to managers the classic "make-versus-buy" decision. Each approach has its pros and cons. Given the choice, corporate management will typically opt for proprietary software or an ASP over in-house development. The best *application portfolios* (an organization's applications software) contain an optimal mix of these.

The material in this chapter describes the process an organization might go through to create an information system. However, the discussion also is applicable to the selection and installation of proprietary software or the use of an ASP.

11-1.1 The best corporate application portfolios contain only proprietary software packages. (T/F)
11-1.2 The information system becomes operational in the birth stage of the system life cycle. (T/F)
11-1.3 Systems are implemented during which stage of the information system life cycle: (a) birth, (b) development, (c) production, or (d) end-of-life?

11-2 System Development Techniques and Concepts

There is no one best analytical technique. In fact, there are dozens of system development and design techniques. The techniques, however, are just tools. It's your skill and imagination that make an information system or a program a reality. However, an understanding of these techniques will help you to understand approaches to applications development.

So, before launching into discussions on approaches to applications development, we need to discuss several fundamental system development techniques, including *structured system design, data flow diagrams, entity relationship diagrams,* and *flowcharting.*

STRUCTURED SYSTEM DESIGN

Information systems, even small ones, can be complex to analyze, design, and implement. It is easier to address the design of a complex information system in small, manageable modules than as one big task. Information systems are designed using the principles of **structured system design.** The structured approach to system design encourages the top-down design technique: That is, the project team divides the system into independent modules for ease of understanding and design. The **structure chart** in Figure 11-3 illustrates how a payroll system can be conceptualized as a hierarchy of modules. Eventually the logic for the modules is represented in detail in step-by-step diagrams that illustrate the interactions between input, processing, output, and storage activities for a particular module.

FIGURE 11–3 **STRUCTURE CHART**
This structure chart breaks a payroll system down into a hierarchy of modules.

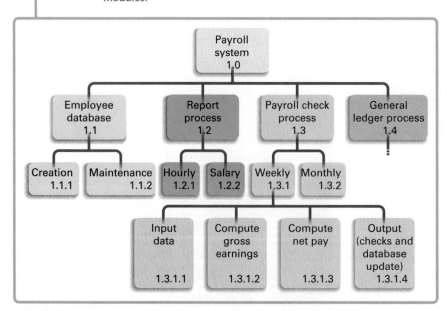

DATA FLOW DIAGRAMS

Data flow diagrams enable systems analysts to design and document systems using the structured approach to system development. Only four symbols are needed for data flow diagrams: entity, process, flow line, and data storage. The symbols are identified in Figure 11-4 and their use is illustrated in Figure 11-5.

- *Entity symbol.* The entity symbol is the source or destination of data or information flow. An entity can be a person, a group of people (for example, customers or employees), a department, or even a place (such as a warehouse).

- *Process symbol.* Each process symbol contains a description of a function to be performed. Process symbols also can be depicted as circles. Typical processes include enter data, calculate, store, create, produce, and verify. Process-symbol identification numbers are assigned in levels (for example, Processes 1.1 and 1.2 are subordinate to Process 1).
- *Flow line.* The flow lines indicate the flow and direction of data or information.
- *Data storage.* Data storage symbols identify storage locations for data, which could be a file drawer, a shelf, a database or file on magnetic disk, and so on.

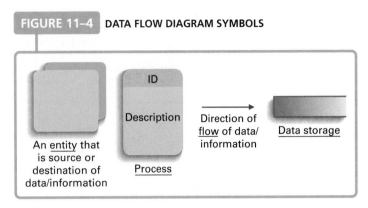

FIGURE 11–4 DATA FLOW DIAGRAM SYMBOLS

An entity that is source or destination of data/information

ID
Description
Process

Direction of flow of data/information

Data storage

The data flow diagram shown in Figure 11-5 is for an enterprise-wide MIS at BrassCo, a manufacturing company with about 1,200 employees at its corporate headquarters and four plant sites. The data flow diagram in Figure 11-5 provides an overview of BrassCo's MIS, showing information flow between its functional components and the integrated database. The functional components of BrassCo's MIS are:

Process 1   Finance and Accounting

Process 2   Human Resources

Process 3   Operations

Process 4   Sales and Marketing

All the MIS component systems share a common database.

In Figure 11-6, the Human Resources Process (2) of the BrassCo MIS (Figure 11-5) is *exploded* to show greater detail. The Human Resources Process (2) is essentially a personnel accounting system that maintains pertinent data on employees. The major processes within this human resources component are Recruiting (2.1), Pay and Benefits Administration (2.2), and Training and Education (2.3). Process 2.1 could be exploded to a third level of processes to show even greater detail (for example, 2.1.1, 2.1.2, and so on).

ENTITY RELATIONSHIP DIAGRAMS

Another similar business modeling tool, the **entity relationship diagram,** is widely used for defining the information needs of a business. Like the data flow diagrams, the entity relationship diagram involves identifying the entities. The focus of the entity relationship diagram is the *attributes* (a description) of the entities and the *relationship* between them. The focus of the data flow diagram is *information flow,* which may also define the relationship between both entities and processes. Also in contrast to data flow diagrams, the resulting entity relationship model is independent of any data storage or access method.

FLOWCHARTING

In **flowcharting, flowcharts** are used to illustrate data, information, and work flow by the interconnection of *specialized symbols* with *flow lines.* The combination of symbols and flow lines portrays the logic of the program or system. The more commonly used flowchart symbols are shown in Figure 11-7. Although flowcharting was initially a program design tool, it is now a common business tool for analyzing and documenting work flow, procedures, and decision processes.

In structured programming, each program has a **driver module,** sometimes called the **main program,** which causes other program modules to be executed as they are needed. The driver module in the payroll program (see Figure 11-8) is a **loop** that "calls" each of the subordinate modules, or **subroutines,** as needed for the processing of each employee. The loop and its subroutines and/or instructions are repeated until a condition is met. The program is designed so that when the payroll program is initiated, the "input data" module (1.1) is executed, or "performed," first. After execution, control is then returned to the driver module unless there are no more employees to be processed, in which case execution is terminated (the "Finish" terminal point). For each hourly or commission employee, Modules 1.2, 1.3, and 1.4 are performed, and at the completion of each subroutine, control is passed back to the driver module.

FIGURE 11–5

MIS OVERVIEW FOR BRASSCO ENTERPRISES
This MIS overview data flow diagram shows the general flow of information within
BrassCo. The database symbol and several entities are repeated to simplify the presentation of the data flow diagram. The diagonal line on the left end of the data storage symbols and the diagonal line in the corner of the entity symbols indicate that these symbols are repeated elsewhere in the data flow diagram.

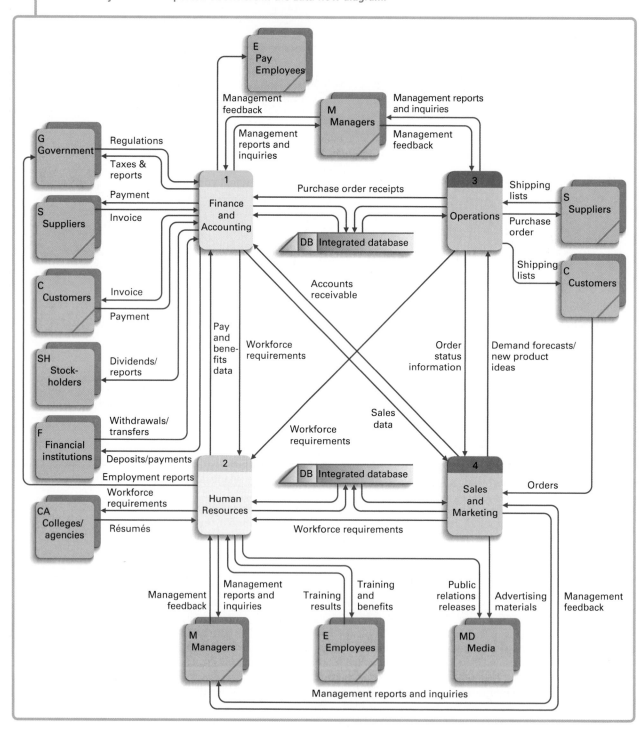

FIGURE 11–6

BRASSCO'S HUMAN RESOURCES SYSTEM
This data flow diagram is the explosion of Process 2 (Human Resources) of the MIS overview data flow diagram in Figure 11-5.

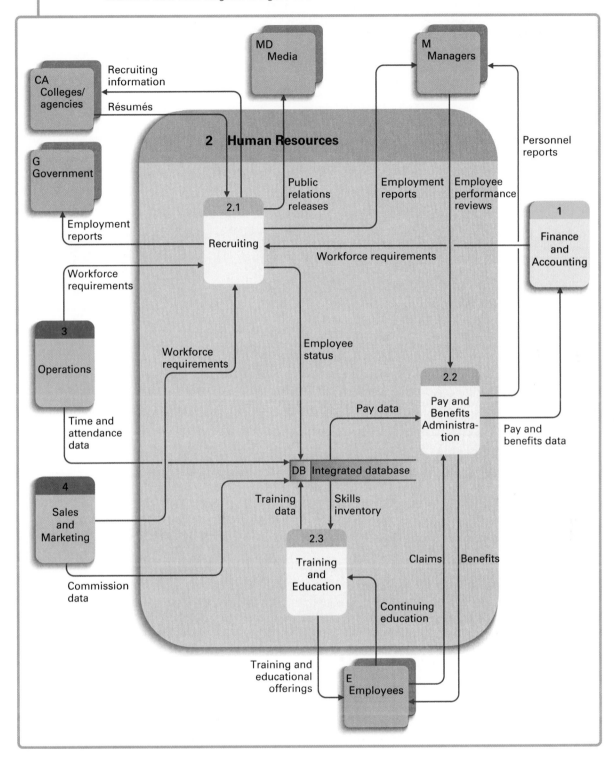

FIGURE 11-7 FLOWCHART SYMBOLS

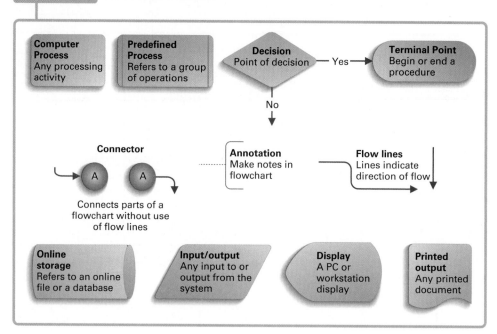

FIGURE 11-8 PROGRAM FLOWCHART

The flowchart presents the logic of a payroll program to compute and print payroll checks for hourly and commission employees. The logic is designed so that a driver module calls subroutines as they are needed to process each employee. Only the "Input Data" subroutine is shown.

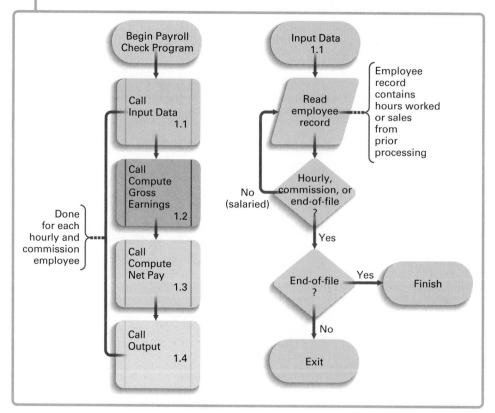

11-2.1 If data flow diagram Process 3.4 were exploded to two third-level processes, the numerical labels of the new processes would be 3.4.1 and 3.4.2. (T/F)

11-2.2 The data flow diagram process symbol is the source or destination of data flow. (T/F)

11-2.3 What is the design philosophy called that enables complex design problems to be addressed in small, manageable modules: (a) planned design, (b) structured design, (c) ordered design, or (d) controlled design?

11-2.4 In a structured program, subordinate modules that are called as needed are called: (a) subroutines, (b) sub par routines, (c) program pieces, or (d) instruction slices.

SECTION SELF-CHECK

11-3 Computer-Aided Software Engineering

The system development process is a cooperative effort of users and IT professionals. On one hand, IT professionals are familiar with the technology and how it can be applied to meet a business's information processing needs. On the other, users have in-depth familiarity with their respective functional areas (marketing, manufacturing, human resources, waste management administration, and so on) and the information processing needs of the organization. Over the past decade, the methods and tools used to create information systems have changed dramatically. Newer methods take full advantage of the technology to coordinate and automate the applications development process.

For years, most people thought the best way to improve productivity in system development was to make it easier for programmers to create programs. *Very high-level programming languages* are an outgrowth of this quest for better programmer productivity. In essence, these languages were designed to let the computer do much of the programming. However, in the early 1980s people began asking, "Why can't the power of the computer be applied to analysis and design work as well?" Now we know that it can. Many of the time-consuming manual tasks, such as creating a database and documenting information flow, can be automated. This general family of software development productivity tools falls under the umbrella of **computer-aided software engineering**, or **CASE**, tools. The term **software engineering** was coined to emphasize an approach to software development that combines automation and the rigors of the engineering discipline. CASE tools have made it possible to automate much of the coordination and work associated with system development. The use of CASE tools can result in higher-quality information systems, reduced cost and time to create information systems, and the elimination of much of the laborious work associated with system development.

CASE tools, which are commercial software packages, provide automated support throughout the entire system life cycle. Several companies market CASE tools. The different proprietary CASE tools use different nomenclature and techniques for the elements of the system development process. Figure 11-9 shows the interface for a CASE tool from Oracle Corporation.

The CASE tool kit continues to grow with the technology, encompassing tools for a variety of applications development tasks. The basic tool kit, however, includes the following:

- Design tools
- Information repository tools
- Program development tools

Each tool is discussed in the following sections. Note that there is some overlap in the functions of the various CASE tools.

Software engineers are developing software products to bridge the gap between design and executable program code. In a two-step process, these tool kits enable project teams to use automated software packages to help them complete the logic design (information flow, input/output) and the database organization; then the CASE software translates the logical design into the physical implementation of the system (executable program code or the software). Some CASE-developed applications emerge ready to implement with little or no actual programming required. CASE tools, however, are seldom that efficient. An operational information system may require anywhere from a little to a considerable amount of **custom programming** (the writing of original programs) to achieve full implementation.

DESIGN TOOLS

Prior to the introduction of CASE technologies, the tool kit for the systems analyst and programmer consisted of flowcharting and data flow diagram templates, lettering templates, rulers, scissors, glue, pencils, pens, and plenty of erasers and "whiteout." The CASE *design tools* provide an automated alternative. They help analysts and programmers prepare schematics that graphically depict the logic of a

WHY THIS SECTION IS IMPORTANT TO YOU

CASE tools, automated system development tools, are changing the way we create, maintain, and upgrade our information systems. This section will help you to become an active participant in future CASE activities within your organization.

FIGURE 11–9

CASE TOOLS EXAMPLES

This figure shows one of Oracle Corporation's CASE tools, Oracle*9i* JDeveloper, which provides end-to-end support for developing, debugging, and deploying business applications and Web services. The software offers an integrated set of system modeling tools that empowers systems analysts, users, and others to work together to construct models that capture business and user needs. Oracle's tightly integrated CASE tools have a shared repository in which technology-independent definitions of applications and business logic are stored. The automated repository makes up-to-date documentation, from entity relationship diagrams to screen layouts, readily available to those working on the project.

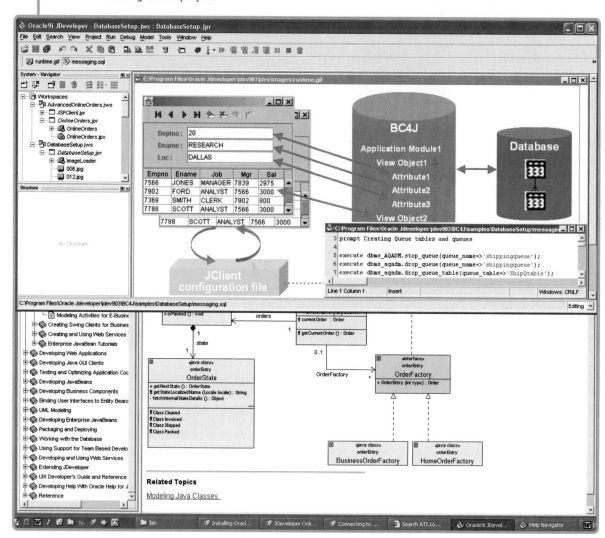

system or program (for example, data flow diagrams, entity relationship diagrams, structure charts). These automated design tools are to a systems analyst as word processing software is to a writer.

Automated design tools enable an analyst or programmer to select and position symbols, such as the data flow diagram process and entity symbols, and to connect these symbols with flow lines. Both symbols and flow lines can be labeled. Because all the design techniques supported by CASE products are structured design techniques, systems ultimately are depicted in several levels of generality.

CASE design tools also help designers prepare the user interface and generate screen and report layouts. The *user interface* capability enables the project team to design and create the system's user interface. The *screen generator* capability provides systems analysts with the capability of generating a mockup, or layout, of a screen while in direct consultation with the user. The **layout** is a detailed output and/or input specification that graphically illustrates exactly where information should be placed, or entered, on a screen or on a printer output. The *report generator* permits the calculation of summary totals by criteria and overall, the creation of graphs and charts, and the editing of output. For example, a report generator can produce a sales report that includes summary totals for each sales region and for overall, plus a bar graph of the information.

INFORMATION REPOSITORY TOOLS

The **information repository** is a central computer-based storage facility for all design information. For example, in an information repository, each field in a database is cross-referenced to all other components in the system. That is, the field *customer number* would be cross-referenced to every screen, report, graph, record/file, database, program, or any other design element in which it occurred. Cross-references also are made to processes in data flow diagrams and entity relationship diagrams. Once the company has had the information repository in place for a while, cross-references can be extended between information systems. The information repository permits all system documentation to be packaged electronically. That is, any part of the system—layouts, database design, notes, project schedules, and so on—can be recalled and displayed for review or modification. In effect, the information repository is the "database" for the system development project.

PROGRAM DEVELOPMENT TOOLS

Program development tools focus on the programming aspect of the system development effort. There is a variety of CASE program development tools, but the **application generators** make the biggest contribution to productivity. Instead of actually coding programs, programmers use application generators in conjunction with the design specifications and the structure of a database to generate software for a particular application. Another program development tool helps the project team with the generation of text data, one of the more laborious tasks associated with applications development.

THE FUTURE OF CASE

The creation of an information system is a cooperative effort between those who use it and IT professionals, with the latter handling most of the technical aspects of systems development. This, however, is changing. Each year, CASE technology makes it possible for us to assign more of the hard-core programming and design work to computers. The next generation of CASE technology may be for the user, giving the user a new level of technical independence. User-friendly CASE software will allow users to describe, in general terms, what they want the system to accomplish. The CASE software will then create a prototype system that can be refined by the user. Once refined, the *user-oriented* CASE software will generate the necessary programs and install the system.

Most of us who work have become, to some degree, slaves to technology. We need computers and their information processing capabilities to accomplish our jobs. Ultimately, it may be CASE technology that frees us from technological bondage, making us masters of technology and our information.

SECTION SELF-CHECK

11-3.1 Many of the manual tasks in system development, such as creating a database and documenting information flow, can be automated. (T/F)

11-3.2 The creation of an information system is a cooperative effort between those who use it and IT professionals. (T/F)

11-3.3 Which CASE tool is a central computer-based storage facility for all design information: (a) design tool, (b) information repository tool, (c) program development tool, or (d) prototype tool?

11-4   Prototyping

The CASE tool kit enables the system development project team to work with users to develop a **prototype system**, a model of a full-scale system. This approach to applications development is called **prototyping.** In effect, a prototype system permits users a sneak preview of the completed system. A typical prototype system

- Handles the main transaction-oriented procedures
- Produces common reports
- Permits typical inquiries to the database

Throughout the twentieth century, manufacturers have built prototypes of everything from toasters to airplanes to integrated circuits (see Figure 11-10). Automobile manufacturers routinely

FIGURE 11–10

PROTOTYPING IN CHIP MANUFACTURING
For years, manufacturers have built physical prototypes, such as this chip, to test product functionality. Only recently has prototyping become popular with information systems development. Now most new systems emerge from prototype systems. Here, these electronics engineers analyze the current situation and identify information needs in the manufacture of semiconductors, two important steps in prototyping.

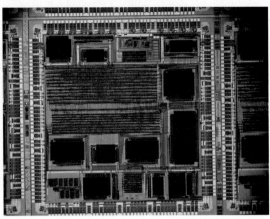

Micron Technology
Photo courtesy of National Semiconductor Corporation

build prototypes according to design specifications. Scaled-down clay models are made to evaluate aesthetics and aerodynamics. Ultimately, a full-size, fully functional prototype is created that enables the driver and passengers to test all aspects of the car's functionality. If engineers see possibilities for improvement, the prototypes are modified and retested until they meet or exceed all specifications. Today, building *scalable* prototype systems is standard procedure in software development. A **scalable system** is one whose design can handle any size database or any number of users. Scalable systems are desirable because they can be implemented at one level, then expanded to keep up with corporate growth by simply adding more hardware (server, PCs, and so on).

THE EMERGENCE OF PROTOTYPING

Most managers have a *good idea* of what they want in an information system, but they do not know *exactly* what they want. This is a problem when it comes to developing information systems. Systems analysts and programmers need precise specifications to give the users what they want in an information system. Prior to the emergence of automated system development tools, users were asked to commit themselves to **system specifications** long before they felt comfortable with the specifications. These **specs** include everything from the functionality of the system to the format of the system's output screens and reports. In this traditional approach, the project team would use feedback from user interviews to formulate **functional specifications** for system input, processing, and output requirements (information needs). The functional specifications describe the logic of the system (input/output, work, and information flow) from the *user's perspective*.

Realistically, though, users cannot know exactly what they want, nor can they recognize the potential of a system, until they have had an opportunity to work with it. In the traditional approach to system development, user familiarity comes after the fact and too late for quick fixes and inexpensive modifications. After system implementation, even small changes to an information system can be time-consuming and expensive.

Today, project team members are able to use CASE tools to create prototype systems that, to the user at a terminal or PC, appear and act very much like the finished product.

THE PROTOTYPE SYSTEM

The three objectives of prototyping are

- To analyze the current situation
- To identify information needs
- To develop a model of the proposed system, often called the **target system**

The prototype system gives users an actual opportunity to work with the functional aspect of the proposed system long before the system is implemented. Once users gain hands-on familiarity with the prototype system, they can relate more precise information processing needs to the project team.

A prototype system can be anything from a nonfunctional demonstration of the input/output of a proposed information system to a full-scale operational system. These models are tested and refined until the users are confident that what they see is what they want. In some cases, the prototype is a scalable system that can be expanded to become a fully operational information system. However, in most cases, the prototype system provides a vehicle for compiling the design specifications.

RAPID APPLICATION DEVELOPMENT

Rapid application development (**RAD**) results in information systems of varying degrees of sophistication. RAD has emerged to be a generic reference to using software tools (CASE) to design, develop, and implement information systems. At the low end, there is the "quick and dirty" RAD prototype, which gives users an opportunity to experiment with the look and feel of a system. This resulting system is just for show and doesn't permit interaction with a database. At this level, RAD focuses on three aspects of the design: the user interface, data entry displays, and system outputs.

At the other end of the RAD spectrum is the fully functional prototype system. This type of prototype system lets users try out the features of the target system during interactive practice sessions. The prototype is modified and refined based on user feedback. Some prototype systems are scalable systems and can be implemented directly at the enterprise level when complete. For example, Wal-Mart information systems are scalable such that all they do is add more computing capacity as stores are opened. Some fully functional systems are for design only and provide specifications for the system development process.

THE PROTOTYPING PROCESS

Both the prototyping and the traditional approaches to system development depend on the efforts of a project team. The composition of the project team is essentially the same for both approaches. The team consists of *systems analysts, programmers,* perhaps the *database administrator,* users who will eventually use the system, and perhaps one or more managers. All work together to develop the system design specifications. The database administrator assists the team in designing and creating the database.

The development of an information system via prototyping is done in four phases (see Figure 11-11).

- Phase I—Define System Specifications
- Phase II—Create Prototype System
- Phase III—Refine Prototype System
- Phase IV—Develop Operational System

Phase I—Define System Specifications

In the traditional approach to system development, system specifications are "frozen" early in the project. That means that no more changes can be made to the specs. In prototyping, the specs do not need to be frozen because the prototype system is easily modified to meet changing needs. It is during this phase (see Figure 11-11) that the current system is analyzed (system analysis) and the target system is designed (system design). What results is the specifications (database structure, input/output layouts, and so on) needed to develop the prototype system. Typically, these specifications are determined during interactive sessions with users. During the sessions, the team will define system specifications for graphical user interfaces, menus, reports, various input/output screens, and the database.

System Analysis: Understanding the System

System analysis produces the following results.

- *Existing system review.* Before designing a new or enhanced information system, the members of the project team must have a good grasp of the existing work and information flow, be it manual or computer-based. Here the team documents the work and information flow of the system by

FIGURE 11–11 THE FOUR PHASES OF THE PROTOTYPING PROCESS

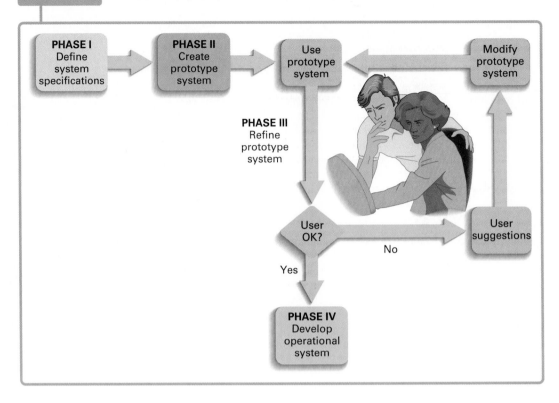

reducing it to its basic components—input, processing, and output. The use of CASE technologies usually encourages a detailed examination of business processes, often resulting in reengineering of existing processes to achieve greater effectiveness and efficiency.

- *System objectives.* Once the existing system is documented, the project team can begin to identify the obvious and not-so-obvious problem areas (for example, procedural bottlenecks, duplication of effort, and so on). This knowledge is formalized as system objectives.

- *Design constraints.* The target system will be developed subject to specific constraints. The purpose of this activity is to detail, at the onset of the system development process, any costs, hardware, schedule, procedural, software, database, and operating constraints that may limit the definition and design of the target system.

- *Requirements definition.* In this activity the project team completes a needs analysis that results in a definition of the information and information processing requirements for the target system.

System Design: Putting It All Together

During system design, the project team takes information from the system analysis and develops a system design for the target system. The design of an information system is more of a challenge to the human intellect than it is a procedural challenge. Just as an author begins with a blank page and an idea, the members of the project team begin with empty RAM and the information requirements definitions. From here they must create what sometimes can be a very complex information system. The number of ways in which a particular information system can be designed is limited only by the imaginations of the project team members.

The system design process involves continuous communication between members of the project team and all affected users. After evaluating several alternative approaches, the project team translates the system specifications into a system design. The documentation completed in the system design stage might include the following:

- A graphic illustration that depicts the fundamental operation of the target system (for example, using data flow diagrams)

- A written explanation of the graphic illustration

- Descriptions of the outputs to be produced by the system, including display screens and hard-copy reports and documents

Eventually the system design documentation depicts the relationship between *all processing activities* and the *input/output associated with them.*

The database must be defined during system design, as well. The database is the common denominator of any system. It contains the raw material (data) necessary to produce the output (information). In manufacturing, for example, you decide what you are going to make, then you order the raw material. In the process of developing an information system, you decide what your output requirements are, and then you determine which data are needed to produce the output. In a sense, output requirements can be thought of as input to database design.

The system design is the cornerstone of the system development process. It is here that the relationships between the various components of the system are defined. The system specifications are transformed with the project team's imagination and skill into an information system. The system design is the *blueprint* for all project team activities that follow.

Phase II—Create Prototype System

To create a prototype system, project team members rough out the logic of the system and how the elements fit together, and then work with the user to define the I/O interfaces (the system interaction with the user). The next challenge is to translate the system design and specifications into instructions that can be interpreted and executed by the computer. This, of course, involves software development.

During this phase (see Figure 11-11), the creation of software becomes the dominant activity. Project team members use CASE tools to create the screen images (menus, reports, inquiries, and so on), to create a database, and to generate much of the programming code (software). Typically, programmers will need to write custom programs to complement automatically generated programs. Programming is discussed later in the chapter. The system specifications resulting from system analysis and design are all that is necessary for programmers to write, or *code,* the necessary programs. The custom programming task is made easier with the well-documented specifications from the design stage. The subsequent programs result in a physical representation of a target system.

Phase III—Refine Prototype System

In this phase (see Figure 11-11), users actually sit down at a terminal or PC and evaluate portions, and eventually all, of the prototype system. Invariably, users have suggestions for improving the user interfaces and/or the format of the I/O. And, without fail, their examination reveals new needs for information. In effect, the original prototype system is the beginning. From here, the system is expanded (if needed) and refined to meet the users' total information needs. The use-and-modify cycle depicted in Figure 11-11 is repeated until users are satisfied with the prototype system.

Phase IV—Develop Operational System

At this point in the prototyping process (see Figure 11-11), users have a system that looks and feels like what they want. If the system is other than a fully functional scalable prototype, the system must be enhanced or another system, based on the prototype system, must be developed. In the latter case, the prototype system is discarded once the specs have been determined. From these specs, the software for an operational information system capable of handling the required volume of work is developed.

Fully functional scalable prototypes are working models of the target information system that can be scaled to meet the information processing needs of the organization. Scalable systems are implemented directly.

11-4.1 A fully functional prototype system is essentially a complete information system but without the capability to access a database. (T/F)

11-4.2 Which results are realized during the system design: (a) description of outputs, (b) existing system review, (c) design constraints, or (d) final system approval?

11-4.3 The target system's specifications are done in which of the four phases of prototyping: (a) Phase I, (b) Phase II, (c) Phase III, or (d) Phase IV?

11-4.4 The functional specifications describe the logic of a target system from whose perspective: (a) systems analyst, (b) CEO, (c) programmer, or (d) user?

SECTION SELF-CHECK

WHY THIS SECTION
IS IMPORTANT
TO YOU

Every knowledge worker at one
time or another will be involved
in many system conversions
and/or system implementa-
tions. When it's your turn you
will know the key options and
considerations.

11-5 | System Conversion and Implementation

Once an information system has been developed and approved by those who will use it, it is implemented within the organization.

SYSTEMS AND ACCEPTANCE TESTING

The first step of the system conversion and implementation process is systems testing. This testing
encompasses everything that makes up the information system—the hardware, the software, the end
users, the procedures (for example, online help documents), and the data. If needed, the interfaces
between the system and other systems are tested as well.

During Phase II, Create Prototype System, programs are generated or written according to
system specifications and are individually tested. Although the programs that make up the software for the system have undergone **unit testing** (individual testing) and have been debugged,
there is no guarantee that the programs will work together as a system. To ensure that the software
can be combined into an operational information system, the project team performs integrated
systems testing.

To conduct the system test, the project team compiles and thoroughly tests the system with *test
data*. In this first stage, tests are run for each subsystem (one of the functional aspects of the system)
or cycle (weekly or monthly activities). The test data are compiled so all program and system options
and all error and validation routines are tested. The tests are repeated and modifications are made
until all subsystems or cycles function properly. At this point the entire system is tested as a unit.
Testing and modifications continue until the components of the system work as they should and all
input/output is validated.

Several of the people who will eventually use the system do the second stage of systems testing with *live data*. Live data have already been processed through the existing system. Testing with
live data provides an extra level of assurance that the system will work properly when implemented.

The system is now subjected to the scrutiny of the user managers whose departments will ultimately work with the system. The managers accept the system as ready for implementation, or they
send it back for further modification and testing.

APPROACHES TO SYSTEM CONVERSION

Once systems testing is complete, the project team can begin to integrate people, software, hardware,
procedures, and data into an operational information system. This normally involves a conversion
from the existing system to the new one. An organization's approach to system conversion depends on
its *willingness to accept risk* and the *amount of time available* for the conversion. Four common
approaches are parallel conversion, direct conversion, phased conversion, and pilot conversion. These
approaches are illustrated in Figure 11-12.

Parallel Conversion

In **parallel conversion**, the existing system and the new system operate simultaneously, or in parallel, until the project team is confident the new system is
working properly. Parallel conversion has two important advantages. First, the
existing system serves as a backup if the new system fails to operate as expected.
Second, the results of the new system can be compared to the results of the existing system.

There is less risk with this strategy because the present system provides
backup. However, it doubles the workload of personnel and hardware resources
during the conversion. Parallel conversion usually takes one month or a major
system cycle. For a public utility company, this might be one complete billing
cycle, which is usually a month.

Direct Conversion

As companies improve their systems testing procedures, they begin to gain confidence in their ability to implement a working system. Some companies forego
parallel conversion in favor of a **direct conversion**, whereby the old system is terminated when the new system goes online. Direct conversion involves a greater
risk because there is no backup in case the system fails.

FIGURE 11–12 **COMMON APPROACHES TO SYSTEM CONVERSION**

Companies select this "cold-turkey" approach when there is no existing system or when the existing system is substantially different. For example, all online hotel reservations systems are implemented cold turkey.

Phased Conversion

In **phased conversion,** an information system is implemented one module at a time by either parallel or direct conversion. For example, in a point-of-sale system, the first phase might be to convert the sales-accounting module. The second phase could involve the inventory-management module. The third might be the credit-check module.

Phased conversion has the advantage of spreading the demand for resources to avoid an intense demand. The disadvantages are that the conversion takes longer and an interface must be developed between the existing system and the new one.

Pilot Conversion

In **pilot conversion,** the new system is implemented by parallel, direct, or phased conversion as a pilot system in only one of the areas for which it is targeted. Suppose a company wants to implement a manufacturing resources planning system in its eight plants. One plant would be selected as a pilot, and the new information system would be implemented there first.

The advantage of pilot conversion is that the inevitable bugs in a system can be removed before the system is implemented at the other locations. The disadvantage is that the implementation time for the total system takes longer than if the entire system were implemented at one time.

THE SYSTEM BECOMES OPERATIONAL

Once the conversion has been completed, the information system enters the production stage of the system life cycle (see Figure 11-1). During the production stage the system becomes operational and is turned over to the users. Once an information system is implemented and goes online, the emphasis switches from *development* to *operations.* In a payroll system, supervisors begin to enter hours worked on their PCs or terminals, and the computer center produces and issues payroll checks. Once operational, an information system becomes a cooperative effort between users and IT professionals.

Just as a new automobile will need some screws tightened after a few hundred miles, an information system will need some fine-tuning just after implementation. Thereafter, and throughout the production stage of the system life cycle, the system will be modified many times. An information system is dynamic and must be responsive to the changing needs of the company and those who use it (see Figure 11-13). The process of modifying an information system to meet changing needs is known as **system maintenance.**

Prior to the emergence of CASE technology, making modifications to operational systems was time-consuming and expensive. CASE tools, however, permit flexibility in system design. For example, when fields are added to the database or screen formats are modified, affected programs are automatically updated to reflect the changes.

An information system cannot live forever. The accumulation of modifications and enhancements eventually will make any information system cumbersome and inefficient. Minor modifications are known as **patches.** Depending on the number of patches and enhancements, an information system will remain operational—that is, be in the production stage of the system life cycle (see Figure 11-1)—from four to seven years.

Toward the end of the useful life of an information system, it is more trouble to continue patching the system than it is to redesign the system completely. The end of the production stage signals the end-of-life stage of the system life cycle (see Figure 11-1). A new system is then born of need, and the system development process is repeated.

FIGURE 11–13 FEDEX INFORMATION SYSTEMS

EMPLOYEE ACCESS TO INFORMATION

Federal Express Corp. (FedEx), an air/ground courier service, is in constant motion. Hundreds of airplanes and thousands of vehicles deliver millions of packages in countries throughout the world. A sophisticated information system provides critical real-time status information on every airplane, vehicle, and package in the system.

ONLINE CUSTOMER SERVICE

Traditionally, information systems involved only the people within the company they serviced. However, more and more companies are using the Internet to expand the reach of their information systems to include customers as well. FedEx customers in more than 200 countries can access a FedEx home page that displays shipping, tracking, and customer service options available in the country where the customer is located.

PACKAGE TRACKING

Packages are scanned at each point en route to their destination and this tracking information is transmitted to a central database. Route drivers use wireless handheld scanners.

11-6 Programming

Once the system has been designed, the software must be created before the system can go online. Some, and sometimes all, of the programs are created as a by-product of the CASE prototyping process. However, most systems require considerable amounts of custom programming by programmers, people who write programs. Perhaps no other element of computing changes as much or as often as the way we program computers (see Figure 11-14).

Programs are made up of instructions that are logically sequenced and assembled through the act of programming. Programmers use a variety of **programming languages,** such as C++, Visual BASIC, Perl, COBOL, and Java, to communicate instructions to the computer. Twenty years ago, virtually all programmers were IT specialists. Today, office managers, management consultants, engineers, politicians, and people in all walks of life write programs to meet business and domestic needs. And, some people do it for fun. Unless you plan to become an IT professional, it is unlikely that you will write

FIGURE 11–14

PROGRAMMING THEN AND NOW
If you ever feel intimidated by the idea of programming a computer, just remember how much easier it is today than in the computer's early days.

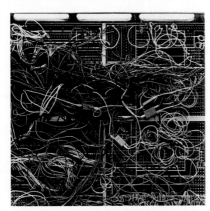

PROGRAMMING ELECTROMECHANICAL ACCOUNTING MACHINES

Prior to the invention of the electronic digital computer, companies relied on electromechanical accounting machines (EAM) for automated data processing. The act of programming these devices was referred to as "wiring the program." Early programmers literally created the circuitry for the devices by inserting wires into interchangeable removable control panels.

Courtesy of International Business Machines Corporation

PROGRAMMING THE FIRST ELECTRONIC DIGITAL COMPUTERS

The quantum leap in technology brought about by the invention of the ENIAC (1946), the first large-scale fully operational electronic digital computer, was offset by the cumbersome method of programming the machine. For each program to be run, switches had to be set manually and wires inserted into a series of panels.

Courtesy of UNISYS Corporation

PROGRAMMING MODERN COMPUTERS

Today CASE tools are able to generate much of the software for an information system. For custom programming, programmers choose the best programming language for the job, then use high-level instructions to interactively create and debug the program. Amsterdam's Schiphol Airport in the Netherlands uses software designed to help meet the growing demands of air traffic control.

Courtesy of Raytheon Company

programs in support of an enterprise-wide information system. You may, however, write programs to perform many personal tasks, such as preparing graphs from spreadsheet data and sequencing displays for multimedia presentations. As you develop expertise and confidence you may tackle more challenging programming tasks.

Many languages have emerged over thousands of years of spoken communication. Although computers have existed for only a short while, there are already as many programming languages as there are spoken languages. In this section, we will sort out these languages and explain what they mean to you, but first, let's put software into perspective.

SOFTWARE IN PERSPECTIVE

Suppose you are sick in bed and you ask a friend to get you a glass of ice water. Your friend then instinctively goes to the kitchen, opens the cabinet door and selects a glass, opens the freezer, gets some ice, turns on the tap, fills the glass with water, returns to your bedside, and hands you the water. Now imagine making the same request to a computer. You would have to tell the computer not only where to get the water but also how to get there, which end of the glass to fill, when to shut off the water, and much, much, more. Now you know why software has to have so many instructions!

We use programming languages to write programs. A single program addresses a particular problem—to compute grades, to monitor a patient's heart rate, and so on. In effect, when you write a program, you are solving a *problem*, which requires you to use your powers of *logic* to develop a procedure for solving the problem. Creating a program is like constructing a building. Much of the brainwork involved in the construction goes into the blueprint. The location, appearance, and function of a building are determined long before the first brick is laid. With programming, the design of a program, or its *programming logic* (the blueprint), is completed before the program is written.

Each programming language has an instruction set with a variety of instructions. For example, input/output instructions direct the computer to "read from" or "write to" a peripheral device. Computation instructions direct the computer to perform arithmetic operations. Control instructions can alter the sequence of the program's execution. With these and a few other types of instructions, you can create software to model almost any business or scientific procedure, whether it is sales forecasting or guiding rockets to the moon.

TYPES OF PROGRAMMING LANGUAGES

We "talk" to computers within the framework of a particular programming language, and the selection of a programming language depends on who is doing the talking and the nature of the "conversation." There are many different types of programming languages in use today.

Machine Language: Native Tongue

In Chapter 4, we learned that all programs are ultimately executed in machine language, the computer's native language. Creating programs in machine language is a cumbersome process, so we write programs in more programmer-friendly programming languages. However, our resulting programs must be translated into machine language before they can be executed.

Procedure-Oriented Languages

The introduction of more user-friendly programming languages (in 1955) resulted in a quantum leap in programmer convenience. Programmers could write a single instruction instead of several cumbersome machine language instructions. These early languages were **procedure-oriented languages,** which require programmers to solve programming problems using traditional programming logic. **COBOL,** shown in Figure 11-15, is a good example of a procedure-oriented language.

Object-Oriented Languages and OOP

In procedure-oriented languages, the emphasis is on *what* is done (the procedure). In **object-oriented languages,** the emphasis is on the *object* of the action. The structure of **object-oriented programming (OOP)** makes programs easier to design and understand. Also, OOP (rhymes with "*hoop*") handles images, videos, and sound better than procedure-oriented languages. Examples of object-oriented languages include **Smalltalk,** one of the first OOP languages, **C++,** one of the most popular languages for developing graphical applications (for example, Windows applications), and **Java,** which is similar to C++.

Because Java is platform-independent and can run on just about any computer, Java has emerged as the foundation programming language for Web-based applications (see Figure 11-16). Until recently, most Web sites presented static content, permitting only crude levels of interaction with the user. Java has enabled Web developers to create dynamic content that lets us trade stocks, purchase almost anything, get online news based on our preferences, and take virtual tours of historic places throughout the world.

THE CRYSTAL BALL:
The Future of Programming The trend is to higher level languages that let computers take on an increasingly important role in programming. The future of programming is toward a natural language interface that allows the computer and a programmer, either an IT professional or a nontechnical knowledge worker, to work as a team to create programs. The "programmer" will articulate processing needs in plain English, Japanese, Spanish, and so on, then the computer will clarify those needs through interactive questioning. Ultimately, the "team" agrees on what is to be accomplished and the computer generates the required program code and the supporting documentation. A crude form of partner programming is available today, but this approach should be mature by the end of the decade.

FIGURE 11-15

A COBOL PROGRAM
This COBOL program accepts the number of hours worked and the pay rate for an hourly wage earner, then computes and displays the gross pay amount. The interactive session below the program listing shows the input prompt, the values entered by the user, and the result.

```
0100    IDENTIFICATION DIVISION.
0200    PROGRAM-ID.              PAYPROG.
0300    REMARKS.          PROGRAM TO COMPUTE GROSS PAY.
0400    ENVIRONMENT DIVISION.
0500    DATA DIVISION.
0600    WORKING-STORAGE SECTION.
0700    01 PAY DATA.
0800          05 HOURSPIC 99V99.
0900          05 RATE PIC 99V99.
1000          05 PAY          PIC 9999V99.
1100    01 LINE-1.
1200          03 FILLER     PIC X(5).       VALUE SPACES.
1300          03 FILLER     PIC X(12).      VALUE "GROSS PAY IS."
1400          03 GROSS-PAY  PIC $$$9.99.
1500    01 PRINT-LINE.      PIC X(27).
1600    PROCEDURE DIVISION.
1700    MAINLINE-PROCEDURE.
1800          PERFORM ENTER-PAY.
1900    PERFORM COMPUTE-PAY.
2000    PERFORM PRINT-PAY.
2100    STOP RUN.
2200    ENTER-PAY.
2300          DISPLAY "ENTER HOURS AND RATE OF PAY."
2400          ACCEPT HOURS, RATE.
2500    COMPUTE-PAY.
2600          MULTIPLY HOURS BY RATE GIVING PAY ROUNDED.
2700    PRINT PAY.
2800          MOVE PAY TO GROSS-PAY.
2900          MOVE LINE-1 TO PRINT-LINE.
3000          DISPLAY PRINT-LINE.
```

```
Enter hours and rate of pay
43, 8.25
                Gross pay is $354.75
```

The Fourth Generation: 4GLs

Most of the programming in procedure- and object-oriented languages is done by IT specialists. Programming in user-friendly **fourth-generation languages (4GLs)** is done by IT specialists and also a growing legion of end users. Fourth-generation languages use high-level English-like instructions to retrieve and format data for inquiries and reporting. In 4GLs, the programmer specifies what to do, *not* how to do it. A few simple 4GL instructions are all that are needed to respond to the following typical management requests:

- Which employees have accumulated more than 20 sick days since May 1?

- Which deluxe single hospital rooms, if any, will be vacated by the end of the day?

- List departments that have exceeded their budgets alphabetically by the department head's name.

Query languages, a subset of 4GLs, let users request information directly from a database. **SQL** (pronounced like *sequel*) is the de facto standard for query languages. The following SQL

FIGURE 11-16

PROGRAM SEGMENT FOR A JAVA APPLET
These are a few of the 400 lines of Java programming code written to create this bouncing ball applet. An applet is a Java program that is run within a Web browser. The applet lets you move and resize a rectangle to manipulate the bouncing balls. Note the hierarchical structure of this program segment.

```
{
        if (collide)
        {
                double xvect=coll_x-getCenterX0;
                double yvect=coll_y-getCenterY0;
                if((xinc>0 && xvect>0) || (xinc<0 && xvect<0))
                        xinc=-xinc;
                if((yinc>0 && yvect>0) || (yinc<0 && yvect<0))
                        yinc=-yinc;
                collide=false;
        }
        x+=xinc;
y+=yinc;
        //when the ball bumps
        against a boundary, it
        bounces off
if(x<6 || x>width-diameter)
{
```

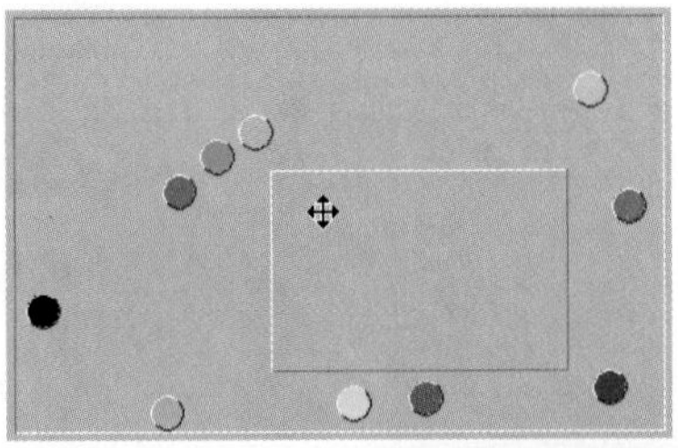

instructions tap the CIA World Factbook database. The first SQL instruction determines the population of the world—6,080,153,149. The second instruction creates a table listing all countries with their region and population.

SELECT SUM FROM cia

SELECT name, region, population FROM cia

Visual Languages: Icons for Words

As they say, a picture is worth a thousand words, and so it is in programming. **Visual programming** takes object-oriented programming to the next level, replacing text-based instructions with symbolic icons, each of which represents an object or a common programming function (see Figure 11-17). Microsoft's **Visual BASIC** is one of the most popular visual languages for both the casual user and the professional software developer.

Macro Languages: The User Language

As end users, we issue commands and initiate operations by selecting activities to be performed from a hierarchy of menus. When we choose an item on a menu, that operation is performed and the applications software causes the system to wait for further commands. We select operations (menu items) one at a time until we have accomplished what we wish to do. This one-at-a-time approach to system interaction is fine for one-time jobs, such as preparing and printing a sales summary bar chart. However, what if you prepare the same charts from an updated spreadsheet at the end of each week? Then, you might wish to consider creating a macro to do the job automatically. A **macro** is a sequence of frequently used operations or keystrokes that can be recalled as needed. A macro is actually a *short program,* containing a sequence of instructions to be performed.

The original macro concept grew from a need to automate repetitive interactions with applications software. The first macros (for spreadsheet and word processing software) simply recorded command interactions for replay at a later time. *Record-and-play macros* are handy for performing interactions that are done over and over. Straightforward macros can be created easily by recording operations as they are entered, then storing their sequence as a named macro for later recall. Once a macro is created, you simply run it whenever you wish to "play" the keystroke sequence.

Record-and-play macros work for most situations. Occasionally, however, you will need to create more complex macros, in which case, you would use a **macro language.** For example, spreadsheet users often create powerful macros to facilitate data entry and the creation of business charts and graphs. The more complex macros use macro languages that enable flow control (decisions and loops), the use of variables, and interaction with users. Most of today's office software (word processing, spreadsheet, database, and so on) have their own powerful macro language (Visual BASIC for Microsoft Office applications). These languages are like procedure-oriented languages, except each is designed to support a particular piece of software. Users can write macros to do simple tasks or to create comprehensive office information systems.

FIGURE 11-17

VISUAL PROGRAMMING
Macromedia Director "movies," which are interactive multimedia images, are the result of a scripting program. A variety of Director visual programming enables the creation of the program (see center of example). When played, the resulting "Using Keyboard Input" (lower right) demonstrates interactively, with sound and motion, the use of a keyboard. The Score window (top left) graphically illustrates the sequencing and play attributes of the elements in the Director "movie." The Internal Cast window (bottom left) shows the member of the cast (elements under program control). Members of the cast can be assigned a particular type of behavior using the Behavior Library Cast window.

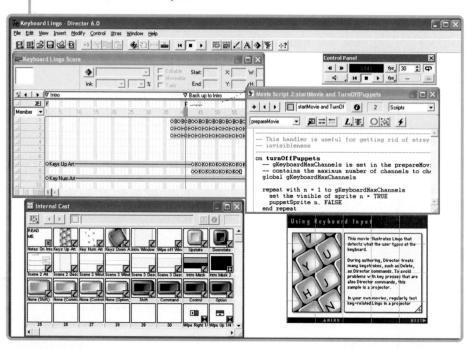

WRITING THE PROGRAM

The challenge to programmers is to translate the system design and specifications created during the prototyping process into instructions that can be interpreted and executed by the computer. To do so, they follow these steps.

System Specifications Review

The system specifications completed during the systems analysis and design are all that is necessary for programmers to write, or *code*, the programs to implement the target information system. But before getting started, programmers should review and study the system specifications (layouts, design, and so on) until they thoroughly understand what needs to be accomplished.

Program Identification and Description

An information system needs an array of programs to create and update the database, print reports, permit online inquiry, and so on. Depending on the scope of the system and how many programs can be generated using applications development tools, as few as three or four or as many as several thousand programs may need to be written before the system can be implemented. At this point, all programs necessary to make the system operational are identified and described (tasks to be performed, input, output, and so on).

Program Coding, Testing, and Documentation

Armed with system specifications and program descriptions, programmers can begin the actual coding of programs. The development of a program is actually a project within a project. Just as there are certain steps the project team takes to develop an information system, there are certain steps a programmer takes to write a program. These seven steps are summarized in Figure 11-18. Several techniques, such as flowcharting, are available to help programmers analyze a problem and design the program.

PROGRAMMING AND YOU

As you continue to gain experience with PCs and PC software, you, like so many before you, will probably begin to seek greater speed, power, and efficiency from your PC and its software. To gain

---

FIGURE 11–18 STEPS IN WRITING A PROGRAM

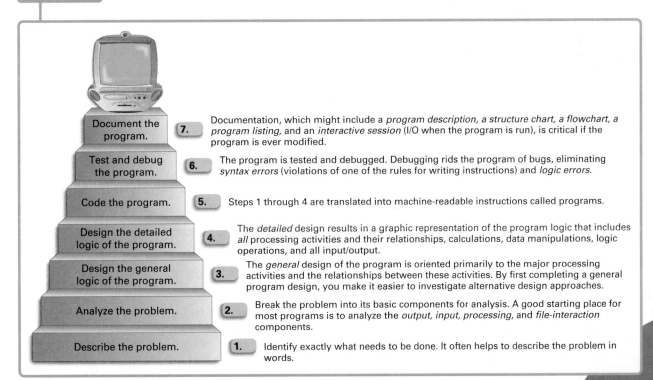

7. Document the program. Documentation, which might include a *program description, a structure chart, a flowchart, a program listing*, and an *interactive session* (I/O when the program is run), is critical if the program is ever modified.

6. Test and debug the program. The program is tested and debugged. Debugging rids the program of bugs, eliminating *syntax errors* (violations of one of the rules for writing instructions) and *logic errors*.

5. Code the program. Steps 1 through 4 are translated into machine-readable instructions called programs.

4. Design the detailed logic of the program. The *detailed* design results in a graphic representation of the program logic that includes *all* processing activities and their relationships, calculations, data manipulations, logic operations, and all input/output.

3. Design the general logic of the program. The *general* design of the program is oriented primarily to the major processing activities and the relationships between these activities. By first completing a general program design, you make it easier to investigate alternative design approaches.

2. Analyze the problem. Break the problem into its basic components for analysis. A good starting place for most programs is to analyze the *output, input, processing*, and *file-interaction* components.

1. Describe the problem. Identify exactly what needs to be done. It often helps to describe the problem in words.

speed and power, you will need to upgrade your hardware with the latest technology. To improve efficiency, you might wish to consider learning to write programs—yes, programs. You do not have to be a professional programmer—most people who program are not. They are users who write programs to accomplish personal processing objectives, often resulting in time savings of up to 15 hours a week!

SECTION SELF-CHECK

11-6.1	C++, Visual BASIC, and Java are programming languages. (T/F)
11-6.2	Record-and-play macros are now obsolete. (T/F)
11-6.3	When you write a program, you solve a problem using your powers of:
	(a) visual interpretation, (b) personality, (c) common sense, or (d) logic.
11-6.4	Which of these programming languages is a query language: (a) Visual BASIC,
	(b) assembler, (c) COBOL, or (d) SQL?
11-6.5	Another term for writing a program is: (a) coding, (b) logicizing, (c) converting, or
	(d) implementing.

11-1 THE SYSTEM LIFE CYCLE

The four stages of a computer-based information system comprise the **system life cycle.** They are birth, development, production, and end-of-life.

There are three basic approaches to satisfying a company's information processing needs. The first is to purchase and install a **proprietary software package.** An alternative is to use company employees and/or outside consultants to create an information system customized to meet user specifications. Some companies obtain information services support from an **applications service provider (ASP),** a company that provides services and solutions via a wide area network or the Internet.

11-2 SYSTEM DEVELOPMENT TECHNIQUES AND CONCEPTS

The system's design includes all processing activities and the input/output associated with them. When adhering to **structured system design,** designers divide the system into independent modules for ease of understanding and design. The **structure chart** enables system designers to conceptualize a system in a hierarchy of modules.

Data flow diagrams enable analysts to design and document systems using the structured approach to system development. The four symbols used in data flow diagrams are entity, process, flow line, and data storage. The focus of the data flow diagram is information flow. Another similar business modeling tool is the **entity relationship diagram.** The focus of the entity relationship diagram is the attributes of the entities and the relationship between them.

Flowcharting is another popular technique for portraying system and programming logic. **Flowcharts** illustrate data, information, and work flow by the interconnection of specialized symbols with flow lines. In structured programming, each program is designed with a **driver module** (which might include a **loop**), or **main program,** that calls **subroutines** as they are needed.

11-3 COMPUTER-AIDED SOFTWARE ENGINEERING

The general family of automated software development productivity tools falls under the umbrella of **computer-aided software engineering,** or **CASE,** tools. The term **software engineering** was coined to emphasize an approach to software development that combines automation and the rigors of the engineering discipline. The basic CASE tool kit includes design tools, information repository tools, and program development tools.

CASE design tools help analysts, programmers, and other project team members prepare schematics that graphically depict the logic of a system. Project team members use CASE design tools to create a physical representation of a target information system. CASE design tools also help designers prepare the user interface and generate screen and report **layouts.** The **information repository** is a central computer-based storage facility for all design information. In an information repository, each piece of system documentation is cross-referenced to all other components in the system. The CASE program development tools, which include **application generators,** use the system design to generate the software for the system. Occasionally,

custom programming is required to complete the system. **Software engineers** develop software products to bridge the gap between design and executable program code.

11-4 PROTOTYPING

The CASE tool kit enables the system development project team to work with users to develop a **prototype system.** This approach to applications development is called **prototyping.** Modern prototyping tools enable the development of a **scalable system,** one whose design can handle any size database or any number of users.

In the traditional approach to system development, the project team would formulate **functional specifications** for system input, processing, and output requirements, but these specs were inaccurate because users had not had an opportunity to work with the **target system.**

The three objectives of prototyping are to analyze the current situation, to identify information needs, and to develop a scaled-down model of the target system.

Ideally, users should experiment and familiarize themselves with the operation of a target system as early in the development process as possible. The prototyping process enables users to relate accurate information processing needs to the project team during the early phases of the project and throughout the project.

Rapid application development (RAD) results in information systems of varying degrees of sophistication.

During Phase I, Define System Specifications, of prototyping, the current system is analyzed (system analysis) and the target system is designed (system design). During system analysis, the team does the existing system review in which it documents the work and information flow of the system. Team members also formalize the system objectives, identify design constraints, and complete a needs analysis that results in a requirements definition.

During system design, the project team takes information from the system analysis and develops a system design for the target system. The design documentation, the **system specification,** might include the following: a graphic illustration of the target system, a written explanation of the graphic illustration, and descriptions of the outputs to be produced by the system. The database is defined during system design, as well.

During Phase II, Create Prototype System, the project team translates the system design and **specs** into instructions that can be interpreted and executed by the computer. During this phase, the creation of CASE-generated and custom software becomes the dominant activity.

During Phase III, Refine Prototype System, a use-and-modify cycle is repeated until users are satisfied with the prototype system.

During Phase IV, Develop Operational System, software capable of handling the required volume of work for an operational information system is developed.

11-5 SYSTEM CONVERSION AND IMPLEMENTATION

Once an information system has been developed, it must be implemented within the organization. Although the programs that make up the software for an information system have been debugged on an individual basis (**unit testing**), they must be combined and subjected to integrated **systems testing** prior to implementation.

The four common approaches to system conversion are **parallel conversion, direct conversion, phased conversion,** and **pilot conversion.** The approach that an organization selects depends on its willingness to accept risk and the amount of time available for the conversion.

An information system is dynamic and must be responsive to the changing needs of the company and those who use it. The process of modifying, or **patching**, an information system to meet changing needs is known as **system maintenance.**

11-6 PROGRAMMING

Programmers use a variety of **programming languages** to communicate instructions to the computer. The design of a program, or its *programming logic*, is completed before the program is written. Each language uses several types of instructions.

All programming languages ultimately are translated into *machine language* in order to be executed. In **procedure-oriented languages,** such as **COBOL,** programmers code the instructions in the sequence in which they must be executed to solve the problem.

Object-oriented languages, such as **Smalltalk, C++,** and **Java,** emphasize the *object* of the action. Java, a platform-independent language, is used for Web-based applications. The hierarchical structure of **object-oriented programming** (OOP) makes programs easier to design and understand.

In **fourth-generation languages** (**4GLs**), the programmer need only specify *what* to do, not *how* to do it. One feature of 4GLs is the use of English-like instructions. **Query languages,** such as SQL, let users request information directly from a database.

In **visual programming,** text-based instructions are replaced with symbolic icons, each of which represents a common programming function. An example of this is **Visual BASIC.**

A **macro** is a sequence of frequently used operations or keystrokes that can be recalled as needed. The more complex macros use **macro languages** that enable flow control, the use of variables, and interaction with users.

Programmers translate the system design and specifications created during the prototyping process into instructions for programs. First, they do a system specifications review. Then they describe all programs necessary to make the system operational. Finally, they write the programs, test them, and document them.

KEY TERMS

application generator (p. 427)
applications service provider (ASP) (p. 419)
C++ (p. 436)
COBOL (p. 436)
computer-aided software engineering (CASE) (p. 425)
custom programming (p. 425)
data flow diagram (p. 420)
direct conversion (p. 432)
driver module (p. 421)
entity relationship diagram (p. 421)
flowchart (p. 421)
flowcharting (p. 421)
fourth-generation language (4GL) (p. 437)
functional specification (spec) (p. 428)
information repository (p. 427)
Java (p. 436)

layout (p. 426)
loop (p. 421)
macro (p. 438)
macro language (p. 438)
main program (p. 421)
object-oriented language (p. 436)
object-oriented programming (OOP) (p. 436)
parallel conversion (p. 432)
patch (p. 433)
phased conversion (p. 432)
pilot conversion (p. 433)
procedure-oriented language (p. 436)
programming language (p. 434)
proprietary software package (p. 418)
prototype system (p. 427)
prototyping (p. 427)
query language (p. 437)

rapid application development (RAD) (p. 429)
scalable system (p. 428)
Smalltalk (p. 436)
software engineer (p. 425)
software engineering (p. 425)
SQL (p. 437)
structure chart (p. 420)
structured system design (p. 420)
subroutine (p. 421)
system life cycle (p. 418)
system maintenance (p. 433)
system specification (spec) (p. 428)
systems testing (p. 432)
target system (p. 429)
unit testing (p. 432)
Visual BASIC (p. 438)
visual programming (p. 438)

MATCHING

1. macro
2. COBOL
3. prototype
4. C++
5. computer-aided software engineering
6. object-oriented programming
7. data flow diagram
8. loop
9. SQL
10. scalable system
11. ASP
12. information repository
13. patch
14. system life cycle
15. parallel conversion

a. automation of system development
b. sequence of instructions to be performed
c. repeated until a condition is met
d. has four stages
e. procedure-oriented language
f. entity, process, flow line, and storage
g. provides software-based services
h. query language
i. OOP
j. minor modification
k. old and new system working together
l. model of system
m. central facility for design information
n. language for developing graphical applications
o. can expand with information needs

CHAPTER SELF-CHECK

11-1.1 System software, such as operating systems, normally is proprietary software. (T/F)

11-1.2 The use of applications service providers (ASPs) is on the downswing. (T/F)

11-1.3 In which stage of the information system life cycle are systems maintained: (a) birth, (b) development, (c) production, or (d) end-of-life?

11-1.4 An organization can progress through the development stage of the system life cycle in all but which of these ways: (a) purchasing proprietary software, (b) using an ASP, (c) relying on government consultants, or (d) creating custom software?

11-2.1 In structured programming, each program is designed with a driver module. (T/F)

11-2.2 Flowcharts can be used to illustrate both information and work flow. (T/F)

11-2.3 Which of the following is not a design technique: (a) flowcharting, (b) data flow diagrams, (c) RE charts, or (d) entity relationship diagrams?

11-2.4 Which of these is not one of the four symbols used in data flow diagrams: (a) entity, (b) process, (c) data storage, or (d) decision?

11-3.1 The application generator is one of the CASE program development tools. (T/F)

11-3.2 Custom programming involves the writing of original programs. (T/F)

11-3.3 Which CASE tool provides systems analysts with the capability of generating a mockup of a screen: (a) design tool, (b) information repository tool, (c) program development tool, or (d) prototype tool?

11-3.4 A detailed output and/or input specification is: (a) a layout, (b) an I/O outline, (c) a screen image spec, or (d) a GUI.

11-4.1 Modern prototyping tools enable the development of a scalable system that can be used by any number of users. (T/F)

11-4.2 A needs analysis results in a definition of the information and information processing requirements for the target system. (T/F)

11-4.3 A model of a full-scale information system is: (a) an archetype, (b) a prototype, (c) a system instance, or (d) a blueprint.

11-4.4 Functional specifications include requirements for system input, output, and: (a) timing, (b) processing, (c) benefits, or (d) feedback.

11-4.5 Which of these includes all processing activities and the input/output associated with them for a target information system: (a) driver module flowchart, (b) blueprint, (c) system design documentation, or (d) system review results?

11-5.1 Systems testing is always completed prior to unit testing. (T/F)

11-5.2 Companies may select the direct conversion approach when there is no existing system. (T/F)

11-5.3 Individual program testing is known as: (a) unit testing, (b) module testing, (c) hierarchical testing, or (d) bullet testing.

11-5.4 In which approach to system conversion do both the full existing system and the full new system operate simultaneously: (a) direct, (b) parallel, (c) pilot, or (d) phased?

11-6.1 There are only five programming languages. (T/F)

11-6.2 Object-oriented programming handles images, videos, and sound better than does COBOL, a procedure-oriented language. (T/F)

11-6.3 In machine language, the programmer specifies what to do, not how to do it. (T/F)

11-6.4 What kind of program instructions alter the sequence of the program's execution: (a) control, (b) computation, (c) input/output, or (d) format?

11-6.5 Which of these programming languages is a procedure-oriented language: (a) Visual BASIC, (b) assembler, (c) COBOL, or (d) SQL?

11-6.6 Because Java can run on just about any computer it is said to be: (a) platform-free, (b) platform-independent, (c) platform-dependent, or (d) platformless.

11-6.7 The seventh and last step in writing a program is: (a) problem description, (b) testing, (c) documentation, or (d) detailed design.

IT ETHICS AND ISSUES

COOPERATIVE DEVELOPMENT OF INFORMATION SYSTEMS

Cooperative development of information systems was unheard of a few years ago. Today, competing companies are cooperating to create Internet-based systems and services that can be shared. For example, several major airlines (American Airlines, Continental Airlines, Delta Air Lines, Northwest Airlines, and United Airlines) have joined together to create a supersite (Orbitz.com) to which travelers can go to obtain airline tickets and to make other travel arrangements. Many other airlines have asked to post fares and schedules to the site, also. The airlines supersite has the potential, in time, to eliminate the need for travel agents, who take a percentage of the value of each ticket they write. Currently, airline tickets, most of which are e-tickets, can be conveniently purchased online, but, apparently, this joint

venture is being viewed by some as an attempt to eliminate the middleman.

Discussion: *Is this cooperative processing venture in violation of any law? If so, which law?*

Discussion: *The American Society of Travel Agents is trying to block further development of the supersite, citing the possibility of price fixing. Does it have a valid argument? Explain.*

Discussion: *If the middleman is eliminated, should the money saved be passed on to the consumer? Explain.*

LOCATIONAL COMPUTING

Wireless connections via telephone and computer are enabling us to become increasingly mobile in our computing. The wireless world creates opportunities for a variety of new applications and information systems, one of which is *locational computing*. A global positioning system (GPS) gives you your geographic position within a few feet anywhere in the world. Integrate GPS with a cell phone, notebook computer, or handheld computer and you have some very interesting and controversial systems. Being geographically connected has obvious advantages, but it has its downside, too. If you are equipped with an integrated GPS and wireless Internet connection and you access a Web site, that Web site knows not only who you are but also about where you are. This opens up many possibilities. For example, your cell phone might beep you when you are near a particular restaurant and offer you a free dessert with any entrée. If you volunteer your whereabouts, you could create a locational "buddy list" such that each person on the list would know the whereabouts of the others. You could even ask the system to notify you if two or more of your friends are gathered at your favorite pub.

Discussion: *Would you give up your locational privacy for the prospects of geographically targeted promotions, such as retail coupons or unsolicited information that might be applicable to a person with your interests?*

Discussion: *Discuss the advantages and disadvantages of a locational buddy list.*

Discussion: *Speculate on other applications of locational computing and discuss their impact on personal privacy.*

DISCUSSION AND PROBLEM SOLVING

11-1.1 Would it be possible for a company with 600 employees to maintain a skeleton information services division of about five IT professionals and use commercially available packaged software for all its computer application needs? Explain.

11-1.2 In general, is it better to change internal procedures to fit a particular proprietary software package or to modify the software to fit existing procedures? Discuss.

11-2.1 Give a system-oriented example, perhaps relating to the registration system at your college, of when you might use each of the flowcharting symbols in Figure 11-7.

11-2.2 Name one way in which data flow diagrams and entity relationship diagrams are alike and one way in which they are not.

11-2.3 Discuss the rationale for the "divide and conquer" approach to system analysis and design.

11-2.4 Break down the registration system at your college into a simple structure chart. Discuss each box in the chart.

11-2.5 Complete a flowchart to illustrate the programming logic for a program that accepts three quiz grades from each of any number of students. The program should compute and display the average for each student. Include a driver module in your logic.

11-2.6 Put yourself in the role of a systems analyst. Draw a first-level data flow diagram depicting your college's student registration system.

11-2.7 Expand on the above question and explode one of the processes in the data flow diagram to show detail.

11-3.1 Twenty years ago, IT professionals didnt have CASE. Discuss how CASE has changed the traditional approach to system development.

11-3.2 Explain how using a CASE information repository during the system development process can have a positive impact on target system quality.

11-3.3 Much of the programming code for an information system can be generated with CASE tools. Nevertheless, the demand for programmers in all areas is high. Explain.

11-4.1 One of the objectives of prototyping is to develop a scaled-down model of the target system. However, some prototype systems are fully functional. Describe how a functional prototype system is scaled down.

11-4.2 What is meant by the remark "Garbage in, garbage out" as applied to system specifications?

11-4.3 Design a screen layout for an online hospital admittance system. Design only that screen with which the hospital clerk would interact to enter basic patient data. Distinguish between input and output by underlining the input.

11-4.4 Software tools are available for rapid application development (RAD), yet many companies continue to use traditional approaches to system development even though system development costs may be greater and project times may be longer. Why do these companies stay with traditional techniques?

11-5.1 Why do information systems need patches? What is accomplished when we patch an information system?

11-5.2 What is the downside of testing a system only with test data and not with live data, too?

11-5.3 What advantage does direct conversion have over parallel conversion? Parallel over direct?

11-6.1 During the last fifty years, hundreds of programming languages have been developed, with over a hundred used widely throughout the world. Why do we need so many programming languages?

11-6.2 Discuss the steps you must take to turn on your TV and select the ESPN channel. Be very specific as you would in a computer program.

11-6.3 Discuss the difference between a procedure-oriented language and a fourth-generation language.

11-6.4 Do you believe that you may eventually write computer programs in your chosen profession? If so, what kind of programs? If not, why?

1. Every productivity software program has built-in keystroke macros in the form of shortcut key combinations. Open Microsoft Word and list these shortcuts. In the *Tools* menu, point to *Macro,* and then click *Macros*. In the *Macros in* box, choose *Word commands*. In the *Macro name* box, choose *ListCommands*. Click *Run,* choose *Current menu and keyboard settings,* and then click *OK* to display a table containing all of the Word shortcut key combinations. Identify at least a dozen (and no more than 30) shortcuts that you feel might be helpful and delete the others. Save and print the table. These shortcut keys can be real time savers when you work with Word documents.

2. Open any software suite productivity tool, such as Word, PowerPoint, or Excel. Tap the F1 key for Help and then enter "macros." Choose the option which tells you how to create or set up a macro. Read about macros, then create a record-and-play macro of your own. The macro can be of any repetitive process (for example, setting up a homework document in accordance with instructor specifications). Describe the macro and, if applicable, print a document that illustrates the use of the macro.

INTERNET EXERCISES @ www.prenhall.com/long

1. The Online Study Guide (multiple choice, true/false, matching, and essay questions)
2. Internet Learning Activities
   - System Development
   - Computers at Work
3. Serendipitous Internet Activities
   - Business

chapter 12

Learning Objectives

Once you have read and studied this chapter, you will have learned:

- The breadth of career opportunities in information technology and for people with IT competency (Section 12-1).

- The rudiments of robots and robotics (Section 12-2)

- Many current and potential applications in information technology and along the information superhighway (Section 12-3).

- The significant challenges posed by information technology as it emerges as a major force in determining how we live, work, and play (Section 12-4).

TECHNOLOGY AND SOCIETY

Why this chapter is important to you

Contrasting the time line of aviation history to that of computing history, computing is about where the Wright brothers were after their first test flight. Just as it was difficult for the Wright brothers to imagine trans-Atlantic passenger planes, moon landings, and permanently inhabited space stations, it's just as difficult for us to imagine the future of information technology.

The *information technology revolution* is changing our lives in ways humanity has seen only twice before—during the *agricultural revolution* and the *industrial revolution*. You don't have to look very far to see the effects of these revolutions. Everything we do is becoming more tightly integrated with computers—robotics in manufacturing, virtual reality in entertainment, and learning without classrooms.

There is no official name for our wired world. The *information superhighway* metaphor is frequently used as a collective reference to these electronic links that have wired our world. The government talks about a *National Information Infrastructure (NII)*, and the media continue to create more descriptors for this virtual frontier, such as *I-way, infobahn,* and *cyberspace*. Whatever it is or will be called, it eventually will connect virtually every facet of our society, and we all need some perspective on where it is taking us.

In this chapter you will learn about working in our information society. What people do for a living and how they do it have changed dramatically during your lifetime. The material in this chapter should provide you with a good overview of career opportunities in information technology and for people interested in working with IT.

Also, you will learn about state-of-the-art applications, emerging applications, and applications that we can anticipate in the near future. After reading this chapter, you'll be better prepared to put each new technological innovation into perspective.

If computing capacity continues to double each year, then we can expect computing capacity to be 1000 times that of today within 10 years. Think about the possibilities. You and everyone else will have access to computing capacity roughly equivalent to all of the computers in New York City during the 1960s! And, there is a good chance that we will wear that power, perhaps on our wrists! The twenty-first century is going to be very interesting.

12-1 Careers in an Information Society

Whether you are seeking employment or a promotion as a teacher, an accountant, a writer, a fashion designer, a lawyer, or in any of hundreds of other jobs, someone is sure to ask, "What do you know about computers?" Today, interacting with a PC is part of the daily routine for millions of knowledge workers and is increasingly common for blue-collar workers. No matter which career you choose, in all likelihood you will be a frequent user of computers and information technology.

Upon completion of this course, you will be part of the IT-competent minority, and you will be able to respond with confidence to any inquiry about your knowledge of computers. But what of that 80% of our society that must answer "nothing" or "very little"? These people are at a career disadvantage and many of them view computers and IT as a continuing source of stress, especially those who work with computers on job-specific tasks.

OPPORTUNITIES FOR IT SPECIALISTS

If you are planning a career as an IT specialist, opportunities remain excellent, even in the face of an economic downturn. Almost every company, no matter how small or large, employs or contracts with IT specialists, and most of these companies are always looking for qualified information technology people. IT specialists have many doors open to them. If they accept employment in an organization's information services department, they often are given the option of working in a traditional office environment or telecommuting to work at least part of the time. Those who prefer working in a variety of environments are working for consulting firms or working as independent contractors. If the trend toward outsourcing (contracting with external personnel to do in-house work) continues, look for the number of consultants and contractors to surpass the number of traditional in-house IT personnel in the near future.

Throughout the past decade, it is estimated that one in every ten jobs for IT specialists was open, waiting to be filled by a qualified applicant. There simply are not enough qualified IT people to fill all jobs. IT workers are in demand not just for their skills but also for what they contribute to the organization. In a recent report, the United States Department of Commerce stated that information technology workers were more than twice as productive as workers in other areas were during most of the 1990s.

Certain IT career fields are in such high demand that an experienced IT specialist can dictate terms of employment including extended vacation time, stock options, telecommuting options, relaxation of dress codes, and, of course, high salaries. The salary table in Figure 12-1 should give you a feel for the salaries that can be expected in familiar IT positions for the year 2004.

The Internet's Impact on the IT Job Picture

The Internet or its predecessor has been around for over three decades, but the World Wide Web and Internet browsers are relatively new (1993). The latter catapulted the Internet into every phase of our information society. The result is that the money flow associated with the Internet industry is growing more than 10 times as fast as the general U.S. economy. The Internet industry is defined by those companies that are wholly online or have a significant presence online in conjunction with traditional bricks-and-mortar companies.

The Internet economy is now larger than the airline industry and is approaching the size of the publishing industry. Over a million new jobs in the U.S. alone can be linked directly to Internet businesses. Tens of thousands of companies are writing job descriptions for the first time for Internet-related jobs. Fortune 500-size companies can have 30 or more job descriptions for Internet-related jobs.

The Growing IT Specialist Fields

For the last decade, people with computer and information technology education have been at or near the top of the "most wanted" list (see Figure 12-2). With millions (yes, millions!) of new computers being purchased and linked to the Internet each year, it is likely that this trend will continue. Of course, the number of people attracted to the booming IT field is also increasing. One of the many reasons for this migration to the IT field is that IT careers are consistently ranked among the most desirable jobs. A recent *Money* magazine article ranked 100 jobs in terms of earnings, long- and short-term job growth, job security, prestige rating, and "stress and strain" rating. The magazine called computer systems analyst the best job in America, with physician, physical therapist, electrical engineer, and civil engineer rounding out the top five. The systems analyst is but one of dozens of IT specialist careers. These are some of the more visible information technology jobs.

THE CRYSTAL BALL:
The Online Doctor Thousands of physicians offer fee-based e-mail consultations for their patients already under their care. The cost of a consultation varies depending on the required response time. Obviously, this form of telemedicine is appropriate only for certain circumstances. The next generation of online patient care will include more sophisticated means of interaction, such as audio/video instant messaging. Used properly, electronic patient care can be just as effective as in-clinic care and can help reduce spiraling medical costs. The electronic patient/physician relation will grow exponentially throughout the decade.

FIGURE 12-1

PROJECTED AVERAGE SALARY AND INDUSTRY SALARY RANGE FOR 2004 (IN $1,000S)

The table shows estimated average salaries (plus bonuses) and salary range for familiar information technology positions. The range is the range of the average salaries by industry. Some industries (for example, high-tech and consulting services) pay higher salaries to IT people than do other industries (for example, education, government, and retail). Actual salaries could be lower or higher. Salaries are projected from year 2002 salary surveys based on historical cost-of-living increases for IT workers and general economic conditions.

TOP MANAGEMENT

Position	Average Salary Range
Chief information officer (CIO)/vice president	$160 ($100–$300)
Chief technology officer	$150 ($95–$180)
Director of systems development	$135 ($90–$172)
Director of IT operations	$115 ($75–$150)
Internet technology strategist	$120 ($60–$140)
Webmaster	$90 ($53–$140)
Director of networks	$120 ($90–$180)

MIDDLE MANAGEMENT

Position	Average Salary Range
Manager of voice and data communications	$85 ($60–$150)
Network manager	$80 ($55–$105)
Manager of Internet/intranet technology	$92 ($55–$134)
Project manager	$96 ($82–$120)
Database manager	$102 ($75–$120)
Computer operations manager	$85 ($67–$125)
Help desk/technical support manager	$82 ($65–$100)

STAFF (INCLUDING ENTRY LEVEL)

Position	Average Salary Range
Network administrator	$70 ($61–$91)
Network engineer	$72 ($55–$85)
Web application developer	$58 ($50–$75)
Senior systems analyst	$85 ($74–$95)
Systems administrator	$71 ($60–$80)
Senior systems programmer	$80 ($69–$95)
Senior programmer	$70 ($55–$90)
Senior programmer/analyst	$80 ($70–$95)
Programmer/analyst	$69 ($60–$82)
Software engineer	$80 ($63–$95)
Database analyst/administrator	$80 ($60–$92)
User liaison	$75 ($60–$90)
Information security specialist	$75 ($49–$90)
Lead computer operator	$55 ($42–$65)
Computer operator	$46 ($38–$55)
PC technical specialist	$60 ($40–$77)
Help desk/technical support specialist	$50 ($40–$60)

FIGURE 12–2 IT-SPECIALIST CAREER OPPORTUNITIES

ROBOTICS ENGINEERS AND PROGRAMMERS
Industrial robots now perform many repetitive tasks, such as those on this automobile assembly line. Although the emergence of industrial robots has eliminated some jobs, they have created thousands of jobs for IT specialists who build and program them.

Courtesy of Sun Microsystems, Inc.

NETWORK ADMINISTRATOR AND WEBMASTER
These IT specialists, a network administrator and a Webmaster, develop and maintain a network and a corporate Internet presence. All of these people need a solid foundation of computer knowledge to accomplish their jobs effectively.

Courtesy of Novell

DESIGN ENGINEERS
Computer-aided design (CAD) has revolutionized the way in which engineers and scientists design, draft, and document a product. With CAD, most of the "bugs" can be worked out of a design before a product or plant (in the example) is built.

Courtesy of Intergraph Corporation

- *Chief information officer.* The director of information services within an organization often is called the **chief information officer (CIO)**. This person is responsible for all the information services activity in the company, from the organization's Web page to its inventory control system. The CIO, often a vice president, must be somewhat futuristic, predicting what information technologies will become reality so the company can position itself to use them as they become available.

- *Systems analyst.* **Systems analysts** analyze, design, and implement information systems. They work closely with people in the user areas to design information systems that meet their information processing needs. These "problem solvers" are assigned a variety of support tasks, including feasibility studies, system reviews, security assessments, long-range planning, and hardware/software selection.

- *Programmer.* **Applications programmers** translate analyst-prepared system and input/output specifications into programs. Programmers design the logic, then code, debug, test, and document the programs. A person holding a **programmer/analyst** position performs the functions of both a programmer and a systems analyst.

- *Network administrator.* **Network administrators** design and maintain networks: LANs, MANs, and WANs. This work involves selecting and installing appropriate system software and appropriate hardware, such as modems and routers, and selecting the transmission media.

- *System programmer.* **System programmers** design, develop, maintain, and implement system software. System software, such as the operating system and system performance management software, is fundamental to the general operation of the computer; that is, it does not address a specific business or scientific problem.

- *Database administrator.* The **database administrator** (**DBA**) designs, creates, and maintains the integrated database. The DBA coordinates discussions between user groups to determine the content and format of the database so that data redundancy is kept to a minimum. The integrity and the security of the database are also responsibilities of the database administrator.

- *Internet site specialist.* The **Internet site specialist** is responsible for creating and maintaining one or more Internet sites. This specialist uses Internet development tools and source material from throughout the organization to create and maintain World Wide Web sites and pages. Occasionally, people in this job function are also responsible for the hardware required at the server site.

- *Webmaster.* The **Webmaster** is an Internet specialist who, depending on the size of the organization, may have a range of responsibilities. Typically, the Web server and its software are the responsibility of the Webmaster. The Webmaster monitors Internet traffic on the server computer and responds to external inquiries regarding Web site operations. Some Webmasters are actively involved in the design and update of Web site pages.

- *Computer operator.* The **computer operator** performs those hardware-based activities needed to keep enterprise-wide systems operational. The operator is in constant communication with the computer(s) while monitoring the progress of online systems, a number of simultaneous production runs, initiating one-time jobs, and troubleshooting.

- *User liaison.* Computer and information processing activity is very intense in companies that seek to exploit the full potential of information technology. In this environment, someone who is working in a particular functional area (perhaps the marketing department) is told to seek ways to take advantage of available IT resources. More often than not, this person is the user liaison. The **user liaison** is a "live-in" IT specialist who coordinates all computer-related activities within a particular functional area.

Computer-related jobs are not nearly as centralized (for example, in an information services department) as they were during the mainframe era (through 1990). The trend toward client/server computing has resulted in the distribution of IT specialists throughout the organization.

The variety and types of IT specialist jobs are ever changing. For example, there's the *information detective*. Companies and individuals call on these high-tech detectives to help them answer such questions as: Has my child's sitter had any driving accidents? Has my materials supplier ever filed for bankruptcy? Did this applicant for the sales manager position really earn an MBA at Harvard? Another related job is the professional *Internet researcher*. Someone who really knows his or her way around the Internet can do in minutes what might take a Net newbie several days to do. A good detective or researcher can make in excess of $100 an hour and never leave the comfort of home!

Women in Information Technology

The Internet explosion has created a new business culture in which women can more easily climb the corporate ladder. In the IT career field, the number of women in senior management positions is approximately that of men. Factors contributing to this shift away from a male-dominated business world include the enormous demand by Internet companies for knowledgeable, talented employees. Also, the hierarchical structure of Internet and high-tech businesses is more loosely defined and ever changing, enabling significant promotions both laterally and into management. Web companies, especially the smaller ones, are under great pressure to achieve quick success, and they face stiff competition in finding the people who will make that happen. The Internet has made IT employment a new game in which traditional patterns of employment no longer apply.

Licensing and Certification

If you are an IT specialist or your chosen career overlaps directly with information technology, you may be in constant contact with sensitive data and may have the power to control events. An implied responsibility to maintain the integrity of the system and its data accompanies such a job. Failure to do so could have a disastrous effect on the lives of individuals and even on the stability of the organization. Trillions of dollars are handled each day by computer-based systems that are created and

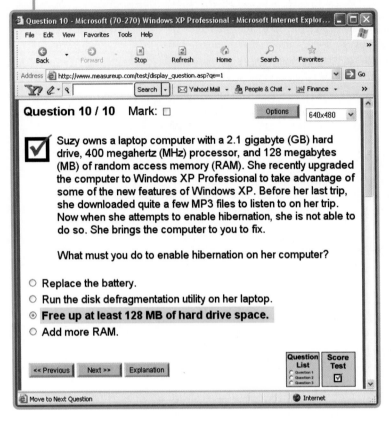

FIGURE 12-3

EXAMS FOR PROFESSIONAL CERTIFICATION
This is an example question for the Windows XP Professional Exam, which is part of several Microsoft certification programs, including the MCP, the MCSE, and the MCSA. The actual exam has 215 questions. Example questions to all Microsoft exams can be found at the Microsoft Web site.

controlled by IT specialists. The lives of millions of air travelers depend on the responsiveness of the computer-based air traffic control system. Life sustaining systems in hospitals are designed, programmed, and maintained by IT specialists.

At present, licensing or certification is usually not a requirement for any IT professional; nor is it required for users of computers. Licensing and certification are hotly debated issues. Many professions require demonstration of performance at a certain level of competence before permission is granted to practice. Through examination, the engineer becomes a registered professional engineer, the attorney becomes a member of the bar, and the accountant becomes a certified public accountant. Many people in the trades, including hairdressers, plumbers, and electricians, must be licensed to practice.

Within the computer community, there are a number of certifications. Several professional organizations provide certification options, including the Institute for Certification of Computer Professionals (ICCP), which awards the *Certified Computing Professional* (*CCP*) and the *Associate Computing Professional* (*ACP*). The CCP and ACP are general certifications in the area of computers and information technology. A growing number of companies whose products have become de facto standards offer certifications. For example, software giants Microsoft and Novell sponsor a range of widely accepted certifications. Microsoft awards these certificates to information technology professionals who have completed a series of rigorous tests (see Figure 12-3).

- *Microsoft Certified Professional.* The MCP credential is for professionals who have the skills to implement successfully a Microsoft product or technology as part of a business solution in an organization.

- *Microsoft Certified Systems Administrators.* MCSAs administer network and systems environments based on the Microsoft Windows platforms.

- *Microsoft Certified Systems Engineer.* The MCSE analyzes business requirements to design and implement an infrastructure solution based on the Windows platform and Microsoft Servers software.

- *Microsoft Certified Database Administrator.* MCDBAs design, implement, and administer Microsoft SQL Server™ databases.

- *Microsoft Certified Trainers.* MCTs are certified by Microsoft to deliver Microsoft training courses to IT professionals and developers.

- *Microsoft Certified Application Developers.* The MCAD uses Microsoft technologies to develop and maintain department-level applications, components, Web or desktop clients, or back-end data services.

- *Microsoft Certified Solution Developer.* MCSDs design and develop business solutions with Microsoft technologies.

- *Microsoft Office Specialist.* Office Specialists are recognized globally for demonstrating advanced skills with Microsoft Office desktop software, such as PowerPoint or Word.

- *Microsoft Office Specialist Master Instructor.* Office Specialist Master Instructors are certified as trainers for Microsoft Office desktop programs.

Novell, a company that specializes in networking products, offers several levels of certification for people who work with its widely used network products.

- *Certified Novell Administrator.* CNAs provide network support for Novell networking products, NetWare and GroupWise.

- *Certified Novell Engineer.* The CNE can provide advanced company-wide networking support, including planning, installation, configuration, troubleshooting, and upgrade.

- *Master CNE.* A Master CNE is a multivendor, multisolution specialist of the network industry.

- *Certified Directory Engineer.* CDEs manage the people, devices, hardware, and applications on a network and the relationships between them.

- *Certified Novell Instructor.* The CNI provides training and performance-based certification for the experienced IT professional on Novell networking products.

- *Novell Authorized Instructor.* The NAI is authorized to teach Novell classes while working toward a CNI.

Novell also awards other IT specialist certificates in such areas as Internet security and database integration.

Sun Microsystems offers several certifications for Java, the "write once, run anywhere" programming language that is so popular with Web-based applications. Certifications are awarded at different skill levels and for Web or enterprise applications. These include the *Sun Certified Programmer for the Java 2 Platform,* the *Sun Certified Developer for the Java 2 Platform,* the *Sun Certified Web Component Developer for the Java 2 Platform (Enterprise Edition),* and the *Sun Certified Enterprise Architect for J2EE Technology.*

People seeking any of these certifications must pass an array of tests. Generally, recruiters and employers view certifications favorably. Often, being certified results in a higher salary. However, certifications are seldom a requirement for employment.

CAREER OPPORTUNITIES FOR THE IT-COMPETENT MINORITY

Information technology competency is becoming a prerequisite for people pursuing almost any career—from actuaries to zoologists (see Figure 12-4). In fact, most professional jobs come with a telephone, a desk, and a PC. The trend toward greater dependence on technology in the workplace has had a dramatic effect on how we do our jobs.

- The terminal or networked PC has become standard equipment at hospital nursing stations and often is found in operating rooms.

- Draftspeople have traded drawing tables for computer-aided design (CAD) workstations.

- Teachers are integrating the power of computers into their instruction and the students' learning experience.

- Economists would be lost without the predictive capabilities of their decision support system (DSS).

- Truck dispatchers query their information systems, which may include the exact location of fleet trucks (via onboard global positioning systems), before scheduling deliveries.

- Construction contractors keep track of on-site inventory on notebook PCs.

- The PC is the administrative assistant's constant companion for everything from word processing to conference scheduling.

- Stockbrokers often have terminals on both sides of their desks. (Some dedicated brokers stay in touch around the clock via Internet-enabled cell phones.)

- An attorney's law library is no longer on the shelf behind the desk, but on CD-ROM and/or the Internet.

- Professional football coaches rely on their play databases to give them insight into what offense or defense to run for given situations.

- Politicians frequently tap Internet-based polls before casting their votes.

Career mobility is becoming forever intertwined with an individual's current and future knowledge of computers and information technology.

Of course, career advancement ultimately depends on your abilities, imagination, and performance, but understanding computers and IT can open doors to opportunities that might otherwise be shut. All things being equal, the person who has the knowledge of and the will to work with computers and IT will have a tremendous career advantage over those who do not.

Our Jobs Are Changing

Automation is causing the elimination of some jobs. For example, the revenue accounting staff at a major U.S. airline was reduced from 650 to 350 with the implementation of a new computer-based system. Those remaining had to be retrained to work with the new system. Those displaced had to be retrained for other work opportunities in an increasingly automated society.

FIGURE 12–4 CAREER OPPORTUNITIES FOR THOSE WITH IT COMPETENCY

THE KNOWLEDGE WORKER'S TOOLS
Knowledge workers in most industries rely on a networked personal computer and access to enterprise systems and information. Here a knowledge worker joins another worker in two ways, via telephone and via a network link. In the business world, PCs are networked to enable the sharing of information and ideas.

Photo courtesy of Intel Corporation

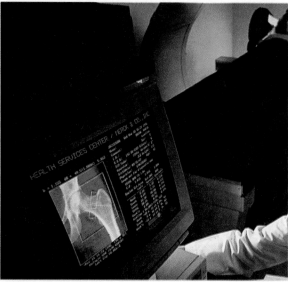

IT IN HEALTH CARE
Hospital and home health care can be easier and more effective when nurses have the patient's complete medical records with them. This nurse reviews the patient's records and updates them on-the-spot as circumstances change, such as a record of tests performed. Here, a nurse is providing a bone densitometry test to detect bone loss, which may indicate osteoporosis.

Courtesy of Merck & Co., Inc.

IT IN EDUCATION
This instructor spends much of his workday interacting with students and computers.

Courtesy of International Business Machines Corporation. Unauthorized use not permitted.

IT solutions have caused all or at least part of many job functions to be replaced with automated systems (see Figure 12-5). Automated telephone systems have eliminated the need for many receptionists. The presence of ATMs means fewer bank tellers are needed. The emergence of e-trading reduces the demand for stockbrokers. E-tailing, much of which is completely automated, affects a variety of retail jobs. Some people get loans from banks online, whereby an expert "loan" system makes the decisions. The explosion of online classes hasn't eliminated the need for professors, but, for some professors, their job function has changed dramatically from in-class instruction to online course development and delivery.

Fortunately, information technology is responsible for the creation of many other jobs. The explosion of information technology has resulted in thousands of new companies that provide a variety of previously unknown products and services. Yahoo! and Netscape were founded in 1994. Dot.com giant America Online was founded in 1985. Many other high-tech companies didn't exist a decade ago. Now they employ hundreds, even tens of thousands, of people in high-paying jobs. Ten years ago, relatively few companies had Web sites. Today, every company desiring to stay in business has a Web site and a site support staff.

As information technology continues to move to the forefront in our society, jobs in every discipline are being redefined. For example, ten years ago sales representatives carried manuals and products to the customer site. Today, they still knock on doors, but to a much lesser extent because much of what used to be personal interaction is now electronic interaction (e-mail, instant messaging, and extranets). When they do make sales calls, they don't carry heavy manuals and products. Instead, they bring their notebook PCs. Thanks to the technology, the sales rep is no longer the sole source of product/service information. Customers can get up-to-date information directly from the vendor via its extranet (an extension of a company's private intranet). Many customers don't deal with sales reps at all. They obtain needed information by browsing the Internet or an extranet, and then they place their orders electronically.

Radical changes in the way we do our jobs are not limited to the business community. Poets, the clergy, politicians, music composers, and others are continually evaluating what they do and how they do it within the context of emerging technology.

Internet Jobs for Nontechnology People

Contrary to what you might imagine, the glamour and high potential of the high-tech Internet world has plenty of room for people who may not consider themselves techies. Millions of workers have asked these questions: What do I need to do to get an Internet-related job? How can I get that job without returning to entry-level work?

To be sure, all job functions in the technology industries require IT-competent people. Many people, however, have the misconception that all jobs in technology companies require programming knowledge. In fact, many positions require relatively little technical knowledge or experience. Large numbers of jobs deal exclusively with Internet content (from creating artistic Web pages to collection and analysis of online surveys). Other jobs focus more on project management than on the specifics of technology.

The high-tech industries are like other companies in that whatever they do is a team effort, requiring all types of skills, both technical and nontechnical. A Web site that exhibits state-of-the-art technological features may be of little value to the organization if it is not presented artistically and does not contain well-written content.

If you consider yourself a nontechnical IT-competent person and want to become a part of the Internet and high-tech industries, be aware that job titles and descriptions vary enormously between companies. A Webmaster in one company may do the same work as an Internet designer in another company. Positions in high-tech companies are evolving at the same pace as the Internet with new types of jobs and titles coming into existence each month. If you are looking for this type of job, pay close attention to the job description and how it relates to your range of experience and salary history.

Information technology continues to steamroll into our lives. Each of us has a choice: We can resist information technology and hope for the best, or we can embrace it and use it to open new horizons for job opportunities. The fact that you are reading this book indicates that you have chosen the latter.

FIGURE 12–5 Keeping Score the Electronic Way
The way tennis is played hasn't changed much in the age of information, but the way players train and the way it is tracked and reported have changed. Every point is documented during the Olympics (shown here), during all professional tennis matches, and during many juniors matches, too. The data are analyzed by players and coaches and reported by broadcasters and reporters.

Courtesy of International Business Machines Corporation.
Unauthorized use not permitted.

GETTING A JOB

Whether you are entering the job market for the first time or seeking alternative employment, resources on the Internet can help you land the position you want.

● *Comprehensive career/employment Web sites.* The Internet now has a number of comprehensive career/employment Web sites designed to help employer and candidate find one another. These include sites like Monster.com and CareerMosaic.com, which offer a wide variety of career services.

● *Industry-specific or professional career/employment Web sites.* These sites offer similar services to the comprehensive sites, but their orientation is to a specific industry, such as health care, oil and gas, or airlines. Or, their orientation is to specific professionals, such as accountants, lawyers, engineers, or physicians.

● *Company job opening pages.* Most company Web sites now have a page called something like "career opportunities" or "job seekers." To find this page from the company's home page, click on *About the Company* or *Company Information.* This page and its links will contain detailed information about available openings, often by geographical location, division, or job function.

The career/employment Web sites offer these types of resources and services.

- *Jobs database.* Potential employers post job openings to a searchable job openings database.
- *Candidates database.* You can post a résumé to the site's candidates database. This database is made available to potential employers.
- *Job search.* A comprehensive site may have hundreds of thousands of job openings in its database. You can search the job-openings database by keyword, industry type, job type, and geographic locale to get a listing of jobs that meet your criteria.
- *Candidate search.* Employers continuously search this candidate database, which contains the résumé of those seeking jobs, to find candidates who can fill their job openings.
- *Career resources.* Major career sites have extensive resources for those people who are contemplating a job or career change or are seeking employment for the first time. These could include: interactive tools that help people prepare a résumé and cover letter templates, tips on preparing for an interview, relocation information (including comparisons between cities), compensation statistics, tips on salary negotiation, information on employers, and much more.

The online jobs search has revolutionized the manner in which those seeking employment find jobs and those companies seeking employees find candidates. The tradition of sending a snail mail résumé in response to a help-wanted ad in a newspaper or magazine may have lost its effectiveness in our connected information society. In this new era the jobs search process is made easier for both employer and candidate. Also, some say that the online process results in a better match for both employee and employer.

SECTION SELF-CHECK

12-1.1	At present, less than half of the companies in the United States employ or contract with IT specialists. (T/F)
12-1.2	Because of privacy concerns, companies rarely post their job opportunities to their Internet Web sites. (T/F)
12-1.3	Which of these is not a Microsoft certification: (a) MCP, (b) CNE, (c) MCAD, or (d) MCSA?
12-1.4	America Online was founded in: (a) 1965, (b) 1975, (c) 1985, or (d) 1995.

12-2   Robots and Robotics

To date, the area of artificial intelligence (AI) having the greatest impact on our society and experiencing the greatest commercial success is robotics. **Robotics** is the field of study that deals with creating robots.

R2D2 and the Terminator can do amazing things, but these Hollywood creations are a lifetime away from reality. As you read this section, you will see that today's robots can do amazing things, too, including working tirelessly to make appliances, clothes, automobiles and a thousand other useful products. Most applications of robotics are in manufacturing and the use of *industrial robots*. Industrial robots are quite good at repetitive tasks and tasks that require precision movements, moving heavy loads, and working in hazardous areas. However, robots are emerging as major players not only in manufacturing but also in nonmanufacturing industries, such as health care and other service industries. Already we can give robots crude human sensory capabilities and some degree of artificial intelligence. As these capabilities mature over the next decade, look for robots in other areas of the workplace, in our homes, and even on stage and in museums.

Robotics offers the potential for increased productivity and better service. These benefits have not been overlooked by the manufacturing and service industries. Progressive organizations are rushing to install more and more applications of robotics as a means of staying competitive in the global economy. Industries throughout the world are looking to robots to help them control costs, respond more quickly to market needs, and reduce labor-related costs.

RUDIMENTARY ROBOTICS

The "steel-collar" workforce is made up of hundreds of thousands of industrial robots (see Figure 12-6). The most common industrial robot is a single mechanical arm controlled by a computer. The arm, called a *manipulator,* has a shoulder, forearm, and wrist and is capable of performing the motions of a human arm. The manipulator is fitted with a hand designed to accomplish a specific task, such as painting, welding, picking and placing, and so on.

The automotive industry is the largest user of robots (for painting and welding) and the electronics industry (for circuit testing and connecting chips to circuit boards) is second. General Motors, for example, now has a robot base of over 20,000. Many of these robots perform operations that are

FIGURE 12–6 THE STEEL COLLAR WORKFORCE

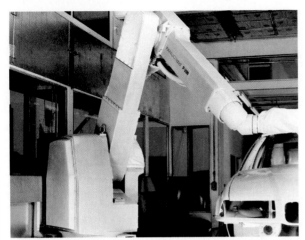

FLEXING MUSCLES

The typical industrial robot has a manipulator arm with a shoulder, forearm, wrist, and hand that is designed for a specific task. Here, this precision industrial robot tirelessly paints automobiles during manufacturing.

Courtesy of FANUC Robotics North America, Inc.

PICK-AND-PLACE

Computer-controlled industrial robots help ensure the flow of work during production. Here a robot transfers boxes between conveyors in a pick-and-place application. This robot can handle 45 boxes up to 130 pounds each per minute.

Courtesy of FANUC Robotics North America, Inc.

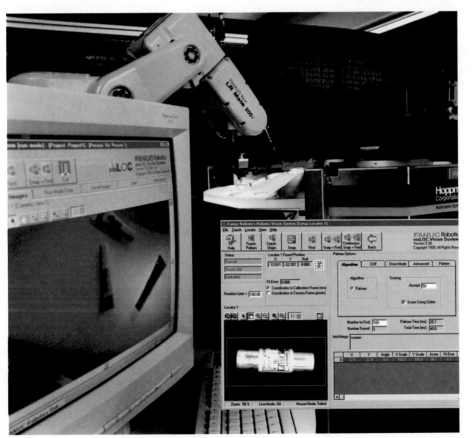

MACHINE VISION

This robotic vision system is used for determining an object's location and orientation. It provides advanced robot guidance capabilities for machine loading/unloading, material handling, packaging, and assembly applications. The robot simplifies the integration of machine vision, as no programming is required to calibrate, train, and run the system (see inset). The system performs visual tasks at a speed and precision unattainable with the human eye.

Courtesy of FANUC Robotics North America, Inc.

FIGURE 12–6 continued

THE ROBOT TEAM
The precise, untiring movement of computer-controlled industrial robots helps assure quality in the assembly of everything from electrical components to automobiles. Here in this DaimlerChrysler Corporation plant, 66 industrial robots apply spot welds. About 300 robots weld, seal, train, paint, clean, and handle material at this plant.

DaimlerChrysler Corporation

difficult or impossible for human workers to perform. For example, robots are used to install sharp windshield glass on cars and trucks. This requires the application of adhesive beads in a precise and uniform manner—something a robot can perform quickly with high repeatability.

TEACHING ROBOTS TO DO THEIR JOB

A computer program is written to control the robot just as one is written to print payroll checks. It includes such commands as when to reach, in which direction to reach, how far to reach, which tool to use, and when to grasp, weld, paint, and so on. Many robots are programmed to reach to a particular location, find a particular item, and then place it somewhere else. This simple application of robotics is called *pick and place*. Instead of a grasping mechanism, other robots are equipped with a variety of industrial tools such as drills, paint guns, welding torches, and so on. Once programmed, robots do not need much attention. One plant manufactures vacuum cleaners 24 hours a day, 7 days a week!

ROBOTS COME TO THEIR SENSES

With the recent innovations in sensor technology, roboticists are outfitting robots with artificial intelligence and human sensory capabilities, such as vision, that enable them to simulate human behavior. A robot with the added dimension of vision can be given some intelligence. Robots without intelligence simply repeat preprogrammed motions. Even though the technology for the vision systems is primitive, a robot can be "taught" to distinguish between dissimilar objects under controlled conditions. With this sensory subsystem, the robot has the capability of making crude but important decisions. For example, a robot equipped with a vision subsystem can distinguish between boxes of differing sizes and shapes as they approach on the conveyor. It can be programmed to place a box of particular dimensions on an adjacent conveyer and let all other boxes pass.

As vision system technology continues to improve, more and more robots will have the ability to move—*navigational capabilities* (see Figure 12-7). Now, most robots are stationary; those that are not

FIGURE 12-7   ROBOTS WITH NAVIGATIONAL CAPABILITIES

ROBOMOW® AT WORK

It may look like a UFO, but this dual-mode (automatic and manual) hands-free lawn mower from Friendly Machines is one smart little robot. Robomow® is environmentally friendly and doesn't need human help to mow a lawn. When Robomow encounters obstacles, it mows around them. Robomow mows in uniformly straight lines to produce a striped, manicured lawn.

Courtesy of Friendly Machines

MOTORING AROUND MARS

The Mars Pathfinder delivered a stationary lander and a surface rover to the Red Planet on July 4, 1997. The rover vehicle, a mobile robot, was manipulated by controllers some 120,000,000 miles away! The six-wheel rover, named Sojourner, explored the area near the lander, testing the soil and sending back pictures of Mars.

Courtesy NASA

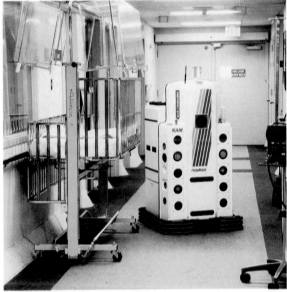

MOBILE ROBOTS CAN DELIVER

The 575 pound HelpMate7 trackless, robotic courier is designed to perform material transport tasks for healthcare facilities. This robot can deliver mail, medication, supplies, and meal trays to the nursing units throughout the hospital. Vision and ultrasonic proximity sensors are used to understand the environment and avoid obstacles as they are encountered. It navigates from point to point by using a map of the building to plan the best route and sensory feedback to follow that route. It can even use the elevator!

Courtesy of HelpMate Robotics, Inc.

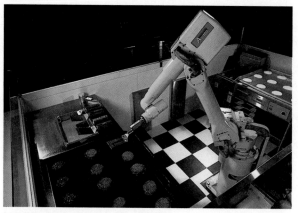

FIGURE 12–8 Flipper the Robot
The number and variety of applications for robots is expanding rapidly. Here, "Flipper," a typical industrial robot, has been programmed to prepare hamburgers and pancakes on two griddles simultaneously. The now famous hamburger-flipping robot was designed originally as a promotional gimmick, but restaurateurs have been so impressed with the speed at which it makes consistently perfect hamburgers and pancakes that we may someday see Flipper and its cousins in commercial kitchens.

Courtesy of AccuTemp Products, Inc.

can only detect the presence of an object in their path or are programmed to operate within a well-defined work area where the positions of all obstacles are known. Service industries using mobile-robot technology applications include hospitals, security and patrol, commercial floor care, hazardous waste handling, bomb disposal, nuclear plant cleanup, janitorial services, rehabilitation programs, and the military.

Autonomous robots can make functional decisions without being guided or remotely piloted by a human operator. These robots can react intuitively to real-world stimuli by using the developing technology of image pattern recognition, mobility, agility, and perceptual cognition. Military self-guided cruise missiles are able to make automatic navigational adjustments in response to changing conditions while constantly reviewing their onboard flight maps. Other potential applications for autonomous robots, especially in situations where human workers would be exposed to great risk, include deep underwater exploration (robots helped in the exploration of the *Titanic*), interior surveillance of nuclear reactors (robots helped clean up after the Chernobyl nuclear incident), and surface navigation of other planets (the Sojourner robot scooted around Mars gathering data).

OPPORTUNITIES FOR ROBOTS ARE GROWING

Each day engineers and entrepreneurs find new ways to use robots (see Figure 12-8). Even surgeons are using robots to help in brain surgery. Robots can be set up to manipulate the surgical drill and biopsy needle with great accuracy, thereby making brain surgery faster, more accurate, and safer. Other surgical applications of robotics include help with hip replacements, knee replacements, and pelvic and spinal surgeries.

Autonomous kinetic sculpture is a new class of robotics and is found in art galleries and in the performing arts. Some robots create works of art, whereas others perform by themselves or with humans. How a performance or robotic sculpture will turn out is often unique because the robots are designed to react in real-time situations and adapt to their environment through their own creative behaviors.

The future of robotics offers exciting opportunities. Companies are sure to take advantage of these opportunities to stay competitive. Robotics suppliers, along with their system integrators, are using Rapid Deployment Automation to expedite the implementation of robotics. This strategy uses computer-aided design (CAD) to shorten the design-to-build cycle and promote a user-friendly "no programming" environment for factory floor personnel. Robotics is being implemented in many nonmanufacturing environments as well (see Figures 12-7 and 12-8). Who knows, we may someday have robots as helpers around the home and as workmates at the office.

SECTION SELF-CHECK

12-2.1	Industrial robots excel at repetitive tasks. (T/F)
12-2.2	Some robots have vision capabilities. (T/F)
12-2.3	Which of these is not a part of a manipulator on an industrial robot: (a) arm, (b) forearm, (c) knuckle, or (d) wrist?
12-2.4	The application where robots find a particular item and then place it somewhere else is called: (a) select and set, (b) move and put, (c) choose and locate, or (d) pick and place.

12-3 Looking Ahead: Future Applications of IT

Let's look down the road at what information technology and the information superhighway might have to offer. The text and the images in this section survey a variety of new and emerging IT applications. Bear in mind that information technology and the Internet are tools. You and other innovators will ultimately determine what applications are created as well as who and what drives along the information superhighway.

Surprisingly, many adults are unaware of the information superhighway, and therefore, the Internet and its impact on society. In fact, millions of people in America and billions worldwide are still waiting at the on ramp. Each day, however, more travelers drive up the ramp and on to the electronic highway. The mode of travel through cyberspace is the computer. A typical Internet session will take you all over the country and often to other countries. The actual traffic along the highway is anything that can be digitized—text (perhaps the morning newspaper), graphic images (an MRI scan of a brain tumor), motion video (a movie), still photographs (a picture of a friend), sound (a radio station in Alaska), and programs (perhaps multiplayer Internet games that load and run on your PC).

The Internet, with its ability to connect people and businesses, will continue to be the basis for innovative new applications of information technology. Some applications will be entirely new to all of us, such as the ability to customize and order automobiles online or the ability to view any previously-aired TV show whenever you want to see it. Other applications will be new to some of us. For example, some of us can shop for groceries online and tap into the online card catalog at the local library. Most of us can't. Eventually shopping for groceries online will be commonplace and you will be able to search a central database that includes the card catalog information for every library in the United States.

A mind-boggling array of information and telecommunication services has been implemented in recent years. Figure 12-9 gives you a feel for the breadth of services, information, and applications currently found on the Net. Many more are planned for the information superhighway, some of which are described in this section.

FIGURE 12–9 **CRUISING THE NET**
The Internet makes a vast treasure trove of information and services available to people all over the world. This figure contains a sampling of a few of the millions of stops along the Internet.

NEWS ONLINE
The Sept. 11, 2001 terrorist attack on the United States has changed everyone's perspective on life. The event let the Internet flex its muscle and show us the awesome capability of this relatively new vehicle for communication. Information on the attacks, including photos, stories, anecdotes, news, and so on, was posted to CBSNews.com (shown here) and thousands of other sites, many of which had little or nothing to do with news. Almost immediately, the FBI began soliciting information on their Web site and within hours, they had thousands of leads. Sadly, there were many hoaxes perpetuated on netizens during this time of crisis, such as the one that told of a man falling 80 stories and, miraculously, living to tell about it. We now know that the Internet can be a wonderful communications tool during times of disaster. We also know that we need to be vigilant about assessing the validity of all information. Fraud was the saddest Internet note in the aftermath of September 11. Criminals set up Web sites supposedly to raise money for worthy organizations, but their entrepreneurial objective, however, was to take advantage of this crisis and the willingness of people to help the victims.

LOOKING FOR A JOB?
The Net has many places, both commercial and nonprofit, that specialize in matching job applicants with employers. Already, most professional positions are listed on the Net. A good place to start your job search is the Monster Job Search, which offers a comprehensive list of online job services and résumé banks. In the example, the user searches the 800,000-job database for an "Information technology" position in "Florida-Miami."

FIGURE 12–9 continued

WEBCAMS AND NETSCAPE

Shown here within the Netscape browser are the images from several San Francisco Webcams. Webcams, which are cameras that capture a live image every few seconds or minutes, are strategically positioned in interesting locations, both inside and outside, all over the world. Webcam sites let you watch the progress of a pregnant rhinoceros; travel around campus with Mike, Gina, or whoever has the mobile camera; follow the goings-on in a radio station; or enjoy the views around San Francisco (shown here).

PRODUCT INFORMATION AND SUPPORT

Customer service has become the byword of corporate America. Competition demands that companies provide customers with the best possible service, including a comprehensive Web site. Hewlett Packard's Web site provides product information and online troubleshooting help (shown here) for every product.

INTERNET GREETING CARDS

E-mail messages far outnumber written messages. It may be only a matter of time before online greeting cards overtake traditional greeting cards. Several Web sites, such as Hallmark.com, give you the facilities to create and send your own "greeting cards." In this card, a personal message is displayed after the frogs finish playing Happy Birthday.

THE BEST OF THE WEB

Cybersurfers are ever vigilant in their search for the best and worst that the Net has to offer. Critics abound on the Internet. People and companies who create Web sites should be aware that cybercritics might eventually pass judgment on the quality of their site, both good and bad. A select few make one of the "best" or "worst" lists. This "How Stuff Works" site is on many "Best of the Web" lists.

FIGURE 12–9 continued

TAKING A VIRTUAL TOUR OF THE WORLD'S GREAT MUSEUMS
Save the plane fare and enjoy virtual museums all over the world, including the Smithsonian's National Air and Space Museum (shown here) and the Louvre.

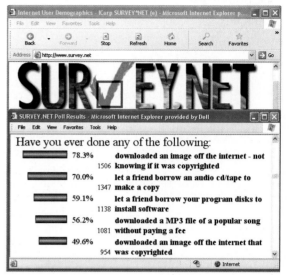

THE ONLINE SURVEY
The Net is a great forum for surveying and polling. Shown here is a survey that taps people's feelings on "Online Intellectual Property." The results of the 17-question survey are continuously updated and made available to online viewers. Many Internet portals have real-time surveys on current events.

SECURITIES ONLINE
Morgan Stanley's brokerage service offers customers quotes, charts, financial planning, online investing, securities research, and more. The Internet has enabled brokerage firms to expand their services and make information accessible to customers that heretofore was available only to brokers. Here, the client requested a chart that compared Wal-Mart's stock performance over the past year with that of the Target Corporation and the Dow Jones Industrial Average.

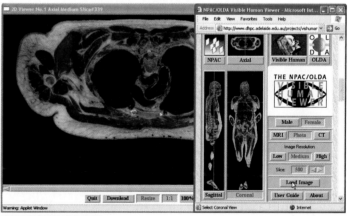

THE VISIBLE HUMAN
This award-winning Visible Human Viewer Web site runs a Java applet that lets you interactively select and view two-dimensional slices of a human body. Selected images can be enlarged (see background image) for viewing.

AT HOME IN 2010

Let's fast forward to the year 2010. Computers are invisible; that is, they are built into our domestic, working, and external environments. Imagine this scenario: B. J. Rogers' invisible computer can be programmed to awaken him to whatever stimulates him to greet the new day. B. J.'s wake up call, which could just as well be yours, can be his favorite music, sports scores, a stock market report, the weather, or a to-do list.

Suppose B. J.'s wake up choice is a *to-do list* for the day. Besides listing the events of the day, his invisible computer, which he calls Rex, might *verbally* emphasize important events (see Figure 12-10). In response to B. J.'s request, the nearest video display, which is prominent in every occupied room in the house, is filled with a list of possible dishes. Just as B. J. notices that all dishes are meatless, Rex, the computer, reminds him of an important consideration. Rex might respond to his inquiry about ingredients by checking the home inventory and ordering as needed (all automatic).

Much of this futuristic scenario is within the grasp of today's technology. Even today, millions of people carry computers with them much of the day, many of which have a wireless link to the Net. Millions more spend most of their day at a computer. Many of these people routinely talk to their PCs via speech-recognition technology. Smart homes now are deemed an economically sound investment. You can shop at thousands of e-tailers from any communications-ready PC. Though expensive, large flat-panel monitors are commercially available. Broadband Internet access is available to most homes in the United States. Hundreds of radio stations now broadcast over the Internet. So you see, we are well on our way to the day when this fictional scenario emerges as reality. The way things are going, the future may be here sooner than we think.

THE ELECTRONIC FAMILY REUNION

Telephones as we know them will probably disappear. In the relatively near future, the function of the telephone will be incorporated into videophones, our PCs, our TVs, our clothing, or perhaps all of these so we can see and hear the person(s) on the other end of the line. The future "telephone" will enable us to pass data and information back and forth, as if we were sitting at the same table. Already some digital cellular telephones permit the sending and receiving of e-mail. Some cell phones have built-in digital cameras that let us take and send pictures.

You will be able to use the Internet, your television, your PC, and multiple videophone hookups to hold an electronic family reunion. Here is how it would work. You would dial, or verbally request, the videophones of your relatives and a real-time video of each family would appear in a window on your wall-size television monitor. The conversation would be in stereo and sound as if all families were in the same room. The members of each family would be able to see the members of the other families. You could even share photos and view family videos. The information superhighway may enable more frequent family reunions, but we will still have to travel on traditional highways to get real hugs and taste grandmother's cherry pie.

Today we have some of these capabilities. Two people with PCs equipped with relatively inexpensive video cameras can hold videophone conversations (see and hear each other) over regular telephone line Internet connections (less than 56 K bps). They can even pass pictures and other still or video images back and forth during the conversation. Only two people can talk to each other at a time, but others can join in the conversation using a chat box (keyed-in text) and share visual information, such as directions to a meeting place.

ENTERTAINMENT EVERYWHERE

Many of the initial e-commerce offerings on the Internet will be aimed at entertaining us. We'll have *video-on-demand*; that is, you will be able to choose what television program or movie you want to watch and when you want to watch it. You will be able to watch any movie, from the classic archives to first runs, at your convenience. The same is true of television programming. If you would prefer to watch this week's edition of *60 Minutes* on Monday, rather than Sunday, you have that option. For that matter, you can elect to watch any past edition of *60 Minutes*. As you might expect, video stores and scheduled TV may become only memories in a few years.

Universal broadband access to the Internet is inevitable and will open the door for a more sophisticated form of entertainment. Already, major television networks are interweaving on-air and online statistics in broadcasts of sporting events. How long will it be before we have interactive soap operas? With the inevitable two-way communication capabilities of your future television/terminal, you can be an active participant in how a story unfolds. The soaps will be shot so they can be pieced together in a variety of ways. Imagine—you can decide whether Michelle marries Clifton or Patrick! You say this sounds far-fetched? Not really. Interactive movies are being produced and shown right now.

Your home entertainment center will become a video arcade, with immediate access to a myriad of games. You can hone your skills on an individual basis or test them, real time, against the best people in the land. Multiplayer games are already very popular on the Internet. Professional players gain

celebrity status and make big money playing games like Quake (from Id Software) and Starcraft™ (from Blizzard Entertainment). Spectators can view the games online. The worldwide gamer community is huge and, in the near future, it is conceivable that online gaming events could have more paying spectators than the Super Bowl or the World Cup.

ELECTRONIC DELIVERY OF NEWSPAPERS, BOOKS, AND OTHER TRADITIONALLY PRINTED MATERIALS

Certainly, books, magazines, newspapers, and the printed word in general will prevail for casual reading and study during the next few years. However, the Internet offers electronic-publishing as an alternative to *hard-copy* publishing. We'll be able to receive virtually any printed matter—books, magazines, newspapers, and reference material—in electronic format. Already you can get online newspapers while the news is hot, with no wait for printing and delivery. This gradual shift to online newspapers is changing the way journalists think and work. Traditionally newspapers have compiled and delivered news once each day, with relatively few exceptions. News, however, happens all day long. Online newspapers post the latest news to the Internet as it happens. Your PC already is a virtual newsstand and it is sure to grow in the future.

Besides having up-to-the-minute online content, online media have several other advantages over print media.

- They are *linked*, enabling related information to be connected via hyperlinks.
- They are interactive.
- They can read to you via *text-to-speech* technology.
- They offer *multimedia* content, such as video and audio.

If people begin to embrace the convenience of dynamically linked, interactive, and multimedia documents, there may be a trend away from print media to online alternatives. Don't be surprised to see novels written specifically for the online market that give readers the flexibility to follow links rather than pages.

The transition to e-publishing is well underway. For example, *The Los Angeles Times* makes "almost the whole newspaper" in an interactive and linked format available for free over the Internet, including the classified ads. Other newspapers make their stories available also, either for free or through an online subscription. The *Encyclopedia Britannica* is now available online—for free. All or part of many traditional magazines, such as *Time* and *People,* and several online only magazines, such as *Slate,* are available to people with access to the Internet. Frequently, stories incorporate text, audio, and video. The trend to e-publishing is evident in other areas also. For example, a number of retailers publish multimedia catalogs on the Internet that are updated almost daily, an option not possible in a print catalog. Any volatile hard-copy document, such as the telephone directory and its yellow pages, is a candidate for e-publishing. Already, continuously updated national white pages and the yellow pages are available online.

Although libraries are far more sophisticated today than they were 50 years ago, we are still in the first generation of libraries. Today's libraries still have shelves of books to be checked out and returned. The new generation of libraries may be all electronic, with no physical facilities for customers. Already thousands of books are made available through traditional libraries and via purely online libraries, such as netLibrary. Each month more and more books are being published in electronic format. The federal government is solidly behind constructing virtual libraries and now, Microsoft, the dominant force in the technology industry, is committed to creating and marketing electronic books. E-books can be viewed on any PC or e-book reader, as well as most handheld PCs. If you wish to purchase a hard-copy version of a book, it will be charged via e-commerce, then printed on your personal high-speed printer.

MAIL AT THE SPEED OF LIGHT

Jokes about the pace of postal delivery will gradually disappear as the Internet matures. Most of what we now know as mail and junk mail will travel electronically over the superhighway. This includes bills, stock summaries, and anything else that can be delivered more cost effectively and quickly over the Net. Personally, we already send e-mail (versus business or personal letters), greeting cards, family photos, and much more over the Internet. Millions of people communicate in real time via instant messaging, which permits real-time interaction via text, audio, and/or video communications. Instant messaging is changing the way people interact in a business environment and is emerging as the preferred means of interoffice communication in many companies.

THE CASHLESS SOCIETY

Each weekday, the financial institutions of the world use business-to-business (B2B) to transfer more than one trillion dollars—that's $1,000,000,000,000! At a more personal level, we use ATMs, have our payroll transferred directly to our bank account, and are beginning to use smart cards (see Figure 12-11). Millions of people now pay utility bills, mortgage payments, and many other bills through automatic electronic bank drafts. E-commerce is exploding. The Internet may be the first step toward a *cashless society*. It provides the necessary link between individuals, businesses, and financial institutions.

If we should move toward a cashless society, the administrative work associated with handling money, checks, and credit transactions would be eliminated. We would no longer need to manufacture or carry money. Each purchase, no matter how small or large, would result in an immediate transfer of funds between buyer and seller. Think of it—rubber checks and counterfeit money would be eliminated. Moreover, with total e-commerce you would have a detailed and accurate record of all monetary transactions.

A cashless society is not feasible until mechanisms are in place to accommodate small retail transactions. That's beginning to happen. A federal task force has been formed to plan for the transition to **electronic money,** or **e-money.** Financial institutions are establishing alliances to prepare for the cashless society. The major players in information technology have agreed on a standard for the *electronic wallet*. The standard, the **electronic-commerce modeling language** (**ECML**), will enable people to make online purchases as easily as they would make in-store transactions in the retail store. With ECML, consumers will no longer need to enter personal information for each purchase. Appropriate information will be stored in an electronic wallet at controlled server facilities.

The use of e-money opens new doors for barter. For example, when payment is entirely electronic, it is administratively possible to pay for goods and services with very small amounts, called **micropayments.** If micropayments catch on, we might be charged each time we play a song, watch a video, or search a database. Micropayments may be a boon to e-commerce, as there are advantages to both seller and buyer. For example, rather than buy a CD for a single artist, you could subscribe to a plan that would let you pay a small amount, perhaps less than a penny a play, to play the songs of 150 artists.

Every day you see more evidence of the move toward e-money. For example, traditional gas pumps are being replaced with ones that accept credit cards—swipe the card and pump the gas. In Phoenix, bus fares can be paid with VISA or MasterCard. All riders have to do is swipe the card and take a seat. Many college students use prepaid debit cards to pay for sodas, photocopying, and concert tickets. One billion U.S. government entitlement checks are distributed electronically each month. Several banks offer a service that will allow a customer to transfer funds from his or her account to

FIGURE 12–11 THE MOVE TOWARDS A CASHLESS SOCIETY

SMART CARDS
Smart cards with their embedded processors can be "loaded" with e-money at an ATM in much the same way you might withdraw cash. Once loaded with e-money, the stored-value smart card can be used to make purchases. The amount of the purchase is transferred electronically from the card's memory to the retailer, thus reducing the card's stored value.

Courtesy of Samsung Electronics Co., Ltd.

THE FUTURE OF WALK-IN BANKING
This prototype Bank of America Financial Center in an Atlanta neighborhood is redesigned to accommodate the trend to greater use of e-money and with the latest in banking technology, such as Web-enabled ATMs, check imaging, and Automated Business Centers (ABCs), providing a one-stop shop where customers can find advice and solutions to help meet their financial needs.

Courtesy of Bank of America

that of someone else via e-mail. In the near future, credit cards may become obsolete. All we will need to do in the future to purchase a candy bar, whether at a vending machine or a checkout counter, is to press a button on our key ring remote to confirm the transaction and transfer the sale amount from our electronic wallet to the store's account. Any sales taxes will be transferred to the appropriate government agency. It looks like the change in your pocket may become collectible items within a very few years.

SHOP AT HOME

The Internet already provides a direct visual and electronic link to many mail-order companies and retail/wholesale establishments via B2C: business-to-consumer. Sales statistics indicate that more and more people are opting for the convenience and value of electronic shopping. It's no longer necessary to drive from store to store to seek a particular style of sneaker in your size. You can go online and get the sneaker you want, often, at a price that is well below that of the bricks-and-mortar stores. We can use our personal computer in conjunction with the Internet to select and purchase almost anything, from paper clips to airplanes. In some cases the items selected will be automatically picked, packaged, and possibly delivered to our doorstep. This type of service will help speed the completion of routine activities, such as grocery shopping, and leave us more time for leisure, travel, and the things we enjoy.

The Internet offers great promise for the retail and wholesale industry. Consider these advantages: a corner bicycle shop in Pomona, California, has access to millions of customers; stores never have to be closed; transactions are handled electronically; and sales and distribution can be done more cost-effectively. Goods frequently are sent directly from the manufacturer to the customer, eliminating the extra stop in traditional retailing.

E-COMMERCE EXPLOSION

The Internet and networking have made it possible for companies and organizations to cooperate via *business-to-business* (B2B) communication. Also, they are expanding their internal intranets to *extranets* and *VPNs* to better deal with an exploding demand for e-commerce. E-commerce can encourage electronic interchange with customers and suppliers and enable all concerned to do business better and more efficiently. E-commerce fosters intercompany cooperation, which helps all involved save money. E-commerce offers a means of electronic cooperation whereby organizations transfer a wide range of information, including e-money, orders, invoices, medical records, real-time POS sales information, and so on via computer networks.

E-commerce is eliminating the need to produce, send, record, and store billions of paper documents. Companies like Wal-Mart are following the trend to greater electronic communication with suppliers. When Wal-Mart computers detect low inventory for toothpaste, its computers communicate that need directly to supplier computers. Supplier computers then issue shipping orders to warehouse computers, and the supplier computers send invoices directly to Wal-Mart computers. Payment is issued via B2B: computer-to-computer.

E-commerce streamlines administrative duties by linking supplier to manufacturer, manufacturer to retailer, and field sales and retail outlets to corporate headquarters. It provides solutions to many common business problems: mountains of paperwork, lost orders, unnecessary delays, lost opportunities, staff overheads, postage costs, paper costs, and data security. This type of networking also provides organizations with greater control of the production, distribution, and payment processes. As these benefits become more widely known, B2B will eventually become standard in most organizations. This is important because intercompany electronic interchange changes the fundamental way that many people do their jobs. Already most organizations, large and small, are cooperating electronically, some to a greater extent than others.

HIGH-TECH VOTING AND POLLING

Local, state, and federal elections might not require an army of volunteers. Politicians might not have to worry about low voter turnout on a rainy Election Day. In the not-too-distant future we will record our votes over the National Information Infrastructure, or whatever our national network will be called. Such a system will reduce the costs of elections and encourage greater voter participation. Plus, we can avoid the confusion that surfaced in the 2000 election when the U.S. presidency hinged on legal opinions, voter recounts, butterfly ballots, and dimpled chads.

The state of Arizona's success with the Democratic presidential primary shows us that online voting by everyone in all elections may be only a matter of time. There was no confusion with the interface (the ballot), the accounting was computer-accurate, and the number of people voting in the election was five times the number in the previous election, which did not permit online voting.

Already television newscasters routinely sample the thinking of viewers by asking them to respond over the Internet. Eventually they will be able to tap the collective thinking of tens of thousands, even millions, of people in a matter of minutes. After they ask the questions, we at home will register our responses over the national network. Our responses will be sent immediately to a central computer for analysis, and the results reported almost instantaneously. In this way, television news programs will keep us abreast on a day-to-day basis of public opinion on critical issues and on attitudes toward political candidates. Many Web sites conduct ongoing polls, asking visitors to respond to timely questions. Results are updated and posted in real-time.

THE NATIONAL DATABASE

The evolution of the Internet will provide the electronic infrastructure needed to maintain a national database. A national database will be a central repository for all personal data for citizens. An individual would be assigned a unique identification number at birth. This ID number would replace the social security number, the driver's license number, the student identification number, and dozens of others. Eventually the ID number probably will be replaced by some kind of unique digital biometric signature, perhaps a fingerprint or iris scan (eye).

A national database would consolidate the personal data now stored on tens of thousands of manual and computer-based files. It could contain an individual's name, past and present addresses, dependent data, work history, medical history, marital history, tax data, criminal record, military history, credit rating and history, and so on. A national database has certain advantages.

A national database could provide the capability of monitoring the activities of criminal suspects; virtually eliminating welfare and food stamp fraud; quickly identifying illegal aliens; and making an individual's medical history available at any hospital in the country. The taking of the census would be done automatically each year (or even each month), rather than every 10 years. The national database would enable us to generate valuable information. Governments at all levels would have access to up-to-date demographic information they could use to optimize the use of our tax dollars. Medical researchers could use the information to isolate geographical areas with inordinately high incidences of certain illnesses. The Bureau of Labor Statistics could monitor real, as opposed to reported, employment levels on a daily basis. The information possibilities are endless.

The national database is among the most controversial information technology issues in that it offers tremendous benefits to society while posing opportunities for serious abuse. In the aftermath of the September 11, 2001 attack on America, the proposal for a more sophisticated national identification system is gaining momentum. A system with biometric identification, such as a digitized fingerprint, can ensure that you are who you say you are, whether you're attending a football game or checking in for a cross-country flight. Opponents of the national database claim it will lead to abuse and the erosion of personal privacy. However, recent polls have shown that people may be more willing to trade a certain level of their privacy for safety.

VIRTUAL REALITY

Imagine that your job is to monitor the operation of a vast telecommunications network. Cables snake underground and underwater. Data flow between communications satellites and earth and across wiring inside building walls. Now imagine that a graphic image of this vast grid and its data flows could be laid out below you, as you float above, an "infonaut" looking for the kink that is blocking service to millions of customers. Far below, you see a pulsing light. There's the problem. With a gestured command, you fix it—without leaving your office. That's the promise of virtual reality, and it's moving from computer fantasy to computer fact. In fact, telecommunications firms are already experimenting with such systems.

Virtual reality (VR) combines computer graphics with special hardware to immerse users in an artificial three-dimensional world, sometimes called a **virtual world.** Instead of passively viewing data or graphics on a screen, users can move about, handle "virtual" representations of data and objects, and get visual, aural, and tactile feedback. The audio, visual, and other stimuli for the virtual world vary, depending on what you do. In the world of computers, the term *virtual* refers to an environment that is *simulated by hardware and software* (for example, virtual memory, virtual department store).

VR Applications

Virtual reality was born in the late 1960s when the U.S. Air Force began experimenting with flight simulators. From there, the technology was picked up by NASA. Today, NASA and a number of universities and corporations are either developing or using virtual reality systems for a variety of applications (see Figure 12-12).

- *Architecture and computer-aided design.* Architects already have access to a number of commercial VR systems that let them conduct electronic "walkthroughs" of proposed buildings.

- *Visualization of data.* NASA has created a virtual wind tunnel that lets a user climb inside an airstream. By gesturing with a data glove, the user can change the airflow and then walk around to experience it from different angles.

- *Exploration of hostile environments.* NASA is using raw data to create a VR version of an Antarctic lake bottom that will let researchers study life forms beneath the frigid waters without risk.

- *Sales.* A Japanese department store uses a "virtual kitchen" for planning custom-designed remodeling projects. After store personnel input a kitchen's existing layout and measurements using CAD software, customers don the VR gear and play around with different appliances, open drawers, turn on faucets, and visualize different arrangements.

- *Exercise.* Exercise bikes and massage chairs are finding a place in the virtual world. With the new lighter headgear, you can add adventure to your exercise as you cycle through virtual towns.

- *Training.* Flight training is one of the most sophisticated and oldest applications of VR. Here is found a world that's almost as realistic as the real world. Pilots can take the controls of a fully loaded passenger plane for their first flight because of the training they received in the simulator. VR researchers are creating VR training systems for firefighters, police officers, and others. Perhaps someday high school drivers' training classes will be conducted in virtual reality.

- *Education.* The learning experience through VR is truly active (versus passive). It allows students to experience first hand such things as life in a medieval village or walking among dinosaurs.

- *Psychology.* A California psychologist is experimenting with VR therapy for acrophobics (those who fear heights). Wearing a VR headset, a patient walks a plank, crosses a bridge, which spans water and hills, and accomplishes other acts that would instill fear. Over 90% of the patients now feel confident enough to climb ladders and cross the Golden Gate Bridge.

- *Virtual weddings.* A bride and groom can join their minister in a virtual world and say their vows amid a virtual re-creation of a significant historical venue, such as the lost city of Atlantis with its palaces, chariots, carousels, and even doves.

FIGURE 12–12 VIRTUAL REALITY IN OUR LIVES

FLIGHT SIMULATORS

This pilot is training in a flight simulator, one of the more mature applications of virtual reality. In the simulator, a pilot can be exposed to many challenging flying situations in a relatively short period of time.

DESIGNING AUTOMOBILES

For this engineer, showing up for work can be as much fun as going to the video arcade. But she's not playing games. She is experimenting with the use of virtual reality to help design cars for the future. This operator wears a helmet and goggles equipped with two small screens (see inset of the 3D image). A special glove fitted with sensors covers her right hand and allows her to manipulate objects during the design process.

Courtesy of Ford Motor Company

THRILLS WITHOUT SPILLS

Virtual reality takes this hang glider to the twenty-first century so he can fly among the skyscrapers of Los Angeles. Virtual hang gliders ride in an actual hang glider harness positioned in front of a box that contains an image generator displaying pictures of a futuristic Los Angeles.

Courtesy of Evans and Sutherland Computer Corporation

Dressing for Cyberspace

To enter the virtual world, users don special hardware for the feeling of total immersion in a three-dimensional world (see Figure 12-12).

● *Headpiece.* The goggles-like head-mounted display (HMD) blocks out visual sensations from the real world and substitutes images presented on *two small video screens*—one for each eye, creating a three-dimensional effect. The headpiece also contains *motion,* or *balance, sensors*—move your head and the computer will shift the view presented on the video screens. Just flip up the visor on your headpiece to see what is going on in the real world. Or, flip it down to enter the virtual world.

● *Headphones.* Headphones block out room noise and substitute three-dimensional *holophononic* sounds. Generally, the headphones are built into the helmet.

● *Data glove.* A data glove outlined with fiber optic sensors and cables completes the ensemble. The glove can be used, like a floating mouse, to "gesture" a command or to grasp and move virtual objects about.

Each piece of hardware is tethered to a computer via wireless or cable links to record the user's movements and provide real-time feedback.

Will the Promise Be Kept?

Virtual reality is still in its infancy, but the breadth and success of existing VR applications have shown us that VR will play an important role in the future. Although some VR applications can be run on PCs, the most realistic experiences are created with sophisticated and expensive computer systems. However, with hardware costs decreasing and software sophistication increasing, virtual reality may emerge as the user interface of the future.

Telemedicine: Networked Health Care

The term **telemedicine** was coined to describe any type of health care administered remotely over communications links. Already, many states are practicing telemedicine (see Figure 12-13). Facilities, such as doctors' offices, nursing homes, and prisons, are networked to regional medical centers. Sophisticated input/output hardware at remote sites, such as digital cameras and medical sensing devices, enable medical personnel and equipment to perform diagnostic procedures on patients.

Federal and state governments are optimistic that telemedicine has the potential to improve health care and reduce its spiraling cost. Recently a consortium of businesses and government agencies demonstrated telemedicine technology for members of Congress. The demonstration simulated a situation in which a car crash victim required doctors in different states to examine medical records, X-rays, and other images quickly. Congress was apparently impressed because millions of federal dollars are being targeted to foster telemedicine. Congress is hopeful that high-tech medicine can reduce overall health-care costs. To realize significant savings, telemedicine must overcome several hurdles. Medical facilities will need to standardize medical records storage and procedures for protection of personal information. Doctors who have been trained in conventional diagnostic methods and are uncomfortable with the high-tech methods will need to be convinced of its value.

Telemedicine has many applications. Mostly it is being used to distribute health-care capabilities to rural areas electronically. Also, it's used in the cities where many ambulances are equipped to administer telemedicine. By the time the ambulance arrives at the hospital, a doctor may have run preliminary diagnostic procedures via telemedicine. The military uses similar systems in the battlefield. As telemedicine matures, look for it to play a major role in home care of the elderly, eliminating the need for costly hospitalization.

THE EDUCATION REVOLUTION

Only recently has information technology begun to have an impact on traditional approaches to education. Our approach to education evolved with the industrial revolution—mass production with students (workers) in rows all doing the same thing at a pace dictated by the teacher (manager). Many

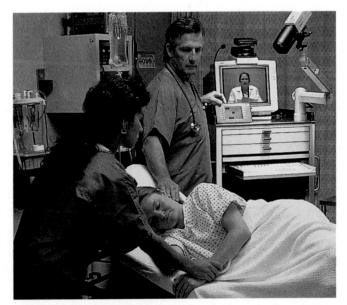

FIGURE 12–13 Telemedicine
This workstation, called F.R.E.D.™ (Friendly Rollabout Engineered for Doctors), is designed for use in health-care facilities such as hospitals, medical centers, clinics, and medical schools. F.R.E.D. provides a telemedicine solution for specialties such as cardiology that gives them virtual bedside access to their patients.

Photo courtesy of VTEL Corporation

educators are questioning the wisdom and effectiveness of traditional techniques in light of recent successes in technology-aided education. The computer has proven a marvelous tool for learning at all levels, from preschool to postgraduate continuing education (see Figure 12-14). The advantages are proving too vivid to ignore.

- Learning is interactive.
- Students can work at their own pace.
- Learning can take place anywhere, anytime, via communications links to available resources.
- Learning materials are more sophisticated (animation, 3-D images, hypermedia links, and so on).

Technology-aided education is being introduced rapidly at all levels of education. Many public school systems are looking to technology-aided education to improve the student/teacher ratio, raise test scores, and ease an ongoing budget crunch. Institutions of higher learning have introduced many ways to leverage information technology in education. Already, the online university is here and growing. You can obtain undergraduate and graduate degrees from reputable colleges and universities through online study. This type of program is sure to appeal to those who are unable to adjust their busy schedules to attend traditional classes. Some universities are using the technology to integrate the teaching of related topics. Rather than teach computers, finance, and ethics in separate courses, they are taught together in concert with applications.

The Internet offers the potential for nationwide uniform testing for elementary and secondary students. With uniform learning standards for each subject at each level, students will be able to advance from one grade to the next based on achievement rather than age. Computer-based uniform testing has another advantage. The system will monitor not only student progress but also the effectiveness of individual teachers and schools.

INTELLIGENT AGENTS AT WORK FOR YOU

Just as we begin to reach electronic saturation with instant messages, voice mail, Internet mailing lists, online newspapers, and so on, along come intelligent agents to help us cope with information overload. We provide *intelligent agents* or *bots,* which are software packages, with instructions detailing what to do. We then give them the authority to act on our behalf, just as we would a human agent. Intelligent agents, which are discussed in more detail in Chapter 10, roam around inside our computer systems, ready to help us whenever they can. They can bring urgent e-mails or instant messages to our attention, page us when our spouse leaves a voice-mail message, alert us to mailing-list messages that contain the keywords *kids* and *games,* and search all East Coast newspapers for articles mentioning *forest conservation.* They can remind us of important birthdays and even order the flowers.

Bots act as intermediaries, filtering the never-ending stream of information to give us only that which we need and want. Today's intelligent agents are still crude, but extremely helpful. We can expect a quantum leap in intelligent agent capabilities in the next five years. In the near future, you will be able to ask your intelligent agent to do some comparison shopping, then make recommendations on which digital camera offers the best value and where to buy it. Intelligent agents will alert us when our favorite music artists release a new album and even download a MP3 sampling of songs from the album. Within a few years, most of us will begin to rely on these cyberbutlers to bring order to our sometimes-hectic lives.

CARS AND THE AUTOMOBILE INDUSTRY GO HI-TECH

Every major manufacturer of automobiles in the world is planning to make computers and Internet access "standard equipment" in the automobile of the future (see Figure 12-15). Some high-end vehicles already have some built-in capabilities, such as the General Motors OnStar global positioning system, which can tell you where you are and how to get to where you are going. OnStar automatically phones police and ambulance services when air bags are deployed. The system can be used to make telephone calls, dinner reservations, and theater reservations, as well.

The soothsayers in Detroit tell us that in the not-too-distant-future we may get in our automobiles and verbally announce ourselves to the car so that it can recall and apply settings from our driver profile. For example, the seat and steering wheel would be repositioned, radio dials would be reset, even selected photographs would be displayed on the dashboard display, and other computer-related settings would be activated such as e-mail preferences, MP3 music play list, and Web site favorites. These automobiles will be continually connected to the Internet, giving us ready access to customized news, weather, stock quotes, thousands of radio stations, and other desired information,

FIGURE 12–14 TECHNOLOGY IN EDUCATION

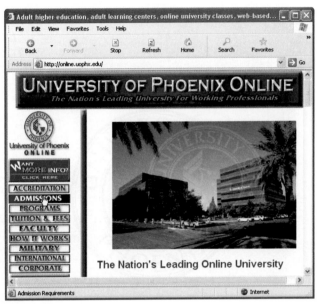

THE VIRTUAL UNIVERSITY
The University of Phoenix exists mostly in cyberspace but it has more students than any other university in the United States. Approximately 150,000 students pursue undergraduate and graduate degree programs via Web-based courses. Hundreds of traditional colleges now offer online courses, and an increasing number are beginning to offer online degrees. The barriers of time and place are eroding and opportunities to learn are everywhere.

THE TOOLS OF EDUCATION
High-tech tools, such as this tablet PC, may never replace paper and scissors in elementary schools; but each year, children spend more time interacting with technology-based learning tools.

Courtesy of Xybernaut

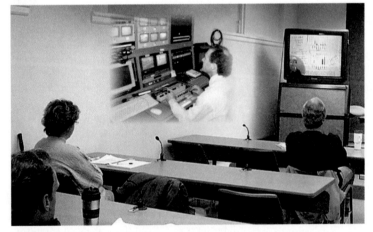

INTERNET2 CLASS
A broadcast technician (inset) controls the picture and sound for an innovative online botany class at Oregon State University. The online class is one of the first in the nation to use the high-speed Internet2 technologies. Internet2, the next generation Internet, is not yet widely available. Students say the class provides a deeper level of understanding because of the interaction between students and professors at several universities.

Copyright 2001 Oregon State University

FIGURE 12–15 AUTOMOBILE ENTERTAINMENT AND PRODUCTIVITY CENTER

THE CONNECTED CAR
The world is changing so quickly that it is difficult to speculate on what it will be like in five years. We know we can expect further integration of computers and cars. Automotive, computer, electronics, and communication industries are working together to develop computing platforms that provide drivers and passengers with an environment that is informative (GPS navigation), productive (cellular communications and onboard computer), entertaining (radio and TV data broadcast, video games), and connected via wireless Internet access.

Photos courtesy of Intel Corporation

IN-DASH WINDOWS-BASED COMPUTER
The Clarion AutoPC, shown here, is an in-dash Microsoft Windows CE-based computer system that integrates communication, navigation, information, and entertainment within an automobile. A navigator leads you to your destination through both visual and audio prompting. Clarion AutoPC's voice-activated control listens to you, so your eyes never have to leave the road.

Courtesy Clarion Corporation of America

via either textual/graphic displays or audio response. The onboard system will even read news and e-mails aloud, if you wish. Of course, auto-based systems will have infrared ports to let users share data with handheld PCs.

Automobile dealers and manufacturers are using IT for sales and service, too. It won't be long before you will be able to shop every showroom and new car lot in the country. You and other consumers will use a *configurator* to identify the exact car and features you want. Such an online system will allow you to pick any car, and then select the exact options you desire. Your cost is adjusted as you add and delete options. This inevitable system is more consumer-friendly. Already several Web sites enable consumers to configure cars with dealer suggested retail pricing. It's a natural extension of the system that will let you simultaneously submit your request to all dealers in a particular region. A fully automated response will include the exact price of the car and when you can expect delivery.

Three major automakers in the United States—General Motors, Ford, and DaimlerChrysler—have agreed to cooperate on an online auto parts exchange that will result in a half trillion dollars in spending by these companies and their suppliers.

THE EMERGING INTERNET

The Internet already offers a seemingly endless variety of services, but in reality, these are just the beginning. We can use our PCs to trade securities, but not all companies offer this service. We can take online courses, but not all colleges offer online degrees. We can view many online newspapers and periodicals, but for the most part, they are by-products of the printed version and have little interactivity. In a few years, you will be able to buy and sell securities with any brokerage company and pursue any degree at any major university. Printed versions of magazines may well be by-products of the online versions.

We can only speculate what amazing applications are coming to the cyberworld. We'll be able to adjust the temperature at home from any remote location. We will be able to view any movie ever made at any time. We'll even be able to talk with someone who is speaking a different language through an electronic interpreter (working prototypes are now in operation). Telecommunications, computers, and information services companies are jockeying for position to be a part of what forecasters predict will be the most lucrative industry of the twenty-first century—information technology.

12-3.1 The volume of traditional mail handled by the postal service is expected to decrease as the information superhighway begins to mature. (T/F)

12-3.2 Instant messaging is emerging as the preferred means of interoffice communication in many companies. (T/F)

12-3.3 What software tool can filter available information to give us only that which we want: (a) an intelligent manager, (b) an intelligent agent, (c) an intelligent diplomat, or (d) an intellectual agent?

12-3.4 The application that delivers video upon request is known as: (a) real video, (b) cybervideo, (c) video-on-demand, or (d) at-the-movies.

12-3.5 Typical VR hardware includes all but which of the following: (a) information vest, (b) data glove, (c) headpiece, or (d) headphones?

12-4 | Our Challenge for the Twenty-First Century

The technology revolution is in its infancy. Only recently are we as an information society beginning to comprehend its vast potential and the vast array of challenges we must overcome to realize its potential (see Figure 12-16).

THE VIRTUAL FRONTIER

We are living in and exploring a *virtual frontier*. The virtual frontier encompasses the electronic highways that comprise the Internet, thousands of newsgroups, scores of information services, and millions of private networks. Already this frontier is expanding to embrace other forms of communication, including television, radio, and cellular telephony.

The *virtual frontier* may be the last great frontier. Much of what lies beyond the virtual horizon is uncharted and potentially dangerous territory. Even so, wagon trains filled with brave pioneers set out each day to blaze new electronic trails. The virtual frontier is likened sometimes to the Wild West because there are few rules and people just keep coming. Responsible pioneers accept and live by society's traditional rules of behavior, but the seedier elements of society are quick to observe that there is no virtual sheriff.

It's difficult to fathom the hardships endured by nineteenth-century pioneers who headed West for a better life. Imagine a hardy pioneer woman pushing a Conestoga wagon through the mud while her husband coaxes their oxen to pull harder. The hardships along the electronic trails are not as physical or life-threatening, but they exist. We're still sloshing through the virtual mud in the virtual frontier. When we find a road, it's more like a trail or a roadway under construction than a highway. The highways that exist are narrow, filled with potholes, and have many detours.

The virtual frontier is growing in the same way the Wild West did. In the western frontier, cities grew from nothing overnight. In the virtual frontier, major services or capabilities unheard of a few years ago are becoming mainstream applications in the cyberworld. In the Wild West, many years passed before the ranchers and the farmers could be friends. Similarly, it might be some time before the various telecommunications, hardware, and software industries in the virtual frontier can become friends. Outlaws roamed the Wild West, creating havoc until law and order were established. Electronic outlaws may have their way in the virtual frontier, as well, until cybercops armed with strict cyberlaws drive them out of town.

The opportunity for a better life enticed pioneers to risk all and follow the setting sun. Eventually the Wild West was tamed, and they realized their dreams. The modern-day version of the Wild West presents us with the same opportunity. Bear in mind, though, that the information superhighway is truly a frontier that may not be tamed in the foreseeable future. The fact that it is a frontier, with all the associated risks, makes it even more exciting.

YOUR CHALLENGE

With your newly acquired base of information technology knowledge, you are now positioned to cope with our virtual frontier and enter the mainstream of our information society. However, the IT learning process is ongoing. The dynamics of rapidly advancing IT demands a constant updating of skills and expertise. By their very nature, computers and IT bring about change. With the total amount of computing capacity in the world doubling every two years, we can expect change that is even more dramatic in the future. Someday in the not-too-distant future computers will be as commonplace in the home and office as telephones, and as commonplace on our person as wristwatches.

WHY THIS SECTION IS IMPORTANT TO YOU

An awareness of where technology, in general, and the Internet are in their evolution will help you to place their potential and the risks you accept when using IT and the Net in perspective. This perspective will better prepare you for the technology challenges in your future.

PERSONAL COMPUTING: The Notebook PC Goes on a Vacation We don't leave home without our notebook PC, the ultimate vacation accessory. We plan our trips and stops with mapping software. A global positioning system helps us navigate unfamiliar cities and locate sites along the way. Each day, we download pictures from the digital camera to the notebook for storage and viewing. The kids enjoy the notebook's gaming programs and we all enjoy watching DVD movies. Of course, the notebook PC is there for general personal computing tasks, as well. Every few days, we check our e-mail, but we ignore it until we return home.

FIGURE 12–16 SMALLER CHIPS MEANS SMALLER COMPUTERS

SMALLER, MORE POWERFUL CHIPS

Jack Kilby's first integrated circuit contained a single transistor. Tens of thousands of engineers around the world have built on Mr. Kilby's invention, such that each year our information society is the beneficiary of smaller, more powerful, cheaper chips. Tomorrow's integrated circuits will be manufactured on 300-millimeter wafers, enabling the more powerful chips to be installed in a greater variety of devices, many of which will be smaller, at lower costs.

Texas Instruments Incorporated

FASHIONABLY UNWIRED

This fashion show features runway models sporting wireless Internet technology products. The belt buckle on the model in the foreground is a wearable PC. Voice-recognition and a head-mounted display (over her right eye) enable communication with the PC. According to a recent national poll, more than half of American adults would, if given the choice, gladly carry around multiple wireless devices. The PC featured in this fashion show support digital cameras, GPS receivers, MP3 music files, and broadband streaming audio/video.

Courtesy of Charmed Technology

It's now apparent that we truly live in a global village. Technology has made it possible for us to communicate with someone on the other side of the world as easily as we would with someone in an adjacent building. International project teams work together via telecommunications to create and support products (from automobiles to video games) and services (from banking services to legal services). From now on, any country's national economy must be considered within the context of a world economy.

Many business traditions are vulnerable to IT: More people are telecommuting; company hierarchies are flattening out; the worker has greater visibility via the Internet and therefore greater mobility; methods of compensation are placing greater emphasis on innovation and productivity; the laws that govern commerce and intercompany relationships are under constant review; business processes are continually changing to integrate the latest innovations in technology; and the way we communicate is changing dramatically every few years. Are we that far away from a speech recognition-enabled wristwatch videophone?

So far, the cumulative effects of these changes have altered the basic constructs of society and the way we live, work, and play. PCs have replaced calculators and ledger books; e-mail and videoconferencing facilitate communication; word processing has eliminated typewriters; computer-aided design has rendered the drawing table obsolete; e-commerce may eventually eliminate the need for money; online shopping is affecting consumer buying habits; the Internet has opened the doors of many virtual universities. . . and the list goes on.

We as a society are, in effect, trading a certain level of computer and IT dependence for an improvement in the quality of life. However, this improvement in the way we live is not a foregone conclusion. Just as our highways play host to objectionable billboards, carjackings, and automobile accidents, the information highways are sure to have back roads lined with sleaze, scams, and cyberthiefs. It is our challenge to harness the immense power of information technology and our wired world so we can direct it toward the benefit of society.

Never before has such opportunity presented itself so vividly. This generation, *your generation*, has the technological foundation and capability of changing dreams into reality.

12-4.1 A decade ago the virtual frontier was like the Wild West, but now it is tamed and tightly controlled by law. (T/F)

12-4.2 E-commerce may eventually eliminate the need for: (a) folding money and coins, (b) intercompany networking, (c) e-money, or (d) VPNs.

12-1 CAREERS IN AN INFORMATION SOCIETY

If you are planning a career as an IT specialist, opportunities remain excellent. Almost every company employs or contracts with IT specialists. IT workers are in demand not just for their skills but also for what they contribute to the organization.

Some of the more visible information technology jobs include **chief information officer (CIO)**, **systems analyst, applications programmer, programmer/analyst, network administrator, system programmer, database administrator (DBA), Internet site specialist, Webmaster, computer operator,** and **user liaison.** The variety and types of IT specialist jobs are ever changing.

An implied responsibility to maintain the integrity of a system and its data accompanies IT jobs; however, licensing or certification is usually not a requirement for any IT professional. However, certification offers career advantages. The Institute for Certification of Computer Professionals (ICCP) awards the *Certified Computing Professional (CCP)* and the *Associate Computing Professional (ACP)*. Microsoft Corporation offers these certificates for IT professionals: *Microsoft Certified Professional (MCP), Microsoft Certified Systems Administrators (MCSA), Microsoft Certified Systems Engineer (MCSE), Microsoft Certified Database Administrator (MCDBA), Microsoft Certified Trainers (MCT), Microsoft Certified Application Developers (MCAD), Microsoft Certified Solution Developer (MCSD), Microsoft Office Specialist,* and *Microsoft Office Specialist Master Instructor*. Novell Corporation offers these certifications: *Certified Novell Administrator (CAN), Certified Novell Engineer (CNE), Master CNE, Certified Directory Engineer (CDE), Certified Novell Instructor (CNI),* and *Novell Authorized Instructor (NAI)*. Sun Microsystems offers several Java-related certifications.

Information technology competency is becoming a prerequisite for people pursuing almost any career. Career mobility is directly related to an individual's current and future knowledge of computers and IT.

IT solutions have caused all or at least part of many job functions to be replaced with automated systems, but IT is responsible for the creation of many other jobs.

Whether you are entering the job market for the first time or seeking alternative employment, resources on the Internet can help you find work. The online jobs search has revolutionized the way job seekers and companies find each other.

12-2 ROBOTS AND ROBOTICS

To date the area of artificial intelligence (AI) having the greatest impact on our society is **robotics,** the field of study that deals with creating robots. Most applications of robotics are in manufacturing and the use of *industrial robots*. Industrial robots are quite good at repetitive tasks and tasks that require precision movements, moving heavy loads, and working in hazardous areas.

The most common industrial robot has a single mechanical arm, called a manipulator, which can be fitted with a variety of hands for painting, welding, and so on. Roboticists are outfitting robots with artificial intelligence and human sensory capabilities, such as vision, that enable them to simulate human behavior. Some robots have navigational capabilities.

12-3 LOOKING AHEAD: FUTURE APPLICATIONS OF IT

The information superhighway is a network of high-speed data communications links that eventually will connect virtually every facet of our society.

During the next decade, computers will be built into our domestic, working, and external environments. Eventually we will talk to our computers within our smart homes. They will help us perform many duties around the house.

A wide range of information and telecommunication services is now available for the Internet and many more are planned. These applications include video communication, video-on-demand, interactive television, virtual libraries, e-publishing, multimedia catalogs, **electronic money (e-money)**, total e-commerce, electronic voting and polling, a national database, **telemedicine**, using configurators to buy cars online, and much more. Professional gaming is gaining steam. Technology-aided education is being introduced rapidly at all levels of education. Intelligent agents, or bots, act as intermediaries, filtering the never-ending stream of information to give us only that which we need and want.

There is now a standard for the **electronic wallet,** the **electronic-commerce modeling language (ECML)**, which ultimately will let us purchase items electronically from retail stores. When payment is entirely electronic, it is possible to pay for goods and services with very small amounts, called **micropayments**. The cashless society may be on the horizon.

Virtual reality (VR) combines computer graphics with special hardware to immerse users in an artificial three-dimensional world, sometimes called a **virtual world.** In IT parlance, the term "virtual" refers to an environment that is simulated by hardware and software. To enter the three-dimensional virtual world, users don special hardware, including a headpiece, headphones, and a data glove.

Eventually the Internet will enable people of all walks of life to interact with just about anyone else, with institutions, with businesses, and with vast amounts of data and information. However, it must be significantly improved to realize its promise.

12-4 OUR CHALLENGE FOR THE TWENTY-FIRST CENTURY

The virtual frontier encompasses the electronic highways that comprise the Internet, thousands of newsgroups, scores of information services, and millions of private networks. It is likened sometimes to the Wild West because there are no rules. The opportunity for a better life is enticing pioneers to explore the virtual frontier.

The computer and IT offer you the opportunity to improve the quality of your life. It is your challenge to harness the power of the computer and direct it to the benefit of society.

KEY TERMS

applications programmer (p. 450)
chief information officer (CIO) (p. 450)
computer operator (p. 451)
database administrator (DBA) (p. 451)
electronic money (e-money) (p. 466)
electronic-commerce modeling language
  (ECML) (p. 466)

Internet site specialist (p. 451)
micropayment (p. 466)
network administrator (p. 451)
programmer/analyst (p. 450)
robotics (p. 456)
system programmer (p. 451)
systems analyst (p. 450)

telemedicine (p. 471)
user liaison (p. 451)
virtual reality (VR) (p. 469)
virtual world (p. 469)
Webmaster (p. 451)

MATCHING

1. robotics
2. Master CNE
3. e-money
4. America Online
5. industrial robot
6. telemedicine
7. CIO
8. VR
9. manipulator
10. MCP
11. Webmaster
12. online candidates database
13. systems analyst
14. e-publishing
15. user liaison

a. artificial three-dimensional world
b. "live-in" IT specialist
c. remote health care
d. good at repetitive tasks
e. a Novell certification
f. robot arm
g. monitors Internet traffic
h. e-books
i. a Microsoft certification
j. founded in 1985
k. responsible for all the information services activity
l. enables cashless transactions
m. ranked as one of the best jobs
n. contains résumés
o. study that deals with creating robots

CHAPTER SELF-CHECK

12-1.1 In general, IT workers are more productive than workers in other areas. (T/F)

12-1.2 Automation does not eliminate jobs. (T/F)

12-1.3 At present, certification is not a requirement to become an IT professional. (T/F)

12-1.4 The director of information services within an organization is called the: (a) DBA, (b) Webmaster, (c) network administrator, or (d) CIO.

12-1.5 The "live-in" IT specialist who coordinates computer-related activities within a particular functional area is called a: (a) user liaison, (b) computer operator, (c) CIO, or (d) Internet site specialist.

12-1.6 Which certification recognizes advanced skills with Microsoft Office desktop software: (a) MCDBA, (b) CDE, (c) Novell Authorized Instructor, or (d) Microsoft Office Specialist?

12-1.7 The focus of certification programs from Sun Microsystems is what programming language: (a) Visual BASIC, (b) Java, (c) Perl, or (d) COBOL?

12-1.8 The career/employment Web sites offer all but which of these types of resources and services: (a) jobs database, (b) job search capability, (c) career resources, or (d) college degree programs?

12-2.1 Industrial robots offer the potential for increased productivity and better service. (T/F)

12-2.2 All robots are stationary. (T/F)

12-2.3 Robots are used in brain surgery. (T/F)

12-2.4 Robotics is an area of: (a) AI, (b) human factors, (c) ergonomics, or (d) remote navigation.

12-2.5 Industrial robots are equipped with a variety of industrial tools that include all of these except: (a) drills, (b) paint guns, (c) welding torches, or (d) pagers.

12-3.1 A national database was approved by Congress and implemented in 1998. (T/F)

12-3.2 Some cellular phones have built-in digital cameras that let us take and send pictures. (T/F)

12-3.3 Internet gaming has begun its decline now that Generation Xers are entering the work force. (T/F)

12-3.4 E-commerce has actually increased the paper flow between cooperating companies. (T/F)

12-3.5 All of these are advantages of online media over print media except: (a) it is interactive, (b) it is linked, (c) it offers text-to-video, or (d) it offers multimedia content.

12-3.6 When health care is administered remotely over communications links, we call it: (a) telemedicine, (b) cybermedicine, (c) health-care magic, or (d) telehealth.

12-3.7 An artificial environment made possible by hardware and software is known as: (a) virtual planet, (b) near reality, (c) virtual reality, or (d) cyberrealism.

12-3.8 Money as we know it may soon be replaced by: (a) e-money, (b) electronic greenbacks, (c) cybercash, or (d) Eurodollars.

12-3.9 A national database has all but which of the following advantages: (a) virtual elimination of welfare fraud, (b) can monitor criminal suspect activities, (c) enables an annual census, or (d) elimination of all abuse of personal information?

12-4.1 The information highway is well-explored and would no longer be considered a frontier. (T/F)

12-4.2 The total computing capacity in the world is increasing at slightly less than 5% per year. (T/F)

12-4.3 A metaphor frequently used as a reference to the wired world is: (a) cyberway, (b) virtual way, (c) information superhighway, or (d) NINI.

IT ETHICS AND ISSUES

MORAL FILTERING OF INTERNET CONTENT

There has been considerable debate in the cyber community among organizations that set policy for the Internet about whether these organizations should provide some level of moral filtering of Web site content and applications. For example, one site published the names of British Intelligence agents, thus putting their lives at risk. Another lists doctors who perform abortions, then crosses them off as they are killed. Then, of course, there is the issue of easily accessible pornography, which currently comprises 1.5% of Internet content.

   Discussion: *What role, if any, should be played by Internet policy-making organizations regarding the assessment of the Internet content and applications?*

   Discussion: *If possible, should cooperative international legislation be enacted to better control access to pornographic content on the Internet?*

PRESCREENING OF ONLINE COMMUNICATIONS

Millions of people have access to and participate in newsgroups, chat rooms, and online forums. Some sponsors and information services feel obligated to give their subscribers an environment that is free of offensive language. These organizations use an electronic scanner to "read" each message before it is posted to a newsgroup or forum. In a split second the scanner flags those words and phrases that do not comply with the information service's guidelines. The scanner even catches words or phrases that may be disguised with asterisks and so on. Generally, the guidelines are compatible with accepted norms in a moral society. These include the use of grossly repugnant material, obscene material, solicitations, and threats. The scanner also scans for text that may be inappropriate for a public discussion, such as the use of pseudonyms, attempts at trading, presentation of illegal mate-rial, and even speaking in foreign languages. Messages that do not pass the prescreening process are returned automatically to the sender.

   Some might cry that their rights to freedom of expression are violated. This, of course, is a matter that may ultimately be decided in a court of law. In the meantime, those who wish a more open discussion have plenty of opportunities. On most international newsgroups and information services, anything goes.

   Discussion: *Is prescreening of electronic communications a violation of freedom of expression?*

   Discussion: *What are the advantages and disadvantages of prescreening online communications from the user's perspective? From the perspective of the organization doing the prescreening?*

INAPPROPRIATE USE OF THE INTERNET AT WORK

Internet usage monitoring at the workplace has revealed what many workers already know, at least some of the Internet surfing is not job related (more than half at the U.S. Internal Revenue Service). Most of this surfing is treated much like nonbusiness telephone calls, such as a call home or to confirm a doctor's appointment. However, management is getting involved when abuse is extensive or "inappropriate" material is viewed or downloaded on company PCs. Although corporate policy on such actions may be nonexistent or unclear, some people are losing their jobs.

   Discussion: *What would be appropriate punishment, if any, for an employee who, against company policy, downloaded and kept "inappropriate" material on his or her PC?*

   Discussion: *What punishment is appropriate for an employee who abuses his or her Internet connection by doing non-job-related surfing at least one hour per day?*

DISCUSSION AND PROBLEM SOLVING

12-1.1 Each year, the IT labor shortage places pressure on the U.S. Congress to open the immigration door for more skilled foreign workers. Those who argue for more visas say that companies in the United States will be unable to fill high-tech jobs from the existing pool of college graduates. There is a group of people who want to protect those jobs and salary levels for American workers and they say that the job shortage may be overstated. Argue for or against allowing greater numbers of foreign IT workers into the United States.

12-1.2 If you plan to pursue an IT career, describe your ideal career path. Or, if you plan to pursue a non-IT career, speculate on how being IT competent might affect your level of success in your chosen career.

12-1.3 Contrast the skills needed to be a good systems analyst with those required to be a good Webmaster.

12-1.4 Relatively few computer professionals have any kind of certification. Is certification really necessary?

12-2.1 Industrial robots are performing tasks formerly done by hundreds of thousands of human beings. Should something be done to curtail this worldwide loss of jobs? Explain.

12-2.2 Industrial robots hands can be outfitted with many tools for painting, welding, and so on. Describe at least two other tools appropriate for industrial robots with manipulator arms.

12-2.3 Robots with navigational capabilities are used routinely in health care and warehousing. In what other industry do you envision the use of mobile robots? Describe what they will be doing.

12-3.1 Continue the story line in the scenario depicted in Figure 12-10 by speculating on other futuristic applications.

12-3.2 Argue for or against a cashless society.

12-3.3 Already, thousands of people choose to do their grocery shopping electronically from their PCs. Typically, groceries are selected, packaged, and delivered to their doorsteps for a charge of about $6 to $8 for orders of more than $100. Would you consider virtual grocery shopping under these circumstances? Why or why not?

12-3.4 Would you feel comfortable voting in a national election via an online link from your home or would you prefer to do it the old-fashioned way? Explain.

12-3.5 A national database would consolidate personal information from scores of databases containing information about you (medical, demographic, work history, and so on). Discuss the upside and the downside of implementing a national database.

12-3.6 Describe the advantages and disadvantages of video-on-demand, a future information superhighway application.

12-3.7 Briefly describe the technology that is expected to replace the telephone over the next few years.

12-3.8 Virtual reality enables us to roam around an artificial world. Discuss the upside and the downside of VR.

12-3.9 Speculate on possible applications for virtual reality in education. In retail. In the government.

12-3.10 Describe at least one scenario where e-publishing might be expected to replace, at least partially, hard-copy publishing.

12-3.11 Describe at least two modern-day applications that support the trend toward a cashless society.

12-3.12 Discuss what types of information might be transferred between a retailer and its suppliers via B2B.

12-3.13 Describe how you think technology-based education will change elementary education by the year 2010. By the year 2020.

12-3.14 Describe how you think technology-based education will change college education by the year 2010. By the year 2020.

12-3.15 On the Web, there's a saying, "no one knows you're a dog," meaning people can remain anonymous. But in the world of e-commerce, your very business may depend on your ability to discern paying customers from the dogs. What can be done to better target Web marketing efforts?

12-4.1 List as many terms or phrases as you can that have been used to refer to our wired world.

12-4.2 Currently the Internet is open and all types of information flow freely, including pornographic text and images. A law enforcement official in Florida calls the Internet a "pedophile's playground." One of the most important issues facing the information superhighway is censorship. Argue for or against censorship.

12-4.3 The federal government is calling for "universal service" such that everyone has access to the "information superhighway." Is this an achievable goal?

12-4.4 Information technology is touching all aspects of your life. Are you prepared for it? Explain.

FOCUS ON PERSONAL COMPUTING

1. Create a pie chart or bar chart that illustrates your current personal computing habits. In the chart, show estimates of what percentage of your personal computing time is spent surfing the Web for no particular reason, surfing the Web for specific information or services, working with office productivity software, engaging in online communication (e-mail, instant messaging, and so on), and doing miscellaneous activities.

2. Within the realm of personal computing, describes three things that you have not done but would like to do.

INTERNET EXERCISES @ www.prenhall.com/long

1. The Online Study Guide (multiple choice, true/false, matching, and essay questions)
2. Internet Learning Activities
   • Jobs
   • New Technology
   • Virtual Reality
3. Serendipitous Internet Activities
   • Worst and Best

Answers to the Section, Chapter, and IT Illustrated Self-Checks

CHAPTER 1

Section Self-Check

1-1.1 A
1-1.2 B
1-1.3 C

1-2.1 F
1-2.2 A
1-2.3 T

1-3.1 T
1-3.2 B
1-3.3 A

1-4.1 T
1-4.2 B
1-4.3 C
1-4.1 F
1-4.2 F
1-4.3 A
1-4.4 D
1-4.5 D
1-4.6 B

1-5.1 T
1-5.2 T
1-5.3 A

1-6.1 T
1-6.2 F
1-6.3 A
1-6.4 D

Matching

1 N
2 O
3 C
4 M
5 L
6 K
7 H
8 F
9 G
10 A
11 J
12 D
13 B
14 I
15 E

Chapter Self-Check

1-1.1 A
1-1.2 C
1-1.3 F

1-2.1 A
1-2.2 C
1-2.3 D

1-3.1 F
1-3.2 C
1-3.3 B

1-4.1 T
1-4.2 F
1-4.3 F
1-4.4 B
1-4.5 F

1-5.1 F
1-5.2 T
1-5.3 B
1-5.4 C
1-5.5 B

1-6.1 F
1-6.2 T
1-6.3 A
1-6.4 C
1-6.5 F

1-7.1 T
1-7.2 B
1-7.3 D
1-7.4 D
1-7.5 T
1-7.6 A
1-7.7 T

IT Illustrated

1 T
2 T
3 F
4 T
5 T
6 B
7 C
8 A
9 B
10 D

CHAPTER 2

Section Self-Check

2-1.1 T
2-1.2 B
2-1.3 D
2-1.4 T
2-1.5 A
2-1.6 B
2-1.7 T
2-1.8 B

2-2.1 F
2-2.2 F
2-2.3 D
2-2.4 D
2-2.5 C
2-2.6 T

2-3.1 F
2-3.2 A
2-3.3 T
2-3.4 T
2-3.5 C
2-3.6 A
2-3.7 T
2-3.8 B
2-3.9 B
2-3.10 F
2-3.11 A
2-3.12 B
2-3.13 B

2-4.1 A
2-4.2 C
2-4.3 A
2-4.4 T
2-4.5 T

Matching

1 D
2 K
3 F
4 L
5 E
6 C
7 I
8 N
9 M
10 O
11 A
12 H
13 G
14 J
15 B

Chapter Self-Check

2-1.1 F
2-1.2 F
2-1.3 B
2-1.4 F
2-1.5 C
2-1.6 F
2-1.7 C
2-1.8 C
2-1.9 B
2-1.10 T
2-1.11 F
2-1.12 F
2-1.13 D
2-1.14 D

2-2.1 T
2-2.2 F
2-2.3 F
2-2.4 C
2-2.5 D
2-2.6 T
2-2.7 D
2-2.8 F

2-3.1 T
2-3.2 T
2-3.3 D
2-3.3 C
2-3.5 B
2-3.6 T
2-3.7 T
2-3.8 T
2-3.9 T
2-3.10 C
2-3.11 A
2-3.12 F
2-3.13 T
2-3.14 F
2-3.15 T
2-3.16 C
2-3.17 C
2-3.18 D
2-3.19 F
2-3.20 F
2-3.21 T
2-3.22 D

2-3.23 A
2-3.24 D
2-3.25 D
2-3.26 T
2-3.27 B
2-3.28 T

2-4.1 C
2-4.2 B
2-4.3 A
2-4.4 C
2-4.5 B
2-4.6 C
2-4.7 B
2-4.8 D
2-4.9 D
2-4.10 T

CHAPTER 3

Section Self-Check
3-1.1 F
3-1.2 T
3-1.3 A
3-1.4 A
3-1.5 B
3-1.6 D
3-1.7 F

3-2.1 T
3-2.2 B
3-2.3 D
3-2.4 A
3-2.5 F

3-3.1 T
3-3.2 F
3-3.3 C
3-3.4 D
3-3.5 B
3-3.6 C

Matching
 1 F
 2 H
 3 B
 4 A
 5 L
 6 K
 7 O
 8 D
 9 C
10 N
11 M
12 J
13 G
14 I
15 E

Chapter Self-Check
3-1.1 T
3-1.2 T
3-1.3 F
3-1.4 F
3-1.5 F
3-1.6 A
3-1.7 C
3-1.8 B
3-1.9 A
3-1.10 B
3-1.11 B
3-1.12 A
3-1.13 B
3-1.14 B
3-1.15 F
3-1.16 B
3-1.17 D
3-1.18 F

3-2.1 F
3-2.2 F
3-2.3 C
3-2.4 B
3-2.5 D
3-2.6 D

3-3.1 T
3-3.2 T
3-3.3 T
3-3.4 B
3-3.5 C
3-3.6 C
3-3.7 B
3-3.8 B

CHAPTER 4

Section Self-Check
4-1.1 T
4-1.2 T
4-1.3 A
4-1.4 D
4-1.5 B

4-2.1 F
4-2.2 T
4-2.3 B
4-2.4 A
4-2.5 B

4-3.1 T
4-3.2 F
4-3.3 B
4-3.4 A
4-3.5 B

4-4.1 T
4-4.2 F
4-4.3 B
4-4.4 C

Matching
 1 N
 2 J
 3 O
 4 K
 5 M
 6 I
 7 A
 8 C
 9 L
10 E
11 D
12 G
13 F
14 H
15 B

Chapter Self-Check
4-1.1 F
4-1.2 F
4-1.3 F
4-1.4 A
4-1.5 B
4-1.6 C
4-1.7 A

4-2.1 T
4-2.2 T
4-2.3 F
4-2.4 D
4-2.5 A
4-2.6 C
4-2.7 B
4-2.8 A

4-3.1 F
4-3.2 F
4-3.3 T
4-3.4 D
4-3.5 A
4-3.6 C

4-4.1 F
4-4.2 F
4-4.3 F
4-4.4 C
4-4.5 C
4-4.6 D
4-4.7 C

IT Illustrated
 1 T
 2 F
 3 T
 4 C
 5 A
 6 D

CHAPTER 5

Section Self-Check
5-1.1 F
5-1.2 T
5-1.3 F
5-1.4 B
5-1.5 A

5-2.1 F
5-2.2 F
5-2.3 B
5-2.4 A
5-2.5 C

5-3.1 T
5-3.2 A
5-3.3 D
5-3.4 T
5-3.5 A

5-4.1 T
5-4.2 D
5-4.3 C
5-4.4 B

5-5.1 T
5-5.2 T
5-5.3 C

Matching
 1 G
 2 D
 3 O
 4 B
 5 E
 6 H
 7 A
 8 C
 9 L
10 K
11 J
12 N
13 M
14 I
15 F

Chapter Self-Check
5-1.1 T
5-1.2 F
5-1.3 T
5-1.4 F
5-1.5 C
5-1.6 D
5-1.7 B
5-1.8 D

5-2.1 F
5-2.2 T
5-2.3 T
5-2.4 F
5-2.5 T
5-2.6 T
5-2.7 F
5-2.8 T
5-2.9 T
5-2.10 T
5-2.11 C
5-2.12 B
5-2.13 A
5-2.14 D
5-2.15 C
5-2.16 B
5-2.17 C

5-3.1 T
5-3.2 T
5-3.3 T
5-3.4 T
5-3.5 A
5-3.6 B
5-3.7 B

5-4.1 F
5-4.2 F
5-4.3 F
5-4.4 F
5-4.5 T
5-4.6 A
5-4.7 A
5-4.8 D
5-4.9 A

5-5.1 F
5-5.2 T
5-5.3 F
5-5.4 F
5-5.5 C
5-5.6 A
5-5.7 D
5-5.8 B

CHAPTER 6

Section Self-Check
6-1.1 T
6-1.2 F
6-1.3 A
6-1.4 A
6-1.5 B
6-1.6 C

6-2.1 T
6-2.2 T
6-2.3 B
6-2.4 C
6-2.5 A

6-3.1 F
6-3.2 T
6-3.3 A
6-3.4 D
6-4.1 T
6-4.2 A

Matching
1 N
2 D
3 F
4 J
5 A
6 K
7 E
8 L
9 G
10 C
11 I
12 B
13 M
14 O
15 H

Chapter Self-Check
6-1.1 F
6-1.2 C
6-1.3 T
6-1.4 F
6-1.5 B
6-1.6 A
6-1.7 F
6-1.8 T
6-1.9 F
6-1.10 T
6-1.11 T
6-1.12 C
6-1.13 D
6-1.14 A
6-1.15 A

6-2.1 F
6-2.2 F
6-2.3 F
6-2.4 A
6-2.5 D
6-2.6 A
6-2.7 C
6-2.8 C
6-2.9 B
6-2.10 C
6-2.11 C
6-2.12 B

6-3.1 F
6-3.2 C
6-3.3 B
6-3.4 A
6-3.5 B
6-3.6 B

6-4.1 T
6-4.1 D

CHAPTER 7

Section Self-Check
7-1.1 T
7-1.2 F
7-1.3 B
7-1.4 C

7-2.1 T
7-2.2 F
7-2.3 F
7-2.4 C

7-3.1 T
7-3.3 F
7-3.3 D
7-3.4 A
7-3.5 B

7-4.1 C
7-4.2 T
7-4.3 C
7-4.4 D
7-4.5 C

Matching
1 M
2 E
3 O
4 C
5 K
6 N
7 L
8 G

9 J
10 B
11 F
12 D
13 I
14 H
15 A

Chapter Self-Check
7-1.1 F
7-1.2 T
7-1.3 T
7-1.4 C
7-1.5 A
7-1.6 B

7-2.1 T
7-2.2 F
7-2.3 F
7-2.4 T
7-2.5 A
7-2.6 C
7-2.7 A
7-2.8 A

7-3.1 T
7-3.2 F
7-3.3 A
7-3.4 C
7-3.5 C
7-3.6 T
7-3.7 T
7-3.8 T
7-3.9 B
7-3.10 D

7-4.1 F
7-4.2 F
7-4.3 F
7-4.4 F
7-4.5 C
7-4.6 A
7-4.7 B
7-4.8 B

IT Illustrated
1 T
2 F
3 F
4 T
5 F
6 T
7 D
8 B
9 D
10 B
11 A

CHAPTER 8

Section Self-Check

8-1.1 F
8-1.2 F
8-1.3 C

8-2.1 T
8-2.2 F
8-2.3 A
8-2.4 B
8-2.5 A

8-3.1 T
8-3.2 F
8-3.3 C
8-3.4 B

8-4.1 T
8-4.2 C
8-4.3 A
8-4.4 D

8-5.1 F
8-5.2 T
8-5.3 A
8-5.4 C
8-5.5 A

Matching

1 N
2 L
3 M
4 K
5 J
6 F
7 G
8 C
9 H
10 O
11 B
12 D
13 A
14 E
15 I

Chapter Self-Check

8-1.1 F
8-1.2 F
8-1.3 C
8-1.4 A

8-2.1 T
8-2.2 F
8-2.3 F
8-2.4 T
8-2.5 F
8-2.6 C

8-2.7 D
8-2.8 B
8-2.9 D

8-3.1 F
8-3.2 F
8-3.3 T
8-3.4 F
8-3.5 C
8-3.6 A
8-3.7 C

8-4.1 T
8-4.2 F
8-4.3 T
8-4.4 D
8-4.5 A
8-4.6 B

8-5.1 F
8-5.2 F
8-5.3 A
8-5.4 D
8-5.5 C
8-5.6 D

CHAPTER 9

Section Self-Check

9-1.1 F
9-1.2 F
9-1.3 C
9-1.4 A

9-2.1 F
9-2.2 T
9-2.3 D
9-2.4 D

9-3.1 F
9-3.2 T
9-3.3 C
9-3.4 D

9-4.1 F
9-4.2 F
9-4.3 B
9-4.4 B

9-5.1 T
9-5.2 F
9-5.3 D
9-5.4 B

Matching

1 N
2 G
3 A

4 I
5 O
6 J
7 H
8 C
9 B
10 F
11 M
12 L
13 K
14 E
15 D

Chapter Self-Check

9-1.1 F
9-1.2 F
9-1.3 T
9-1.4 D
9-1.5 B

9-2.1 T
9-2.2 F
9-2.3 T
9-2.4 A
9-2.5 C
9-2.6 D
9-2.7 A

9-3.1 F
9-3.2 F
9-3.3 A
9-3.4 B
9-3.5 B

9-4.1 T
9-4.2 T
9-4.3 F
9-4.4 T
9-4.5 D
9-4.6 B

9-5.1 T
9-5.2 F
9-5.3 C
9-5.4 A
9-5.5 A

CHAPTER 10

Section Self-Check

10-1.1 T
10-1.2 T
10-1.3 D

10-2.1 F
10-2.2 T
10-2.3 T
10-2.4 D

10-3.1 F
10-3.2 T
10-3.3 C
10-3.4 C

10-4.1 F
10-4.2 T
10-4.3 B

10-5.1 F
10-5.2 T
10-5.3 B

10-6.1 T
10-6.2 F
10-6.3 B

10-7.1 T
10-7.2 D

Matching

1 G
2 M
3 I
4 C
5 F
6 A
7 E
8 J
9 H
10 K
11 N
12 B
13 L
14 O
15 D

Chapter Self-Check

10-1.1 F
10-1.2 F
10-1.3 B

10-2.1 T
10-2.2 F
10-2.3 T
10-2.4 C
10-2.5 A

10-3.1 F
10-3.2 T
10-3.3 A
10-3.4 C
10-3.5 B

10-4.1 C
10-4.2 T
10-4.3 F

10-4.4 A
10-4.5 D

10-5.1 F
10-5.2 D
10-5.3 C
10-5.4 A

10-6.1 F
10-6.2 T
10-6.3 F
10-6.4 D

10-7.1 F
10-7.2 C
10-7.3 C

CHAPTER 11
Section Self-Check
11-1.1 F
11-1.2 F
11-1.3 B

11-2.1 T
11-2.2 F
11-2.3 B
11-2.4 A

11-3.1 T
11-3.2 T
11-3.3 B

11-4.1 F
11-4.2 A
11-4.3 A
11-4.4 D

11-5.1 T
11-5.2 F
11-5.3 B

11-6.1 T
11-6.2 F

11-6.3 D
11-6.4 D
11-6.5 A

Matching
 1 B
 2 E
 3 L
 4 N
 5 A
 6 I
 7 F
 8 C
 9 H
10 O
11 G
12 M
13 J
14 D
15 K

Chapter Self-Check
11-1.1 T
11-1.2 F
11-1.3 C
11-1.4 C

11-2.1 T
11-2.2 T
11-2.3 C
11-2.4 D

11-3.1 T
11-3.2 T
11-3.3 A
11-3.4 A

11-4.1 T
11-4.2 T
11-4.3 B
11-4.4 B
11-4.5 C

11-5.1 F
11-5.2 T
11-5.3 A
11-5.4 B

11-6.1 F
11-6.2 T
11-6.3 F
11-6.4 A
11-6.5 C
11-6.6 B
11-6.7 C

CHAPTER 12
Section Self-Check
12-1.1 F
12-1.2 F
12-1.3 B
12-1.4 C

12-2.1 T
12-2.2 T
12-2.3 C
12-2.4 D

12-3.1 T
12-3.2 T
12-3.3 B
12-3.4 C
12-3.5 A

12-4.1 F
12-4.2 A

Matching
 1 O
 2 E
 3 L
 4 J
 5 D
 6 C
 7 K
 8 A

 9 F
10 I
11 G
12 N
13 M
14 H
15 B

Chapter Self-Check
12-1.1 T
12-1.2 F
12-1.3 T
12-1.4 D
12-1.5 A
12-1.6 D
12-1.7 B
12-1.8 D

12-2.1 T
12-2.2 F
12-2.3 T
12-2.4 A
12-2.5 D

12-3.1 F
12-3.2 T
12-3.3 F
12-3.4 F
12-3.5 C
12-3.6 A
12-3.7 C
12-3.8 A
12-3.9 D

12-4.1 F
12-4.2 F
12-4.3 C

GLOSSARY

1394 bus A recent bus standard that supports data transfer rates of up to 400 M bps, over 30 times faster that the USB bus. (See also *FireWire*.)

1394 port Enables connection to the 1394 (FireWire) bus.

Absolute cell address A cell address in a spreadsheet that always refers to the same cell.

Access arm The disk drive mechanism used to position the read/write heads over the appropriate track.

Access point A communications hub that enables a link to a LAN via short-range radio waves.

Access time The time between the instant a computer makes a request for a transfer of data from disk storage and the instant this operation is completed.

Accumulator The computer register in which the result of an arithmetic or logic operation is formed. (Related to *arithmetic and logic unit*.)

Active window The window in Microsoft Windows® with which the user may interact.

ActiveX controls A program that uses Microsoft's ActiveX technology that can be downloaded and executed by a browser to enable multimedia in Web pages. (See also *applet*.)

Address (1) A name, numeral, or label that designates a particular location in RAM or disk storage. (2) A location identifier for nodes in a computer network.

Address bus Pathway through which source and destination addresses are transmitted between RAM, cache memory, and the processor. (See also *data bus*.)

AGP (Accelerated Graphics Port) board A graphics adapter that permits interfacing with video monitors.

AGP bus A special-function bus designed to handle high-resolution 3-D graphics.

All-in-one peripheral device A peripheral device that handles several paper-related tasks: computer-based printing, facsimile (fax), scanning, and copying.

Alpha A reference to the letters of the alphabet. (Compare with *numeric* and *alphanumeric*.)

Alphanumeric Pertaining to a character set that contains letters, digits, punctuation, and special symbols. (Related to *alpha* and *numeric*.)

America Online (AOL) An online information service.

Analog signal A continuous waveform signal that can be used to represent such things as sound, temperature, and velocity. (See also *digital signal*.)

Animation The rapid repositioning of objects on a display to create movement.

Anonymous FTP site An Internet site that permits FTP (file transfer protocol) file transfers without prior permission.

ANSI The American National Standards Institute is a non-government standards-setting organization that develops and publishes standards for "voluntary" use in the United States.

Antivirus program A utility program that periodically checks a PC's hard disk for computer viruses then removes any that are found.

Applet A small program sent over the Internet or an intranet that is interpreted and executed by Internet browser software. (See also *ActiveX controls*.)

Application generator A system development tool used to actually generate the system programming code based on design specifications.

Application icon A miniature visual representation of a software application on a display.

Application window A rectangular window containing an open, or running, application in Microsoft Windows.

Applications programmer A programmer who translates analyst-prepared system and input/output specifications into programs. Programmers design the logic, then code, debug, test, and document the programs.

Applications service provider (ASP) An ASP is a company that provides software-based services and solutions to customers via the Internet from a central server computer.

Applications software Software designed and written to address a specific personal, business, or processing task.

Argument That portion of a function that identifies the data to be operated on.

Arithmetic and logic unit That portion of the computer that performs arithmetic and logic operations. (Related to *accumulator*.)

Arithmetic operators Mathematical operators (add [+], subtract [-], multiply [*], divide [/], and exponentiation [^]) used in programming and in spreadsheet and database software for computations.

Artificial intelligence (AI) The ability of a computer to reason, to learn, to strive for self-improvement, and to simulate human sensory capabilities.

ASCII [American Standard Code for Information Interchange] A 7-bit or 8-bit encoding system.

ASCII file A generic text file that is stripped of program-specific control characters.

Assembler language A programming language that uses easily recognized symbols, called mnemonics, to represent instructions.

Assistant system This knowledge-based system helps users make relatively straightforward decisions. (See also *expert system*.)

Assistive technology Enabling input/output peripherals and software for people with disabilities.

Asynchronous transmission A protocol in which data are transmitted at irregular intervals on an as-needed basis. (See also *synchronous transmission*.)

Attached file A file that is attached and sent with an e-mail message.

Audio file A file that contains digitized sound.

Audio mail An electronic mail capability that lets you speak your message instead of typing it.

Authoring system Software that lets you create multimedia applications that integrate sound, motion, text, animation, and images.

Automatic teller machine (ATM) An automated deposit/withdrawal device used in banking.

B2B (business-to-business) An e-commerce concept that encourages intercompany processing and data exchange via computer networks and the Internet. (Contrast with *B2C*.)

B2C (business-to-consumer) An e-commerce concept that encourages electronic interactions between businesses and consumers via Internet server computers. (Contrast with *B2B*.)

Backbone A system of routers and the associated transmission media that facilitates the interconnection of computer networks.

Back-end applications software This software on the server computer performs processing tasks in support of its clients, such as tasks associated with storage and maintenance of a centralized corporate database. (See also *front-end applications software*.)

Background (1) That part of RAM that contains the lowest priority programs. (2) In Windows, the area of the display over which the foreground is superimposed. (Contrast with *foreground*.)

Backup file Duplicate of an existing file.

Backup Pertaining to equipment, procedures, or databases that can be used to restart the system in the event of system failure.

Backward compatible Reference to a modern platform's ability to run programs written for legacy platforms.

Badge reader An input device that reads data on badges and cards.

Bandwidth Generally the range of frequencies in a communications channel or, specifically, the number of bits the channel can transmit per second.

Banner ad Horizontal Internet advertisement that entices users to click on them to link to the site being promoted.

Bar code A graphic encoding technique in which printed vertical bars of varying widths are used to represent data.

Bar code scanner A device that scans and interprets text and codes.

Bar graph A graph that contains bars that represent specified numeric values.

Batch processing A technique in which transactions and/or jobs are collected into groups (batched) and processed together.

Baud (1) A measure of the maximum number of electronic signals that can be transmitted via a communications channel. (2) Bits per second (common-use definition).

Binary A base-2 numbering system.

BIOS (Basic Input Output System) Flash memory-based software that contains the instructions needed to boot a PC and load the operating system.

Bit A binary digit (0 or 1).

Bit-mapped graphics Referring to an image that has been projected, or mapped, to a screen based on binary bits. (See also *raster graphics*.)

Bits per second (bps) The number of bits that can be transmitted per second over a communications channel.

BMP A popular format for bit-mapped files.

Boilerplate Existing text in a word processing file that can in some way be customized for use in a variety of word processing applications.

Bold A font presentation attribute that thickens the lines of a character.

Boot The procedure for loading the operating system to RAM and readying a computer system for use.

Bots See *intelligent agent*.

Broadband access Generic term for high-speed Internet access.

Broadband connection Typically, a reference to a high-speed Internet link via cable, satellite, or DSL.

Browsers Programs that let you navigate to and view the various Internet resources.

Bug A logic or syntax error in a program, a logic error in the design of a computer system, or a hardware fault. (See also *debug*.)

Bus An electrical pathway through which the processor sends data and commands to RAM and all peripheral devices.

Bus topology A computer network that permits the connection of terminals, peripheral devices, and microcomputers along an open-ended central cable.

Business-to-business See *B2B*.

Business-to-consumer See *B2C*.

Button bar A software option that contains a group of pictographs that represent a menu option or a command.

Byte A group of adjacent bits configured to represent a character or symbol.

C A transportable programming language that can be used to develop software.

C++ An object-oriented version of the C programming language.

Cache memory High-speed solid-state memory for program instructions and data.

CAD See *computer-aided design*.

Carpal tunnel syndrome (CTS) A repetitive-stress injury.

Carrier Standard-sized pin connectors that permit chips to be attached to a circuit board.

Cascading menu A pop-up menu that is displayed when a command from the active menu is chosen.

Cascading windows Two or more windows that are displayed on a computer screen in an overlapping manner.

Cathode-ray tube See *CRT*.

CBT See *computer-based training*.

CD production station A device used to duplicate locally produced CD-ROMs.

CD-R [Compact Disc-Recordable] The medium on which CD writers create CDs and CD-ROMs.

CD-ReWritable (CD-RW) This technology allows users to rewrite to the same CD media.

CD-ROM disc [CompactDisk Read-Only Memory disc] A type of optical laser storage media.

CD-ROM drive A storage device into which an interchangeable CD-ROM disc is inserted for processing.

CD-RW See *CD-ReWritable*.

Celeron A line of Intel®microprocessors designed for low-cost PCs.

Cell The intersection of a particular row and column in a spreadsheet.

Cell address The location—column and row—of a cell in a spreadsheet.

Central processing unit (CPU) See *processor*.

Centronics connector A 36-pin connector that is used for the electronic interconnection of computers, modems, and other peripheral devices.

CGM A popular vector graphics file format.

Channel The facility by which data are transmitted between locations in a computer network (e.g., terminal to host, host to printer).

Channel capacity The number of bits that can be transmitted over a communications channel per second.

Chat An Internet application that allows people on the Internet to converse in real time via text or audio.

Chief information officer (CIO) The individual responsible for all the information services activity in a company.

Chip See *integrated circuit*.

Chipset A motherboard's intelligence that controls the flow of information between system components connected to the board.

Choose To pick a menu item or icon in such a manner as to initiate processing activity.

CISC [Complex Instruction Set Computer] A computer design architecture that offers machine language programmers a wide variety of instructions. (Contrast with *RISC*.)

Click A single tap on a mouse's button.

Client application (1) An application running on a networked workstation or PC that works in tandem with a server application. (See also *server application*.) (2) In object linking and embedding, the application containing the destination document. (See also *OLE*.)

Client computer Typically a PC or a workstation that requests processing support or another type of service from one or more server computers. (See also *server computer*.)

Client program A software program that runs on a PC and works in conjunction with a companion server program that runs on a server computer. (See also *server program*.)

Client/server computing A computing environment in which processing capabilities are distributed throughout a network such that a client computer requests processing or some other type of service from a server computer.

Clip art Prepackaged electronic images that are stored on disk to be used as needed in computer-based documents.

Clipboard An intermediate holding area in internal storage for information en route to another application.

Clone A hardware device or a software package that emulates a product with an established reputation and market acceptance.

Cluster The smallest unit of disk space that can be allocated to a file.

Coaxial cable A shielded wire used as a medium to transmit data between computers and between computers and peripheral devices.

COBOL [Common Business Oriented Language] A third-generation programming language designed to handle business problems.

Code (1) The rules used to translate a bit configuration into alphanumeric characters and symbols. (2) The process of compiling computer instructions into the form of a computer program. (3) The actual computer program.

Color depth The number of bits used to display each pixel on a display.

Command An instruction to a computer that invokes the execution of a preprogrammed sequence of instructions.

Common carrier A company that provides channels for data transmission.

Communications channel The facility by which data are transmitted between locations in a computer network.

Communications protocols Rules established to govern the way data in a computer network are transmitted.

Communications server The LAN component that provides external communications links.

Communications software (1) Software that enables a microcomputer to emulate a terminal and to transfer files between a micro and another computer. (2) Software that enables communication between remote devices in a computer network.

Compact disc-recordable See *CD-R*.

Compatibility Pertaining to the ability of computers and computer components (hardware and software) to work together.

Compile To translate a high-level programming language into machine language in preparation for execution.

Compiler A program that translates the instructions of a high-level language to machine language instructions that the computer can interpret and execute.

Compound document A document, such as a word processing document, that contains one or more linked objects from other applications.

CompuServe An online information service.

Computer An electronic device capable of interpreting and executing programmed commands for input, output, computation, and logic operations.

Computer-aided design (CAD) Use of computer graphics in design, drafting, and documentation in product and manufacturing engineering.

Computer-aided software engineering (CASE) An approach to software development that combines automation and the rigors of the engineering discipline.

Computer-based training (CBT) Using computer technologies for training and education.

Computer competency A fundamental understanding of the technology, operation, applications, and issues surrounding computers.

Computer literacy See *computer competency*.

Computer matching The procedure whereby separate databases are examined and individuals common to both are identified.

Computer monitoring Observing and regulating employee activities and job performance through the use of computers.

Computer network An integration of computer systems, terminals, and communications links.

Computer operator One who performs those hardware-based activities needed to keep production information systems operational in the server computer environment.

Computer system A collective reference to all interconnected computing hardware, including processors, storage devices, input/output devices, and communications equipment.

Computer virus See *virus*.

Computerese A colloquial reference to the language of computers and information technology.

Configuration The computer and its peripheral devices.

Connectivity Pertains to the degree to which hardware devices, software, and databases can be functionally linked to one another.

Context-sensitive Referring to an on-screen explanation that relates to a user's current software activity.

Control unit The portion of the processor that interprets program instructions, directs internal operations, and directs the flow of input/output to or from RAM.

Cookie A message given to your Web browser by the Web server being accessed. The cookie is a text file containing user preference information.

Cooperative processing An environment in which organizations cooperate internally and externally to take full advantage of available information and to obtain meaningful, accurate, and timely information. (See also *intracompany networking*.)

Coprocessor An auxiliary processor that handles a narrow range of tasks, usually those associated with arithmetic operations.

CPU See *processor*.

Cracker An overzealous hacker who "cracks" through network security to gain unauthorized access to the network. (Contrast with *hacker*.)

Cross-platform technologies Enabling technologies that allow communication and the sharing of resources between different platforms.

CRT [*Cathode-Ray Tube*] The video monitor component of a terminal.

Cryptography A communications crime-prevention technology that uses methods of data encryption and decryption to scramble codes sent over communications channels.

CSMA/CD access method [*Carrier Sense Multiple Access/ Collision Detection*] A network access method in which nodes on the LAN must contend for the right to send a message.

Cumulative trauma disorder (CTD) Repetitive motion disorders of the musculoskeletal and nervous systems that, often, are a result of poor workplace design.

Current window The window in a GUI in which the user can manipulate text, data, or graphics.

Cursor-control keys The arrow keys on the keyboard that move the cursor vertically and horizontally.

Cursor, graphics Typically an arrow or a crosshair that can be moved about a monitor's screen by a point-and-draw device to create a graphic image or select an item from a menu. (See also *cursor, text*.)

Cursor, text A blinking character that indicates the location of the next keyed-in character on the display screen. (See also *cursor, graphics*.)

Custom programming Program development to create software for situations unique to a particular processing environment.

Cyberphobia The irrational fear of, and aversion to, computers.

Cyberstalking Technology-based stalking where the Internet becomes a vehicle by which the stalker directs threatening behavior and unwanted advances to another person.

Cylinder A disk-storage concept. A cylinder is that portion of the disk that can be read in any given position of the access arm. (Contrast with *sector*.)

Data bits A data communications parameter that refers to a timing unit.

Data bus A common pathway between RAM, cache memory, and the processor through which data and instructions are transferred. (See also *address bus*.)

Data cartridge Magnetic tape storage in cassette format.

Data communications The collection and distribution of the electronic representation of information between two locations.

Data compression A method of reducing disk-storage requirements for computer files.

Data entry The transcription of source data into a machine-readable format.

Data file This file contains data organized into records.

Data flow diagram A design technique that permits documentation of a system or program at several levels of generality.

Data mining An analytical technique that involves the analysis of large databases, such as data warehouses, to identify possible trends and problems.

Data path The electronic channel through which data flows within a computer system.

Data processing (DP) Using the computer to perform operations on data.

Data processing (DP) system Systems concerned with transaction handling and record-keeping, usually for a particular functional area.

Data transfer rate The rate at which data are read/written from/to disk storage to RAM.

Data warehouse A relational database created from existing operational files and databases specifically to help managers get the information they need to make informed decisions.

Data warehousing An approach to database management that involves moving existing operational files and databases from multiple applications to a data warehouse.

Data/voice/fax/modem A modem that permits data communication with remote computers via a telephone-line link and enables telephone calls and fax machine simulation via a PC.

Data Representations of facts. Raw material for information. (Plural of *datum*.)

Database The integrated data resource for a computer-based information system.

Database administrator (DBA) The individual responsible for the physical and logical maintenance of the database.

Database software Software that permits users to create and maintain a database and to extract information from the database.

DDR SDRAM A "double data rate" SDRAM. (See also *SDRAM*.)

Debug To eliminate bugs in a program or system. (See also *bug*.)

Decision support system (DSS) An interactive information system that relies on an integrated set of user-friendly hardware and software tools to produce and present information targeted to support management in the decision-making process.

(Contrast with *management information system* and *executive information system*.)

Decode To reverse the encoding process. (Contrast with *encode*.)

Decoder That portion of a processor's control unit that interprets instructions.

Dedicated keyboard port A port built into the system board specifically for the keyboard.

Dedicated mouse port A port built into the system board specifically for the mouse or other similar device.

Default options Preset software options that are assumed valid unless specified otherwise by the user.

Defragmentation Using utility software to reorganize files on a hard disk such that files are stored in contiguous clusters.

Density The number of bytes per linear length or unit area of a recording medium.

Desktop The screen in Windows upon which icons, windows, a background, and so on are displayed.

Desktop PC A nonportable personal computer that is designed to rest on the top of a desk. (Contrast with *laptop PC* and *tower PC*.)

Desktop publishing software (DTP) Software that allows users to produce near-typeset-quality copy for newsletters, advertisements, and many other printing needs, all from the confines of a desktop.

Destination application, Clipboard The software application into which the Clipboard contents are to be pasted. (Contrast with *source application*.)

Detailed system design That portion of the systems development process in which the target system is defined in detail.

Device controller Microprocessors that control the operation of peripheral devices.

Device driver software Software that contains instructions needed by the operating system to communicate with the peripheral device.

Dialog box A window that is displayed when the user must choose parameters or enter further information before the chosen menu option can be executed.

Dialup connection Temporary modem-based communications link with another computer.

Dialup line See *switched line*.

Digicam See *digital camera*.

Digital A reference to any system based on discrete data, such as the binary nature of computers.

Digital camcorder Portable digital video camera.

Digital camera A camera that records images digitally rather than on film.

Digital certificate An attachment to an electronic message that verifies that the sender is who he/she claims to be.

Digital convergence The integration of computers, communications, and consumer electronics, with all having digital compatibility.

Digital ID A digital code that can be attached to an electronic message that uniquely identifies the sender.

Digital jukebox An Internet-based software application that enables the selection, management, and playing of Internet-based music.

Digital signal Electronic signals that are transmitted as in strings of 1s and 0s. (See also *analog signal*.)

Digital Subscriber Line See *DSL*.

Digital video camera A camera that enables the capture of motion video directly into a PC system (used for Webcam applications).

Digital video disc See *DVD*.

Digital video disc plus RW See *DVD+RW*.

Digitize To translate data or an image into a discrete format that can be interpreted by computers.

Digitizer tablet and pen A pressure-sensitive tablet with the same *x-y* coordinates as a computer-generated screen. The outline of an image drawn on a tablet with a stylus (pen) or puck is reproduced on the display.

DIMM [Dual In-line Memory Module] A small circuit board, capable of holding several memory chips, that has a 64-bit data path and can be easily connected to a PC's system board. (Contrast with *SIMM*.)

Dimmed A menu option, which is usually gray, that is disabled or unavailable.

Direct access See *random access*.

Direct-access storage device (DASD) A random-access disk storage.

Direct conversion An approach to system conversion whereby operational support by the new system is begun when the existing system is terminated.

Disc, optical A storage medium which uses lasers for the data read/write operations.

Disk address The physical location of a particular set of data or a program on a magnetic disk.

Disk caching A hardware/software technique in which frequently referenced disk-based data are placed in an area of RAM that simulates disk storage. (See also *RAM disk*.)

Disk defragmenter A utility program that consolidates files into contiguous clusters on a hard disk.

Disk density The number of bits that can be stored per unit of area on the disk-face surface.

Disk drive icon Graphical representation of a disk.

Disk drive, magnetic A magnetic storage device that records data on flat rotating disks. (Compare with *tape drive, magnetic*.)

Disk optimizer A program that reorganizes files on a hard disk to eliminate file fragmentation.

Disk, magnetic A storage medium for random-access data storage available in permanently installed or interchangeable formats.

Diskette A thin interchangeable disk for secondary random-access data storage (same as *floppy disk*).

Docking station A device into which a notebook PC is inserted to give the notebook PC expanded capabilities, such as a high-capacity disk, interchangeable disk options, a tape backup unit, a large monitor, and so on.

Document A generic reference to whatever is currently displayed in a software package's work area or to a permanent file containing document contents.

Document file The result when work with an applications program, such as word processing, is saved to disk storage.

Document icon A pictograph used by Windows within an application to represent a minimized document window.

Document window Window within an application window that is used to display a separate document created or used by that application.

Domain expert An expert in a particular field who provides the factual knowledge and the heuristic rules for input to a knowledge base.

Domain name That portion of the Internet URL following the double forward slashes (//) that identifies an Internet host site.

DOS [Disk Operating System] See MS-DOS.

Dot-matrix printer A printer that arranges printed dots to form characters and images.

Dot pitch The distance between the centers of adjacent pixels on a display.

Double-click Tapping a button on a point-and-draw device twice in rapid succession.

Download The transmission of data from a remote computer to a local computer.

Downsizing Used to describe the trend toward increased reliance on smaller computers for personal as well as enterprise-wide processing tasks.

Downstream rate The data communications rate from server computer to client computer.

Downtime The time during which a computer system is not operational.

DP See data processing.

Drag A point-and-draw device procedure by which an object is moved or a contiguous area on the display is marked for processing.

Drag-and-drop software Software that lets users drag ready-made shapes from application-specific stencils to the desired position on the drawing area to do drawings for flowcharting, landscaping, business graphics, and other applications.

Draw software Software that enables users to create electronic images. Resultant images are stored as vector graphics images.

Driver The software that enables interaction between the operating system and a specific peripheral device.

Driver module The program module that calls other subordinate program modules to be executed as they are needed (also called a main program).

DSL (Digital Subscriber Line) A digital telecommunications standard for data delivery over twisted-pair lines with downstream transmission speeds up to 9 M bps.

DSLAM (Digital Subscriber Line Access Multiplexor) A device that communications companies use to multiplex DSL signals to/from the Internet.

DTP See desktop publishing.

Dual in-line memory module See DIMM.

DVD (Digital video disc) The successor technology to the CD-ROM that can store up to about 8.5 gigabytes per side.

DVD+RW (Digital video disc plus RW) One of the rewritable standards for high-capacity DVD. (Contrast with DVD-RAM and CD-RW.)

DVD-R The capability to record data to a DVD disc. (Contrast with CD-R.)

DVD-RAM One of the rewritable standards for high-capacity DVD. (Contrast with CD-RW and CD+RW.)

DVD-ROM High-density read-only optical laser storage media.

DVD-RW One of the rewritable standards for high-capacity DVD. (Contrast with DVD-RAM and DVD+RW.)

DVD-Video DVD format for playing movies.

Dynamic IP address A temporary Internet address assigned to a user by an ISP.

EBCDIC [Extended Binary Coded Decimal Interchange Code] An 8-bit encoding system.

Echo A host computer's retransmission of characters back to the sending device.

ECML (electronic-commerce modeling language) A standard that will enable people to make online purchases via an electronic wallet.

E-commerce (electronic commerce) Business conducted online, primarily over the Internet.

E-commerce hosting service A company that creates and maintains e-commerce Web sites for a fee.

EDI See electronic data interchange.

Edutainment software Software that combines education and entertainment.

Electronic book An electronic version of a book (also called e-book).

Electronic commerce See e-commerce.

Electronic data interchange (EDI) The use of computers and data communications to transmit data electronically between companies.

Electronic dictionary A disk-based dictionary used in conjunction with a spelling-checker program to verify the spelling of words in a word processing document.

Electronic document See online document.

Electronic mail A computer application whereby messages are transmitted via data communications to "electronic mailboxes" (also called e-mail). (Contrast with voice message switching.)

Electronic messaging A workgroup computing application that enables electronic mail to be associated with other workgroup applications.

Electronic money (e-money) A payment system in which all monetary transactions are handled electronically.

Electronic publishing (e-publishing) The creation of electronic documents that are designed to be retrieved from disk storage and viewed.

Electronic ticket (e-ticket) An electronic alternative to the traditional paper ticket for airlines, movies, and so on.

Electronic trading (e-trading) Making online investments electronically through an online brokerage service.

Electronic wallet An electronic version of a wallet/purse, which can be used to make online purchases.

E-mail See electronic mail.

E-mail server A host or network that services e-mail.

E-money See electronic money.

Emoticons Keyboard emotion icons used to speed written interaction and convey emotions in online communications.

Encode To apply the rules of a code. (Contrast with decode.)

Encoding system   A system that permits alphanumeric characters and symbols to be coded in terms of bits.

Encryption/decryption   The encoding of data for security purposes. Encoded data must be decoded or deciphered to be used.

Enhanced television   A TV presentation combining video and general programming from broadcast, satellite, and cable networks.

Enterprise computing   Comprises all computing activities designed to support any type of organization.

Enterprise-wide information system   Information systems that provide information and processing capabilities to workers throughout a given organization.

Entity relationship diagram   A business modeling tool used for defining the information needs of a business, including the attributes of the entities and the relationship between them.

EPS   (*Encapsulated PostScript*) A vector graphics file format used by the PostScript language.

Ergonomics   The study of the relationships between people and machines.

E-signature   An electronic method of placing a legal signature on an electronic document.

E-tailing   Online retailing.

Ethernet   A local-area-net protocol in which the nodes must contend for the right to send a message. (See also *token access methods*.)

Ethernet card   An Ethernet-standard network interface card.

E-ticket   See *electronic ticket*.

E-time   See *execution time*.

E-trading   See *electronic trading*.

Exception report   A report that has been filtered to highlight critical information.

Executable program file   A file that contains programs that can be executed and run on a computer.

Execution time   The elapsed time it takes to execute a computer instruction and store the results (also called *E-time*).

Executive information system (EIS)   A system designed specifically to support decision making at the executive levels of management, primarily the tactical and strategic levels.

Exit routine   A software procedure that returns you to a GUI, an operating system prompt, or a higher-level applications program.

Expansion board   These add-on circuit boards contain the electronic circuitry for many supplemental capabilities, such as a fax modem, and are made to fit a particular type of bus (also called *expansion cards*).

Expansion bus   An extension of the common electrical bus that accepts the expansion boards that control the video display, disks, and other peripherals. (See also *bus*.)

Expansion card   See *expansion board*.

Expansion slots   Slots within the processing component of a microcomputer into which optional add-on circuit boards may be inserted.

Expert system   An interactive knowledge-based system that responds to questions, asks for clarification, makes recommendations, and generally helps users make complex decisions. (See also *assistant system*.)

Explorer   Windows software that enables the user to do file management tasks.

Export   The process of converting a file in the format of the current program to a format that can be used by another program. (Contrast with *import*.)

Extranet   An extension of an intranet such that it is partially accessible to authorized outsiders, such as customers and suppliers. (See also *intranet*.)

E-zine   An online magazine.

Facsimile (fax)   The transferring of images, usually of hardcopy documents, via telephone lines to another device that can receive and interpret the images.

FAQ   A frequently asked question.

Fault-tolerant   Referring to a computer system or network that is resistant to software errors and hardware problems.

Fax   See *facsimile*.

Fax modem   A modem that enables a PC to emulate a facsimile machine. (See also *modem*.)

Feedback loop   A closed loop in which a computer-controlled process generates data that become input to the computer.

Fetch instruction   That part of the instruction cycle in which the control unit retrieves a program instruction from RAM and loads it to the processor.

Fiber optic cable   A data transmission medium that carries data in the form of light in very thin transparent fibers.

Field   The smallest logical unit of data. Examples are employee number, first name, and price.

File   (1) A collection of related records. (2) A named area on a disk-storage device that contains a program or digitized information (text, image, sound, and so on).

File allocation table (FAT)   MS-DOS's method of storing and keeping track of files on a disk.

File compression   A technique by which file size can be reduced. Compressed files are decompressed for use.

File format   The manner in which a file is stored on disk storage.

File server   A dedicated computer system with high-capacity disk for storing the data and programs shared by the users on a local area network.

File Transfer Protocol (FTP)   A communications protocol that is used to transmit files over the Internet.

Filtering   The process of selecting and presenting only that information appropriate to support a particular decision.

Filtering program   A program that denies Internet access to specified content.

Firewall   Software that is designed to restrict access to an organization's network or its Intranet.

FireWire   The Apple Computer Company name for the 1394 bus standard.

Fixed disk   See *hard disk*.

Flaming   A barrage of scathing messages from irate Internet users sent to someone who posts messages out of phase with the societal norms.

Flash memory   A type of nonvolatile memory that can be altered easily by the user.

Flat files   A file that does not point to or physically link with another file.

Flat-panel monitor A monitor, thin from front to back, that uses liquid crystal and gas plasma technology.

Floating ad Internet advertisement that "floats" over the requested page for a few seconds.

Floating menu A special-function menu that can be positioned anywhere on the work area until you no longer need it.

Floppy disk See *diskette*.

Floppy disk drive A disk drive that accepts either the 3.5-inch or 5.25-inch diskette.

FLOPS [*Fl*oating point *op*erations *p*er *s*econd] A measure of speed for supercomputers.

Flowchart A diagram that illustrates data, information, and work flow via specialized symbols which, when connected by flow lines, portray the logic of a system or program.

Flowcharting The act of creating a flowchart.

FMD-ROM Very high density, multilayer disc that holds up to 140 GB of data. (Contrast with *DVD-ROM*.)

Folder An object in a Windows® graphical user interface that contains a logical grouping of related files and subordinate folders.

Font A typeface that is described by its letter style, its height in points, and its presentation attribute.

Footprint (1) The evidence of unlawful entry or use of a computer system. (2) The floor or desktop space required for a hardware component.

Foreground (1) That part of RAM that contains the highest priority program. (2) In Windows, the area of the display containing the active window. (Contrast with *background*.)

Form factor Refers to a computer's physical shape and size.

Formatted disk A disk that has been initialized with the recording format for a specific operating system.

FORTRAN [*FOR*mula *TRAN*slator] A high-level programming language designed primarily for scientific applications.

Fourth-generation language (4GL) A programming language that uses high-level English-like instructions to retrieve and format data for inquiries and reporting.

Frame A rectangular area in a desktop publishing-produced document into which elements, such as text and images, are placed.

Frames (Web page) The display of more than one independently controllable sections on a single Web page.

Freeware Copyright software that can be downloaded and used free of charge.

Front-end applications software Client software that performs processing associated with the user interface and applications processing that can be done locally. (See also *back-end applications software*.)

Front-end processor A processor used to offload certain data communications tasks from the host processor.

Full-duplex line A communications channel that transmits data in both directions at the same time. (Contrast with *half-duplex line*.)

Function A predefined operation that performs mathematical, logical, statistical, financial, and character-string operations on data in a spreadsheet or a database.

Function key A special-function key on the keyboard that can be used to instruct the computer to perform a specific operation.

Functional specifications Specifications that describe the logic of an information system from the user's perspective.

Function-based information system An information system designed for the exclusive support of a specific application area, such as inventory management or accounting.

Gb See *gigabit*.

GB See *gigabyte*.

General-purpose computer Computer systems that are designed with the flexibility to do a variety of tasks, such as CAD, payroll processing, climate control, and so on.

General system design That portion of the system development process in which the target system is defined in general.

Geosynchronous orbit An orbit that permits a communications satellite to maintain a fixed position relative to the surface of the earth.

GFLOPS A billion FLOPS. (See *FLOPS*.)

GIF A popular format for bit-mapped files.

Gigabit (Gb) One billion bits.

Gigabyte (GB) One billion bytes.

Gigahertz (GHz) Billions of clock cycles per second

GIGO Garbage in, Garbage out.

GPS (global positioning system) A system that uses satellites to provide location information.

Grammar and style checker An add-on program to word processing software that highlights grammatical concerns and deviations from effective writing style in a word processing document.

Graphical user interface (GUI) A user-friendly interface that lets users interact with the system by pointing to processing options with a point-and-draw device.

Graphics adapter A device controller that provides the electronic link between the motherboard and the monitor.

Graphics conversion program Software that enables files containing graphic images to be passed between programs.

Graphics file A file that contains digitized images.

Graphics software Software that enables you to create line drawings, art, and presentation graphics.

Gray scales The number of shades of a color that can be presented on a monochrome monitor's screen or on a monochrome printer's output.

Green computing Environmentally sensible computing.

Grid computing Using available computing resources more effectively by tapping the unused processing capabilities of many PCs via a network and/or the Internet.

Groupware Software whose application is designed to benefit a group of people. (Related to *workgroup computing*.)

Hacker A computer enthusiast who uses the computer as a source of recreation. (Contrast with *cracker*.)

Half-duplex line A communications channel that transmits data in one direction at the same time. (Contrast with *full-duplex line*.)

Half-size expansion board An expansion board that fits in half an expansion slot.

Handheld PC Any personal computer than can be held comfortably in a person's hand (usually weighs less than a pound). (See also *personal digital assistant*.)

Handshaking The process by which both sending and receiving devices in a computer network maintain and coordinate data communications.

Hard copy A readable printed copy of computer output. (Contrast with *soft copy*.)

Hard disk A permanently installed, continuously spinning magnetic storage medium made up of one or more rigid disk platters. (Same as *fixed disk*; contrast with *interchangeable magnetic disk*.).

Hard disk drive See *hard disk*.

Hardware The physical devices that comprise a computer system. (Contrast with *software*.)

Help command A software feature that provides an online explanation of or instruction on how to proceed.

Help desk A centralized location (either within an organization or outside of it) where computer-related questions about product usage, installation, problems, or services are answered.

Hexadecimal A base-16 numbering system.

HiFD disk A storage technology that supports very high-density diskettes up to 200 MB. (Contrast with *Zip disk* and *SuperDisk*.)

High-level language A language with instructions that combine several machine-level instructions into one instruction. (Compare with *machine language* or *low-level language*.)

Hit When a Web page is retrieved for viewing or is listed in results of a search.

Home network A network of PCs in a home or small office.

Home page The Web page that is the starting point for accessing information at a site or in a particular area.

Horizontal scroll bar A narrow screen object located along the bottom edge of a window that is used to navigate side to side through a document.

Host computer The processor responsible for the overall control of a computer system.

Hot plug A universal serial bus (USB) feature that allows peripheral devices to be connected to or removed from the USB port while the PC is running.

Hoteling Providing on-site office space that is a shared by mobile workers.

Hotkey A seldom used key combination that, when activated, causes the computer to perform the function associated with the key combination.

HPNA (HomePNA) A Home Phoneline Networking Alliance standard that allows the elements of the network to communicate over a home's existing telephone wiring or via wireless links.

HTML (HyperText Markup Language) The language used to compose and format most of the content found on the Internet.

HTTP (HyperText Transfer Protocol) The primary access method for interacting with the Internet.

Hub A common point of connection for computers and devices in a network.

Hyperlinks Clickable images or text phrase that let you link to other parts of a document or to different documents together within a computer system or on the Internet.

I/O [Input/Output] Input or output or both.

IBM Personal Computer (IBM PC) IBM's first personal computer (1981). This PC was the basis for PC-compatible computers.

Icons Pictographs used in place of words or phrases on screen displays.

Identity theft When a person gathers personal information to assume the identity of another person for illicit reasons.

IEEE 802.11a A wireless communications standard capable of 11 M bps up to about 300 feet from an access point.

IEEE 802.11b (Wi-Fi) A wireless communications standard capable of 54 M bps up to about 50 feet from an access point.

iMac An Apple Computer personal computer.

Image processing A reference to computer applications in which digitized images are retrieved, displayed, altered, merged with text, stored, and sent via data communications to one or several remote locations.

Image scanner A device that can scan and digitize an image so that it can be stored on a disk and manipulated by a computer.

Impact printer A printer that uses pins or hammers that hit a ribbon to transfer images to the paper.

Import The process of converting data in one format to a format that is compatible with the calling program. (Contrast with *export*.)

Inactive window A Windows window that displays an application that is running but not being used by the user. (Contrast with *active window*.)

Industrial espionage Theft of proprietary business information.

Industrial robot Computer-controlled robots used in industrial applications.

Information Data that have been collected and processed into a meaningful form.

Information-based decision A decision that involves an ill-defined and unstructured problem.

Information repository A central computer-based database for all system design information.

Information resource management (IRM) A concept advocating that information be treated as a corporate resource.

Information service A commercial network that provides remote users with access to a variety of information services.

Information society A society in which the generation and dissemination of information becomes the central focus of commerce.

Information superhighway A metaphor for a network of high-speed data communication links that will eventually connect virtually every facet of our society.

Information system A computer-based system that provides both data processing capability and information for managerial decision making.

Information technology (IT) A collective reference to the integration of computing technology and information processing.

Information technology competency (IT competency) Being able to interact with and use computers and having an understanding of IT issues.

Infrared port See *IrDA port*.

Ink-jet printer A nonimpact printer in which the print head contains independently controlled injection chambers that squirt ink droplets on the paper to form letters and images.

Input Data entered to a computer system for processing.

Input/output (I/O) A generic reference to input and/or output to a computer.

Input/output-bound application An IT application in which the amount of work that can be performed by the computer system is limited primarily by the speeds of the I/O devices.

Instant messaging Internet application in which personal communications are sent and displayed in real-time.

Instruction A programming language statement that specifies a particular computer operation to be performed.

Instruction cycle Defines the process by which computer instructions are interpreted and executed.

Instruction register The register that contains the instruction being executed.

Instruction time The elapsed time it takes to fetch and decode a computer instruction (also called *I-time*).

Integrated circuit (IC) Thousands of electronic components that are etched into a tiny silicon chip in the form of a special-function electronic circuit.

Integrated information system An information system that services two or more functional areas, all of which share a common database.

Integrated Services Digital Network (ISDN) A digital telecommunications standard for data delivery over twisted-pair lines with transmission speeds up to 128 K bps.

Intelligent agent Artificial intelligence-based software that has the authority to act on a person or thing's behalf. (Also called *bot*.)

Interactive Pertaining to online and immediate communication between the user and the computer.

Interchangeable magnetic disk A magnetic disk that can be stored offline and loaded to the computer system as needed. (Contrast with *hard disk* or *fixed disk*.)

Intercompany networking Companies cooperating with customers and other companies via electronic data interchange and extranets. (Contrast with *intracompany networking*.)

Internet (the Net) A global network that connects more than tens of thousands of networks, millions of large multiuser computers, and tens of millions of users in more than one hundred countries.

Internet appliance An inexpensive communications device for Internet applications.

Internet Protocol address See *IP address*.

Internet Relay Chat (IRC) An Internet protocol that allows users to join and participate in group chat sessions.

Internet service provider (ISP) Any company that provides individuals and organizations with access to or presence on the Internet.

Internet site specialist A person responsible for creating and maintaining one or more Internet sites.

Interoperability The ability to run software and exchange information in a multiplatform environment.

Intracompany networking Computer networking within an organization. (Contrast with *intercompany networking*.)

Intranet An Internet-like network whose scope is restricted to the networks within a particular organization. (See also *extranet*.)

Invoke Execute a command or a macro.

IP address (Internet Protocol address) A four-number point-of-presence (POP) Internet address (for example, 206.28.104.10).

IRC See *Internet Relay Chat*.

IrDA port Enables wireless transmission of data via infrared light waves between PCs, printers, and other devices (also called *infrared port*).

ISP See *Internet service provider*.

Itanium® High-end Intel processor.

I-time See *instruction time*.

Java Platform-independent language used for Web-based applications.

Joystick A vertical stick that moves the mouse pointer on a screen in the direction in which the stick is pushed.

JPEG A bit-mapped file format that compresses image size.

JPG The Windows-based extension for JPEG files, a bit-mapped file format that compresses image size.

Jukebox A storage device for multiple sets of CD-ROMs, tape cartridges, or disk modules enabling ready access to vast amounts of online data.

Kb See *kilobit*.

KB See *kilobyte*.

Kernel An operating system program that loads other operating system programs and applications programs to RAM as they are needed.

Key field The field in a record that is used as an identifier for accessing, sorting, and collating records.

Keyboard A device used for key data entry.

Keypad That portion of a keyboard that permits rapid numeric data entry.

Kilobit (Kb) 1024, or about 1000, bits.

Kilobyte (KB) 1024, or about 1000, bytes.

Knowledge base The foundation of a knowledge-based system that contains facts, rules, inferences, and procedures.

Knowledge-based system A computer-based system, often associated with artificial intelligence, that helps users make decisions by enabling them to interact with a knowledge base.

Knowledge engineer Someone trained in the use of expert system shells and in the interview techniques needed to extract information from a domain expert.

Knowledge worker Someone whose job function revolves around the use, manipulation, and dissemination of information.

LAN operating system The operating system for a local area network.

LAN server A high-end PC on a local area network whose resources are shared by other users on the LAN.

Landscape Referring to the orientation of the print on the page. Printed lines run parallel to the longer side of the page. (Contrast with *portrait*.)

Laptop PC Portable PC that can operate without an external power source. (Contrast with *desktop PC* and *tower PC*; see also *pocket PC*.)

Large-format ink-jet printer See *plotter*.

Laser printer   A page printer that uses laser technology to produce the image.

Layout   A reference to the positioning of the visual elements on a display or page.

Leased line   See *private line*.

LindowsOS   A Linux-based operating system for PCs that has a Windows-like interface.

Linux   An open source spin off of the UNIX operating system that runs on a number of hardware platforms and is made available for free over the Internet.

Listserv   A reference to an Internet mailing list.

LMDS   A fixed line-of-sight wireless technology designed to enable high-bandwidth "last mile" connectivity.

Load   To transfer programs or data from disk to RAM.

Local area network (LAN or local net)   A system of hardware, software, and communications channels that connects devices on the local premises. (Contrast with *wide area network*.)

Local bus   A bus that links expansion boards directly to the computer system's common bus.

Local net   See *local area network*.

Log off   The procedure by which a user terminates a communications link with a remote computer. (Contrast with *logon*.)

Logic bomb   A harmful set of instructions that are executed when a certain set of conditions are met.

Logic error   A programming error that causes an erroneous result when the program is executed.

Logical operators   AND, OR, and NOT operators can be used to combine relational expressions logically in spreadsheet, database, and other programs. (See also *relational operators*.)

Logical security   That aspect of computer-center security that deals with user access to systems and data.

Logon   The procedure by which a user establishes a communications link with a remote computer. (Contrast with *log off*.)

Loop   A sequence of program instructions executed repeatedly until a particular condition is met.

Low-level language   A language comprising the fundamental instruction set of a particular computer. (Compare with *high-level language*.)

Mac OS X   The operating system for the Apple family of microcomputers.

Machine cycle   The cycle of operations performed by the processor to process a single program instruction: fetch, decode, execute, and place result in memory.

Machine language   The programming language that is interpreted and executed directly by the computer.

Macintosh   An Apple Computer personal computer.

Macro   A sequence of frequently used operations or keystrokes that can be invoked to help speed user interaction with microcomputer productivity software.

Macro language   Programming languages whose instructions relate specifically to the functionality of the parent software.

Macro virus   A program written in the macro language of a particular application.

Magnetic disk   See *disk, magnetic*.

Magnetic disk drive   See *disk drive, magnetic*.

Magnetic-ink character recognition (MICR)   A data entry technique used primarily in banking. Magnetic characters are imprinted on checks and deposits, then scanned to retrieve the data.

Magnetic stripe   A magnetic storage medium for low-volume storage of data on badges and cards. (Related to *badge reader*.)

Magnetic tape   See *tape, magnetic*.

Magnetic tape cartridge   Cartridge-based magnetic tape storage media.

Magnetic tape drive   See *tape drive, magnetic*.

Mail merge   A computer application in which text generated by word processing is merged with data from a database (e.g., a form letter with an address).

Mailing list   An Internet-based capability that lets people discuss issues of common interest via common e-mail.

Main menu   The highest-level menu in a menu tree. (See also *menu*.)

Main program   See *driver module*.

Mainframe computer   A large computer that can service many users simultaneously in support of enterprise-wide applications.

MAN   See *Metropolitan Area Network*.

Management information system (MIS)   A computer-based system that optimizes the collection, transfer, and presentation of information throughout an organization, through an integrated structure of databases and information flow. (Contrast with *decision support system* and *executive information system*.)

Mass storage   Various techniques and devices used to hold and retain electronic data.

Massively parallel processing (MPP)   An approach to the design of computer systems that involves the integration of thousands of microprocessors within a single computer.

Master file   The permanent source of data for a particular computer application area.

Mb   See *megabit*.

MB   See *megabyte*.

Megabit (Mb)   1,048,576, or about one million, bits.

Megabyte (MB)   1,048,576, or about one million, bytes.

Megahertz (MHZ)   One million hertz (cycles per second).

Memory   See *RAM*.

Menu   A display with a list of processing choices from which a user may select.

Menu bar   A menu in which the options are displayed across the screen.

Menu tree   A hierarchy of menus.

Message   A series of bits sent from a terminal to a computer, or vice versa.

Metafile (WMF)   A class of graphics that combines the components of raster and vector graphics formats.

Metropolitan Area Network (MAN)   A data network designed for use within the confines of a town or city.

MHZ   See *megahertz*.

MICR   See *magnetic-ink character recognition*.

Microcomputer (or micro)   A small computer (See also *PC*.)

Micropayment   Electronic payment for goods and services in very small amounts.

Microprocessor   A computer on a single chip. The processing component of a microcomputer.

Microsecond   One millionth of a second.

Microsoft Network (MSN)   An information service provider sponsored by Microsoft Corporation.

Microwave signal   A high-frequency line-of-sight electromagnetic wave used in wireless communications.

MIDI   [*Musical Instrument Digital Interface*] An interface between PCs and electronic musical instruments, like the synthesizer.

MIDI file   A nonwaveform file result for MIDI applications.

Millisecond   One thousandth of a second.

Minicomputer (or mini)   A midsized computer.

Minimize   Reducing a window on the display screen to an icon.

MIPS   Millions of instructions per second.

MMDS   A fixed line-of-sight wireless technology designed to deliver network access at fiber-optic speeds.

Mnemonics   A memory aid often made up from the initials of the words in a term or process.

Modem   [*MOdulator-DEModulator*] A device used to convert computer-compatible signals to signals that can be transmitted over the telephone lines, then back again to computer signals at the other end of the line.

Monitor   A television-like display for soft-copy output in a computer system.

Moore's Law   The density of transistors on a chip doubles every 18 months.

Morphing   Using graphics software to transform one image into an entirely different image. The term is derived from the word *metamorphosis*.

Motherboard   See *system board*.

Mouse   A point-and-draw device that, when moved across a desktop a particular distance and direction, causes the same movement of the pointer on a screen.

Mouse pointer   A symbol that indicates the positioning of the point-and-draw device pointer on the screen.

MP3   A sound file format that enables CD-quality music to be compressed to about 8% of its original size while retaining CD sound quality.

MPEG   A video file format with the extension MPG or MPEG.

MPP   See *massively parallel processing*.

MS-DOS   [*MicroSoft-Disk Operating System*] The pre-Windows PC operating system.

Multifunction expansion board   An add-on circuit board that contains the electronic circuitry for two or more supplemental capabilities (for example, a serial port and a fax modem).

Multifunction printer   Multifunction machines that can handle several paper-related tasks such as computer-based printing, facsimile, scanning, and copying.

Multimedia   Computer application that involves the integration of text, sound, graphics, motion video, and animation.

Multimedia projector   An output peripheral device that can project the screen image (display) onto a large screen for group viewing.

Multiplatform environment   A computing environment that supports more than one platform. (See also *platform*.)

Multiplexor   A communications device that collects data from a number of low-speed devices, then transmits the combined data over a single communications channel. At the destination, it separates the signals for processing.

Multitasking   The concurrent execution of more than one program at a time.

Multiuser PC   A microcomputer that can serve more than one user at any given time.

Nanosecond   One billionth of a second.

National Information Infrastructure (NII)   Refers to a futuristic network of high-speed data communications links that eventually will connect virtually every facet of our society. (See also *information superhighway*.)

Native file format   The file format normally associated with a particular application.

Natural language   A programming language in which the programmer writes specifications without regard to the computer's instruction format or syntax—essentially, using everyday human language to program.

Navigation   Movement within and between a software application's work areas.

Net PC   Same as *network computer* (*NC*).

Netiquette   Etiquette on the Internet.

Network address   An electronic identifier assigned to each computer system and terminal/PC in a computer network.

Network administrator   A data communications specialist who designs and maintains local area networks (LANs) and wide area networks (WANs).

Network bus   A common cable in a bus topology that permits the connection of terminals, peripheral devices, and microcomputers to create a computer network.

Network computer (NC)   A single-user computer, usually diskless, that is designed to work with a server computer to obtain programs and data (also called *Net PC*).

Network interface card (NIC)   A PC expansion card or PCMCIA card that facilitates and controls the exchange of data between the PC and its network.

Network topology   The configuration of the interconnections between the nodes in a communications network.

Network, computer   See *computer network*.

Neural network   A field of artificial intelligence in which millions of chips (processing elements) are interconnected to enable computers to imitate the way the human brain works.

Newbie   A new user on the Internet.

Newsgroup   The electronic counterpart of a wall-mounted bulletin board that enables Internet users to exchange ideas and information via a centralized message database.

Node   An endpoint in a computer network.

Nondestructive read   A read operation in which the program and/or data that are loaded to RAM from disk storage reside in both RAM (temporarily) and disk storage (permanently).

Nonimpact printer   A printer that uses chemicals, lasers, or heat to form the images on the paper.

Nonvolatile memory   Solid-state RAM that retains its contents after an electrical interruption. (Contrast with *volatile memory*.)

Non-Windows application A computer application that will run under Windows but does not conform to the Windows standards for software.

Notebook PC A notebook-size laptop PC.

Numeric A reference to any of the digits 0-9. (Compare with *alpha* and *alphanumeric*.)

Object A result of any Windows application, such as a block of text, all or part of a graphic image, or a sound clip.

Object linking and embedding See *OLE*.

Object-oriented language A programming language structured to enable the interaction between user-defined concepts that contain data and operations to be performed on the data.

Object-oriented programming (OOP) A form of software development in which programs are built with entities called objects, which model any physical or conceptual item. Objects are linked together in a top-down hierarchy.

Object program A machine-level program that results from the compilation of a source program. (Compare with *source program*.)

OCR See *optical character recognition*.

Offline Pertaining to data that are not accessible by, or hardware devices that are not connected to, a computer system. (Contrast with *online*.)

OLE [*Object Linking and Embedding*] The software capability that enables the creation of a compound document that contains one or more objects from other applications. Objects can be linked or embedded.

Online Pertaining to data and/or hardware devices accessible to and under the control of a computer system. (Contrast with *offline*.)

Online document Documents that are designed to be retrieved from disk storage (locally or over a network) and viewed on a monitor. (Same as *electronic document*.)

Online thesaurus Software that enables a user to request synonyms interactively during a word processing session.

Open application A running application.

Open source software Referring to software for which the actual source programming code is made available to users for review and modification.

Operating system The software that controls the execution of all applications and system software programs.

Optical character recognition (OCR) A data entry technique that permits original source data entry. Coded symbols or characters are scanned to retrieve the data.

Optical disc See *disc, optical*.

Optical laser disc A storage medium that uses laser technology to score the surface of a disc to represent a bit.

Optical scanner A peripheral device that can read written text and hard-copy images, then translate the information into an electronic format that can be interpreted by and stored on computers.

Option buttons Circle bullets in front of user options that when selected include a dot in the middle of the circle.

Output The presentation of the results of processing.

Packet Strings of bits that contain information and a network address that are routed over different paths on the Internet according to a specific communications protocol.

Page (Web) The area in which information is presented on the World Wide Web.

Page printer A printer that prints a page at a time.

Paint software Software that enables users to "paint" electronic images. Resultant images are stored as raster graphics images.

Palmtop PC See *pocket PC*.

Parallel conversion An approach to system conversion whereby the existing system and the new system operate simultaneously prior to conversion.

Parallel port A direct link with the microcomputer's bus that facilitates the parallel transmission of data, usually one byte at a time.

Parallel processing A processing procedure in which one main processor examines the programming problem and determines what portions, if any, of the problem can be solved in pieces by other subordinate processors.

Parallel transmission Pertaining to the transmission of data in groups of bits versus one bit at a time. (Contrast with *serial transmission*.)

Parameter A descriptor that can take on different values.

Parity checking A built-in checking procedure in a computer system to help ensure that the transmission of data is complete and accurate. (Related to *parity error*.)

Parity error Occurs when a bit is dropped in the transmission of data from one hardware device to another. (Related to *parity checking*.)

Password A word or phrase known only to the user. When entered, it permits the user to gain access to the system.

Patch A modification of a program or an information system.

Path The hierarchy of folders that lead to the location of a particular file.

Pattern recognition system A device that enables limited visual input to a computer system.

PC [*Personal Computer*] A small computer designed for use by an individual. (See also *microcomputer*.)

PC card Same as *PCMCIA card*.

PC specialist A person trained in the function and operation of PCs and related hardware and software.

PCI local bus [*Peripheral Component Interconnect*] Intel's local bus. (See also *local bus*.)

PCMCIA card A credit-card-sized module that is inserted into a PCMCIA-compliant interface to offer add-on capabilities such as expanded memory, fax modem, and so on (also called *PC card*).

PCX A bit-mapped file format.

PDF See *portable document format*.

Peer-to-peer computing A type of computing in which people allow their stored data to be shared.

Peer-to-peer LAN A local area network in which all PCs on the network are functionally equal.

Pen-based computing Computer applications that rely on the pen-based PCs for processing capability.

Pen-based PC A portable personal computer that enables input via an electronic pen in conjunction with a pressure-sensitive monitor/drawing surface.

Pentium® An Intel microprocessor.

Pentium® II Successor to the Intel® Pentium Pro microprocessor.

Pentium® III   Successor to the Intel® Pentium II microprocessor.

Pentium® 4   Successor to the Intel® Pentium III microprocessor.

Pentium® Pro   Successor to the Intel® Pentium microprocessor.

Peripheral device   Any hardware device other than the processor.

Personal computer (PC)   See *PC*.

Personal computing   A computing environment in which individuals use personal computers for domestic and/or business applications.

Personal digital assistant (PDA)   Handheld personal computers that support a variety of personal information systems.

Personal home page   A Web site for an individual.

Personal identification number (PIN)   A code or number that is used in conjunction with a password to permit the user to gain access to a computer system.

Personal information management (PIM) system   Software application designed to help users organize random bits of information and to provide communications capabilities, such as e-mail and fax.

Phased conversion   An approach to system conversion whereby an information system is implemented one module at a time.

Photo illustration software   Software that enables the creation of original images and the modification of existing digitized images.

Physical security   That aspect of computer-center security that deals with access to computers and peripheral devices.

Picosecond   One trillionth of a second.

Picture element   See *pixel*.

Pie graph   A circular graph that illustrates each "piece" of datum in its proper relationship to the whole "pie."

Pilferage   A special case of software piracy whereby a company purchases a software product without a site-usage license agreement, then copies and distributes it throughout the company.

Pilot conversion   An approach to system conversion whereby the new system is implemented first in only one of the several areas for which it is targeted.

Pipelining   When a processor begins executing another instruction before the current instruction is completed, thus improving system throughput.

Pixel   [Picture *element*] An addressable point on a display screen to which light can be directed under program control.

Platform   A definition of the standards by which software is developed and hardware is designed.

Plotter   A device that produces high-precision hard-copy graphic output (also called *large-format ink-jet printer*).

Plug-and-play   Refers to making a peripheral device or an expansion board immediately operational by simply plugging it into a port or an expansion slot.

Plugin   A complementary application to an Internet browser.

PNG   A license-free bit-mapped file format, similar to GIF.

Pocket PC   A handheld personal computer (also called *palmtop PC*).

Point-and-draw device   An input device, such as a mouse or trackpad, used to *point* to and select a particular user option and to *draw*.

Pointer   The highlighted area in a spreadsheet display that indicates the current cell.

Polling   A line-control procedure in which each terminal is "polled" in rotation to determine whether a message is ready to be sent.

POP (point-of-presence)   An access point to the Internet.

Pop-out menu   A menu displayed next to the menu option selected in a higher-level pull-down or pop-up menu.

Pop-under ad   Internet advertisement that opens in a separate browser window "under" the requested page.

Pop-up menu   A menu that is superimposed in a window over whatever is currently being displayed on the monitor.

Port   An access point in a computer system that permits communication between the computer and a peripheral device.

Port replicator   A device to which a notebook PC can be readily connected to give the PC access to whatever external peripheral devices are connected to its common ports (keyboard, monitor, mouse, network, printer, and so on).

Portable document   An electronic document that can be passed around the electronic world as you would a print document in the physical world.

Portable Document Format (PDF)   A standard, created by Adobe Corporation, creating portable documents.

Portable hard disk   External hard disk device that is easily connected to any PC.

Portal   A Web site or service that offers a broad array of Internet-based resources and services.

Portrait   Referring to the orientation of the print on the page. Printed lines run parallel to the shorter side of the page. (Contrast with *landscape*.)

Post Office Protocol (POP)   Refers to the way an e-mail client software gets e-mail from its server.

POTS   Short for *plain old telephone service*, the standard voice-grade telephone service common in homes and business.

Power up   To turn on the electrical power to a computer system.

PowerPC processor   A RISC-based processor used in Apple iMac and other computers.

PPP (Point-to-Point Protocol)   A method by which a dialup link is connected to an ISP's local POP.

Presentation software   Software used to prepare information for multimedia presentations in meetings, reports, and oral presentations.

Prespecification   An approach to system development in which users relate their information processing needs to the project team during the early stages of the project.

Print server   A LAN-based PC that handles LAN user print jobs and controls at least one printer.

Printer   A device used to prepare hard-copy output.

Private line   A dedicated communications channel provided by a common carrier between any two points in a computer network. (Same as *leased line*.)

Procedure-oriented language   A high-level language whose general-purpose instruction set can be used to produce a sequence of instructions to model scientific and business procedures.

Process/device control   Referring to a computer-based system that controls processes and/or devices.

Processor   The logical component of a computer system that interprets and executes program instructions.

Processor-bound application   The amount of work that can be performed by the computer system is limited primarily by the speed of the computer.

Product stewardship policy   A policy that encourages responsible consideration of products.

Program   (1) Computer instructions structured and ordered in a manner that, when executed, causes a computer to perform a particular function. (2) The act of producing computer software. (Related to *software*.)

Program register   The register that contains the address of the next instruction to be executed.

Programmed decision   Decisions that address well-defined problems with easily identifiable solutions.

Programmer   One who writes computer programs.

Programmer/analyst   The title of one who performs both the programming and systems analysis function.

Programming language   A language programmers use to communicate instructions to a computer.

Programming   The act of writing a computer program.

PROM   [Programmable *Read-Only Memory*] ROM in which the user can load read-only programs and data.

Prompt   A program-generated message describing what should be entered.

Proprietary software package   Vendor-developed software that is marketed to the public.

Protocols   See *communications protocols*.

Prototype system   A model of a full-scale system.

Prototyping   An approach to systems development that results in a prototype system.

Proxy server computer   A computer between the client PC and a actual server that handles many client requests before they reach the actual server.

Pseudocode   Nonexecutable program code used as an aid to develop and document structured programs.

Public-domain software   Software that is not copyrighted and can be used without restriction.

Public-key encryption   Communications-based encryption that requires a private key and a public key.

Pull-down menu   A menu that is "pulled down" from an option in a higher-level menu.

Pull technology   Technology where data are requested from another program or computer, such as with an Internet browser. (Contrast with *push technology*.)

Pumping and dumping   A scam where someone floods the Internet with bogus information about a particular company.

Push technology   Technology where data are sent automatically to an Internet user. (Contrast with *pull technology*.)

Query by example   A method of database inquiry in which the user sets conditions for the selection of records by composing one or more example relational expressions.

Query language   A user-friendly programming language for requesting information from a database.

QuickTime   Software that lets you view videos, listen to music, and view panoramas.

Radio signals   Signals that enable data communication between radio transmitters and receivers.

RAID (Redundant Array of Independent Disks)   An integrated system of disks that enables fault-tolerant hard disk operation.

RAM   [*Random-Access Memory*] The memory area in which all programs and data must reside before programs can be executed or data manipulated.

RAM disk   That area of RAM that facilitates disk caching. (See also *disk caching*.)

Rambus DRAM   See *RDRAM*.

Rambus in-line memory module   See *RIMM*.

Random access   Direct access to records, regardless of their physical location on the storage medium. (Contrast with *sequential access*.)

Random-access memory   See *RAM*.

Random processing   Processing data and records randomly. (Contrast with *sequential processing*.)

Range   A cell or a rectangular group of adjacent cells in a spreadsheet.

Rapid application development (RAD)   Using sophisticated development tools to create a prototype or a functional information system.

Raster graphics   A method for maintaining a screen image as patterns of dots. (See also *bit-mapped graphics*.)

RDRAM (Rambus DRAM)   A new RAM technology capable of very high-speed transfer of data (600 MHz) to/from the processor.

Read   The process by which a record or a portion of a record is accessed from the disk storage medium and transferred to RAM for processing. (Contrast with *write*.)

Read-only memory (ROM)   A memory chip with contents permanently loaded by the manufacturer for read-only applications.

Read/write head   That component of a disk drive or tape drive that reads from and writes to its respective storage medium.

Record   A collection of related fields (such as an employee record) describing an event or an item.

Register   A small high-speed storage area in which data pertaining to the execution of a particular instruction are stored.

Relational database   A database, made up of logically linked tables, in which data are accessed by content rather than by address.

Relational operators   Used in formulas to show the equality relationship between two expressions (= [equal to], < [less than], > [greater than], <= [less than or equal to], >= [greater than or equal to], <> [not equal to]). (See also *logical operators*.)

Relative cell address   Refers to a cell's position in a spreadsheet in relation to the cell containing the formula in which the address is used.

Resolution   Referring to the number of addressable points on a monitor's screen or the number of dots per unit area on printed output.

RGB monitor   Color monitors that mix red, green, and blue to achieve a spectrum of colors.

RIMM   [Rambus In-line Memory Module] The circuit board designed to hold rambus in-line memory module memory chips.

Ring topology   A computer network that involves computer systems connected in a closed loop, with no one computer system the focal point of the network.

RISC   [Reduced Instruction Set Computer] A computer design architecture based on a limited instruction set machine language. (Contrast with CISC.)

Robot   A computer-controlled manipulator capable of locomotion and/or moving items through a variety of spatial motions.

Robotics   The integration of computers and industrial robots.

ROM   [Read-Only Memory] RAM that can be read only, not written to.

Root directory   The directory at the highest level of a hierarchy of directories.

Routers   Communications hardware that enables communications links between LANs and WANs by performing the necessary protocol conversions.

RS-232C connector   A 9-pin or 25-pin plug that is used for the electronic interconnection of computers, modems, and other peripheral devices.

Ruler bar   In the document window, a line that shows appropriate document measurements.

Run   To open and execute a program.

Scalable system   A system whose design permits expansion to handle any size database or any number of users.

Scalable typeface   An outline-based typeface from which fonts of any point size can be created. (See also typeface.)

ScanDisk   A Windows utility program that enables the repair of lost clusters on a hard disk.

Scanner   A device that scans hard copy and digitizes the text and/or images to a format that can be interpreted by a computer.

Scheduler   Someone who schedules the use of hardware resources to optimize system efficiency.

Screen-capture programs   Memory-resident programs that enable users to transfer all or part of the current screen image to a disk file.

Screen name   Another name for user ID at logon.

Screen saver   A utility program used to change static screens on idle monitors to interesting dynamic displays.

Script   A small scripting language program downloaded with a Web page and run on the client PC.

Scripting language   A programming language for creating scripts.

Scroll arrow   Small box containing an arrow at each end of a scroll bar that is used to navigate in small increments within a document or list.

Scroll box   A square object that is that is dragged along a scroll bar to navigate within a document or list.

Scrolling   Using the cursor keys to view parts of a document that extend past the bottom or top or sides of the screen.

SCSI bus   [Small Computer System Interface] This hardware interface allows the connection of several peripheral devices to a single SCSI expansion board (or adapter).

SCSI controller   The add-on circuitry needed for a SCSI port.

SCSI port   A device interface to which up to 15 peripheral devices can be daisy-chained to a single USB port. (Contrast with USB port.)

SDRAM (Synchronous Dynamic RAM)   RAM that is able to synchronize itself with the processor enabling high-speed transfer of data (600 MHz) to/from the processor.

Search engine   An Internet resource discovery tool that lets people find information by keyword(s) searches.

Sector   A disk-storage concept of a pie-shaped portion of a disk or diskette in which records are stored and subsequently retrieved. (Contrast with cylinder.)

Sector organization   Magnetic disk organization in which the recording surface is divided into pie-shaped sectors.

Secure Sockets Layer (SSL)   A protocol developed by Netscape for transmitting private documents via the Internet.

Select   Highlighting an object on a windows screen or a menu option.

Self-extracting zip file   An executable zip file that, when executed, unzips itself.

Sequential access   Accessing records in the order in which they are stored. (Contrast with random access.)

Sequential files   Files containing records that are ordered according to a key field.

Sequential processing   Processing of files that are ordered numerically or alphabetically by a key field. (Contrast with random processing.)

Serial port   A direct link with the microcomputer's bus that facilitates the serial transmission of data.

Serial representation   The storing of bits, one after another, on a storage medium.

Serial transmission   Pertaining to processing data one bit at a time. (Contrast with parallel transmission.)

Server   A LAN component that can be shared by users on a LAN.

Server application   (1) An application running on a network server that works in tandem with a client workstation or PC application. (See also client application.) (2) In object linking and embedding, the application in which the linked object originates.

Server computer   Any type of computer, from a PC to a supercomputer, which performs a variety of functions for its client computers, including the storage of data and applications software. (See also client computer.)

Server program   A software program on the server computer that manages resources and can work in conjunction with a client program. (See also client program.)

Shareware   Copyrighted software that can be downloaded for free, with its use based on an honor pay system.

Shortcut icon   A graphic icon that represents an application or document that when chosen causes the application to be run or the document to be opened.

Shortcut key   A key combination that chooses a menu option without the need to display a menu.

Shut down   The processes of exiting all applications and shutting off the power to a computer system.

SIMM   [Single In-line Memory Module] A small circuit board, capable of holding several memory chips, that has a 32-bit data path and can be easily connected to a PC's system board. (Contrast with *DIMM*.)

Simultaneous click   Tapping both buttons on a point-and-draw device at the same time.

Skyscraper ad   Vertical Internet advertisement that entices users to click on them to link to the site being promoted.

Slides   One of the images to be displayed in presentation software.

Smalltalk   An object-oriented language.

Smart card   A card or badge with an embedded microprocessor.

Soft copy   Temporary output that can be interpreted visually, as on a monitor. (Contrast with *hard copy*.)

Soft font   An electronic description of a font that is retrieved from disk storage and downloaded to the printer's memory.

Soft keyboard   A keyboard displayed on a touch-sensitive screen such that when a displayed key is touched with a finger or stylus, the character or command is sent to memory for processing.

Software   The programs used to direct the functions of a computer system. (Contrast with *hardware*; related to *program*.)

Software engineer   A person who develops software products to bridge the gap between design and executable program code.

Software engineering   A term coined to emphasize an approach to software development that embodies the rigors of the engineering discipline.

Software installation   The process of copying the program and data files from a vendor-supplied master disk(s) to a PC's hard disk.

Software package   One or more programs designed to perform a particular processing task.

Software piracy   The unlawful duplication of proprietary software. (Related to *pilferage*.)

Software portfolio   The mix of software on a PC.

Software suite   An integrated collection of software tools that may include a variety of business applications packages.

Sort   The rearrangement of fields or records in an ordered sequence by a key field.

Source application, Clipboard   The software application from which the Clipboard contents originated. (Contrast with *destination application*.)

Source data   Original data that usually involve the recording of a transaction or the documenting of an event or an item.

Source-data automation   Entering data directly to a computer system at the source without the need for key entry transcription.

Source document   The original hard copy from which data are entered.

Source program file   This file contains high-level instructions to the computer that must be compiled prior to program execution.

Source program   The code of the original program (also called *source code*). (Compare with *object program*.)

Spam   Unsolicited junk e-mail.

Spammer   A person who distributes spam.

Speech-recognition system   A device that permits voice input to a computer system.

Speech synthesis   Converting raw data into electronically produced speech.

Speech synthesizers   Devices that convert raw data into electronically produced speech.

Spelling checker   A software feature that checks the spelling of every word in a document against an electronic dictionary.

Spreadsheet file   A file containing data and formulas in tabular format.

Spreadsheet software   Refers to software that permits users to work with rows and columns of data.

SQL   A type of query language.

Star topology   A computer network that involves a centralized host computer connected to a number of smaller computer systems.

Start button   Permanent button on the Windows® task bar.

Stop bits   A data communications parameter that refers to the number of bits in the character or byte.

Streaming audio   Internet-based audio that is received and played in a steady, continuous stream.

Streaming video   Internet-based video that is received and played in a steady, continuous stream.

Structure chart   A chart that graphically illustrates the conceptualization of an information system as a hierarchy of modules.

Structured system design   A systems design technique that encourages top-down design.

Stylus   A pen-like point-and-draw device.

Subroutine   A group or sequence of instructions for a specific programming task that is called by another program.

Supercomputer   The category that includes the largest and most powerful computers.

SuperDisk   A disk-storage technology that supports very high-density diskettes.

Switched line   A telephone line used as a regular data communications channel (also called *dialup line*).

Switching hub   A type of hub that accepts packets of information sent within a network, then forwards them to the appropriate port for routing to their network destination, based on the network address contained in the packet.

Symmetric-key encryption   Communications-based encryption that requires each computer in a loop to have the key.

Synchronous dynamic RAM (SDRAM)   RAM that is able to synchronize itself with the processor enabling faster throughput.

Synchronous transmission   A communications protocol in which the source and destination points operate in timed alignment to enable high-speed data transfer. (See also *asynchronous transmission*.)

Syntax   The rules that govern the formulation of the instructions in a computer program.

Syntax error   An invalid format for a program instruction.

System   Any group of components (functions, people, activities, events, and so on) that interface with and complement one another to achieve one or more predefined goals.

System board   A microcomputer circuit board that contains the microprocessor, electronic circuitry for handling such tasks as input/output signals from peripheral devices, and memory chips (same as *motherboard*).

System check   An internal verification of the operational capabilities of a computer's electronic components.

System life cycle A reference to the four stages of a computer-based information system—birth, development, production, and end-of-life.

System maintenance The process of modifying an information system to meet changing needs.

System programmer A programmer who develops and maintains system programs and software.

System prompt A visual prompt to the user to enter a system command.

System software Software that is independent of any specific applications area.

System specifications (specs) Information system details that include everything from the functionality of the system to the format of the system's output screens and reports.

System unit An enclosure containing the computer system's electronic circuitry and various storage devices.

Systems analysis The examination of an existing system to determine input, processing, and output requirements for the target system.

Systems analyst A person who does systems analysis.

Systems testing A phase of testing where all programs in a system are tested together.

T-1 line A high-speed digital link to the Internet (1.544 M bps).

T-3 line A high-speed digital link to the Internet (44.736 M bps).

TAN See *tiny area network*.

Tape backup unit (TBU) A magnetic tape drive designed to provide backup for data and programs.

Tape drive, magnetic The hardware device that contains the read/write mechanism for the magnetic tape storage medium. (Compare with *disk drive, magnetic*.)

Tape, magnetic A storage medium for sequential data storage and backup.

Target system A proposed information system that is the object of a systems development effort.

Task The basic unit of work for a processor.

Taskbar In a Windows session, the bar shows what programs are running and available for use.

TCP/IP [*Transmission Control Protocol/Internet Protocol*] A set of communications protocols developed by the Department of Defense to link dissimilar computers across many kinds of networks.

Telecommunications The collection and distribution of the electronic representation of information between two points.

Telecommuting "Commuting" via a communications link between home and office.

Telemedicine Describes any type of health care administered remotely over communication links.

Telephony The integration of computers and telephones.

Template A model for a particular microcomputer software application.

Terabyte (TB) About one trillion bytes.

Terminal Any device capable of sending and receiving data over a communications channel.

Terminal emulation mode The software transformation of a PC so that its keyboard, monitor, and data interface emulate that of a terminal.

Text cursor A symbol controlled by the arrow keys that shows the location of where the next keyed-in character will appear on the screen.

Text-to-speech software Software that reads text and produces speech.

TFLOPS A trillion FLOPS. (See *FLOPS*.)

Thesaurus, online See *online thesaurus*.

Thin client A networked workstation that depends on a server computer for much of its processing and for permanent storage.

Third-generation language (3GL) A procedure-oriented programming language that can be used to model almost any scientific or business procedure. (Related to *procedure-oriented language*.)

Thread (newsgroup) An original Internet newsgroup message and any posted replies to that message.

Throughput A measure of computer system efficiency; the rate at which work can be performed by a computer system.

Throwaway system An information system developed to support information for a one-time decision, then discarded.

Thumbnail A miniature display of an image or a page to be viewed or printed.

TIF The Windows-based extension for TIFF files, a bit-mapped file format often used in print publishing.

TIFF A bit-mapped file format often used in print publishing.

Tiled windows Two or more windows displayed on the screen in a nonoverlapping manner.

Tiny area network (TAN) A term coined to refer to very small local area networks, typically installed in the home or small office.

Title bar A narrow Windows screen object at the top of each window that runs the width of the window.

Toggle The action of pressing a single key on a keyboard to switch between two or more modes of operation, such as insert and replace.

Token access method A local-area-net protocol in which an electronic token travels around a network giving priority transmission rights to nodes. (See also *Ethernet*.)

Toolbar A group of rectangular graphics in a software package's user interface that represent a frequently used menu option or a command.

Top-level domain (TLD) The highest level in the Internet URL (com, org, edu, and so on).

Touch-screen monitors Monitors with touch-sensitive screens that enable users to choose from available options simply by touching the desired icon or menu item with their finger.

Tower PC A PC that includes a system unit that is designed to rest vertically. (Contrast with *laptop PC* and *desktop PC*.)

Track, disk That portion of a magnetic disk-face surface that can be accessed in any given setting of a single read/write head. Tracks are configured in concentric circles.

Track, tape That portion of a magnetic tape that can be accessed by any one of the tape drive's read/write heads. A track runs the length of the tape.

Trackball   A ball mounted in a box that, when moved, results in a similar movement of the mouse pointer on a display screen.

Trackpad   A point-and-draw device with no moving parts that includes a touch-sensitive pad to move the mouse pointer or cursor.

Trackpoint   A point-and-draw device that functions like a miniature joystick, but is operated with the tip of the finger.

Tracks per inch (TPI)   A measure of the recording density, or spacing, of tracks on a magnetic disk.

Transaction   A procedural event in a system that prompts manual or computer-based activity.

Transaction file   A file containing records of data activity (transactions); used to update the master file.

Transmission medium   The central cable along which terminals, peripheral devices, and microcomputers are connected in a bus topology.

Transaction-oriented processing   Transactions are recorded and entered as they occur.

Transparent   A reference to a procedure or activity that occurs automatically and does not have to be considered by the user.

Trojan horse   A virus that masquerades as a legitimate program.

TSR   [Terminate-and-Stay-Resident] Programs that remain in memory so they can be instantly popped up over the current application by pressing a hotkey.

Tunneling   The technology where one network uses the channels of another network to send its data.

Turnaround document   A computer-produced output that is ultimately returned to a computer system as a machine-readable input.

Twisted-pair wire   A pair of insulated copper wires twisted around each other for use in transmission of telephone conversations and for cabling in local area networks.

Typeface   A set of characters that are of the same type style.

Unicode   A 16-bit encoding system.

Uniform Resource Locator (URL)   An Internet address for locating Internet elements, such as server sites, documents, files, bulletin boards (newsgroups), and so on.

Uninterruptible power source (UPS)   A buffer between an external power source and a computer system that supplies clean, continuous power.

Unit testing   That phase of testing in which the programs that make up an information system are tested individually.

Universal product code (UPC)   A 10-digit machine-readable bar code placed on consumer products.

Universal Serial Bus (USB)   A bus standard that permits up to 127 peripheral devices to be connected to an external bus.

UNIX   A multiuser operating system.

Upload   The transmission of data from a local computer to a remote computer.

Upstream rate   The data communications rate from client computer to server computer.

Uptime   That time when the computer system is in operation.

URL   See *uniform resource locator*.

USB 2.0   A second generation USB standard that is 40 times faster than the original.

USB hub   A device that expands the number of available USB ports.

USB port (Universal Serial Bus port)   A high-speed device interface to which up to 127 peripheral devices can be daisy-chained to a single USB port. (Contrast with *SCSI port*.)

USENET   A worldwide network of servers, often hosting newsgroups that can be accessed over the Internet.

User   The individual providing input to the computer or using computer output.

User-friendly   Pertaining to an online system that permits a person with relatively little experience to interact successfully with the system.

User ID   A unique character string that is entered at logon to a network to identify the user during personal communications and to the server computer. (See also *screen name*.)

User interface   A reference to the software, method, or displays that enable interaction between the user and the software being used.

User liaison   A person who serves as the technical interface between the information services department and the user group.

User Location Service (ULS)   Internet-based listing of Internet users who are currently online and ready to receive Internet telephone calls.

User name   Same as *user ID*.

Utility software   System software programs that can assist with the day-to-day chores associated with computing and maintaining a computer system.

Vaccine   An antiviral program.

VDT   [Video Display Terminal] A terminal on which printed and graphic information are displayed on a television-like monitor and into which data are entered on a typewriter-like keyboard.

Vector graphics   A method for maintaining a screen image as patterns of lines, points, and other geometric shapes.

Vertical scroll bar   A narrow screen object located along the right edge of a window that is used to navigate up and down through a document or list.

VGA   [Video Graphics Array] A circuit board that enables the interfacing of very high-resolution monitors to microcomputers.

Video capture card   An expansion card that enables full-motion color video with audio to be captured and played on a monitor or stored on disk.

Video display terminal   See *VDT*.

Video editing   The process of manipulating video images.

Video file   This file contains digitized video frames that when played rapidly produce motion video.

Video for Windows   Software that lets you view videos and listen to music.

Video mail (V-mail)   Mail that is sent as video rather than as an electronic document.

Video operator's distress syndrome (VODS)   Headaches, depression, anxiety, nausea, fatigue, and irritability that result from prolonged interaction with a terminal or PC.

Video RAM (VRAM)   RAM on the graphics adapter.

Videophone   An Internet-based capability that permits two parties to both see and hear one another during a conversation.

Virtual file allocation table (VFAT) Windows® method for storing and keeping track of files on a disk.

Virtual machine The processing capabilities of one computer system created through software (and sometimes hardware) in a different computer system.

Virtual marketplace A generic reference to the whole of Internet-based retailing.

Virtual private network (VPN) A private network over the Internet.

Virtual reality An artificial environment made possible by hardware and software.

Virtual world An environment that is simulated by hardware and software.

Virus A program written with malicious intent and loaded to the computer system of an unsuspecting victim. Ultimately, the program destroys or introduces errors in programs and databases.

Visual Basic A visual programming language.

Visual C++ A visual programming language.

Visual programming An approach to program development that relies more on visual association with tools and menus than with syntax-based instructions.

V-mail See *video mail*.

Voice message switching Using computers, the telephone system, and other electronic means to store and forward voice messages. (Contrast with *electronic mail*.)

Voice-response system A device that enables output from a computer system in the form of user-recorded words, phrases, music, alarms, and so on.

Volatile memory Solid-state semiconductor RAM in which the data are lost when the electrical current is turned off or interrupted. (Contrast with *nonvolatile memory*.)

VPN See *virtual private network*.

WAN See *wide area network*.

Wand scanner A handheld OCR scanner.

Wave file A Windows sound file.

Wearable display A display that is worn on a wireless headset.

Wearable PC A small personal computer that is worn.

Web See *World Wide Web*.

Web hosting company A company which maintains a network of interconnected Web servers for the Web sites.

Web page A document on the Web that is identified by a unique URL.

Web page design software A Web site authoring system.

Web presence providers A company that hosts individual and corporate Web site on their Internet server for a fee.

Webcam A digital video camera that sends still and video imagery over the Internet.

Webcast The broadcasting of real-time audio and/or video streams over the Internet.

Webmaster An individual who manages a Web site.

Wheel mouse A mouse with a "wheel" to facilitate scrolling.

Whiteboarding An area on a display screen that permits a document or image to be viewed and worked on simultaneously by several users on the network.

Wide area network (WAN) A computer network that connects nodes in widely dispersed geographic areas. (Contrast with *local area network*.)

Wi-Fi See *IEEE 802.11b*.

Window A rectangular section of a display screen that is dedicated to a specific document, activity, or application.

Windows® A generic reference to all Microsoft Windows operating system products.

Windows .Net Server A server-side Microsoft operating system.

Windows® 2000 A 32-bit operating system by Microsoft Corporation (successor to Windows NT).

Windows® 2000 Server The server-side portion of the Windows 2000 operating system.

Windows® 95 An operating system by Microsoft Corporation.

Windows® 98 An operating system by Microsoft Corporation (the successor to Windows 95).

Windows® application An application that conforms to the Windows standards for software and operates under the Microsoft Windows platform.

Windows® CE A Microsoft operating system whose GUI is similar to that for Windows 9x operating systems, designed to run on handheld PCs, PDAs, and other small computers.

Windows Me (Millennium Edition) A consumer-oriented operating system by Microsoft Corporation (the successor to Windows 98).

Windows® NT A 32-bit operating system by Microsoft Corporation.

Windows® terminal An intelligent terminal that can run Windows operating systems, but is not designed for stand-alone operation.

Windows XP An 32-bit operating system by Microsoft Corporation (successor to Windows 2000).

Windows XP 64-Bit Edition A 64-bit version of Windows XP.

Windows XP Home Edition The client-side operating system for home and small business.

Windows XP Professional Edition The client-side operating system for businesses.

Wintel PC A personal computer using a Microsoft Windows® operating system in conjunction with an Intel® or Intel-compatible processor.

Wireless LAN PC card A device to enable a wireless link between a PC and a LAN.

Wireless transceiver Short for *transmitter-receiver*, a device that both transmits and receives data via high-frequency radio waves.

Wizard A utility within an application that helps you use the application to perform a particular task.

WMF (Windows metafile) A popular format for metafiles.

Word (1) For a given computer, an established number of bits that are handled as a unit. (2) Word processing component of Microsoft Office.

Word processing software Software that uses the computer to enter, store, manipulate, and print text.

Workgroup computing Computer applications that involve cooperation among people linked by a computer network. (Related to *groupware*.)

Workspace The area in a window below the title bar or menu bar containing everything that relates to the application noted in the title bar.

Workstation A high-performance single-user computer system with sophisticated input/output devices that can be easily networked with other workstations or computers.

World Wide Web (the Web, WWW, W3) An Internet server that offers multimedia and hypertext links.

Worm A virus that invades computers via e-mail and IRC.

WORM disk [Write-Once Read-Many disk] An optical laser disc that can be read many times after the data are written to it, but the data cannot be changed or erased.

WORM disk cartridge The medium for WORM disk drives.

Write To record data on the output medium of a particular I/O device (tape, hard copy, PC display). (Contrast with *read*.)

WYSIWYG [*What You See Is What You Get*] A software package in which what is displayed on the screen is very similar in appearance to what you get when the document is printed.

X terminal A terminal that enables the user to interact via a graphical user interface (GUI).

XHTML The new standard for Web page development, replacing HTML.

Yahoo An Internet portal.

Year 2000 problem (Y2K) An information systems problem brought on by the fact that many legacy information systems still treat the year field as two digits (98) rather than four (1998).

Zip disk The storage medium for Zip drives. (Contrast with *HiFD disk* and *SuperDisk*.)

Zip drive A storage device that uses optical technology together with magnetic technology to read and write to an interchangeable floppy-size 100, 250, or 750 MB Zip disks.

Zip file A popular file compression format.

Zoned recording Disk recording scheme where zones contain a greater number of sectors per track as you move from the innermost zone to the outermost zone.

Zoom An integrated software command that expands a window to fill the entire screen.

INDEX